Restoring the Jews to Their Homeland

RESTORING THE JEWS TO THEIR HOMELAND

NINETEEN CENTURIES IN THE QUEST FOR ZION

JOSEPH ADLER

JASON ARONSON INC.
Northvale, New Jersey
Jerusalem

This book was set in 9-½ pt. English Times by Aerotype, Inc., in Amherst, New Hampshire.

Copyright © 1997 by Joseph Adler

10 9 8 7 6 5 4 3 2 1

Library of Congress Cataloging-in-Publication Data

Adler, Joseph, 1923–
    Restoring the Jews to their homeland : nineteen centuries in the quest for Zion / Joseph Adler.
        p.   cm.
    Includes bibliographical references and index.
    ISBN 1-56821-978-4 (alk. paper)
    1. Palestine in Judaism—History of doctrines. 2. Jews—Restoration—History of doctrines. 3. Jews—Migrations—History. 4. Palestine—Emigration and immigration—History. 5. Pseudo Messiahs—Biography. 6. Christian Zionism—History.
7. Zionism—History. 8. Jewish nationalism—History. I. Title.
  BM729.P3A35   1996
  320.5'4'095694—DC20   96-20616

Manufactured in the United States of America. Jason Aronson Inc. offers books and cassettes. For information and catalog write to Jason Aronson Inc., 230 Livingston Street, Northvale, New Jersey 07647.

For Lunita, Michael, and Sara

"Blood and fire and pillars of smoke,
this is the whole history of the Jews,
the rest is commentary;
study it."

Contents

Preface

On May 14, 1948, the State of Israel was born, and for the first time in nineteen centuries—since Jerusalem fell to the Roman legions of Titus—the Jewish people could point with pride to a national home of their own. The renewal of this ancient polity among the nations was an event of universal significance, as well as one of the most dramatic milestones in the long course of Jewish history.

Political or Herzlian Zionism, the movement that led to the creation of the modern State of Israel, came into being in the summer of 1897 when the First Zionist Congress, under the leadership of Theodor Herzl (1860-1904)[1] adopted the Basle Program. The Congress proclaimed to the world that "Zionism seeks to secure for the Jewish people a publicly recognized, legally secured home in Palestine."[2] Herzl's charismatic personality and diplomatic forays to achieve this goal stirred the imagination of Jews everywhere.[3] Indeed, his efforts tended to cast into the shadows the fact that the groundwork for the nationalistic program advanced in his book *Der Judenstaat* (*The Jewish State*)[4] had been preceded by almost 2,000 years of yearning for Zion on the part of Jews throughout the Diaspora.

Most scholars are in agreement that the term "Zion" originally signified the easternmost of the two hills of ancient Jerusalem. This designation was gradually extended to symbolize the city of Jerusalem and eventually the whole of the Land of Israel. The Israelites in exile could not forget Zion. The Hebrew psalmist sat by the waters of Babylon and swore: "If I forget thee O Jerusalem, let my right hand lose her cunning."[5] Thus as the prominent Israeli diplomat Chaim Herzog has written, ". . . for Jews the name Zion, very early on came to mean the ancient Jewish homeland, symbolic of Judaism and of Jewish national aspirations."[6]

It is not the intention of this book to present a definitive study of all the predecessors of Herzl who advocated or toyed with the idea of a Jewish restoration in Palestine. Such a task would require a lifetime of effort. Rather, the intention is to render an account of some of the more interesting benchmarks on the long, winding road that led to Basle, Switzerland, in the last decade of the nineteenth century.

Emphasis throughout the work has been placed primarily on individuals (Jewish and Christian) who either by their thoughts or deeds sought to restore Jewry to the Promised Land. In addition, movements and events tending toward this same goal have been included and explored.

In retrospect, in the wake of the current drive to find a permanent and peaceful solution to the Israeli-Arab conflict there has been a flood of books and articles dealing with the problem. Unfortunately, the majority of writers responsible for this verbal deluge take the position that Israel is a freak of history, a recent phenomenon lacking roots in the chronicle of Judaism and the Jewish experience. Contemplating the State of Israel as a creation of the mid-twentieth century without taking into account the past, particularly the numerous efforts through the centuries following the Roman destruction of Jerusalem and the Temple in the first century C.E., is a deliberate distortion of history. It is a crude effort by Israel's detractors to portray her as an interloper in the Arab world of the Middle East. This trivialization of Jewish history must not go unchallenged. It is the earnest hope of this scribe to correct this misapprehension.

I

EARLY MESSIANIC MOVEMENTS

1

The First Millenium

Judas the Galilean

The belief in the "ingathering of the exiles," first referred to in the Bible, exerted a powerful sway on Jewish thought, which was constantly augmented in the liturgy by a yearning for Eretz Israel – and particularly for the holy city of Jerusalem. Down through the ages Jews who were sometimes inspired by messianic aspirations were not content merely to hope and pray for the restoration of Zion, and as individuals or in groups, made the decision for *aliyah* (i.e., to immigrate to Israel) or sought to hasten the redemption of the ancient homeland by the use of magic or force.

For centuries, in every corner of the Diaspora, Jews awaited the Messiah, and many valiant men and many false prophets were hailed as the long-awaited liberator. The hope for a personal Messiah received considerable impetus following the incursion into Judean affairs by the Roman general Pompey (106–48 b.c.e). In 6 c.e. Judea was annexed and incorporated into the Roman Empire as a procuratorial province with Caesarea Maritima as its capital, and a census was ordered for purposes of tax assessment. Almost immediately, however, a fierce resistance led by a fiery prophet erupted in the hills of Galilee. Known to history as Judas the Galilean, or Judas of Gamala, he is believed to have perished fairly early in the prolonged series of guerrilla activities he inaugurated against Roman domination. Around 46 c.e. two of Judas' sons were crucified by the Roman procurator, but the movement he had created survived and its adherents became known as Zealots. The Zealots' philosophy was straightforward enough: Rome was the enemy; no Jew should pay tribute to Rome; no Jew should acknowledge the Roman Emperor, a mortal man, as their master; there was no other master than God, who had conferred a unique birthright on Israel. The patriotic duty, therefore, of every Jew was to fight for the reinstatement of this birthright, and the restoration of the rightful rulers of Israel. During the years of the Zealots, activity they were frequently referred to by the historian of the period, the turncoat Flavius Josephus, as "Lestai" (brigands) or as "Sicarii" (daggermen), a name derived from the *sica,* a small curved dagger especially favored by the Zealots for political assassinations.[7]

Theudas

By the middle of the first century (46 C.E.) the Jews were ready to welcome almost any self-proclaimed Messiah. Thus it was not unusual that a certain Theudas was able to persuade about 400 Judeans to gather up their possessions and follow him to the Jordan River where, at his command, the waters would part and provide easy passage to escape Roman domination. The Roman procurator, Cuspius Fadus, on learning of the plan, sent a squadron of cavalry in pursuit of the group, and many of the Jews were slain or captured. Theudas himself was caught and decapitated and his head was sent to Jerusalem. Twelve years later an Egyptian-Jewish claimant to messiahship promised an eager audience that the walls of Jerusalem would fall at his command, as Jericho had fallen for Joshua. He led his followers to the Mount of Olives, where they were attacked and dispersed by the troops of the Roman garrison.

In 63 C.E. severe earthquakes shook southern Italy, and again stimulated messianic expectations among the Jews (Rome's destruction had come to be regarded by many as a precursor for the coming of the Messiah). Indeed, in the following year Rome was laid waste by fire; ten of the fourteen sections of the city were partially or totally destroyed. Fuel was added to the messianic bonfire in Judea by the actions of the Roman procurator, Gessius Florus, a Greek from Asia Minor. When fighting broke out between Greeks and Jews in Caesarea Maritima, Florus detained a Jewish deputation that had come to see him and placed its members under arrest. He then seized a large sum from the Jerusalem Temple's treasury. Rioting followed, along with a house to house search that resulted in pillaging and the crucifixions of a number of eminent Jews. Troops from Caesarea called in to control the situation made the matter worse. Upon the procurator's return to Caesarea, Eleazer, son of the former High Priest Ananias and captain of the Temple proclaimed that henceforth no sacrifices would be accepted from any foreigner. This meant that the twice-daily offerings for Rome and the emperor would have to be discontinued. It was an action tantamount to a declaration of war. The First Jewish Revolt, or as the Jews came to call it, the First Roman War, had become inevitable.

Menahem, the Zealot

Foremost among the early participants in the "great revolt" against Rome was Menahem, the son (or grandson) of Judas the Galilean, the founder of the Zealot Movement. Menahem stormed and captured the Dead Sea fortress at Masada. After distributing the contents of the fort's armory to his followers, he led them to Jerusalem where they joined the insurgents led by Eleazer in besieging the Romans and the Jewish auxiliaries holed up in Herod the Great's former royal palace. Taking command of the situation, Menahem accepted the surrender of the Jewish soldiers in the palace, while the Roman troops retreated into its three strong towers. Flushed by his initial success, Menahem tried to establish control over all the insurgent forces in the city. He comported himself like a king, and encouraged the impression that he was the Messiah. However, the assumption of power by Menahem was unacceptable to his rival Eleazer. When Menahem murdered Eleazer's father Ananias, the die was cast for a bloody showdown. Eleazer's opportunity came when the would-be Messiah dressed in royal garb and accompanied by a band of armed men came to pray in the Temple court. Eleazer and his followers attacked the Zealots and in the ensuing fray Menahem was captured, and killed (66 C.E.). Eleazer then allowed the Roman soldiers to move out of the palace towers, telling them they were free to withdraw. But he broke his promise and slaughtered all of them except their commander, who agreed to accept circumcision.

Menahem's men were forced to flee Jerusalem. Some regrouped and joined their comrades at Masada where they were led by Eleazer, the son of Jair, who may have been a grandson of the freedom fighter Judas the Galilean, and a nephew of the murdered leader, Menahem. The Zealots of Masada continued to hold out for three years after the Romans had reconquered Jerusalem. When the Roman army under the command of Flavius Silva finally breached the Zealot stronghold they found that the 960 members of the garrison had committed suicide rather than surrender.

The opposition of the Jerusalem insurgents to the leadership of Menahem, which led to his untimely death, was due to several factors. Many of the Jerusalemites feared the revolutionary social changes that the Zealot leader wished to introduce; others resented his seizure of power. According to Josephus they did not want to fight for their freedom against the Romans, only to be enslaved under a despot of lowly origins. However, at the heart of the opposition was the fact that most of them were disturbed by the messianic pretensions of Menahem. Curiously, the messianic element in the Menahem story has led some modern scholars to believe that the Zealot leader may have been "the teacher of righteousness" referred to in one of the Dead Sea Scrolls.[8]

The Roman conquest of Judea resulted in great physical and human destruction, the enslavement of many thousands, and the widespread confiscation of property. Although apocalyptic and messianic tendencies persisted, a far-ranging spiritual revival was launched. The outstanding figure of the postwar period was Johanan ben Zaccai who had escaped from Jerusalem during the siege of the city and assembled, with Roman permission, those Pharisaic sages and scribes who had survived the fighting. In the town of Yavneh, near the Judean seacoast, Johanan and his followers articulated a rabbinic blueprint for Jewish survival.

Despite the rabbinic reformation, messianic agitation in Judaea and the Diaspora led to further Jewish revolts. In 114 C.E. the Roman Emperor Trajan launched an invasion of the East with the intention of spreading the Roman Empire to the Persian Gulf. His efforts, however, were seriously hampered by a chain of violent, unprecedented Jewish uprisings in many parts of the Jewish Diaspora (Egypt, Mesopotamia, Cyrenacia and Cyprus). These outbreaks were caused by a mixture of religious hostility, messianic yearnings, and lingering bitterness over the Roman destruction of the Jerusalem Temple several generations earlier. The risings, for all their ferocity, stood no chance of success. History is silent about the fighting in Judea itself, but Jewish tradition has applied to the rebellion the name "the war of Quietus" (*Polemos shel Kitos*) after the Moorish general Lucius Quietus. He ruthlessly suppressed the revolt in Mesopotamia, and was then sent to Judea to deal with the insurgency there. He had not completely pacified Judea when Trajan died, and his kinsman Aelius Hadrian was named Emperor in 117 C.E.

Hadrian, envious of the reputation of his predecessor and anxious to put an end to the disturbances that threatened his rule, abandoned the effort to expand the Roman frontier eastward. Indicating a willingness to make concessions, he also removed the hated Quietus from his post as governor of Judea, and had him executed for having exceeded his powers. Hadrian also promised the Judeans that he would rebuild Jerusalem and the Temple. He did not keep his word and relations between ruler and ruled rapidly disintegrated. The mutual antipathy manifested itself openly during the Emperor's journey through Judea in 130 C.E. Hadrian's change of heart toward the Jews remains, even today, a matter of speculation. He may have feared the political consequences of allowing the Jews to regain control of Jerusalem. Some historians are of the opinion that the non-Jewish inhabitants of the region turned the Emperor against the Jews, and that the constant uprisings against Roman rule fueled Hadrian's animosity. The Emperor's championship of Hellenism, and hatred of Oriental religions may also have contributed to his change of attitude toward the Jews. Whatever the reasons, Hadrian's plans to rebuild Jerusalem as a pagan Roman colony, under the name Aelia Capitolina (the Emperor belonged to the Aelian family), and to build a shrine to Jupiter on the site of the destroyed Temple triggered a new revolt known as the Second Judean Revolt, or Second Roman War (132–135 C.E.).[9]

Bar Kochba

This time the Jewish rebels carefully prepared for the fighting by storing up arms, carving out underground passages and places of refuge in the region's mountains, and establishing a unified command. The talented, vigorous leader of the rebellion appears to have been the national commander of the Jewish forces from the beginning of hostilities. Not a trace exists of his origins, early life, or background. Even his real name was shrouded in mystery, and a subject of much speculation, until a few decades ago when letters naming the leader were discovered in caves near the Dead Sea. The letters revealed that his original name was Simeon bar Kosiba (son of Kosiba, or perhaps referring to the village of his birth), and that he was styled "Prince of Israel." The great rabbi of the period, Akiba ben Joseph, hailed him as Simeon Bar Kochba, "son of the star", a messianic allusion to the biblical passage "There shall go forth a star out of Jacob" (Balaam's prophecy, Numbers 24:17).[10] Indeed, tradition has it that Bar Kochba possessed many of the qualities of the expected Messiah. He is reported to have been tall and powerfully built, and to have slept on the bare ground and shared the coarse food of his soldiers. He fought at the most dangerous points, showed great courage, and for a long time out-maneuvered experienced Roman commanders. In addition, he hated Rome, loved his country, and was modest and receptive to advice. These qualities earned the respect and loyalty of rich and poor, learned and simple, who flocked to his banner and served him obediently. Impressed by his personality, the aged Akiba was convinced that Simeon Bar Kochba would suc-cessfully defeat the Romans, restore Jewish independence, and speedily inaugurate the messianic era. Not all rabbis shared Akiba's beliefs or pious enthusiasm. To Akiba's assertions that Bar Kochba was the Messiah, Rabbi Yohanan ben Tortha retorted, "sooner shall grass grow from your chin before the Son of David (i.e., the Messiah) comes."[11] However, Yohanan and the other skeptics were few.

Although there is no record of any messianic miracles performed by Bar Kochba, extraordinary legends of his toughness and bravery abound. There is, for example, the fanciful tale of how he used to bounce ballistae stones back against the Romans with his knee; another story relates how, when recruiting his army, he compelled each volunteer to cut off a finger as evidence of loyalty. When about two hundred soldiers had been enrolled, the rabbis inquired how long he intended to maim the Jewish youth. His explanation that he was trying to prevent the entry of traitors into the army was accepted. Those recruits who refused to submit to this test had to prove they could uproot a cedar of Lebanon while riding a horse at full speed. Some legends ascribe to Bar Kochba certain undesirable traits: conceit and a penchant for blasphemy. He is supposed to have exclaimed once when going into battle, "Oh God! Neither help us nor disgrace us."[12] Most allusions in Jewish sources to Bar Kochba are ambivalent in nature. Admiration for his military prowess is combined with animosity toward a false messiah. Some talmudic references are particularly harsh in their judgment of the military leader, and refer to him as Bar-Kozivah, "son of deceit," a name clearly reflecting the disillusionment that followed his defeat at the hands of the Romans. Yet there is no evidence that he pursued any selfish end by his messianism; he seems to have been motivated solely by the desire to win back freedom for his people and to restore the tarnished glory of the Jewish state.

Details on the war itself, which lasted over three years, are lacking, as the Second Roman War had no chronicler of the stature of Flavius Josephus who left a vivid account of the first revolt. Narrative accounts are confined to a few brief references by Roman historians, and in the Talmud. References to the conflict also appear in the work of the church historian Eusebius (260–340? C.E.). However, there is no question that in the early phases of the war the Jewish forces enjoyed considerable success. Tinnius Rufus, the Roman governor of Judea, was caught off-guard by the rebellion and suffered a series of humiliating defeats. He was forced to withdraw from one citadel to another, and an entire legion (the 22nd) was trapped and annihilated. Bar Kochba also forced the Roman governor to evacuate the Tenth Legion, the troops that formed the garrison of Jerusalem. The Jews reoccupied the city, and gradually extended their control over the whole of Judea, Samaria, and the Galilee. In order to demonstrate and commemorate the achievement of national independence, Bar Kochba had new coins minted. The old ones had displayed on one side a Roman, and on the other side a Jew standing by a palm tree, his hands tied behind his back, and a weeping Jewess nearby. The triumphal coin issued by Bar Kochba displayed on one side his first name "Simeon," a star, and a representation of the entrance to the Temple which the Romans had destroyed. On the reverse side were the words "Year one of the Redemption"[13] and a representation of citron fruit and a palm tree.

Alarmed by developments in Judea, Rome reacted quickly. According to the early third-century historian Dio Cassius, fresh legions from Syria, Egypt, and Transjordan were dispatched to Judea. Julius Severus, then governor of Britain and Hadrian's best general, was given the task of crushing the rebellion and destroying the newly formed independent state. Severus, on arrival with additional troops from the Danube provinces, found the military position of the Jews so secure that he did not dare give them battle immediately. Instead he adopted a strategy which avoided costly seek and destroy engagements. The wily Roman general used the forces at his disposal to regain control of the country by cutting off and starving out one village after another, a tactic that eventually succeeded. It is estimated that in this manner Severus destroyed fifty fortresses and more than 1,000 villages, and in the process killed hundreds of thousands of Jews. Bar Kochba was steadily forced to give ground under the constant pressure of the Roman legions. With the loss of the border citadels and Jerusalem, Bar Kochba retreated with the remnant of his army into the fortress of Betar, a few miles south of the Jewish capital. The Romans built a siege wall around Betar, and in the summer of 135 C.E. they broke through the citadel's defenses and massacred the defenders and inhabitants of Betar. Jewish tradition has it that the event occurred on the ninth of Ab, the anniversary of the destruction of Jerusalem's first and second Temples.

The Jews paid heavily for Simeon Bar Kochba's effort to launch the messianic kingdom. Historians estimate that half a million lost their lives and many of the survivors were sold into slavery. Some were shipped to Rome, Gaza, and Egypt; and many succumbed to famine or shipwreck. Judea was nearly devastated. Rabbi Akiba and a number of other sages who had supported Bar Kochba were cruelly tortured and put to death. They later became hallowed prototypes of the Jewish martyr in liturgical poetry and medieval writings on this theme.

A vindictive Hadrian abolished the name of Judea with its potentially subversive overtones, and called the province Syria Palaestina (a reference to the land of the Philistines). Following old Roman custom a plow was drawn over the ruins of Jerusalem and the Temple mount, and the new city of Aelia Capitolina was built on the site and populated with Roman soldiers who had served their term of enlistment. Jews were forbidden to set foot in Aelia Capitolina or in the surrounding district. Additional edicts forbade Jews from practicing circumcision, observing the Sabbath, or following Jewish law.

Roman losses in the Second Roman War were also heavy and may account for the severity of Hadrian's decrees. Dio Cassius, the most important classical source on this even states that Hadrian in his message to the Roman Senate did not dare to employ the traditional formula, ". . . I and the army are well."[14] Bar Kochba had sustained his rebellion for three and one-half years; not since the days of Hannibal had any man defied for so long the armies of Rome.

Hadrian died in 138 C.E. and early in the reign of his successor Antonius Pius prohibitions on the practice and teaching of Judaism were dropped. The Bar Kochba defeat set the stage for a pacific and concilatory policy of the Jewish authorities toward the Romans and for the resumption of the rapid development of rabbinic Judaism. The center of Jewish intellectual life in the Roman Empire shifted to Galilee, still densely populated by Jewish farmers and townspeople. Nevertheless messianic thought persisted among Jewish rabbinical leaders as well as among the masses.

Moses of Crete

Early in the fifth century, hopes of the approach of the millennium once again gained ground. The expectation was supported by a prediction in the *Sibylline Oracles* (Hellenistic-Jewish literature written in Greek hexameter and designed to convert pagans to Judaism) that the Messiah would come between 440 and 470 C.E. Claimants appeared in various parts of the Jewish Diaspora. However, unlike Menahem or Bar Kochba the new pretenders were not cast in a heroic mold. Most were enthusiasts or charlatans who attempted to persuade their audiences that redemption was at hand. Moses of Crete (about 431 C.E.) was such an individual.[15] He promised to lead the Jews of Crete across a dry Mediterranean Sea back to the Promised Land, thus ending their exile from their ancient homeland. His message came at a time when Rome, beset by barbarian invasions, had experienced a rapid decline, and messianic fever was again running high.

For an entire year Moses of Crete (he had adopted the name of the great lawgiver; his real name is unknown) traversed the island persuading Jews that he was the Messiah.

Convinced by his persuasive oratory, the Jews of Crete neglected their daily pursuits, abandoned their property, and eagerly awaited the promised day of redemption. When the designated day arrived, Moses led the entire Jewish population of Crete onto a promontory overlooking the sea. He then ordered the faithful to fling themselves headlong into the waters below, assuring them that the waters would part, and that they would not suffer any injuries. Those who were at the head of the procession obeyed Moses' command and were dashed to death on the rocks below the precipice or drowned in the swirling waters. More would have perished but for the efforts of some fishermen and merchants who saved many Jews from the sea. Those rescued stopped others from plunging to their death. When the Jewish survivors came to their senses they sought to lay hold of their deceiver, but he was nowhere to be found. Moses of Crete had vanished without a trace.

Severus of Syria

In 640 c.e. a Jew from the village of Pallugia on the Euphrates announced that the Messiah had come. He collected a force of 400 men (mostly weavers and carpenters) who burned three Christian churches and killed the superintendent of the district. Troops brought in to quell the disturbance routed the band, and killed them and their wives and children. The false messiah was crucified.

A similar messianic role was adopted by Severus of Syria (also known as Serene, Serenus, or Zonaria).[16] About 720 c.e. he appeared in northern Mesopotamia. His timing was excellent, as a series of Muslim victories in the seventh century culminating in the siege of Constantinople in 717–18 c.e. provided a climate for an upsurge of messianic expectations.

Severus is described in some sources as an adventurer, a Syrian Christian who converted to Judaism. The chronicler Pseudo-Dionysis states that the conversion was not motivated by religious feelings. Nevertheless, Severus managed to attract a large following of Jews with the promise that he would bring about an imminent return to Zion. Although they freely gave to him their money, assets, and bodies, many of his followers were not certain whether Severus was the Messiah or only a messenger and forerunner of the Redeemer. However, all were convinced that he would somehow defeat the Muslims, and renew Israel's ancient glory.

Severus introduced ritual innovations contrary to talmudic law, which greatly upset the rabbinical authorities. According to a responsum of Natronai I, head of the Babylonian Talmudic Academy of Sura, Severus had urged his disciples to abandon talmudic Judaism, and to conform only to the precepts of the Bible. He had, for example, instructed them not to observe the prescribed forms of prayer, and encouraged celebrations of marriage without any need for a *ketubah* ("marriage contract"). Similarly, Severus saw no need for formal writs of divorce, and favored the abolishment of certain incest laws established by the rabbis. In addition, he advocated the abrogation of the Jewish laws pertaining to food, and the custom of abstaining from work on the second day of a festival.

Severus gained many supporters beyond the borders of Mesopotamia and Syria. His influence among Byzantine Jews, and the risk that they would affect the loyalty of his other subjects may have been the motivating factor for their persecution by the Emperor, Leo III. Spanish Jews, smarting from centuries of oppression together with general disappointment in Arab rule, were also eager to enlist under his banner. When reports of

Severus' activities reached the Iberian Peninsula, many Jews liquidated their affairs, and sailed east to become participants in the expected return to Zion.

In spite of his early successes, Severus' messianic career was shortlived. His financial exploitation of credulous adherents came to light, and he was unmasked and apprehended by Maslama, brother and active collaborator of the Caliph, Yazid ibn Abd al-Malik (720–24 C.E.). Closely questioned by the Caliph as to the nature of his messianic mission, Severus was unable to supply satisfactory answers. He is reported to have confided to the Muslim ruler that he had only intended to make game of the Jews, and that he had never entertained any designs against the regime. Released from prison after Maslama had confiscated all his property (other sources state that he was turned over to the Jewish establishment for punishment), Severus resumed his messianic preaching. Most of his followers had remained loyal to the pretender in spite of his exposure by the Muslim authorities. His activities continued into the reign of Caliph Hisham (724–43 C.E.) who put an end to the turmoil by executing Severus.

Following the death of their leader the majority of his followers applied for readmission into the Orthodox Jewish community. Their appeal was granted by the Gaon, Natronai I. However, the Spanish disciples of Severus who had left their homelands to join the pretender were not so fortunate. They had left behind in Spain their valuables and property. The Muslim rulers, provided with a splendid opportunity to augment their treasuries, confiscated the abandoned properties.

Severus had left neither a military nor a sectarian heritage. So disillusioned were those Jews who had blindly followed his lead that neither they nor those who had remained loyal to talmudic teaching made any effort to preserve for posterity his proposed reforms or even his name.

Abu Isa al-Isfahani and the Isawites

During the stormy period of the Umayyad—the Abbasid struggle for supremacy in the Islamic world of the eighth century—a new messianic figure arose among the Jews of Persia. Ishak ben Ya'kub Obadiah Abu Isa al-Isfahani[17] was of lowly origin, a tailor by profession, and probably illiterate (a claim disputed by the prominent nineteenth century German-Jewish historian Heinrich Graetz). Considerable disagreement between historians exists as to when Abu Isa al-Isfahani lived. The Karaite scholar Jacob al-Kirkisani in his *Book of Gardens and Parks* (938 C.E.) places him in the reign of the Umayyad Caliph, Abd al-Malik ibn Marwan (685–705 C.E.), while the Arab historian Shahrastani, states in his *Book of Religions and Sects* (1128 C.E.) that Abu Isa-Isfahani was active during the reign of the last Umayyad Caliph, Marwan II (744–49 C.E.), and well into the reign of the second Abbasid Caliph, Al Mansur (754–75 C.E.).

Abu Isa al-Isfahani did not claim to be the Messiah, but asserted that he was the forerunner and awakener of the Davidic Messiah. He taught that five harbingers had been destined to precede the coming of the Messiah, and that he was the last of the group (which included Abraham, Moses, Jesus, and Mohammed) and was the Messiah's herald, summoner, and prophet whom the Lord had sanctified. Tradition claims that Abu Isa al-Isfahani was made aware of his call by being suddenly cured of leprosy, and that in colloquy with God he was entrusted with the mission of freeing the Jewish people from the yoke of exile, and making them once again politically independent.

The self-styled messianic messenger found many followers among the Jews of Persia. In a rather short time he succeeded in establishing a new sect, the members of which were called after their leader Isawites (or Isunians, Iswanites, Isfahanites). Although the practices and ideology of the sect cannot be determined in detail, it is known that they followed an unusual form of Judaism. Abu Isa al-Isfahani, for example, insisted that his followers abstain from meat and wine and that they pray seven times a day. He cited the verse of the psalm, "Seven times a day do I praise Thee"[18] in support of the prayer. In addition, he abolished all grounds for divorce (even in cases involving adultery). His recognition of Jesus and Mohammed as legitimate prophets to the Gentile nations, on the other hand, may have been dictated by a practical assessment of his situation, for had he not recognized these religious figures he would have immediately encountered dangerous opposition (particularly from the Muslims). Curiously, in spite of his religious innovations, the Orthodox rabbinate did not consider them a serious enough threat to put Abu Isa al-Isfahani or his adherents under a ban.

Although there is no hard evidence that Abu Isa considered himself as anything more than a herald of the Messiah, there is little doubt that his followers believed that he was the Messiah. Indeed, the latter believed that he composed books under divine inspiration (even though by most accounts he could not read or write). In fact, there is no record of any literary legacy that can be ascribed to Abu Isa al-Isfahani.

As the Isawites grew in numbers, their leader threw caution to the wind and raised the standard of revolt against the Caliph. His goal was nothing less than the liberation of the Jews of Persia and the resurrection of a Jewish state in the Land of Israel. The moment seemed favorable for an attempt to gain freedom. Throughout the Islamic empire the spirit of rebellion was alive, fostered by dynastic disputes and ambitious men. Abu Isa and his army, estimated as 10,000 strong, began their campaign in the vicinity of Isfahan. After much skirmishing a decisive battle was fought at Rai (ancient Rhagae), and the Jewish forces were routed and dispersed. Abu Isa was killed in the engagement, but his followers refused to believe that he was dead. Some maintained that when Abu Isa witnessed the tide of battle turning against him, he entered a nearby cave and disappeared. The Isawites were convinced that he would reappear at a more propitious time to resume the struggle. This mystic fancy in many ways complemented Jewish folklore about events surrounding the coming of the Davidic Messiah, as well as the Christian account of the death and resurrection of Jesus, and the Muslim sectarian teachings of the concealed and ever reappearing Mahdi. According to another legend, during the height of the battle with the Muslims, Abu Isa encircled his camp with a rope, and assured his men that they would be safe as long as they remained within the enclosed area. In a slightly different version Abu Isa placed his followers in a circle which he drew with a myrtle branch. The Muslim army could not break through the circle and were forced to retreat. Abu Isa then rode out and single-handedly dealt the enemy a mighty blow, thereby achieving a miraculous victory. Afterwards he supposedly went into the desert to announce the word of the Lord (i.e., his prophetic mission) to the Bene Moshe, the mythical Jews who were reputed to be descendants of Moses, before withdrawing to a mountain cave from which he would stage a comeback at some later date.

The Yudghanites and Other Persian Sects

Shortly after the Muslim victory at Rai, a disciple of Abu Isa named Yudghan[19] formed a new sect from the surviving Isawites. A native of the Persian highlands around Hamadan,

Yudghan was more prudent than his predecessor. He did not openly claim to have been selected by God to liberate the Jews, but instead assumed the role of a prophet and teacher (to emphasize his calling he adopted the surname al-Ra'i [the Shepherd]. In spite of these precautionary measures, most of Yudghan's followers considered him to be the Messiah or a forerunner of the expected liberator.

Yudghan was deeply influenced by the doctrine of Sufism, which at that time was making great inroads in the Islamic world. Thus he set aside the literal meaning of the Torah in favor of a more mystical or spiritual interpretation. Like the Sufis he taught that all religious beliefs relating to paradise or hell were allegories. Yudghan, however, rejected the Sufi concept of predestination, and stressed instead that man was absolutely free in the choice of good and evil, and therefore responsible for his actions. He also believed that man should not represent God with material attributes (i.e. anthropomorphically).

The Yudghanites attached great importance to praying and fasting, which they considered more important than the observance of ceremonial law. They also believed that the laws concerning the Sabbath and the festivals were not binding in the Diaspora, but nevertheless should be observed as a reminder of the ancient Jewish homeland (Judea).

As in the case of Abu Isa al-Isfahani the Yudghanites maintained their faith in their prophet long after his demise. They also insisted that Yudghan had not really died, and that he would eventually reappear. When Yudghan, like Abu Isa, failed to materialize, a new leader arose to take his place. His name was Mushka, and building on the following of Yudghan he founded a sect called "al-Mushkaniyyah."[20] Its tenets were identical to those of the Yudghanites except for one major addition, an injunction to forcibly impose their ideology upon all Jews. In an attempt to carry out this policy Mushka and a handful of his supporters marched out of their base in Hamadan to begin their campaign among the Jews. Although the fate of this band is not clear it is believed by historians that they were massacred by the Muslims in the vicinity of Koom, an Arab garrison city southwest of Teheran. The influence of the Isawites, Yudghanites and al-Mushkaniyyah persisted until the tenth century, especially in such cities as Isfahan, Hamadan and Damascus. The doctrines of these sects also played an important role in the thought of Anan ben David (second half of the eighth century) the founder of the Karaite sect which would provide rabbinical Judaism with its greatest challenge and schism.[21] The Karaites rejected the Talmud and insisted that Jewish law should adhere as literally as possible to the Bible.

In retrospect, the Jews of these centuries regarded the successes of Islam as the first indication since the fall of Rome that the messianic kingdom would be realized. They believed that Islam would relieve them of oppression in Christian countries and in Persia. When this hope failed they attempted, as we have noted, on several occasions to rid themselves of the new oppressor, Islam. Disappointed by the defeats of the would-be Messiahs they voiced the conviction that the power of the Roman Empire would be revived and that Rome would vanquish Islam. The Jewish apocalypse work, the *History of Daniel*, written probably in the first half of the ninth century (although some historians believe it dates back to the early Hellenistic period) predicts the victory of a Roman ruler over Islam. Then, according to the *History of Daniel*, there would arise a false Messiah who, when asked to perform miracles, would fail. Later the archangels Michael and Gabriel would appear to the Israelites in the desert, along with Elijah and the Messiah ben David who would slay the false Messiah with the breath of his mouth. The dead would then rise, and the Israelites would be gathered together from the four quarters of the earth bringing the exile to an end. The ensuing period of rejoicing and domination would last for 1,000 years.

2

Revival of Messianism

The struggle between the Crescent and the Cross (the Crusades) stimulated messianic movements among the Jews. Both in Christian and Muslim lands Jews looked forward to the coming of the Messiah, and a return to the Promised Land. In 1096, in the midst of the First Crusade, a powerful messianic movement arose among German Jews, who had long looked toward that year as the time of deliverance. Thousands set out for the Holy Land by way of the Byzantine Empire, firmly believing that beyond the dark mountains in the East the lost ten tribes were waiting to unite with their brethren from the West. From the Byzantine Empire emanated reports that 17 Jewish congregations, defying the dangers of the Syrian desert, were traveling to Palestine. A Messiah appeared in France about 1087, another in Cordova in 1177, and at Fez in 1127. In his work *Sefer ha-Kuzari* ("the Book of the Khazars") Judah Halevi, the "sweet singer of Zion" declared Christianity and Islam were the preparation and preface to the expected Messiah, and that all men would be the fruit of God's seed when they acknowledged Him, and all would then become one mighty tree (c. 1141).

The conquest of Palestine and the establishment there of a Latin kingdom by the Christian crusaders and the massacres, persecutions, and oppressive taxation that followed this event were interpreted by the Jews of the East as the pangs heralding the advent of the Messiah. These feelings were heightened considerably in the period immediately preceding the Second Crusade (1146–47). The Muslim caliphate, failing to oust the crusaders, was showing signs of disintegration and this afforded an opportunity for adventurous souls to stir up the restive masses. Everywhere in the Muslim world local leaders arose who took advantage of the weakening of authority to set up independent entities in defiance of their paramount rulers. The anarchy and turmoil associated with these events provided a fertile breeding ground for self-proclaimed prophets and messianic pretenders.

David Alroy

Most celebrated of the Jewish false Messiahs of this period was David Alroy[22] whose life was dramatized centuries later in a novel by Lord Beaconsfield (Disraeli).[23] Alroy was born in Amadiya (date uncertain), east of Mosul (modern Iraq). His real name seems to have been Menahem ben Sulayman ibn Abruhi. Menahem in the Hebrew language means "the comforter", and has messianic implications; Alroy may mean "the inspired one", but more likely is an Arabic corruption of the family name Abruhi. The name David was obviously appropriated to bolster Alroy's messianic claims.

Although there is a lack of hard historical evidence, the generally accepted belief is that the movement that Alroy was destined to lead began before the year 1121 among the warlike mountain Jews of northeast Caucasia (and lasted until 1147, or perhaps even beyond that year). Some historians (e.g., Cecil Roth) believe it was triggered off by an invasion of nomadic Kipchaks from the steppes of the Black Sea.[24] The first leader of this Jewish messianic movement was Alroy's father Sulayman (Solomon) who declared that he was the prophet Elijah. He was assisted in his pretensions by Ephraim ben Azariah, "the Jerusalemite", a scribe who had emigrated from Palestine. In time, Sulayman's son, a youth possessing great charm and a handsome appearance, took over the leadership of the group from his father. He was also a talented and scholarly individual who had excelled in his studies under the Exilarch, Hisdai, and Ali, the head of the Talmudic Academy in Baghdad. In addition, David Alroy was skilled in magic, and thoroughly familiar with Muslim literature and customs, as well as learned in talmudic law and Jewish mysticism.

Confident of his destiny, Alroy called upon the oppressed Jews to regard him as the long-awaited Messiah, and raised the banner of revolt against the Seljuk Sultan, Muktafi. He promised to lead his brethren to victory and to Jerusalem. Alroy's appeal to wage war against the Muslims went out to all the major Jewish communities of the region, including Baghdad and Mosul and even reached the remote provinces of Persia. However, before his movement could gain momentum it was suppressed by the Muslims, and Alroy was forced to flee to the mountains of Kurdistan. At the same time he tried to gain a firm foothold in his native city of Amadiya. Amadiya's strategic importance as a Muslim springboard for operations against the Crusader kingdom had also been recognized by Zanzi, the ruler of Mosul, who had taken steps to strengthen its fortifications. Alroy was determined to capture the citadel of Amadiya. If successful, he planned to attack and conquer Edessa. From there, taking full advantage of the ongoing hostilities between the resuscitated Muslim armies and the slowly disintegrating powers of the Crusader principalities, Alroy hoped to proceed to Palestine and to capture Jerusalem.

Alroy knew that the Muslim inhabitants of Amadiya feared him because they were convinced he was a sorcerer who possessed great magical powers. He was also aware that he could expect encouragement, if not actual support, from a group of Muslim sectarians (the Yezedis), who also desired to control the city. With these factors in mind Alroy conceived a plan to take the city by surprise. He instructed his supporters to assemble on a given day in Amadiya, with weapons concealed in their garments. If questioned by the authorities, they were to give as a pretext for their presence in the city that they had come to study Talmud at the feet of the distinguished master, David Alroy.

What followed next is unclear as the two chief sources on the life of Alroy, one by the traveler Benjamin of Tudela, and the other by a contemporary, Samuel ibn Abbas, a Jewish physician and mathematician who had converted to Islam, are contradictory and interwoven with legendary material. The legends are fascinating and probably contain some kernels of historical truth. Benjamin of Tudela relates in his *Sefer ha-Massa'ot* ("Book of Travels")[25] that when the news of Alroy's planned revolt reached the ears of the sultan, the Jewish leader was summoned to appear before the Muslim potentate. When he complied, the sultan asked, "Are you the King of the Jews?" and "Do you believe that God wants you to take Jerusalem from us and lead your people there?" Alroy answered both questions in the affirmative and the sultan had him imprisoned in Tabaristan (Azerbaijan). Three days later, while the sultan and his advisors were deliberating the fate of Alroy and his followers, the psuedo-Messiah suddenly appeared in their midst, having miraculously escaped from prison. The sultan immediately ordered his soldiers to seize him, but Alroy, employing his magical skills, became invisible and left the council chamber. Guided by the voice of Alroy, the sultan and his men followed him out of the palace to the banks of a nearby river. Here the wizard made himself visible again, and was seen to cross the water on a shawl to make good his escape. On the same day he returned to Amadiya, a journey which ordinarily took 10 days from Tabaristan, and appeared before his followers to relate to them what had transpired in the sultan's court.

Meanwhile, the sultan, in his anger over the conjurer's escape threatened to put all the Jews in his domain to the sword if David Alroy was not delivered into his hands. The Jewish authorities, fearing a massacre, attempted without success to induce Alroy to abandon his messianic pretensions and to submit to the Muslim ruler. Finally, the governor of Amadiya, Sayf al-Din, bribed Alroy's father-in-law to kill the so-called Messiah of the Jews. The dastardly deed was carried out while Alroy slept, bringing to an end the revolt against the Muslims.[26] A vindictive sultan, still unappeased, decreed a persecution of the Jews of those provinces which had supported Alroy. In an effort to deflect the decree and placate the sultan's wrath the Jewish exilarch presented the Muslim ruler with a gift of 100 talents of gold.

The account of Alroy's career by Samuel ibn Abbas is equally interesting. Full of zeal for Islam, Samuel wrote a scathing attack of Judaism (about 1169) and included in his work a satirical description of the messianic agitation for the sole purpose of poking fun at the gullible Jews.[27] Biased though this account is, there are historical nuggets interspersed among his anti-Jewish diatribe. He recounts basically the same tale as Benjamin of Tudela of the origins of the messianic movement, the character of its leader, the plan to capture Amadiya, and Alroy's death (which he believes occurred at the hands of the Muslim commander of the Amadiya citadel).

Samuel ibn Abbas also notes that the death of David Alroy did not completely dampen the enthusiasm of his followers, or their belief that he was the Messiah. Many Jews, especially in the province of Azerbaijan, continued to revere his memory, and to invoke his name in the most holy of oaths. Like earlier groups they were convinced that David Alroy would reappear to lead them once again.

Samuel ibn Abbas also relates that at the time that Alroy was making his plans to seize Amadiya, two crafty individuals claiming to be his messengers arrived in Baghdad. They carried forged letters bearing Alroy's name, which stated that redemption was at hand, and specified the date and time when the great event would occur.[28] In addition, the letters instructed the Jews that on the appointed date the Jews were to put on green garments (the Moslem symbol of resurrection and of God's mercy) and assemble on their rooftops. They were then to await the angels who would convey them on their wings from Baghdad to Jerusalem (probably a reference to the messianic hope expressed in Isaiah 60:8 "who are those that fly as a cloud").[29] To hasten the expected miracle, many Jews gave the two imposters their money, jewelry, and other valuables, so that they might distribute this wealth to the needy – an act of charity intended to ensure the coming of the messianic age. The denouement of this cunning scheme can be imagined. On the prescribed night for the flight to Jerusalem, the Baghdad Jews followed the instructions indicated in the forged letters and waited in eager expectation on their rooftops for the arrival of the angels. At dawn they realized that they had been duped. Meanwhile, the messengers to whom they had entrusted their money and other valuables had decamped and were nowhere to be found. Samuel ibn Abbas concludes his account by mocking the credulity of the Baghdad Jews, and notes how it made them the laughing stock of both the Muslims and the Christians. He adds that the people of Baghdad referred to this incredible affair as "the year of flying,"[30] and thereafter reckoned time from it.

Abraham Abulafia

A century after the downfall of David Alroy a remarkable eccentric and self appointed liberator of the Jews arose in Spain. His name was Abraham ben Samuel Abulafia (1240–91),[31] a member of a large and influential family that had produced rabbis, poets, statesmen, and scholars. Born in Saragossa (Aragon) he was taken as a child to Tudela, in the province of Navarre, where he received his early education. Abulafia's father taught his son the Bible and its commentaries, as well as some Talmud and grammar. Two years after his father's death, Abraham Abulafia began a lifetime of wandering. His first journey took him to Palestine where he hoped to find the legendary river of Sambatyon on whose banks the remnants of the lost ten tribes of Israel were said to live. Hampered by the desolation wrought by the Crusaders and Muslims, he was able to get no further than Acre. Returning to Europe, he went to Greece where he lingered long enough to get married. Ever restless he moved on to Capua, Italy where he undertook with a passionate zeal the study of philosophy. Under the tutelage of the philosopher and physician Hillel ben Samuel ben Eliezer of Verona, Abulafia delved deeply into the work of Maimonides, especially the great opus, *Guide to the Perplexed*.[32] At this time he was introduced to the Jewish mystical tradition (the Kabbalah) by Baruch Togarini, the author of a commentary on the *Sefer Yetzirah* ("Book of Creation").[33]

About 1270 Abulafia returned to Spain and immersed himself in mystical studies. In Barcelona, during a session of intensive examination of the *Sefer Yetzirah* and its commentaries, he was overcome by a prophetic spirit. He had visions that he believed were sent by demons to confuse him, and would later note that he had "groped about like a blind man at midday for fifteen years with Satan to his right."[34] Entirely convinced of the truth behind his mystic experiences and of his newly acquired prophetic knowledge, Abulafia at age thirty-one began to teach his views to a small circle of disciples.

Abulafia's teachings formed the basis for a new school of mysticism that had as its chief objective the attainment of the spirit of prophecy. He called it "prophetic Kabbalah" to distinguish it from other Jewish schools of mysticism. Abulafia's system stressed the need to "unseal the soul" through intensive contemplation with the aim of achieving spiritual ecstasy. The main object to be contemplated was the Hebrew alphabet, especially the letters that constituted the secret names of God. Abulafia called this science of letter combinations *hokhmat ha-tzeruf,* and it included such methods as *gematria* (the symbolic employment of letters as numbers), *notarikon* (regarding each letter in a word as the initial letter of some other word, and so making it an acrostic), *temurah* (substitution of one letter for another), and *tzeruf* (connecting various letters of the same word). Although Abulafia claimed to have derived his system from the famous Spanish rabbi, Moses ben Nachman (Nahmanides), he was probably also influenced by the work of the German kabbalistic school of Eleazer of Worms and his successors. By the proper use of *hokhmat ha-tzeruf* and by the observance of certain rites and ascetic practices, Abulafia was convinced one could reach the highest degree of perception (i.e., become a prophet). Such an accomplishment would make it possible to draw closer to the Deity, and better understand the riddles of nature and the problems of human life.

Abulafia's ecstatic trend, a strange amalgam of emotionalism and rationalism, would later play an important role in influencing the sixteenth-century kabbalists centered in Safed, Palestine. Baffling as it may at first seem, the Spanish-born mystic regarded his ideas as a logical continuation to Maimonides' *Guide to the Perplexed,* which he deeply admired, and for which he wrote a mystical commentary. The affinity of Abulafia the mystic to Maimonides the great rationalist of the Middle Ages has its astounding parallel in the relationship of the Christian mystic Meister Eckhart to Maimonides. Certain points of contact can also be found between Abulafia's thoughts and the doctrine of the Moslem Sufis.

In 1273 Abulafia left Spain for the last time to wander through southern Europe (Italy, Sicily, and Greece). While living in Patras, Greece, he wrote the first of his prophetic books. A prolific writer, he would in the course of his lifetime produce twenty-six kabbalistic tracts and twenty-two prophetic works.

In 1279 or 1280 Abraham Abulafia published a book in Sicily predicting that the messianic era would begin in 1290. Many Jews believed his prognostication and made preparations for the return to Eretz Israel. However some of Abulafia's opponents, alarmed by this turn of affairs, decided on drastic action to silence him. They appealed to the most influential rabbinical authority of the day, Solomon ben Abraham Adret of Barcelona (Rashba), and accused Abulafia of being a false prophet with messianic pretensions. Adret addressed a letter to the Palermo Jewish community in which he viciously condemned the mystic's conduct. Fearing persecution Abulafia was compelled to take up the pilgrim's staff. He left Sicily and took up residence on the desolate island of Comino, near Malta (about 1288), where he continued to produce mystic tracts on esoteric subjects.

Undaunted by his lack of success as a prophet, Abulafia decided on a dangerous mission. In 1290, urged on by an inner voice, he went to Rome to present himself before Pope Nicholas II, and to call the pontiff to account for the suffering of the Jews throughout Christendom. Many historians believe that Abulafia intended to convert Nicholas II to Judaism on the day before the Jewish New Year 5041.[35] Indeed, Gershom Scholem, the outstanding authority on Jewish mysticism, was of the opinion that Abulafia's action was definitely the result of his messianic persona. He surmises that the mystic may have been influenced by a popular and widely circulated booklet dealing with the disputation between Rabbi Moses ben Nahman and the apostate Pablo Christiani in the year 1263. In this publication Moses ben Nahman states, ". . . when the time of the end will have come, the Messiah will at God's command come to the Pope and ask of him the liberation of his people, and only then will the Messiah be considered really to have come, but not before that. . . ."[36]

After being informed about Abulafia's mission, the Pope refused to grant him an audience and ordered that on his arrival he was to be arrested and taken out of Rome to be burned at the stake. Although aware of what was in store for him, Abulafia did not attempt to escape. While passing through the outer gate of Suriano he learned that the Pope had died of an apoplectic stroke during the preceding night. On entering Rome, Abulafia was arrested and held in the College of the Franciscan Minorites. After languishing twenty-eight days in prison he was released. Abulafia credited his miraculous deliverance to God who as he expressed it, ". . . had caused a double mouth (or tongue) to grow in him."[37] This rather obscure remark may refer to Abulafia's deft recourse to mystifying language when questioned by his captors. In 1291 Abulafia wrote his last work, *Imre Shefer* ("Words of Beauty"). Nothing more is known of his life after this date.

Asher Lämmlein (the Lamb)

The expulsion of the Jews from the Iberian Peninsula at the close of the fifteenth century brought to a close one of the most cultured and creative of all Jewish communities. Two centuries earlier (1290), England had expelled her Jews, and in 1394 France had followed suit, thus ushering in for most of Western European Jewry a period of stagnation. For the Jews of Central Europe the First Crusade (1096) had been the turning point in history, entailing a condition of constant deterioration, so that by the close of the Middle Ages they were left with insecurity of residence and a stunted inner life. The one exception to this dire picture of Jewish communal disintegration was in Italy, where Jews had continued their long tradition of interaction with the larger world well into the sixteenth century and beyond. Under the stimulating atmosphere of the Renaissance, this Jewish community, among the oldest in Europe, had produced a remarkable legacy of literary and scholarly works.

Even in Italy, the opening years of the sixteenth century were marked by a feeling of uneasiness on the part of the Jewish community. Like their coreligionists everywhere, the Italian Jews yearned for an explanation of the tragedy that had befallen their Spanish and Portuguese brethren. They sought an interpretation that might invest what had transpired on the Iberian Peninsula with deeper significance. Since neither rabbinic tradition or rationalist philosophy seemed to be able to supply an answer, many Italian Jews turned to mysticism to fill the gap.

In 1502 a German Jew named Asher Lämmlein (the Lamb)[38] appeared in Istria, near Venice, and proclaimed to a receptive audience that he was the forerunner of the Messiah. He added that if the Jews immediately adopted a strict program of repentance and mortification the Messiah would appear within six months' time. No one knew where Lämmlein had come from, and history has left us in the dark as to his life before his mysterious manifestation in Istria. It is clear, however, that his prophetic call attracted many followers and stimulated an ascetic movement.

Shortly after Lämmlein's initial pronouncement, the rumor spread that the Messiah had already come, and that the expected savior was none other than the prophet himself. Lämmlein did nothing to discourage these reports. Instead, he traveled to Austria and Germany to preach his message that redemption was imminent. In both countries "the Lamb" was well received. Invariably, his appearances were followed by fasting, alms giving, and a heightened desire to begin the long journey to Eretz Israel. Jewish audiences were so swayed by Lämmlein's messianic utterances that the year of his manifestation in Italy became known as "the year of penitence." As 1502 approached its end, the messianic ferment among the Jews intensified. Many Jewish communities completed their preparations for "aliyah" to Eretz Israel. The chronicler David Gans (1541–1613) relates how his grandfather was so moved by Lämmlein's promises of redemption that he demolished an oven for the baking of unleavened bread, firmly believing that he had no further need for it since he expected to celebrate the next Passover in the Promised Land.[39] Those Jews not taken in by the false messiah did not dare to check the fanaticism of "the Lamb's" followers. Many Christians were also swept up by the enthusiasm which had taken hold of the Jews. At the height of this mass hysteria, as the date for the promised redemption approached, the instigator of the messianic convulsion, Asher Lämmlein, vanished. With his disappearance, disillusion set in and the agitation came to an end. Some historians speculate that Lämmlein had not deserted his followers, but had suddenly died.

3

David Reubeni
and Solomon Molcho

In the two-and-one-half centuries between the last of the crusades and the beginning of the Reformation, a profound, if gradual, transformation occurred in the character of European civilization. This period was an age of transition in which medieval institutions were crumbling. However, in spite of the explosive forces released by the growth of humanism and nationalism, and the new vistas opened up by the Renaissance propelling man to escape the bondage of ecclesiastical authority and corporate society, vestiges of the old medieval outlook toward one group in Europe, the Jews, remained basically unchanged.

Exclusions, expulsions, and persecutions of the Jews had increased markedly during the declining years of the fifteenth century and had engendered among the Jews a passionate longing for the fulfillment of the ancient predictions of redemption and a return to the Land of Israel. A generation after the disappearance of Asher Lämmlein many Jews still remained convinced that the time of the Messiah was approaching, and with his arrival, an end of suffering and the exile. This vision of a savior continued to inspire rabbis, preachers, laymen, and bold adventurers. Amid this general expectation there appeared in Italy, in the second decade of the sixteenth century, a mysterious figure with a story that fanned the embers of messianism into blazing flames.

He called himself David Reubeni,[40] and claimed that his elder brother was King Joseph, the ruler of the biblical lost tribes of Gad, half Manasseh, and Reuben (hence David's surname). Joseph's kingdom was supposedly located in the desert of Khaybar in the Arabian peninsula. His mission, he declared, was to convince the papacy and the powerful Christian states of Europe of the benefits they could derive from the formation of a military alliance with his brother's kingdom against the common enemy, the Muslims (notably the Ottoman Empire). Through this cooperation with the Christians, Reubeni believed the Jews would be able to reestablish a Jewish state in Palestine.

If his diary[41] is to be believed, Reubeni traveled widely in the East prior to his appearance in Europe (in disguise to Jeddah on the Red Sea, then across to Ethiopia, and to the Sudan and Egypt). At one point along this perilous journey he was captured and sold as a slave to Arabs who brought him to Alexandria where he was ransomed by fellow Jews. From Egypt, Reubeni made his way to Jerusalem and Safed where he secretly met with Jewish community leaders and informed them of his mission. After carrying his message to Damascus he returned to Alexandria, and after a brief stay embarked for Italy.

In the autumn of 1523 Reubeni arrived in Venice. Contemporary accounts describe him as about 40 years old, and carrying himself in a regal manner that admitted no familiarity. He was of swarthy complexion and of exceedingly short stature. Although very thin (perhaps as a result of constant fasting), he was wiry, an expert horseman, and courageous to the point of being fearless. Some historians believe that Reubeni may have been a Falasha Jew, or an Indian Jew from Cranganore.[42] Other scholars stress that Reubeni's diary, written in corrupt Hebrew, abounds in Germanisms, thus precluding the claim that his origins were in the East.[43]

Most of the Venetian Jews doubted Reubeni's story, but he found support among a few community notables. Partly through these contacts he was able to continue his journey, and carry his mission to Rome. In 1524, accompanied by a servant and an interpreter, David Reubeni ostentatiously entered the Eternal City riding on a white horse. He received an audience with the humanist Cardinal, Egidio da Viterbo, a student of Jewish lore (especially of Kabbalah). The prelate, who understood Hebrew, displayed great interest in Reubeni's proposals and introduced him to other high ranking officials of the church. The attention lavished upon the "Jewish ambassador" by the Christian clerics enhanced his status among the Jews of Rome. Representatives of the Jewish community, among them Obadiah Sforno and the physician Judah Ascoli, visited him. Particularly impressed was one of community's most powerful personages, Samuel Abrabanel, the son of the former leader of Spanish Jewry, and the head of a banking house with strong ties to the debt-ridden papacy. Of even greater import for Reubeni, Cardinal Egidio da Viterbo managed to procure for him an audience with the Pope.

Clement VII was an unusual pontiff. The illegitimate scion of the Florentine Medicis, he dreamed of liberating Italy from the "barbarians," the Germans. He reigned at a time when Europe was experiencing traumatic political and religious changes. The Protestant Reformation threatened to undermine the papacy; and on the other hand the Pope's enemy, the Holy Roman Emperor, Charles V, ruler of Germany, Burgundy, and Spain had about crushed Italy into servile dependency (his German troops would sack Rome in 1527). If this was not enough, the Ottoman Turks had recently conquered two bulwarks of Christendom, Belgrade in 1521, and Rhodes in 1522, and were threatening Hungary and Austria. Clement VII's hopes of recouping the territory lost to the Muslims was rapidly fading. Eager to find a way out of these dilemmas, the Pope was willing to listen to any proposal—even from a strange-looking Jew who had emerged from obscurity with a scheme that might resolve his problems.

During Reubeni's audience with the Pope he presented the pontiff with letters of introduction from his imaginary brother, the king of the lost Jewish tribes, and from Portuguese captains and business agents. The latter credentials Clement VII sent to the Portuguese court and when they were declared trustworthy, Reubeni was treated with the greatest distinction and accorded all the honors due an ambassador.

He proposed to the Pope a grand military alliance between his brother's kingdom and allies and the Christian world to be directed against the Muslims, particularly the Ottoman Turks. If the Christian powers agreed to the pact and supplied Reubeni with weapons and military specialists (cannon founders and gunsmiths), then he, as commander-in-chief of his brother's army, would lead 300,000 Jewish warriors against the common enemy. The Jewish envoy's plan envisioned an assault against Mecca and Egypt, and a campaign to drive the Turks out of the Holy Land. The Portuguese and Venetian fleets would supply the allied force, and support operations by sweeping the seas of Muslim shipping. Simultaneously, the Hapsburg forces would keep the Turks occupied by invading their Balkan provinces. It was a bold and daring scheme conceived in the best spirit of the Renaissance. Reubeni concluded his discussions with the Pope by requesting from him letters to various European rulers entreating their help in carrying out his "grand design."

However, not everyone at the Vatican favored Reubeni's talks with the Pope. Portugal's ambassador to Rome could not have been more displeased with the timing of the Jew's visit. He had received a bribe to obtain a papal bull to authorize the Inquisition in Portugal. The ambassador feared that the pontiff would consider it more important to prevent the Mediterranean and Black Seas from becoming Turkish lakes and therefore support Reubeni's plan. Clement VII, however, was uncertain what action to take. Finally, after almost a year had gone by, he furnished Reubeni with two letters of introduction—one to the legendary Ethiopian ruler "Prester John," and the other to King John III of Portugal.

During the hiatus caused by the Pope's vacillation, Reubeni had strengthened his ties with Italian Jewry. Even the most skeptic Jew could not help but notice the attentions and honors bestowed on the Jewish envoy by the Vatican. Soon his coreligionists began to take him more seriously, and he was showered with costly gifts and money. Reubeni, who seems to have possessed a keen sense of the theatrical, played his part in a masterly manner. He rode through the streets of Rome, usually mounted on a mule, and always accompanied by an escort of ten Jews, and often by a crowd of 200 or more Christians.[44]

In 1525 Reubeni received a formal invitation from King John III of Portugal to visit his court in Lisbon. The wife of Samuel Abrabanel, and the wealthy family of Jehiel of Pisa supplied him with the means for his voyage to Portugal. The galleon they provided, as a tribute to Reubeni, flew the flags of the ancient tribes of Israel. The Jewish envoy was received by the Portuguese with ambassadorial honors and with great respect. In the ensuing discussions with the Portuguese considerable thought was given to the logistics involved in transporting munitions and weapons to the East. The very presence of Reubeni in Portugal forced John III to temporarily halt the persecution of the country's Marranos (forcibly converted Jews who secretly maintained Jewish beliefs and rituals).

The Marranos, astonished by the king's sudden change in attitude toward them, hailed David Reubeni as their "deliverer." They flocked to see him and to kiss his hand. They swelled with pride when they heard that Reubeni had told an envoy of the sultan of Fez that the time had come for the Jews to wrest control of the Holy Land from the Ishmaelites. The feeling that redemption was imminent spread rapidly among the Marranos of Portugal even though Reubeni made no moves to encourage such sentiments. Nevertheless, a few individuals among the Nuevos Cristianos (New Christians, also known as "Conversos," i.e., Jews who had converted to Catholicism voluntarily or because of expediency) made the decision to abandon Christianity and return to the faith of their ancestors. Among the latter was a highly imaginative and talented youth named Diogo Pires (1500–32),[45] whose path was destined to cross that of David Reubeni several times and who would share the envoy's final adventures.

Pires, who was born into a New Christian family, had acquired a good education and had risen to be a royal secretary in one of the high courts of justice in Lisbon. During the highly charged atmosphere created by Reubeni's negotiations with the Portuguese king, the impressionable Pires underwent a deep religious experience and decided to return to the faith of his forefathers. Embarking on a strict regimen of ascetic exercises, the young man began to have mystic visions tinged with messianic overtones. Alarmed, Pires approached Reubeni to ascertain whether the latter's mission tallied with his visionary revelations. Sensitive to the danger posed by Pires' religious confession, Reubeni warily and rather cooly informed the excitable youth that his mission had nothing to do with messianic prophecies. Believing that Reubeni's aloofness was due to the fact that he had not yet accepted the sign of the covenant, Pires had himself circumcised. He completed his conversion to Judaism by changing his name to Solomon Molcho (a surname derived from *melech,* the Hebrew word for king). Molcho now intensified his ascetic practices, and his visions became more frequent and pronounced. According to his own account, Molcho spoke in his visions to a heavenly messenger (a *Maggid*),[46] who charged him to leave Portugal. Reubeni, fearing that Molcho's acceptance of Judaism would wreck his own plans as well as endanger his stay in Portugal, encouraged the former royal secretary to abandon his native land.

Forsaking Lisbon, Molcho began an odyssey that took him to various parts of the Ottoman Empire. Wherever he wandered his captivating personality, good looks, eloquent speech, romantic disposition and religious fervor gained him new friends and followers. Many Jews believed he was an emissary of David Reubeni. In Salonica, Molcho studied with and made a deep impression on the city's kabbalistic circle, led by Rabbi Joseph Taytazak. This group of mystics included among its members Joseph ben Ephraim Karo (1488–1575) who was later to win fame as the author of the standard code of rabbinic law and practice known as the *Shulhan Arukh* ("The Prepared Table"). As a result of his kabbalistic studies, Molcho became convinced that the arrival of the Messiah was at hand and that his reign would begin in the year 1540.

In 1529, after traveling and preaching in Palestine (mostly in Jerusalem and Safed), Molcho suddenly appeared in the Italian city of Ancona. His fiery sermons in the synagogues of the city attracted large numbers of Jews and Christians. Molcho's words and deeds seemed to suggest that he regarded himself as either the Messiah or his precursor. This development became more evident when Molcho left Ancona for Rome. Dressed in dirty, tattered clothes, he sat at the gates of the city opposite the Pope's palace among the beggars and the maimed for thirty days. By this bizarre behavior, he seemed to be reenacting a talmudic legend relating to the conduct of the Messiah before his final triumph.[47] Emboldened by his continuing visions and new confidence, the impetuous mystic began to preach in public, and soon gained the ear and favor of Pope Clement VII. He predicted before the pontiff and his court that Rome and Flanders would soon be inundated by floods, and that Lisbon would suffer a severe earthquake. The Pope was deeply impressed by the young prophet and provided him sanctuary in his palace, and thus shielded him from the prying eyes of the Inquisition.

As the date forecast by Molcho for the natural disasters approached, he slipped out of Rome and traveled to Venice. Here he encountered Reubeni who was still pursuing his mission. Much had transpired since their first meeting. Molcho no longer regarded himself a follower of Reubeni, and the latter could not forget that the circumcision, conversion, and flight of the former royal secretary had deeply offended the Portuguese king and greatly weakened his own position. Indeed, prior to the Molcho affair, Reubeni had received the promise that eight ships and 4,000 firearms (including cannons) would be placed at his disposal to enable his brother to wage war against the Muslims.[48] Following Molcho's conversion, King John III's enthusiasm for Reubeni's plan waned as suspicions mounted that the Jewish envoy was responsible for the messianic fervor and unrest among the Marranos and Conversos of Portugal. This view gained additional support when the commission entrusted to establish the Inquisition in Portugal informed the king that by dealing with the "Jewish prince" the Marranos were encouraged in their unbelief and in their secret adherence to Judaism. Convinced that he had erred, the Portuguese monarch summoned Reubeni to appear before him and accused him of suborning the Marranos to abjure Christianity. He then ordered Reubeni to leave the country.

The vessel carrying Reubeni and his retinue ran aground off the Spanish coast and Reubeni was imprisoned by the local authorities. After a rather lengthy incarceration, he was released on instructions from the Emperor, Charles V, and betook himself to Avignon, which was under papal jurisdiction. Later, Reubeni made his way to Venice in still another attempt to convince the republic of the merits of his "grand design." The Venetian Senate, always sensitive to suggestions that might affect trade or profits, chose a representative to meet with Reubeni. However, nothing resulted from their discussions.

The presence of David Reubeni and Solomon Molcho in Venice disturbed many Jews who sensed danger for themselves and their community. They were aware, for example, that while Molcho was in Ancona he had engaged a Catholic prelate in a public disputation that had placed him and the entire Jewish community in jeopardy. On that occasion Molcho had narrowly escaped punishment by accepting the invitation of the Duke of Urbino to take shelter in Pesaro before proceeding to Rome. Similarly, the Doge of Venice had Reubeni investigated by Gian Battista Ramusio, a well known traveler with pretensions to a knowledge of many Oriental tongues. The fears of the Venetian Jews soon led to action. Molcho was poisoned, but slowly recovered after coming close to death.

Meanwhile, the flood he had predicted occurred on October 8, 1530, turning Rome into one gigantic lake. At the same time, a comet appeared in the sky giving an eerie effect to the scene and further alarming the superstitious populace, causing them to believe that "the end of days" was upon them. Incredibly, a few months later in Portugal (January 26, 1531), the earth shook thrice, and destroyed a considerable number of houses in Lisbon, burying many people under the ruins. Upon recovering his health, Molcho returned to Rome where he was now regarded as a true prophet and messenger of God. Reubeni accepted an invitation from the Marquis of Mantua to visit his city.

Although most Jews ignored Molcho's messianic pretensions, a few considered him a menace that had to be removed. Among his uncompromising opponents was Jacob Mantin (or Mantino), a physician, a favorite of powerful princes and Church dignitaries, and a translator of philosophical and medical books into Latin. Mantin chanced upon some writing of Molcho in which the latter had used offensive language against Christianity. He translated the passages into Latin and placed the material in the hands of the Inquisition. He also informed the inquisitors that Molcho had lived as a Christian in Lisbon. The Holy Office accordingly cited Molcho as a renegade from Catholicism. Clement VII, who liked the young prophet, tried to protect him, but was compelled to acquiesce to the inquisition court when Mantin produced witnesses confirming his accusations. Molcho was convicted and condemned to be burnt at the stake. At the hour of execution the funeral pyre was built up, the faggots kindled, and the wretched victim, covered by a penitential shroud, was thrown into the fire. However, it was not Solomon Molcho. The pope, unwilling to sacrifice the young man, had hidden him in one of his chambers, and at the last moment substituted a condemned criminal in Molcho's place. Later, escorted by a few faithful servants of the pope, he was spirited out of Rome in the dead of the night.[49]

A few months later the pope, no longer able to resist the combined pressure of the courts of Spain and Portugal and the reactionary elements within the Catholic Church, issued a bull formally establishing the Inquisition in Portugal (December 17, 1531). When the Inquisition began its execrable work many of the Portuguese Marranos attempted to flee, but in most cases were either caught or perished at sea. Others were drawn from their hiding places, tried, and burned to death. Few who managed to escape from Portugal found relief or refuge from persecution (the one great exception was in the Ottoman Empire, where the unfortunate refugees were welcomed).

As these tragic events were unfolding, Molcho rejoined Reubeni in northern Italy where they conceived a plan to alleviate the plight of the Marranos. They journeyed to Ratisbon where the Emperor was meeting with the Imperial Diet (summer of 1532) on the question of war with Turkey. With a flying banner bearing (in initials) the legend, "Who is like unto Thee, O Lord, among the mighty?" they appeared before Charles V. They pleaded with the Holy Roman Emperor to allow the Marranos in his realm to arm themselves, and to permit them to join the Jewish tribes in the East in a crusade against the Turks. The remonstration against their folly by the sagacious official lay-head of the German Jews, Joseph (Joselmann) of Rosheim, was in vain. But the stubborn persistence of Molcho and Reubeni eventually led to their undoing. The emperor would not listen to their pleas (he had recently been warned by the Marquis of Mantua that Reubeni was a charlatan), and he ordered both men to be placed in chains and imprisoned. When Charles V returned to Italy from Ratisbon, he took his Jewish prisoners back with him and had them incarcerated in Mantua.

For Reubeni this was the second time that he had felt the wrath of Charles V. According to one fanciful tale, during Reubeni's detention in Spain (following his departure from Portugal and shipwreck) the emperor had showed him the legendary spear of Longinus. In medieval Christian mythology the spear was portrayed as having been thrust into the side of Jesus by a German mercenary officer in the Roman army, thus ending Jesus' suffering on the cross. The spearhead had supposedly been forged by Phineas, wielded by Joshua, thrown by Saul at David, kept by each Judean king, and treasured by the Roman emperors and later by the Holy Roman emperors. Expecting a sudden thrust from Charles V, Reubeni managed, like King David, to narrowly escape being impaled by the fabled spear.

Shortly after Reubeni and Molcho's incarceration in Italy, their fate was already being decided. Subsequently, an ecclesiastical court met and condemned Molcho to death by fire for relapsing from Christianity and heresy. Fearing his eloquence might have an effect upon the mob, they led him to the place of execution with a gag in his mouth. At the very last moment a courier appeared, and in the emperor's name offered Molcho a pardon if he would recant his transgressions, renounce Judaism, and return to the Church. Molcho flatly refused, and is reported to have replied that he longed to die as a martyr, ". . . a burnt sacrifice, of a sweet savor unto the Lord,"[50] and that he repented only of having been a Christian in his youth. Unable to persuade him to repent, the courier withdrew, and Molcho was cast into the fire and perished.

Legends about Solomon Molcho, especially in kabbalistic circles, began to circulate soon after his demise. Many admirers of the prophet in Italy and Turkey believed that he had escaped death a second time, and had gone to Safed to visit his intended bride. Another version of this romantic legend had it that on every Friday evening, Molcho would recite to his beloved in Safed the benediction over the kiddush cup of wine that initiated the Sabbath.[51]

David Reubeni was destined to suffer a different fate than Molcho. Since he was an Orthodox Jew, not a Marrano or Converso, the Inquisition theoretically had no power over him. Nevertheless, he was charged with having seduced Conversos into embracing Judaism. Eventually he was taken to Spain and confined in Badajoz. He languished there for several years until his death (probably by poison) in 1538.[52]

4

Shabbetai Zevi

Belief in a Messiah who would fulfill biblical prophecies and restore the Jews to their ancient homeland has been a constant theme in Jewish thought since the time of the Babylonian captivity. False Messiahs, like shooting stars, have flashed across the skies of Jewish history, glowing brightly for a moment, then gradually fading into oblivion. In the wake of each falling star came disillusionment. However, the Jewish people continued to yearn for a Redeemer, and this desire became an obsession that gained in intensity with each passing generation. This golden dream reached its apogee with the expulsion of the Jews from the Iberian Peninsula, and the phenomenal turn toward mysticism (especially the study of the Kabbalah) among Jews in the Diaspora. The wave of persecutions of the sixteenth and seventeenth centuries led many Jews to regard the catastrophes as the:

> . . . birth pangs of the Messiah—a time out of which only redemption could issue. So hellish was present reality that only a supernatural miracle seemed the appropriate response of a beneficent Deity to the suffering of a faithful people. And indeed collective craving did produce a redeemer in whose person the unbearable tension of an existence strung between the poles of exile and redemption was temporarily resolved. The redeemer, in whom all Jewry took hope, was Shabbetai Zevi.[53]

Born in Smyrna, supposedly on the Ninth of *Av*, the traditional date of the destruction of the first and second Temples in Jerusalem, Shabbetai Zevi (1626–76)[54] was the son of a poor Sephardic merchant who later became wealthy as an agent for Dutch and English trading firms. He received a thorough religious education, first under Isaac de Alba who taught him Talmud, and later under the most illustrious rabbi of Smyrna, Joseph Escapa. Destined for the rabbinate, Zevi, according to one source, left the yeshiva at age fifteen to begin a life of abstinence, solitude, and study, without the help of teachers.[55] While still in his teens, he embarked on an intensive study of Kabbalah accompanied by a vigorous program of mortification that included fasting, flagellations, and frequent bathing in the sea, day and night, summer and winter. Although attracted to solitude, Shabbetai possessed a magnetic personality. He was tall, well formed, and had fine dark hair, a splendid beard, and a pleasant voice that won hearts by speech and song. A contemporary, Abraham Cuenqui, on first meeting Shabbetai Zevi could not refrain from admiring his physical appearance and princely demeanor. He would later write, "I looked on spellbound unable to turn my eyes from him."[56] Cuenqui's impression of Zevi was representative of the effect Zevi had on people.

Zevi was physically appealing, but his emotions and imagination seem to have been greater than his intellect. In early manhood he presented a contrast to his companions (he had already attracted a circle of disciples who studied the mystical texts of Lurianic Kabbalah with him), as he felt no attraction to the opposite sex. Nevertheless, according to custom, he married early, but deliberately avoided his wife, so that she applied for a divorce, which he willingly granted. The same thing happened with a second wife.

Between 1642 and 1648 Shabbetai Zevi lived in semiseclusion, and it was during this period that he began to display behavioral patterns of profound depression separated by intervals of normality. The late Gershom Scholem (the acknowledged authority on Kabbalah and its adherents) termed Zevi's condition, "an extreme case of cyclothymia or manic-depressive psychosis. . . ."[57] Shabbetai's disciples, on the other hand, tended to describe their leader's affliction in theological terms as "illumination" and "fall or hiding the face" (i.e., a state in which God hid his face from Zevi). During his periods of "illumination" in his exalted state Shabbetai had a predilection for strange and bizarre rituals and acts that ran counter to Orthodox religious law and behavior.

Shortly after the horrors of the Chmielnicki massacres (1648–49), which had decimated Polish Jewry and had left an indelible imprint on Jewish consciousness, Shabbetai Zevi was moved by a messianic spirit. In a Smyrna synagogue, in the midst of services, he suddenly cried out the full name of God, an act that in ancient times only the High Priest was permitted to do, and then only on the Day of Atonement, and which, according to tradition, the Messiah would utter at the end of time. Zevi climaxed his antinomian performance by publicly proclaiming that he was the long-awaited Redeemer, who would restore the Jews to Palestine. Because he was known to be mentally afflicted, none of the congregation took him seriously. However, his compulsion to violate Jewish law during his illuminated states, which were often accompanied by experiences of levitation and by frequent claims to be the Messiah, finally led the Smyrna rabbis (including his teacher Joseph Escapa) to intervene. He was excommunicated and banished from his native city.

Far from intimidating Zevi, exile gave him a sense of dignity. The idea of a suffering Messiah had been transplanted from Christianity, and it was the accepted view among many Jews that humiliation was the precursor of the Messiah's exaltation and glorification. During the period of his banishment Shabbetai wandered through Greece and Thrace (his father Mordecai had originally come from the Peloponnesus). For a time he sojourned in Salonika. His stay in the city, however, was cut short as a result of a bizarre incident. While in one of his exalted states he prepared a solemn festival to which he invited a number of his friends and followers. At the height of the affair Zevi sent for the sacred books of the law (Torah), and intimated to those present that he was about to celebrate a mystical marriage with the Torah. In the language of the Kabbalah this meant that the Torah, the daughter of heaven, was to be united indissolubly with the Messiah, the son of heaven (En-Sof).[58] After committing other antinomian acts, which were considered intolerable by the Jewish community of Salonika, Zevi was once again banished.

In 1658 Shabbetai found himself in Constantinople where he made strenuous efforts to shed his demonic obsessions. These efforts proved fruitless, and things gradually got out of hand. This time Zevi's relapse into erratic behavior was the direct result of the machinations of a crafty preacher named Abraham Ha-Yahini. The latter forged a manuscript in archaic characters and in a style reminiscent of the ancient apocrypha, and alleged that it bore testimony to Shabbetai's messiahship. Zevi seems to have taken this document for a genuine revelation. In the ecstatic mood that followed, Shabbetai celebrated the three Jewish festivals of Passover, Shavuot, and Sukkot in one week, and for good measure declared the abolition of all the Torah commandments. This unacceptable conduct aroused the Jewish community's passions and he was denounced to the Turkish authorities. Sensing that his life was in danger, Zevi fled the Turkish capital.

In 1662 Shabbetai decided to settle in Jerusalem. He reached the Holy City after brief stopovers in Rhodes, Tripoli, and Egypt. During this entire period he showed little trace of messianic agitation, and his conduct and kabbalistic scholarship won for him universal respect. He fasted much, prayed devoutly, wept copiously, and chanted psalms through the night while pacing up and down the floor of his chamber. Indeed, in the fall of 1663, when the Jerusalem community was confronted by a severe financial crisis due to a rapacious pasha who was clamoring for funds, and pious gifts ceased to flow from Poland because of the terrible Chmielnicki massacres, they selected Zevi as their emissary (*shaliah*) to seek aid in Egypt. He performed his mission successfully, and while in Cairo became closely associated with the circle around Raphael Chelebi of Aleppo, mint master, tax farmer, and the acknowledged head of Egyptian Jewry. Chelebi like Zevi was a great admirer of the Kabbalah. At his table fifty scholars and kabbalists sat down daily and entertained their host with spiritual conversation.

In Cairo, Shabbetai's messianic pretensions returned. It is probable that in one of his fits of illumination he made the decision to marry Sarah, an Ashkenazi girl of doubtful reputation. Sarah was a survivor of the Chmielnicki massacres of 1648 in Podolia. Six years old at the time, and an orphan wandering in the streets, she had been found by Christians, and sent to a Catholic nunnery. After ten years of confinement she escaped, and with the help of some Jews was taken to Amsterdam. Some years later she traveled by way of Frankfort-am-Main to Leghorn where she led an irregular life (rumors that she was a woman of easy virtue were current even later in the intimate circle of Zevi's admirers). Being of a very eccentric disposition, Sarah conceived the notion that she was destined to become the bride of the Messiah. Shabbetai seized on this report, which fitted in with his own fantasies, and claimed that such a consort had, indeed, been promised to him in a dream. Possibly influenced by the example of the biblical prophet Hosea who married a harlot, Zevi had Sarah brought to Egypt from Italy and married her in Cairo on March 31, 1664. Her beauty and easy manners gained for him many followers, and her lewd life was looked upon as an additional confirmation of Zevi's messiahship. Chelebi, in whose house the marriage of the would-be Messiah and his consort had occurred, placed his fortune at the disposal of Shabbetai and became his first influential supporter.

However, the turning point in Shabbetai Zevi's life came with the news that a man of God had appeared in Gaza who possessed great powers and who was "a physician of the soul."[59] His name was Nathan Benjamin Levi (1644–80), better known as Nathan of Gaza. He was the son of an immigrant from Germany, and sent by the community of Jerusalem as a messenger to North Africa and Europe to collect funds for the support of the Jews making their homes in the Holy City. Nathan grew up in Jerusalem, where he attended the talmudical school of Jacob Hagiz, an Italian scholar. On the recommendation of Hagiz, a rich Portuguese Jew named Samuel Lisbona, who had moved from Damascus to Gaza, gave Nathan his daughter for a wife (she was pretty, but blind in one eye). The marriage enabled him to pursue his mystic studies.

Zevi lost little time in seeking out the wonder worker of Gaza. Instead of curing Shabbetai of his illusions, Nathan claimed that he had experienced an ecstatic vision of Zevi as the Redeemer, and convinced his visitor that he was, indeed, the true Messiah. Evidently considering himself the forerunner of the Messiah (i.e., Elijah come down to earth to pave the way for the Messiah), Nathan became Shabbetai Zevi's foremost propagandist. Imbued with a new spirit of confidence Shabbetai again proclaimed publicly that he was the Messiah, and with the help of Nathan convinced the Jewish community of Gaza. Weeks of frenzied excitement followed as the news of the emergence of a Redeemer spread like wildfire to other communities in Palestine. Only a handful of rabbis in Jerusalem (notably Nathan's teacher Jacob Hagiz, and his son-in-law, the highly esteemed Moses Galante) remained doubtful. Zevi's attempts to overcome this resistance by kabbalistic means failed, and the opposition succeeded in expelling him from the Holy City.

Nathan of Gaza now came into his own as Zevi's herald and prophet, courier and advisor. He proclaimed the need for a mass movement of repentance to facilitate the coming redemption. He wrote letters to various Jewish communities telling them of the wondrous deeds of Shabbetai Zevi, and fanned the messianic flames with cryptic references to the coming redemption. In a long letter to Chelebi (September, 1665), Nathan outlined the course of events leading to the glorious day of redemption. Shabbetai, he wrote, would seize the crown from the Turkish sultan and make the sultan his servant. He would then proceed to the mythical river Sambayton, and bring back the 10 lost tribes of Israel and lead them to the Holy Land. Afterwards he would take for his spouse the thirteen-year-old daughter of the resuscitated Moses. While engaged in these activities, Shabbetai would put the deposed sultan in charge, but the sultan would rebel against him. This event would usher in the birth pangs of redemption, and a time of great tribulation. A year and several months would then elapse before the actual redemption—an interval devoted to penance (Nathan composed special prayers and liturgy to be used during this time span). Nathan concluded his letter to Chelebi by designating 1666 as the year of redemption.

The first extravagant reports about Shabbetai Zevi reached Europe in the fall of 1665, largely through the stories of travelers and the highly imaginative letters of Nathan of Gaza. Special messengers were also dispatched to herald the advent of the Messiah, among them Sabbatai Raphael of Morea and Mattathiah Bloch, a kabbalist from Germany. Zevi himself, after visits to Safed and Aleppo where he was greeted enthusiastically, returned to his native city of Smyrna. His homecoming had been smoothed by his wealthy brothers, who ensured a good reception by distributing alms among the poor and needy. The whole city was thrown into an uproar by Zevi's appearance, and his earlier banishment was completely forgotten.

Sir Paul Rycaut, the English Consul in Smyrna, an eyewitness to these events reported that men, women, and children, many in a highly emotional state, were all caught up in the messianic madness which seized the city. "They . . . spoke of visions in which Zion and the triumph of Shabbetai had been revealed to them."[60]

Zevi, basking in his newly found popularity, soon began to show signs of a state of ecstasy. Once again he performed antinomian acts (pronouncing the Ineffable Name, and violating the dietary laws). He also attracted considerable attention by his eccentric deportment. This behavior included appearing in the synagogue in royal apparel, enthralling the congregation with his ecstatic singing, rising at midnight for ritual immersions in the sea, and distributing sweetmeats to the children of Smyrna.

The three members of Smyrna's rabbinic court were appalled by Shabbetai's behavior, but were powerless to act in face of his popular support among the Jewish masses. A crowd tried to storm the house of one of Zevi's severest critics, but failed to gain entry. On the following day Shabbetai took personal control of the mob. He led them to the Portuguese synagogue, the headquarters of his opposition, and taking up an axe, attempted to smash in the bolted doors. His adversaries, shocked by this act of desecration, opened the doors and let him into the sanctuary. An astonishing scene followed. Ignoring tradition, Shabbetai read the portion of the Torah for that day from a printed copy instead of the customary scroll, and disregarding the priests and levites present, called up to the reading of the law his brothers and many other men and women. He then, like a ruling monarch, distributed imaginary fiefdoms to them and demanded that all so honored pronounce the Ineffable Name. Turning to his opposition, Zevi verbally attacked them, and compared them to unclean animals. He then informed the so-called unbelievers that the Messiah ben Joseph, who according to tradition, must precede the Messiah ben David, had already come. According to Shabbetai he had been a man named Abraham Zalman, who had died a martyr's death in 1648.[61] Following his harangue of the congregation, Zevi went up to the synagogue's ark, took a holy scroll in his arms and sang a coarse Castilian song about "Meliselda the emperor's daughter." In this song (his favorite throughout his life) Zevi envisioned kabbalistic mysteries. After explaining the mystic meaning of the song to the congregation, he once again proclaimed himself the anointed of the God of Jacob, and the Redeemer of Israel. He then fixed the date of the redemption for the 15th of Sivan, 5426 (June 18, 1666). This was in conformity with Nathan of Gaza's predictions, and with notions set forth by Christian writers who considered 1666 to be the apocalyptic year. This belief was so prevalent that the famous rabbi Menasseh ben Israel (1604–57), in his petition to Cromwell and the English parliament, did not hesitate to cite it as a motive for his plea for the readmission of Jews into England. Shabbetai concluded his wild performance in the Portuguese synagogue by announcing that he would shortly leave for Constantinople to claim the crown of the sultan.

In the tumultuous jubilation that followed all discipline was cast aside. The aged rabbi Aaron Lapapa attempted to restore order, and was speedily deposed by Shabbetai and replaced with one of his own supporters (Hayim Benveniste, 1603–74). Messianic fever now raged unchecked in the Jewish community of Smyrna. Trade and commerce came to a standstill. Dancing in the streets and festive processions alternated with the penitential exercises prescribed by Nathan of Gaza. All opposition was borne down, if necessary by force. Thus Hayim Pena, a wealthy and influential member of the community who was not taken in by Zevi's antics, was forced to flee from the synagogue to escape Zevi's followers. However, when his own daughters joined in the general madness, Pena could do no less than acquiesce to Shabbetai's domination of the Jewish community. Zevi, in the meantime, in his role as Redeemer set about appointing counterparts to the ancient kings of Judea (as he had previously done in the Portuguese synagogue). The appointees were mainly his key supporters in Smyrna, but also included some of his devotees in Palestine, Egypt, and Syria.

From Smyrna the messianic excitement spread to other nearby communities, and gradually throughout the Jewish Diaspora. Samuel Primo, Shabbetai's secretary, and Nathan of Gaza flooded the Jewish communities the world over with messages concerning the appearance of the Messiah and his wonderful accomplishments. Christian sources added to the frenzy. The many broadsheets and pamphlets that appeared in English, Dutch, Italian, and German were also read by the Jews and often taken as independent sources confirming their own news. Christian millenarian circles helped spread the Shabbetaian propaganda as they looked on 1666 as the year of grace in which the Jews would be restored to Palestine—an event that would herald the Second Coming of Christ. As a youth Shabbetai may have heard stories brought home by his father of the millenarian dreams nurtured by the fanatical Fifth Monarchy Men of England.

A distinguished German savant, Heinrich Oldenburg, writing to the philosopher Spinoza about the agitation among the Jews noted, ". . . all the world is talking of a rumor of the return of the Israelites . . . to their own country. . . . Should the news be confirmed it may bring about a revolution in all things."[62] Curiously, when questioned about these developments Benedict de Spinoza saw no rational reason for doubting the possibility of a restoration of the temporal rule of the Jews. In London Samuel Pepys was told by a Jew that he was willing to wager 100 pounds against ten that within two years Shabbetai would be anointed king of Jerusalem.[63]

The most fantastic reports circulated in many Jewish communities and were accepted by otherwise dispassionate men. For example, rumors spread that in the north of Scotland, a ship had been sighted that carried silken sails and ropes manned by sailors who spoke Hebrew. On its main mast flew a flag bearing the inscription, "the twelve tribes of Israel." Other accounts spoke of ships crammed with Jews sailing for Palestine, and of an army composed of the ten lost tribes conquering Mecca, or assembling in the Sahara desert for a campaign to wrest the Holy Land from the Turks. Those individuals more mystically inclined spoke of many signs and portents that had been witnessed in the evening skies. Others trembled in fear and awe in the belief that the end of days was approaching, and that the messianic age was about to begin.

In some parts of Europe, Jews began to unroof their houses and prepare for the exodus to the Promised Land. The Jewish community of Avignon, for example, carried away by the mass hysteria, actually concluded plans to emigrate to Palestine in the spring of 1666. In the Iberian Peninsula interest in Zevi and adherence to his cause among the Marranos was so intense that the authorities instituted a special watch at all seaports to apprehend those individuals who sought to smuggle themselves out of the country in order to join Shabbetai and participate in the Great Deliverance. A Marrano physician who managed to escape to the Levant was rewarded by Zevi with the "throne of Portugal." In Hamburg the Jewish council introduced the custom of praying for Shabbetai Zevi several times a week. Also in Hamburg Jewish youths wearing green sashes, the livery of the Shabbetaians, danced madly in the synagogue led by Benito de Castro, physician to the queen of Sweden, and Manoel Texeira, an important financial magnate. On the bourses of Hamburg large sums were wagered that soon Zevi's claims would be officially recognized in European countries.

In Moravia the messianic excitement reached such a pitch that the government was forced to intervene; while in Sale (North Africa) the Emir, alarmed by the turn of events, ordered a persecution of the Jews. At Venice, Moses Zacuto, a fellow student of Spinoza, inflamed the minds of the credulous Jews; in Leghorn, one of Shabbetai's early adherents, Moses Pinheiro, acted with equal zeal.

Gluckel von Hameln, describing in her diary the effect of the Shabbetaian agitation upon her community wrote: "Many individuals sold their houses and everything they owned, and expected salvation to come any day. My late father-in-law who lived in Hameln . . . sent two great casks filled with linen stuffs to us in Hamburg. Amidst the linens were packed all sorts of foods, such as peas, beans, dried meat, prunes and similar things that keep well for the old man thought that we would depart at once from Hamburg to the Holy Land."[64]

Similarly, Jacob Sasportas, a highly articulate scholar and one of the individuals who was skeptical of Shabbetai's claims, described the impact of Shabbetai's propaganda in Amsterdam. The city, he wrote, ". . . seethed and roared. Great throngs of people moved in prancing step to the pounding of drums, through the squares and streets. . . ."[65]

Indeed, among the leading supporters of Shabbetai in Amsterdam were the rabbis Isaac Aboab and Raphael Moses d'Aquilar and the wealthy philanthropist and theological writer Abraham Pereyra, for several years president of the Jewish community. Even rationalistic circles were drawn into the messianic maelstrom. Benjamin Mussafia, philosopher and one time physician to King Christian of Denmark, was among the first to sign the address of homage sent to the "Messiah Shabbetai Zevi" by the Jews of Amsterdam.

In almost all of the Jewish communities where the messianic fever raged, repentance alternated with public manifestations of joy. Penitents, crazed by the excitement, went to excessive lengths of mortification. Some fasted for days on end; others adopted more radical measures such as stripping naked and burying themselves up to their shoulders in the frozen earth, or dropping hot melted wax on their bodies. Still others used thorns to inflict pain and then submitted themselves to lashing. At the height of the winter season many individuals chose to deny their bodily passions and appetites by rolling in the snow or by diving into the frigid waters of the Mediterranean Sea.[66]

Some wealthy believers made arrangements for renting ships to transport the poor to Palestine. Many communities sent delegates to Smyrna to indicate their support of Shabbetai Zevi. The madness reached such proportions that Shabbetai's adherents in Smyrna and elsewhere married off their children (aged 12, 10, and younger) to one another so that, according to kabbalistic thinking, ". . . souls not yet born to enter into life, and thereby remove the last obstacle to the commencement of the time of grace."[67]

A new era in Jewish affairs was inaugurated as letters and even some published books were dated from "the first year of the renewal of the prophesy and the kingdom." In many prayer books, Shabbetai Zevi's picture was printed alongside that of King David, and his kabbalistic statements incorporated in the text. "Shabbetaianism" as the agitation would come to be called, had with breathtaking suddenness become the largest and most momentous messianic movement in Jewish history, subsequent to the Bar Kochba revolt. Although there were hardly any differences in the reactions of Ashkenazi, Sephardi, Italian, and Oriental Jewry, the movement found its strongest support in those communities composed largely of former Marranos.

A mounting wave of terrorism threatened those who spoke derisively of Shabbetai Zevi, and who refused to take part in the general excitement. Nevertheless, there were a handful of skeptics who would not succumb to the mass hysteria that swept many of the

Jewish communities. Outstanding in this respect were the religious leaders Samuel Aboab of Venice; Joseph ha-Levi, the preacher of the Leghorn community; and the indomitable Jacob Sasportas, who had left London because of the Great Plague and had settled in Amsterdam.[68]

At the beginning of the mystic year 1666, Shabbetai, having secured his position in Smyrna, announced that he was called upon by God to set out for Constantinople to remove the Sultan from his throne—the first step in ushering in the messianic age. Accompanied by his most devoted adherents he set sail for the Turkish capital. The Ottoman Grand Vizier, Ahmed Köpruliis, alarmed by rumors of Shabbetai's intentions, and anxious to avoid any disturbances on the eve of his departure on a military expedition to Crete, ordered the sailing ship bringing Zevi to Constantinople to be boarded and the Jewish agitator arrested. The vizier's instructions were carried out and Zevi was cast into a dungeon in one of the capital's prisons. Two months later he was removed to the Castle of the Dardanelles at Abydos where important political prisoners were kept. Shabbetai's imprisonment heightened the belief in his messiahship. It seemed to confirm the view that the Redeemer had to suffer tribulations before his final triumph. The removal of Shabbetai to a more favorable place of confinement seemed to bear out this widely held conviction, because such leniency on the part of the Turks was unusual. By means of bribes the believers soon converted Zevi's detention into honorable confinement. The immense sums sent to Zevi by his rich adherents, the charms of the queenly Sarah, and the reverential admiration shown him even by the Turkish officials, enabled Shabbetai to live in royal splendor in the castle at Abydos, which was given the mystical name Migdal Oz (the tower of strength), a reference to Proverbs 18:10. Hundreds of Zevi's followers from neighboring communities and also from Germany, Poland, Italy, Holland, flocked to the castle, which took on the appearance of a royal residence. So great was the number of people visiting Abydos that the governor of the castle and his men decided to take advantage of the situation to enrich themselves. Accordingly, they raised the price of their provisions and other necessities, and set fees for all persons seeking admittance to Shabbetai Zevi's presence. To prolong this windfall the Turkish governor made certain no complaints reached the ears of his superiors.

Shabbetai, swayed by the adoration of the believers and by a prolonged state of "illumination" now went from one extravagance to another. He began to sign his letters with such grandiose titles as "The first born son of God," "Your father Israel," "The bridegroom of the Torah, and the Messiah of the God of Jacob, the Lion of the mountain recesses." As the Jewish fasts of the seventeenth of *Tammuz* and the ninth of *Ab* approached, Zevi's euphoria mounted. He proclaimed the abolition of the fasts and instituted new festivals in their place. The ninth of Ab was to henceforth be observed as a major festival in commemoration of his birthday. In addition, Zevi gave expression to the abrogation of the laws of Moses and the rabbis by pronouncing a benediction: "Blessed be God, who looseth (permits) that which is bound (forbidden)."[69]

The Shabbetaian movement reached its climax in the summer of 1666, and the turning point came in a most unexpected manner. A delegation of Polish Jews led by Isaiah and his stepbrother, the sons of the celebrated rabbi of Lemberg, David Halevi, came to Abydos to see for themselves the Redeemer. They were received with marked attention by the pretender. They told him that a Polish kabbalist named Nehemiah ha-Kohen had predicted the near advent of the Messiah, but not with Shabbetai as the messianic person. Zevi was miffed by this information. In an enigmatic letter that he gave to Isaiah for his father (it offered mystical instructions to cure the ailing rabbi, and also promised the Polish Jews vindication for the suffering they had recently endured) Zevi peremptorily ordered that Nehemiah be sent to Abydos forthwith. The prophet came and met with Shabbetai in a private conference that lasted for two days and ended in a bitter dispute. Nehemiah failed to see any connection between Zevi's claims and the predictions of older aggadic writings about the Messiah. He stressed the absence of a visible Messiah ben Joseph who, according to tradition, would precede the actual Redeemer. Nehemiah may have even asserted to be the Messiah ben Joseph, a claim that certainly would have been rejected by his host. It is not clear what happened next, but with Shabbetai's repudiation of Nehemiah's arguments, Nehemiah was placed in great danger. Zevi's adherents now considered the Polish kabbalist a schismatic and an enemy, and secretly plotted to do away with this dangerous rival to their leader. Sensing that his life was in jeopardy, Nehemiah escaped from the castle by suddenly declaring in the presence of the Turkish guards his willingness to become a Muslim. He was taken to Adrianople where he accused Shabbetai of fomenting sedition against the sultan.

Following these charges Zevi was removed from Abydos and brought to Adrianople. In the presence of the divan and the sultan, Mohammed IV, who watched the proceedings from behind a latticed alcove, Shabbetai was questioned about his beliefs and activities. The accounts of what transpired during this investigation are contradictory. According to one version the sultan accused Shabbetai of blasphemy and treason (plotting to remove Palestine from Ottoman control), but offered him an opportunity to escape a death sentence if he accepted Islam. Seeing no way out, Zevi replied that he was contented to be a Muslim, and that he had for a long time considered such a conversion.

Gershom Scholem, an authority on Zevi's life, viewed his conversion to Islam somewhat differently. Shabbetai, he believed, when brought before the sultan was in one of his melancholy moods and behaving with utter passivity. In this state of mind, he was easily influenced to convert to Islam by an apostate Jew named Mustapha Hayatizade, the sultan's personal physician. Accordingly, Shabbetai cast off his Jewish headgear and accepted a white turban, a sign of his conversion to the Muslim religion (September 16, 1666). The Turks were delighted by Shabbetai's decision, for they did not wish to make a martyr out of him. For them Shabbetai the "Jewish Messiah" was no more, for he left the sultan's presence as Aziz Mehmed Effendi, the grand signior's pensioner. He was rewarded with title *Kapiei Baski* (keeper of the palace gates, i.e., doorkeeper of the *seraglio*). Several of the believers who had accompanied him into Adrianople followed their leader into apostasy, as did Zevi's wife Sarah. Nehemiah ha-Kohen, who had been responsible for the would-be Messiah's downfall returned to Poland, took off his turban and disappeared from public view.

The apostasy of Shabbetai Zevi produced a profound shock wave throughout the Jewish world. For a time, a sense of bewildering disenchantment and shame prevailed. Muslims and Christians, many of whom had previously been swayed by Shabbetai's oratory and behavior, were now quick to point with scorn at the credulous Jews. The street boys of Constantinople and Smyrna openly jeered at Jewish passers-by. But the ridicule was not all. So widespread had been the Shabbetaian commotion that it could not die out easily. Indeed, the Turkish sultan was not so forgiving, and for a time seriously contemplated a plan to annihilate all adult Jews in his empire, and taking all Jewish children under the age of seven to be brought up as Muslims. Fortunately for the Jews he was dissuaded from carrying out this plan by his mother and a handful of his councilors, who pointed out that not all Jews had rebelled against his authority, and that in general the Jews had been duped. This has led some historians to speculate whether Shabbetai's courage had really failed him, or whether he converted because he feared that a terrible catastrophe would befall the Jews of the Ottoman Empire because of his actions.

After Zevi's apostasy many Jews regretted their support of the false Messiah and quietly returned to their former orthodoxy. However, the most remarkable part of the whole episode was still to take place. Belief in Shabbetai's messianic mission among many of his staunch supporters persisted even after his conversion to Islam. Some insisted that it was not Zevi who had become a Turk, but a phantom who had assumed his likeness; and that Shabbetai himself had ascended to heaven, or had gone to the habitat of the lost ten tribes, and would return in glory to complete the work of redemption.

Nathan of Gaza, who had remained in Palestine while these events were transpiring, clung to the notion that Shabbetai's conversion was part of an unfathomable mystery. When he had recovered from his initial shock he offered a theological explanation for the apostasy. Using kabbalistic terminology, Nathan argued that the amazing turn about (i.e., the conversion) was in reality part of the messianic blueprint—a further step in the mythical descent to struggle for the sparks of goodness imprisoned in the demonic power. In brief, Shabbetai had to take upon himself the shame of being called a traitor before revealing himself in all his glory as the true Messiah. Shabbetai's secretary, Samuel Primo, argued along similar lines, maintaining that the "deliverer" must have the experience of every side of human life, even the lowest and most un-Jewish aspects, before he could successfully accomplish his mission.

By placing the paradox of an apostate Messiah, a tragic but still legitimate redeemer, at the center of their Shabbetaian theology, Nathan, Primo and others laid the foundations for the ideology of the "believers" for the next century. These men and their successors searched the Bible, Talmud, Midrash and kabbalistic literature for evidence to support their theories and came up with daring, audacious, and often outright heretical interpretations of the sacred texts. Once the basic paradox was accepted, everything seemed to fall in place. All the objectionable acts of the biblical heroes, and strange tales of the Talmud, as well as the enigmatic passages of the Zohar, seemed to point to a type of exegesis useful for explaining the scandalous behavior of Shabbetai Zevi. With the latter's acquiescence these ideas were given wide circulation among the remaining believers.

Nevertheless, the excitement generated by the Shabbetaian movement gradually ebbed. When Nathan of Gaza tried to see Zevi in Adrianople, he was met by a delegation of rabbis who on pain of excommunication forced him to sign a promise that he would not meet with the apostate. In spite of this vow Nathan did visit Zevi, and continued to see him from time to time. On one occasion, on direct orders from Shabbetai, Nathan undertook a mission to Rome to carry out a secret magical ritual designed to bring about the downfall of the Pope. Following this fiasco, he traveled though Asia Minor, the Balkans, European Turkey, the Greek islands, and Italy, everywhere heartening the believers not to lose faith in Shabbetai's messianic mission. However, the saner people and especially the rabbis had come to their senses, and the false prophet was frequently expelled from the cities he visited. He is believed to have died in Sofia in 1680.

Shabbetai Raphael, another prophet who sponsored the Shabbetaian cause, had better fortune than Nathan of Gaza and was welcomed in many cities as he wandered through Germany, Holland, and Poland. In Leghorn, Moses Pinheiro initiated into the mysteries of Kabbalah a Portuguese Marrano who had returned to the Jewish fold, the physician

Abraham Michael Cardosa. This visionary became an ardent Shabbetaian and won over many individuals to the lost cause, particularly in North Africa.

Shabbetai himself, it seems, lived a dual life. At times he would assume the role of a pious Muslim and revile Judaism; at other occasions he would enter into relation with Jews as one of their own faith, and observe large parts of the Jewish ritual. The Turks expected him to act as a Muslim missionary, but the 200 heads of families he drew to Islam were all secret Shabbetaians. Zevi continued to have periods of illumination and depression, and during the former state he acted in the same manner as before his conversion. In March of 1668 he said that he had been filled with a holy spirit during Passover and had received a revelation. At about the same time a mystic work was published suggesting that the true objective of Shabbetai's conversion was to bring thousands of Muslims to Judaism. However, outside the circle of believers these claims were no longer taken seriously.

Although the Shabbetaians retained a strong following in the Balkans and Turkey, they were eventually driven underground. The borderline between the apostates and those who remained Jews gradually widened. Shabbetai, who for a time enjoyed the sultan's favors, added to the process of complete separation by forming connections with Muslim mystics among the Dervish orders.

Zevi's double existence came to an abrupt end in 1672 when he was surprised by the Turks in a village near Constantinople singing psalms and participating in religious rites with a small group of Jewish friends. Accused of being unfaithful to Islam, he was arrested. The Grand Vizier wavered between executing or deporting him, but finally decided to banish Shabbetai to Dulcigno, a small Albanian town. Although allowed relative freedom, Zevi disappeared from public view. His key supporters, apparently disguised as Muslims, continued the practice of making pilgrimages to his place of exile.

In 1674 Zevi's wife Sarah died, and he married Esther, the daughter of one of his most fervent supporters, Joseph Filosof of Salonika. The marriage was short-lived, as two months after his fiftieth birthday, on the Day of Atonement (September 17, 1676), Shabbetai suddenly expired. Nathan of Gaza, loyal to the last, immediately fostered the fanciful tale that Shabbetai's death was merely an occultation, and that he had actually ascended toward heaven and had been absorbed into the "supernal lights." This theory of apotheosis was in line with his earlier speculations on the gradual deification of the Messiah, but left unanswered who would represent the Messiah on earth.

Outside the circle of believers, Zevi's demise went largely unnoticed. Nevertheless, a fairly large number of Shabbetai's former supporters accepted Nathan of Gaza's views and the cult survived. A new set of vigorous leaders arose to claim the messianic mantle, among them Abraham Michael Cardosa, Mordecai of Eisenstadt, Daniel Israel Bonafoux, Judah Hassid, Hayyim Malakh, and Herschel Zoref. However, most prominent among the would-be successors was Joseph Filosof, the father-in-law of Shabbetai, and his son Jacob Querido who was passed off by his sister Esther as the posthumous offspring of Shabbetai Zevi. Devotees in Salonika rallied about Querido as the reincarnated Messiah, but when the Turkish authorities learned of the new movement, Querido and his followers converted to Islam to save themselves. After Querido's death his adherents acclaimed his son Berechiah as a reincarnation of both Shabbetai and Jacob. These Shabbetaians professed and practiced Islam in public, but adhered to a strange mixture of traditional and heretical Judaism in secret. Known as the "Doenmeh," they have survived in their traditional bastions in Turkey down to the present day.

II

THE UNBROKEN COVENANT: JEWISH ATTEMPTS TO RETURN TO THE PROMISED LAND

5

The Lure Of Zion

The Karaite Movement

Concomitant with the messianic currents released in the distant provinces of Islamic Persia by the Isawites and Yudghanites during the eighth century, an intensified longing developed among Jews throughout the Islamic world to return to their ancestral homeland. Aware that magic and force had failed to achieve redemption, many pious Jews undertook pilgrimages to the Holy Land, and some decided to settle there permanently. Spearheading this movement was a sect which threatened not the Islamic state, but Judaism itself.

According to most accounts, the occasion for the schism was a disputed succession to the exilarch (Resh Galutha, head of the captivity, the highest official of Babylonian Jewry). Anan ben David, passed over in favor of a younger brother (he had lived for some time in Persia at the center of Jewish heresies), found consolation in resisting the decision. The caliph, who had confirmed the election of the new exilarch, got wind of the rebellion and threw Anan into prison. Tradition suggests that Anan was incarcerated with the famous Muslim scholar of jurisprudence, Abu Hanifa, who advised him to bribe the vizier, seek trial in the presence of the caliph, and pray for recognition as the representative of another body of Jews. Thus the open breach with the main body of Jews was effected, and the Ananite sect was born (about the year 767).

The Ananites rejected the authority of the rabbis and branded the Talmud as an imposture and those who followed it as hypocrites. They refused to admit the weight of tradition in interpreting Jewish law and practice, and recognized only the authority of the Bible. Anan and his followers tended toward asceticism and were extremely pietistic and severe in their religious observance. They considered the rabbinical practices that emphasized the joy of the Sabbath and the festivals to be contrary to the mourning that should mark Jewish life in exile. Therefore no lights might be kindled to illumine the home on the eve of Sabbath, and all food was to be eaten cold. Fast days were multiplied. The eating of almost any kind of meat was forbidden, recourse to physicians in time of sickness was considered an impiety, and the prohibited degrees of marriage were greatly extended. In addition, the Ananites criticized excessive rabbinic leniency in carrying out kashrut (dietary laws) and the regulations concerning ritual impurity.

The movement started by Anan was solidified by Benjamin ben Moses al-Nahawendi of Persia (9th century), who was the first to use the term "Karaites" (from the Hebrew word *mikrah,* i.e., scriptures) to designate followers of the Bible only, in contrast to the Rabbanites (those Jews who adhered to rabbinic tradition). Benjamin abandoned artificial opposition to the Rabbanites and now and then even ranged himself on the side of the latter, against the decisions of Anan. He taught that Jews should decide individually which practices were implied by biblical legislation. Personal freedom of interpretation thus became a fundamental Karaite principle.

The Jerusalem Karaites (Shoshanim)

By the early tenth century the Karaites could be found throughout the Middle East. The metamorphosis of this fringe group from mainline Judaism was further helped by the establishment of a Karaite academy in Jerusalem. Daniel son of Moses al-Kumisi (9th–10th century), a Persian Karaite, seems to have been the first to call on the sectarians to settle in Jerusalem in order to pray constantly that Israel's sins be forgiven and to appeal to God for redemption.

Called "Shoshanim" (roses) by their admirers, the Jerusalem Karaites ordered their lives according to the customs of their ancient forebearers, the *Avelei Zion* (Mourners for Zion), who had been prominent in the period immediately following the destruction of the second Temple by the Romans.[70] Like their predecessors, the Shoshanim devoted their energy to praying and to ascetic practices designed to hasten redemption. As a sign of their grief that the Temple no longer existed and the majority of Jews lived in exile, the Jerusalem Karaites always added to their signature the word "mourner" in their correspondence. Intercourse with non-Jews was shunned by these sectarians who would not buy bread from Gentiles or eat anything touched by a Gentile. Commerce and trade was also eschewed by the group, who depended on the charity of Jewish pilgrims and Diaspora communities for their meager existence (as the social composition of the movement gradually changed many Karaites, particularly in Egypt, became prosperous merchants).

Daniel al-Kumisi in his messages to Karaite communities throughout the East exhorted them to return to the Holy City. "But if you do not come," he added, "for you are engrossed in running after your trades, send five men from each city, and provide them with a livelihood. In this manner we shall become a united people, dedicated to constant prayer on the mountain of Jerusalem."[71] As a result of his call and those of his successors, the Mourners for Zion formed a considerable segment of the city's population during this period of Jerusalem's history.

In the tenth and eleventh centuries the Jerusalem Karaites included some of the most distinguished literary figures of eastern Jewry. Karaite scholars in Jerusalem composed handbooks of law, wrote commentaries on the Bible, furthered the growth of Hebrew philology, and engaged in theological and philosophical speculation. Throughout their sojourn in Jerusalem they thought of themselves as the "remnant of Israel," destined by their ascetic practices to bring about an end to the exile and redemption. However, with the conquest of Palestine by the Seljuks (1071), and later by the Crusaders (1099), the Mourners for Zion disappeared from Jerusalem. The center of Karaite activity shifted to the Byzantine Empire; from there the sectarians founded settlements in Crimea, Poland, and Lithuania.

Judah ha-Levi (the Singer of Zion)

Renowned for his songs of Zion, Judah ha-Levi (1075–1141),[72] physician, philosopher, and Hebrew poet, like the prophets Ezekiel, Isaiah, and Jeremiah believed in the eternity of Israel and the national restoration of the Jews to the Promised Land. He was born in either Toledo or Tudela, Spain, to a wealthy and learned family. His childhood years were spent during a relatively peaceful period for the Jews of the Iberian Peninsula, but the so-called golden age of Jewry was already showing signs of danger and decline. The "Reconquista", the reconquest of Spain by the Christians, had begun in earnest. From 1035 to 1065, Ferdinand I of Castile had gradually increased his holdings and power to the extent that the Muslim rulers of Saragossa, Toledo, and even Seville were paying him tribute. His successors continued his policies of expansion. As the Christians took over parts of Muslim Spain, they slaughtered the Muslim rulers, but allowed the peasants to remain on the land. The Jews were also permitted to stay, and in some instances were even entrusted with high offices in the some Christian realms. Political and economic considerations, rather than any change of heart on the part of the descendants of the antisemitic Visigoth rulers dictated this policy of toleration. Indeed, as long as the southern region of Spain remained under Muslim control, the Jews were needed, especially for diplomatic missions to the Muslim emirates.

In 1085, after a five year siege, Sultan Kader surrendered Toledo to the Castilians, thus restoring to the Christians the ancient Visigoth capital of Spain. The Muslim princes of Andalusia, unable to fend off the steady advances of the Christians, asked for help from their fellow Muslims in North Africa. Yusuf ibn Tashfin, leader of the Berber sect of the Almoravides, crossed the Straits of Gibraltar with a large army and marched into Andalusia. On October 23, 1086, the armies of the crescent and the cross clashed at Zallaka, near Badajoz. Both armies contained Jewish soldiers (the greater number, however, served on the Muslim side). The battle ended with a complete rout of the Christian forces – Andalusia had been saved for Islam. The victory proved to be a hollow one for the Muslim Emirs who had invited Yusif ibn Tashfin, for the latter gradually seized power and made them his vassals.

In the years just prior to the Almoravide invasion, young Judah ha-Levi went south to study in the great centers of Jewish learning in Andalusia. Among the communities he passed through was Cordoba, where he was destined to spend the greater part of his life. After winning a poetry contest, he was invited by the scholar Moses ibn Ezra (1055–1135?) to his home. A close friendship developed between the two men. Through Ibn Ezra, the young poet was introduced into an intellectual circle that included many of the celebrities of the age.

With the coming of the fanatical Almoravides from North Africa, the position of the Jews rapidly disintegrated. Judah ha-Levi, who was enjoying a stay in Granada in the company of Ibn Ezra, decided the time had come to leave the province. For the next 20 years he traveled incessantly. Gifted in many fields, Judah ha-Levi became a master of the

Hebrew and Arabic languages (particularly their poetic forms). He was also conversant with Castilian poetry, Greek philosophy, metaphysics, the natural sciences, and the Talmud (as a youngster he had studied at Lucena in the school of the famous talmudist Isaac Alfasi). Nevertheless, in Toledo, Judah ha-Levi chose to practice medicine, apparently in the service of the Christian king and his court. Like many of his coreligionists he believed that the influence of Jews who were close to the royal house would provide security for the entire Jewish community. However, disillusionment soon set in when in 1108 his patron and benefactor, the courtier Solomon ibn Ferrizuel, who had achieved high rank under Alfonso VI, was murdered. As a result of this incident Judah left Toledo and resumed the life of a wanderer.

Aside from his profession as a physician, Judah ha-Levi engaged in trade with Jewish merchants in Egypt for a short period. But throughout his life, his true avocation remained that of a poet. About 800 of his poems have survived. It has been said of these poems that since the end of the biblical age no such lyrical notes have sounded in Jewish literature. Many of Judah's early poems were songs of love or songs in praise of wine and its pleasures. A second group of secular poems can be classified as eulogies and laments. Many of the laments were written for the poet's friends and some of the Jewish community's outstanding figures (e.g., Moses ibn Ezra, Joseph ibn Migash, Joseph ibn Zaddik). A third and by far larger group of poems are religious, and consist mainly of compositions of a liturgical character (*piyyutim*). Composed for all the Jewish festivals the *piyyutim* include poems dealing with the Diaspora. Many of these poems reflect the tragic suffering of the Jewish people. "Is there not in the East or West," the poet cries, "one place where we might live in peace? How much longer, O God, must I burn in the consuming flames between Edom and Arab, whom you have set above me for judges?"[73]

The most famous of Judah ha-Levi's poems are the *Shirei Ziyyon* (also known as the *Zionides*).[74] These 35 nationalistic verses, written over a period of several decades, speak of the unquenchable longing of the Jews for their ancient homeland. In these lyrics the beauty and luxury of Spain are depicted as unreal in contrast to the one place where the Jewish people can fulfill their special destiny, where they first realized they were God's people, where patriarchs and prophets received divine revelations, and where the Temple stood. Throughout the *Zionides* the poet contrasts the current status of the Jews (and his own situation) with the emptiness of life in exile under alien rulers. In these verses Judah ha-Levi had become a spokesman for the return of the Jews to the Holy Land, which he felt would restore them to their rightful place in history.

From the *Zionides,* it is obvious that for Judah ha-Levi life in Spain had become impossible, as well as a betrayal of God. However, he was not yet ready to take the final step of emigrating to Eretz Israel. Instead, he completed his magnum opus, *The Kuzari* (*Book of the Khazars*),[75] a theological work that had taken the author 20 years to write. The Arabic title, *Book of Argument and Proof in Defense of the Despised Faith* clearly indicated the work's thesis. It was a classical defense of Judaism, cast in the form of a dialogue between a king of the Khazars (Bulan), ready to relinquish paganism, an Aristotelian philosopher, a Muslim, a Christian, and a Jewish sage. This literary device enabled Judah ha-Levi to compare the teachings of the various protagonists. When the king discovers that both Christians and Muslims rest their appeal upon the Jewish scriptures he agrees to convert to Judaism. During the course of the dialogue with the Jew the king had taunted the sage with the lip service his people gave to a future restoration in Palestine. They pray for it daily, the king noted, yet are loath to relinquish their possessions in exile. In shame, the Jewish sage thereupon resolves to expatriate himself and settle in the ancestral home.

Judah ha-Levi practiced what he preached. Immediately after his completion of *The Kuzari* he made ready to fulfil the vow he had uttered through the mouth of his fictional character. His friends tried in vain to persuade him not to undertake the hazardous journey (Palestine at this time was under crusader control). At last, on September 8, 1140, he set out for the Holy Land. His passage through Spain was like a triumphal procession. Jewish communities such as those of Cordova and Granada vied with each other in honoring the great poet and philosopher. Finally, in the company of faithful friends, he embarked for Egypt. A great reception awaited him in Alexandria, where he arrived after a stormy sea voyage at the time of the Feast of the Tabernacles. In spite of his desire to press on to Jerusalem he was delayed for several months by his Alexandrian host, the chief rabbi and physician Aaron Benzion ibn Alamani. After enjoying unlimited hospitality and fully recovering his health, which had suffered during the sea crossing to Egypt, Judah ha-Levi managed to tear away at last from his host. He hastened to Damietta where he hoped to board a vessel bound for Palestine. Once again the journey was interrupted because an invitation awaited him from the Jewish *nagid* (prince) at Fustat, Samuel son of Hananiah Abu Manzur, to visit him. With much reluctance, the poet accepted the invitation of the head of Egyptian Jewry. Judah ha-Levi was charmed with the *nagid* and his household, but after a brief stay, armed with letters of introduction, he returned to the port of Damietta. What happened next is mainly conjecture. From elegies written in Egypt and some Genizah letters that mention Judah ha-Levi's death, it could be concluded that he never reached Jerusalem, and that he had expired some six months after reaching Alexandria.[76] Some scholars, on the other hand, believe that, saddened by the Christian occupation of Eretz Israel, he wandered to Tyre and Damascus. Still other writers insist that the poet-philosopher achieved his life-long quest to see Jerusalem. Legend suggests that when Judah ha-Levi saw Jerusalem in the distance (some versions say when he stood in front of the Western Wall), he threw himself to the ground and began to pour out his soul in stirring verses for Zion when he was trodden underfoot and stabbed to death by an Arab horseman.

Moses ben Nahman (Nahmanides)

Throughout the Middle Ages, the vast majority of Jews were convinced that if they did not waiver in their faith, redemption was inevitable. These sentiments were frequently augmented by the utterances and writings of prominent rabbinical leaders. One of the most distinguished of a long line of rabbis to advocate the resettlement of the Land of Israel was Moses ben Nahman (acronym Rambam), also known as Nahmanides, or by his Spanish name Bonastruc de Porta (1194–1270).[77] He was the spiritual leader of Spanish Jewry, and the foremost talmudist of his time. Nahmanides' youth was spent in an environment not radically different from his Christian contemporaries in the urban society of southern Europe—a setting in which the songs of the troubadours, the lore of the gnostics, and the preaching of ascetics all found a hearing. Moses ben Nahman himself wrote poetry, and studied philosophy, medicine, rabbinics, and Kabbalah.

However, for the young scholar eager to absorb all that Judaism had to offer, the Talmud was the ultimate authority. Indeed, Moses ben Nahman was barely beyond the age of puberty when his name began to be counted among the great talmudic scholars of

Europe. Both his early writings and later works were distinguished by unusual acumen and profundity, as well as by a distinctive conservative trend. He was, for example, opposed to the Greco-Arabic philosophy that had made great inroads into Judaism. Neither did he sympathize with the rationalism of the great Jewish philosopher Maimonides (1135–1204). Unlike Maimonides, Nahmanides refused to regard philosophy as the touchstone of religious truth. He believed that miracles were the foundation of Judaism on which rested its three pillars: the creation from nothing, the omniscience of God, and Divine Providence.

In 1238 he was called upon for support by Solomon of Montpellier who had been excommunicated by the Maimonists (the faction favoring the doctrines of Moses Maimonides). It was expected by the anti-Maimonists that since Nahmanides was so diametrically at variance with Maimonides intellectually and emotionally, that he would lean to the side of the opponents of philosophical studies. However, Nahmanides disliked the quarrel and pleaded for a hearing of both sides to the controversy before a court. In this sense, he addressed a letter to the Jewish communities of Aragon, Navarre, and Castile in which he harshly criticized the Maimonists. However, the great respect he professed for Maimonides as a scholar kept Moses ben Nahman from allying himself completely with the anti-Maimonist party. He preferred the role of a conciliator. He emphasized that Maimonides' great work the *Guide to the Perplexed,* which was the focal point of the controversy, was not intended for those of unshaken faith, but was meant for those Jews who had been led astray by the works of Aristotle and Galen. To placate both parties, Nahmanides proposed that the ban imposed by the anti-Maimonists against some portions of Maimonides' work be revoked, but that the ban against the study of the *Guide,* and against those persons who rejected talmudical interpretation of the Bible should be maintained and strengthened. The differences, however, were too fundamental to be settled by compromise and were accordingly rejected by both parties.

In spite of the turbulent religious controversies of his age, Moses ben Nahman, first as a rabbi of Gerona, and later as chief rabbi of Catalonia, seems to have led a quiet and happy life, surrounded by his family and disciples, and enjoyed a universal reputation as a talmudic master. When well-advanced in years this idyllic existence was shattered by an event which compelled him to leave his family and native land. In 1263 he was called upon by King James I of Aragon (1213–1276) to engage in a religious disputation with Pablo Christiani, a Jewish apostate who had become a Dominican friar. In order to better understand the dilemma in which Nahmanides was placed it is essential to digress and examine in some detail the historical events leading up to the "disputation of Barcelona."

In 1233 Pope Gregory IX, bent upon destroying the last vestiges of the Albigensians (members of a Catharistic sect of southern France), had conferred upon the Dominican order inquisitorial powers to ferret out and repress heresy. In all the large communities of Provence where Dominican cloisters were located special tribunals were created which condemned heretics, or those suspected of heresy. Quite often in the process innocent people were imprisoned or condemned to die at the stake. This religious frenzy was carried by the mendicant friars from France into Aragon where they sought to extend their antiheretic campaign to cover the Jews.

The Maimonidean controversy, which had rent apart the Jewish communities of Provence (and Spain), provided the Dominicans (some historians claim with the aid of the anti-Maimonist party of Montpellier) with the pretext for moving against the Jews. It began with a call to examine Jewish books (especially the Talmud) for blasphemous passages. This cry was picked up by the French scholastics and teachers in the University of Paris, and soon was echoed all over Europe. The established Church had largely ignored the Talmud until Nicholas Donin, a Jewish apostate to Christianity, denounced the work to Pope Gregory IX and provided the ecclesiastical tribunals with excerpts from the Talmud for scrutiny. Accordingly, the Pope addressed letters to the prelates and friars, and to the kings of France, England, and the Iberian Peninsula directing them to seize all Jewish books (on the Sabbath morning of March 3, 1240, when the Jews would be in their synagogues) and to turn them over to the Dominican and Franciscan orders. As far as is known the papal command was carried out only in Paris where, after a mock hearing, the Talmud was condemned to be burnt (also included were the writings of Maimonides). The wanton destruction of the volumes was finally halted by Gregory's successor Innocent IV, who reminded his flock that Judaism was a tolerated faith, and that the Talmud was essential to its practice.

As the mid-thirteenth century approached, the mendicant friars embarked on an intensive campaign directed mainly against the Jews. They turned from condemnation of the Talmud to drawing upon it for support of Christian doctrines. The Talmud, they now contended, contained implicit corroboration of Christian teachings, but the rabbis, through ignorance and ill will, had deliberately concealed these facts. The key propagandist for this new approach was the apostate Pablo Christiani who, as a member of the Dominican order, had been sent by his general, Raymond de Penyaforte (appointed by Gregory IX as chief agent of the Inquisition for Aragon and Castile, and confessor of King James I of Aragon), to proselytize among the Jews of Provence. Christiani's mission met with little success, and the Dominican general decided that better results could be achieved in Aragon by forcing the most famous rabbi in Spain to participate in a public disputation on the relative merits of Judaism and Christianity. If Nahmanides lost the debate, Raymond de Penyaforte hoped to effect without difficulty the wholesale conversion of the Jewish communities of Aragon to the Christian faith. The Dominican prelate informed the Aragonese king (James I) of his plan and persuaded the latter to call for the disputation.

Unable to ignore the king's command, the aged Jewish scholar agreed to debate Pablo Christiani before the royal court at Barcelona. However, he stipulated that complete freedom of speech be granted him so that he might meet his opponent on an equal footing. The king consented. At the very beginning of the disputation (it would last four days from July 20 to 24, 1263) Nahmanides defined the points to be discussed. The topics were: whether the Messiah had appeared or not; whether according to the prophecies of the Bible the Messiah was to be considered as God, or as man born of human parents; and whether the Jews or Christians were in possession of the true faith. From the start of the debate Nahmanides overwhelmed his opponent and the efforts of Raymond de Penyaforte to disconcert him. When the Dominican general admonished the Jewish disputant not to cast aspersions on the Catholic Church, Nahmanides retorted that he was familiar with the rules of propriety.

During the course of the debate, Christiani contended that the Messiah had already come, and asserted as proofs certain haggadic passages (Jewish lore forming especially the non-legal part of the Talmud). In reply Nahmanides pointed out that a Jew is bound to believe in the truth of the Bible, and in the exposition of the Talmud in all points of religious practice, but he was perfectly at liberty to accept or reject haggadic interpretations whether found in the Talmud or in Midrash literature. Haggadic expositions,

Nahmanides emphasized, represented only homilies, which a Jew might accept or reject as private opinions. These were startling words to Christiani, who immediately accused the elderly sage of heresy, but Nahmanides was not to be intimidated by his opponent's attack. Instead, he went on the offensive by proving that the biblical prophets had thought of a Messiah as a man of flesh and blood, and not as a divinity. Furthermore, the messianic promises of a reign of universal peace and justice had not yet been fulfilled. On the contrary, since the appearance of Jesus the world had become filled with violence and injustice.

As the disputation turned in favor of Moses ben Nahman, the Jews of Barcelona, fearing the resentment of the Dominicans, entreated him to discontinue. Many knights, clergymen, and burghers also warned the rabbi, and urged the closure of the dangerous spectacle. But the king, in spite of the apprehensions that prevailed among the Jewish and Christian inhabitants of Barcelona, desired the disputation to continue. Accordingly, after a recess of several days the debate was resumed. Nahmanides continued to hold his own against Christiani until the abrupt conclusion of the disputation. The king, in a private audience with the rabbi, acknowledged the latter's performance, and ruefully remarked, "I have never seen a man defend a wrong course so well."[78] The Dominicans, however, refused to accept defeat and spread the rumor that Pablo Christiani had outwitted his opponent so decisively that Nahmanides, overcome with shame, had fled the city. In reality, the rabbi remained in Barcelona for a whole week after the disputation in order to attend synagogue on the Sabbath and to hear a Christian sermon forced upon the Jewish community by the Dominicans. James I, accompanied by members of his court, also came to the synagogue to listen to Raymond de Penyaforte deliver a talk on the Christian trinity to his reluctant audience. In response Nachmanides forced the confessor of the king to acknowledge that the idea of the trinity was so profound that even the angels were unable to understand it. Seeing his opportunity, the rabbi added, ". . . if this is really the case, then no reproach ought to be made to men, if they cannot surpass the angels in wisdom."[79] The next day Nachmanides took his leave of the king, who dismissed him with a friendly farewell and gave him a gift of 300 *maravedis* as a mark of respect.

Despite their setback the Dominican friars redoubled their efforts to convert the Jews. The king supported the friars on some occasions, and at other times took measures to protect the Jews. However, less than a month after the disputation, James I issued a series of rescripts designed to facilitate the missionary work of the friars, notably the work of Pablo Christiani. He was given permission to renew his disputations with the Jews throughout Aragon and the royal dominions beyond the Pyrenees. The Jews were ordered to defray the expenses of Christiani out of the taxes due to the king, and to supply the convert with books. Unable to make headway in winning over the Jews and bitter over his repeated failures, he decided to follow in the footsteps of the apostate Nicholas Donin by denouncing the Talmud as a repository of derogatory and blasphemous references to Jesus and Christianity. Christiani presented these charges in person to Pope Clement IV who, at the request of the friar, issued a papal bull (1264) commanding officials once again to seize copies of the Talmud and to submit them to the Dominicans and Franciscans for examination. When the bull reached Aragon the king complied with the edict by creating a panel of censors to expurgate all objectionable passages from the confiscated books. However, to counter the zeal of the Dominicans, Raymond de Penyaforte, and Christiani, the king included on the panel of censors the Bishop of Barcelona and the Franciscan,

Peter de Janus, both of whom were more restrained in their religious ardor than the fanatical friars.

Nahmanides, alarmed by these developments and the false rumors circulated about him by the Dominicans, decided to write an accurate account of what had transpired during the contest. At the request of the bishop of his native town Gerona, he furnished the latter a copy of the final manuscript, which he had entitled *Sefer ha-Vikuach* ("The Book of the Debate"). When the bishop raised no objections to the book's publication, copies were made and widely circulated among the Jewish communities of Spain. As might have been expected Nahmanides' account of the contest aroused the ire of the Dominicans. Pablo Christiani accused the rabbi of having written a work replete with blasphemous passages against Christianity. The Dominican general lodged a formal complaint with the king against the rabbi from Gerona. James I was obliged to entertain the charges made by the Dominican leader, and called into being an extraordinary commission to hear the case. The proceedings were held in April of 1265, and conducted in the king's presence. Moses ben Nahman freely admitted that his pamphlet contained statements antagonistic to Christianity, but insisted that he had written nothing that had not been stated at the Disputation of Barcelona. He reminded the commission that the king had granted him freedom of speech for the duration of the disputation. The justice of his defense was recognized by the king and the commission, but to satisfy the Dominicans, Nahmanides was condemned to two years' exile, and an order was given to burn his pamphlet. The Dominicans, however, were not appeased by the sentence. They had planned to summon the rabbi before their own tribunal where they would have undoubtedly condemned him to death. Angry at the king for the mild punishment he had meted out to Nahmanides, the Dominicans turned to Rome for assistance. They obtained from Pope Clement IV letters reaffirming the stand taken by Gregory IX against the Talmud. A short time later Clement IV issued the bull *Turbato Corde,* which became the basic doctrine of the Inquisition for the prosecution of Judaizing heresies. The bull empowered the inquisitor to proceed against false converts, and against Jews who proselytized among Christians or converts. The pope also addressed a stern letter to James I demanding the most rigorous punishment of, ". . . the man who had composed a tract full of falsehood concerning his disputation with Pablo Christiani . . . and even circulated copies of the book in order to disseminate his erring faith."[80] Unable to withstand such papal pressure the king reversed his commission's earlier decision and condemned Nahmanides to perpetual banishment.

Compelled to abandon his native land, family, disciples, and friends, Nahmanides left Aragon and sojourned for some time in Castile and southern France before making his way to the Holy Land. For most of his life the rabbi of Gerona had, like his spiritual kinsman Judah ha-Levi, been filled with an intense longing for Zion. He believed it was the religious duty of every Jew to dwell in Eretz Israel. Fate, he believed, had done him a kindness for his banishment gave him the chance to fulfill this religious command.

In the summer of 1267, Nahmanides finally achieved his most cherished desire. He arrived in the Holy Land at Jean d'Acre, which was still under the control of the Christians. From Acre he traveled to Jerusalem. His feelings were deeply stirred on seeing the condition of the city. The Tartar invasion of 1260 had devastated Jerusalem, and transformed the city into a heap of ruins. Buildings had been demolished, and Jerusalem had become depopulated. Astonishingly, Jewish survivors connected this extraordinary event with their hopes for the advent of the Messiah.[81] This expectation, however, soon expired with the expulsion of the invaders by the sultan of Egypt.

Nahmanides was saddened by what he observed. All of Judea was devastated. The Jewish population of Jerusalem, he discovered, had either been slain or scattered to the four winds; only two self-supporting Jews were to be found in the city. The scrolls of the law had been rescued by some Jews who had fled to Shechem. Following the catastrophe 2,000 Muslims and 300 Christians had settled again in Jerusalem, but only a few Jews had returned.[82]

Moses ben Nahman bent all his efforts to revitalize the Jewish community of the Holy City. He organized the Jewish returnees, had the sacred scrolls brought back to Jerusalem, and established a synagogue in one of the demolished residences. In addition, he encouraged pilgrims from Damascus, Aleppo, and elsewhere in Syria to participate in the rebuilding of a viable Jewish community. Slowly, the mild mannered rabbi with an iron will gathered about him a circle of pupils and founded an academy for talmudic studies. Reports of his activities circulated rapidly, and many Jews streamed into Jerusalem. People came to hear him speak from as far away as the Euphrates, and even Karaites, the bitter enemies of Talmudism, forgot their animosities to sit at his feet.

In 1268 Nahmanides moved to Acre, where he became the spiritual leader of the Jewish community following the death that year of his predecessor Jehiel ben Joseph of Paris. Here he completed his commentary on the Pentateuch, which he had begun while still in Spain. Nahmanides had in mind the layman who possessed both the prerequisite schooling and the interest to desire an exposition of the Scriptures. The commentary was an eloquent blend of philological precision, rabbinical tradition, and mysticism.

From the first day of his arrival in Eretz Israel until his death in 1270, Nahmanides maintained a correspondence with the land of his birth. He sent copies of his writings to his sons and friends in Spain, and provided them with vivid descriptions of conditions in the ancestral Jewish homeland. His correspondence awoke among some Spanish Jews an ardent longing for the Promised Land, and induced them to follow Nahmanides' example and emigrate. More importantly, Nahmanides' efforts had ensured a continuing presence of Jews in Jerusalem, and had in the process prevented the age-old dream of a Jewish return to Eretz Israel from becoming a mere chimera.

The site of Moses ben Nahman's tomb, like that of the first Moses, remains a mystery. Some scholars believe he was interred in Haifa, alongside the grave of Jehiel of Paris, while others claim he was buried at the foot of Mount Carmel. Still others assert his tomb is in Hebron. A few writers believe the village of Silwan, near Jerusalem, to be the final resting place of the great talmudic savant.

Obadiah ben Abraham di Bertinoro

The love of, or rather yearning for, the Promised Land, was at all times markedly strong among Italian Jews. It was easier for them, than for most other European Jews, to make pilgrimages to Eretz Israel. They lived so much nearer to its shores, and communication between the two countries was, especially during the Renaissance, generally good. Except for the years between 1427 and 1430, and 1467 and 1487, when Italian sea captains were forbidden by the papacy to transport Jews to Palestine, there was a constant stream of Jewish pilgrims traveling to their ancient homeland. Although few, they played a disproportionately large part in the renewal of Jewish life in Palestine that took place in the sixteenth century. The groundwork for this upsurge in Jewish immigration, however, was laid in the closing decade of the preceding century with the arrival in the Holy Land, at the time a Mameluke province, of the Italian talmudist, Obadiah ben Abraham di Bertinoro (1450–1510).[83]

Born in northern Italy at Bertinoro (in the province of Flori), Obadiah, also known as Yare (a Hebrew acrostic meaning "Let him be the favored of his brethren"), was trained from childhood for the rabbinate. Little is known of his family background, except that prior to his emigration to Palestine Obadiah lived in the small community of Citta di Castello. Early in his rabbinical career he began work on a popular commentary on the Mishnah—the legal codification containing the core of the postbiblical oral Torah, compiled and edited by Rabbi Ha-Nassi at the beginning of the third century of the common era. This magnum opus of Obadiah, which he would complete years later in Jerusalem, would win for him great fame as a talmudic scholar. Indeed, the importance of his contribution is best attested to by the fact that since the original publication of the commentary (Venice, 1519), hardly an edition of the Mishnah has been printed without its inclusion.

Having determined to live out his days on holy ground, Obadiah set out for Eretz Israel on October 29, 1486. From his home in Citta di Castello he traveled south through Italy and Sicily, and thence to Rhodes, Egypt, and finally Palestine. Traveling at a leisurely pace, the journey took the Italian rabbi over one and one-half years. Thus the inquisitive talmudist had ample time to observe the conditions of the Jewish communities though which he passed. His letters to his relatives describing his experiences are among the classics of Jewish geographical and travel literature. Written in the pungent, nervous Hebrew prose characteristic of the Italian Jews of the Renaissance, Obadiah's graphic descriptions, although intended only as private correspondence, are of great historical value. Unlike his medieval predecessors, who merely listed sites of holy places, Obadiah observed and commented on everything. He presents a lively record of the foreign lands he visited; of the political, economic, and social life of the inhabitants and of their customs; and records his personal experiences as well as places of interest worthy of a tourist's inspection.

On his arrival in Jerusalem (March 25, 1488), Obadiah was bitterly disappointed. Instead of the earthly paradise that he had expected, he found corruption, rampant oppression, and poverty. There was a complete lack of Jewish communal organization; cultural and moral life was at a low ebb; and the Muslim population was hostile.

The Mameluke officials and tax collectors were particularly rapacious and dishonest, and their Jewish agents no less venal. In a long letter to his father, Obadiah described the ungenerous spirit of Jerusalem's community organization. In vivid terms he portrayed how the wicked elders oppressed Jewish refugees and the poor by placing upon them intolerable tax burdens, and by making residence in Jerusalem a great hardship. Incredibly, these greedy and unprincipled men, Obadiah noted, had sold the synagogue furnishings, the crowns and ornaments of the Torah scrolls, and the scrolls themselves in order to fulfill their own avaricious appetites and to please their Mameluke masters. As a result of these excesses the Jerusalem Jewish community had been reduced to 70 poverty-stricken households

Corruption, poverty, and moral decay, however, could not completely suppress Obadiah di Bertinoro's basic optimism. His faith remained unshaken, and he found much to be grateful. Unlike many of the newcomers to Palestine who were unable to adjust to the country's climate and fell ill, Obadiah's health remained robust. In addition, his strong personality, in combination with his scholarship and eloquent oratory, led to his immediate acceptance as spiritual head of the Jewish community of Jerusalem. He used this position to bring about badly needed reforms, and to infuse new hope in what had been a moribund society.

In rapid order he set about suppressing corruption and improving relations with the Muslims, as well as with the Karaites and Samaritans. Obadiah also created new philanthropic agencies, and raised the educational levels of the community by instituting regular courses of instruction, and by the establishment of a talmudic academy. He also secured the removal of the onerous annual tax of 400 ducats, which had afforded the elders the opportunity for self-aggrandizement at the expense of the community. In its place a simple poll tax was substituted, payable directly to the government. Obadiah also made himself responsible for the collection of funds from Italy for support of the poor. Emanuel Hai Camerino of Florence to whom Obadiah had entrusted his property, and who promised to send him 100 ducats, added twenty-five more ducats for charity. The wealthy brother of Obadiah di Bertinoro also sent him contributions for the poor Jews of Jerusalem.

Whereas before the advent of Obadiah men of wealth and piety had tended to leave Jerusalem, now with the improvement of conditions brought about by his reforms, many returned to the city. This trend would continue in the decade following Obadiah's demise. Isaac Solal, for example, the last head (*nagid*) of Egyptian Jewry transferred his wealth and beneficent activity to Jerusalem (1517), leaving the rabbinate of Cairo in the hands of David ibn Abi Zimra

In the years of Obadiah di Bertinoro's leadership of the Jewish community of Jerusalem harmony and justice prevailed. No longer were the poor harassed, or the members of the community driven to despair or voluntary exile by rapacious and tyrannical representatives. A host of benevolent institutions such as hospitals, burial and relief societies, and educational facilities were overhauled, reinvigorated, and placed under competent management. This was a far cry from the situation that existed when Obadiah had arrived in Jerusalem. Indeed, on one occasion shortly after settling in the Holy City, he had been compelled to dig a grave because the community had provided no one to perform that labor.

Most importantly, Obadiah's presence in Jerusalem contributed to an improvement in the moral tone of the Jewish community. For over two decades he taught the growing community genuine piety and nobility of sentiment by precept and example. Almost imperceptibly Obadiah's fame spread throughout the Holy Land and the neighboring countries. He came to be looked upon as the guardian angel of Jerusalem. Even the Muslim population acknowledged his merits and frequently called upon him to decide judicial cases. An Italian pilgrim, reflecting on Obadiah's sway over the Jewish community of Jerusalem, noted that everything was done according to his orders, and that no one dared gainsay his instructions.

As a result of Obadiah's efforts the groundwork was prepared for an expansion of the Jewish community in Palestine. The trigger for such a population increase was provided by the expulsion of the Jews from Spain in 1492. It was natural that many of the refugees turned to the land that had been associated with their hopes and prayers for so many centuries. In a relatively short time the Jewish population of the Holy Land increased dramatically. The newcomers included not only those who had left Spain as practicing Jews, but also New Christians and Marranos who were drawn to Palestine to be able to return to Judaism. Obadiah greeted the first refugees from the Iberian Peninsula with open arms. He became their leader, and they supported his reforms and continuing campaign to raise the moral and intellectual standards of the community.

Obadiah di Bertinoro died in 1510 just as large-scale immigration to Palestine of Spanish and Portuguese Jews was about to begin. The Italian rabbi who had done so much to stabilize the Jewish community was buried on the Mount of Olives in Jerusalem. Conditions favoring Jewish immigration to the Holy Land had come about as a result of the conquest of Jerusalem by the Ottoman sultan, Selim I. The sultan, who had also annexed Syria and Egypt, was acclaimed by many Jews as the "scion of Cyrus the Great." Unlike the Mamelukes, he was exceedingly tolerant toward the Jews, whose commercial and intellectual talents he valued. Under Selim's benevolent rule many Jewish refugees from Spain and Portugal, as well as elsewhere in Europe, flocked to the Holy Land. Soon large communities of Jews were in Jerusalem, Safed, Tiberias and Hebron—the so-called four holy cities of Palestine.

Some of the new immigrants earned a living as artisans and merchants; others supported themselves as manual laborers. Many were ardent pietists and mystics. The latter group, having arrived in the Promised Land, considered it an impiety to engage in any occupation and devoted themselves completely to the study of Torah. They depended on the generosity of Jews in the Diaspora for material support. Year after year representatives known as "emissaries of the merciful" were sent by Palestinian Jewish communities to the four corners of the earth to collect funds on behalf of the pious. The efforts of these representatives helped to bring the latest currents of scholarship to the Diaspora and kept alive the memory of the Holy Land. [84]

6

The House Of Mendes

More pragmatic than Obadiah di Bertinoro in attempting to promote Jewish interests and to restore the Jews to their ancient homeland were two outstanding members of a powerful and influential Marrano household known as Nasi-Mendes.[85] The family had left Spain for Portugal at the time of the expulsion, and had been subjected to forcible baptism in 1497. Some scholars believe that the Nasi family, who changed their name to Mendes after accepting Christianity, somehow were able to smuggle a large fortune out from Spain to Portugal. Although converted, they continued to live their lives as secret Jews. By the beginning of the sixteenth century the Mendes family was well established in Portugal, and its members moved in the highest circles of the country. Their business firm, "The House of Mendes" was regarded as the leading trading company in the land, with extensive links to Levantine, Asian, and African trade, and agents in England, France, Italy, and Flanders.

The founder of this trading and banking empire was Francisco Mendes. He was married to the daughter of another distinguished Marrano family, the Benveniste, who had been financial advisors to the kings of Aragon for many years. Francisco's wife, a woman of great charm and beauty, concealed her Jewishness under the adopted name, Beatrice de Luna (1510–69). A younger brother of Francisco, called Samuel, had been baptized Agostinho Miguez, and had become a body-physician to the Portuguese king, and a teacher of medicine at the University of Lisbon. His son Joao Miguez (1524–79) and Beatrice de Luna would become the guiding lights of the House of Mendes.

While Francisco lived, Lisbon remained the headquarters of his firm. However, the company's most thriving branch was in Antwerp and it was under the direct supervision of Diego Mendes, another brother of Francisco. The choice of Antwerp as the most important of the Mendes family establishments was anything but fortuitous as the city had become the leading port in Europe. British, French, Spanish, and Portuguese mercantile

54

firms were well represented in the city, as were the powerful German banking houses of Fugger, Welser, and Hochsteller. Conversos such as the Mendes family were encouraged to settle in Antwerp and enjoyed all the rights, freedoms, and franchises accorded to foreign merchants.[86]

The demise of Francisco in 1534 created a crisis in the House of Mendes. His wife Beatrice, then 24 years old and the mother of a beautiful daughter named Reyna, became the head of the family's Portuguese undertakings. Fearing the Inquisition would eventually confiscate their property, she decided to quietly liquidate the firm's headquarters in Lisbon and seek a safer environment elsewhere. Because the Portuguese were suspicious of all Conversos, and frowned on any flight of wealth from the country, Beatrice, for reasons of security, gave out that she intended to make an inspection tour of the family's various foreign enterprises. Beatrice soon turned her plan to abandon Portugal into action. Accompanied by a large entourage of servants, a younger sister, and several nephews she left Lisbon and traveled to England where she was welcomed as a noblewoman. Eventually, she moved on to Antwerp, the real goal of her journey, to join her late husband's brother, Diego. Some time earlier, Joao Miguez had also joined his uncle in Antwerp.

In Antwerp, Beatrice and her household settled down in one of the great mansions of the city. Her upbringing, extraordinary intelligence, beauty, and social graces, as well as great wealth, attracted both nobility and merchant princes. Shortly after her arrival in the port city she was introduced to the regent Mary, the former Queen of Hungary and sister of the Emperor Charles V (who had granted the Marranos the right of residence in the Netherlands). Mary, quite taken with the beautiful Beatrice, gave her a position as a lady in waiting, and Joao was given a comparable post in the court of Charles V.

However, Beatrice was by no means at ease in Antwerp. Her deep love for Judaism, which she was compelled to deny, and her desire to find a place where she could practice it openly, made Flanders just as hateful to her as Portugal had been. Oppressed by the pretense of passing as a Christian, and disturbed by the frequent outbursts of hostility against Jews and Marranos, she became convinced that the Mendes family was again in great danger. Even Joao, whose winning personality and talents had made him a court favorite was not immune from these fears. He had been arrested twice for Judaizing, and had only gained his freedom after the Emperor and his sister had personally intervened on his behalf. During his incarcerations several attempts had been made by officials to confiscate the Mendes fortune (after studying at the University of Louvain, Joao had become an active member of the family's banking establishment). Beatrice became further alarmed when Queen Mary personally solicited the hand of her daughter Reyna for one of the court favorites. It is reported that she replied without mincing words that she would rather see the maiden dead than sanction such a marriage. The incredible refusal made it advisable for the family to seek a new home.

Beatrice importuned her brother-in-law Diego, who had married her younger sister (in the Cathedral of Nôtre-Dame) either to go elsewhere with her, or buy out her share of the family business. Diego agreed to the latter proposal, but died before the projected parting of the ways. This unexpected turn of events left Beatrice as sole head of the Mendes family and fortune. The new responsibilities forced her temporarily to postpone plans to find a more tolerant home, and to concentrate on protecting the family interests. Indeed, the large holdings of the House of Mendes had attracted the attention of Charles V. An accusation was made that the recently deceased Diego Mendes had secretly practiced

Judaism, and therefore the whole of his property, being that of a heretic, was subject to confiscation by the Imperial treasury. Although an order was issued that the books and goods of Diego Mendes be seized, Beatrice was able by a series of bribes and judicious loans to forestall its implementation. However, it was now impossible to leave Antwerp without arousing the suspicion of the authorities.

At length the hour of deliverance seemed at hand, but things did not go as planned. Just as large trunks and cases of the House of Mendes, filled with valuables, were being loaded aboard ships, government agents intervened. Three coffers containing gold, diamonds, and pearls were seized. A charge was brought against Beatrice for smuggling and Judaizing. Beatrice, however, could not be found. She and her household had quietly left Antwerp ostensibly to take the cure in Aix-la-Chappele. From there the group had dispersed and gradually made their way to Venice, Italy. On her arrival in Venice (1544), Beatrice and her daughter were denounced and arrested as secret Jews. They had been betrayed to the authorities by the widow of Diego Mendes who was anxious to wrest her husband's estate from Beatrice. This reckless and scatter-brained younger sister of Beatrice had asked the Venetian government to assist her in obtaining possession of the Mendes wealth so that she might use it as a good Christian for the benefit of the residents of the Adriatic port. She also sent an agent to France to take possession of the Mendes property in that country. The avaricious envoy, seeing an opportunity to enrich himself, denounced his employer to the French authorities (he accused her of being a heretic). The French court, following the example of the greedy Venetians, confiscated the Mendes property. The French King, Henry II, who had previously borrowed large sums from the Mendes family, used the affair as an alibi to cancel his debt.

For two years Beatrice remained incarcerated in Venice. She was, however, treated with respect and deference, probably because the Venetian government feared international repercussions. Throughout this period, Joao Miguez labored to set his aunt free. After many false starts, he finally found a way to induce the Turkish sultan, Suleiman the Magnificent to embrace his cause. With the help of the sultan's physician, Moses Hamon, a refugee from Granada, Joao planted the idea that Beatrice and the Mendes fortune had been destined for Constantinople. Joao suggested that the Venetian Republic, which existed only by Ottoman forbearance, had illegally detained Beatrice and deprived the sultan's treasury of this wealth. Once aroused, the sultan gave instructions that a special envoy be sent to the Doge of Venice demanding the immediate release of Beatrice and her daughter and that their confiscated property be returned. The Venetians, fearful of the Turks, eventually complied.

Following her release, Beatrice found a temporary refuge in Ferrara under the protection of its liberal duke, Hercules of Este. Here she resided for several years, and declared herself openly as a Jewess. Beatrice de Luna now became Gracia Mendes (she chose the name Gracia because it was the Spanish version of the Hebrew name Hannah which means grace). In Ferrara she resumed her role as a great lady, living in grand style and keeping an open house for scholars, aristocrats, merchant princes, and ordinary Jews in need of a helping hand. The famous translation of the Bible, published by Abraham Usque and Yomtob Athias in 1553 (known as the Ferrara Bible), was largely the result of her patronage, and was in fact inscribed to Gracia Mendes. Samuel Usque, a kinsman of Abraham, dedicated to Gracia his great Portuguese chronicle *Consolations in the Tribulations of Israel*. The inscription read, "To your excellence, as the heart of the body [i.e., of the Jews of Portuguese origin who had escaped the fires of the Inquisition] in whose bones your name and your happy memory will be carved forever."[87] This tribute was well-deserved for Donna Gracia had organized an incredible underground organization that assisted hundreds, perhaps even thousands, of Marranos to escape from the Iberian Peninsula.

During this same period, Gracia's gifted nephew, Joao Miguez, was engaged in overseeing the Mendes business interests in Lyons, Marseilles, Rome, and Sicily, and preparing for the family's final move. Eventually, in 1553, after taking care that the needs of all the members of the Mendes family were met (including those of the sister who had betrayed her) Gracia left for Constantinople. She was warmly received by the Jews of the Ottoman capital, and by the sultan, who expected to gain commercial and financial advantages from her residence in Turkey.

Of the 100,000 Jews in Constantinople at that time at least 10,000 were Marranos. The Ottoman Empire had become the most secure refuge from Christian persecution and intolerance. The Ottoman Turks could not understand Spain and Portugal's expulsion of the Jews, a practice which, as the sultan noted, had impoverished Spain and enriched Turkey. Under the wise rule of Suleiman the Magnificent, the Ottoman Empire had greatly expanded. Hungary, Rumania, Tabriz, Rhodes, Algiers, Baghdad, and Aden had all come under the aegis of the Ottoman Turks. The Mendes family was destined to play a role in the Empire's continuing expansion.

Not long after Donna Gracia had settled in Constantinople, Joao Miguez followed her lead. His arrival in the city, with a large entourage of servants, aboard a Mendes family vessel was treated as an affair of state. A German contemporary, named Hans Dernschwam, an employee of the Fuggers, the richest international business concern in sixteenth-century Europe, and an individual hostile to Jews noted the event in his diary.

> This rogue, whom I have just mentioned, came to Constantinople in 1554 with over twenty well dressed Spanish servants. They attend him as if he were a prince. He himself wore silk clothes lined with sable. Before him went two janizaries with slaves, as mounted lackeys, as is the Turkish custom, in order that nothing should happen to him. . . . The servants who came with him and with the women have also all been circumcised and have become Jews.[88]

Joao Miguez now also proclaimed his allegiance to Judaism and was at last able to discard his Christian name. He became Joseph Nasi, and shortly afterwards married his young cousin, the much-courted Reyna, daughter of Donna Gracia. The marriage bound even more tightly the bonds between Joseph Nasi and his mother-in-law. The Jewish inhabitants of the Ottoman Empire, and especially the Marranos scattered throughout the Diaspora, soon benefited from the generosity of the pair. Donna Gracia and Joseph Nasi helped the poor, established houses of prayer and schools, and made every effort to rescue those Jews confronted by hostile rulers or governments.

Thus when news came that Pope Paul IV had launched a campaign of persecution against the Jews of Italy, and had imprisoned a number of Marranos who lived in Ancona, Donna Gracia joined with Joseph Nasi in an effort to save them.[89] Ancona, an old Roman port city, was part of the Papal States, and the well being of the Jewish community, which dated back to the thirteenth century, depended on the policies of each succeeding pope. A few of the popes had enforced the Church doctrine that called for social separation and degradation of the Jews. Others had administered the Papal States as a secular government and had considered not only the spiritual values, but also the economic welfare of their subjects. Under the latter popes the Jewish community lived unmolested. Because the periods of freedom were more frequent than those of persecution, Ancona had become a magnet for Marranos from Spain and Portugal. They enjoyed papal protection, and with official consent discarded their Christian names for Jewish ones and were allowed to erect synagogues. Indeed, they were held in high esteem by most of the Christian community of Ancona. However, in May of 1555 the last of the benevolent popes, Julius III died and was succeeded by Giovanni Pietro Caraffa (Paul IV) a fanatic anti-Semite. Disregarding the assurances and promises given to the Marranos by his predecessors, he brought the Inquisition to Ancona. Trials were held, Marranos were tortured, and many were sentenced to die in autos-da-fé (i.e., burnt at the stake).

Donna Gracia and Joseph Nasi appealed to the Turkish sultan for help to succor the victims of the Inquisition. They entreated him to at least demand that the Marranos from Turkey who had been imprisoned in Ancona while on business there be released. Suleiman the Magnificent agreed to this request, and addressed a letter to the pope indicating that his subjects had been unjustly incarcerated, and if they were not immediately freed he would jail all Christians in his dominions. The pope, fearing the threatened retribution, immediately complied with the sultan's request and the Marranos from Turkey were set free. The remaining prisoners, however, had no such powerful voice to speak on their behalf. As a result 25 Marranos who remained steadfast in their loyalty to Judaism were condemned to the stake and 27 more confessed under torture that they had strayed from the Church. These were sentenced to hard labor on the island of Malta, but managed enroute to escape.

The Ancona affair shocked Jews everywhere. After several family meetings, Donna Gracia and Joseph Nasi decided to engage in a commercial war against the Papal States. They took the lead in a boycott that had been launched by some Marrano merchants against the port of Ancona. The boycott was designed not only to economically punish the pope, but also to reward Duke Guido Ubaldo of Pesaro, who had received some of the Marranos who had escaped from Ancona. All agents of the House of Mendes were instructed to bypass Ancona and send their goods to Pesaro. Other merchants took their cue from the Mendes family and joined the boycott. Sultan Suleiman also took a personal interest in the execution of this commercial war. Soon countless business establishments in Ancona went bankrupt, and the once busy harbor was almost completely empty. Though the boycott seemed effective, opposition to it soon developed from an unexpected quarter. The Jews of Ancona, who were neither Conversos nor Marranos, felt threatened by the boycott. They faced not only economic ruin, but also the wrath of the pope. The question of continuing the strangulation of the port of Ancona was placed in the hands of the rabbis. A unanimous decision was required, but was impossible to obtain. While the boycott debate was going on, the Duke of Pesaro, pressured by the Vatican, had a change of heart and expelled the Marannos from his realm. This development, and their inability to achieve Jewish solidarity for the boycott compelled Donna Gracia and Joseph Nasi to accept the inevitable, and bring to a conclusion the commercial war against the Papal States.

As Donna Gracia became more involved in her philanthropic causes and rescue efforts, endeavors that would occupy her remaining years, Joseph Nasi found a new arena for his considerable talents. Highly recommended by various foreign diplomats and by the Jewish personal physician to the Ottoman ruler, Joseph gained entry into the inner circle of Suleiman the Magnificent. Through his contacts and agents he was well informed about the activities in various European courts, and was able to keep the sultan current on political and military affairs in these countries. The sultan recognized Joseph Nasi's usefulness and ability. Court intrigue also played a role in heightening the importance of Joseph Nasi in Ottoman affairs. Hatred and jealousy were rife among the sons of Suleiman the Magnificent, all of whom were anxious to succeed him. The sultan favored a younger son named Bajazet because of the son's military prowess. As a result, Selim, the eldest son, was ignored by courtiers who were convinced that he would never inherit his father's throne. Only Joseph Nasi supported Selim and pressed his legitimate claims with Suleiman. On the strength of Joseph's arguments the sultan relented and made amends to his oldest son by presenting him with a gift of 50,000 ducats in cash and 30,000 more in valuables. He chose Joseph Nasi to be the bearer of these gifts to Selim's residence in Asia Minor. Selim, overwhelmed by the change in attitude of his father, assured Nasi of his gratitude and made him his favorite and confidant. Selim also showered Nasi with gifts and honors, including an appointment to the *Mutafarrica* (the imperial life-guard).[90]

Suleiman the Magnificent, who had ruled the Ottoman Empire for forty years and had made it the most powerful state of the age, died in 1566. His son Selim, who had defeated Bajazet in the decisive battle of Konia, inherited the throne. Bajazet fled to Persia and was later murdered, along with his four sons. Soon after his accession as Selim II the new sultan appointed Joseph Nasi Duke of the islands of Andros, Milo, Paros, Santorina, and the other islands of the Cyclades chain. These islands had previously been ruled by a Christian duke who had been deposed by the Turks. Joseph, who favored the title Duke of the Aegean Sea, Lord of Naxos, did not take up residence in his duchy as it was too far from the Ottoman capital. Instead, he remained in his palace, Belvedere, in Constantinople, and governed the islands through a deputy, a Spanish nobleman named Francisco Coronello. Coronello's father, a descendant of the Converso Abraham Senior, had been governor of Segovia. By this indirect method of governing, Nasi avoided any antipathy on the part of the Greek inhabitants of his domain. He also sought to gain the favor of the islanders by moderating their taxes—a step made possible by the generosity of the sultan, who demanded only from Nasi 14,000 ducats a year for the privilege of ruling the dukedom. Selim II further alleviated any possible financial burden for his favorite by allowing Joseph Nasi to collect duties on wine imported to Turkey by way of the Black Sea.

Despite the jealousy and intrigues of Nasi's chief enemy at court, the Grand Vizier Mohammed Sokolli, he remained so influential with the sultan that representatives of European powers often found it necessary to seek his advice and help. No Jew of his time, or probably of any period prior to the emancipation of the eighteenth century, played such an important role in European affairs. When an Austrian embassy arrived in Constantinople to sue for peace (after a series of victories gained by the Turks in Hungary) it was under instructions from the emperor, Maximillian II, to give lavish gifts to Nasi, and to solicit his aid for their cause.

In 1566 Joseph Nasi encouraged the Protestant Council of Antwerp to defy the Catholic king of Spain. William of Orange sent a confidential note to the Duke of Naxos asking him, in view of the revolt the Dutch were planning, to urge the sultan to declare war on Spain. Although Nasi sympathized with the Dutch he was not able to convince the sultan to take such a drastic step. The Jewish duke also carried on an active and friendly correspondence with Sigismund Augustus II of Poland, who frequently asked Nasi to support his emissaries in their negotiations with the Sublime Porte.

However, it was France and Venice, the two states that constantly sought Joseph Nasi's downfall, that were destined to feel the most his power and wrath. The French King had steadfastly refused to pay the debt contracted with the House of Mendes. In 1569 the Duke of Naxos decided to take action against the French monarch. Accordingly, he obtained a firman from Selim II which granted him permission to seize all ships flying the French flag that sailed into Turkish waters. Nasi sent privateers as far afield as Algiers to raid French merchant shipping. In the harbor of Alexandria his raiders succeeded in capturing several French vessels. The cargoes aboard these ships were sold to the amount of the debt owed the Mendes family, despite the protests lodged with the Sublime Porte by the French ambassador.[91]

The humiliated French king sought revenge. An opportunity to discredit the Duke of Naxos soon presented itself. A Jewish physician in the service of Nasi was bribed by the French ambassador to betray his employer. Lured by hopes of quick riches and feeling a personal animosity toward his employer, he accused the duke of treason. The French ambassador, convinced that he had successfully entrapped Nasi, passed on in cipher details of the plot to the French court. However, the entire intrigue was uncovered by Nasi, and he brought it to the attention of the sultan. Selim had no doubts as to the loyalty of his advisor, and the accuser was banished for life to the island of Rhodes. He was also excommunicated by the rabbis of Constantinople. The French, who had often boasted in European councils that their word carried the greatest weight at the Turkish court, were placed in disrepute and lost much of their influence.

The Duke of Naxos dealt even more severely with Venice. He had not forgotten the ill treatment his mother-in-law had received at the hands of the Venetian government. During the difficult years of the House of Mendes the Venetian government had refused his request for safe conduct through its territory for himself and his brother. In addition, Venice had acted in a dastardly manner toward the Marranos who sought refuge in the republic. Indeed, the policy of the Venetian government toward Jewish refugees, especially Marranos, had fluctuated wildly. In 1550 a hostile administration expelled all the Marranos in the republic. Joseph Nasi, who with his mother-in-law, had become the spokepersons for Marranos everywhere, now saw an opportunity to repay Venice for the indignities suffered by his people and family.

In 1571 a gunpowder explosion wreaked havoc in the arsenal of Venice, and destroyed much of the city's harbor. It was later asserted that the House of Mendes had paid arsonists to set the blaze. On learning the extent of the damage Nasi advised the sultan to take advantage of the situation by dispatching a fleet against the island of Cyprus (Venetian territory). Selim, who was not well disposed toward the Venetians, ignored the warnings of his grand vizier and agreed to Nasi's plan. In his excitement, or perhaps in his cups, Selim promised to make Joseph Nasi king of Cyprus if the expedition proved successful. The attacking Turkish fleet captured the island's capital, Nicosia, in the first assault, and the second important city of Famagusta fell after a difficult siege. Joseph Nasi had achieved his revenge against Venice, but not his kingdom. Although the Turks managed to complete their conquest of Cyprus, they later suffered a disastrous naval defeat at Lepanto, in consequence of which the peace party led by Nasi's rival, the Grand Vizier Sokolli gained the ascendancy and the sultan's ear.

Joseph Nasi had long cherished the idea of founding a Jewish state. Years earlier, while still a Marrano, he had requested of the rulers of the Republic of Venice one of its many islands which he planned to populate with Jews.[92] Though his plan was rejected by the

Venetians, Nasi did not abandon the idea. The plan took on new life soon after his arrival in Constantinople when Donna Gracia obtained from Sultan Suleiman the Magnificent concessions in Palestine near Tiberias (the city itself was in ruins). In the orders sent to the governor of Damascus and the director of the Wafq (lands designed for Muslim religious purposes), informing them of the concessions, some of the advantages that would accrue to the concessionaires were also spelled out. The region, it noted, contained considerable water resources, including a large lake as well as a number of hot springs. There were also abundant date palms and other fruit bearing trees. The site was also suitable for sugar cane planting and the manufacture of silk. To assuage the local authorities the orders also indicated that the concessionaires were willing to pay a sum for the rental of Tiberias.

Joseph Nasi obtained an extension of the grant, with some important additions in 1561. Under the new arrangements he was given plenary authority in Tiberias and seven nearby villages, with the understanding that he was to pay the Sublime Porte a fixed annual sum of 1,000 gold pieces for these privileges. It seems that both Suleiman and his successor Selim had little interest in Palestine as long as the Muslim shrines of the region were not endangered.

Joseph Nasi envisioned creation of a viable Jewish colony that would serve as a haven for refugees from Europe. His first step in carrying out his plan was to appoint Rabbi Joseph ben Ardut as his agent to supervise the rebuilding of Tiberias. Because Tiberias had once been a great city there was an abundance of building stone. There was also plenty of sand for mixing mortar as the Sea of Galilee was nearby. Labor, on orders of the Turkish sultan, was to be supplied to Rabbi Ardut from the villages leased to Nasi.

Work on the walls of Tiberias progressed slowly as opposition to the project mounted among the Arab laborers. They stalled partly from envy, and partly from fears aroused by an old sheik who warned that if the city was rebuilt, they and their religion would suffer dire consequences.

Joseph ben Ardut complained to the pasha of Damascus that the orders of the Turkish sultan were being ignored, and the Arab workers had stopped all work on the city walls of Tiberias. Terrified that the sultan's wrath would fall upon him, the pasha immediately sent his men to Tiberias to restore order. The soldiers promptly seized two of the Arab leaders and executed them. All resistance to the restoration of the city collapsed and construction resumed (the walls of Tiberias were completed in the winter of 1564–1565).

During the rebuilding of the city walls the diggers found a large stone, and under it an opening with a ladder descending to a chamber. It in turn led to a large Crusader church full of marble statues, and three large bells which the Christians had hidden in the days of Guy, the last Christian king of Jerusalem (he had been defeated in (1186–1187). The bells were eventually melted down and cast into cannon to be used for the defense of the new city.

With security achieved, Joseph Nasi turned his attention to developing the city's economy. He attempted to foster textile and silk manufacturing in the colony. Hundreds of mulberry trees were planted for the raising of silkworms; and wool was imported from Spain to make garments which would rival the products of Venice. In addition, Nasi sent a letter to Jewish communities inviting all who were willing to labor as farmers or artisans to settle in Tiberias. His proclamation was directed especially to the Jews of the Papal States driven to desperation by Pope Paul IV. A little community of 200, Cori in the Campagna, decided to emigrate en-masse when they heard that Nasi was asking for

Jewish craftsmen to resettle and restore Tiberias. It was the community's belief that the settlement of Tiberias represented the first sign of the coming of the messianic age.

The longing for a refuge from persecution reached new heights following the issuance of a papal bull (February 26, 1569) banishing the Jews from the Papal States. The Italian Jewish community of Pesaro also decided to accept Joseph Nasi's offer of an asylum in Tiberias, and 102 Jews from Pesaro boarded a ship in Venice bound for Palestine. The ill-fated vessel, however, was seized by Maltese pirates who sold their victims into slavery.

Although a small number of emigrants managed to reach Tiberias safely, the city did not grow as rapidly as Nasi had expected. The Marranos did not flock to Tiberias as the Duke had hoped. They evidently preferred urban life, however dangerous or tenuous, to life in isolated Galilee. Arab opposition to the settlement also played a role in frightening away potential colonists. Most crucial was the fact that these were years in which Joseph Nasi was completely preoccupied by his labors for the Sublime Porte, and could not personally preside over the Tiberias project. Indeed, the intrigues of his rivals in Constantinople led him to concentrate his efforts on survival. In spite of his inability to devote sufficient time to Tiberias he remained titular head of the city and surrounding region until the end of his life, when the venture was taken over by Don Solomon Abenaes, Duke of Mytilene, another Turkish-Jewish courtier who was originally from Spain. Don Abenaes entrusted the community's affairs to his son, who was more enthusiastic than practical. By 1598 the Tiberias experiment was in a state of crisis. Slowly the city reverted to its previous ruinous condition. The houses, which had been erected for the expected flood of refugees, remained empty, and the untended mulberry trees withered and died.[93]

After the death of Sultan Selim II, Joseph Nasi retired from public life to his Belvedere palace, and devoted himself almost exclusively to furthering Jewish scholarship. Like his mother-in-law Donna Gracia (who is believed to have died in Palestine), Joseph was patron of many scholars, including Moses Almosnino, the author of a treatise on dreams; and the famous physician Amatus Lusitanus. At Belvedere, Nasi maintained a fine library, a Hebrew printing establishment, and a yeshivah presided over by Joseph ibn Lab. During these years Nasi seems to have thought no more about Tiberias. Curiously the great nineteenth-century Jewish historian, Heinrich Graetz was convinced that had Selim II kept his promise to make Joseph Nasi king of Cyprus, Nasi would have attempted to transform this island of the "goddess of beauty" into a Jewish state.

Although his closing years were marked by a steady decline in influence, Nasi managed to retain his offices and income. Following the Turkish naval defeat at Lepanto, Nasi's islands were reconquered by the Venetians, but not long afterwards his authority over this territory was restored. In compensation for the initial loss of his dukedom some historians believe he was appointed Voivode of Wallachia (Rumania), though the details concerning this event are obscure. More certain is the incontrovertible fact that until his death in 1579, Joseph Nasi remained the great champion of the Marranos and of Jewish interests in general.

7

A Shabbetaian Odyssey

The Shabbetaian movement had stimulated in Jews a new wave of longing for a return to Eretz Israel. However, much of this enthusiasm waned with the apostasy of Shabbetai Zevi. Nevertheless, his missionaries managed to carry the messianic infection into many European Jewish communities, and when attacked by the guardians of tradition, remained active by forming underground cults. In this way individuals materialized in many communities with the message that redemption was close at hand. Among the crypto-Shabbetaians in Poland a group arose that had as its leaders two extraordinary personalities, Judah Hassid (1660–1700) and Hayyim Malakh (1660–1717).[94]

Judah Hassid ha-Levi and Hayyim ben Solomon Malakh

Judah Hassid ha-Levi (also called Judah the Saint) was born in Dubno. Nothing is known of his early life, although it is widely believed that he studied Kabbalah in Italy. In 1695 he was teaching in Szydlowiec, Lithuania, when a wandering Shabbetaian preacher (*maggid*) visited the town. Impressed by the preacher's message Judah became a believer. Following this shift in his religious orientation, Judah Hassid traveled throughout Poland and Lithuania preaching the importance of repentance, mortification, and good deeds. A stirring speaker (although not a man of high intellectuality), his sermons found an appreciative audience, and the circle of his adherents and disciples steadily widened. Within a relatively short span of time Judah consolidated his following into an association or sect (1697), which later became known as the Hassidim, the Pious Ones. The sect engaged in ascetic practices to hasten the coming of the Messiah. They also made public confessions of their sins, inserted mystical prayers into the liturgy, dressed in white shrouds as a symbol of penitence, and like Christian flagellants of old, distinguished themselves by constant fasting and mortifications.

As the Hassidim grew in numbers, the Orthodox rabbis became alarmed and began to persecute the sectarians. Stimulated by the persecution, Judah and his followers decided to leave Poland and immigrate to Palestine. Early in 1700 the Hassidim began their odyssey. They stopped enroute in Nikolsburg (Moravia), where there were many secret Shabbetaians, to regroup and find financial support for their long trek to the Promised Land. During their sojourn in the city they were joined by a band of radical Shabbetaians led by Hayyim Malakh, who had played a prominent role in helping Judah establish the "Association of Hassidim." Hayyim ben Solomon Malakh was born in Kalish, Poland. As in the case of Judah Hassid, almost nothing is known of Malakh's early years. A rabbinic scholar, kabbalist, and preacher, Malakh was attracted to Shabbetaian doctrines, and became closely associated with Herschel Zoref—a fellow believer, and self styled prophet of Vilna, Lithuania. In 1690 Hayyim Malakh went to Italy, most likely on a mission on behalf of the Polish Shabbetaian sects, and while there studied in depth the teachings of the kabbalist Isaac Luria, and the writings of Nathan of Gaza. He also received from his hosts, the Italian Shabbetaian leaders, their traditions concerning Shabbetai Zevi. On his return to Poland (1692), Malakh became active as a crypto-Shabbetaian missionary among rabbinic circles. Later, possibly because of a ban placed upon him by rabbinical authorities, he went to Adrianople (Turkey). Here he stayed with Samuel Primo for several years, receiving from Shabbetai Zevi's former secretary the customs and secrets of the circle that had been closest to the false messiah. Under the influence of Primo, Malakh renounced the moderate faction of Shabbetaianism and became a spokesman for the more radical elements in the movement. According to Jacob Emden, a bitter rabbinical foe of the sectarians, it was during this period of his life that the Polish-born Shabbetaian received the name Mehallek (the wanderer), which was afterwards changed by his followers to Malakh (angel).

From Adrianople, Malakh eventually traveled to the Turkish city of Bursa, where some prominent leaders of the sectarians lived. However, a vision caused him to cut short his stay in the city, and to return to Poland. He arrived in Zolkiew, late in 1696, and began to secretly preach that Shabbetai Zevi had indeed been the Messiah. Furthermore, like Moses who had kept the Israelites wandering in the desert for 40 years before bringing them to the Promised Land, Zevi would rise from the dead and redeem the Jewish people in 1707, 40 years after his conversion to Islam. Incredibly, Malakh's fiery exhortations announcing the return of Zevi were well received, especially among the ignorant masses of Poland's most backward provinces, Podolia and Galicia.

Perhaps in an effort to drink still deeper of the waters of the authentic spring of Shabbetaianism, Hayyim Malakh returned to Turkey in 1697. It is believed that on this trip he met with Abraham Cardoza, one of the more prominent claimants to Zevi's movement, and that he came in contact with Baruchiah Russo (also known as Osman Baba), the acknowledged leader of the most radical wing of the Doenmeh sect of Salonika.

On his return to Poland, Malakh and his adherents joined forces with the moderate faction of Shabbetaians, led by Judah Hassid to form the "Association of Hassidim." While the group waited in Nikolsburg before resuming their journey to the Holy Land, Malakh and Judah Hassid participated in a secret meeting of Poland's Shabbetaian leaders. At this meeting the memory of Shabbetai Zevi was extolled, and a strategy adopted to combat rabbinical opposition to the sect. Soon after the conclave, while Hassidim were still assembling in Moravia and Hungary, Judah Hassid and Hayyim

Malakh left Nikolsburg separately with their respective groups to continue their propaganda campaign and to seek additional financial aid. Malakh went to Vienna where his debates with various Orthodox opponents won him recognition and support. Judah Hassid, with a second body of adherents, passed through Germany by way of Altona and Frankfort-on-the-Main to the Austrian capital. Along the way his powerful voice, theatrical gestures, and tears gained for him many new believers. His appeal was especially strong to women, to whom, contrary to custom, he preached (usually with a Torah scroll under his arm as he walked among them in the women's gallery of a synagogue).

While in Vienna the wealthy banker and court Jew, Samuel Oppenheim supplied the Hassidim with the means to continue their journey to the Holy Land. The emigrants travelled in small groups, stopping frequently in various communities to rest and to give their leaders opportunities to harangue the crowds that came to hear their exhortations to repent. On the road the Hassidim were frequently joined by individuals anxious to associate with the sectarians, and by pilgrims desirous of visiting Eretz Israel. As a result the original band swelled from 31 families of Hassidim to about 1,500 people. Once again the Hassidim split into two groups. One party headed by Malakh was dispatched with the help of the charitable Jews of Vienna from that city to Constantinople, and from the Turkish capital made their way to Palestine. Judah Hassid and the second group took a different route. They traveled through the Tyrol to Venice where they took ships to the Holy Land.

The hazardous journey took its toll among both groups. Approximately 500 of the emigrants died enroute. On October 14, 1700 the remnant reached Jerusalem, only to be confronted with new disappointments. Judah Hassid died soon after setting foot in the Holy City, leaving his followers leaderless and totally unprepared to cope with the harsh realities facing them. Instead of redemption the Hassidim found only misery, poverty, and corruption. The majority of the old Jewish community of Jerusalem, themselves living on the charity of their European brethren in the Diaspora, were not able to help the new arrivals, who found themselves without any means of subsistence, plagued by disease, and harassed by venal Turkish officials.

Rabbi Gedalia of Siemiatycze, a member of Judah Hassid's party, has left a graphic account of conditions in Jerusalem during this difficult period.[95] The poor people among the Hassidim, he noted, tended to hide in their homes during the week, for fear of being caught by the rapacious tax collectors, emerging only from necessity on Sabbaths and holidays. Many Hassidim did not even have enough to buy a loaf of bread. Others in desperation were forced to resort to begging alms, but soon found that they were unable to support themselves by such means as the community lacked charitable prosperous householders.

Discouraged and disillusioned, the sectarians rapidly lost their unity. Dissension broke out between the moderates and the radical element led by Malakh. Malakh and his supporters were expelled from the Association of Hassidim, but even this move did not dispel the unrest among the moderates or resolve their dilemma. Many decided to return to Europe where they mystified the credulous with tales of marvels; others joined existing Turkish Shabbetaians who posed as Muslims; and some, persuaded by German missionaries, embraced Christianity (including two of Judah Hassid's nephews).[96]

Hayyim Malakh and a few adherents lingered in Jerusalem. In this circle of believers symbolic services, patterned after the rituals of the Turkish radical Shabbetaians, were secretly practiced. Jacob Emden, a foe of all antinomian sects, believed that Malakh carried a wooden image of Shabbetai Zevi which his followers danced around and worshipped. At length the bizarre behavior of Malakh aroused the rabbinical authorities of Jerusalem and he was banished from the Holy City.

Malakh returned to Turkey and renewed relations with the radical wing of the Doenmeh. He took part in their rituals and for a while openly preached their doctrines in Jewish communities. These acts led to a prolonged persecution by the traditional rabbinate. In 1709 he was excommunicated at Constantinople, and wandered in Germany before returning to his native Poland. In Podolia, a fertile ground for sectarianism, Malakh succeeded in establishing another radical Shabbetaian cell. Aware of the growing hostility in most Jewish communities to these sectarians, Malakh in public denied any connection with the Shabbetaian heresy. However, his reputation as an agitator had preceded him, and he was once again forced to move on. Rabbinical bans followed Malakh wherever he went, and after several years of roving around Germany and Holland he returned to Poland (1716). His death shortly after (date uncertain) is believed to have been caused by excessive drinking.

Although the aliyah of the Hassidim ended in failure, it was the first organized Ashkenazi immigration to Eretz Israel. It left an indelible impression on Jews everywhere, and there are many testimonies in songs and dance to its lasting influence. The place in which the Hassidim had established themselves and their synagogue in Jerusalem was destroyed by the Arabs in 1720; the enclosure was long known as the "Ruin" (*Hurbah*) of Judah the Saint, and the chief synagogue of the Ashkenazi community in Palestine was subsequently erected there and named after Judah Hassid. This synagogue stood until destroyed by the Arabs in the 1948 War of Independence. It has since been rebuilt by the State of Israel.[97]

Hayyim ben Moses Attar

Natural disasters, political instability, and economic decay transformed seventeeth century Palestine into a desolate corner of the Ottoman Empire. The Jewish population of this Turkish province, small in number and imbued with an otherworldly mysticism, struggled to survive. In the eighteenth century there was a slight improvement. Following the disenchantment and disintergration of the Hassidim led by Judah Hassid and Hayyim Malakh, serious efforts were made to consolidate the Jewish community of the Holy Land. In 1740 the chief rabbi of Izmir (Turkey), Hayyim Abulafia (1660-1744), set off a new wave of immigration to the Holy Land. Abulafia settled in Tiberias, and under the protection of Daher el Omar, the governor of the Galilee, he sought to renew Jewish settlement in the city and surrounding area. Stimulated by Abulafia's example, a small group of scholars led by the prominent talmudist and kabbalist, Rabbi Hayyim ben Moses Attar (1696-1743)[98] also decided to emigrate to Palestine.

Attar was born in Sale, Morocco, the descendant of a family of Spanish origin that had fled the Iberian Peninsula during the persecutions of the fourteenth and fifteenth centuries. He received his early education at the feet of his grandfather. After the death of a great-uncle, Attar settled in the city of Menkes in order to manage the deceased man's business. In spite of the demands of his commercial enterprise, he found the necessary time to complete his rabbinical studies. A downturn in the economic and political climate in Morocco and a conviction that redemption was imminent led Attar to consider emigrating to Palestine. News of the work of Abulafia in Tiberias reinforced his resolve to undertake aliyah. He also dreamt of establishing in the Holy Land a great yeshivah, a citadel of Jewish learning, that would attract students from every quarter of the Diaspora, and by its accomplishments hasten the coming of the Messiah.

Gathering about him a small group of disciples, Attar set his plan in motion in 1739. Moving at a leisurely pace, the group traveled to Leghorn, Italy, where they tarried for many months. Here the Moroccan rabbi's saintly nature and reputation as a preacher won for him many new followers. His residence in Leghorn became a gathering place for students and scholars. Attar's personality seemed to radiate religiosity, and his behavior reflected his sincerity. One of his disciples would later describe these traits in the following glowing terms:

> . . . his heart pulsated with Talmud; he uprooted mountains like a resistless torrent; his holiness was that of an angel of the Lord . . . having severed all connections with the affairs of this world.[99]

The Jewish community of Leghorn was enthralled by the preacher who had come into their midst. Groups were organized to raise funds for Attar's proposed yeshivah, and for the trip to Palestine. In addition, the Maecenases of the community financed the publication of some of the Moroccan rabbi's religious writings. During his long stay in Leghorn, Attar used the city as a base to spread his message throughout Italy, urging Jews to immigrate to Eretz Israel.

Finally, in 1741 he decided the time had come to move on. Accompanied by a small band of thirty disciples, Attar embarked from the port of Leghorn for the Holy Land. The group reached Acre in the late summer, and were prevented from pushing on to Jerusalem because of an epidemic raging in the Holy City. Eager to make his life-long dream a reality, Attar decided to set up a temporary yeshivah in Acre. A year later he transferred his academy to Peki'in, because of a widely held belief that Acre was unlucky for Jews. According to the Talmud, Acre had not been included within the historic boundaries of Eretz Israel.[100] During a visit to Hayyim Abulafia, Attar was entreated by the former chief rabbi of Izmir to reestablish his school in Tiberias, but he decided to keep to his original plan. He eventually moved the yeshivah to Jerusalem after the last vestiges of the epidemic that had struck the city had subsided.

The academy, which became known as the Midrash Kenesset Yeshivah, consisted of two divisions; one for advanced students and the other for beginners. Almost from its inception the yeshivah acquired a reputation for ascetic practices. Many of the students would spend night after night in supplication and prayer for the redemption of Jewry. Others would prostrate themselves in prayer on the graves of holy men to achieve the same end. Hayyim ben Moses Attar did not live long enough to see the school he had founded take root, for he died approximately one year after settling in Jerusalem. His major works, however, including novellas on Talmud, and a commentary entitled *Or ha-Hayyim* ("Light of Life") survived. The commentary enjoyed an extensive circulation in Germany and Poland, and became a favorite in Hassidic circles. Legend suggests that the founder of the eighteenth century Hassidic movement, Israel Ba'al Shem Tov, at one point in his life considered traveling to the Holy Land in order to study under Attar, but that circumstances prevented him from going.[101] Without a doubt Attar's most important contribution to Judaism, and to the hope of a Jewish return to Eretz Israel, was his Jerusalem yeshivah. Long after his demise it continued to act as a lodestar, drawing students from the Diaspora, and in numerous instances provided these individuals the raison d'etre to settle permanently in the Promised Land.

8

Hassidism

Israel ben Eliezer (The Ba'al Shem Tov)

Victimized by political, social, and economic discrimination; persecuted and hounded; and periodically threatened with expulsion, most Jews in the Diaspora found stability by clinging fiercely to their faith. Often, when under relentless stress, the Jews turned inward by seeking solace in mysticism and messianic movements. The expulsion of the Jews from Spain, Portugal, Sicily, southern Italy, Provence, and some of the cities of Germany during the course of the fifteenth and sixteenth centuries drew many Jews to the kabbalistic doctrines taught by Isaac Luria and his disciples at Safed, Palestine. Similarly, the bloody massacres of 1648–1649 in the Ukraine, and the pogroms in Greater Poland created the atmosphere that helped spread the Shabbetaian heresy that caused such upheaval in the Jewish world that its consequences were in evidence for generations. During the eighteenth century in Eastern Europe, where the progressive impoverishment of the Jews continued unchecked, a great revivalist movement known as Hassidism[102] attracted a large number of Jews. The name for this religious movement was derived from the biblical noun *hassidim* (i.e., the pious ones). The name had been used to designate Jewish groups of great piety and fervor, such as the Hassideans in the days of the Maccabees, the Hassedei Ashkenazi of medieval Germany, and the kabbalistic followers of Judah Hassid in the last half of the seventeenth century. However, there was no historic link between these earlier pietistic groups and the eighteenth century movement. The new Hassidism had its roots in the Saxon period of Polish history when the Jews were all but overwhelmed by continuous rounds of oppression and persecution. During this period Poland was beset by the chaos that preceded its partitions by Russia, Prussia, and Austria. The noblemen who dominated the private cities and the towns and villages treated the Jews callously; the Catholic clergy encouraged religious fanaticism and made the Jews their particular target. Students and guild members, inflamed by Jesuit rhetoric, assaulted Jews in the Crown cities; ritual murder and desecration of the host charges directed against the Jews became more commonplace. The Christian merchant class used every means possible to subvert and discredit their Jewish rivals. The king and his court were no longer able to protect their Jewish wards. As if all this was not enough, the Haidamak peasant revolt of 1768 brought new terrors to the Jewish population. Once again they became the victims of senseless killings reminiscent of the Cossack outbreaks of the previous century. In addition, the Jews found themselves caught up in the struggle of the Union for the Defense of the Faith and the Fatherland (better known as the Bar Confederation). This organization composed of Polish nobles rampaged through the provinces for several years leaving a path of destruction in their wake. Their policy of extorting war levies from the Jews raised havoc among the Jewish communities struggling to survive in a state on the edge of anarchy.

Internal forces at work in the Jewish communities also played a role in preparing the way for the Hassidic movement. As pressures from the Polish state increased, the Jewish communal structure was considerably weakened. Opposition to the community regimes (the *kehillot*) on the part of the Jewish masses became more strident. The Jews longed for relief from the grinding poverty and the corruption of their community leaders. The kehillot administrations had long ago ceased to function as defenders of the rights of their people. Nor were they able or willing to adequately meet basic communal and cultural needs. They had become tools of the monarchy and of the noblemen who owned the towns. Most of the kehillot had come under the control of oligarchic cliques. These cliques were usually supported by the scholar class (i.e., the rabbis) who had become tightly linked to the wealthy individuals who ruled the kehillot.

The craving for community reforms and for redemption fused to provide the impetus for a religious revival. Jewish religious life had lapsed into a state of rigidity and obscurantism. The indifference of the scholar class toward the masses was symptomatic of the spiritual crisis that had enveloped the Jews of Eastern Europe. Pilpul, an analytical method used in talmudic study, which often tended to degenerate into casuistry, dominated yeshivot education. The prominence of this method in the academies tended to negate the traditional role of the Torah, which ceased to be a rule for living, and therefore less of a guide for the Jewish masses. Students and scholars used pilpul as a means to gain distinction in the hierarchy of Jewish community life, thereby advancing their social as well as economic careers. Neglected by their spiritual leaders, the poverty-stricken masses labored under a sense of religious inadequacy. Contemporary ethical literature that might have provided some guidance had become debased and permeated by the "practical Kabbalah," which was overly concerned with demons, spirits, and the transmigration of souls. Instead of lifting the spirits of the Jewish masses, the moralists urged them to forswear the vanities of the world, praised the virtues of asceticism, and threatened damnation and the tortures of hell for the slightest transgression. It was to these downtrodden and neglected masses that Israel ben Eliezer (1700–60),[103] the founder of modern Hassidism, brought the message of serving God with joy. He assured the ordinary Jew that mystical communion with God was within their reach.

Israel ben Eliezer was born in Poland in the village of Ukop on the border between the provinces of Podolia and Wallachia. His parents were of humble origin and were quite old at the time of his birth. Left an orphan at a tender age, Israel was brought up by kindly neighbors. His boyhood years are veiled in obscurity and legend—no reliable documents exist. Nevertheless, all accounts of Israel's early life stress that he did not display any great enthusiasm for study, and that he spent most of his time in the forests and fields surrounding his village. As a lad of 12 he took service as a helper to the schoolmaster. His duties were to take children from their homes to school and back. As he grew older Israel ben Eliezer held down a variety of odd jobs. Legend suggests that while employed as a synagogue sexton he would complete his work in a short time, sleep the rest of the day, and then remain awake the whole night studying and praying. He concealed this studying from the congregation and townspeople, and affected the personality of a simple unlettered Jew. While still in his teens, Israel received what would become known in Hassidic circles as "a disclosure" (Hebrew *hitgalut,* a concept signifying a revelation of one's true worth and message). This revelation made Israel feel he was called to a sacred mission.

At the age of twenty, Israel married the sister of Rabbi Abraham Gershon Kutower of Brody. For the next 16 years he lived an austere life in various places—as a lime digger at the foot of the Carpathian mountains, as a teacher, and as the proprietor of an inn. The latter enterprise was managed by his wife, while Israel studied the whole week in the solitude of a woodland cottage from which he returned only for the Sabbath. Wandering about in the mountains and the forests, he was frequently carried away by ecstatic experiences. At age thirty-six, Israel ben Eliezer came to the conclusion that the time had come to reveal his miraculous powers and to begin his mission. He became a *ba'al shem,* (i.e., a practitioner of the healing and miracle working arts), and began to travel around the countryside prescribing herbal remedies and ointments, exorcising demons, and writing out charms, amulets, and talismans to cure and ward off disease. The adherents of this profession, much of whose wisdom was derived from the "practical Kabbalah" received the title *Ba'al Shem* (Master of the Name), because they were presumed to possess knowledge of the secret names of God, which they would invoke in their incantations and prayers. Israel, however, did not resort to the use of the holy names of God in the charms he distributed, but employed only his own name and that of his mother. He was highly successful as a *ba'al shem.* In addition to his fame as a wonder-worker, Israel gained a wide reputation throughout Podolia, Galicia, and the Ukraine for his inspiring personality, religious enthusiasm, generosity, and keen personal interest in those he served. By virtue of these accomplishments, he received from the grateful people he had ministered to the appellative *Ba'al Shem Tov* (Master of the Good Name), commonly abbreviated to *Besht.*

Around 1745 the *Ba'al Shem Tov* gave up traveling and settled in the town of Medzhibozh in Podolia. Here he established a *bet-ha-midrash* (house of study and prayer) to which many admirers, among them some prominent rabbis and scholars were attracted by his teaching and personality. The majority of his congregation were simple God-fearing folks, for the *Besht* was of the people and mixed among them. It was his belief that it was given to the commonest man to find God; for the Deity was diffused throughout the entire creation. Accordingly, it was mostly the ordinary folk who came to seek the *Besht's* guidance and blessings, and to seek his intercession with God for their spiritual and physical welfare. Although he drew heavily upon the mystical doctrines of Isaac Luria, the Besht did not practice the lugubrious mortifications of the Safed school of Kabbalah. Instead, the *Ba'al Shem Tov* tried to bring to the meanest life a consciousness of spiritual power and make of religion a joyous immersion in the all-pervading, ever present God-head. In defining his mission he stated that it was, ". . . to stir the hearts of those seeking communion with God. This contains nothing new. It adds nothing. It is merely a reminder, a strengthening of the faith which has somehow been forgotten."[104] Indeed, his

Hassidism was not a sectarian movement, and the Hassidim had not the least intention of forming a sect. There would be no concerted attempt to modify cardinal doctrines or to do away with the smallest detail of accepted observance. Emphasis was placed upon a new way of serving God, and this method addressed itself to the individual concerned with his own personal salvation. Curiously, apart from a few letters, the *Besht* never committed his teachings to writing; they were handed down orally, and preserved by his disciples who recorded many of his sayings. Twenty years after the *Ba'al Shem*'s death, Rabbi Jacob Joseph of Polonnoye (d. 1782) would publish a book incorporating most of the Hassidic founder's teachings and aphorisms.

The *Besht's* cardinal doctrine was the omnipresence of God. He is reported to have said, "God, blessed be He, fills the entire world with His glory, and every moment, even every thought comes from Him."[105] He also believed that everyone could be redeemed. Intimate union with the God-head could be achieved by concentrating on devotion and ecstasy in prayer to such a degree that a person became unconscious of existence. The *Besht* did not reject observance of the law prescribed in the Talmud or of the traditional codes. He was, on the other hand, not as rigorous in his demands as were the traditional rabbis. The *Besht* believed that assiduous study of the Torah and exact obedience to its commandments carried no greater promise of acceptance than the sincere faith and intention (*kavvanah*) of the humble Jew. Though the latter could not study much or always pray at the designated time and place, he freely surrendered himself and his life to God in simple trust and confidence.

Israel ben Eliezer preached three principal virtues: humility (*shiflut*), cheerfulness (*simhah*), and enthusiasm (*hitlahavut*). For an individual to achieve the supreme goal of life, the state of adhesion, or cleaving to God (*devekut*), it was essential to overcome natural egotism and self assertion, and remove from himself all vanity and conceit. For the *Besht* it was clear that the inability to overcome these traits constituted a barrier to the sense of the omnipresence of God, and the experience of communion with Him.

Israel ben Eliezer also rejected the obsession with sin and retribution in hellfire that was characteristic of many sermons of the traditional preachers of his day. He opposed asceticism and mortification of the flesh and sought instead to infuse joyousness into the religious life of Jews, whose surroundings were so drab and whose outlook was so bleak. Eating, drinking, sleeping, and other ordinary functions of the body, when carried out in the proper spirit of joyfulness and directed toward God, could also be considered sacramental acts. In later years, cheerfulness and love of life, frequently expressed in the fondness of the Hassidim for song and dance, became one of the hallmarks of the movement.

The *Ba'al Shem Tov* was also convinced that religious enthusiasm would lead to a better knowledge and love of God. Perfunctory role performance of any commandment unaccompanied by burning enthusiasm or fervor, and an intense feeling of love for God was of little consequence. The Hebrew word *hitlahavut*, used to describe this intense enthusiasm, literally means a kindling, or setting on fire. Prayer especially was regarded by the Besht as pointless, if offered mechanically. He believed true prayer was a state that freed the individual from the trammels of the body and allowed fusion of the soul with God. To obtain ecstatic fervor in prayer the Hassidim made use of all available stimuli, including swaying movements, gesticulations, loud singing, dancing, and even somersaulting. Through prayer the *Besht* taught that disease may be cured, wealth obtained, misfortune averted, and all kinds of blessings secured. Although he felt that every individual had the capacity to offer prayers of such efficacy, his successors taught that this capacity was beyond the abilities of the average person, and inherent only in the saint or perfectly righteous man. This idea was largely the basis of the Hassidic institution of the *Tzaddik* (the just or righteous man).

Dov Ber of Mezeritch (1710–72), also known as the "Great *Maggid*", because of his extraordinary preaching ability, inherited the mantle of leadership after the demise of the *Ba'al Shem Tov* in 1760. Believing that the ordinary Hassid could not attain the level of communion with God at which prayer was efficacious, Dov Ber urged each individual to attach himself to a *Tzaddik*. Through such an allegiance, and by following the *Tzaddik's* example, the Hassid would rise to a higher degree of holiness and also obtain the benefits of his leader's intercessory powers. This concept of an intermediary between the people and God became a distinctive feature of Hassidism. It eventually led to an almost idolatrous devotion of the *Tzaddik*, and to the growth of Hassidic dynasties.

Dov Ber's greatest talent was his ability as an organizer. He turned Hassidism into a mass movement by attracting hundreds of disciples and dispersing them throughout Eastern Europe as emissaries of the new doctrine. These dedicated disciples founded Hassidic centers wherever they went, and won adherents to the movement by the thousands. Eventually, Hassidism branched off into three major divisions: the popular Ukrainian offshoot, which carried on the traditions of the *Ba'al Shem Tov* and Dov Ber; the philosophical and rationalist *Habad* wing founded by the disciple of the Great *Maggid*, Shneour Zalman of Lyady (1747–1812), and centered in Lithuania and White Russia; and the Polish Galician branch established by Elimelech of Lizensk (1717–86), which played an important role in elevating the *Tzaddik* as an intermediary between man and God.

The Hassidic centers founded in Lithuania and White Russia encountered bitter resistance from traditional Orthodox Jews who became known as *Mitnagdim* (opponents, or protestants). The *Mitnagdim* resented the extremism of the Karliners (the name given to the Hassidim in White Russia following the establishment of the first Hassidic congregation in Karlin, a suburb of Pinsk). A group of Hassidim led by Abraham ben Alexander Katz of Kalisk, a future key figure in a mass migration to the Holy Land, succeeded in arousing the traditionalists to a fever pitch by their contempt for scholars and by their erratic behavior in the market places and streets (turning somersaults and engaging in other bizarre antics).

Reacting to *Mitnagdic* opposition, the Hassidim withdrew from the synagogues of the traditionalists to form their own private prayer rooms (*Klausen*). Although Hassidism seemed to possess all the characteristics of a redemption movement, it did not advocate social change. It did, however, leave its mark on the leadership and structure of Jewish society and on ritual and prayer. In those regions where Hassidism held sway, the importance of the traditional rabbi waned. He was no longer the paramount spiritual leader, becoming instead more of a teacher and expert on *Halakhah* (religious law), and living in the shadow of the *Tzaddik* who enjoyed supreme authority. The *Tzaddik* or *rebbe* (not necessarily a halakhic scholar or teacher) acted as a guide to his followers by virtue of the spiritual power and holiness thought to be inherent in him. This development seriously weakened the ruling groups of oligarchs and scholars, who forfeited much of their importance and influence to the *Tzaddikim*.

The rapid spread of Hassidism also renewed the age-old longing for redemption in the Holy Land. The way of life, entirely enveloped in sanctity, that Hassidism prescribed demanded exodus from the profane lands of the Diaspora, and settlement in Eretz Israel. The motivation to make aliyah (immigration to Israel) was reinforced by a desire of the Hassidim to establish a center in Palestine. Early on, however, it became obvious to some of the Hassidic leaders that only a select few could fulfill this objective. The social passiveness that stamped Hassidic doctrine precluded consideration of any practical program for settlement of large numbers of Hassidim in the Holy Land. Moreover, the scope of Hassidic immigration was circumscribed from the outset by the rapid rise of the *Tzaddikim*. Since it was the *Tzaddik* who acted as an intermediary with God to accelerate salvation, his support or opposition to aliyah was critical. Nevertheless, in spite of a rather ambiguous attitude on the part of many of the early Hassidic leaders, the movement managed to send more immigrants to Eretz Israel, at more frequent intervals, than had any of its predecessors.

Hassidic Immigration to the Holy Land

The aliyah of Hassidim to Palestine began during the lifetime of the *Ba'al Shem Tov*. Hassidic legend is replete with accounts of how the *Besht* had his heart set on immigrating, and of his burning desire to meet with the great rabbi, Hayyim ben Attar. Two stories, obvious fantasies, tell of the *Besht's* futile attempts to reach the Holy Land. In one version he supposedly manages to get as far as Constantinople, and in another account a band of robbers endeavor to lead him to Palestine, but once again he is compelled to turn back before reaching his destination. This inability or unwillingness of the *Ba'al Shem Tov* to make a successful aliyah did not extend to some members of his inner circle. Rabbi Abraham Gershon Kutower, the brother-in-law of the *Besht* emigrated with his family to Eretz Israel in 1747, and many Hassidim from Galicia and Volhynia followed his example. Kutower settled first in Hebron, and six years later moved to Jerusalem. In the Holy City he established contact with the circle of mystics known as "Beth El" (a group founded by the Yemenite kabbalist Sar Shalom Sharabi).

Abraham Gershon Kutower was disappointed by the failure of the *Besht* to emigrate to the Holy Land, and at one point accused the founder of the Hassidic movement of preferring his synagogue in the Diaspora to life in the Promised Land. In a letter to Abraham Gershon Kutower (circa 1750) the *Besht* provided a clue to his strange behavior. He writes his brother-in-law that some years earlier, in a dream, he had seen and talked with the Messiah. "When will you come?" the *Besht* had asked the Messiah, and had received the answer, "After your teachings have spread and become known in the world."[106] This reply had saddened the *Ba'al Shem Tov* for he now understood that a long period of time would elapse before the redemption of the Jewish people. A prominent Jewish historian analyzing this strange letter has pointed out that the *Besht's* words seem to indicate that he had taken upon himself a messianic task.

Other historians differ on this point. They see the *Ba'al Shem Tov*, in his letter, as being more focused on individual salvation of souls rather than on messianism. Preparations for redemption in the *Besht's* eyes became a matter of prayer and meditation—not very different from traditional practices throughout the centuries. This view seems logical when Hassidism is considered in a historical perspective. Although Hassidism was heir to all of the religious folk movements in the history of the Jewish people, it did not possess the attributes of a straightforward messianic movement. On the contrary, from its inception Hassidism opposed Shabbetaianism and its offshoots, despite the fact that some of Hassidism's earliest adherents may have been secret Shabbetaians. Hassidism even adopted some of the mystic elements, trappings, and customs of the Shabbetaian mode of life.

Still others believe that the *Besht's* letter to his brother-in-law may have been intended for a wider audience. The assertion that the Messiah would not come before Hassidism had spread throughout the Diaspora was a powerful argument for attracting Jews to the movement.

With the passage of time the *Ba'al Shem Tov's* thoughts concerning aliyah to the Holy Land became still more ambiguous. When one of his most able followers, Rabbi Jacob Joseph, indicated a desire to settle in Palestine, the *Besht* at first favored the idea. He even wrote to Abraham Gershon asking the rabbi to personally befriend Jacob Joseph, and to look out for his welfare. But shortly afterwards the *Besht* changed his mind and actively opposed emigration to Palestine, considering it a form of escapism. He then cautioned Jacob Joseph, who had not yet left for the Holy Land, not to emigrate.

Hassidic legends also reveal that another of the movement's first generation leaders wanted to settle in Eretz Israel. Pinhas of Korecz (1728–91) was prepared to leave in 1768, and had already hired wagons for the journey. However, he suddenly fell ill, and during the course of his sickness he had a conversation with God. "Perhaps," Pinhas inquired, "you do not want me to go to Palestine—then I will not go."[107] Following this discourse, Pinhas of Korecz immediately recovered from his illness. This story, like those about the *Ba'al Shem Tov* and Jacob Joseph, seem to symbolize the conflict between the strong pro-Palestine yearnings of the Hassidic leaders and the demands made upon them by their followers, and the realities of life in the Diaspora.

Eventually, for the *Ba'al Shem Tov* and many of his disciples, the concepts of exile, the Promised Land, and the Messiah lost their original meanings and underwent a process of spiritualization. The Holy Land became identified with Torah study, or the *Shekhinah* (the Divine Presence), while failure to study or say one's prayers was equated to life in exile. The Great *Maggid* carried this thought process one step further. He played down messianism, and emphasized that serving God in exile was more within the grasp of the devout than serving Him in the Holy Land. Dov Ber was convinced that holy inspiration (*ruah hakodesh*) was more readily attainable in *galut* (exile) than at the time of the Temple in ancient Judea. According to Shneur Zalman, the Great *Maggid* also believed that there were souls that especially needed the Holy Land, and others who needed the *galut*. The two were, therefore, equally important. Other Hassidic leaders picked up on Dov Ber's theme and expanded it still further. They stated repeatedly to their followers that wherever an individual fulfills God's will, this is called redemption. Furthermore, they stressed, the quality of the Diaspora was equal to that of the Holy Land, and that Zion connoted anywhere that halakha was studied.

This trend to empty the concepts of Eretz Israel and Zion of their physical context continued among Hassidic leaders of the second generation. They sought to convert Zion into a spiritual state (Eretz Israel on high, i.e. heaven), and to equate it with the work of the *Tzaddikim*. These ideas were best summed up by Nahum of Czernoby (1730–98), another disciple of the Great *Maggid*. He declared that even though a physical Eretz Israel exists, its true quality and vitality are spiritual. All synagogues, he insisted, are invested by the Creator with the life of Eretz Israel, and by praying in a house of worship one was in Israel.

In spite of all of the efforts to spiritualize Zion, many Hassidim, including some *Tzaddiks,* remained unconvinced. Indeed, besides the *Ba'al Shem Tov's* brother-in-law, there were other prominent Hassidim who settled in Palestine during the founder's lifetime. Most eminent were Nahman of Horodenka (d. 1780),[108] and Menachem Mendel of Przemyslany (1728–72),[109] who led a small group of Hassidim to the Holy Land. The band of fifteen adult males (most of whom were of an advanced age), and fourteen women and children, after a long and arduous journey from Europe, settled in Tiberias. Their motives for making aliyah were basically traditional – deference for the holiness of the land and the "mitzvah" (literally, commandment, i.e., a religious act or deed of piety) gained by living or being buried in the Holy Land. These fundamental beliefs were reinforced by hope that these acts of faith would hasten the coming of the Messiah.

The strong religious feelings of the group were best exemplified by Menachem Mendel of Przemyslany, who rebuked his brother in Poland for not undertaking aliyah. Menachem, however, noted sadly that many people believed it was not good to stay in the Promised Land while one was still alive. On the other hand, the belief that residing in Eretz Israel would hasten the coming of the Messiah was a common theme in Hassidic legend. A story is told of two Hassidic friends who agree to meet in Palestine in order to help bring about the advent of the Messiah, but alas, they miss each other.[110]

Menachem Mendel of Przemyslany, the driving spirit behind the 1764 emigration to Eretz Israel, was representative of the extreme enthusiasts among the first generation of Hassidic leaders. Like other disciples of the *Ba'al Shem Tov* he considered devotion to God the pivotal point of Hassidic doctrine and conduct. However, in contrast to most of his Hassidic peers, he believed that Torah study and the practice of devotion were not compatible. Study, Menachem felt, should be restricted so as not to restrain the process of approximation to the Creator. "If we divert our thoughts from devotion to God, and study excessively, we will forget the fear of Heaven . . . study should therefore be reduced and one should always meditate on the greatness of the Creator."[111] Menachem Mendel considered prayer to be the most suitable method to achieve devotion. "May it be granted me to pray," he once declared, "but one prayer properly during my lifetime."[112] Prior to making aliyah to the Holy Land, Menachem Mendel had been involved in ransoming Jewish captives in town along the Dniester River. His decision to go to Palestine may have been dictated by the popularity he had gained as a result of his good works. Some historians believe that he emigrated because Hassidim started to consider him a *Tzaddik* and miracle worker, and he refused to assume such a role.[113] Settlement in Palestine received new impetus in 1777 with a Hassidic migration from Lithuania and White Russia. It was led by Menachem Mendel of Vitebsk (1730–88), and his associates, Israel ben Perez of Polotzk (d. about 1785) and Abraham ben Alexander Katz of Kalisk (1741–1810). All three men were disciples of Dov Ber of Mezeritch and had originally been instructed by him to establish Hassidic centers in Lithuania and White Russia. In carrying out their mission they had encountered the first wave of opposition to Hassidism to sweep the region (1772). Seeking means to avoid conflict, Menachem Mendel of Vitebsk attempted on several occasions to meet with Elijah ben Solomon (1720–97), the Gaon of Vilna and the acknowledged leader of the Mitnagdim. The Gaon, however, refused to recognize or receive the Hassidic leader.

Hassidic tradition regards Menachem Mendel of Vitebsk to have been one of the chief participants at a critical meeting convened by the Great Maggid, and held in his home. The assemblage faced a crisis as a result of a ban (*herem*) placed on the Hassidic movement by the Gaon of Vilna. In considering how best to respond to the attacks of the Mitnagdim some consideration was given to establishing a Hassidic center in Palestine. It was felt that such a settlement would act as a counter-weight to the Mitnagdim accusations of heresy and greatly enhance the prestige of the Hassidic movement. However, the issue of a Palestinian center was temporarily tabled in order to deal with the immediate problem of the ban. After much discussion, the Hassidic conclave adjourned without reaching agreement on a common policy.

Mitnagdic pressure on the Hassidim in Lithuania and White Russia continued unabated, and Menachem Mendel, who at the time headed a congregation in Minsk, was compelled by the ferocity of his opponents to abandon his post and the city. He settled in the province of Vitebsk, and from his new base resumed his proselytizing on behalf of Hassidism.

The idea of immigrating to the Holy Land, however, had become deeply ingrained in Menachem Mendel's psyche, and throughout the years of persecution he dreamed of making it a reality. In 1777 the opportunity presented itself, and the Hassidic leader, accompanied by a large number of followers, set out for Palestine. The eminent rabbi and future head of Lithuanian and White Russian Hassidism, Shneur Zalman of Lyady (1747–1813),[114] a disciple of Menachem Mendel of Vitebsk (he had accompanied the latter on his second attempt to see the Gaon of Vilna), also joined the party of emigrants. Later, Shneur Zalman had a change of heart and turned back. It is believed that he had second thoughts about leaving the Hassidim of Lithuania and White Russia leaderless.

The trek from White Russia through Volhynia and Podolia to the Moldavian frontier took five months. The Hassidim stopped at various Jewish communities to solicit funds and to establish links with sympathetic congregations, whom they hoped would support their settlement efforts in Eretz Israel. The expedition was attended by a good deal of publicity, and large crowds of Hassidim escorted the emigrants on the successive stages of their journey. News of the caravan's progress reached Eastern European Jewry at a time of crisis and political anarchy. Poland had already suffered its first partition in 1772, and the years immediately following were marked by uncertainty as to the future of the Jews of the former state. New borders had been created, and parts of Poland had come under different regimes with new laws and regulations concerning Jews. Austria and Prussia, which had swallowed large areas of Poland, were seeking to expel impoverished Jews from their newly annexed territories. Some Jews, in desperation, had sought refuge in the Russian occupied zone. Some of these uprooted people joined the Hassidic party winding its way to Palestine. The newcomers, mostly paupers, were anxious to escape their hostile environment. The prospect that they might be able to exist in the Holy Land on manual labor or charity, or both, appealed to their imagination.

Efforts of Menachem Mendel of Vitebsk and other Hassidic leaders to halt this migration of the poor, which threatened to become a burden on their own followers, proved fruitless. Many of the paupers who did not feel the need to physically join the Hassidic band preceded the band like the vanguard of an army.

The Hassidim gradually made their way to the port of Galatz (Rumania) on the Black Sea, and took ships to Constantinople. One vessel of this small armada was wrecked at sea near the Crimean Peninsula, and only thirty of the eighty Hassidic passengers on board escaped. For the rest of the Hassidim, the journey from Europe, which had taken four months, finally came to an end in the summer of 1777. In spite of the vicissitudes encountered enroute, over 300 people had managed to reach Palestine. They traveled by donkey from Acre to their final destination—Safed.

The initial feeling of the Hassidim upon reaching the Holy Land was one of exultation and joy. In their letters to the Diaspora, they gave vent to the happiness that had overwhelmed them when they had first seen the cherished land. They were excited not only by the holiness of the land, but also by its fertility (the region had made an amazing recovery from a series of devastating wars that had ended two years prior to the arrival of the Hassidim). In addition, the Hassidim did not have to face a housing problem. Safed had not been fully repopulated after the earthquake of 1760, and the emigrants were able to find many large and good houses that had been abandoned by their original owners.

Adjustments to the country, however, proved extremely difficult for most of the Hassidim. Differences in climate, language, customs, and above all, the necessity of earning a livelihood accentuated the task of creating a permanent settlement. Abraham ben Alexander of Kalisk, for example, firmly believed that only true love for the Holy Land could enable the Hassidim to overcome the formidable obstacles. He emphasized patience and noted that a considerable time would have to elapse before everyone felt at home in their new environment. At the very least, despite the harsh conditions, the ruins, the stones and dust of the Land of Israel, he felt, it was far preferable to living in the Diaspora. Abraham ben Alexander urged those in Eastern Europe who were thinking of making aliyah to come to the sacred land with the feeling that they had been raised anew from infancy, in order to appreciate the land and bind their souls.

From the outset, the Hassidic leaders made an all-out attempt to alleviate the suffering of the poor who had accompanied them to the Holy Land. They were particularly concerned that the poor would quickly exhaust the funds of the Hassidic congregation and severely strain the limited resources of the older Jewish community. Confronted with these economic problems, the Hassidic leadership issued proclamations warning would-be immigrants not to come to Palestine without some means of support. In letters to the Diaspora, and by the use of special couriers, the Hassidim appealed for financial help. A year after their arrival in Palestine, the Hassidim decided to send one of their most distinguished members, Israel ben Perez of Polotzk, back to Europe to organize the collection of funds, and to arrange for regular maintenance of the settlement. Israel's talents as a speaker and organizer made him ideally suited for this mission. His first stop was Constantinople, where he succeeded in raising a considerable sum of money. From the Turkish capital he traveled to his native Belorussia, where he joined forces with Rabbi Shneur Zalman and other Hassidic notables in a campaign to obtain funds for the Palestine center. With the help of these men, Israel was instrumental in introducing the practice of *ma'amadot* (the establishment of a special fund for the maintenance of the Hassidim in the Holy Land). His activities were, however, somewhat curtailed by a second round of persecution initiated by the Mitnagdim (the Hassidic movement was once again banned in 1781). However, having successfully accomplished his mission, Israel made plans to return to Palestine. Enroute, fate intervened and he died in Fastov in the Ukraine, where he was buried.

In spite of many obstacles, the Hassidic community in Palestine gradually took root. Most of the settlers, however, were dependent on the philanthropic contributions from the European Diaspora. A few managed to achieve a measure of financial stability within a relatively short time. There were also a few well-to-do individuals among the Hassidic emigrants, who required no support at all.

To their chagrin, the Hassidim encountered considerable hostility from the older established Jewish residents of Safed, as a result of a letter writing campaign launched by their Mitnagdic foes in the Diaspora. Violence followed on the heels of this agitation, causing a group of the Hassidic settlers under the leadership of Menachem Mendel of Vitebsk, to abandon Safed and settle in Tiberias. A smaller number of Hassidim moved to Pe'kiin. The remainder of the original group of Hassidim led by Alexander Katz of Kalisk chose to stay in Safed.

Even after coming to Palestine, Menachem Mendel maintained his position as spiritual leader of the Hassidim of White Russia. By means of couriers and correspondence he continued to guide and advise his followers. Nevertheless, the Hassidic leader did not consider himself to be a *Tzaddik*. He believed that a *Tzaddik*'s function should be limited to teaching and guidance in divine worship. Menachem Mendel was particularly repelled by the growth of *Tzaddik* dynasties. Following his demise in 1788 at Tiberias, the leadership of the Lithuanian and White Russian Hassidim passed into the capable hands of his disciple, Rabbi Shneur Zalman, who at the eleventh hour of the migration to Palestine had opted to remain in Europe.

The aliyah of 1777 was not followed by a mass movement of Hassidim to Eretz Israel. Although the deep stirring among the masses of Eastern Europe for redemption in the Holy Land was strong, they were not able to overcome the economic, political and cultural conditions that held them fast in the lands of their birth. Menachem and his associates however, feared an unorganized mass emigration. They had been deeply disturbed by the paupers who had come to Palestine with them, and tried desperately to discourage such immigration in the future.

In the years that followed the 1777 migration, economic and political circumstances in Eastern Europe negated any possibility of large scale immigration to the Holy Land, but individual Hassidim continued to make aliyah. The latter were often inspired by the statements of prominent Hassidic leaders who had not completely accepted the concept of the spiritualization of Zion. Rabbi Jacob Isaac Hurwitz (1745–1815),[115] better known for his saintliness as *Ha-Hozeh* (the Seer) of Lublin, the acknowledged leader of Polish Hassidism, strongly advocated emigration and urged the repossession by Jews of the Land of Israel. Even more emphatic was Rabbi Simha Bunam (1765–1827),[116] a disciple of the Seer of Lublin. A widely traveled Hassidic leader who wore modern European clothes, spoke Polish and German, visited the theatre occasionally, engaged in commerce, and enjoyed playing cards, Bunam was also an outspoken advocate of messianic nationalism. He often compared the love of the Jews for Eretz Israel to that of the love of a bride for her bridegroom.

Still another Hassidic leader, Isaac Meir of Gur (1799–1866),[117] throughout his life made strenuous financial efforts to preserve the *Yishuv* (the Jewish community of Palestine). During the Polish rebellion of 1863 he tried desperately to arouse the nationalistic instincts of his coreligionists to think of Eretz Israel in the same way that the Poles thought of their homeland. He pointed to the efforts being made by the Poles to liberate their country from the hands of the Russians, and rhetorically posed the question as to what the Jews were doing to regain Eretz Israel. A prophet as well as a political realist, Meir of Gur had grave forebodings about the future of Jewry in Europe.

Sporadic attempts by small bands of Hassidim to colonize the Holy Land would continue into the modern era, but would not equal the intensity or the numbers of the 1777 migration until after World War II. The eighteenth century Hassidic aliyah brought new life to the Galilee and paved the way for the future Jewish settlement of this region. It also marked the initial stage of the historic role that the largest Jewish center in the European Diaspora was destined to play in the resettlement of the ancient homeland in the nineteenth and twentieth centuries.

9

The Perushim

A new epoch in the history of Jewish immigration to Eretz Israel began during the last quarter of the eighteenth century and the opening years of the nineteenth century. Once again it originated in the populous heartland of Eastern Europe's Jewish Diaspora. However, whereas the earlier flow of immigrants had been Hassidim, the new migration stemmed from the camp of their opponents, the Mitnagdim.

The Hassidim had stressed the blessings inherent in living on the sacred soil of the Promised Land. Their opponents entertained similar beliefs. The Mitnagdim were also motivated by a burning desire to neutralize the foothold that the Hassidic movement had managed to establish in Palestine and to create a viable Torah center for their own movement. In addition, the age-old yearning for redemption had taken on new meaning in the Pale of Settlement with the adoption by the Russian Government of a policy designed to drive Jewish lessees from the villages.

Elijah ben Solomon Zalman (the Gaon of Vilna)

In a manner strongly reminiscent of the Hassidic emigrations, which had been largely led by the disciples of the *Ba'al Shem Tov*, the Mitnagdic aliyah was spearheaded by pupils of Rabbi Elijah ben Solomon Zalman (1720–97),[118] the renowned Gaon of Vilna (the title of Gaon, Hebrew for eminence, originally designated the heads of the Babylonian academies; later used for great scholars). Born in Selets, a little town near Brest, Elijah was descended from a family rich in scholarship and rabbinical tradition. From his earliest years he showed unusual gifts, and was considered a child prodigy (*ilui*). At age six, Elijah delivered a homily in the Great Synagogue of Vilna, and a few years later participated in talmudic discussions, amazing scholars and laymen alike with his erudition. Although he studied briefly with some of the prominent rabbis of the age, Elijah acquired most of his immense knowledge on his own, and was thus spared from the fruitless casuistry (*pilpul*) that so enthralled most of his contemporaries. His memory was so remarkable that he was able to read a book, and then recite it by heart several years later.[119]

Elijah studied not only the Bible and the Talmud, but Kabbalah as well; even prior to age thirteen he was reputed to have indulged in mystic experiments. By his own admission he once sought to create a *golem* (a formless mass, i.e., an automaton, usually in human form, produced by supernatural means).[120] His intense interest in mysticism did not, however, prevent Elijah from also exploring secular subject matter. Indeed, in range of knowledge, intellectual grasp, profundity of thought, and originality, the future Vilna Gaon towered above his contemporaries.

At eighteen, Elijah married the daughter of Rabbi Judah Leib of Kaiden. A few years later he undertook a long journey through Poland and Germany. This odyssey, which lasted eight years, was part of a self-inflicted penance commonly known as "going into exile" (*galut uprichten*). Later hagiographic accounts of the Vilna Gaon's life would recount how the young scholar astonished learned professors in the Prussian capital (Berlin) with his profound knowledge of the sciences. After returning from his voluntary exile, Elijah settled with his family in Vilna, where he would spend the rest of his life.

Elijah ben Solomon Zalman's personal life resembled that of a hermit, nevertheless through his influence on a select circle of disciples he exerted considerable power over Lithuanian Jewish communal life. Rarely leaving his home, the Gaon spent most of his waking hours studying. He is believed to have authored seventy books before the age of forty (none were published during his lifetime). An ascetic as well as a recluse, legend has it that to prevent himself from falling asleep while studying, Elijah kept his feet in a basin of cold water in an unheated room.[121] The shutters of his study were always closed, and he pursued his studies by candlelight. Only on the eve of the Sabbath and festivals would Elijah interrupt his work to join his wife and children. According to his sons, he slept no more than four hours, taken in four periods of one hour each. Not until he was forty years old did the Gaon modify his hermit-like regimen to give lectures to the chosen group of scholars who gathered at his home to sit at the master's feet.

The Gaon refused to accept rabbinic office in Vilna. Nevertheless, large sums of communal money passed through his hands as he received about 1,400 gulden annually from the Vilna Kahal (organized apparatus of the Jewish community that exercised autonomous powers and collected taxes for the secular government). The funds received by Elijah were then distributed to the poor and used for community educational purposes. The Gaon, however, supported his own family on a small weekly allowance from a legacy left by an ancestor (Rabbi Moses Rivkes) for the maintenance of any of his descendants who devoted themselves to the study of Torah. The Kahal, keenly aware of the prestige of having in their midst a great scholar, supplemented the Gaon's meager stipend by providing him with housing for most of the period of his residence in Vilna.

The major exception to the Gaon's policy of not becoming directly involved in community affairs was his participation in the battle against Hassidism. He was convinced that the movement was a menace to Judaism, and several times authorized excommunication of its members. Elijah was particularly disturbed by the Hassidic claim that God could be worshipped in the temporal world through both the good and evil impulses that exist in man. He felt that this approach blurred the limits between the secular and the sacred, and the forbidden and the permitted. Emphasis on inner devotion, and deviation from clearly designated law, the Gaon believed, would lead the Hassidim to transgress against the Torah, and eventually undermine Judaism completely. The concept of the *Tzaddik* as an intermediary between God and the people appalled Elijah. The Gaon considered such behavior to be idol worship, particularly since he regarded many of the Hassidic leaders, including the *Ba'al Shem Tov*, to be ignoramuses. In addition, he objected to the changes the Hassidim introduced into the religious service, and in dress, as well as their tendency to separate themselves from the rest of the Jewish community. Lastly, the Gaon felt that the entire Hassidic Movement was riddled by moral laxity, and smacked of Shabbetaianism.

To the end of his life the Vilna Gaon remained steadfast in his opposition to Hassidism. In 1796 the Hassidim spread a rumor that the Gaon had come to regret his years of implacable hostility to their movement. On learning of this deception, the aged Elijah ben Solomon Zalman dispatched a circular letter to the Jewish communities of Lithuania and White Russia. It reiterated his firm opposition to Hassidism, and stressed the duty of every believing Jew to repudiate and actively persecute all followers of the movement.

By his life and pursuit of knowledge the Gaon set a pattern for others to follow. His range of interests were remarkable. Besides the Bible, Talmud, and Kabballah, his Jewish studies included Hebrew grammar, and *midrashim* (literally expositions, i.e., books of talmudic and post-talmudic times that deal with homiletical exegesis of the Scriptures). Elijah also delved into astronomy, algebra, geometry, trigonometry, geography, biology, and medicine. When the physician Baruch of Shklov translated Euclid's *Elements* into Hebrew, the Gaon heartily approved the project. He encouraged Baruch to translate other scientific works into Hebrew and deeply deplored the total neglect of the physical sciences by most of the talmudic savants of his time. He believed that such intentional ignorance was the cause of much mockery of the Jews among the nations. Although he encouraged secular studies as useful auxiliaries to the understanding of the Bible and the Talmud, the Gaon did not share the modernizing tendencies of the Berlin *Haskalah* (Jewish Enlightenment), which in his twilight years were beginning to attract adherents among the Jews of Western Europe.

For the Vilna Gaon, the Torah and its commandments were the ultimate values, the omega of human existence. In all of his biblical and talmudic studies he preferred literal interpretation of the material (*peshat*) to the more popular method of his day, *pilpul* (dialectics). Knowing by heart almost the entire body of talmudic and rabbinical literature, the Gaon had no difficulty in solving the most complicated questions of Jewish law. Indeed, in the hyperbolic language of one biographer, ". . . with a single shaft of the light of truth he would illumine the darkness, and with a single word overthrow heaps of pilpulim hanging by a hair."[122]

Settlements in Eretz Israel

Like the *Ba'al Shem Tov,* the Vilna Gaon longed to emigrate to the Holy Land, and as in the case of the founder of Hassidism, he never achieved his goal. On one occasion Elijah actually set out unaccompanied for Eretz Israel, with the intention of sending for his family when he reached Jerusalem. While passing through Germany he had a change of heart. Accordingly, he abandoned the journey, and returned to his home in Vilna. Although the reason for this has never been satisfactorily explained, legend has it that the

Gaon turned back because he realized that he would not be able to observe the dietary laws aboard any vessel bound for Palestine.

Unlike the *Ba'al Shem Tov* the Gaon did not object to the emigration of his disciples, and encouraged his followers to build a Mitnagdic center in Eretz Israel. This idea took hold and a steady stream of Mitnagdic emigration began during the Gaon's lifetime, and continued intermittently after his demise. In 1772 the first organized group of Mitnagdim reached the shores of Palestine, and succeeded in establishing a small community. A second band, headed by Rabbi Menahem Mendel of Shklov (d. 1827),[123] a well known kabbalist, and one of the Gaon's favorite disciples, arrived in Eretz Israel in 1808. Menahem Mendel had been a member of the Vilna Gaon's innermost circle and worshipped his teacher. He would later recall: "I did not withdraw from his presence; I held onto him and did not leave him; I remained in his tent day and night. I went where he went, slept where he slept, and never left his hand."[124] Following the demise of the Gaon, Menahem Mendel helped his sons to arrange and publish some of their father's manuscripts, and only then did the faithful disciple make plans for emigrating to Palestine.

Menahem Mendel settled in Safed where he established a center for study and prayer, and became the leader of the Mitnagdic settlers. Anxious not to be confused with the Hassidic community, the Mitnagdim called themselves *Perushim,* (i.e., the "secluded" or "separatists"), a name associated in ancient Israel with the Pharisees. The 150 Perushim included many artisans and scholars. In an effort to strengthen the community, Menahem Mendel maintained an active correspondence with the Diaspora. A good deal of this communication was directed at his old friend Rabbi Israel ben Samuel Ashkenazi of Shklov (1770–1839).[125] Menahem entreated the rabbi to act on behalf of the Safed Perushim in the Diaspora.

In 1813 a plague broke out in Safed, and Menahem Mendel and most of the Perushim fled to Jerusalem. Three years later Menahem decided to permanently settle in the Holy City. His example led other Perushim to follow suit, and marked the renewal of the Ashkenazi community of Jerusalem after a lapse of about a century.

A third group of the Vilna Gaon's followers led by Hayyim ben Tobiah, journeyed to Palestine in 1809 and merged with the Perushim of Safed. Almost immediately the new arrivals experienced financial difficulties, as none of them could engage in local trade because of their inability to understand Arabic. An assembly of elders seeking a way out of this dilemma decided, as the Hassidim had done before them, to send an emissary to Europe to organize regular financial support for the Perushim of Safed. The man chosen for this important mission was Israel ben Samuel Ashkenazi of Shklov the good friend of Menahem Mendel.

Israel had been one of a group of talmudic scholars from his native city of Shklov who had come to Vilna to study at the feet of the Gaon. A late member of the circle, Israel attended the great sage's court for less than one year. After the death of the Gaon, Israel returned to Shklov where he served as a preacher for twelve years before deciding to settle in Eretz Israel.

The fund raising mission to the Diaspora encountered unexpected difficulties. The Napoleonic wars had come to Russia, and travel had become hazardous. Nevertheless, despite the unsettled conditions, Israel of Shklov traversed White Russia and managed to successfully establish financial support institutions for the Perushim of Safed. He was aided in these efforts by Rabbi Haim of Volozhin who accompanied Israel through Lithuania to Vilna. Amazingly, the energetic Israel still found time in his fund raising activities to publish the Gaon's notes to a tractate of the Jerusalem Talmud, together with a commentary of his own.

Returning to Safed in 1813, Israel and his family were forced by a raging epidemic to join other Perushim fleeing the city. On the road to Jerusalem his wife succumbed to the plague. In Jerusalem the pestilence claimed his two sons, two of his daughters, and a son-in-law. Israel's father and mother, who had remained in Safed also perished. Of his entire family only Israel and his youngest daughter survived the epidemic. Help from the Diaspora failed to arrive in time to help any of the stricken Perushim. Despite this ordeal, which had tested their innermost convictions and faith, the Perushim congregation persevered, and in time recovered from the tragedy that had claimed so many lives.

Israel of Shklov returned to Safed in 1816 and was chosen by the Perushim, whose numbers had grown to 600 souls, to serve as head of the community. He organized and regulated the system of financial assistance, founded a yeshivah, maintained amicable relations with the Hassidic and Sephardic communities, established a rapport with the local Arab tribes, and represented the Perushim before the Ottoman authorities. When reports reached Safed in 1830 of the existence of Jewish tribes in Yemen, the indefatigable Perushim leader sent a special envoy to investigate whether they were remnants of the ten lost tribes.

In 1832 a Hebrew printing establishment was founded in Safed, and Israel entrusted it with the publication of his opus, *Pe'at ha-Shulhan* ("Corner of the Table") a codification of the rabbinic laws dealing with Eretz Israel that had been omitted from Joseph Karo's classic code, the *Shulhan Arukh* ("The Prepared Table"). Israel's masterpiece, however, did not come off the presses until 1836, its printing having been interrupted by an attack by the Arabs of the Upper Galilee on the Jews of Safed. During this difficult period, Israel managed to hold the community together, and to organize help for the victims of the Arab assault (the attack, which lasted for over a month, resulted in considerable loss of life and extensive property damage).

Crises seemed to mark Israel of Shklov's long tenure as leader of the Perushim. In 1837 Safed was struck by an earthquake. The city was reduced to a rubble and 2,000 Jews perished. Israel, who was in Jerusalem when the tremors occurred, immediately organized aid for the Jewish survivors of the stricken city, and appealed to the Diaspora for additional help in the way of funds and supplies. The survivors were brought to Jerusalem, and efforts were made by Israel of Shklov and other Jewish leaders to find them new homes. In the aftermath of the disaster, Israel's health began to fail. Two years later (1839), while seeking a cure in Tiberias, he died.

The Perushim immigration, in comparison to their Hassidic predecessors, represented a great step forward in the Jewish march to reclaim the Holy Land. In organization, and in numbers involved, the Perushim outshone their rivals. The followers of the Gaon of Vilna managed to create communities containing a broader spectrum of occupations and skills. This diversity increased the communities' chances for survival and growth. That this development was the result of policy rather than chance can be detected from the congregational regulations of the Perushim for the 1820s. The statutes, for example, granted special privileges for craftsmen in the community's distribution of charitable funds.

Of equal importance was the administrative skill of the Perushim leadership, notably that of Israel of Shklov, which provided a solid basis for the community's growth. Unlike the Hassidic leaders, who were inordinately absorbed with pietism and mysticism, the heads of the Perushim were more level headed and realistic. Being practical minded, the Perushim built solid links with the Diaspora, which in turn acted as a reservoir for funds and manpower. The immigration of the Perushim, which began during the Vilna Gaon's lifetime, would continue unabated well into the nineteenth century, when it would be overshadowed by secular inspired movements.

10

The Jews of Leghorn
and Jerusalem

During the course of the eighteenth century, Italian Jewry was particularly sensitive to events in the Holy Land. The geographical proximity of the Middle East, an undercurrent of messianic fever, and conditions in Italy itself (such as the prevalence of the ghetto system) all played a role in heightening interest in the ancient Jewish homeland. Throughout the Italian peninsula pious brotherhoods of Shomrim la-Boker (Morning Watchers) existed, who prayed daily at sunrise for the speedy redemption of the Jewish people. Members of the Italian *kehillot* (plural of the term *kehillah,* which designates the Jewish community as a whole, or the elected board that ran the affairs of each community) from the seventeenth century on were also required to contribute a fixed annual sum for establishing settlements in Palestine.[126] These strong attachments to Eretz Israel were strenuously tested in the 1770s, with the unfolding of a bizarre event involving the Jews of Leghorn and an international cast of characters. To fully understand this curious affair, it is essential to digress for a moment to examine the history of the Ottoman Empire and Palestine during this period.

The reign of the Turkish Sultan, Mustafa II (1659–1703) witnessed a sea-change in the political status of the Ottoman power in Europe. The Treaty of Karlowitz (1699) forced the Turks to make many concessions. Russia, for example, demanded control of the holy places in Jerusalem, and of all Orthodox Christians in the Ottoman Empire. The decline of Turkish military power also created havoc within the Ottoman system of government. No longer able to depend on the Janissaries (Turkish elite troops) for domestic control, the Sublime Porte was forced to recruit soldiers from its far-flung provinces. Accordingly, Albanians, Bosnians, and Maghrebi mercenaries were enrolled in large numbers. Their salaries were paid from the income of government estates and special taxes levied on the population. The provincial governors also created private armies and used them along with the imperial troops for tax collection, extortion, and for personal aggrandizement at the expense of their weaker neighbors. The proliferation of these private armies and the ever increasing corruption of the central and local governments were largely responsible for the anarchy that beset the Ottoman Empire and made it the "sick man of Europe." It also brought to the foreground the so-called Eastern Question which would come to play a prominent role in the politics of the major European powers. These European powers, whose attentions were increasingly drawn to the Eastern Mediterranean by nationalist movements among the Christian populations of the Ottoman Empire, began to seriously consider a possible collapse of the Turkish regime. Accordingly, each power began to develop policies which would either bolster the Turkish administration by urging reforms, or hasten the demise of the Ottoman Empire by encouraging nationalistic elements and supporting internal rebellions. The Jews were destined to play a role in this diplomatic maelstrom. The historian Ben Halpern, in describing this development, has written:

> As the notion of restoring the Jews to Palestine was current at the time . . . it began to be woven into the strategies devised by some European politicians to deal with the Eastern Question. The Jews were thought of both as possible pawns in schemes to dispossess the Turks of Palestine and on the other hand as new settlers who could help bolster up the Turkish power.[127]

Palestine reflected in microcosm some of the problems confronting the Ottoman regime. The area was administratively under the control of the pashalik of Damascus, and the pashalik of Sidon (the latter's capital was shifted to Acre in the middle of the eighteenth century). The pashalik of Damascus included southern Syria, a part of the Upper Galilee, Samaria, Judea, the Negev, and northern Transjordan. The pashalik of Sidon-Acre encompassed southern Lebanon, the Bay of Acre, Lower Galilee, and part of Upper Galilee, and at the height of its influence the entire coastal area of Palestine. The relationship between the pashaliks was usually one of mutual mistrust and hostility. Indeed, warfare between the two entities was commonplace until the Egyptian conquest of the pashaliks in 1831.

Zahir al-Omar

A century prior to the Egyptian takeover, a bold attempt had been made by a Bedouin sheik named Zahir al-Omar (1688?–1775) to liberate Palestine from Turkish rule and unify it as an independent state.[128] Zahir was a member of a prominent family (the Zeidans), and a few years after the death of his father had gained a reputation among the Bedouins and the Druze by capturing large areas of the Upper Galilee from the rapacious officials of the Pasha of Sidon. In an effort to forestall further encroachments upon his province, the Pasha of Sidon granted Zahir the right to collect taxes in the areas he had captured. This privilege enabled Zahir, in time, to gain control of the entire Tiberias district. The wily sheik used the tax revenues he received to enlarge his army, and to gradually extend his rule over all of the Galilee down to the Valley of Jezreel. Zahir's aggressive policy continued, and by 1735 he was in control of the city of Nazareth and his forces had reached the Nablus district on the border of the Pashalik of Damascus.

In 1742 the Pasha of Damascus, Suleiman el-Adem received permission from the Turkish sultan to wage war against Zahir al-Omar, and to put an end to his depredations.

The following year Suleiman set out with a large force into Zahir's territory, and succeeded in destroying several villages in the vicinity of Tiberias. However, he was unable to wrest Tiberias from Zahir's control, and withdrew his army to Acre, where he expected to receive reinforcements and supplies from Constantinople. Shortly after reaching Acre, Suleiman el-Adem died.

The new Pasha of Damascus made peace with Zahir, who took advantage of the new situation by crushing his remaining opponents among the Arabs, and by advancing his plans for further conquests at the expense of the Turks. The sheik subsequently turned his attention to Acre, which he eventually took over, and shortly afterwards established dominion over the entire region surrounding Acre Bay by capturing the fortress of old Haifa. Zahir's campaigns were made easier by his influential connections with officials of the Sublime Porte in Constantinople, who turned a blind eye to his encroachments. Consolidating his gains, Zahir was able in 1761 to repulse an attempt by Othman, the new Pasha of Damascus, to recapture Haifa. Zahir's seizure of Acre and Haifa gave him an access to the Mediterranean Sea and brought him into direct contact with the merchants and agents of Europe, who had established bases in the coastal towns to conduct trade with the inland regions.

The rule of Zahir al-Omar, in comparison to his Turkish predecessors, was benevolent, and in general marked a period of unprecedented economic growth for the entire region. Keenly aware of his rather insecure position in the midst of the Ottoman Empire, Zahir embarked on a large-scale military construction program. He fortified Tiberias, erected strongholds along the southern border of the Galilee, repaired the walls of Acre, strengthened the fortifications of Haifa, and built watch towers throughout his realm as a defensive measure against a surprise attack by a hostile force.

When war broke out between Turkey and Russia in 1768, the crafty Bedouin sheik saw an opportunity to execute his plan for establishing an independent state in Palestine. The Turkish-Russian conflict had encouraged uprisings throughout the Ottoman Empire (most notably in Egypt), and Zahir's position as master of the Galilee now appeared as a dangerous threat to the ability of the Turks to retain control of their Egyptian and Syrian dominions. To remove this threat, the Turkish sultan ordered his military commanders to dislodge Zahir from his strongholds.

The Mameluke Ali Bey

At the same time as these events were unfolding, the Mameluke governor of Cairo, Ali Bey,[129] one of the twenty-four beys who ruled Egypt in the name of the Turkish sultan's pasha, stopped sending taxes to Constantinople. Shortly after this act of defiance, Ali Bey declared himself ruler of all Egypt, and embarked on a campaign in the Arabian Peninsula, adding the Hedjaz, with the holy city of Mecca, to his newly acquired realm. Zahir al-Omar, now over eighty years old, saw in the Mameluke rebellion an opportunity to gain a powerful ally in his own struggle against the Turkish sultan. United by a common interest, Ali Bey agreed to an alliance with the Bedouin chieftain. Their cause received additional support with the arrival of a Russian fleet in the Mediterranean Sea.

Responding to Zahir's call for immediate assistance, Ali Bey dispatched some advance units of his army to Palestine. By March of 1771 these troops had been reinforced, and had grown into a Mameluke army of over 40,000 men. Joining Zahir's forces the invading army quickly overran and subdued most of Palestine. The joy in Zahir's camp, however, was soon dashed by an unexpected turn of events. The military commander of the Mameluke expeditionary force, an individual named Abu Daheb suddenly, without consulting his Arab allies, withdrew his army from Palestine and returned to Egypt. Apparently encouraged by the Turkish Sublime Porte he had decided to openly challenge Ali Bey for control of Egypt.

The Pasha of Damascus (Othman) aware of what had transpired quickly raised an army and set out to crush Zahir al-Omar. The old sheik rose to the challenge, and in a surprise attack before dawn on September 1, 1771, dealt a mortal blow to the pasha's army which had been encamped near Lake Huleh in the Galilee. Zahir captured the entire army of the pasha, together with its equipment and ammunition. Following up on his great victory Zahir marched up the coast and captured Sidon. The Sublime Porte in Constantinople, seeking a way out of an embarrassing situation, attempted to come to terms with Zahir, but the old warrior, expecting to be momentarily reinforced by Ali Bey, rejected the Turkish peace offer. Zahir's expectations, however, never materialized. His ally, Ali Bey, was defeated by his rival, Abu Daheb, and was forced to flee Egypt, with a few hundred men, to southern Palestine. On learning that the residents of Jaffa and Nablus had risen against this Mameluke remnant, Zahir came to their rescue and brought them safely to Acre.

Emboldened by Ali Bey's defeat, the Turks turned their full attention on Zahir. They laid siege to Sidon, forcing the Bedouin chieftain to seek help from the Russians. The latter's fleet sailed for Sidon and joined the fray. The combined efforts of Zahir and his Russian and Mameluke allies met with success and the siege of Sidon was broken. As the Ottoman forces retreated, Zahir and Ali Bey launched a new campaign to conquer southern Palestine. By the spring of 1773 all of Palestine, with the exception of Jerusalem, was in their hands.

A Proposal to Buy Jerusalem

During the period 1771–73, when Russia was acting in consort with the forces of Zahir and Ali Bey, a coterie of German officers attached to the Russian fleet sought to enlist the support of the Jews in the anti-Turkish alliance. These officers approached the Jews of Leghorn, where the fleet was anchored at the time, and proposed that the Jewish community leaders offer Ali Bey their financial backing. If accepted, they were to propose an agreement with the Mameluke leader for the purchase of Jerusalem. The Jews of Leghorn responded with alacrity to these suggestions, and asked the German officers to act as mediators. Incredibly, Ali Bey accepted the offer for the Holy City made by the Jews through their agents. Although the price agreed upon was enormous, the Jews of Leghorn were elated by their accomplishment, and immediately set about to raise the required sum. Jewish communities throughout Italy, Holland, and England were alerted and asked to contribute to the purchase price. In Leghorn itself, messianic aspirations were rekindled, and many members of the community became convinced that God had chosen them to play a role in rebuilding the Temple in the redeemed city of Jerusalem.

In the midst of these speculations, Ali Bey set out from Palestine with a small force to retake Egypt from his enemy, Abu Daheb. Once again the fates proved unfavorable and Ali's army was defeated near Cairo and he himself taken prisoner. A few days later he died of the wounds he had received during the battle, and with his demise vanished the dreams of the Jews of Leghorn to redeem Jerusalem.

Ali Bey's ally, the wily Zahir al-Omar managed to survive until the signing of a peace treaty between the Ottoman Empire and the Russians (July, 1774) left him alone to defy the Turks. The following year, with Turkish warships in Acre Bay, and confronted by large scale defections among his troops, the aged sheik prepared for the end. Unable to flee because of his infirmities, he was captured and killed by Moroccan mercenaries. He was decapitated and his head was displayed in front of the Turkish sultan's palace in Constantinople. Ottoman rule was restored to Zahir's former realm, and the sultan appointed a Bosnian mercenary, Ahmed Pasha al Jazzar (better known as "the butcher") to be the Pasha of Sidon and Acre.

III

CHRISTIAN ZIONISTS

11

Voices of Conversion

$\mathbf{T}$he Era of Enlightenment, the eighteenth-century European philosophic movement was characterized by a revolt against dogma and authority. It placed emphasis upon reason and the empirical method to discover truth, and attempted to reshape institutions to make them more conducive to social progress and harmony. The Enlightenment, in its wake, also brought forth a renewed interest in the Jews. Politicians and pamphleteers, philosophers and prophets, missionaries and monarchs suddenly discovered the "Jewish Question." Although the Enlightenment occasionally produced individuals who were totally unsympathetic to the Jews (e.g., Voltaire),[130] there were others, notably a handful of Christian writers and theologians who, for a variety of religious beliefs, were inclined to act as apologists for the Jews. Indeed, from the time of the Reformation, the belief that the Jews were destined to return to the Holy Land in accordance with certain biblical prophecies was widely accepted among Protestant pietists. This view was closely interwoven with the millenarian concept that the Second Coming of Christ was at hand, and that after the Advent he would rule from Jerusalem for 1,000 years. The millenarians anticipated not only the return of the Jews to the Promised Land, but also their conversion to Christianity—a "sign of the times" that would precede the Second Coming. In order to hasten the fulfillment of these eschatological prophecies, many millenarians exhibited great enthusiasm in their efforts to foster a Jewish restoration in Palestine.

Messianic hopes among many Christians had reached new heights in the seventeenth century. Thus in 1644 much excitement was aroused by the report that the lost ten tribes had been found in America. Many Christians and learned Jews believed that the time of a return to the Promised Land was near. In the *New Atlantis*, written about 1619, Francis Bacon referred to the messianic era and the part the Jews were destined to play in bringing it about. Bacon's contemporary, Tommaso Campanella, predicted that social and political changes would culminate in the reign of the Messiah. John Sadler, the town clerk of

London, referred to the prediction in the *Zohar* that the Messiah would come in 1648. The Puritans were interested in messianic prophecies, for they were intent upon a new communion of saints, and they found scriptural confirmation for associating their new kingdom with the restoration of Israel. The great English poet, John Milton, believed that the twelve tribes would return to Zion. Similar views were expressed by Samuel Hartlib in *Macaria: The Prosperous Kingdom,* by John Durie in *Israel's Call to March to Jerusalem* (1646), and in his *Commonwealth of Israel* (1650). In 1649–50 Manasseh ben Israel's *The Hope of Israel* was published in Spanish and Latin, and almost immediately was translated into English. Throughout Europe the work aroused considerable interest. Manasseh argued that because the natives of the New World were Jews, only the presence of Jews in the British Isles was necessary to fulfill the prophecy of a complete dispersion. Accordingly, Manasseh sent to Cromwell, the Lord Protector of England, a Latin petition to be presented to Parliament, asking that Jews be admitted into England. With their admission, the Messiah would appear and summon his followers to the Holy Land. Cromwell was agreeable to Manasseh's suggestion, but the Parliament opposed the plan. Nevertheless, Cromwell unofficially allowed many Spanish Jews to settle in London.

Holger Paulli

A Dane, Holger Paulli (1644–1714),[131] displayed unusual zealousness for the return of the Jewish people to their ancient homeland. Little is known of his early life except that he studied theology and amassed a fortune in the slave trade in the West Indies and on the coast of Guinea. In 1694 Paulli underwent a religious experience. As a youth he had often dreamed of the coming greatness of Israel, in which he was to play a part. Following his transfiguration, he announced that God had commanded him to proclaim himself King of the Jews. He had been chosen by God, Paulli claimed, to convert His people (i.e., the Jews) to Christianity. In order to convince the doubtful of his credentials the eccentric Dane maintained that his grandfather had been a Jew, and that he himself was a direct descendant of the royal line of David. All evidence, however, indicates that Paulli was of Christian stock, and came from a Danish family of noble rank.

Leaving his wife and children, the would-be King of the Jews traveled to France and later to Holland, where he wrote and published religious tracts. In all of his writings, Holger Paulli sought to arouse the Jews from their spiritual lethargy, and to move them closer to a union with Christianity. Like other millenarians he was convinced that the Second Coming of Christ was not possible without a return of the Jews to the Promised Land. In addition to his religious tracts, Paulli incorporated his ideas in letters, replete with prophetic and mystical statements, addressed to King William III of England, and to the dauphin of France. The Danish zealot assured these royal personages that Jerusalem (and the Temple) was to be rebuilt in the year 1720, and that the Messiah himself would return to officiate as High Priest of the Holy City. In his correspondence he urged the British monarch and the French prince to use their great powers for assembling and restoring the Jews to Palestine. Those Jews, Paulli emphasized, who would not embrace Christianity following redemption were to be forcibly baptized. By showing enthusiasm for the Jews, the Danish millenarian wrote the dauphin, France could atone for the bloody Saint Bartholomew Massacre of the country's Huguenots.

While propagandizing his religious convictions in regard to the Jews in Holland, his fanaticism aroused the authorities and he was imprisoned in Amsterdam (1701). The following year Paulli's relatives were able to secure his release after promising the Dutch officials to keep him away from the Netherlands. Undaunted by his recent incarceration, Paulli resumed his religious mission. From 1702 to 1706 he concentrated his efforts on Germany. Although he lavishly expended funds to propagate his millenarian beliefs, the German public showed little interest in the messenger or in his prophecies. Desperate for recognition, Holger Paulli decided in 1706 to return to his native city, Copenhagen. Here, using his home as a meeting place, he was able to attract a small group of followers. Word of his activities reached the ears of the Danish king, Frederick IV, who was greatly disturbed by what he heard. Denmark was a strict Protestant country (Lutheran) and anyone who deviated from the predominant religion was regarded with suspicion. Paulli's messianic utterances and his insistence that God had commanded him to be King of the Jews had angered many of the citizens of the Danish capital, and had created a religious backlash that threatened to get out of hand. Fearing an outbreak of violence, King Frederick IV moved swiftly to put an end to Holger Paulli's activities. He ordered the police to prevent any more meetings from taking place in Paulli's home, and to admonish the latter from further preaching until the agitation he had stirred up subsided. These strong measures on the part of the King succeeded in defusing an explosive situation. Holger Paulli never fully recovered from the setback he had received. He did manage to publish a few more tracts, but then as suddenly as he had begun his preaching, Paulli abandoned his missionary efforts. The would-be King of the Jews was not heard from again.

Phillipe Gentil de Langallerie

Although Phillipe Gentil de Langallerie (1656–1717),[132] a contemporary of Holger Paulli, was not a millenarian in the strict meaning of the word, his bizarre attempt to found a new religion and a state which would provide a refuge for European Jewry deserves our attention. The scion of an ancient and noble French family, Langallerie had distinguished himself as a Lieutenant General in the army of the Sun King, Louis XIV. After thirty-two military campaigns, disillusionment set in (exacerbated by bitter quarrels with the king's Minister of War, Chamilar) and the veteran soldier decided on a radical change of allegiance. To the consternation of the French court, Langallerie joined the ranks of his country's arch-enemy, the Hapsburg Emperor, Joseph I. This volte-face so enraged his former benefactress, Madame de Maintenon, the wife of the French king, that she insisted that he be hanged in effigy.

Rewarded by the Emperor with a field marshal's command for his decision, Langallerie served his Hapsburg masters with great elan and gallantry in the Italian Wars. However, he once again became disenchanted with his lot in life. He was convinced that his military prowess was not fully appreciated or properly recognized by the Hapsburg regime. These feelings, which Langallerie openly voiced, alienated the Austrian court. Aware of the growing hostility toward him, the disgruntled field marshal, in the tradition of the condottieri of an earlier age, suddenly left Austria to seek his fortune in Dresden (1710). Augustus the Strong, Elector of Saxony and King of Poland, always eager to augment his military with seasoned officers, conferred upon Langallerie a command, and eventually placed him at the head of his regiments in Lithuania.

With the passage of time the ever restless mercenary, finding his talents totally unsuited for peacetime, tired of his new post and left the service of Augustus the Strong to seek greener pastures elsewhere. Wandering through the German states of Prussia and Hesse-Cassel, Langallerie underwent a religious transformation, and came to the conclusion that the existing churches, both Catholic and Protestant, were no longer viable and should be cast aside. He visualized in their place the creation of a theological republic based solely on the Word of God—an entity rooted in revelation in which priests, judges, and lawyers would be strictly proscribed. Langallerie called his ecclesiastical blueprint "The Theocracy of the Divine Word", and appealed for support to the Jews, whom he hoped would constitute the nucleus of his theological republic.

Many German Jews responded favorably to the Frenchman's call. This response was not entirely unexpected as Langallerie, while still in the employ of the Elector of Saxony, had made important contacts with court Jews. One of them, Behrend Lehmann, had played a prominent role in obtaining the large sums required by the Elector to purchase the throne of Poland. Lehmann had introduced the professional soldier to his circle of friends, thus making him known to the Jewish community. Indeed, a Jew of Frankfort named Joseph Latere provided Langallerie's "new religion" with a mystic underpinning. He pointed out that the cognomen Langallerie literally meant "the angel", and that according to his interpretation of certain kabbalistic prophecies the founder of the "Theocracy of the Divine Word" was destined to reestablish a Jewish kingdom. Langallerie did nothing to discourage Latere, as it made his own views more palatable among the elements of the Jewish community more inclined toward mysticism.

Where and how did Langallerie hope to establish his theological republic? The answer is startling. While on a visit to Holland, Langallerie became intimate with Osman Ago, a minister plenipotentiary of the Turkish sultan. Ago had come to the Hague to reclaim from the General Estates, a Turkish vessel captured by the Dutch. Langallerie and his chief disciple, the Margrave of Linange (a relative who had served in the army of the Russian Czar, Peter the Great) disclosed to the Ottoman diplomat their plans to found a new religion and state. The Turk at first considered the two professional soldiers as mad and their project as hare-brained, but as the talks progressed over a long period he changed his mind.

Almost imperceptibly the discussions evolved into serious negotiations. The end result was a formal agreement between Langallerie and the envoy of the Sublime Porte. Incorporated into the accord was a plan proposed by Langallerie to raise and lead an army of mercenaries into Italy. Disguised as pilgrims this force would infiltrate the Vatican, depose the pope, seize papal treasures, and then capture the rest of Rome. The Eternal City would be turned over to the Turks, and in return Langallerie was to be granted a territory in the Greek Archipelago, or possibly be ceded Palestine. In either case, Langallerie hoped to settle Jews in his territory, and firmly establish his new religion.

The pact also specified that the Turks would assist the former field marshal in the recruitment of 10,000 mercenaries and the equipping of a fleet of fifty men-of-war. Linange was designated as the grand admiral of the proposed fleet, and was assigned the additional responsibility of seeking assistance from the pirates who plied the waters of the Greek Archipelago. Langallerie and his handful of kabbalistic followers assumed the task of appealing directly to Jewish communities for manpower and financial support.

Incredibly, a number of Jews responded to Langallerie's call for assistance. Most notable among those who answered his appeal was the kabbalist Alexander Susskind of Metz, a former employee of the court Jew, Behrend Lehmann. Susskind's talents as a secretary, translator, and treasurer were quickly recognized by Langallerie who decided to make him seneschal of his new republic.

However, before the agreement with the Turks could be fully implemented, fate intervened. Langallerie, while on the road to Hamburg, was captured by soldiers of the Hapsburg Emperor, Charles VI. Brought to Vienna he was accused of conspiring with the Turks and of high treason. During the course of his trial the plot to depose the pope was uncovered, and a roundup of Langallerie's followers ensued. Convicted and incarcerated, his movement ruthlessly suppressed, Langallerie realized he was doomed. When an escape plan devised by the remnant of his followers failed, the former field marshal resorted to a hunger strike. Although force fed by his jailers, Langallerie continued to refuse all nourishment. Death finally came to his rescue on September 18, 1717. Linange and Susskind, who had also been taken into custody by the Austrians, were eventually released, bringing to a close the entire extraordinary affair.

Moses Mendelssohn and the "Christian Man of Rank"

Haskalah, the Jewish Enlightenment movement, was an offshoot of the European Age of Enlightenment. The singularity of the Haskalah lay in its emergence against a backdrop of the social and cultural integration of the Jews with their surroundings. Although the basic tenets of Judaism constituted the focal point of the Jewish enlighteners (the *maskilim*), their efforts were marked by a spirit of extreme rationalism and a definite tendency to downplay Jewish nationalism. In pursuing these objectives the *maskilim* gradually discarded the ancient dream of redemption in the Holy Land in favor of civic emancipation in the European countries in which they lived. Thus without fully realizing the consequences of their actions they sowed the seeds of assimilation, and undermined venerable Jewish religious traditions.

The father of the Haskalah was the prominent philosopher Moses Mendelssohn (1729–86),[133] and his life exemplified the struggle of the *maskilim* for the hearts and minds of European Jewry (particularly Western Jewry). Born in the ghetto of Dessau, the capital of the small German principality of Anhalt-Dessau, he was the youngest son of a Torah scribe, who, although impoverished, claimed descent from a long line of scholars. Young Moses possessed an agile mind and a capacity for study, and his father, who was his first instructor, placed him under the wing of the Dessau rabbi, David Fraenkel. Unremitting application to his studies brought on an illness that left Moses Mendelssohn with a curvature of the spine and permanent damage to his nervous system. When his teacher, David Fraenkel, left Dessau in 1743 to become chief rabbi of Berlin, the fourteen-year-old Moses, with little money or recommendations, followed him to the Prussian capital. Knocking on the only gate into Berlin through which Jews were allowed to pass, he convinced the gatekeeper that he was worthy to enter the city, paid the required *leibzoll* (body tax imposed on Jews and cattle moving from town to town), and was admitted. Enrolling in Fraenkel's academy, Mendelssohn continued his talmudic studies. The gifted and eager student soon attracted the attention of Jewish intellectuals of the Berlin community who introduced him to secular studies. Prior to coming to Berlin, Mendelssohn spoke only Yiddish and Hebrew, but under his new mentors he studied philosophy, mathematics, and several languages, notably German, French, Latin, and English.

After seven years of struggle, often hungry and in rags, Mendelssohn found a patron. In 1750 a wealthy Jewish silk merchant named Isaac Bernhard offered him the post of tutor in his household, and Mendelssohn accepted with alacrity. In time he would become a partner in Bernhard's firm.

Recommended by one of his former instructors as a chess player of considerable talent, Mendelssohn, in the year 1754, was introduced to the famous dramatist and critic Gotthold Ephraim Lessing (1729–81).[134] The German writer, the first strong Christian voice in Germany to speak out on behalf of the Jews during the eighteenth century, became Mendelssohn's life-long friend. He encouraged the shy ghetto scholar to write on philosophical and literary themes, and on his own initiative published Mendelssohn's *Philosophical Dialogues,* the first book by a Jew in the German language, and the beginning of his career as an author.

A period of great activity followed, and Mendelssohn contributed many articles to magazines published by Lessing and Friedrich Nicolai, a literary critic and book dealer. He also reviewed novels and poetry. One such critique brought him to the brink of disaster. The King of Prussia, Frederick the Great, fancied himself a poet, and often published verses written in French. Mendelssohn, commenting on some of the king's work noted that it was a pity that the royal poet preferred a foreign language to his mother tongue. Summoned to Sans Souci for his impudent remarks, Mendelssohn managed to placate the monarch's ire with a witty analogy. "Writing verses", he informed the ruler, "is like bowling, and anyone who bowls, whether he be king or peasant, must submit to having the pin boy say how well or ill he bowls."[135]

Two years after this incident, Mendelssohn enjoyed a unique triumph. He was awarded first prize in a contest sponsored by the Berlin Academy of Sciences. His winning essay eclipsed a contribution by the great German philosopher, Immanuel Kant. Mendelssohn's success earned him the plaudits of Berlin's savants, the so-called coffee house of the learned. However, in spite of his newly won fame it took a special appeal by an aristocratic admirer to convince the Prussian King to grant Mendelssohn the privilege of being a *shutzjude* (protected Jew).[136] By this act Mendelssohn's fear of expulsion from Berlin was forever removed.

Moses Mendelssohn reached his apogee as a philosopher in 1767 with the publication of his book *Phaedon,* an eloquent defense of the immortality of the soul modeled after a work by Plato. It became the most widely read book of the age, and its author was hailed as "the Jewish Plato", and "the Socrates of Berlin." The Berlin Academy of Sciences, wishing to honor Mendelssohn's accomplishments, proposed him for membership in their society, but the king obstinately refused to confirm the nomination. Some historians believe that Frederick did not wish to offend Catherine the Great of Russia who had expressed a desire to be elected to the academy, and would not be at ease with a Jewish member.[137]

In answer to a challenge from a Swiss pastor named John Casper Lavater to convert to Christianity, Mendelssohn in an open letter to the minister reaffirmed his Judaism. The confrontation with Lavater struck a responsive chord in Mendelssohn's psyche and impelled him to a deeper and more intensive concern with Jewish community life. Henceforth, much of his work was to be directed toward bringing about a total revolution in the life of his coreligionists by changing those aspects that prevented the individual Jew from gaining acceptance as a Jew within the framework of the larger society. Mendelssohn advocated a reconstruction of the political foundation of that society to allow a Jew to participate fully in its life and yet remain loyal to his religion. To break down the cultural isolation of the Jewish world, and to allow the spirit of the Enlightenment to penetrate, Mendelssohn undertook his celebrated translation of the *Pentateuch* into German. To make it understandable to his Jewish audience the elegant German was printed in Hebrew characters, and accompanied by a commentary in Hebrew, known as the *Biur*. The translation proved to be a major contribution to the Jewish Enlightenment, providing as it did a key to the German language, European culture, and to life beyond the ghetto.

Mendelssohn's efforts on behalf of his co-religionists also included cultural projects: most notably support of a parochial school in Berlin for Jewish children in which the curriculum encompassed modern languages, science, and the arts. He also encouraged a group of Jewish scholars to publish a Hebrew magazine called *Ha-Meassef* (the Gatherer). Equally important was the Jewish Plato's involvement in the protracted struggle for civil rights for the Jews of Germany, Switzerland, and Alsace. It led to Mendelssohn's exploration and expansion of a principle long favored in European circles, namely the separation of state and religion. In a work entitled *Jerusalem,* Mendelssohn advocated a society where all members would enjoy religious freedom as well as political equality. He argued that a man's religious beliefs ought to be regarded as his personal affair, and that neither civil nor religious authority should be granted the power to compel conformity by expelling individuals from the community (i.e., excommunication) or by otherwise punishing dissidents. Mendelssohn concluded his book with an eloquent appeal for tolerance—a view he had earlier stressed in a preface to a German translation of an essay by Manasseh ben Israel entitled *Vindiciae Judaeorum.*

Although keenly aware of the Jews' marginal position in the German states and elsewhere in Europe, Mendelssohn, the rationalist philosopher, had grave doubts as to the possibility of the revival of a Jewish state. In 1770, shortly after his reply to the Swiss pastor Lavater, he received, through an intermediary, a memorandum on how to solve the Jewish Problem. It was accompanied by a letter that asked him to refrain from trying to discover the identity of the writer and from communicating the contents of the memorandum to anyone. The anonymous author urged Mendelssohn to give serious consideration to his proposal, and if he thought the scheme foolish or impractical to indicate why by means of the intermediary. The go-between was George Detlef Friedrich Koes, the Director-General of the Royal Bank of Berlin, who acted as a courier only and knew nothing of the contents of the mysterious memorandum. When questioned by Mendelssohn, Koes would only say that the nameless correspondent was "a man of rank," whom he knew and loved as a friend of humanity.[138]

Some historians believe that the author of the memorandum was Count Rochus Friedrick zu Lynar,[139] a former Danish minister to St. Petersburg. The count, who was deeply involved in religious studies, may have been influenced by chiliastic ideas, such as those advocated by the Danish zealot Holger Paulli and the Swiss pastor Lavater, both of whom expected the restoration of a Jewish state as essential for the Second Advent of Christ.

The "man of rank's" memorandum was not preserved, but the essentials of the nobleman's plan can be surmised from Mendelssohn's reply. He began by stressing his incompetence to judge a project that presupposed a profound knowledge of matters important to a state, such as population, taxation, natural resources, and trade. Mendelssohn, however, acknowledged the majesty of the idea, and the audacity of the memorandum's author. He was especially impressed by the writer's tolerance and by his views on religion and morality. Having disqualified himself from passing judgment on a scheme of such magnitude, Mendelssohn then cited the difficulties, which in his opinion, precluded the restoration of a Jewish state in Palestine.

The greatest obstacle, he believed, was the character of the Jewish people. The long centuries of exile and persecution had taken a toll on the spirit and vigor of the Jews. The desire for freedom had been stifled, and the "nation" had been transformed into a people who expressed themselves in prayer and patience rather than in action. Mendelssohn also expressed doubts that the widely dispersed Jewish people were willing or able to implement such a grand design as restoring a state in the Holy Land. The unity required for an endeavor of that scale hardly existed. In addition, such a plan would require large sums of money and access to sources of credit. Apart from all of these factors, such a project could only be realized if the European Powers were distracted by a war or other major crisis. In a quiet period, a single jealous state could derail any Jewish hopes for a restoration in Palestine.[140]

Mendelssohn's rejection of the proposal of the "man of rank" may have been influenced by the writings of the philosopher Baruch Spinoza (1632–77), who had expressed similar views in his *Tractatus Theologico-Politicus*. Spinoza, in particular, had felt that the psychological characteristics that had come to the foreground during the nation's long period of exile militated against the successful restoration of a Jewish state.

Mendelssohn's pessimism and lack of Jewish nationalistic ardor was largely due to a conviction that the most important issue facing the Jews of his day was that of emancipation in the countries in which they lived. This belief, which negated any possibility of the Jewish people actively seeking to return to their ancient homeland as an independent nation, was shared by most of the outstanding personalities of the Berlin Haskalah.

Karl Friedrich Gustav Seyfart

Jews instinctively regarded with suspicion the appeals made to them by Christians to participate in schemes to create a polity in Palestine. Such was the fate of a call by a Berlin-born evangelist named Karl Friedrich Gustav Seyfart.[141] On Christmas Eve of 1830, in a proclamation written in the biblical style, he pleaded with European Jewry to awaken and redeem their ancestral home in Palestine. God, he wrote, had removed the curse that had been placed on them, and it was the sacred duty of every individual who belonged to the House of Israel to gather together, organize, and plan for the great exodus out of Europe. With a flourish indicative of the grandiose nature of his character, he signed his proclamation with the imperial sounding name, Siegfried Justus I.

Soon after the appearance of this document, Seyfart launched a campaign to make his appeal a reality. He traveled throughout Germany, spreading his message of the need for a Jewish restoration in Palestine, before alighting in Cracow, Poland, in 1832. He intended to make Cracow his campaign headquarters because of its unique geographical location and its political status. At the time, Cracow was a free state, a commonwealth created in the wake of the Napoleonic era by the Congress of Vienna. The city and its environs contained a large number of Jews and provided easy access to Galicia, which also had a sizable Jewish population.

Seyfart now redoubled his efforts. He sent memoranda, letters, and pamphlets, replete with biblical phraseology, to prominent personalities, and to most of the monarchs of Europe. In English, French, and German he emphasized the inevitability of a Jewish restoration in Palestine. At the same time he tried, with very little success, to contact and persuade Jewish community leaders to join in his efforts to hasten their people's redemption. In time Seyfart's proclamations began to take on an even more majestic tone and gave the impression that they originated in the Holy Land. He frequently enlarged on his self-assumed royal title, and signed his letters and announcements as Siegfried Justus I, King of Israel and High Priest of Jerusalem.

In moves designed to attain the sympathy and support of Cracow's administration, as well as that of the Jewish population, Seyfart suggested several novel proposals. To the Jews of the city he announced his intentions of creating an institution to take care of the community's widows and orphans. Almost with the same breath he proposed a plan to aid the refugees of the unsuccessful Polish Insurrection of 1830–31. In addition, Seyfart set forth a scheme to petition the government of Greece for permission to organize on its territory a new Polish army.

However, Seyfart's main efforts continued to be directed toward Jewish redemption in the Holy Land. He constantly stressed the "oneness of the Jewish people," and the need for a "Society of Zion," which would form the apex of a pyramid of Jewish communal organizations in every nation where Jews lived. The deputies elected by the communal organizations to the "Society of Zion" would in turn act in concert with the King of Jerusalem on all matters concerning Jewry. The Jewish communities, for example, would provide the society with lists of all Jews interested in serving the movement, or in immigrating to Palestine.

Seyfart was convinced that a reconstituted Jewish state would eventually become a commercial and industrial center for the entire Middle East. To accelerate this development, he advocated, in 1833, the establishment of Jewish trade missions, or consulates, in every major European city. In the manner of modern philanthropic campaigns, Seyfart suggested the sale of bonds to those individuals dedicated to the restoration of a Jewish state in Palestine. By such means, Seyfart believed the Jews could cover the costs of the proposed network of trade missions and other expenses incurred by the Society of Zion.

Seyfart's activities attracted the attention of the Cracow senate, and on May 1, 1832, he was summoned to testify before that august body. In the proceedings that followed he informed the senate that he was thirty-three years old, a Christian, and a merchant by profession. He also described his diplomatic work on behalf of the Jews as his duty as a "plenipotentiary of the king of Jerusalem" (an obvious retreat from his previous statements and correspondence in which he claimed to be the king and high priest of the Holy City). Seyfart also told the senators of his hopes for the Society of Jews, which would have the major responsibility for assisting the Jews to return to Palestine. Lastly, he spoke of why he had chosen Cracow as his headquarters, and of his correspondence with the various monarchs of Europe and with Jewish leaders. Among the latter individuals contacted by Seyfart was the Cracow rabbi and Polish patriot, Dov Berush Meisels (1798–1870). Indeed, Meisels had promised to call a meeting of the Cracow Jewish community to discuss Seyfart's plans for a return to Zion, but the gathering was postponed in order to allow the "legate of the King of Jerusalem" time for an intensive educational campaign.

The Cracow senate, somewhat bewildered by Seyfart's testimony and by his personality, continued to press him for more details as to his mission, background, profession, and relations to the so-called King of Jerusalem. When the questioning revealed that the senators considered him as some sort of mystic charlatan, Seyfart became upset. Nevertheless, recovering his composure, he requested that he be granted permission to freely publish his pamphlets and proclamations. The senate hesitated to grant Seyfart's petition, and suggested instead that he turn over his writings to the Cracow censor for further examination. The censor would determine if the material contained anything harmful to the Free State of Cracow. Unbeknown to Seyfart, the senate also requested assistance from the three major powers occupying Poland—Prussia, Austria, and Russia—all of whom launched investigations into Seyfart's background and activities.

The Prussian official report portrayed Seyfart as a harmless crank; the Russians, aware of the pamphleteer's sympathy for the Polish insurrectionists, advocated that Seyfart's proclamations be banned, and the printing of any new publications forbidden. The Governor of Galicia went even further, and suggested that all of Seyfart's printed material be confiscated. He considered Seyfart to be an adventurer and an agent of a dangerous conspiratorial committee (perhaps an indirect reference to the proposed Society of Zion). Paradoxically, the governor's report also noted that Seyfart had little if any contact with Jews. Still another official, the police director of the city of Lemberg, after a preliminary investigation, decided that Seyfart was a religious fanatic with dangerous liberal tendencies.

During the course of these probes Seyfart realized that the Cracow senate would never give him permission to publish his pamphlets and other material or even allow him to remain in the Free State. He somehow managed to get back his writings from the censor and quietly left Cracow before a final decision on his status was made by the senate.

In 1836 Seyfart resurfaced in France (Nice). Once again he told the Jewish communities of Europe that the time had come for a major change in their state of affairs. He stressed that in the struggle of all nations for freedom and justice the Jews also had a right to think of their future. It was their moral obligation to demand of the European powers support in obtaining a state. The restoration of the Jews in Palestine, Seyfart insisted, was a historical necessity. Furthermore, once this Jewish entity was achieved, it would serve as a model for other peoples to emulate. As in his previous proclamations, the author bolstered his arguments with biblical quotations (mostly from the writings of the Hebrew prophets). Sensitive to the winds of change unleashed by the Haskalah, Seyfart condemned those Jews who sought a solution to the Jewish Question through emancipation or assimilation.

Attached to his 1836 proclamation was a pamphlet outlining the goals of the "Society of Zion." In it Seyfart reiterated his earlier ideas on the subject in greater detail. He particularly stressed how best to organize the Jewish communities and the importance of immediately establishing trade missions in London and Leipzig. He also suggested the need to reward those who served the cause of Zion. In an earlier publication, Seyfart had proposed a series of awards consisting of three grades, each with special privileges, namely the Order of David, the Order of Solomon, and the Order of Siegfried. In addition, Seyfart recommended the adoption by the Jews of a new calendar, and toyed with the idea of inviting all people of good will—Jews, Christians, and Muslims—to help in the rebuilding of the Temple in Jerusalem.

Following the 1836 proclamation and pamphlet, Seyfart was not heard from again. Like the biblical Korah, the would-be legate of the King of Jerusalem had vanished. His impact upon Jewry was negligible, a fact clearly brought out in the dossiers of the Austrian, Prussian, and Russian authorities, as well as in the reports of the investigators of the Free State of Cracow. The final verdict on Seyfart was rendered by Josef Perl (1773–1839), an author of satirical works and a leading figure of the Galician Haskalah. He was called upon by the Galician authorities to examine Seyfart's writings, and to determine what effect they had on the Jewish community. Perl undertook the assignment with some trepidations fearing that a positive assessment would trigger an anti-Jewish reaction. Nevertheless, he came to the conclusion that Seyfart had not aroused the slightest interest among Jews. Perl attributed this reaction to the suspicion of many Jews that Seyfart was following in the footsteps of the false Messiah, Shabbetai Zevi. Ignorance of Jewish life on the part of the Christian pamphleteer had also played a part in preventing the development of a viable movement around him. With the acceptance of Josef Perl's report by the Galician authorities, the bizarre episode of "the legate to the King of Jerusalem" was officially closed.

Charles F. Zimpel

Christian voices continued to be raised on behalf of a Jewish restoration in Palestine throughout the nineteenth century. Most unusual were the exhortations of a German-born physician named Charles F. Zimpel[142] — a deeply religious man who claimed that he was neither Catholic nor Protestant. An ardent individual, Zimpel thought of himself as "a pupil and disciple of Christ." He showed no interest in converting Jews to Christianity, but firmly believed in the Bible. The Jews alone, he felt, were the rightful heirs of Palestine, the homeland promised them by God.

In 1852 Zimpel toured Palestine, and was shocked by the state of stagnation that prevailed in the land. He was especially appalled by the horrid conditions under which the Jews of Jerusalem lived and resolved to bring their plight to the attention of the world at large. Upon his return to Germany, Zimpel published a pamphlet giving a full account of his experiences in the Holy Land and his thoughts on how to revive the country from the political, economic and social morass brought about by Ottoman misrule. His central theme, which reflected strong messianic overtones, accentuated the need for a positive Jewish role to make Palestine once again a crossroads of civilization. Zimpel, however, differed slightly from the millenarians who believed that the establishment of a Jewish entity in Palestine must precede the Second Coming of Christ. He favored instead the creation of a republic in the Holy Land under the joint rule of Jews and Christians (the Muslims had no place in his projected state).

Zimpel was convinced that his ideas were viable, and that the seeds required to make his plan a reality had already been sown. He took note of the efforts made by the various Christian societies in England, Germany, and France to establish schools and hospitals in Palestine, and the renewed interest among Jews in the land of their ancestors. The efforts of Christians and Jews acting in unity, Zimpel believed, could provide the required resources to establish the mixed republic he had in mind.

Nevertheless, Zimpel was of the opinion that a true Jewish renaissance in the Holy Land was not possible as long as the system of *halukkah* (distribution of charity funds from the Diaspora) prevailed. This method of providing financial support for the pious Ashkenazi Jews in the four holy cities of the Land of Israel — Jerusalem, Hebron, Safed, and Tiberias — had become institutionalized at the end of the eighteenth century. Originally the creation of the Ashkenazi rabbi of Jerusalem, Isaiah Horowitz (1565–1630), who had managed to obtain steady funds from Jewish communities in Central Europe, the *halukkah* system was further developed and firmly entrenched in the aftermath of succeeding waves of Hassidic and Mitnagdic immigrants to Palestine. Zimpel viewed the entire charity system as an obstacle to the economic and political development of the *Yishuv* (the Jewish community in the Holy Land). He was convinced that the system was perpetuated by the directors of *halukkah,* who for self-serving interests, saw fit to keep the Jewish population in a state of idleness and poverty. It was ironic, Zimpel noted, that the Jews who had, during their early history, been cultivators of the soil had become beggars who lived off of charity and spurned agriculture. To remedy this situation he urged the promotion among the Jews of a "return to the land movement."

To improve the moral, social, and economic climate of the Yishuv, Zimpel recommended moral and ethical education for Jewish youth (boys and girls), emphasis on religious principles, agricultural instruction for all able-bodied adults, the establishment of health centers to meet the medical needs of the population, centers for the care of the sick and the aged who were no longer able to work, and the establishment of a central committee (as well as local committees) to be responsible for raising the necessary funds and for guiding the actual work on the land.

The physician's plan failed to arouse the Jewish public, but the religiously motivated reformer persisted in his efforts. Seeking a practical demonstration of his ideas, he contributed a large sum of money to an American-Christian sect who had in 1850 founded a colony in Palestine in the Wadi-Turtash region near Bethlehem. Although the colonists exhibited missionary tendencies, in obvious violation of Zimpel's plan, he supported the venture because of the sect's willingness to instruct Jerusalem Jews in farming. In their zeal, which bordered on utopianism, the sectarians chose as their site for a settlement land leased from a converted Jew known as J. Meshulam. Quarrels soon arose between the settlers and their landlord. The latter decided on drastic action and drove the colonists off his property. This setback plus the inability of the sect to recruit many Jews or to find sufficient funds for their agricultural experiment soon brought the entire project to an inglorious end.

Although saddened by the failure of the Wadi-Turtash colony, Zimpel remained resolute and confident that his plans were sound. After a second visit to Palestine in 1864, he published an essay in pamphlet form addressed to all of Christendom and Jewry. Going far beyond his previous position, the author now called for a Great Power crusade to liberate Palestine from Turkish rule. He also expected the Jews to play a key role in this struggle to remove the Ottoman yoke from the promised land. A potent inducement for their participation would be the realization that the return to the ancient homeland, with Great Power backing, was no longer an impossible dream.

Not all of the European nations, Zimpel felt, would be willing to partake in the campaign against the Turks. Russia, Austria, and Prussia would probably remain indifferent to the crusade. England and France, however, could be expected to play major roles. Napoleon III of France, in particular, Zimpel believed, would be anxious to become involved, as he was ambitious to fulfill the thwarted plans of Napoleon Bonaparte for the East, including those concerning Palestine.

After the liberation of Palestine had been attained, the Jews were not to immediately press for the establishment of a purely Jewish state. Instead, Zimpel, in his essay, returned to his earlier conception of a pact between Christians and Jews for the formation in the Holy Land of a "mixed republic." In many ways this entity would resemble the government of the United States. Zimpel's pamphlet struck a popular chord and sold over 10,000 copies, but its ideas found few supporters among the Jews of Europe or America.

In 1865 the physician–pamphleteer published still another essay on his favorite subject. Changing his tactics he approached the issue of the future of Palestine from a completely different angle. He outlined a scheme to link the Dead Sea and Damascus by railroad with the Mediterranean Sea. This rail system would incorporate in its network Jerusalem, Bethlehem, Tiberias, and Nazareth. Zimpel, who had some practical experience with railroad construction in America, had, prior to the release of his pamphlet, approached the Turkish government with a similar suggestion. He estimated that the railroad project would cost $4 million to construct, and predicted that it would greatly facilitate the tourist and pilgrim trade. Edhem Pasha, the Turkish Minister of the Interior indicated to Zimpel that the sultan had expressed an interest in his proposal, and was willing to offer the physician a concession if he could raise the necessary capital for the railroad project within six month's time. This stipulation proved insurmountable and the Turks withdrew their offer.

Zimpel's railroad scheme was merely a facade for his earlier proposals. Aside from the technical suggestions, the text of his pamphlet dealt with the importance of the proposed railroad for European Jewry. He urged Jewish capitalists to throw their considerable influence behind the project for their own salvation and that of the Jewish people.

Once again Zimpel's appeal for Jewish support received little attention and, in a few instances, actually aroused considerable opposition. Ludwig Philippson (1811–89), a leading spokesman of German Jewry and strong advocate of Jewish emancipation, vehemently attacked Zimpel's ideas in his newspaper the *Allgemeine Zeitung des Juden-thums*. Philippson was particularly disturbed by the physician's prediction that Europe would one day witness a general persecution of the Jews, and that their only choice of finding a haven would be to flee to Palestine.

Although Charles F. Zimpel's efforts to revive Jewish interests in their ancestral home failed, his thoughts on Christians and Jews sharing a common government in the Holy Land uncannily reflected the situation that developed during the period of the British Mandate for Palestine in the second quarter of the twentieth century. However, to most of Zimpel's contemporaries, Christians and Jews alike, his message seemed remote, his plans impractical, and his vision of a Jewish return to the Land of Israel a phantasmagoria.

12

Sects and Sectarians

Darbyites and Thomasites

By the mid-nineteenth century, millenarian sects had markedly proliferated, but their message had become less strident than the groups that had preceded them. Conversion of the Jews, however, remained a key element of most of these sects, and emphasis was placed on acts designed to bring about their redemption in Palestine in order to hasten the Second Coming of Christ. Typical of this new breed of millenarians were the Plymouth Brethren or Darbyites founded in England (1830) by John Nelson Darby (1800–82),[143] a clergyman of the Anglican Church of Ireland. Darby, a prominent Bible scholar, was a strong advocate of "premillenialism," the doctrine that asserts that all biblical prophecies relate to the return of the Jews to the Land of Israel prior to the Second Advent of Christ. Following a period of tribulation, during which the Jews would be judged, the Second Coming would occur, and Jesus would rule over all the nations from Jerusalem.

Millenarianism, however was not a European monopoly. In 1832 John Thomas (1805–71), an English physician who had settled in the United States, established a sect known as the Christadelphians or Thomasites.[144] This group made a valiant attempt to return to a primitive form of Christianity, and, from the very outset of its existence, campaigned for the restoration of the Jews in Palestine. The Christadelphians offered practical assistance to several Jewish organizations and during the Nazi period attempted to rescue Jews from the Holocaust.

Mormons

The best known, and the most successful, of the American sects that arose in the second quarter of the nineteenth century was the Church of Jesus Christ of Latter-Day Saints (the

Mormons).[145] Joseph Smith (1805–44),[146] the founder and prophet of this sect, was convinced that a Jewish return to the Holy Land would precede the Second Coming of Christ. Born in Sharon, Vermont, Smith was the fourth in a family of ten children. Both his mother and father's families had been established in New England since the middle of the seventeenth century. However, both sides of Smith's family had suffered economic reversals, and had declined in status to frontier drifters. After relocating an estimated ten times in nineteen years, Smith's parents finally settled down in Palmyra, New York (1816).

Joseph Smith's boyhood was spent in an environment notable for producing a great many experimental societies and religious sects. His immediate family reflected the intense revivalism common to the region and exhibited behavior that, at best, can be described as eccentric or peculiar. Joseph's father, a failed farmer, storekeeper, and root digger, believed in witchcraft and frequently had visions. His mother believed in faith healing and considered dreams as warnings from heaven. She also suffered from hallucinations during which she heard supernatural voices and saw luminous faces. Smith's maternal grandfather, an infirm beggar, was subject to "falling fits", and his paternal grandfather was a man with unusual religious convictions.

An attack of melancholy at age fifteen, coincident with one of his family's periodic religious conversions, had a traumatic effect on Joseph Smith. Confused by the conflicting claims of the various Christian denominations, the young lad prayed to God for guidance, and was rewarded with a vision (spring of 1820). A series of vivid visions, extending over seven years, would follow, in which Smith claimed to see and be instructed by a heavenly being. During these visitations Joseph would be subjected to dazzling color sensations, dizziness, vacuity, and occasionally suffer body bruises. The crux of the visions conveyed to him by the angelic messenger, whom he identified as Nephi (later corrected to Moroni), an ancient prophet of the American continent, was that no existing sect represented God's will. Furthermore, the original church of Christ, owing to apostasy, had been withdrawn from earth. He was also informed by the angel that in the near future the fullness of the Gospel would be made known to him.

In September of 1827 Joseph Smith proclaimed that the heavenly messenger had directed him to a certain cave on a hillside near Manchester, New York, where he had found "golden plates" bearing hieroglyphics, which he alone, through the gift and power of God, could decipher. Over a period of two years, with the aid of instruments supposedly found with the plates, which he had dubbed "Urim and Thummim" (objects of divination used by the ancient Hebrews), Smith undertook the task of translating the mysterious writings. Hidden behind a blanket and usually in a state of reverie, he would dictate the contents of the golden plates to several scribes. The result of this effort was The Book of Mormon.[147] Begun in 1827 at Manchester and continued at Harmony, Pennsylvania, the work was finally completed at Fayette, New York, in June, 1829. Shortly before publication of the volume, Smith, supposedly following the instructions of the angel Nephi, founded the Church of Jesus Christ of Latter-Day Saints (April 6, 1830). The church members consisted largely of Smith's relatives and neighbors. In time the church would come to accept The Book of Mormon as the scriptural base of Smith's teaching, along with three other books: the King James version of the Bible, a work entitled Doctrine and Covenants (outlining the government of the new church), and The Pearl of Great Price (a work containing "lost" ancient scripture and a revised twenty-fourth chapter of Matthew, as well as Smith's account of his visions, and his sect's articles of faith).

According to Joseph Smith, *The Book of Mormon* not only contained the complete Christian Gospel as revealed by Jesus Christ, but also chronicled the events of ancient America from the earliest ages after the flood to the fifth century of the Common Era. It told of several migrations from the Middle East to the New World. The first group of emigrants were the so-called Jaredites, some of the builders of the Tower of Babel who had been dispersed when God had confounded their ability to understand each other. The second emigration came from Jerusalem just prior to the city's conquest by the Babylonians. They were, according to the *Book of Mormon,* principally Israelites, descendants of the Hebrew tribes of Ephraim and Manasseh, and were led by a righteous man named Lehi. Christ, after his crucifixion, was resurrected in the New World, and appeared before these transplanted Israelites and gave them his teachings. At about the time the Israelites arrived in America, the Jaredites were destroyed, and the newcomers occupied their lands. During the fourth century of the Common Era the principal tribe (or nation) of the second migration, known as the Nephites, were annihilated after a sixty-five-year struggle with the Lamanites. The latter, a dark skinned people related to the Nephites, were supposedly the ancestors of the American Indians.

The Mormon belief that the Indians were the descendants of the Lamanites reflected a commonly held view that the American natives were the offspring of the ten lost tribes of Israel. Like many others of his time, Joseph Smith believed that the ancient Indian burial and temple mounds in the mid-west and in the south-eastern United States had been built by a fair-skinned race, rather than by the dark-skinned natives found by Columbus. Many of Smith's followers were convinced that Jesus Christ had been resurrected in the New World as the god Quetzalcoatl. Topiltzin Quetzalcoatl was an actual tenth-century ruler of the Toltecs. He supposedly had fair skin and a beard and identified his reign with the beneficent ancient Indian god Quetzalcoatl (thus his surname). After losing a civil war, Topiltzin Quetzalcoatl left his capital in the year 987 and migrated with his followers to Chichen Itza in the Yucatan. The Aztecs coming onto the scene a few centuries later worshipped Topiltzin Quetzalcoatl as a god. Legend foretold that he would return someday in a boat from the east. When the Spaniard Cortez appeared in Mexico with his pale skin and beard, he was taken for the returning god and was welcomed by the Aztec leader Motecuhzoma. It is the figure of the Toltec chieftain Topiltzin Quetzalcoatl who has emerged as Jesus in some of the Latter-Day Saints' literature.[148]

According to Joseph Smith, the records of the experiences of the Nephites in the New World were kept by certain prophets. Finally they were compiled, edited, and hidden in the earth by the prophet Mormon from whom *The Book of Mormon* derives its title, and its believers their name. Throughout the *Book of Mormon* references are made to the Jews (i.e., the Israelites) as a "lonesome and solemn people, wanderers out of Jerusalem."[149] They are constantly portrayed as yearning for the eventual restoration of the House of Israel. In one particular section of the volume entitled "Third Nephi," prophetic passages dealing with "the return" abound. Elsewhere the book admonishes Gentiles (i.e., non-Mormons) to refrain from anti-Semitic activities, and speaks of the role their nations will play in the final ingathering of the Jewish people.

The complex Mormon hierarchy, which developed very early in the church's history, borrowed much of its terminology from the Old Testament. Smith as the first elder and apostle of the new church bore the title of prophet, and stood at the head of a priesthood called the "Melchizedeks." This group chose three presiding high priests, who in turn formed a quorum of the presidency of the Church. A lesser priesthood known as the

"Aaronic" was also established. The entire community of Mormons (in their final home in Utah) were divided into twenty-one divisions called the "Stakes of Zion."

Mormon doctrine, as expounded by Joseph Smith, taught that the true covenant with God was recorded on the first set of stone tablets that Moses brought down from Mount Sinai—the tablets he broke when confronted with the golden calf. According to Smith the second set of tablets, which the Jews received and still follow, contained lesser commandments. Nevertheless, the Mormon leader emphasized, even though the Jews had proved themselves unworthy, because of the golden calf incident, to receive the higher covenant, they were still more deserving than the Gentiles, as they did accept and observe the second set of commandments.

When an individual converted to Mormonism, Smith stressed, his or her blood was transformed so that they literally became descendants of those ancient Israelite emigrants who had fled from the Babylonians to America. Carrying this point even further, the Mormon Church, at one stage in its turbulent history, gave serious consideration to the introduction of circumcision. The early Church also believed that at some future date Jews and Mormons would unite. Biblical proofs, especially from Isaiah and Ezekiel were frequently cited to verify that two branches of truth exist, which must eventually coalesce. "Let them therefore," wrote Smith, "who are among the Gentiles [non-Mormons] flee unto Zion, and let them who be of Judah flee unto Jerusalem, unto the mountains of the Lord's House."[150] The founder of the Mormon Church repeatedly assured his flock that not only would the Jews return to the Land of Israel, but that the Temple would be rebuilt, and Jesus Christ would reappear. At Christ's Second Coming, all Jews would recognize Jesus as the Messiah and convert.

In preparation for these great events, Smith encouraged the establishment of a Hebrew school at Kirtland, Ohio. He also initiated a special mission to go to Palestine to help speed Jewish redemption. The man chosen to carry out this assignment was Orson Hyde, one of the Prophet's close associates.[151] Enroute to the Holy Land, the Mormon elder stopped over in England where the Church, from its inception, had enjoyed considerable success in winning over converts from other Christian denominations. While in England, Hyde also tried to persuade Jewish community leaders that restoration in Palestine was close at hand. In connection with this effort he arranged, in Holland, for the publication of a work entitled *Address to the Hebrews,* in which the position of the Mormon Church toward the Jews was delineated. Having accomplished his recruitment drive in England, Hyde resumed his journey to the Middle East. He arrived in Beirut in the midst of a war between the Druse and the Maronite Christians, but managed after some further unanticipated delays to reach Jerusalem on October 21, 1841. A few days later, on a Sunday morning, he ascended the Mount of Olives, and offered up a special prayer to God. He petitioned the Almighty to remove the curse of barrenness which had descended over the Promised Land, and to speed the redemption of the Jews, "the rightful heirs to Palestine." In a rather lengthy letter to twelve apostles of the Mormom Church concerning his mission, Hyde recounted his adventures and predicted that England was destined to play a key role in the restoration of the Jews in Palestine.[152]

On his return trip to the United States, Orson Hyde stopped over once again in England to reap the harvest of his previous missionary work. Finally, in 1842 the Mormon elder left Liverpool at the head of 214 converts and sailed for America. The group landed in New Orleans and traveled up the Mississippi, and then overland to the Mormon settlement at Nauvoo, Illinois.

From the outset, the doctrines postulated by Smith and his associates had encountered bitter opposition and outright persecution. Most Christians were offended by such Mormon beliefs as: the rejection of hell; a hereafter through which souls progress; the concept of preexistence; the idea of a spirit world in which people lived while waiting their turn on earth; the conception of a God with corporeal attributes; the view that there must be a female deity in whose image women were created since God was male and man was made in his image; the tenet that Jesus and Satan were brothers; that black skin was a curse acquired by some spirits when they would not choose sides in the struggle between Jesus and Satan; the concept of celestial marriage, the belief that in heaven the family would be reunited if here on earth it was "sealed for time and eternity" by certain secret marriage rites; the notion of baptism of the dead; a firm belief in polygamy; and that other churches did not represent God's will.

Hatred on the part of their Christian neighbors had forced Smith to move his followers from New York State to Kirtland, Ohio, in 1831. Here the sect had remained for a short interval before taking up residence in Independence, Missouri. After two years of relative peace and prosperity the Latter-Day Saints succeeded in arousing the ire of the local population. Continuing pressure on the Mormon community, and on Smith who had become a fugitive from justice as a result of wildcat banking, forced the sectarians to once again seek a safe haven elsewhere. They settled in Clay County, Missouri. In this outpost of civilization which Smith declared to be the site of the Garden of Eden, the Mormons established a semi-socialistic community (1833). A few years later history repeated itself. Neither the new faith nor the socialistic organization of the community appealed to their non-Mormon neighbors who were individualistic frontier farmers. A systematic persecution of the Mormons culminated in 1838 with their expulsion from Missouri. They found refuge in Illinois where they purchased an abandoned frontier village called Commerce, and renamed it Nauvoo (i.e., beautiful place). By thrift and hard work they acquired neighboring farms, engaged in manufacturing various items, and slowly but steadily accumulated wealth. Converts from the eastern states, as well as from Great Britain, Scandinavia, and Germany swelled the population of Nauvoo making it the largest city in Illinois. With the growth of the city, the Mormons became a power in state politics. Joseph Smith, exploiting the situation, extracted from the state legislature local autonomy for Nauvoo, and permission to establish a military unit (the Nauvoo Legion). His increasing prominence led him to announce his candidacy for the office of the President of the United States. However, Smith's political intrigues, his sanctioning of polygamy, together with the charges of the non-Mormons that the sect harbored cattle thieves, counterfeiters, and other criminals led to turbulence within and without Nauvoo. When Smith suppressed a newspaper, the Nauvoo Expositor, which had been severely critical of his policies, the city's non-Mormon population exploded. Joseph Smith and his brother Hyrum were arrested and lodged in the jail of nearby Carthage. On June 27, 1844, a mob broke into their cell and killed the two brothers. Following the prophet's murder, the crazed rioters burned the homes of the Mormons living in Nauvoo, plundered their property, and desecrated and destroyed their temple. In the end the Mormons were driven from the city that they had built and enriched.

Brigham Young (1801–77), the forceful President of the Council of Twelve Apostles was chosen as Smith's successor. Under his direction the Mormon survivors from Nauvoo migrated to Council Bluffs, Iowa (the spring and summer of 1846). The following year, Brigham Young, with a company of picked men, set out in quest of the long sought

"Promised Land." They pushed rapidly up the north bank of the Platte River, past Fort Laramie to South Pass, and then southward until they reached a narrow semi-desert valley west of the Wasatch Mountains in Utah. Here they came upon a tableland overlooking a saline body of water (the Great Salt Lake) fed by a river flowing out of a more distant fresh water lake. This accident of nature presented to their minds an obvious parallel to the Holy Land's geography, namely the salt-laden Dead Sea fed by the waters of the Jordan, emanating from the Sea of Galilee. The Mormon leader and his party accordingly named the river they had discovered the Jordan, and staked out a site for the new Zion they planned to build. At the time the entire region lay within Mexican territory, but following the Mexican War it was ceded to the United States. By the end of 1847 the first contingent of Mormons arrived at the chosen location for the settlement; others soon followed, and by 1850 the colony had a population exceeding 11,000.

The rank and file of the Mormons thought their experiences seemed to parallel the history of the ancient Israelites. The sect's founder and prophet and his successor were, for the believers, equated with the biblical figures of Moses and Joshua. The Mormons' remarkable trek across the Great American Desert was similar to the exodus of the Israelites from Egypt and their wandering in the wilderness of Sinai until they could enter the Promised Land. Mormon identification with ancient Israel became even more pronounced with the passage of time. The Colorado River, for example, was renamed the "Bashan," after a river mentioned in the Bible, and much of the Utah landscape received similar biblical place names.

Under Brigham Young's leadership the Mormon colony prospered. Although completely absorbed with reclaiming the wilderness and with missionary work, the Mormons never forgot Joseph Smith's prophecies concerning the return of the Jews to the Holy Land. Indeed, support for a Jewish restoration remained strong well into the fourth decade of the twentieth century, and only showed signs of weakening after the establishment of the State of Israel

Adventists

Still another Christian movement with strong millenarian views, which arose during the nineteenth century was that of the Adventists.[153] The Adventists appeared under various guises and included such diverse groups as the United Society of Believers (better known as the Shakers), the Rappites, the Dunkers, the Quakers, the Moravians, Schwenkfelders, Millerites, Campbellites, Universalists, and some Mennonites such as the Amish and Old Amish.

The Adventists came into prominence in 1831 when William Miller (1782–1849), an earnest New England farmer, began to warn people that the end of the world was at hand. He began to attract wide attention when he set the Second Coming of Christ for the year 1843. As the time specified by Miller approached, mass hysteria spread among believers and non-believers alike. Meetings discussing Miller's prophecy were held in churches, public buildings, tents, fields and groves. Dawn on March 21, 1843, found Miller's followers, estimated as numbering between 50,000 and 1 million individuals, in graveyards, on rooftops, and on hills and mountainsides awaiting the end of days. Some were clad in white robes, others wore their best clothes. The failure of Jesus to appear at the appointed time nearly overwhelmed Miller, and in the disillusionment that ensued his following decreased dramatically. However, a remnant remained loyal, and Miller forged them into a sect in 1845 that became known as the Adventists. The following year a group calling themselves the Seventh Day Adventists broke away from the original sect over the question of observing the seventh day on Saturday instead of Sunday.

The obscure visions delineated in the *Book of Daniel* and in *Revelations* served as the main source of Adventist theology. These sectarians believed that the Jews would return to their ancestral homeland before the Second Advent, and would participate in the last battle between God and Satan. The victory of God would usher in the Kingdom of God, headed by Jesus, who would be proclaimed King in Jerusalem.[154] As a direct result of these eschatological beliefs, many Adventist groups moved their headquarters to Palestine, and took a positive stand toward the Political Zionist movement initiated by Theodor Herzl in the last quarter of the nineteenth century.

Warder Cresson

A number of American millenarians played active roles in promoting Jewish settlement of the Holy Land. Prominent among this group was Warder Cresson (1798–1860),[155] a religious zealot and visionary. Born into an old Philadelphia Quaker family, Warder Cresson became in turn a Shaker, a Mormon, a Millerite, and a Campbellite. In 1844 Cresson decided to visit Palestine, and received an honorary appointment to be the American Consul in Jerusalem. His nomination was immediately challenged by Samuel D. Ingham, a former Secretary of the Treasury who was convinced that Cresson was deranged. Following this charge, the appointment was withdrawn. However, Cresson, unaware of the change in his status, had already left for the Holy Land, where he served for a brief period as the official representative of the American government.

During his four year residence in Jerusalem, Cresson became convinced that he could only find spiritual truth in Judaism. In 1848 he converted and took the name Michael Boaz Israel. Returning to Philadelphia to settle his affairs, Cresson was, at the instigation of his wife and son, declared insane. He appealed the decision and a jury found him sane. Soon after his acquittal, Cresson returned to Palestine to begin his new life as a Jew. He remarried (his first wife had divorced him) and became very active in Jewish community affairs. One of Cresson's earliest efforts on behalf of his adopted community was to have circulars printed and distributed throughout Europe and America in a campaign designed to solicit colonization funds, ". . . for the land given by the Almighty in covenant to Abraham and his seed forever."[156] In 1852 he helped found a Jewish agricultural colony near Jerusalem. Although his hopes for a Jewish restoration in Palestine did not material-ize during his lifetime, Warder Cresson was an authentic precursor of modern Zionism.

Millenarian Colonies in Palestine

Noteworthy attempts by millenarians to establish colonies in the Holy Land marked the efforts of George J. Adams and Clorinda S. Minor.[157] In 1852 Minor led a group of sectarians to Palestine, and established an agricultural settlement, which they named Mount Hope, near Jaffa. It survived for six years before going under.

Adams had accompanied the Mormon elder, Orson Hyde, on his mission to Jerusalem. Following the death of Joseph Smith, he recruited a small following of his own and convinced them to emigrate to Palestine. In 1866 this group also chose a site close to Jaffa to establish their colony. However, like the Mount Hope experiment, they failed after a few years. More persistent were colonists of the German Templars movement. This sect originated in southwest Germany in 1851 in the little village of Wurtemberg. One of their chief goals was to settle in Palestine, and to restore the land to the fertility it had enjoyed in biblical times. Plots of land were purchased near Haifa and Jaffa and later in the vicinity of Jerusalem. Excellent farmers, the Templars established a solid foothold in the Holy Land, and succeeded where others had failed.[158]

William Eugene Blackstone

The most famous of the American Christian-Zionist millenarians was William Eugene Blackstone (1841–1933),[159] a native of Adam, New York. Blackstone was largely self-educated and an avid reader of the Bible. Turned down for active military duty during the Civil War, he served, for the duration of the conflict, with the United States Christian Commission, a religious social-service organization. Following his marriage, Blackstone moved to Chicago where he became a highly successful businessman. A religious experience in which, ". . . for several hours he wrestled with God in prayer"[160] brought about a radical change in his life. He began to devote much of his time to missionary and evangelistic activities. It was during this period that Blackstone became interested in the Jews, ". . . a people chosen by God to manifest His power and His love to . . . a world steeped in deepest idolatry."[161]

In 1888, together with his daughter Flora, Blackstone toured Europe and visited the Holy Land. While traveling in Europe his sympathy and compassion for the Jewish people was aroused. He was particularly disturbed by the precarious situation confronting the Jews of Russia (the recurring pogroms and the hostile attitude of the government toward its Jewish subjects). Upon his return to the United States, Blackstone successfully organized a conference of Christian clergymen and Jews (mostly Reform rabbis). He hoped that the conferees would work together to bring relief to the oppressed Jews of the Russian Empire. Acting as chairman of the conference, Blackstone suggested to the assembled clergymen that a solution to the Jewish Problem was possible if they used their pulpits to pressure the United States government and the governments of the world to help restore the Jews to Palestine. Amazingly, this proposal angered some of the Reform rabbis as it ran counter to their credo. Rabbi Emil G. Hirsch speaking for the rabbis declared:

> We modern Jews do not wish to be restored to Palestine . . . the country wherein we live is our Palestine. . . . We will not go back . . . to form a nationality of our own.[162]

Undaunted by this unexpected opposition, which he suspected represented a minority view, Blackstone managed to force through a resolution expressing sympathy with the plight of Russian Jewry. Copies of the resolution were sent to the Russian czar and to a number of other European monarchs and prominent public figures. Blackstone, however, unhappy with the results of his ecumenical conference launched a one-man campaign to arouse American public interest to the plight of Russian Jewry. Aware of the need for a long range solution to the Jewish Problem, he continued to stress that the only realistic solution to this vexing issue was the restoration of the Jewish people to Palestine. Eventually he incorporated this proposal in a formal document on behalf of Russian Jewry that became widely known as "the Blackstone Memorial."[163] The sincerity and passionate plea of Blackstone's appeal influenced many important and powerful individuals to lend their names as signatories to the memorial. Among the 400 signers of the document were all of Chicago's prominent newspaper publishers and editors, as well as several national public figures. On March 5, 1891, Blackstone presented his memorial to the President of the United States, Benjamin Harrison, and to the Secretary of State, James G. Blaine.

The memorial raised the question of what could be done to help Russian Jewry? In analyzing the problem, the memorial suggested that it was both unwise and futile to dictate to Russia concerning her internal affairs. The Jews had lived as foreigners in her dominions for centuries, and the czarist regime fully believed they were a burden on the nation's resources, and prejudicial to the welfare of the peasantry. Indeed, the Russian government was determined that the Jews must go; hence they must emigrate. But to where? Europe was crowded and could ill afford taking in millions of poor people. To bring them to America would entail a tremendous expense and require years to accomplish.

Why not give Palestine to them again, the memorial asked? After all, it was their ancient home from which they were expelled by force. It had in the past sustained millions of Israelites, who industriously tilled its hillsides and valleys. Indeed, they had been agriculturists and producers, as well as a nation of commercial importance—a center of civilization and religion.

The memorial went on to point out that the major European powers under the terms of the 1878 Treaty of Berlin had given Bulgaria to the Bulgarians and Serbia to the Serbians. These lands as well as Rumania, Montenegro, and Greece had been wrested from the Turks and given to their natural owners. Could not the same be done for the Jews? If they could have autonomy in Palestine, the land, under their care, would rapidly recover its ancient fertility. The Jews of the world would rally to transport and establish their long-suffering brethren in their time-honored habitation. They have waited for over seventeen centuries for such a privileged opportunity. Whatever vested rights, by possession, may have acquired to Turkey can easily be compensated.

Blackstone concluded the memorial with a strong appeal to all the nations, especially the Christian nations of Europe, for sympathy, justice, and humanity in restoring the Jews to the land from which they were so cruelly expelled by the Romans.

The memorial aroused considerable public interest throughout the United States. Its author followed up on the enthusiasm generated by the document with a series of speeches and articles. In an article dealing specifically with the question whether America had the right to intercede for the Jews, Blackstone answered the query in the affirmative, noting that the country had precedents for such a policy.[164]

In the period immediately following the presentation of the memorial to President Harrison, the State Department distributed the document to its embassies and to the governments of the principal nations of the world. Not all American diplomats were happy about the solution suggested by Blackstone. Particularly disturbed was the chief of the Jerusalem consulate, Selah Merrill. A graduate of a theological seminary and a former army chaplain, he was convinced that the memorial would alienate the Ottoman regime. Merrill was not impressed by the large number of eminent Americans who had affixed their signatures to the memorial. He firmly believed that those individuals were abysmally ignorant of Near East and Middle East realities and politics. Merrill's superiors took into consideration his objections and forebodings but did nothing to stop the distribution of the memorial or to disown its proposed solution to the Jewish Problem.

During the administration of President McKinley, Blackstone approached John Sherman, the Secretary of State, and inquired whether the United States would be willing to join with the Great Powers of Europe in obtaining Palestine for the Jews on some basis acceptable to the Turkish sultan. Accordingly, Sherman instructed the American minister in Constantinople to find out if the Turks would be amenable to such a course of action. The minister reported back to the secretary of state that the Turks would not part peaceably with any of their territories. The rejection by the Ottoman regime of the solution to the Jewish Problem highlighted in Blackstone's memorial brought to an abrupt end all further American diplomatic efforts in this matter.

Blackstone, however, refused to acknowledge defeat. In May of 1916 he produced a second memorial, which he addressed to President Woodrow Wilson. He reminded the administration of the past activities of the American government on behalf of the Jews and urged that these efforts be resumed and pressed vigorously. Like its predecessor, the second memorial received the endorsement of many prominent personalities. Among them were Andrew D. White, president of Cornell University and former ambassador to Russia; Samuel Gompers, the head of the American Federation of Labor; and John Wanamaker, the merchant king. The memorial also had the blessing of the Federal Council of Churches of Christ in America, the Presbyterian Ministerial Association, the Baptist Minister's Conference, and the Jewish Kehillah of New York.

In spite of its considerable support, the second memorial failed to produce any results. However, Blackstone's efforts did succeed in bringing before the American public, in a rather dramatic fashion, the Jewish Problem and the proposed Zionist solution. Blackstone would remain a fervent Christian Zionist for the remainder of his life. Addressing a Zionist meeting in Los Angeles (January 27, 1918), the fiery evangelist summed up his life work, and the forces which had motivated him. He indicated that for over thirty years he had been a staunch advocate of Zionism and that his support was based on the belief that true Zionism was part of God's plan as reflected in the Bible.

William Henry Hechler

Not quite so prominent as Blackstone, but of great importance to the fledgling Zionist Movement initiated by Theodor Herzl in the last decade of the nineteenth century, was the British clergyman and millenarian, William Henry Hechler (1854–1931).[165] He was born in Bernares, India, where his father served as a missionary of the Evangelical Church. Following in his father's footsteps, William Hechler, in 1871, worked as a missionary in Lagos, Nigeria. On the recommendation of the British royal house, he was chosen to become the tutor of Prince Ludwig, the son of Friedrich, the Grand Duke of Baden. While serving in this capacity, Hechler became acquainted with some of the members of German royalty, including the grand duke's nephew, the future emperor, Wilhelm II.

After the premature death of his pupil, Hechler returned to England. In 1882 he participated in a conference of Christian clergy and laymen which had as its objective the possibility of settling Jewish refugees from Rumania and Russia in Palestine. Subsequently, Hechler visited Russia in an attempt to determine first hand what could be done for the Jewish victims reeling from the recent wave of pogroms. Deeply disturbed by the misery he witnessed, the former missionary became convinced that the evils that had befallen the hapless Jews were signs that the biblical prophecies relating to their redemption were close at hand. Putting his thoughts on paper, Hechler, in 1884, published a treatise entitled, *The Restoration of the Jews to Palestine* in which, on the basis of certain messianic calculations, he predicted the return of the Jewish people to the Holy Land in or about 1897–98.

Soon after the appearance of his treatise, the English reverend applied for the post of Anglican Bishop in Jerusalem. Failing in his bid he accepted instead a position as chaplain to the British Embassy in Vienna. While posted in the Austrian capital, Hechler learned from a Jewish acquaintance (Saul Raphael Landau, 1870–1943) of Theodor Herzl's provocative book *Der Judenstaat*. After reading this work, Hechler became electrified by its message of a Jewish state and was thoroughly convinced that Herzl had been designated by God to fulfill the very prophecies that he himself had written about. Galvanized into actions by these thoughts, Hechler went out of his way to establish a close relationship with Theodor Herzl. The two men met for the first time on March 10, 1896, and until Herzl's demise in 1904, Hechler remained a staunch friend, as well as an important agent in the Jewish leader's diplomatic efforts to interest Germany in the Zionist cause. He introduced Herzl to his former employer, the Grand Duke of Baden, who paved the way for subsequent interviews with prominent individuals, including the German kaiser, Wilhelm II.

Hechler was Herzl's guest at the First Zionist Congress (1897), and accompanied the Zionist leader on his trip to Palestine in 1898. The Christian minister, on several occasions, also tried to arrange a meeting with the czar of Russia though the good graces of the czar's brother-in-law, the Grand Duke of Hesse. Although the proposed audience never materialized, the efforts to obtain an interview with the czar made Herzl's name known among highly-placed officials of the Russian court. Later, Herzl would meet and personally negotiate with some of these officials, most notably with the minister of the interior (Plehve), to alleviate Jewish suffering and to tolerate Zionist activity in Russia. Hechler also attempted to interest the Prince of Wales (later King Edward VII) in Herzl's plans, but as in the case of the Russian czar, his efforts were unsuccessful.

The Christian evangelist's support of the Zionist Movement remained steadfast until his death at the ripe old age of eighty-six. This in itself was quite remarkable considering the fact that Theodor Herzl, the man that Hechler firmly believed to be a second Moses sent by God to redeem his people, had died without having achieved his goal. Nevertheless, although shocked by Herzl's untimely death, Hechler never lost faith in the efficacy of his predictions, or enthusiasm in the Jewish cause he had espoused.

IV

EUROPEAN RESTORATIONISTS

13

The Napoleonic Era

The Age of Enlightenment in Western Europe was a period of ferment, but most of the unrest was expressed in words rather than action. Not until the close of the eighteenth century did the arguments erupt into revolution and war. The flash point came on July 14, 1789, when an enraged Parisian mob stormed the city's most conspicuous symbol of royal absolutism—the fortress prison known as the Bastille. Following this defiant act the French people became the first European nation to raise the cry of liberty, equality, fraternity for all. By the end of that same year the French Revolution had swept away most of the inequalities and abuses of the *ancien regime*. Indeed, in the brief ten years before the century ended, France would form a republic; execute a king; build a formidable army; and establish an effective, although faction ridden, revolutionary government. Following these events, the nation would pass through a period of confusion that would culminate in a coup d'etat, and the accession to power of Napoleon Bonaparte. These turbulent years also marked a watershed for French Jewry.

The revolutionary National Assembly, which convened in Paris in 1789, proceeded in August of that year to issue its celebrated "Declaration of the Rights of Man and of Citizens." This document established, among other things, the principles of religious freedom and civic rights. But the logical consequences of this declaration in favor of Jewish emancipation were not immediately drawn. On the eve of the revolution some 35,000 Jews were living within the boundaries of France. In the southwestern corner of the country, about 3,500 Sephardim and Avignonnais Jews were to be found. The latter group, closer to the French language and culture, less observant than their co-religionists elsewhere in France, and partially assimilated, were granted full citizenship by the National Assembly on January 28, 1790.

Emancipation for the second and much larger body of French Jewry, the so-called German nation, the Yiddish speaking Ashkenazim, proved more difficult. Numbering over 30,000 individuals, the Ashkenazim were mainly concentrated in Alsace–Lorraine on the northeastern border of France. Poor and engaged chiefly in petty trade and money lending, they seemed to the majority of the members of the National Assembly a completely alien element who had made no effort to adapt their way of life to French culture. Nevertheless, twenty months later, after the Sephardim had achieved citizenship, and after much heated debate, the opposition to the Ashkenazim was overcome and a decree was promulgated granting all the Jews of France complete civic rights (September 27, 1791).

The price to be exacted for emancipation, however, had been made quite clear by the Deputy Clermont-Tonnere, one of the key protagonists in the struggle for Jewish rights. He reassured those members of the National Assembly inconsolable over the grant of civic equality to the Jews by noting that his intentions were to make the Jews Frenchmen, yet at the same time allow them to practice their religion without abuse or molestation. The Jews were to be denied everything as a nation, but granted everything as individuals.

Although the French National Convention remained active for three years (1792–95), it failed in the primary task for which it had been summoned: to provide a permanent and satisfactory constitution for the nation. Consequently, the convention evolved into a revolutionary assembly with no constitutional limits to its authority. It conducted the affairs of the state with despotic assurance, repressing criticism, and crushing its opponents. Gradually, in the conflict that developed for control of the revolution between the bourgeoisie and the radical elements, the latter (better known as the Jacobins) gained power. Under their leader, Robespierre, measures were adopted that today would be classified under the rubric of state socialism. Property of emigre nobles was seized, and a special revolutionary tribunal was established (1793) to judge so-called enemies of the state.

The Reign of Terror that ensued claimed hundreds of victims and lasted until the overthrow of Robespierre on the Ninth of Thermidor, as the date was styled in the revolutionary calendar (July 27, 1794). The death of Robespierre, himself a victim of the guillotine, ushered in a period in which the revolution seemed frozen or stagnant. From 1795 to 1799 the executive power of the government would remain concentrated in the hands of a committee of five individuals known collectively as the "Directory."

At the height of the Reign of Terror an all out effort had been made by the Jacobins to suppress all religious institutions. Synagogues as well as churches were closed down. Particularly offensive to Orthodox Jews were the efforts by extremists to have the Abrahamic rite of circumcision prohibited by law. Equally disturbing was the introduction of the revolutionary calendar, which treated every tenth day as a feast. Under this arrangement the Sabbath fell awkwardly at variable points, and those Jews who sought to honor the Sabbath in the traditional manner were forced to do so secretly, for discovery was rewarded with imprisonment.

In spite of these setbacks, in the two decades that followed the emancipation of French Jewry, the armies of France, sweeping across Europe, brought some degree of temporary civic equality to the Jews of almost every state and territory the forces occupied. Not everywhere, however, was the gift of civic equality accepted with unalloyed enthusiasm by its recipients. Many Jews feared the price to be paid—loss of communal authority, increased susceptibility to assimilation, and a weakening of the traditional way of life— was far too high. The apprehensions of these Jews increased markedly with the arrival on the French scene of Napoleon Bonaparte.

From the Directory, which he had helped put into power, Bonaparte, after a successful campaign in Italy, received permission for a military expedition in the East. His plan was to strike at Great Britain indirectly by invading Egypt, Palestine, and Syria, and then moving overland to attack British posts in India. While Napoleon was preparing for the Egyptian campaign, proclamations and articles began to circulate in France urging the establishment of an independent Jewish state in Palestine.

In one announcement entitled, "A Jew's Letter to his Brethren,"[166] the anonymous author pleaded with the Jews of the world to organize and to hold conversations with the Directory on the possibility of opening negotiations for Palestine with the Sublime Porte at Constantinople. The substance of the manifesto was fully in accord with the objectives of Napoleon's master plan, and was probably intended to win the sympathy of Jews at home and those living in areas near the forthcoming battlegrounds in North Africa and Asia. Even more significant, the manifesto clearly revealed France's economic interests in the regions it was secretly preparing to conquer.

In an article written in response to "A Jew's Letter to his Brethren" published in the semiofficial periodical *La Decade* on April 19, 1798, the "Jewish option" open to France is explored in greater detail. The author, at first, reminds his readers of the enthusiasm shown by the Jews of Leghorn, Italy, in their abortive attempt to purchase Jerusalem from Ali Bey, the Mameluke governor of Cairo. Jews everywhere, he notes would react more favorably to a French-sponsored program for the restoration of a Jewish population in Palestine.

In addition, considerable commercial advantage would accrue to France from such a venture as the Jews were an exceptional and talented economic force already well established in all the ports that traded with the Levant. By resettling Palestine, the Jews would inject new capital into the entire region. They could also be expected to exert considerable influence on their coreligionists in North Africa, and thereby play a role in opening up for France economic exploitation of the interior of the Dark Continent. A Jewish revival in the Holy Land would also bring in its wake European culture and technology that would greatly enrich the entire Levant.

Following an easy conquest of Egypt, Napoleon, cut off from France by the destruction of his fleet by the English Admiral, Lord Nelson (Battle of the Nile, August 1, 1798), decided to concentrate his forces on Palestine. About a week after he had launched this new campaign (February, 1799) a memorandum from Thomas Corbit was sent to Paul Barres, a member of the Directory ruling France.[167] The author, obviously unaware that the invasion of Palestine had already begun, stressed the need for a Jewish restoration in their ancient homeland. He envisaged a step by step plan. France would first take upon itself the responsibility of helping the Jews organize. This could best be accomplished if the Directory designated some Jewish notables to institute a mass movement among their coreligionists at home and abroad. A specially convened congress of world Jewry would then undertake the task of raising funds for the purchase of land from Egypt in the vicinity of the Suez Isthmus and the Red Sea. Eventually this settlement would serve as a springboard for the conquest of Palestine. The military skills essential for such an enterprise could easily be acquired, Corbit suggested, if the Jews would enroll in Napoleon's army in Egypt. A select number of Jews could also be sent to French and Italian ports to master navigation and the art of shipbuilding. The knowledge thus obtained would enable the Jews to engage in trade and other commercial enterprises, and to build vessels for ferrying immigrants and for carrying troops designated for the conquest of the Holy Land.

Similar plans advocating a Jewish state seem to have originated from circles close to Napoleon. By and large propaganda pieces disseminated by Bonaparte's staff were designed to arouse the Jews of North Africa and Asia to rally under the French flag in the struggle against Great Britain and the Ottoman Empire.

Napoleon Bonaparte's Manifesto

Soon after conquering a major part of Palestine in the spring of 1799, Napoleon considered the time ripe for a public pronouncement specifically intended to win over the Jews of the East to his campaign. Accordingly, four days after a French victory at Mount Tabor, a manifesto was issued in the name of Napoleon Bonaparte, Commander-in-Chief of the French Republic in Africa and Asia. It was addressed to the Jews and called upon them to rise and conquer their patrimony, and to show the courage of the ancient Maccabees in holding the land (i.e., Palestine) against all comers. In addition, it appealed to Jews everywhere to end their exile, and to return to the Holy Land. The French government's newspaper *Moniteur Universal de Paris* carried the story that Napoleon had issued a manifesto that promised the restoration of Palestine to the Jews, and many European newspapers reproduced the article.

Attached to Napoleon's manifesto was a letter from Jerusalem signed by Aaron ben Levi, supposedly a rabbi, stating that the glorious biblical prophecies of Joel, Zephaniah, and Malachi were about to be fulfilled by the victorious French army, and urged all Jews able to bear arms to help finish the task. The letter concluded with a cry to the Lord to, "remember for good all that the great nation has done unto us," and raised the slogan, "a sword for the Lord and for Napoleon."[168]

The manifesto clearly reflected Napoleon's growing need for additional manpower (it is estimated that several thousand North African Jews served in the French general's Egyptian campaign). At this juncture Napoleon was still engrossed in his master plan to conquer the Ottoman Empire. He hoped to capture Acre and then march to Damascus. From Syria, Bonaparte hoped to launch a lightning thrust against Constantinople. His failure to reduce Acre (1799), and the hasty retreat from Palestine to Egypt that followed, thwarted all his carefully laid plans to outdo Alexander the Great. Years later in recalling the Palestine campaign, Napoleon would categorically deny that he ever contemplated creating a Jewish state, and attributed the idea to rumors circulated by the Jews for their own gain. Indeed, considerable controversy surrounds the entire issue of Napoleon's Jewish manifesto.

Some historians point out that the proclamation was said to have originated in Jerusalem—a very unlikely proposition because the French never captured the city. Furthermore, the letter of Aaron ben Levi seems to be an obvious fraud as the Jews of Jerusalem labored resolutely to strengthen the defenses of the city against a potential French attack. An open letter by a prominent rabbi would surely have attracted the attention of the Turks and jeopardized the position of the writer as well as the entire Jewish community.

At the zenith of his career, Napoleon once again occupied himself with the affairs of Jewry and Judaism, still somewhat spectacularly, but now with a well-defined purpose. Thus not long after the disastrous Palestinian campaign, Bonaparte, leaving his marooned army to waste away in Egypt, slipped through the British blockade and returned to France (October 9, 1799). A month later, by means of a coup d'etat, he was master of France. As first consul, and later as emperor of the French (1804–14), instead of favoring the restoration of Jews to Palestine, he embarked on a program designed to eradicate the memory of Zion among French Jews by securing their integration and assimilation within the French nation.[169] In the Concordat with the papacy, Napoleon had left no room for the domination of Catholicism, the religion of the majority of the French people. Similarly, he framed the constitution of French Protestantism so as to prevent the infiltration of foreign influences into France. In the same manner he set out to deal with the Jews.

Shortly after the Battle of Austerlitz (1805), Bonaparte gave ear to complaints that Jewish money lenders were extorting usurious rates of interest and foreclosing mortgages among the peasants of Alsace. In addition, it was alleged that Jews generally were evading military conscription. Although the charges appeared to Napoleon to be greatly exaggerated, he reacted quickly to the situation by issuing a rescript declaring a one-year moratorium on all debts held by the Jewish creditors in the eastern departments of France. At the same time he felt the time was ripe for completely transforming the Jewish way of life, as their emancipation had not produced the anticipated result of furthering their fusion with the French people.

Accordingly, Napoleon gave orders for the convening of an Assembly of Jewish notables to serve as a sort of states-general of French Jewry.[170] The task of the notables would be to produce specific answers to the questions troubling the Emperor (e.g., on usury, the role of religion, citizenship, loyalty), and offer suggestions as to the regulation of Jewish life. Many leaders of the Jewish community were apprehensive of Napoleon's motives because his personal attitude toward the Jews had always been rather ambivalent. They disliked the idea that the Assembly of Notables was being convened by edict and not of their own volition; they were also disturbed that they would have little if any input in choosing the delegates (delegates were to be nominated by France's departmental prefects). Most of all, they feared the loss of the Jewish community's ethnic religious autonomy and traditional way of life.

The Assembly of Notables numbering 111 delegates, mostly laymen, met in Paris from July 15, 1806, to April 6, 1807. A government commission of three individuals headed by Count Louis Mathie Mole, a man who had previously drafted a memorandum inimical to the Jews, was appointed by Napoleon to oversee the deliberations of the notables. The agenda of the Assembly of Notables consisted of twelve questions designed to explore every facet of the status of the Jews in France. The first three queries dealt with Jewish attitudes toward polygamy, divorce, and intermarriage between Jews and Christians; underlying the three queries was the basic issue of whether Jews were willing to be governed by the civil legislation of France rather than by their own religious laws in these matters. A second set of three questions focused on Jewish attitudes toward non-Jews and the degree of their loyalty to France. The remaining questions dealt with the nature and scope of religious authority within the Jewish community, and the permissibility of lending money on usurious terms.

The delegates were instructed by the commissioners to give unanimous and unequivocal replies. It was made crystal clear that Napoleon desired assurances that the jurisdiction of rabbinic law in civil and judicial matters would give way before the supremacy of French law, and that he expected a complete renunciation of all claims to Jewish nationhood and separate corporate status within France.

The Assembly of Notables rose to the occasion and were able to give satisfactory answers to virtually all the questions posed to them. Of course they were opposed to polygamy, which had been abolished by a synod of European rabbis in the eleventh century. Of course they considered Frenchmen their brothers and would fight to the death in defense of France. Of course the authority of the rabbis was only spiritual. To the thorniest question, that of usury, the notables stressed that only fair rates of interest were permitted in accord with the principles of Jewish law. Only on the subject of intermarriage did the delegates feel compelled to give an evasive answer.

In order to give the work of the Assembly of Notables doctrinal force, Napoleon convoked a Grand Sanhedrin,[171] an institution modeled after the ancient tribunal of Israel. Composed of seventy-one members, of which forty-six were rabbis, and twenty-five laymen, the Sanhedrin met in Paris on February 9, 1807. During the course of eight sessions over a period of two months it endorsed the answers of the Assembly of Notables, thus conferring upon their conclusions the authority of a court of religious law. Having accomplished this task the Grand Sanhedrin was summarily dissolved by order of the Emperor, Napoleon Bonaparte.

Although the resolutions of the Assembly of Notables and the Grand Sanhedrin were gratifying to Napoleon, they did not lead to any expansion of Jewish rights in France. Quite the contrary. On March 17, 1808, Bonaparte signed a decree (dubbed by the Jews the Infamous Decree) incorporating a series of regulations arbitrarily restricting for ten years the economic activities and rights of domicile of French Jewry. All debts contracted with Jews were either annulled, reduced, or postponed. Jews interested in engaging in trade or commerce had to obtain a license, which was renewed annually by the prefect of the department in which they resided. Still other regulations sought to weaken the ethnic cement which kept the Jews apart from their neighbors. Thus prayers for the imperial family were made a regular feature of synagogue service, Jews were no longer allowed to discharge their military service by proxy, and the adoption of surnames was made obligatory.

At the same time, the French Emperor promulgated an "organic statute on the Mosaic religion," pronouncing Judaism one of the official religions of France and establishing a state supervised consistorial system to regulate Jewish religious life.[172] Seven consistories were established in France itself, six in the German provinces of the Empire, five in Italy, and four in Holland. Each local consistory included three laymen and one rabbi (the law called for two rabbis where possible) elected by notables appointed by the prefects, but subject to the approval of the central consistory in Paris, in agreement with the minister of religions. The central consistory itself was made up of three rabbis (the original group of three had been members of the Grand Sanhedrin) and two laymen. Contrary to the provisions governing the organization of the other recognized religions, expenses for religious purposes were still to be met by the Jews. Although the central consistory was empowered to exercise absolute authority over Jewish affairs, in practice it chiefly concerned itself with religious matters. This development won for it the support of the rabbinate who, under the consistorial system, were charged with the responsibility of teaching Jewish religion and upholding the decisions ratified by the Grand Sanhedrin promoting obedience to the civil law. Apart from occasional intervention against affronts to Jews, the energies of the consistories were taken up with the promotion of patriotism and insuring an adequate supply of young men for conscription into the French army.

Prince Charles Joseph de Ligne's Memorandum

Napoleon had, in a few short years, succeeded in completely reversing the trend for Jewish restoration in Palestine, which had prevailed under the rule of the Directory.

Nevertheless, the idea of a Jewish entity had also found favor with some of the Emperor's aristocratic opponents. Most notable among the latter was Prince Charles Joseph de Ligne (1735–1814).[173] The Belgian-born nobleman, who was both a grandee of Spain and an Austrian field marshal, was a true cosmopolitan. He was as much at home at Versailles as at Schönbrunn, as happy in his beautiful gardens of Beloeuil as at a military camp in Germany, and equally at ease with Marie Antoinette or with Voltaire. A discreet diplomat and an exemplary soldier, the prince was also renowned for possessing a quick and witty tongue whose "bon mots" circulated widely in the salons of Europe. Traveling about the continent, Charles de Ligne had come in contact with many Jews, especially in Eastern Europe, and his attention had been drawn to the Jewish Question. His ideas on the subject gradually coalesced, and in 1797 he authored a memorandum in which he proposed a solution to this complex and perennial issue. Although written in the aftermath of the French Revolution and a few years after the granting of civic rights to all of French Jewry, these events left no visible imprint on the prince's views. On the contrary, the memorandum reflected the opinions of an educated and sophisticated aristocrat of the earlier era of enlightened despotism. Seemingly unaware of the paradox, in his memorandum Charles de Ligne combined elements from the theories of Voltaire and Rousseau with evangelical prophecies.

His solution to the Jewish Question hinged on two basic ideas—the institution of a broad range of reforms in the countries where the Jews lived and the reconstitution of a Jewish state in Palestine. De Ligne's program of reforms contained no startling innovations, and varied little from the suggestions expressed by enlightened circles of the era preceding the French Revolution. Like other spokesmen of the European Enlightenment he placed emphasis on the need for Jews to engage in productive activities. Somewhat novel was his suggestion that the Jews of Eastern Europe be directed into agriculture on the southern steppes of the Ukraine (De Ligne had served as a field marshal in the army of Catherine the Great and was familiar with the region). However, having personally witnessed the indifference and outright hostility of the Russian regime to their poverty stricken Jews, the prince had no illusions as to the difficulties involved in bringing about reforms in this vast empire. The canny soldier–diplomat also anticipated that his suggestions for Jewish enfranchisement in Eastern Europe would be vehemently opposed. Church and state and merchant and artisan alike in this backward region viewed the Jews as the progeny of the devil as well as unwelcome competitors and rivals. Although Charles de Ligne in his memorandum made no implicit decision in favor of his alternative (i.e., a territorial solution of the Jewish Question) it was quite obvious that he believed it to be the most likely plan to succeed.

De Ligne was convinced that the restoration of the Jews to Palestine would infuse new life into the Ottoman Empire. The Jews would revive the empire's stagnant economy, strengthen provincial administration, and introduce European technology. Above all, the Jews would bring prosperity to Palestine, which should be returned to them as a kingdom under the Turkish sultan or placed under the administration of one of his pashas (governors). If these steps were taken, De Ligne visualized, Jerusalem, which had become a seedy village, would be rapidly restored to its former glory and the desert wastes of the Holy Land reclaimed, settled, and cultivated. In addition, the holy places would become accessible to all, Solomon's Temple would be rebuilt, and the Garden of Eden rediscovered.

The return to Zion, Charles de Ligne noted, would not appeal to all segments of Jewry. It would, however, definitely attract the poor and the middle class as well as those individuals without any hope for the future in the lands of their birth. Wealthy and enlightened Jews steeped in European culture would no doubt choose to remain put.

The prince, after committing his thoughts on the Jewish question to paper, did nothing to bring them to a wider audience. His memorandum was not published until 1810. Curiously, although Charles de Ligne's ideas failed to arouse much interest among his peers, his mortal enemies in France's revolutionary entity—the Directorate—as noted previously came to similar conclusions in regard to restoring the Jews to Palestine.

Reactions to Napoleon's Jewish Overtures

British theological literature on Jewish redemption during the period of the French Revolution and the Napoleonic era gradually took on a distinct political and nationalistic aspect. In 1790 a pastor named Richard Beere had submitted a memorandum to England's Prime Minister, William Pitt, in which he urged the use of the British fleet to restore the Jews to the Holy Land. More representative of the clerical supporters of Jewish redemption was Reverend James Bicheno. In a booklet written in 1799, before any news of Napoleon's Palestinian campaign had reached England, Bicheno intimated that the wars and revolutions shaking the world heralded the advent of the Kingdom of Heaven. It would begin, the reverend wrote, with the overthrow of Catholic and Protestant hierarchies, and the destruction of the Ottoman Empire. These events would be followed by the return of the Jews to Palestine. The miracle of the return would be made possible by the assistance of a Great Power, who would in the process be fulfilling a divine mission. It was therefore, according to Bicheno, incumbent upon England to be that power and to prove by its actions that it was the chosen instrument of Providence. By restoring the Jews to Zion, Great Britain would also in the process thwart its enemy, France. There were grounds to believe, the reverend wrote, that France might assume the role of assisting the Jews, not in order to fulfill biblical prophecies, but rather for narrow and selfish political ends. The creation of a Jewish state under French auspices would prove fatal to British interests in the East, as well as to the nation's commerce. In concluding his theological–political treatise, Bicheno recommended that the British government use its influence to persuade the Turks to give up Palestine. The Ottoman Empire, the author emphasized, derived little benefit from this province, and would stand to gain considerable economic advantage by returning Palestine to its rightful owners—the Jews.

Soon after Napoleon Bonaparte issued his call for a Grand Sanhedrin, new suspicions as to the Emperor's motives swept across the British Isles. Pamphlets appeared warning against French duplicity. Some of these works were directed toward the Jews. In one such publication written by a preacher named L. Mayer, the Jews were informed that deliverance was at hand but cautioned against hastening the end by revolting against reigning monarchs.

The Austrian, Prussian, and Russian regimes, with their large Jewish populations, were also alarmed by the rumors that reached them concerning Napoleon's courting of the Jews. They strenuously opposed the idea of a Jewish state in Palestine sponsored by the French. In addition, they feared even more the repercussions to their administrations that might result if reforms were granted to the Jews in the lands of their birth. Austria, at the time a bastion of conservatism, reacted to these fears by imposing strict police surveillance upon its Jewish community. By these draconian measures it hoped to counteract any sympathy for a Jewish state in Palestine. Russia's reactionary regime, equally concerned by Napoleon's actions, conceived a plan to offset the French Emperor's overtures to the Jews. The Russian government decided to offer their Jewish subjects a territory within the empire for settlement. Such a proposal was actually submitted to Czar Alexander I in 1806 as part of a project for the colonization of under-populated regions of the realm. The territory suggested for Jewish settlement was a vast area between the Don and Dnieper Rivers. Although the project failed to materialize, it did stimulate the Russian Government to accelerate an agricultural program for the Jews in the Ukraine that had been launched that same year.

Reports of Napoleon's plans to create a Jewish state also crossed the Atlantic. Many Americans shared their English cousins' concerns about the Second Coming of Christ, and the belief that a Jewish restoration in the Holy Land was a prerequisite for ushering in the Kingdom of Heaven. In general, however, they were not motivated by the political and economic rivalry that had prompted many Englishmen to react so strongly to Bonaparte's Jewish policies. Members of the Jeffersonian party, for example, advocated friendship with France and, in many parts of the United States, Napoleon's manifesto concerning a Jewish restoration in Palestine received considerable attention. In Virginia a dialogue on these subjects was carried on in the state's press for two years (1806–08). Most notable was a series of articles by a journalist using the pseudonym of "Pacificator." After advancing the usual arguments in favor of a Jewish restoration he affirmed France's right to undertake the liberation of the oppressed people of the Ottoman Empire and especially to correct the ancient wrong done to the Jews.

How did the Jews of Europe react to the stories emanating from Napoleon's France? The evidence seems contradictory. Certainly, western Jewry caught up in the struggle for civil rights did not, on the whole, consider the possibility of a restoration in Palestine as being imminent. The Jews of Central Europe, in particular in Bohemia and Moravia, on the other hand, placed great hope in revolutionary France and Napoleon and were favorably inclined toward the establishment of a Jewish state. In the vast hinterland of the Russian Empire, rumors of Napoleon's manifesto received a mixed reception in Jewish townlets and villages. Hassidic opinion, for example, in relation to the French Emperor, was divided. Some Hassidic leaders regarded Napoleon Bonaparte as the harbinger of the Messiah; others considered him to be a demagogue and were loyal to the house that ruled over their lives.

In retrospect, though most Jews had no clear grasp of it at the time, the net result of the Napoleonic policies was to reinterpret Judaism in individualistic terms. It also prepared the way for the disassociation among significant segments of Western Jewry in the nineteenth and twentieth centuries from the distinctive communal organization that for ages had been the foundation and the chief source of Jewish vitality. Bonaparte's insistence on a price to be paid for the Jews' entrance into the modern world had some unforeseen consequences. Thus when the ghetto walls finally fell and the Jews walked out to freedom, they found they were entering a new, less tangible but equally hostile environment of suspicion. They had exchanged ancient disabilities for modern anti-Semitism.

With Bonaparte's demise, the Jewish Question did not again become the subject of a wide discussion in France until the reign of Napoleon III.

14

French Champions
of a Jewish State

The Jewish restoration movement experienced a revival in France in the aftermath of the Crimean War. Statesmen, journalists, and theologians increasingly adopted the concept of the redemption of the Jews in the Holy Land as a corollary to their country's renewed interest in the Levant. The regime of Napoleon III (1852–70) was marked by an enhancement of French prestige throughout the East as a result of the construction of the Suez Canal by the French diplomat and engineer, Vicomte Ferdinand-Marie de Lesseps.

Ernest Laharanne

In 1860 Ernest Laharanne, a member of Napoleon III's secretariat, and former editor of the newspaper *L'Etat*, published a pamphlet entitled *La Nouvelle Question d'Orient*,[174] proposed the establishment of a Jewish state in Palestine. The author appealed to European Jewry to undertake the rehabilitation of the Holy Land under the aegis of France.

A Roman Catholic, Laharanne considered his proposed solution to the Jewish Question to be of the utmost importance to Christianity and to France's future in the Levant. Curiously, his thesis, which championed a Jewish state extending from Suez to Smyrna, also included a plea for the creation of an Arab entity which would encompass Syria, Mesopotamia, and Anatolia. The Ottoman sultan, Laharanne stressed, should be left only with his European possessions.

The return to the Promised Land, Laharanne believed, would prove therapeutic for the Jews, and would enable them to discard forever the crown of age-long martyrdom. In addition, it presented the Jews with a rare opportunity to serve humanity as bearers of civilization to peoples less cultured and to act as mediators between Europe and Asia.

The pamphleteer's romantic outlook and facile pen failed to impress the French Emperor. Napoleon III, preoccupied with grandiose plans of his own, had no time for his secretary's musings. Nevertheless, Laharanne's proposals managed to find a receptive audience with the Emperor's wife, Eugenie. In 1867 she gave her blessings and patronage to the establishment of a committee dedicated to encouraging Jewish immigration to the Holy Land, and to efforts to rehabilitate the region.[175]

Joseph Salvador

More novel in his approach to resolving the Jewish Question was the eminent historian, Joseph Salvador (1796–1873).[176] Born at Montpellier, he claimed descent, on his father's side, from the Maccabees of ancient Israel. According to family tradition, Salvador's ancestors had migrated from Palestine to North Africa, and from there to Spain in the ninth century. During the fifteenth century, the family fled the Spanish Inquisition and found refuge in France where they gradually assimilated into the life of their adopted country. Joseph Salvador's mother was a Roman Catholic; his brother married a Hugenot, and his sister wedded a Jewish lawyer. Joseph himself, although far removed from any formal religion, seems nevertheless to have been extremely proud of his Jewish heritage. He was, however, buried at his own request in the Protestant cemetery of Le Vigan, near Montpellier.

Although part of an assimilated and multiconfessional family, Joseph Salvador received a Jewish as well as secular education. In 1816 he graduated as a physician, but very early on in his career abandoned the medical profession to devote himself entirely to literature and history.

Shortly after settling in Paris, Salvador gained a reputation as a scholar of the history of religions, a field to which he applied the techniques of historical criticism. Following the anti-Semitic Hep! Hep! riots of 1819, Salvador's fascination with Judaism quickened and he began to concentrate his research on Jewish history. As a result of his studies, he came to the conclusion that the Torah was an ideal body of laws, corresponding favorably with the ideals of the French Revolution. He elaborated on this theory in a series of books in which Salvador sought to prove that the basic ideas of Judaism emphasized the unity of the human race. He also envisaged the development of a newer and higher form of messianism dedicated to the establishment of a universal order—one in which Caesars and Popes would no longer hold sway. Salvador summed up his philosophical and historical religious thought on Judaism in a book entitled *La Loi de Moise, au Système Religieux des Hebreux*. In this work the author attempted to find a rational basis for the Mosaic legislation of the Old Testament. Strongly influenced by the rationalistic outlook of eighteenth century French philosophy, Salvador tried in his book to prove that the inclination of Mosaic legislation was to curb the powers of the priest, and to place the king (or leader) on constitutional grounds. This theme continued to captivate Salvador throughout his remaining years, and he would follow up his initial effort by devoting three volumes to a *Histoire des Institutions de Moise et du Peuple Hébreu*.

Undaunted by adverse criticism, and acutely aware of the sensitivity of his subject matter, Salvador continued to explore Jewish religion, law, and history as well as the roots of early Christianity. His book *Jesus Christ et Sa Doctrine* (1838), a history of the origins and early organization of the Christian Church, aroused the ire of the Papacy and was placed on the its index of forbidden works. In still another tome (*Histoire de la Domination Romaine en*

Judee et de la Ruine de Jerusalem) published in 1846, Salvador expounded on the fall of Jerusalem to the Romans from the point of view of universal history. He theorized that the destruction of the Temple was essential for the spread of the Christian form of Judaism. Salvador elaborated on this theme in a controversial book written in 1859, but not published until years later. The work, entitled *Paris, Rome, Jerusalem, ou la Question religieuse au XIX Siecle,*[177] was condemned by the Roman Catholic Church, which rejected outright the author's prognostications on the future of religious thought. Salvador's central theme, which so irritated the Church, was his attempt to outline a universal religion based on a fusion of Judaism and Christianity—a kind of Reform Judaism. The author believed that the natural center for this syncretistic religion was Jerusalem, and visualized the evolution of this universal faith as a lineal outgrowth of what he imagined classical Judaism to have been.

To achieve this fusion of religions, Salvador advocated the establishment of a new state, a bridge between the Orient and the Occident, encompassing the borders of ancient Israel. He also believed that there were only two groups capable of bringing civilization to the East: the Greeks and the Jews. Notwithstanding the deep degradation suffered by the Jews, Salvador felt they were best suited to infuse new life into the mountains of Judea. Permeated with a belief in the future, deeply rooted in the tradition of mid-nineteenth century speculative philosophy of history, the author did not bother to spell out in any great detail how his sketch of a syncretistic religion would come about. Most importantly, Salvador did not consider why the Turks who controlled the Holy Land would agree to an infringement of their territory or sovereignty.

Salvador's emphasis on Jerusalem, and his constant references to the Jewish people later led a number of historians to regard him as a precursor of Zionism. However, it must be noted that his dreams were chiefly of a "heavenly Jerusalem", and the society or state of which the city was to be the center was of a universalist nature, and not of a restored Jewish people. It has also been postulated that Joseph Salvador, in his quest for a genuine religious synthesis, was probably motivated by a desire to resolve his own spiritual dilemma. Many writers have also pointed out a strange similarity between Salvador's ideas and those of the French utopian socialists known as the "Saint-Simonians."

John Henri Dunant

Jean Henri Dunant (1828–1910),[178] philanthropist, founder of the International Red Cross, and the guiding spirit of the First Geneva Conference was born in Switzerland. Highly respected at the court of Napoleon III, Dunant, an avid Christian Zionist, tried strenuously to interest the French Emperor in a plan for the Jewish settlement of Palestine. He also attempted to gain the support of other European leaders for his scheme, as well as that of Western Jewry. In a letter addressed to the editor of the *London Jewish Chronicle* (1867), he entreated Jews everywhere to throw their support behind a committee formed in Paris for the express purpose of encouraging Jewish immigration to the Holy Land. Dunant sought and obtained for the Paris committee the patronage of the Empress Eugenie.

A tireless organizer, Dunant also played a conspicuous role in the founding, in London, of the Palestine Colonization Society. He intended that this organization, which was to be an international institution, bear the responsibility for Jewish immigration and for the establishment of settlements in Palestine. The society would also help in the creation of an infrastructure for the colonists (i.e., roads, seaports, railways etc.), and administer the settlements under the nominal authority of the Turkish sultan. Diplomatically, the colonies would be neutral, on the pattern of the Swiss cantons, so as not to antagonize the European Powers. Dunant was convinced that this unusual arrangement would put an end to the squabbles of European nations over the holy places, as well as resolving the Jewish Question.

Dunant promoted his plan at every opportunity, especially at international conferences and among the power brokers of Europe. In addition, he approached leading Jewish personalities such as the Anglo-Jewish philanthropist Moses Montefiore, and Adolphe Crémieux, the Parisian lawyer who had played a key role in the establishment of the Alliance Israelite Universelle. In spite of his forceful arguments, Dunant was unable to convince these Jewish leaders that his plan was feasible.

Jean Henri Dunant remained a staunch friend of the Jews throughout his lifetime. When the political Zionist Movement came into being he supported its objectives, which closely paralleled many of his own ideas. Dunant attended some of the sessions of the First Zionist Congress (1897) which met in Basle, Switzerland. The Zionist leader, Theodor Herzl acknowledged his presence in the hall, and made a point in his closing remarks to refer to the great Swiss humanist as a Christian Zionist.[179]

Alexandre Dumas-fils and Leon Bourgeois

Among the prominent French voices raised on behalf of a Jewish revival in Palestine were those of the novelist Alexandre Dumas-fils (1824–95), and the statesman Leon V. A. Bourgeois (1857–1925). Dumas eloquently expressed his views on the subject in his novel *La Femme de Claude* (1873).[180] Bourgeois, like Dunant, was an early advocate of a Jewish restoration in Palestine. He served as prime minister of France during the epochal years that witnessed the dawn of the modern Zionist Movement. In an exchange of views with the famous Austrian writer and pacifist Bertha von Suttner (1843–1914), Bourgeois vigorously attacked anti-Semitism and stressed the need for a Jewish homeland. The existence of such an entity, he stressed, would satisfy an age-old yearning on the part of the Jews, and at the same time provide a refuge for Jewish victims of persecution. A Jewish nation, newly reconstituted in Palestine, would also bring about a renaissance in the East.

Except for their obvious humanism, Laharanne, Salvador, Dumas, and Bourgeois were, to a large extent, representative of France's traditional interest in the Levant—a concern that dated back to the Crusades. From the middle of the eighteenth century onwards, France actively participated in the struggle of the Great Powers (brought on by the decadence of the Ottoman Empire) for control of this vital region. The so-called capitulations by which the Turkish government ceded rights to France made the latter the chief protector of Christian pilgrims in the Holy Land. France's early interest in Palestine was motivated by religious as well as nationalistic and commercial considerations. Political and economic concerns eventually replaced the religious impulses. By the last quarter of the nineteenth century, France's attitude to Palestine, and to Jewish national aspirations was largely molded by its rivalry with Great Britain, and a desire to placate the Arabs.

15

Lord Palmerston
and the Jewish Question

The middle years of the nineteenth century were years of exceptional prosperity for England. As the greatest manufacturing, colonizing, and naval power in the world, Great Britain enjoyed a unique position in international affairs. A spirit of complacency permeated the nation's ruling class that neither political blunders nor the murmurs of an exploited working class could seriously disturb. It was chiefly among elements of this elite English society that the concept of "Zion redeemed" first arose and won the approbation of a handful of prominent statesmen, religious enthusiasts, poets, and novelists.

Events in the Near and Middle East also played a role in bringing the idea of Jewish redemption to the foreground. Britain had watched with anxiety Napoleon's invasion of Egypt and his campaign in Palestine. The meteoric rise to power in Egypt of a Muslim adventurer named Muhammed Ali[181] had done little to allay British apprehensions. A man of no education but with vast ambition, Ali (an Albanian by birth) had stepped into the vacuum created by the French departure from Egypt, and made himself undisputed master of the country. He had engineered this feat by first getting the Turkish sultan to name him pasha (governor). Then he disposed of his opposition, Egypt's old-guard Mameluke aristocracy, by inviting 300 of its leading members to a reception in Cairo and having them massacred. After building up his armed forces, Muhammed Ali added Nubia and Sudan to his holdings, and at the behest of the Turkish sultan put down a rising against the Ottomans in Greece and on Crete. For these services Ali was awarded Crete by the Turks. He was also promised Syria (including Palestine), but the pledge was never fulfilled. Angered by what he considered a betrayal, Ali in defiance of his overlord, the Turkish sultan, used his army to wrest Syria and Palestine from Ottoman control. Only the threatened intervention of the British prevented Muhammed Ali from attacking Constantinople itself, deposing the sultan and setting himself up as the head of a new Islamic state.

With the Ottoman Empire torn by internal dissensions and shaken by constant rebellions at its extremities, the Great Powers once again began to consider Palestine as an object of strategic importance. In this context the Jews were recognized as possible pawns in the political game to either divest the Turks of their territories or as a means of strengthening Ottoman rule. Great Britain tended to favor the latter scheme, and this policy coincided with the ideas set forth by various branches of the British Protestant evangelical and millenarian movements. Theological concern by these groups once again focused on the Jews, this time in an entirely new light, i.e., as hapless exiles separated from the sacred soil of their ancient homeland. They were also convinced that the Second Advent of Christ was impossible without the return of the Jews to Palestine and considered the restoration as a prerequisite for the eventual mass conversion of the Jews to Christianity. Some of these religious zealots combined their theology with British domestic politics, and sought to forestall emancipation as a possible solution to the Jewish Question by advocating Jewish settlement elsewhere, notably in Palestine. Less hypocritical were a small number of Christian writers who were deeply imbued with the romantic vision of a restored Zion, and some hardheaded statesmen who saw in Jewish restoration a chance to serve both religion and country.

Representative of the latter group was the English statesman Henry John Temple (1784–1865),[182] Third Viscount Palmerston. Elected to the House of Commons in 1807, Lord Palmerston, who would later become affectionately known as "Old Pam," remained a member of Parliament almost continuously until his death six decades later. Party labels meant little to Palmerston. Originally a Tory, he was at odds with his party by 1826, although a member of Wellington's cabinet. Thereafter, he served with the Whigs, and, in the final stages of his political life, with the Liberals. Astute, perceptive, and self-confident, Palmerston, during his lengthy career, held many important posts, including Junior Lord of the Admirality (1807), Secretary for War (1809–28), Foreign Secretary (1830–34, 1835–41, 1846–51), Home Secretary (1852–55), and Prime Minister (1855–58 and 1859–65).

As foreign secretary, Lord Palmerston pursued imaginative and frequently daring policies largely inspired by the conviction that Great Britain's interests were best served by peace. To accomplish this objective he favored the preservation of a balance of power policy and the presence of liberal regimes in Europe.[183] His statesmanship in 1830–32 brought modern Belgium into being, and in the process probably prevented a European war. Similarly, his diplomacy in 1839–41 forced France to back down in a Near East crisis, and saved Turkey from being conquered by the rebellious Pasha of Egypt, Muhammed Ali. Even today, this feat, in which Palmerston used the British Navy to accomplish his objectives, is considered as one of the classic examples of decisive policy execution in the annals of the Foreign Office. The foreign secretary employed the fleet again in 1847 to end a Portuguese civil war and, during the same period, his diplomatic maneuvering kept Austria from intervening in Swiss affairs. A year later, Palmerston prevented France and Austria from warring over Italy, and his open sympathy for Italy played a role in that nation's drive for unification.

Lord Palmerston's interest in Palestine and the Jews reflected his overall policy of curtailing French influence in the Levant, and his desire to stabilize the Ottoman Empire. His opportunity to accomplish both of these objectives came with the notorious Damascus blood libel of 1840.[184] In February of that year, Father Thomas, superior of the Franciscan convent, and his servant vanished without a trace. Although it was known that a Turkish muleteer had threatened to kill the priest, his fellow monks spread the rumor that he had been slain by the Jews for ritual purposes. The French Consul, a ruthless and unprincipled individual named Ratti Menton, seized on the incident as a way of consolidating his own position locally and with his superiors in France. He did everything to hamper a thorough investigation of the crime, brought forth false witnesses, and aroused the Muslim population to a fever pitch. The Jewish community was terrorized and Menton, with the aid of the governor, Sherif Pasha, had several arrests made in the Jewish quarter. The innocent victims were subjected to the most barbarous tortures in an effort to wring from them confessions of guilt, and the entire Jewish community was threatened with violence. Finally, a confession was extorted from one of the detainees, a Jewish barber, and seven notables of the community were in turn arrested and subjected to torture. One of them, Joseph Lanado, a feeble old man, died under the cruel treatment. Another of the notables, Moses Abulafia, embraced Islam; and several others, unable to endure the torture, took upon themselves the blame for a crime that neither they nor their fellow Jews had committed. As a result, more Jews were detained, including sixty small children who were confined in jail and left without food. Three of the rabbis and other prominent Jews, arrested at the instigation of the French consul, remained steadfast; and Isaac Levi Picciotto, an Austrian subject, escaped as a result of the interposition of the Austrian Consul, Merlato.

The French consul did his worst to poison public opinion abroad by libelous publications in the French press. He prepared to make short shrift of the detained Jews. The governor, equally desirous of executing them, sought authorization from his master, Muhammed Ali, the Pasha of Egypt, who had possessed himself of Palestine and Syria in 1832.

Aroused by these developments in Damascus, a handful of prominent French and English Jews met and appealed to their respective governments to intercede and use their influence with Muhammed Ali and the Ottoman government to put a stop to the inhuman proceedings taking place in Syria. The French government, headed by Louis-Philippe and his minister, Thiers, who were pursuing a policy friendly to the usurper Muhammed Ali, ignored the pleas to intercede, and expressed full support of their representatives in the East. On the urgent request of the British and Austrian governments, Muhammed Ali indicated a willingness to turn over the Damascus case to a special court of the consular agents of England, Austria, Russia, and Prussia. The French consul general in Alexandria persuaded the Egyptian Pasha not to reopen the case or succumb to the pressure of any of the Great Powers.

In England a Jewish deputation asked for and received an audience with Lord Palmerston. The foreign secretary promised the deputation, which had laid before him full proofs of the innocence of the Jews of Damascus, that he would empower the English ambassador at Constantinople and the English consul at Alexandria to continue to use every means at their disposal to stop the Damascus Affair from proceeding any further. In a speech in the House of Commons (June 22, 1840),[185] Palmerston announced that he had duly served notice on Muhammed Ali concerning the continuing barbaric treatment of the Jews of Damascus, and outlined the diplomatic steps already taken to obtain the release of the unfortunate victims.

However, when it transpired that the authorities in Damascus had no intention of reopening the investigation, or even of conducting an open and fair trial for the accused Jews, public opinion the world over was aroused, In London, a great meeting was held in

Mansion House, at which members of Parliament and Christian clergy vigorously protested against the medieval blood libel. Similar meetings occurred in New York City and Philadelphia, and on behalf of President Van Buren, Secretary of State John Forsyth had letters sent to the consul at Alexandria and the minister to Turkey to use their good offices in mitigating the horrors that were taking place in Damascus.

An assembly of representative Jews in London decided to send a delegation of three prominent Jews (Moses Montefiore, Adolphe Cremieux, and Solomon Munk) to Egypt to make a last appeal to Muhammed Ali to intercede on behalf of the accused Jews. Once again the French consul interposed all possible obstacles. Finally, after nearly three weeks of negotiations with the Jewish delegation and a collective note from nine other European consuls, the pasha ordered the release of those Jews who had not succumbed to death. He refused, however, to reopen the investigation or to declare the Jews innocent of the charges that had resulted in their incarceration and torture. Muhammed Ali's procrastination in resolving the affair cost him dearly, for he had lost the opportunity to forestall British designs against his rule. Palmerston was adamant in his determination that Ali should not succeed, with French connivance, in remaining master of Syria and, from that position of strength, making further inroads on the Ottoman dominions in Asia. Ali's successful defiance of the Turkish sultan had to be checked, if the integrity of the rickety Ottoman Empire was to be preserved. Only in this way, the British foreign secretary believed, would the French be compelled to relinquish their dreams of a great Muslim state under Egyptian leadership and French patronage.

The Damascus Affair provided Palmerston the smokescreen he needed. It discredited Muhammed Ali and his Great Power supporter, France, in the eyes of the civilized world. With Palmerston's prodding, a quadruple alliance consisting of England, Russia, Prussia, and Austria was formed in July of 1840. Directed against France, the pact members all agreed that Syria must be restored to the Turkish sultan. By October, 1840, a British naval force had succeeded in forcing Muhammed Ali out of Syria. France, realizing she had been out-maneuvered by Palmerston, was not prepared to back the Egyptian Pasha at the risk of a general European conflagration. In the months that followed, Muhammed Ali's position worsened, and he was forced to acquiesce to a settlement in which his claim to Syria (including Palestine) was for once and all set aside. Ali was left to content himself with the status of hereditary Viceroy of Egypt.

Palmerston now began to consider other means of strengthening the Ottoman regime. During the height of the Syrian crisis, the idea of the restoration of the Jews to Palestine had received strong support among certain religious circles in England. In the summer of 1840, Palmerston, fully aware of the diplomatic possibilities inherent in the restoration idea, gradually adopted it as part of his overall plan for the Near and Middle East. In a dispatch dated August 11, 1840, to the British ambassador in Constantinople, Lord Ponsonby, he wrote:

> The Jewish people, if returning (to Palestine) under the sanction and protection of the sultan, would be a check upon any future evil designs of Muhammed Ali or his successor. . . .[186]

A few weeks later, the British foreign secretary returned to the subject by impressing upon Lord Ponsonby that a sympathetic response by the sultan, aimed at the Jews, could gain him the goodwill of many of England's religious groups, as well as enriching his realm by attracting wealthy Jewish immigrants.[187] In still another dispatch to Ponsonby, the ambassador was reminded that the Jews, ". . . were a sort of Free Mason fraternity whose goodwill would be useful to the sultan."[188] A few months later, Palmerston went even further and informed his ambassador to Turkey that he was convinced that the Jews who are scattered throughout the European and African continents should be induced to go and settle in Palestine. He stressed, however, that for such a movement to take place, the Jews would require real and tangible security. Accordingly, Palmerston felt they should be able to count on Britain's protection. In addition, Britain could serve as a conduit for any complaints that Jews might bring against the Turkish authorities.[189]

In 1839, while Palestine was still occupied by Muhammed Ali's forces, Palmerston succeeded in establishing a British vice-consulate in Jerusalem. This office was instructed to "afford protection to the Jews generally."[190] The motivation behind this order, other than the obvious political one, can be detected in the man chosen to serve as vice-consul. He was an individual dedicated to the conversion of Jews to Christianity—a favorite hope of the English missionary societies.

Following up on his instructions to Ponsonby, Palmerston authorized Moses Montefiore to write to the Jews of the East, that if they had any serious complaints to make, the English consuls would forward them to the British ambassador in Constantinople, who would represent them before the ministers at the Porte. In line with this policy, the foreign secretary, shortly after Syria and Palestine were restored to the Turks, formally asked the sultan to agree to recognize the region's Jewish inhabitants as British proteges.

There is little reason to doubt that in "Old Pam's" solicitude for the Jews, there was an element of concern for their security but it is not unduly cynical to believe there were other forces at work behind his actions. France, as the leading European Catholic power had large numbers of ready-made clients in the Levant. Britain had next to none. Palmerston seems to have aimed, as a matter of good policy, at encouraging the Jews in Palestine, and ultimately throughout the Ottoman Empire, to look to Great Britain for protection in much the same way as the Catholics of the East were being encouraged to look to France, and the Orthodox Christians to Russia.

Indeed, there was a definite relationship between these ideas, and those underlying the proposal that took shape about this time to establish a Protestant bishopric in Jerusalem. The initiative came from Prussia, but the British government quickly agreed that the project was worthwhile. In the summer of 1841 the powers reached an accord on the establishment of the Jerusalem bishopric. Once again Great Power competition in the Levant was fused with a desire to establish a genuine Protestant claim to a recognized status in the Holy Land. Although not openly expressed in the pact, the religious impulse to convert Jews could be detected behind the diplomatic verbiage. As in the case of the British vice-consul in Jerusalem, the man chosen under the Prussia–British agreement to serve as the first Protestant bishop in the Holy City was a converted Jew named Michael Alexander.[191] He had been born in the part of Poland seized by the Prussians. After immigrating to Great Britain, Alexander was part of a Jewish congregation in Plymouth before joining the Church of England. If the choice of a converted Jew as bishop was significant, the comment of the Prussian diplomat (de Bunsen) who had carried out the successful negotiations with Palmerston was equally revealing of the religious motivations behind the pact. "So the beginning is made, please God," he declared, "for the restoration of the Jews."[192] In de Bunsen's mind, the return of the Jews to Palestine was to be followed by their eventual conversion to Christianity—essential steps leading to the Second Advent of Christ.

Palmerston's efforts to gain recognition of the Jews in Palestine as de facto British proteges encountered stiff opposition from the Sublime Porte. The Turkish sultan stubbornly refused to concede a special status to Great Britain in relation to the Jews. In spite of a considerable amount of cajoling, Palmerston was forced in the end to abandon his "protege scheme." It was, however, not entirely extinct, for in 1849 British consular officials were instructed to afford protection to those Russian Jews in Palestine who, having divested themselves of their Russian nationality, ". . . and so forfeited the protection to which prima facie they were entitled. . . ."[193] Curiously, this rather strange arrangement was sanctioned by the Russian consul-general, and appears not to have been challenged by the Turks. This protection agreement lasted until 1890, when it was terminated at the request of the Russian government.

With the failure of his efforts to induce the Turks to open Palestine for Jewish settlement, Palmerston turned his attention to other pressing matters. Although the Jewish Question had become a secondary issue, an incident involving a Jew would make "Old Pam" one of England's most popular figures, and help to gain for him the prime minister's office. The "Don Pacifico Affair",[194] as it became known, involved a Jewish merchant and diplomat named David Pacifico. Pacifico was a British subject born in Gibraltar. In 1812 his business activities took him to Lagos, Portugal where he was appointed Portuguese consul to Morocco (1835–37), and later to Greece (1837–42). In 1847 the Greek minister, Coletti, in deference to one of the Rothschilds who happened to be visiting Athens at the time, prohibited the populace of the capital from burning a wooden effigy of Judas Iscariot on the Friday before Easter. The cancellation of this annual custom caused a riot during which Pacifico's house was attacked by the crazed mob and completely destroyed. Pacifico, who barely escaped with his life, demanded a sum of 800,000 drachmas from the Greek government as compensation for his loss of property and personal papers. The Greek regime refused to consider his claim, and added further insult to injury by confiscating Pacifico's remaining property. Pacifico then turned to the British government for help. Palmerston, in a move designed to defend Pacifico's rights as a British subject, and eager to avenge other acts on the part of the Greek regime against English citizens, instructed the British navy to blockade the port of Piraeus (1850). After 200 ships had been captured, the Greek government had a change of heart and decided to pay David Pacifico for the damages and indignities he had suffered. His claim settled, Pacifico retired to London where he spent the remainder of his life.

Palmerston's high-handed action, which almost led to a war with France and Russia (both, along with England, protectors of the recently created Greek state), aroused a furor at home. He was censored by the House of Lords, and was called upon to defend his actions in the House of Commons. Ordinarily an unimpressive speaker, Palmerston on this occasion rose to the challenge and delivered a brilliant five-hour speech ("Civis Romanus sum"), in which he spelled out a policy that any British subject, in any location, was entitled to the same respect and protection that the citizens of Imperial Rome had enjoyed.[195] This oration, the most dramatic in his long career, silenced his critics and made Palmerston a national hero. When Prime Minister Aberdeen was forced to resign during the Crimean War, "Old Pam" was immediately named his successor (1855). Some years later, after being defeated on a comparatively unimportant measure, he was compelled to resign his prime minister's post. However, Palmerston remained active in parliamentary affairs and was able to regain the prime minister's office under the first Liberal government in English history (1859). During this administration, which ended with his death in 1865, Palmerston was successful in building up the nation's defenses, and keeping England neutral throughout the American Civil War.

"Old Pam's" policies helped place the Jews of Palestine in a different and rather unaccustomed light. In some English circles the events that had brought Palestine to the forefront of the Eastern Question were believed to have an apocalyptic significance, and to foreshadow the end of the Jewish exile. Others more politically inclined saw in Palmerston's Jewish moves a new approach to extending the power and prestige of the British Empire.

16

The Seventh Earl of Shaftesbury: An Evangelical Restorationist

In England one of the major driving forces behind Lord Palmerston's efforts on behalf of the Jews was the so-called "religious party" – a group of devout and influential evangelical Christians. Keenly aware of the ferment and turmoil prevailing in the Ottoman Empire they were convinced that the restoration of the Jews to the Holy Land was close at hand. Imbued with a uniquely Victorian brand of pietism, they also nurtured a compelling vision that it was God's will that the British nation was destined to be His instrument for achieving Jewish restoration. The accomplishment of this goal would in turn set in motion a chain of events leading to the Second Coming of Christ.

The most prominent advocate of this school of thought was the social reformer Lord Anthony Ashley Cooper (1801–85),[196] who would, following the death of his father, assume the title of Seventh Earl of Shaftesbury. As a member of Parliament from 1826 onwards, Cooper fought vigorously for various social reforms. His efforts won for him a well-deserved reputation as England's most ardent champion of social change.

A deeply religious person, Shaftesbury's parliamentary program was largely the product of his evangelical Christian outlook. He strongly believed that a man's religion, if it was worth anything at all, must permeate every aspect of his life and behavior. The ability of Shaftesbury to live by this idealistic code in the realistic world of British politics was greatly abetted by his station in society and his family connections. He was related on his mother's side to the Duke of Marlborough, and by marriage to Lord Palmerston (he had wed Palmerston's step-daughter).

Like the Puritan leaders in Cromwell's time, the earl looked forward to the conversion of the Jews, "God's ancient people", as an essential step in hastening the Second Advent. "Our church and nation," he declared, "have been called to the glorious service of making known the Gospel of Christ to the many thousands of Israel."[197] Thus from 1848 until his death, he strove to lead the Jews to the font in his capacity as president of the London

Society for the Promotion of Christianity (known in popular parlance as the Jews' Society).[198] Established in 1809, the society was the first missionary organization in Great Britain devoted exclusively to the conversion of Jews. It included among its list of patrons prominent members of the nobility, and such famous people as Wilbur Wilberforce, the evangelical leader who led the fight for the abolition of the slave trade, and Zachary Macaulay, the father of the celebrated historian.

Although Shaftesbury venerated the Jews for their sacred writings, there was another side to his religiosity that suggested hypocrisy. He was, for example, convinced that as a practicing Christian he was duty bound to oppose the recognition of Jews as full citizens of England. In a diary entry of March 12, 1841, the earl noted that though he would not oppose the admission of Jews to municipal offices, he regarded their claims to be eligible to sit in parliament as "an insult to Christianity."[199] Some years later (1847) during a debate in the House of Commons over a motion to relieve the Jews of their remaining disabilities, Shaftesbury arose and spoke against the proposal. He argued that the Jews were voluntary strangers in England, and therefore had no claim to become citizens, " . . . except by conforming to our moral law, which is the Gospel."[200]

If, in English domestic politics, the Seventh Earl of Shaftesbury was no friend of the Jews, his religious convictions, on the other hand, spurred him on to act as their staunchest supporter for restoration in Palestine. It was these intense religious feelings that motivated him in 1838 to urge Lord Palmerston to appoint a British vice-consul for Jerusalem, and to extend the consulate's protection to the Jews of Palestine. A few years later, Shaftesbury played a major role in influencing the British government's decision that culminated in the Anglo-Prussian Agreement, establishing a Protestant bishopric in the Holy City. Very early in his parliamentary career, the earl realized that it was advisable at times to suppress his evangelical enthusiasm if he was to win for his proposals the support of the Jews and England's power brokers. How well he was able to disassemble his innermost religious impulses when dealing with a pragmatic and hardheaded statesman such as Lord Palmerston can be deduced from a diary entry made during the period when Shaftesbury was pressuring the British foreign secretary to approach the Turkish sultan on behalf of the Jews of Palestine. It read:

> I am forced to argue politically, financially, and commercially; these considerations strike him home; he weeps not like his Master over Jerusalem, nor prays that now, at last, she may put on her beautiful garments.[201]

By 1840 the Earl of Shaftesbury's ideas on a Jewish restoration had crystallized into a definite plan for resettling Jews in Palestine.[202] With single-minded tenacity, he campaigned for its sponsorship by the British government. He stressed that the returning Jews would revitalize the entire region. They would once more become the husbandmen of Judea and the Galilee, ". . . as long ages of suffering have trained [them] . . . to habits of endurance and self denial [and] they would joyfully exhibit them in the settlement of their ancient country."[203] Great Britain, the earl believed, should provide the capital, skills, and security required to ensure the success of such a settlement. He was also careful to point out that Jewish restoration in the Holy Land would also best serve England's imperial interests in the East.

Palmerston accepted many of Shaftesbury's suggestions but, as noted previously, his efforts failed to persuade the Turkish sultan of the benefits to be derived from a Jewish settlement of Palestine. Undeterred by such setbacks, Anthony Ashley Cooper continued to goad British officials to renew their diplomatic efforts with the Sublime Porte. At Cooper's instigation, Palmerston instructed the British vice-consul in Jerusalem to take a census of the Jews in the Holy Land, for the purpose of taking them under his protection. However, this concern for the Jews in the 1840s gradually dissipated in the decades that followed. The British government, although still prepared to take a benevolent attitude toward the betterment of conditions for the Jews of Palestine was no longer so eager to repeat Palmerston's efforts to pressure the Turks to open the Holy Land to Jewish settlement.

In spite of this reluctance to bear down too hard upon the Ottoman regime, Shaftesbury continued to urge on British officialdom on behalf of the Jews. In May of 1854, just after the outbreak of the Crimean War, Shaftesbury approached the new British foreign Secretary, Lord Clarendon and suggested to him that, ". . . the sultan should be moved to issue a firman granting the Jewish people power to hold land in Syria or any part of the Turkish dominions."[204] This proposal was accordingly passed on by Clarendon to the British ambassador in Constantinople, and may have influenced the Sublime Porte's issuance of a firman, a year later, to the prominent Jewish philanthropist Sir Moses Montefiore enabling him to buy some land in Jerusalem and Jaffa.

The indefatigable Earl of Shaftesbury continued to speak out in favor of a Jewish restoration in Palestine, whenever and wherever an occasion presented itself. Toward the end of his parliamentary career, events in Eastern Europe seemed, for awhile, to breathe new life into his appeals. On March 31, 1881, a bomb put an abrupt end to the life of Alexander II, the Czar of Russia, who had emancipated the Empire's serfs. Under his successor, Alexander III, a wave of pogroms (the Russian word for "devastation") descended on Russian Jewry. It was obvious to all impartial observers that the bloodletting had the blessings of the government. Indeed, the riots were instigated from a central headquarters, and erupted simultaneously at different locations throughout southern Russia. Even more incriminating, the rioters followed an identical pattern everywhere, both in regard to the actions taken, and the inaction of the police.

News of these frightful events shocked the Western world. In England there were vehement public protests, and calls for government action to put a stop to the atrocities being carried out against the Jews. The *Times* of London added fuel to the public outcry by publishing a series of articles describing the horrors and barbarisms committed during the pogroms. At a public meeting in the Mansion House, the official residence of the Lord Mayor of London, the Earl of Shaftesbury boldly declared that an appeal be immediately directed to the czar.

The pogroms sowed fear among the Jewish population of Russia. For many, the only course of action seemed to be flight. Emigration committees formed with unprecedented speed and set to work to rescue the hapless victims of Russian persecution. However, thousands of Jews were too frightened to await the formalities involved in securing permission to emigrate. They left everything behind them in panic flight, and a vast flood of refugees began to pour towards the borders. Soon hordes of the hopeless and impoverished were to be found in all the capitals of the West. Before the century had ended, over 1 million Jews had left their former homes in Eastern Europe. The overwhelming majority found asylum in the United States, Canada, South America, and Australia. A large group settled in England. In London's East End alone immigration rapidly increased the number of Jewish inhabitants from 47,000 to 150,000. For the octogenarian Earl of

Shaftesbury, the Russian pogroms, which he publicly denounced as brutal acts of terror, must have appeared as signs confirming his evangelical beliefs. The "end of days" foretold by the ancient biblical prophets seemed at hand, and with it the beginning of the long-awaited millennium and the Second Coming of Christ. But when many of the Jewish refugees chose to make England their permanent home, and few succumbed to the preachments of the Christian missionaries, Shaftesbury's vision of the Second Coming must have seemed more remote than ever. Unfortunately, history has not recorded the social reformer's reactions to these developments during the closing years of his life.

17

Laurence Oliphant

Jewish restoration in Palestine strongly appealed to Laurence Oliphant (1829–88),[205] one of the most paradoxical figures of the Victorian era. Author, journalist, lawyer, traveler, diplomat, politician, adventurer, and mystic—the world was his stage. Born in Cape Town, South Africa, he was the son of Sir Anthony Oliphant, at the time the Attorney General of the Cape Colony and Maria Campbell, the daughter of the colonel of the 72nd Highlanders Regiment. Both of Laurence's parents were religious enthusiasts (evangelicals). After a boyhood spent in England, Laurence Oliphant journeyed to Ceylon (1841) to rejoin his father, who had been appointed chief judge of the island two years earlier. As a result of these radical shifts in residence, Laurence received a desultory education. Nevertheless, he managed to be called to the bar, and by age twenty-two had participated in twenty-five murder cases. However, travel, rather than law, proved more enticing to Oliphant. He accompanied his parents on a tour of France, Germany, the Tyrol, Italy, and Greece (1846–48). A few years later he traveled on his own to Nepal, Russia, and the Crimea before returning to the British Isles. While in England, Oliphant became involved in various projects sponsored by the Earl of Shaftesbury. Always restless, he eagerly accepted a position as a private secretary to James Bruce (Lord Elgin), and accompanied the veteran diplomat on a mission to Canada and the United States (1853–54). The results of these peregrinations provided Oliphant material for two books, *A Journey to Katmandu,* and *The Russian Shores of the Black Sea.* They were the first of a number of descriptive works that he would produce during the course of his adventurous life.

In 1855 Oliphant's wanderlust took him to Constantinople and to the Crimea, where he witnessed the siege of Sebastopol. He later served under Omar Pasha in the latter's Transcaucasian military expedition—a highpoint of the Crimean War. Seeking new adventures, Oliphant joined the American filibuster, William Walker, in New Orleans and participated in Walker's campaign to overthrow the government of Nicaragua. Returning to England he joined Lord Elgin as a member of a special mission to China and Japan (1857–59). Oliphant would later render a fascinating account of nineteenth-century gunboat diplomacy, based on his experiences during these years.

In 1860 Oliphant was again in Europe, this time as a war correspondent covering the activities of Garibaldi in Italy. After a side trip to Montenegro, he accepted a diplomatic assignment as first secretary of the British legation in Yeddo, Japan. However, his diplomatic career was literally cut short when he was attacked and severely wounded by a Japanese assassin wielding a two-handed sword (Oliphant had attempted to fend off the attacker with a hunting whip). Recovering from his wounds, Oliphant returned to England. Subsequently, he would recall with verve his experiences in the Far East in a book entitled *Episodes in a Life of Adventure.* [206]

Never content to stay in one place for any length of time, Oliphant accompanied the Prince of Wales on a visit to Corfu (1862). This trip was followed by journeys to Herzegovina, Moldavia, Egypt, and Poland where he observed first hand the Insurrection of 1863. Resuming the occupation of a war correspondent, he next reported on the Schleswig-Holstein conflict, and also found time to write a satirical novel on London society which he called, *Picadilly: A Fragment of Contemporary Biography.*

In 1865 Oliphant began a new career as a member of Parliament. Two years later, influenced by the American spiritualist Thomas Lake Harrison, he gave up his seat and joined the *Brotherhood of New Life,* an odd spiritual, mystical, and esoteric society centered in New York State's Chautauqua County at Brocton. The brotherhood's creed was a curious mixture of philosophy, popular science, and religious mysticism. Harrison, the founder of the group, believed that marriage should be platonic. He also cast out devils and formed "magnetic circles" around his disciples to protect them from evil forces. While at Brocton, Oliphant was compelled by the spiritual leader to perform the community's most menial tasks. His mother later joined the society, but was forbidden by Harrison to hold any confidential conversations with her son. Both mother and son bequeathed considerable fortunes to the brotherhood while under the spell of Harrison.

At the outbreak of the Franco-Prussian War, Oliphant took leave of the society and returned to Europe as a war correspondent for the London *Times.* Two years later, a married man, he went back to Brocton, accompanied by his wife and mother. All three now came completely under the spell and control of Harrison, who frequently called on Oliphant to engage in various commercial enterprises for the good of the community, while his wife and mother were routinely assigned servile chores. Incredibly, at the insistence of Harrison, Oliphant was eventually persuaded to separate from his wife. She was sent to a branch of the sect located in California. Disillusionment gradually set in, but it was not until 1882 that the Oliphants were able to break free from Harrison's clutches and successfully recover some of the fortune they had squandered on the sect's prophet.

Throughout his years at Brocton, Oliphant had retained a lively interest in British politics and foreign relations. At the height of the Russo-Turkish War (1878) he began to give serious thought to the Eastern Question. He became convinced that Palestine was the key to the revitalization of the Ottoman Empire. The Holy Land, he felt, could serve as a bridge between Europe and Asia if the Turks allowed Jews to freely settle there. In the process, the Jews would enjoy a rebirth in their ancient homeland and at the same time provide the Turkish sultan with a resourceful and loyal population.

There is little doubt that Oliphant's concern for the Jews was motivated by the religious convictions he had imbibed from early childhood, and which had been reinforced by his experiences as a war correspondent. He had also been greatly moved by George Eliot's novel *Daniel Deronda*, which first appeared in *Blackwood's Magazine*, a favorite outlet for his own writings, and by the literature of the Palestine Exploration Fund. Curiously, Oliphant was always careful to disparage suggestions that his solution to the Jewish question was motivated by religious impulses and liked to claim that his ideas were purely practical, and reflected political and commercial considerations.

> It is somewhat unfortunate that so important a political and strategic question as the future of Palestine should be inseparably connected in the public mind with a favorite religious theory [the Second Advent].[207]

He went on to note that the mere accident that a measure involving the most important consequences, was advocated by a large section of the Christian community, from a purely biblical point of view, did not necessarily impair its political value.

Eager to implement his ideas concerning both the Eastern Question and the Jewish Problem, Oliphant brought them to the attention of the Prime Minister of England, Lord Beaconsfield (Disraeli). Beaconsfield directed him to formulate his ideas in writing and to forward them to the foreign office. In November of 1878 Oliphant sent a letter to Lord Salisbury, the British Foreign Secretary, outlining his plan. It consisted of a proposal to create a Palestine Development Company which would seek to obtain a land concession from the Turkish government for a period of twenty-five years or more. The company would build settlements and operate them with Jewish immigrants from Rumania and Russia.

Lord Beaconsfield and Lord Salisbury unofficially gave their blessings to Oliphant's scheme, but were unwilling to commit the government to carry it out. Unfazed by the lack of official government recognition, Oliphant decided to look on his own for a suitable site for establishing a colony. Armed with letters of recommendation from the British foreign office and the French foreign ministry, he sailed in 1879 for Beirut. From there he made his way overland, with a small party, to northern Palestine. After weighing several possibilities, Oliphant concluded that the most promising site for a settlement was the area east of the Jordan River at the upper end of the Dead Sea. It was a region abundantly fertile and semitropical. He called the territory the "Land of Gilead," and was particularly struck by the realization that the western section of the proposed colony would be within an easy day's journey of Jerusalem. A railway running through Jericho, Oliphant visualized, would put the colony in direct communication with Jerusalem, which already had a Jewish population of about 15,000. Similarly, a railway connection between the "Land of Gilead" and the port of Haifa would provide the settlement with an outlet for its produce.

After completing his Palestine survey, Oliphant traveled to Constantinople to persuade key members of the sultan's government of the soundness and beneficial aspects of his plan. During his initial conversations with the Sublime Porte he was encouraged by the interest shown in the settlement plan by the Turkish officials. His request for tenancy rights and concessions for Jewish settlement within the Ottoman Empire's Asian regions received the consent of the Turkish cabinet. However, at the very last moment of negotiations the decision of the cabinet was overruled by the sultan, who feared that the proposed project masked a clever British intrigue.

In spite of the sultan's rejection of his plan, Oliphant continued to propagate his views in a series of articles in *Blackwood's Magazine*, and in a provocative book entitled *The*

Land of Gilead.[208] Analyzing the Eastern Question, he noted that the Treaty of Berlin had set a precedent that would make inevitable future Great Power interference in the affairs of Turkey. The only way to prevent such interference, Oliphant believed, was to reform the administration of the Ottoman Empire. Because it was doubtful that the Turks were willing to adopt the necessary reforms, Oliphant thought that perhaps an experiment might be made on a small scale. Evidence might then be presented to the sultan of the advantages that would attend the development of a single province, however small, under conditions that should increase the revenues of the empire, add to its population and resources, and enlist the sympathy of Europe, without affecting the sovereign rights of the Ottoman regime. It seemed to Oliphant that such objectives could best be achieved by the establishment of a colony in one of Turkey's sparsely populated districts. The project itself would be managed and developed, under the auspices of the sultan, as a commercial enterprise, with headquarters based in Constantinople.

Elaborating on this idea, Oliphant considered the sensitive questions of the locality best-suited for the colonization experiment and the class of people who should be invited to come as colonists. The objections to foreigners, who were at the same time Christians, seemed insurmountable. Existing Turkish law required that any colonists permanently settling in Turkey in Asia had to become Ottoman subjects—a provision with which most foreign Christians were extremely unlikely to comply.

Oliphant also considered the possibility of an asylum for the thousands of Moslem refugees who, driven from their homes in Bulgaria and Rumania, were starving in various parts of the Empire. The difficulty in this case arose from the extreme improbability of finding the financial resources in Christian Europe that would be required for the aid of these Moslem victims.

As far as Oliphant could see there was only one group in Europe, the Jews, who had the necessary capital and did not need to appeal to Christian capitalists for money to carry through the undertaking. Since they were not Christians, the objection of the Sublime Porte to the introduction of more rival Christian sects did not apply. In addition, the Jews had always proved themselves loyal and peaceful subjects of the sultan.

Because the Jews had strong historical associations to a province in Asiatic Turkey (i.e., Palestine) the inducement of once more becoming proprietors of its sacred soil might prove strong enough to tempt them to comply with the probable conditions of the Turkish government. A further incentive was the fact that they were frequently subjected to persecution by some European governments, which contrasted sharply with the toleration they experienced in Turkey. Oliphant concluded that it was logical that the locality of the colonization experiment should be Palestine, and the colonists Jews.

The pogroms of 1881 in Russia, like the Rumanian excesses of 1879, which he had personally witnessed, stirred Oliphant's deepest emotions. An activist by nature, he quickly called together a group in London of influential Christian leaders to cope with this latest outrage against Russian Jewry. In addition, Oliphant, acting as an agent of the mayor of London's Mansion House Relief Fund, helped provide assistance for Russian refugees in Galicia. When representatives of the Alliance Israélite Universelle reacted to the Russian pogroms by directing refugee immigration to the United States, Oliphant tried to persuade the relief organization to change its policy, and to channel the flow of refugees to Palestine. The Alliance, as well as the other major relief organizations of the West, ignored his suggestions and in the process indirectly undermined his second attempt to convince the Turkish government to accept his plan for the Jewish colonization of Palestine.

Acutely aware that his negotiation with the Turks was leading nowhere, Oliphant changed his tactics. In June of 1882, accompanied by a committee of Rumanian Jews (on a visit to Rumania some years earlier, he had established contacts with the Jewish Palestinian movement, the Love of Zion) Oliphant approached Lewis Wallace, the American Minister at Constantinople. A former Civil War general and the author of the novel *Ben Hur,* Wallace was a man touched by Protestant messianism and receptive to Oliphant's new approach to the Jewish Problem—to bring American pressure on the Turkish sultan to grant Jewish refugees colonization rights in Syria. The new plan was purposely ambiguous as to the geographic area covered by the term Syria and whether it included northern Palestine. Wallace, adhering to the chain of command, forwarded Oliphant's proposal to his superior, Frederick Frelinghuysen, the United States' Secretary of State. The secretary, after consulting with the President, Chester Arthur, gave Wallace permission to use his good offices on behalf of finding a haven for Jewish refugees. Not long after notifying Wallace of the new policy, Frelinghuysen had second thoughts about his decision. He had received a strongly worded letter from a Georgia clergyman who urged the administration to submit a proposal to the Sublime Porte for the purchase of the Holy Land by the oppressed Hebrews of all nations. The secretary of state alerted Wallace, who agreed with his superior that the clergyman's suggestion was unrealistic and impractical.

In spite of the secretary of state's doubts, Wallace remained impressed by Oliphant's plan. Oliphant had aroused the general's sympathies with his vivid descriptions of the flight of Jews from Russia and Rumania. During further discussions between Wallace, Oliphant, and an individual named James Alexander, who also was representing Rumanian Jewish societies interested in colonization projects, agreement was reached that the American minister would try to wrangle a colonization permit from the Sublime Porte. If successful in obtaining the permit, Wallace would then sever all connections with the colonization scheme.

Unknown to Wallace, James Alexander was not only an agent of the Rumanian Jewish societies, but also a personal representative of British industrialist Edward Cazalet, who was trying to obtain a railroad concession from the Turkish government. In Cazalet's mind the idea of Jewish settlements along the railroad's right of way was an important factor in his negotiating strategy.

When Wallace finally called on the Turkish minister of foreign affairs and presented Oliphant's plan, he was informed that the proposal had already been discussed by the council of ministers and had been ruled on favorably. However, certain conditions had to be met before the scheme could be implemented. The Jewish refugees would be allowed to settle in any of the unoccupied areas of Mesopotamia and in Syria, in the vicinity of Aleppo; or in the territory adjacent to the Orontes River. Palestine, however, was to be excluded from the lands that could be colonized by the Jews. In addition, the refugees would be obliged to pay the authorities a set sum for each family, and each settlement was to be formed of approximately 250 families. Lastly, the existing Turkish law on immigration could not be ignored, and every colonist was expected to become an Ottoman subject.

The American minister was jubilant. He felt that he had helped make a major breakthrough in resolving the refugee problem, although the Turkish policy differed very little from what the Sublime Porte had offered some months earlier. A cautious diplomat, Wallace asked the Turks to confirm their offer in writing, but the Turks, always wary of formal documents, were only willing to give him oral assurances.

Oliphant and the committee of Rumanian Jews did not share Wallace's joy over the Turkish offer. They felt that the minimum financial requirement of 1,350 francs for each immigrant family was inordinately high. Moreover, the exclusion of Palestine from the areas of settlement was a major deterrent to the would-be colonists who were either active members, or deeply steeped in the spirit of the Love of Zion movement.

News of Oliphant's efforts to extract a colonization permit from the Ottoman regime attracted the attention of a small group of Russian Jewish students, who had sworn to emigrate to Palestine and form a colony. Known by the acronym "Bilu" from Isaiah 2:5, "House of Jacob come and let us go," the group waited anxiously for some sign that Oliphant was succeeding in his negotiation with the Sublime Porte. The sign never came, and following the Wallace initiative, the sultan nullified the council of ministers' offer and issued a series of edicts reinforcing his earlier rulings forbidding Jews to purchase land or to settle in Palestine.

Rebuffed once again, an enraged Oliphant decided to take his case to the public. He published a diatribe highlighting the duplicity of the sultan and his ministers and in general made himself unwelcome at the Porte. Even more devastating for him than the failure of his various stratagems to gain a colonization permit from the Turks, was the new attitude to the entire Eastern Question adopted by the British government. Having occupied Cyprus a few years earlier, Great Britain was distinctly reluctant to further provoke Turkish suspicions of territorial aggrandizement by standing four-square behind Oliphant's refugee settlement plan. This change in British policy had come about rather suddenly. Lord Beaconsfield, on whom Oliphant had counted for political support, died on April 19, 1881, and after six years in opposition, Gladstone, Disraeli's rival, was back in power as prime minister. Any scheme that smacked of imperial adventurism was taboo to Gladstone and his colleagues. Strangely enough, in spite of his strong feelings on imperialism, Gladstone, in 1882, would abandon his principles and send an army into Egypt, supposedly to resolve a political crisis. Great Britain would remain in Egypt for the next seventy-four years.

By July of 1882 tidings of Oliphant's lack of success in his Turkish negotiations reached Russia, and members of the Bilu group decided to take independent action. Believing that the Englishman's setback might only be of a temporary nature, they shifted their headquarters from Kharkov to Odessa on the Black Sea. From Odessa a small band of seventeen Biluim sailed for Constantinople, where they received the melancholy intelligence that Oliphant had exhausted all his resources and that nothing more could be expected from him as far as obtaining a colonization permit from the Sublime Porte. All but three of the Biluim decided to take their chances and journey on to Palestine. These adventurous youths, after incredible hardships, managed to establish a foothold in the Holy Land, and became the vanguard of the "First Aliyah" i.e., the first wave of Jewish immigration to Palestine in modern times.

With the realization that Great Britain had lost interest in his grand design and that there was little hope of reviving his American card, Oliphant was forced to abandon his colonization plans. At the end of 1882, he retired with his wife to Haifa in the Bay of Acre region of Palestine. He continued, however, his efforts on behalf of Jewish refugees and provided advice and assistance to the early Jewish pioneers in Palestine. In addition, Oliphant solicited the help of prominent Jewish philanthropists such as Baron Edmund de Rothschild, and Baron Maurice de Hirsch for the struggling Palestinian Jewish settlements established by the Love of Zion movement.

In 1887 Oliphant played a pivotal role in the purchase of 2,100 *dunams* of land on which the Jewish colony of B'ne Y'huda was founded. More importantly, he kept alive the idea of a Jewish restoration in the Holy Land by his articles on the new settlements and by such personal accounts as his book, *Haifa, or Life in Modern Palestine.* [209]

Among the small band of enthusiasts who rallied around Oliphant in his declining years was the poet Naphtali Herz Imber (1856–1909), [210] who acted as the Englishman's secretary. Imber's early poems appeared in a volume entitled *Barkai* and were dedicated to Laurence Oliphant. In this book were two poems that were to achieve great popularity among the Jews of Palestine and the Diaspora, "Mishmar Hayarden" and "Hatikvah." The latter poem would later become the State of Israel's national anthem.

During a trip to Lake Tiberias in 1886, Oliphant's wife contracted a fever and died a short time afterwards. Following her death, the bereaved Oliphant turned inwards and devoted himself almost exclusively to religious and mystic subjects. He tried to communicate with the spiritual world and believed that his wife had returned in spirit form. Even prior to the death of his wife, the deep religious impulses that had marked most of his youth and manhood surfaced in an esoteric work which he entitled *Sympneumata.* A strange amalgam of spiritualism, mysticism, and religion the book reflected the major influences in Oliphant's life – Christian evangelicalism, the theories of Thomas Lake Harrison, the mysticism of the Kabbalah, and Oriental philosophies.

The last years of Oliphant's life were relatively quiet. He remarried and continued his interest in the Jewish communities of Palestine. His travels and religious beliefs had made him sensitive to the cries of an ancient people for justice, and he had tried desperately to find a solution that would alleviate their suffering. With his death on December 23, 1888, Jewry lost an eloquent Christian voice and a staunch friend, while Great Britain was deprived of its most ardent advocate for commercial domination of the Near and Middle East.

18

Colonel Charles Henry Churchill

The British movement for restoration of the Jews to Palestine reached its zenith during the nineteenth century. It had come a long way from the sermons of Thomas Brightman (1525–1607), who had first propagated the idea in England. Similar views had struck responsive chords among such prominent public figures as Oliver Cromwell, the Lord Protector of England; Edmund Bunny, the Secretary of the London Municipality, and the highly respected jurist Henry Finch. Almost from its inception, the restoration movement drew its main support from pious Protestants who believed in a fundamental interpretation of the Bible. By the eighteenth century, the movement had gained many adherents among writers, romantics, and statesmen, as well as theologians and ordinary folk. Most notable among the clergy favoring a restoration of the Jews to their ancient homeland were Thomas Newton, the Bishop of Bristol, and Robert Lowth, the Bishop of London. The advent of the nineteenth century brought dramatic changes to the character and composition of the restoration movement. There now appeared on the scene millenarian sects among whom the belief in the return of the Jews to the Holy Land was a central tenet. Political and military events had also pushed Palestine onto center stage, and had made the Near and Middle East a subject of Great Power concern.

In 1838, Mohammed Ali, an Albanian adventurer who had made himself master of Egypt, threw caution to the wind and launched a powerful attack against his overlord, the Turkish sultan. His ultimate target was Constantinople and the overthrow of the Ottoman Empire. Ali's army, under the able command of his son Ibrahim Pasha, achieved a great victory over the Ottoman forces near Nizib, which led to the surrender of the Turkish fleet. The fate of the sultan seemed sealed. At this juncture the Great Powers—England, Russia, Austria, and Prussia intervened on the side of the Ottoman regime. An ultimatum was drawn up and delivered to Mohammed Ali demanding immediate withdrawal of Egyptian forces from the territory seized from the Ottoman Empire: Syria, Lebanon,

Palestine, Aden, and the island of Crete. When Mohammed Ali rejected these demands, the Great Powers resorted to armed force. Beirut was bombarded by a British fleet under the command of Sir Charles Napier, and Admiral Sir Robert Stoppard shelled Acre (November 3, 1840), causing the city to capitulate to the besieging Turkish troops. British, Austrian, and Turkish troops led by Napier, and later by the German general August von Jochmus, applied steady pressure on Ibrahim Pasha's army. By February of 1841 Ibrahim Pasha's forces were in full retreat and the allied army had captured Damascus, thus putting an end to Egyptian rule over Syria, Lebanon, and Palestine, as well as to the threat to Constantinople.

Among the English officers who participated in the military expedition against Mohammed Ali and his son was Colonel Charles Henry Churchill (1807–69).[211] Born in Madras, India, Charles was the son of an official of the East India Company, a descendant of the brother of the first Duke of Marlborough. A professional soldier, Churchill, prior to the Syrian-Palestinian campaign had served with distinction in Portugal and Spain.

Although it cannot be ascertained with any certainty whether Churchill entertained any thoughts about the Jewish Problem before his arrival in the East, there is some indirect evidence that he might have been influenced by a distant relation. The Churchill family was related by marriage to Lord Anthony Ashley Cooper, the Seventh Earl of Shaftesbury, a leader in the movement for Jewish restoration in Palestine.

Charles Henry Churchill's participation in restoration activities began on the island of Malta, and were linked to Sir Moses Montefiore[212] and the infamous Damascus blood libel. Montefiore, returning to England after a successful audience with the Turkish sultan, in which he had obtained a firman expressing the sultan's disapproval of the Damascus Affair and a promise to grant the Jews the same privileges enjoyed by other subjects of the empire, stopped over on Malta. The firman ("Hatti Sherif") had aroused considerable interest and admiration among diplomatic circles in the West, and Montefiore was received by the British authorities on Malta with great honor.

The philanthropist's stopover coincided with that of a group of British officers preparing to leave for Syria. Churchill was one of the group, and he, along with two other officers decided to call on Sir Moses Montefiore. They praised him for his accomplishment and asked if they could be of any service. Montefiore availed himself of their kindness and entrusted Churchill with copies of the firman "Hatti Sherif," and other documents for transmission to the Jewish community of Damascus.

The entry of the victorious allied army into Damascus received a tumultuous welcome from the city's Jewish residents. Churchill, the bearer of Montefiore's documents and the sultan's firman, was especially singled out by the Jewish elders and honored. Raphael Farhi, acknowledged leader of the Jewish community, gave a reception for Churchill in his home, to which he invited all the British and Austrian staff officers, as well as the surviving victims of the blood libel. Rising to the occasion, Churchill delivered an emotional speech in which he touched upon the historic aspiration of Israel's political existence. The spellbound audience interrupted him several times with cries of *Inshallah! Inshallah!* (May God grant it! May God grant it!).[213]

Churchill's Damascus address, considering the time and place, was unusual. In some ways it paralleled the appeal to the Jews made by Napoleon Bonaparte during his Egyptian–Palestinian campaign. However, the British colonel's talk placed emphasis on humane rather than political factors. Unlike his family relation, the Earl of Shaftesbury, who was motivated by evangelical doctrines relating to the Second Coming of Christ,

Churchill was free of any conversionist tendencies. Indeed, he reversed the prevailing Christian evangelical doctrine by insisting that the Jewish nation itself had to be the prime mover in the struggle for Jewish restoration in Palestine. In promulgating this concept, Churchill foreshadowed the Jewish nationalist movement which a century later would culminate in the establishment of a Jewish state.

While British resident officer in Damascus, Churchill attempted to implement some of his novel ideas in relation to the Jews. He became the protector of the Jews in the Syrian capital, regarding them not only as proteges, but as the linchpin in his scheme to rally world Jewry to the idea of a mass movement back to Palestine. His efforts encountered considerable resistance from the Ottoman authorities, forcing Churchill to change his tactics. He decided to appeal directly to the Jews of Western Europe for support. To this end he forwarded a long letter to Sir Moses Montefiore (June 14, 1841) in which he outlined his thoughts on the creation of a Jewish nationalist movement. Clearly and forcefully, Churchill informed the philanthropist of his desire to see Montefiore's countrymen resume their existence as a nation. He considered the objective to be perfectly attainable.

The goal could be reached, Churchill emphasized, if the Jews took up the matter universally and unanimously and tried to win over the European Powers to the idea of a Jewish restoration. It was essential, however, that the Jews take the lead in initiating the process. This could best be done if the leaders of the Jewish communities placed themselves at the head of the restoration movement. They should meet, organize, and petition. In fact the agitation must be simultaneous throughout Europe. The ferment arising from such actions, Churchill believed, would introduce a new element into the Eastern Question that would inevitably attract the attention of the Great Powers. In summing up, the British colonel insisted that if the resources available to the Jews were directed toward the regeneration of Syria and Palestine, there could be little doubt that these countries would amply repay the undertaking, and that the Jews would end by obtaining sovereignty of at least Palestine.

Churchill was also convinced that Great Power efforts to prop up the Ottoman Empire were futile, and that areas like Syria and Palestine had to be rescued from the grasp of ignorant and rapacious Turkish officials. He further felt that under the blundering and decrepit despotism of the Turks real progress and commercial enterprise were impossible. It was therefore essential that regions like Syria and Palestine be taken under European protection and administration. The role of the Jews, Churchill informed Montefiore, was to make certain that when the Eastern Question came again before the Great Powers, they put forth their claims to their ancient homeland.

A pragmatist, Churchill recognized that the Turkish presence in Palestine could not be easily eliminated. He therefore suggested that if the Jews wished to gain a foothold in the Holy Land, they should first become subjects of the sultan. Following this move, the Jews, Churchill felt, should concentrate on convincing the Great Powers of their desire to return to Palestine and getting them to act as intermediaries with the Turks. The Great Powers could make it clear to the Turks that they would accept responsibility for the protection of the Jews if the sultan allowed them to colonize part of Syria or Palestine. If permission was given, the European Powers would then ask the Ottoman regime to grant the Jewish settlers the privilege of regulating their own internal affairs and of exemption from Turkish military service. For these privileges the Jews would pay a tribute to the Sublime Porte.

In his letter to Montefiore, Churchill acknowledged that his plan would require, on the part of the Jews, an extraordinary output of capital, enthusiasm, perseverance, and intelligent leadership. However, political events seemed to warrant the conclusion that the time was on hand for the Jews to take the initiative in the work of national regeneration. The prospect of success was now clearly within reach if the Jews remained steadfast in their resolve to become a viable nation-state once again.

Colonel Churchill's grandiose scheme contained a serious flaw. It failed to take into account that Western Jewry, the pool from which he expected leadership and money to come, was not prepared to rally behind the idea of a return to the Holy Land. Indeed, many of these Jews were still involved in a struggle for civic equality or were already assimilated. If concerned about their coreligionists, Western Jewish resources were largely directed toward philanthropic causes and the improvement of Jewish conditions in Eastern Europe and elsewhere in the Jewish Diaspora. Sir Moses Montefiore, in many ways, exemplified the thinking and philosophy of the philanthropic Jewish leaders of the West. Churchill's call for a mass political movement clearly ran counter to Montefiore's belief in the merits of quiet diplomacy by prominent individuals as the best way to achieve the restoration of the Jews in Palestine.

It was therefore not surprising that Montefiore failed to respond to Churchill's letter, and instead passed it on to the Board of Deputies of British Jewry without comment. While the board considered the matter, the great opportunity for a Jewish revival slipped away. In November of 1840 Sir Charles Napier concluded an agreement with Mohammed Ali, which was later ratified by the London Conference (January 10, 1841). Under the terms of these pacts, the fates of Syria and Palestine were sealed. Both areas were evacuated by the Egyptian army and returned to Ottoman rule.

Unperturbed by his failure to win over Montefiore and by the course of events, Churchill began to consider new schemes to stimulate Jewish interest in Palestine. In his new posts as assistant adjutant general, and soon thereafter as British vice-counsel in Damascus, he frequently extended protection to Jews. His efforts on behalf of the Jews irritated the Turkish administration, who were already smarting from Churchill's charges that the pasha and his minions were corrupt. The pasha countered by vilifying Churchill's character, and by organizing a well-orchestrated campaign to depose him from his post. A board of inquiry called to investigate Churchill's conduct found no wrong doing and cleared him of all allegations. However, soon after the conclusion of this unsavory affair he returned to England.

Never one to give up a fight easily, Churchill again tried to interest Montefiore in his Jewish restoration schemes. In a letter to the Jewish philanthropist dated August 13, 1842, he enclosed a document addressed to the Jews of Europe, in which he set forth his views on the status of Syrian and Palestinian Jewry. After briefly describing the deplorable and precarious conditions under which these Jews of the East lived and the outrages committed upon them and their property, for which no redress was possible, Churchill posed a rhetorical question. Were the instructions sent out to British consuls in the East authorizing them to receive any complaints made to them by Jews and to forward such charges to Constantinople, a sufficient guarantee for their peace and security? And if not, what could be done to strengthen the work of the consuls. Churchill's answer was simple and straightforward. He proposed that the Jews of England, jointly with their brethren on the continent of Europe form a committee and petition the British government to accredit and send out a person to reside in Syria or Palestine for the sole purpose of representing and watching over the Jews residing in that region. The duties and powers of such an official to be a matter of agreement between the secretary of state for foreign affairs and the committee of Jews conducting the negotiations with the British government. The benefits of such an arrangement would accrue to the Jewish nation at large. The spirit of confidence in the breasts of Jews all over the world would be raised if an acknowledged agent for the Jewish people resident in Syria and Palestine operated under the auspices and sanctions of Great Britain. This would also go far to remove the fear of the insecurity of life and property that has rested so long on the Jewish residents of Syria-Palestine, which the British consulates, burdened by other duties, could not alone resolve.

The key element in Churchill's plan was his concept of a Jewish Committee that would be recognized as an equal partner with the British government in matters of vital concern to the Jews. He was convinced that such an alliance would inevitably lead to a Jewish restoration in the Holy Land. It was, in a way, a diplomatic device for getting around the terms of the London Conference which had restored Syria and Palestine to the Ottoman Empire.

Shortly after the dispatch of his letter and memorandum to Montefiore, Churchill left England for the East. He had previously married a young widow in Damascus and had decided to make Syria his permanent home. Before departing from the British Isles, he met with Montefiore, who entrusted him with another mission on behalf of the Jews of Damascus. Incredibly, on this occasion as well, the philanthropist made no attempt to discuss Churchill's memorandum. Montefiore again passed on the document for review to the Board of Deputies of British Jewry. The board, more concerned with civil rights than restoration in Palestine, was at a loss on how to respond to Churchill's proposals. After considerable hesitation, the board members sought to escape their dilemma by enacting a resolution that straddled the issue. They resolved that, in their opinion, great benefits could arise from the realization of Churchill's plan, but that any measure in reference to the subject should emanate from the general body of Jews throughout Europe. If the latter favored the proposition, Great Britain's Jewry would be prepared to throw their full support behind their European counterparts.

On January 8, 1843, the secretary of the Board of Deputies formally notified Churchill of their resolution. Although the board had not outright rejected his proposals, it was obvious to Churchill that his plan was a dead letter. Disillusioned and keenly aware that without the backing of respected leaders such as Montefiore, he had no way of reaching the Jewish masses, Churchill accordingly surrendered his vision of becoming an instrument for the restoration of the Jews in Palestine. He compensated for the loss of his dream by focusing his attention and considerable energy on the aspirations of ancient Israel's neighbors to the north in Lebanon and Syria.

An astute political observer, Churchill sensed that another storm against Turkish rule was brewing, and that its epicenter would be the region around Mount Lebanon. It would begin, he felt, as a clash between the two main segments of the population that inhabited the area, the Christian Maronites and the Druses. The Druse, inferior to the Maronites in number but superior in courage, prudence, and military and political skills, were friends of the Turks only as long as the latter helped them maintain ascendancy over their Christian rivals. Churchill was strongly attracted to the Druse (nominally a Muslim sect that had broken away from the mainstream of Islam in the eleventh century). He decided to live among them, and to actively participate in their affairs. He bought a small village (Bihwarah), 8,000 feet above sea level, on the slopes of Mount Lebanon, and erected a permanent residence there. He changed his name to Sharshar Bey and adopted completely the ways and customs of his new homeland. Living among the residents of Lebanon, linked to them by his own marriage and those of his children, and speaking their language, Churchill became a trusted counselor and military advisor to the local sheiks.

A brilliant organizer, as well as first rate soldier and diplomat, Churchill played a prominent role in improving the educational system of the region, and was personally responsible for the establishment of a number of schools. In addition, he embarked on a literary career which made his name known throughout Europe. His book, *Mount Lebanon*,[214] aroused the fears of the Turkish and the British governments. Both regimes were apprehensive about Churchill's thesis that the Ottoman Empire would eventually lose its Asiatic possessions, and that the region dominated by Mount Lebanon would either come under British control or form part of an independent state.

In the late 1860s Churchill's dire predictions on the political instability of his adopted homeland became a reality. The intense rivalry between the Christian Maronites and the Druse erupted into open warfare. Churchill, fearing that the larger Maronite population would attempt to exterminate their Druse neighbors, tried to use his influence on behalf of the Muslim sectarians to defuse the conflict. However, when the Druse, with the aid of Turkish officers, gained the upper hand in the fighting and exhibited an increasing lust for power, Churchill became disenchanted with his former favorites. This feeling intensified when the Druse began to disarm and slaughter the Christian population. In spite of the prestige of his name and his reputation as a friend to all the peoples of the region, Churchill was unable to stem the rising tide of hatred and bloodshed.

By July of 1860 the fighting had become a full-fledged religious war that had spread to Damascus and other Syrian cities. Scenes of horrible massacres became commonplace. Thousands of innocent people were murdered, mutilated, or violated. Churchill, living in the midst of this carnage was shattered by the brutal acts of inhumanity that he had witnessed. Although his earlier admiration of the Druse had undergone a radical change, he remained reluctant to pass judgment on either of the parties involved in the conflict. Instead, he accused the Turkish administration of instigating the Druse to disarm and murder the Christians. In a book entitled *The Druse and the Maronites Under the Turkish Rule from 1840–1860*,[215] Churchill told the story of the bloody sectarian war and of the ominous part played in the conflict by the Turks. During this period, Churchill also began work on what would be his last major literary creation. It was a biography of the Algerian sultan, Abdel Kader, who had distinguished himself in the Druse-Maronite struggle by saving 15,000 Lebanese Christians from certain death at the hands of their traditional foes. Two years after the publication of *The Life of Abdel Kader*,[216] Churchill died (February 2, 1869) in the home that he had built in Bihwarah. The fact that Colonel Churchill, for the last three decades of his life did not, except for brief allusions in his writings, return to his former favorite theme of a Jewish restoration in Palestine, remains a mystery that has never been adequately explained. With the passage of time, Churchill's pro-Zionist efforts were forgotten by Jew and Gentile alike.

19

Other English Restorationists

George Gawler and Son John Cox Gawler

Colonel Churchill's advocacy of Jewish restoration was emulated by his fellow countryman, George Gawler. Soldier, pamphleteer, and administrator, Gawler fought hard to convince the British government to adopt a policy favoring the establishment of Jewish colonies in the Holy Land.[217] Educated at the military academy of Great Marlow, Gawler entered the British army at the tender age of fourteen. He served with distinction with a light infantry regiment in the Spanish Peninsular Campaign and was wounded at Badajoz and again at San Munos. At the Battle of Waterloo, Gawler was awarded for gallantry in action and promoted to colonel. He would later claim that his regiment was largely responsible for Napoleon's defeat during this crucial battle.

In 1838 Colonel Gawler was made governor of the South Australian colony. Torn apart by dissension between the former governor and the resident commissioner of the South Australian Colonization Society, the colony had come upon hard times. Faced with internal administrative strife, a diminution in the colony's sources of revenue, and ever increasing expenditures Gawler was unable to extricate the settlement from its financial difficulties. In 1840 he was replaced by another governor.

Returning to England, Gawler devoted himself to religious and philanthropic causes, and in particular to the idea of restoring the Jews to their ancient homeland. In an effort to bring his views on the subject before the public he published in 1845 a pamphlet entitled *Tranquillisation of Syria and the East*. In this curious amalgam of religious and political themes Gawler argued strongly for the return of the Jews to Palestine, but expressed reservations against granting them sovereignty over the country because of strategic considerations. In his search for a permanent solution to the East's perennial unrest, Gawler, a patriotic Englishman, firmly believed that all interests would best be served if

Great Britain extended its influence over Syria and Palestine. By encouraging Jewish colonization of the region, Great Britain would gain a stable and loyal population on the vital lines of communication and trade to India.

To further popularize his views among Jews, Gawler accompanied Sir Moses Montefiore on his third trip to the Holy Land (1849) and tried to persuade the philanthropist to support the establishment of several Jewish agricultural settlements. Three years later the colonel was instrumental in the formation of The Association for Promoting Jewish Settlement in Palestine. This organization, in conjunction with the British consul in Jerusalem, helped train a small number of local Jews for agricultural work.

The colonel's son, John Cox Gawler, followed in his father's footsteps and in 1874 published a detailed plan for Jewish colonization of Palestine based on sound business and technological principles. His endeavors, like those of his father, to win Montefiore's financial backing for his scheme proved unsuccessful. A Hebrew translation of John Cox Gawler's plan inspired a small group of Jewish residents of Jerusalem in 1878 to follow his blueprint for establishing a settlement. Some six years earlier, members of this same group had purchased a strip of land near Jericho but had been compelled by the Turkish authorities to abandon their efforts to found a colony. The Turks had voided the land sale on the pretext that the purchasers were foreign subjects (they were mostly Hungarian Jews). In a second attempt to establish a settlement the group bought some land on the coastal plain near the sources of the Yarkon River, and founded a colony, which they named *Petah-Tikva* (Gate of Hope). The following year the colonists purchased additional land, and more Jews from Jerusalem joined the original settlers. The newcomers ignoring the warnings of the old-timers settled quite close to swamps infested with malaria-carrying mosquitoes near the Yarkon River. Inevitably, malaria took its toll and decimated the hapless settlers.

The original group of colonists also suffered great hardships. Their buildings collapsed in the rainy season, and the local Arabs harassed them day and night. By 1881 conditions in the colony had deteriorated to such an extent that the settlers were forced to abandon the site. The very next year a new group of Jews returned to the area and bought land close to the Arab village of Yahud, in the vicinity of Petah-Tikva. They succeeded in planting a colony that, in a relatively short span of time, expanded and recolonized Petah-Tikva. With funds provided by the Love of Zion movement and later by the philanthropist, Baron Edmund de Rothschild, the settlers were able to drain the swamps and eliminate the threat of malaria. The dream of creating a permanent Jewish settlement outside the walls of Jerusalem had become a reality.

At about the same time as Colonel Gawler and his son were thinking and planning a Jewish restoration in Palestine, other Englishmen were entertaining similar ideas. Outstanding among these Englishmen were Reverend Thomas Crybace Tully and a colonial official named Edward L. Mitford. The reverend helped popularize the concept of Jewish redemption throughout England. In a stirring address to a London audience in 1884, Tully proposed the immediate formation of a British society to promote the restoration of the Jewish nation in Palestine. Although his suggestion was well received, the society never materialized.

Edward L. Mitford's Levant Plan

Less vocal but far more realistic and politically aware than most of his contemporaries among the restorationists, was the seasoned traveler and civil servant, Edward L.

Mitford. An adventurous soul, Mitford had, during the years 1839–42, journeyed over 7,000 miles on horseback from Trieste to India. He was also thoroughly familiar with North Africa and the Levant. While a resident of Morocco he had become conscious of the cruelties and outrages endured by the Jews in Muslim lands. In a pamphlet published in 1845 entitled *An Appeal on Behalf of the Jewish Nation in Connection with British Policy in the Levant,* Mitford described in great detail the pitiful status of the Jews in the Barbary states and suggested a possible solution to the Jewish Problem.[218] Like British restorationists before him, he advocated the reestablishment of the Jewish nation in Palestine as a protected state under the guardianship of Great Britain. After the national spirit of the Jews as well as their institutions had sufficient time to develop, British tutelage could be withdrawn and the people allowed to govern themselves within an independent state. Such a polity would not only prove beneficial to the Jewish people who would again rejoin the nations of the world on an equal footing, but would also prove of immense importance to British strategic and political interests. The policy would go a long way toward restoring the balance of power in the Levant and assure Great Britain uninterrupted communication with her possessions east of Suez.

If Great Britain would not act to bolster its position in the Levant, other nations would certainly fill the power vacuum. Russia, for example, had already greatly increased its influence in the region, and was threatening British interests.

According to Mitford's reasoning France also posed a serious challenge in the region to Great Britain. Any incident that might arise to disturb the existing state of affairs in the Levant would, he felt, endanger communication with India. Certainly, Mitford stressed, England could not depend on Turkey to protect its interests in the East, for the Ottoman Empire was in a state of disintegration. Furthermore it was ridiculous for a power like Great Britain, upon whom so many nations depended on for their peace and security, to allow one of the most vital arteries of its system to remain at the mercy of enemies or doubtful friends. England had to take steps to safeguard its own interests. Mitford was certain that the best way to attain this objective in the Levant was to insert into the region a people united by religion and nationality and possessed of sufficient good sense to act under good counsel. The reestablishment under British guidance of a Jewish nation in Palestine would not only provide England the means it needed to preserve its national interests, but would also provide a commanding position to check the encroachment into the region of enemies. Was Mitford's plan feasible or just the musings of an individual with a fertile imagination?

Mitford was convinced there would be little difficulty in persuading Turkey to cede the territory (Palestine), required for implementing his plan. He was not adverse, if Turkey objected, to forcing the Sublime Porte to relinquish the necessary territory because the advantages that would accrue, he believed, were vital to civilization and humanity.

What boundaries should the new polity have? Mitford felt that the question did not require an immediate answer, but nevertheless suggested the following demarcations. In the north a line could be drawn beyond the town of Acre from the vicinity of the waters of Merom to the sea coast. On the east, the boundary line could parallel the eastern bank of the Jordan River, the lake of Tiberias, and the Dead Sea. To ensure the security of the border against attacks by predatory Arabs, a chain of small forts could be established along the entire eastern boundary line. The coastline of the Mediterranean Sea extending to the Gulf of Suez would form the western border of the territory. To further secure these boundaries and to bolster the economy of the entire region, Mitford proposed the development of port facilities at El Arish, Gaza, and Jaffa. He also recommended the construction of a railroad to connect the ports.

Unlike most restorationists, Mitford gave serious consideration to the thorny problem of what should be done about the existing population of Palestine—the Arabs and Turks. He noted that most of the Turks had fled the country following its conquest by Ibrahim Pasha, and that the Arab population was basically nomadic. In addition, a deep antipathy existed between the Arabs and the remaining Turks. All of these elements, Mitford felt, lent themselves to his proposed solution of the Jewish Problem. Nevertheless, certain factors had to be carefully considered before any action could be taken. It would be foolhardy to foist a large body of strangers on the existing population without preparing the ground for such an operation.

The Ottoman regime, Mitford suggested, might be persuaded to have the Moslem inhabitants of Palestine removed to neighboring regions of the Empire's extensive Asian territories. As an inducement, the transplanted population could be given tracts equal, or far superior to the lands they had been compelled to abandon. Although a rather arbitrary proposal by Western standards, Mitford felt it was not inconsistent with the manners, customs, and traditions of the East. The proposed move would pose little hardship for the nomadic population of Palestine, the Bedouins. Mitford, however, recognized that the Christian Arab population might present a problem. They were scattered in several towns, with heavy concentrations in Bethlehem and Nazareth. To overcome this possible source of conflict, which could seriously impede a peaceful settlement of the Jews, Mitford suggested that the Christian powers had an important role to play. As the traditional protectors of Christian institutions, their influence was considerable. On one point, however, Mitford was adamant: that churches and convents were not to be permitted to acquire more property in land than they already possessed, and whether ecclesiastical or civil, all were subject to the laws that might be framed by the new state.

A stickler for detail, Mitford also addressed the question of the forces that would be required to protect the new entity's frontiers and to maintain internal order. After acknowledging that he was not a military expert, the sagacious civil servant, drawing from his experience, suggested that three regiments of infantry, two of cavalry, and some artillery units would probably suffice to protect the borders and keep the peace. He also recommended that the country be divided into three military provinces—northern, midland, and southern. The northern province, with its headquarters at Acre, would have military detachments stationed at Tiberias, Nazareth, and Jenin; the midland province, with its headquarters in Nablus, would assign detachments of troops to Jaffa, Jerusalem, and Jericho; the southern province, with headquarters at Hebron, would have units stationed in Gaza, El Arish, and along the Red Sea. In addition to the deployment of these units, Mitford suggested that an armed steamer be used to patrol the Dead Sea, and that the Bay of Acre serve as a station for the British Mediterranean fleet.

Although Palestine was mostly barren and desolate, Mitford was convinced that the Jews would be able to successfully restore the land to its original fertility. He strongly believed that once the country was settled by the Jews, agriculture and commerce, no longer under the thumb of corrupt Turkish officials, would flourish. In time, with judicious encouragement by their British protectors, the Jewish entity might come to monopolize the trade of the entire Levant, and even compete with Russia on its own southern frontier.

In summing up his arguments for a restoration of the Jews in Palestine, Mitford did not neglect the humane aspects of his plan. The Jews, he observed, in all parts of the world had kept their attention and hopes fixed on Palestine and would eagerly embrace the opportunity, if offered, to return to their ancient homeland. Their gratitude to the nation that helped them gain this objective would be unbounded. As the instrument for such a restoration Great Britain would also greatly benefit—commercially, strategically, and morally. Most importantly, restoration would provide a bulwark against further encroachment by England's enemies into this vital corner of the Levant.

Mitford's pamphlet proved to be a prophetic document. The author had uncannily anticipated the Balfour Declaration of 1917, the British Mandate over Palestine following the conclusion of World War I, and the eventual emergence of a Jewish state.

Edward Cazalet

The issue of Jewish colonization of Palestine was also conspicuously thrust before the British public as a result of a vigorous campaign waged by the industrialist and economist Edward Cazalet (1827–83).[219] While engaged in business ventures in Russia, he came in contact with Jewish workers. Shocked by the conditions under which they labored, their lack of civil rights, their grinding poverty, and the recurring pogroms and constant persecutions, Cazalet decided to devote his energies to finding a solution to the Jewish Problem. He was quick to recognize the potential of Palestine as a possible refuge for the Jews of Eastern Europe, and the political, economic, and strategic importance of the region for Great Britain. Having reached this conclusion, Cazalet in his correspondence, speeches, and personal contacts advocated a Jewish mass settlement in Palestine under British sponsorship and protection. His views commanded public attention and received wide circulation in 1879 following his publication of a pamphlet entitled, *England's Policy in the East: Our Relations With Russia and the Future of Syria.*

When Cazalet came to the realization that the British government was turning a deaf ear to his proposals, he decided to change his tactics. In 1881 he sent his agent James Alexander to negotiate directly with the Turkish regime for a concession to build a railroad from Syria to Mesopotamia. Alexander was also instructed to arrange for the purchase of land adjacent to the route of the proposed railroad. Cazalet's intention was to employ Jews in the construction of the railroad, and then to settle them along the right of way following the completion of the transportation system. The negotiations with the Turks dragged on for years without any tangible results. Finally, in 1883, the talks were abruptly terminated when Great Britain consolidated its control over Egypt.

The Palestine Exploration Fund

The efforts of various English advocates of Jewish restoration in the Holy Land were greatly aided by the voluminous literature on Palestine that came into being during the second half of the nineteenth century. Outstanding in this regard was the work of the Palestine Exploration Fund. Established in 1865, the Fund was dedicated to exploring the land and historical background that had produced the Bible. In 1867 the Fund sent Charles Warren (1840–1927),[220] a lieutenant in the Royal Engineers, to Jerusalem to conduct archaeological soundings in an attempt to determine the exact locations of the ancient Jewish Temple and the Holy Sepulchre. In the years that followed, the Fund supported numerous studies, field surveys, and archaeological digs throughout the Holy Land (e.g., at Jerusalem, the Shephelah, Gezer, and Beth Shemesh). It also produced the first modern map of Palestine, and added greatly to the store of knowledge of the region's topography, geology, anthropology, and archaeology. Among the many personalities who contributed their talents to the work of the Palestine Exploration Fund were the cartographer and orientalist Claude Reignier Conder (1849–1910),[221] a staunch supporter of Zionism; Horatio Herbert Kitchener (1850–1916), a future British field marshal; the archaeologist Leonard Wooley (1880–1960); and Thomas Edward Lawrence (1888–1935) who would achieve fame for his exploits in World War I as Lawrence of Arabia.

Some of the Fund's explorers, notably Warren, Conder, and Lawrence, would also publish personal and less formal accounts of their discoveries and experiences. In Warren's treatise, *The Land of Promise: Or Turkey's Guarantee* (1875), the author actually anticipated many of the ideas of Theodor Herzl, the founder of the modern Zionist movement. He proposed, for example, the colonization of Palestine by the Jews under the auspices of a British chartered company that would in turn compensate Turkey by assuming a portion of the latter's national debt.

Benjamin Disraeli

English advocates to restore the Jews to Zion were not limited to theologians, military men, civil servants, and adventurers. The idea also attracted a few members of the literati. Into this category one must place Benjamin Disraeli (1804–81),[222] whose writings contain some allusions to the restoration of Israel. One of the most exotic figures to reach the summit of British politics, Disraeli was also a prominent novelist. His father Isaac D'Israeli, the scion of a Sephardic family of Italy, was a historian and essayist of some note who, early in life, had turned his back on commerce to devote himself entirely to literary pursuits. Following a dispute with the Bevis Marks Sephardi synagogue (he had refused to serve as a warden and had been fined), Isaac resigned as a member of the congregation. Convinced that his daughter and three sons would have a better prospect of advancement in life if they were Christians, he had them baptized as Anglicans. Benjamin, the eldest, was thirteen years old at the time.

At the age of seventeen, Disraeli was apprenticed to solicitors in London and a few years later entered Lincoln's Inn. After a series of unsuccessful business ventures, including an abortive attempt to publish a newspaper, he turned to literature. He wrote several satirical novels on English society. His 1826 novel, *Vivian Grey,* attracted wide attention and gained Disraeli entry into London society where his eccentricities in dress, flamboyant manner, and other extravagances made him a conspicuous figure.

His health failing, Disraeli spent the years 1828–31 traveling in the East. He was fascinated by the Holy Land and in particular by Jerusalem. The impressions gained during this journey would be reflected in his novels and later in the policies he pursued as a politician and statesman. The immediate literary harvest of Disraeli's wanderings was the novel *The Wondrous Tale of Alroy* (1833), a story about Jewish messianism in twelfth-century Persia. The hero of the tale, David Alroy (an actual historical figure) assures his followers that God had sent him to free the Jews from the yoke of Islam and to effect their ingathering in the land of their forefathers. He raises the standard of revolt, but his army is crushed in battle. Alroy himself is eventually murdered. Some critics believe that the novel symbolized a debate between Jewish nationalists and assimilationists. Whatever the case may be, it is interesting to note that the book, with its messianic overtones and theme of a Jewish restoration in Zion, would remain Disraeli's sole work dealing entirely with a Jewish subject.

Disraeli's social ambitions inevitably drew him into politics. However, his initial attempts to gain a seat in Parliament were unsuccessful. In the contest of 1835 he attacked the policies of the Irish patriot O'Connell who reciprocated with verbal abuse. Never one to take insults lightly, the fledgling politician challenged the son of O'Connell to a duel on behalf of his father, but nothing came of the affair. Throughout his public career, Disraeli never denied his Jewish roots. He saw no conflict between his Christian affiliation and Jewish ancestry, as he considered the former to be a further step in the development of Judaism.

In 1837 Disraeli's political fortune changed and he was elected to Parliament as a Tory from Maidstone, Kent, along with a Mr. Wyndham Lewis. His challenging, eloquent, and carefully crafted maiden speech resulted in a fiasco. His unusual attire and, above all, the enmity of the O'Connell faction robbed him of the leniency usually afforded new members of the House of Commons. Drowned out by the jeers and laughter he was not allowed to finish his speech. It was a cruel blow to his ego, but his natural ability and oratorical talents would soon gain the attention of friend and foe alike.

Two years after his election to Parliament, Disraeli married the widow of his late colleague, Wyndham Lewis, and was then free from the pecuniary problems that had marked his early years. During the entire decade of the 1830s, Disraeli continued to write and publish literary works. An acute political thinker, he also wrote trenchant essays on various aspects of government. In two of these tracts, *Letters from Runnymede,* and *Vindication of the English Constitution,* he spelled out for the first time his political ideology—a curious expansion of the conservatism enunciated by Bolingbroke and Burke in the previous century.

In 1841, after failing to receive a cabinet appointment in the Robert Peel administration, Disraeli became a member, and eventually the leader of a band of dissident conservatives known as the Young England Movement. This group favored policies tinged with a nostalgia for a mythical golden age harking back to a simpler period in British history. They dreamed of rallying the public around Crown and Church, under aristocratic leadership.

Having reached a plateau in what was proving to be a brilliant but unorthodox career, Disraeli fell back on his earlier calling as a writer of fiction. In rapid succession, he wrote three major novels, *Coningsby* (1844), *Sybil* (1845), and *Tancred* (1847), in which, in thinly disguised form, he promulgated the theories and programs of the Young England Movement. The third novel of the trilogy, *Tancred,* centers attention on an amalgam of ideas including Jewish messianism, Church of England Christianity, and old-fashioned imperialism. Jewish restoration of Zion is considered against the backdrop of the author's rather odd concepts of race and religion. The hero of the novel, young Lord Montacue, whose Christian name, Tancred, is significantly that of a famous knight of the Crusades, decides to go on a pilgrimage to the Holy Sepulcher. He is seeking spiritual inspiration and escape from the emptiness of his privileged position. The wisdom of the East is summoned to the aid of the bewildered occidental in the form of two characters, a Jew named Sidonia (who first appeared in Disraeli's novel *Coningsby*), and the Arab, Fakredeen. As Tancred's adventure proceeds, he discovers himself to be a "Hebrew" in every aspect except race. He falls in love with a beautiful Jewess and becomes involved in the political intrigues of the Levant. Tancred exhorts his Jewish friends to strive for a "Semitic" revival in Palestine. The task, he informs them, is to free the country from Turkish domination and make it an independent nation in which Jews will share power along with Muslim and Christian Arabs. Through the character of Tancred, Disraeli is voicing his belief that all of these people belong to the same race. As one character explains, Arabs are only Jews on horseback, and Jerusalem will remain the appanage of Israel or Ishmael, either one, but not anyone else, having a right to sit upon the throne of David.

How could the goal of a Semitic restoration in Palestine be accomplished? Disraeli, speaking through his characters, outlines a fantastic scenario. First, the French must be kept out of the region. Their attempt, starting with the Crusades, to force themselves on the people of Syria-Palestine was without racial or moral justification. So far out of sympathy with everything Semitic was the French nation, that in its great revolution it even attempted to discard the Judeo-Christian faith. Tancred, who dreams of a theocratic form of government for Palestine, is informed by his Arab friend, Fakredeen, that everything is possible if the English would only recognize their own interests in the region. Fakredeen suggests a threefold alliance involving the ambitious ruler of Egypt, Mohammed Ali, the Arabs, and the British. Ali would seize Mesopotamia and the Arabs would take care of Syria and Asia Minor. The Queen of England would, at the same time, muster all her resources to aid her allies. This could best be achieved by transferring the seat of her government from London to Delhi, where there already existed a first-rate army and large revenue sources. For her assistance, the allies would acknowledge the queen of England as empress of India.

Although in his book *Tancred,* Disraeli expressed Jewish aspirations for a rebirth in Palestine, it was tempered by his racial theories, his unusual concept of Judaism in relation to Christianity, and his desire to expand the British Empire. His outlook on Judaism, in particular, was reflected through a distorting lens that allowed him to adhere to the Anglican faith and still have pride in his Jewish ancestry. It also enabled him to stress, as he did so often in *Tancred,* that Christianity was an offshoot of Judaism, and that the laws and institutions of Western society were based on moral values derived from Hebrew roots.

Following the publication of his trilogy, Disraeli returned invigorated to the political fray. With Prime Minister Robert Peel's resignation in 1846, Disraeli emerged as one of the shining stars of the protectionist wing of the Conservative Party. Two years later he assumed the leadership of the party. That same year (1848) Baron Lionel de Rothschild was elected to Parliament, but was not permitted to take his seat because he refused to take the required oath, which was offensive to a professing Jew. Disraeli strongly supported Rothschild's fight to be seated, even though Rothschild belonged to the opposition party. Curiously, Disraeli's position on this issue was not dictated by tolerance, but rather by his firm conviction that European civilization owed Jewry a special debt, because many European institutions, laws, ethics and morals were derived from Jewish sources.

In his biography of Lord George Bentinck, Disraeli returned to his favorite theme of the link between Judaism and Christianity. He also attributed the preservation of Jewish vitality from ancient times onward to their natural conservative attitude toward religion, aristocratic privilege, and property—the very foundations of his own political philosophy.

The year of the publication of the Bentinck biography also witnessed the return of the Tory Party to power. Under Lord Derby, Disraeli was made chancellor of the exchequer (1852) and leader of the House of Commons. His first budget, in which he was forced to announce his party's abandonment of protectionism, led to the downfall of the Derby government and the formation of a coalition cabinet. During the second administration of Lord Derby (1858–59), Disraeli had another brief taste of power, and in June of 1866 he again was awarded the post of chancellor of the exchequer. The following year he proposed and carried through the Commons an electoral reform bill extending the franchise to the industrial classes, and in the process doubled the number of eligible voters. This so-called leap in the dark was in conformity with Disraeli's long-held view of establishing Toryism as a national and popularly based movement. At the retirement of Lord Derby, Disraeli became prime minister. Ironically, that same year he was defeated at the general election, largely because of the extension of the suffrage that he had worked so hard to put in place.

Some years later, in 1874, after a decisive Conservative victory, Disraeli again became prime minister. During the next six years he diligently applied the principles of government for which he had always stood. Disraeli tried to bridge the gap between capital and labor by social and factory legislation and strove to follow a foreign policy designed to restore to England the glory he felt had been eroded by previous administrations.

In Disraeli's mind India was the key to the success of the British Empire, and he set about securing the vital access routes to the subcontinent. Thus it was not accidental that a renewed interest in the Near and Middle East occurred during his tenure as prime minister. In November of 1875, six years after the opening of the Suez Canal, Disraeli purchased for Great Britain forty-four percent of the shares in the canal company from Mohammed Ali's grandson, the insolvent Khedive of Egypt. This audacious act was made possible by a loan of 4 million pounds sterling from the bank of Lionel de Rothschild, whose long struggle to sit in Parliament had been championed by Disraeli. Only after the canal shares had been purchased, did the prime minister seek parliamentary approval.

The plan of empire that Disraeli had outlined in his novel *Tancred* came one step closer in 1876 when he successfully ushered through Parliament a Royal Titles Bill officially proclaiming Queen Victoria Empress of India. The grateful queen reciprocated by making her prime minister a peer of the realm with the title of Earl of Beaconsfield. British interest in the Near East was further stimulated that same year by events within the Ottoman Empire. Insurrection against Turkish rule had broken out among the Christian population of Bosnia and Herzegovina and had spread to other parts of the Balkans. In Bulgaria the revolt had been suppressed with particular cruelty by troops of irregulars, and reports of atrocities had reached the British press. A public outcry arose, especially among members of the Liberal Party, who favored the people trying to break away from Turkish domination. Disraeli, whose Oriental policy was based on preserving the Ottoman Empire, sought desperately to minimize the newspaper reports of atrocities. However, when his rival William Ewart Gladstone emerged from retirement with a pamphlet entitled *The Bulgarian Horrors and the Question of the East,* the issue refused to fade away. Disraeli remained adamant, refusing to change his policy even when accused by the opposition that his inflexibility was the result of his "Judaic bias", i.e., his sympathies were with the Turks because they were traditionally tolerant of the Jews.

In April of 1877 the crisis reached a climax when Russia, in defiance of existing treaty obligations, declared war on Turkey. The following year Russian troops reached the gates of Constantinople, and it was widely assumed that Disraeli would enter the conflict to save the Turks. The wily prime minister managed to avoid actual combat, but instituted instead an aggressive policy designed to check Russian access to the Mediterranean Sea and thereby pose a barrier to the heartland of the Ottoman Empire. However, when the Russian forces had practically effaced the Ottoman Empire in Europe, and attempted to secure their gains by compelling the Turks to sign the hastily drawn up Treaty of San

Stefano (1878), Disraeli reacted swiftly. He sent the British fleet into the Dardanelles and Indian troops to Malta. These signs that Great Britain was prepared for an all-out war alarmed the Russians. A similar mobilization by Austria, who feared Russian activities in the Balkans, had the same effect. Both England and Austria now called for a convocation of the Great Powers to revise the Treaty of San Stefano. Realizing the futility of a wider conflict, the Russians suddenly gave in to these demands for a special congress and Berlin was chosen as the site for the proposed meeting.

At the Congress of Berlin, Disraeli again proved his diplomatic prowess. Russia was compelled by the assembled powers to modify the treaty it had imposed on the Turks. The Russians were permitted to annex the provinces of Bessarabia, on the Black Sea between the Danube and the Dniester deltas, and the Armenian districts of Kars, Ardahan, and Batum. Austria-Hungary received the right to administer the late Turkish provinces of Bosnia and Herzegovina, and Great Britain, by a separate convention with Turkey, assumed possession of the island of Cyprus.

The wishes of the Balkan peoples who were most vitally concerned with the decisions of the Congress were scarcely considered. Bulgaria was split into three parts, the northernmost section winning political independence, the middle section administrative autonomy, while the southern section was restored to Turkish control. For Rumania, Serbia, and Montenegro, the Congress of Berlin decreed complete independence, and the Greeks were permitted to add Thessaly to their diminutive peninsular kingdom. Capping off their work, the Great Powers repeated their solemn determination to respect and to preserve the territorial unity of the Ottoman empire (literally, what remained of it).

Disraeli also supported the inclusion into the treaty that emerged from the Congress of Berlin a clause granting rights to the Jews of the newly created Balkan states. Some historians have also attributed to the prime minister the authorship of an anonymously published memorandum, intended for submission to the congress, proposing the creation of a Jewish state in Palestine. Current scholarship, however, tends to believe that Disraeli was not the author of the memorandum. The document itself was never circulated to all of the delegates of the congress because of the opposition to the proposal of a Jewish state by the German Chancellor, Bismarck, and the Austrian foreign minister.

The Berlin Congress was the climax of Disraeli's career. The years that followed brought new crises in Africa and Central Asia and finally saw the defeat at the polls of the Conservative party (1880) and the resignation of the Disraeli government. Gladstone was returned to power as prime minister, and Disraeli, now in his late seventies, knew there was little prospect of surviving his rival's administration. He resumed his career as a writer, completing the novel *Endymion,* a vivid portrayal of Whig and Tory politics set against the background of high society. Disraeli would retain his fascination with the political process to his death in 1881. Described by some of his contemporaries as "the old Jew gentleman sitting on top of the chaos", Disraeli, as a novelist and politician, was largely responsible for harnessing the turbulent political forces that marked the England of his day, and using them to convert Great Britain into a world power.

George Eliot

Although in his novels and politics Benjamin Disraeli frequently skirted the idea of a Jewish restoration in the Holy Land, a contemporary novelist, George Eliot (pseudonym of Mary Anne Evans, 1819–80), was more forthright. Eliot was destined to take her place among the great Christian precursors of the Zionist idea. Her books, *Adam Bede, Mill on the Floss, Silas Marner,* and *Middlemarch,* had established her reputation as a gifted writer, but it was her last novel, *Daniel Deronda*[223] that startled the literary world. For the first time in English fiction, Jewish figures were cast in a favorable light and as nationalists. In this ground-breaking novel, the author revealed an unusual insight into Jewish life and aspirations, and accurately forecast the force that Zionism would become in the near future.

Eliot's interest in Jewish subject matter went back to her youthful years when she had been fully in the grip of the evangelical fervor of the era. While still in her teens, she had begun compiling a chronological "chart of ecclesiastical history" designed to show, in parallel columns, the principal dates in the histories of Rome, Christianity, and Judaism from the birth of Christ to the Reformation. In 1846, while a professional translator of German, she had produced the first English version of David Strauss's *The Life of Jesus,* a pioneer work in historical criticism of the Bible. In the decade that followed, Eliot became intrigued by the Hebrew language and embarked on a serious study of the ancient tongue, under the tutelage of a Berlin-educated Jewish scholar named Emanuel Deutsch.

In 1869 Deutsch made a journey to Palestine that deeply stirred his emotions. Four years later, while again traveling in the East, he suddenly died. At the time of his death, George Eliot had already begun a novel whose contents were to a large extent modeled on the life and dreams of her Hebrew tutor, Emanuel Deutsch. Eliot, during the years preceding the writing of *Daniel Deronda,* had also greatly expanded her knowledge of Jewish history and was familiar with the renewed interest in Palestine resulting from the work of the Palestine Exploration Fund. She was also aware of the various agricultural experiments in the Holy Land undertaken by various Jewish groups (e.g., the founding of the Mikveh Israel Agricultural School in 1870), and of British sponsorship of similar enterprises. Agricultural settlements in Palestine owed much to a fellow countryman of Eliot, James Finn. Finn, a devoted friend of the Jews, was British Consul in Jerusalem from 1845 to 1862, and during his tenure in office actively promoted the idea of Jewish agricultural development. In 1852 Finn purchased twelve acres of land outside the walls of Jerusalem to be set aside as an industrial plantation for the employment of Jews. The project eventually failed and led to Finn's bankruptcy. A few years later the Jewish philanthropist Sir Moses Montefiore, emulating Finn's pioneer efforts, purchased land near Jerusalem, Jaffa, and Safed for the purpose of establishing Jewish agricultural and industrial settlements. By the time George Eliot had completed her novel, *Daniel Deronda,* the indefatigable Montefiore had made seven trips to the Holy Land. On each trip he provided assistance to the Jewish community or encouraged new projects to be undertaken.

Daniel Deronda first appeared in installments during the spring and summer of 1876. Its plot centers around two major characters. Young Daniel Deronda, one of the two protagonists is raised in the home of Sir Hugo Mallinger, whom he calls uncle, but knows nothing of who his parents were or of his Jewish descent. In love with the beautiful Mirah, Deronda is deeply moved by the Jewish learning and idealism of her brother Mordecai (a character based on Eliot's tutor, Emanuel Deutsch). As a result of his friendship with Mordecai, Deronda becomes absorbed in the study of Jewish life and literature, even before he learns the truth of his origins.

The sickly Mordecai, who has the qualities of an ancient Hebrew prophet, is imbued with the idea of Jewish national regeneration, but realizes that he is physically ill-equipped to bring such a mission to fruition. From his first meeting with Daniel Deronda, however, he is convinced that he has found the man to carry out his dream. Mordecai alone as the story unfolds, is convinced that Deronda is a Jew even before the latter learns of his origins. As for the mission that Mordecai has in mind, it is nothing less than the restoration of the Jewish people to the Land of Israel.

> There is a store of wisdom among us to found a new Jewish polity, grand, simple just like the old, – a republic where there is equality of protection. . . . Then our race shall have an organic center, a heart and a brain to watch, guide and execute; the outraged Jew shall have a defense in the court of nations . . . and the world shall gain as Israel gains. For there will be a community in the van of the East which carries culture and the sympathies of every great nation in its bosom; there will be a land set for a halting-place of enmities, a neutral ground for the East as Belgium is for the West.[224]

Deronda perceives that the mission outlined by Mordecai is most suitable in providing meaning to his search for a fulfilling life. Nevertheless, he is keenly aware that his education and his Christian upbringing have made it impossible for him to be like his orthodox grandfather. Only as a secular nonreligious Jew can he identify with his people and give his soul and heart to them. Accordingly, Daniel Deronda marries Mirah and resolves to travel to the East to become better acquainted with the conditions of the Jews in these regions. He intends eventually, just as Mordecai had visualized, to participate in the restoration of the political existence of his people, to make them again a nation with a national center in Palestine. As the novel ends, Mordecai dies and Daniel Deronda and his wife prepare for their journey to the East and the great adventure that lies before them.

Although Zionist sentiments were already afloat at the time of the publication of *Daniel Deronda,* George Eliot's novel kindled a new awareness and pride among the younger generation of Western Jewry. By an odd coincidence, Eliot's views also anticipated many of the ideas that would decades later be developed by the essayist Ahad Haam, the father of Cultural, or Spiritual Zionism, and by Eliezer ben Yehudah, the pioneer of the restoration of Hebrew as a modern language.

Great Britain, however, was not alone in producing Christian Zionists. Other nations also produced a number of individuals who, for a variety of reasons, advocated a Jewish return to the Holy Land. Among the many calls for such a movement were two that came from nations that were politically poles apart. The first originated in reactionary Czarist Russia; the second in Risorgimento Italy.

20

Russian and Italian Advocates of Jewish Restoration

$\mathbf{D}$uring the reign of Czar Nicholas I of Russia (1825–55), two Jews were condemned to death in Odessa because, from fear of the plague, they had attempted to escape across the frontier. At the last moment the czar commuted the death penalty and issued the following instructions to the jailers. "The prisoners are to run a gauntlet [of] 1,000 men, twelve times. God be thanked, that with us the death penalty has been abolished, and I will not reintroduce it."[225] In this barbaric land, a citadel of autocracy and reactionary policies, one would hardly expect to find people sympathetic to the Jews, or even rarer, Christian Zionists. Yet, in spite of an environment steeped in medieval practices and permeated with anti-Semitism, there were some individuals, who for a variety of reasons, favored the idea of an independent Jewish state. A rather unusual source for such a radical solution arose among some of the leaders of the Decembrists, a conspiracy of army officers and gentry who, following the death of Czar Alexander I and the assumption of power of his younger brother Nicholas I, attempted a coup d'etat.[226]

The Decembrists

The Decembrists (their revolt took place on December 26, 1825, hence the name of the movement) were following a course of action that had become commonplace in the preceding century. All Russian palace revolutions of the eighteenth century had been the work of the Guard, the elite regiments of the gentry class. Prior to the Napoleonic Wars members of this class had enjoyed a monopoly of Russia's contacts with Western Europe. After 1812, elements of the Russian army, including Guard units, spent years in Germany and France as part of an army of occupation. The conditions produced in France by the revolution were constantly discussed among the Guard units in the barracks, at mess, and around the camp fires. Comparisons were made to the situation in Russia (especially the total absence of personal liberty under the czars). By 1816 these informal discussions led to regular meetings of reform-leaning officers of the Guard under the chairmanship of Prince Trubetskoy, Colonel of the crack Preobrazhensky Regiment. The following year these officers formed the nucleus of a secret organization known as the "Society of Salvation."[227]

The prevailing voices in the society were those of Nicholas Turgenev; Nikita Muravyov, a high ranking staff officer; the poet Ryleyev; and Pavel Pestel. Turgenev was an eminent authority on taxation and a strong advocate of free trade and liberal reforms. He also favored the emancipation of the serfs, which he believed could best be achieved by the autocracy. However, if the latter proved unwilling or unable to carry out emancipation, Tugenev was ready to work with others who sought a more radical solution to accomplish the objective.

Muravyov and Ryleyev favored a constitutional monarchy for Russia, while Pavel Pestel, the most radical member of the society, advocated the elimination of the autocracy and its replacement with a republican form of government. Pestel was adamant that the removal of the czar and the establishment that supported him was essential as the first step in the introduction of a vast reform program that would include the emancipation of the serfs, land distribution, and the abolishment of all class distinctions.

In an effort to obtain public support for their ideas, the Society of Salvation decided to change its tactics. The original organization was abolished and replaced by a Society of Welfare, which stressed a more modest program of reform than its predecessor. However, this turnabout alienated some of the more radical members and led to increasing friction. With the posting of Pavel Pestel to military duty in southern Russia, the split between the radicals and the moderates widened and the Society of Welfare disbanded. There remained, however, intact two underground groups of the former organization in the army: the Northern Union headed by Muravyov and Ryleyev, and based in St. Petersburg; and the Southern Union based in Kiev and led by Pavel Pestel.

On December 18, 1825, Czar Alexander I died and, in the period of confusion that followed his demise the secret societies decided to act. Two thousand soldiers of the Guard regiments formed in a square outside the council of state in St. Petersburg shouting for "Constantine and Constitution." The troops were unaware that Constantine, a brother of Alexander I had abdicated in favor of Nicholas, a still younger brother of the late czar. Nicholas, shaken by the demonstration of the Guard soldiers sent the Governor-General of St. Petersburg, Miloradovich, to reason with the insurgents. Unable to persuade them, the governor-general turned to retire and was mortally wounded. At this point Nicholas gave the order to troops loyal to him to bring cannon up and to use them against the insurgents. Several volleys of grape cleared the square, putting an end to the coup d'etat. Nicholas I was quick to follow up on his initial victory. The leaders of the conspiracy were captured and tried. Five were hanged, and 120 exiled to Siberia or sentenced to life service in the ranks of the army.

In general, the attitude of the rank and file of the Decembrists toward the Jews reflected the xenophobic society in which they lived. The utter estrangement in language, religion, manners, and culture between Russians and Jews bred hostility and anti-Semitism. Educated Russians and, in particular, the military aristocracy looked with suspicion on the exclusiveness of Jewish life. Nevertheless, in formulating programs of reform for their country some of the Decembrists gave serious thought to possible solutions to the Jewish Problem.

Most interesting in this respect were the proposals of Gregory Peretz (1788–1855),[228] a converted Jew. The son of a prominent tax farmer, contractor, and ship builder, Gregory, through his father's connections, was on familiar terms with powerful court officials and was rewarded with an important administrative post in the czarist government. From 1820 to 1822 he actively participated in the Decembrist conspiracy. While a member of the secret organization he proposed a number of projects, including the establishment of a society for the liberation of the Jews of Russia and the rest of Europe. He suggested their resettlement in the Crimea or the East, where they could live as an autonomous nation. Following the failure of the Decembrist revolt, Gregory Peretz was imprisoned and banished to northern Russia, where he remained in exile for twenty years before being permitted to live in Odessa.

Nikita Muravyov, one of the leaders of the Northern Union also gave some thought to the Jewish Problem. In a constitution drafted for his group, he originally proposed granting political rights only to those Jews living within the Pale of Settlement. In a second draft he reconsidered his position and applied the principle of perfect equality without limitation as to residence. Unlike Gregory Peretz, Muravyov was not willing to opt for complete Jewish autonomy.

Pavel Pestel, the leader of the Southern Union, best articulated the views of the majority of the Decembrists towards the Jews.[229] He approached the Jewish Problem with the arguments of the typical anti-Semite. In a book entitled *Russian Truth,* he enumerated the peculiar Jewish characteristics that, in his opinion, rendered the Jews unfit for membership in the Russian social order. Pestel accused the Jews of fostering among themselves incredibly close ties that hindered integration with other nations. Their religion, he stressed, instilled in them a belief that they were an elect group, predestined to conquer all nations. The rabbis of the Jews, Pestel felt, wielded unlimited power over the masses and kept them in spiritual bondage (he no doubt based this conclusion on the Hassidic Tzaddiks, whom he had observed in Tulchyn, his Podolian place of residence). Lastly, he was convinced that the belief held by the Jews in the coming of the Messiah led them to regard whatever land they lived as a temporary residence, and inevitably led to a concentration on commerce rather than on agriculture.

In his analysis of the Jewish Problem, Pestel showed little awareness of life within the Pale of Settlement. He seemed totally blind to the perennial persecutions as well as the legal, economic, political, and social restrictions confronted by Russia's Jews every day of their lives. Amazingly, he considered the Jews a privileged class because they did not furnish recruits for the army (this would change radically under Nicholas I), enjoyed the prerogative of their own rabbinical tribunals, and the right to educate their own children.

After presenting this rather dismal portrait of Russian Jewry, Pestel suggested two possible solutions to the Jewish Problem. One resolution of the problem was to break up the unity of the Jews. To accomplish this objective, the Decembrist leader recommended a convocation of the most learned and influential rabbis and lay leaders who, after considering all ramifications of their people's situation, would adopt measures for eradicating Jewish exclusiveness (Pestel was evidently familiar with Napoleon Bonaparte's summoning of an Assembly of Jewish Notables and a Grand Sanhedrin).

The second possible solution to the Jewish Problem advocated by the Russian conspirator and revolutionist was to assist the Jews to form a separate commonwealth of their own in some portion of Asiatic Turkey. As a first step, Pestel suggested that it was essential that a rallying point be chosen for the concentration of Russian and Polish Jews. Once gathered at this site, such a mass of people could more easily overcome any obstacles that might be placed in their way. They would then proceed to leave the Russian Empire and to cross European Turkey into Asiatic Turkey (namely Palestine) and, having occupied an adequate area, form an independent state.

Pestel tended to favor the second of his solutions, and may have been influenced in this direction by the views of his fellow Decembrist, Gregory Peretz. The idea of an independent Jewish entity also bore striking resemblance to a proposal put forth by Gregory Potemkin, Catherine the Great's favorite field marshal. In 1784 Potemkin, then at the height of his power, formed a Jewish battalion known as the Israelovsky and envisaged the day that both Constantinople and Jerusalem would be wrested from the Turks, and the Jews restored to their ancient homeland.[230]

Benedetto Musolino

Unlike Russia, the Italian Peninsula, from the earliest of times, had a Jewish Diaspora, always small in number, and for most of its existence rarely persecuted. Moreover, Italy was a region in which the Jews, in the course of a history spanning more than 2,000 years, had never experienced a country-wide expulsion. When the Jews were forced by a local ruler to leave his city or territory, they were as a rule hospitably received elsewhere on the peninsula. Despite sometimes papal, and more rarely ducal, anti-Jewish measures, the relationship between Jew and Gentile was generally friendly. In this Catholic enclave and seat of the papacy, the church was less able to translate its anti-Jewish decrees into a reality of everyday life than elsewhere in Christian Europe. Even when the Inquisition was at its height, the Jews of Italy continued to live in relative security and peace. Nor did the Protestant persecution of Jews in Northern and Central Europe following the Reformation have any counterpart in Italy, which remained a Roman Catholic stronghold. This tolerant attitude toward the Jews made Italy a favorite place of refuge during the Middle Ages, and inspired in the Italian Jewish communities a cultural explosion of considerable magnitude during the Renaissance. However, beginning in the sixteenth century, especially after the ascendancy of Cardinal Caraffa to the papacy as Pope Paul IV, the position of the Jews began to rapidly deteriorate. The new pontiff introduced the strictest canonical restrictions, which crippled the Jews of the papal dominions economically and spiritually. In addition, Jews were confined within cramped quarters in ghettoes, and watches were set to regulate the closing of the gates at night and opening at dawn. No real estate could be owned by Jews and they were kept from the exercise of the professions; none but the meanest occupations remained open to them. In spite of these drawbacks, Italy's division into many states allowed Jews throughout the seventeenth and eighteenth centuries to find refuge in other areas of the peninsula where the ducal rulers were not willing, chiefly for economic reasons, to take the drastic measures enacted in the papal states.

Napoleon's conquest of Italy gave the peninsula the semblance of unity for a few years and broke down the ghetto walls. However, following the Congress of Vienna, Italy was again divided into several states, many of which were dominated by Austria or ruled by reactionaries who tried to wipe out the reforms introduced during the Napoleonic era.

The first half of the nineteenth century witnessed a rebirth of Italian nationalism spurred on by intellectuals, writers, adventurers, and statesmen, who pointed with pride to Italy's long history and traditions. The nationalistic movement that emerged had as its goals liberation from foreign elements and unification of the peninsula. The Risorgimento, as the movement was called, through the efforts of three men (Giuseppe Mazzini, Count Camille Benso di Cavour, and Giuseppe Garibaldi), succeeded in unifying the Italian Peninsula after a long and protracted struggle.

The philosopher, statesman, and author Benedetto Musolino (1809–85)[231] was an active participant in the march toward unification. Born in Pizzo, Calabria, he was exiled in his youth for his revolutionary activities. In 1861 after serving in Garibaldi's army, Musolino became a member of the special Italian parliament that was convoked in Turin, which would confirm Victor Emmanuel II as King of Italy. In later years, Musolino would represent his country as a senator.

During his long and active career, Musolino published seven books on philosophy, law, and social justice. He visited the Holy Land four times and predicted that the Jews, like the Italians had done, would eventually close their ranks and make their dream of returning to Jerusalem a reality. Musolino elaborated on this conviction in a work entitled *Gerusalemme ed il Popolo Ebreo* (1851).[232] Remarkably, the book anticipated many of the ideas later expressed by Theodor Herzl in *Der Judenstaat*.

Musolino, practical as well as visionary, suggested in his writings that Great Britain take the lead in supporting the establishment of a Jewish entity in Palestine under the Turkish crown. He also proposed a possible constitution for the new Jewish polity. Power would reside in a prince, assisted by a bicameral parliament. The official religion of the country would be Judaism, and the language of the land, Hebrew. The right to vote and run for office would be granted only to those individuals who could read and write Hebrew. All public offices, including judicial posts would be determined by elections, and all office holders would serve for one year. Citizenship would automatically be granted to all Jews settling in Palestine, and to non-Jews who requested citizenship in the Jewish entity. Freedom of speech would be guaranteed. In addition, compulsory education would be instituted for all children between the ages of four and sixteen. The right to work for all citizens of the principality would also be guaranteed. Lastly, polygamy was to be forbidden.

Benedetto Musolino's book calling for a Jewish principality in Palestine did not reach a wide audience, but his bold approach to the Jewish Problem was novel and prophetic. It spoke of things to come. Indeed, the broad range of Jewish activities that emerged in Western Europe as a result of the European Enlightenment and the French Revolution (e.g., the movement for civil rights, the Haskalah [Jewish Enlightenment], Reform Judaism, and Neoorthodoxy) together with the ever deteriorating position of the Jews of Eastern Europe tended to act as catalytic agents in producing champions of a Jewish national revival among the Jews themselves.

V

THE REBIRTH OF JEWISH NATIONALISM

21

In Victorian England

A staunch advocate of the need for a Jewish presence in Eretz Israel was Moses Montefiore (1784–1885), the most famous Anglo-Jew of the nineteenth century. His efforts on behalf of his coreligionists made him a legend during his own lifetime. The scion of a well-to-do Sephardi family, Montefiore was brought to England from Italy as an infant (he had been born in Leghorn while his parents were visiting the city). Everything about Montefiore seemed larger than life. He was tall with a massive physique and a formidable personality that matched his boundless energy. Montefiore was also extremely pious and enjoyed great wealth. Early on in his life he had amassed a fortune as a broker, largely through close collaboration with the English branch of the Rothschilds, to whom he was related by marriage. At the age of forty, after having become one of London's most successful financiers, he retired from business affairs to devote all of his time to communal and philanthropic work.

Moses Montefiore

In 1837 Montefiore became Sheriff of London, and was knighted by Queen Victoria. Less than a decade later he was made a baronet. Throughout these years Montefiore remained a strict Orthodox Jew, and actively participated in Jewish communal life. Indeed, in his capacity as president of the Board of Deputies of British Jewry (1838–74) he donated large sums to charity, pleaded with various officials and governments for Jewish civic rights, and took a special interest in the welfare of the Jewish community of Palestine.

Incensed by the eruption of violence against the Jews of Syria in the Damascus Affair, Montefiore led a Jewish delegation to Cairo to plead with Mohammed Ali, whose forces under the command of his son, Ibrahim, controlled Syria and Palestine. Soon after these talks the surviving imprisoned Damascus Jews were released, and further harassment of the Jewish community ceased. Not content with this accomplishment, and cognizant that Turkey, with Great Power help would soon regain control over Syria and Palestine, Montefiore traveled to Constantinople to seek an audience with the Ottoman sultan, Abdul-Medjid I. In the negotiations that followed, Montefiore obtained from the sultan a firman (the Hatti Sherif) pronouncing ritual murder charges a base libel on the Jewish people, and confirming the inviolability of Jewish people and their property in the Ottoman Empire.

In 1846 and again in 1872 Montefiore visited St. Petersburg, Russia. On both occasions he beseeched the reigning czars (Nicholas I and Alexander II respectively) to rescind the laws and edicts that pressed so heavily on the lives of their Jewish subjects. Similarly when news of the infamous Mortara forced baptism case reached England, Sir Moses hastened to Rome (1859) to plead with the Pope for justice.[233] The pontiff, Pius IX, refused to receive him and threatened the leaders of the Jewish community of Rome with retaliatory measures for having publicized the incident. This shameful affair, which riveted the attention of the world on the Papacy, involved the six-year-old son of a Jewish family, Edgardo Mortara, who had been forcibly taken from his parent's home in Bologna, at night, by papal agents. The stunned parents could only look on helplessly while their son was taken from them to be raised as a Christian. The pretext given for this dastardly act was that some years earlier, the child's Christian nurse, believing Edgardo to be on the point of death, had secretly baptized him. It made no difference to the pope that Montefiore and other prominent people as well as governments raised their voices in protest. He remained obdurate even to the pleas of the Catholic monarchs Napoleon III and Francis Joseph and is reported to have replied to his critics, ". . . that he snapped his fingers at the whole world."[234] Edgardo Mortara remained in the hands of his captors who systematically imbued him with hatred for Judaism, so that when he attained majority he refused to return to the faith of his parents.

The Mortara Affair reinforced Montefiore's conviction that Jews everywhere must stand together in the face of persecution and injustice. This belief was shared by many of Western Jewry's leaders and led to the establishment by French Jewry of the Alliance Israélite Universelle.[235] The goals of the Alliance were to ". . . work everywhere for the emancipation and moral progress of the Jews; to give effectual support to those who are suffering persecution because they are Jews; and to encourage all publications calculated to promote these ends."[236]

Montefiore, a firm believer in the principles outlined by the Alliance frequently extended his personal influence and wealth to help endangered Jewish communities. Thus when Montefiore learned of the harsh oppression under which 200,000 Jews of Morocco lived, he was outraged. Constantly harassed, poverty stricken, and demeaned, the Jews of this Maghreb state were forced to exist under medieval conditions. They could not marry without the sultan's permission, possess land or property outside the *mellah* (Jewish Quarter), or wear brightly colored clothes. The Jews also had to prostrate themselves before officials and present the sultan with costly gifts on the four major festivals of Islam and on occasions of birth or matrimony in the imperial household. In addition, they could not bear witness before a judge or raise their hands against a Muslim, even in self defense (except if attacked under their own roof). Lastly, they were compelled to carry their dead to the cemetery at a run and had to be within their quarter at sunset.

In 1863 Montefiore, despite his advanced age, traveled to Morocco to seek justice from the sultan after receiving word of a murder case in which Jews were condemned without evidence. The seventy-nine-year-old philanthropist was well received, and the sultan responded to his pleas by issuing an edict proclaiming the full equality of Jewish subjects in his realm. The sultan's pashas, however, paid little attention to their master's decree, and the condition of the Jews remained basically unchanged.

The situation of the Jews in Persia was strikingly similar to conditions in Morocco. Here the intolerant and fanatical Moslem sect of Shiites were all-powerful, and treated Jews and Christians alike with extreme contempt and cruelty. When reports of persecutions and atrocities from this region reached London in 1865, Moses Montefiore, who never turned down appeals from his coreligionists for help, at once made ready to journey to the East to petition the ruler, Shah Nazr el Din. The British foreign office, on learning of Montefiore's intentions, advised the elderly philanthropist not to undertake such a hazardous journey, but to allow his representations to be submitted through official channels by Great Britain's envoy to the shah. Montefiore agreed to this approach and his petition, which asked for an edict similar to that granted by the Ottoman sultan to his Jewish subjects was delivered to the shah. The latter, aware that the British government was solidly behind Sir Moses conceded to the requests made of him, and forbade further violence against his Jewish subjects.

When new complaints of oppression of Jews in Persia reached Montefiore following a severe famine that devastated the Shiraz and Isfahan regions, Montefiore made plans to set out for the troubled land. However, at the eleventh hour he was compelled to abandon his mission when informed by the British foreign office of an outbreak of guerilla warfare in the area, which threatened to engulf all of Persia.

In 1873 the Shah of Persia visited London, and a memorandum on the untenable position of the Jews in his realm was submitted to him. The ruler responded to the note with both oral and written assurances that he would take steps to improve the lot of his Jewish subjects. Except for the creation of a special commission to protect Jews (1878), the shah's promises remained unfulfilled.

Moses Montefiore's concern for his coreligionists also reached out to the beleaguered Jews of Rumania. Although Jews represented about ten percent of the country's population, they were considered aliens and were frequent targets of discrimination and violence. When Carol von Hohenzollern acceded to the throne of Rumania, Montefiore and the Franco-Jewish lawyer Adolphe Crémieux visited the country and attempted to persuade the new regent to grant the Jews civil equality with the rest of the population. In 1866, while the Rumanian government was considering the Jewish Problem, a fanatical mob attacked the parliament building interrupting the legislative session and threatening the deputies. The frightened legislators yielded to the mob's demands and voted against granting the Jews civil rights and against freedom of religion. Fired up by their triumph, the mob then ran wild through the city of Bucharest assaulting Jews and destroying synagogues. Some weeks later when Carol von Hohenzollern entered the city of Jassy he witnessed Jews being hunted down and assaulted. Nevertheless, neither the regent nor his government possessed the courage to condemn such behavior or to condemn the wanton acts of destruction that followed in the wake of the mob. The Rumanian government completely ignored Jewish complaints, and added insult to injury by acknowledging that the granting of Jewish rights was not on their agenda. Protests from the Great Powers that had helped create Rumania from the former principalities of Moldavia and Wallachia fell on deaf ears (the Rumanian government would not win recognition as a sovereign state until 1878, following the decisions of the Congress of Berlin). Ignoring all denunciations of their anti-Jewish actions, the Rumanian government continued to support a policy of anti-Semitism well into the twentieth century. Jews were denied basic civil rights, frequently attacked, beaten, murdered, and on one occasion forced at bayonet point across the Danube into Turkish territory. Montefiore and Crémieux's efforts to persuade the Rumanians to abandon their anti-Semitic policy, like those attempts made by the Great Powers, failed.

In spite of his activities on behalf of Jewish people everywhere, Palestine dominated Montefiore's thought and philanthropy. The name of Jerusalem was emblazoned on his escutcheon and was an outward expression of the profound spiritual bond that united him with Eretz Israel and its holy city. He was completely dedicated to the Promised Land with the fervor of a pious Jew. His deep faith pictured the desolate countryside as it would appear once the Jews returned to their ancient homeland to renew its soil with love and devotion. In furtherance of this conviction Sir Moses made seven trips to the Holy Land (the first in 1827 and the last in 1875). On most of these visits he was accompanied by his wife, Judith Cohen Montefiore (1784–1862), who shared her husband's belief in a Jewish restoration in Palestine.

During the period of Mohammed Ali's rebellion against the Turkish sultan, Montefiore formulated a plan to lease land from the Egyptian Pasha whose forces had overrun Palestine. He visualized the establishment of a colonization company that would be responsible for the large-scale settlement and cultivation of the leased lands by Jewish settlers. The leased land and the lease holder were to be free from all taxes. Montefiore was to have the right to send experts to educate, guide, and otherwise assist the Jewish settlers. Emphasis was to be placed on agriculture and viniculture and would include the planting of cotton, olives, grapes, and mulberry trees, as well as the breeding of sheep. Rental for the lease, which would run fifty years, was to be paid annually to the Egyptian ruler at Alexandria.[237]

Montefiore's proposal also embodied a provision ensuring special status and considerable autonomy for the Jewish settlers. This proviso, he felt, would encourage the Jews of Eastern Europe, the Balkans, and the Islamic world who were in need of a haven from persecution to flock to the Holy Land.

Economic benefits, Montefiore stressed in his negotiations with Mohammed Ali, would also accrue from the establishment of Jewish settlements in Palestine. Increased production brought about by the new immigrants would create additional revenue for the Muslim ruler and stimulate further economic growth. As an additional inducement for the acceptance of his plan, Montefiore offered to expand the credit system in Mohammed Ali's realm by establishing a joint stock bank with a capital of one million pounds sterling. The bank would also have branch offices in Alexandria, Cairo, Beirut, Damascus, Jaffa and Jerusalem.

Although Montefiore received oral assurances from Mohammed Ali that he favored the plan, the lease never materialized. Unexpectedly, military developments radically altered the geopolitical structure of the region. In 1840 Ali's son, Ibrahim, was encamped with his army on the coast of Lebanon when a British-Austrian fleet taking up the Turkish cause landed troops near Beirut. In the ensuing battle, Ibrahim's forces were defeated, compelling his father to come to terms with the Turkish sultan. The resulting pact of 1841 obliged Mohammed Ali and his son to abandon Syria and Palestine and withdraw their army to Egypt. The Turkish sultan and his administration were not interested in ceding or leasing any land in the recovered territories, no matter how small, to foreigners.

Disappointed by the Ottoman refusal to lease land, Montefiore decided to concentrate his efforts on helping the existing Jewish community of Palestine survive. He began by sponsoring a census of the Jews living in the Holy Land—the first such polling to be taken since ancient times. Having ascertained that about 6,500 Jews were residing in the land, mostly in Jerusalem, Sir Moses then set about improving their living conditions. At his own expense he sent a Jewish physician to Jerusalem, established a pharmacy, and planned a hospital (subsequently built by the Paris branch of the House of Rothschild). Montefiore also initiated a fund for the relief of famine victims, and during his 1855 visit to the Holy Land provided funds to assist Jewish families from Safed and Tiberias to resettle in rural areas. He also sought and obtained permission from the Ottoman authorities to purchase land outside the walls of Jerusalem. Four years, however, would elapse before the local authorities would allow Montefiore to build on the land he had purchased. His persistence finally prevailed, and a row of houses were erected for the Jewish poor just outside of Jerusalem's Jaffa Gate. The Jews who ventured to occupy the new quarter (it was called *Mishk'not Sha'ananim*) were considered hardy souls because the conditions of security made it dangerous to live outside the walls of Jerusalem.[238]

The need to improve the Jewish educational system of the Holy City also attracted the attention of Sir Moses. However, his very modest suggestions and plans for school reform met with the opposition of Jerusalem's Ashkenazi rabbis who feared that the changes would undermine their authority in the community. Although frustrated by the rabbinate's opposition, Montefiore did manage to establish a girls' school in which the students were taught home economics in addition to traditional subject matter.

In general all of Montefiore's efforts in Palestine were directed toward making the Jewish community more productive and self supporting. His 1849 visit was followed by the founding of a textile mill in Jerusalem. In 1855 he purchased an orange grove near Jaffa, and helped hundreds of Jews in the Galilee who were desirous of becoming farmers to acquire land. In 1874 Montefiore returned to his original idea of establishing new agricultural settlements in Palestine. He wrote letters to the rabbis and communal leaders of Eretz Israel outlining his plans, but received very little encouragement from these individuals. That same year Sir Moses retired as president of the Board of Deputies of British Jewry. In recognition of his years of dedicated service the Board established in his honor a testimonial fund and, in accordance with Montefiore's wishes, earmarked the sums raised for the construction of industrial and residential units in Jerusalem.

At the age of ninety-one, Sir Moses paid his last visit to Eretz Israel. His life long support of the Jewish community of Palestine encouraged other philanthropists to emulate his example. Judah Touro (1775–1854) of New Orleans was representative of this development. He bequeathed funds for the Jewish poor of Palestine, and made Montefiore joint trustee for the disposition of the monies. A portion of this benefaction was used in the construction of the new quarter outside the walls of Jerusalem. Similarly the pattern set by Montefiore was later followed on a larger scale by the Jewish philanthropists Baron Maurice de Hirsch (1831–96) and Baron Edmund de Rothschild (1845–1934).

In the closing years of Moses Montefiore's life, the Hibbat Zion movement (Love of Zion)[239] came into being and succeeded in founding a number of agricultural settlements in Palestine. As the hundredth birthday of the Anglo-Jewish philanthropist approached, the Lovers of Zion (Hoveve Zion), keenly aware that the event would be widely celebrated throughout the Jewish world, saw an opportunity to exploit the occasion for their own needs. They called for a special conference to honor Montefiore by founding in his name a society for the promotion of agriculture in Palestine. David Gordon, the editor of the Hebrew weekly newspaper *Ha-Maggid* (The Narrator), was dispatched to Montefiore's home in Ramsgate, England, to seek the philanthropist's blessing and support for the proposed society (Sir Moses had already made substantial contributions to the existing Hibbat Zion settlements). Gordon found Montefiore too feeble to be receptive to new projects, and his relatives and associates unwilling to allow the old man to assume additional responsibilities. Undaunted by this setback, the Lovers of Zion went ahead with their plans for the proposed convention. The Kattowitz conference[240] of 1884 that ensued (named for the city where the conference was held, at the junction point of the Russian, Austrian, and German empires) marked a turning point in the Love of Zion movement. The thirty-six delegates who attended the conference came from all over Europe and represented a wide spectrum of professions as well as a variety of religious and secular viewpoints. Most importantly, the group openly endorsed a policy of return-ing Jews to agriculture and the Jewish colonization of Palestine.

Eight months after the Kattowitz Conference, Sir Moses Montefiore passed away (July 25, 1885). He was buried on his estate at Ramsgate, beside his wife in a mausoleum that is a replica of the edifice on the Bethlehem road in Eretz Israel known as the Tomb of Rachel. Eighty-eight years later the remains of Sir Moses and his wife would be exhumed and reburied in Israel as a grateful state and people remembered and honored the great Jewish philanthropist and benefactor of Zion.

Abraham Benisch

Sir Moses Montefiore's mission to Egypt during the height of the Damascus Affair and his negotiations with Mohammed Ali kindled renewed interest in Palestine among a number of Jewish students in Western and Central Europe. When Adolphe Crémieux, who had participated with Montefiore in the efforts to obtain the release of the imprisoned Jews of Damascus, returned to France, he was presented with a project for Jewish colonization of Palestine by a young man named Abraham Benisch (1811–78).[241] Benisch had been raised in Drossau, Bohemia, and attended the University of Prague as a medical student. While in Prague he had written a commentary on Ezekiel, with a view to prepare himself spiritually for a journey to the Holy Land. In addition Benisch, in conjunction with two other students, Albert Löwy and Moritz Steinschneider[242] (the future great bibliographer of Judaica) organized a discussion group to consider ideas for restoring Jewish indepen-dence in Eretz Israel.

In 1836 Benisch decided to continue his studies at the University of Vienna. A popular student, he soon drew about him many admirers who were attracted by his ideas on Jewish nationalism. Eventually a secret society was formed among the students and Benisch was chosen to act as the group's spokesman and leader. His major responsibility was to visit Jewish communities to find support for the society's goal of initiating a Jewish restoration movement in Palestine. It was in this capacity that Benisch met with Crémieux upon the latter's return from Egypt.

Frustrated by Crémieux's lack of interest in his plans and by the lack of any visible progress among the Jewish community of France, Benisch, in 1841, with a letter of recommendation from the House of Rothschild, proceeded to London. He had come to the conclusion that the influential Anglo-Jewish community could best provide the political and financial backing essential for a successful revival in the Promised Land. Receiving no encouragement or assistance from the leaders of English Jewry, Benisch was forced to lay aside his plans to stimulate among British Jewry a revival of Jewish nationalism. In order to earn a living he turned to Jewish journalism and literature.

From 1841 to 1848 the disillusioned nationalist promoted his views in the periodical *The Voice of Jacob.* In 1853 seeking a wider audience Benisch founded a newspaper, *The Hebrew Observer.* The following year the *Hebrew Observer* merged with the prestigious *Jewish Chronicle* (still in existence), and Abraham Benisch became its editor. He would hold this position from 1854 to 1867, and again from 1875 until his death three years later.

As editor of the most important Jewish newspaper in England, Benisch used his influence to oppose all forms of assimilation. He took an active part in communal affairs and helped establish several learned societies, the Biblical Institute, the Syro-Egyptian, and the Biblical Chronological Society. Later these three entities were fused into the Society of Biblical Archaeology. During his long tenure as editor of *The Jewish Chronicle,* Benisch seized every opportunity to raise the question of a Jewish return to Eretz Israel. He collaborated with Charles Netter (1826–82), one of the founders of the Alliance Israélite Universelle, in establishing in Palestine the Mikve Israel Agricultural School – a first step toward the attainment of the hopes and aspirations of his youth. A few years later Benisch played a prominent role in the creation of the Anglo-Jewish Association and became its first director. During his tenure the association carried on an aggressive campaign for the rights of Jews in Russia and elsewhere in Eastern Europe.

A prolific writer, Benisch contributed weekly articles to *The Jewish Chronicle* during his tenure as the newspaper's editor. He also produced essays, articles, and books on religion, archaeology, politics, Jewish nationalism, travel, and bibliography. In many of his articles, and especially in those dealing with the deliberations of the Congress of Berlin, Benisch stressed Jewish restoration in Palestine as the ideal way of resolving the Jewish Problem. Fame and fortune had not in any way modified the convictions of his youth.

Adversely, the compatriot of his student days at the University of Prague, Moritz Steinschneider, who had shared the same Zionist dreams, underwent a complete change of heart. By 1842 he had completely broken his links with the Benisch circle, and had come to believe that the latter's goals were unrealistic as well as unattainable. With the passage of years the schism widened as Steinschneider became one of the foremost protagonists of Die Wissenschaft des Judenthums (the Science of Judaism), a movement of scholars and reformers dedicated to investigating every facet of Jewish religion, history, and literature. Steinschneider's catalogues of the Hebrew books and manuscripts in the libraries of Leyden, Berlin, Hamburg, Munich, and most important of all, in the Bodleian collection at Oxford University, marked a radical breakthrough in the field of Jewish bibliography. His work in this field led to the discovery of literary treasures whose very existence had previously been unknown. Similarly his research into Judeo-Arabic literature and Hebrew translations of the Middle Ages won for Steinschneider universal recognition as one of the great scholars of the nineteenth century. However, by the turn of the century, the great bibliographer was far removed from a belief in Jewish nationalism and was actually saddened when one of his students spoke to him of Zionist aspirations. Looking longingly at his collection of Jewish books he turned to the student and said, ". . . my dear fellow, it is too late. All that remains for us to do is to provide a decent funeral."[243] For Abraham Benisch such a belief was unthinkable.

Although a precursor of modern Zionism, Benisch is best remembered for his work as an editor, and for his contributions to Jewish scholarship. Most notable were his lectures on the life and times of Maimonides (1847), a translation into English of the Pentateuch, and a rendition into English of the travels and adventures of Pethahiah b. Jacob of Regensburg. Benisch also produced an elementary Hebrew grammar, a manual on scriptural history, a dissertation on Bishop Colenso's criticism of the Bible, and a volume tracing the development of Judaism from the time of Moses to the modern era. Capping off his voluminous writings are thirty-three letters that were published posthumously by *The Jewish Chronicle* under the title *Why I Should Remain a Jew.*

Abraham Benisch did not live long enough to witness the rise of Herzlian Zionism, and during his lifetime never considered himself to be numbered among those gallant souls who through the ages had strived for a Jewish restoration in Eretz Israel. Nevertheless, his pen earned for him a rightful place in the gallery of those individuals who fought tirelessly for Jewish redemption.

22

Rabbinical Nationalists

Jewish nationalism in its early phases drew much of its strength from the messianic aspirations of the Jewish people. It was therefore not surprising that among the first individuals in the nineteenth century to transform messianic fervor into a more contemporary framework were a handful of rabbis and scholars. Among the latter was Rabbi Judah Bibas (1780–1852),[244] the descendant of a long line of rabbinical scholars and physicians. The Bibas family originated in Spain and following the expulsion of the Jews in 1492 managed to find asylum in Morocco. Eventually, members of the family settled in Egypt and Palestine (Safed and Jerusalem), and in Europe (Leghorn, Amsterdam, and Gibraltar).

Judah Bibas

Judah Bibas was born in Gibraltar. He received a religious and a secular education and was apparently granted a doctoral degree by an Italian university. Between 1805 and 1832 he slowly gained a reputation as an outstanding scholar (during this period he resided in Gibraltar, England, and Italy). In 1832 Bibas was appointed Rabbi of Corfu, the northernmost of the Ionian Islands. At the time the island's Jewish community consisted of three distinct groups, Greek, Spanish, and Apulian. Acutely aware of these divisions and of the basic need for reform, Bibas attempted to reorganize the community along more modern lines. His efforts, however, antagonized many members of the community, creating a schism between those favoring reform and those anxious to keep the status quo. The reform party led by Bibas persisted in their demands for change and succeeded in improving the educational and philanthropic institutions of the community. The reform victory was short-lived because the traditionalists eventually regained control over the community's affairs. In spite of this setback, Bibas managed to retain his office. His interest in community affairs remained strong, but he attempted to escape the stifling insularity of his post by traveling throughout Europe. Deeply impressed by the upsurge of nationalism that he had witnessed among the peoples of the Balkans, Bibas felt that the time was now ripe for a Jewish nationalistic movement with Palestine as the final objective. He boldly proclaimed to all who would listen that Jews should learn to use arms so that, like the Greeks, they might take advantage of the nationalistic tide to regain sovereignty in their ancient homeland. Underpinning his thesis with quotations from the Pentateuch and the Talmud, Bibas stressed that the future of the Jews was dependent on their return to Eretz Israel, for God would only redeem them if they would make an effort of their own to reclaim the Promised Land. The Jews, he furthermore insisted, had to undergo a radical transformation of their traditional way of life if they were to achieve a restoration of their sovereignty. It was essential, for example, that they pursue secular as well as religious studies. Indeed, circumstances might even demand neglecting the sacred for the secular, ". . . for the Torah was like a normal diet for Jews, to be taken regularly when well, but the secular sciences were a medicine which they must take when ill."[245]

The nationalistic arguments of the Rabbi of Corfu found few supporters during his lifetime. By and large the Orthodox masses and their leaders continued to believe in a messianic redemption unaided by human hands. Worn out by his failure to convince his fellow Jews that a restoration in Palestine was possible, Bibas decided on aliyah. In 1852 he settled in Hebron, where he died shortly afterwards, a disillusioned man.

Yehudah ben Salamo Hai Alkalay

The nationalistic views expressed by Judah Bibas were elaborated and expanded on in the succeeding generation by the Sephardi rabbi, Yehudah ben Salamo Hai Alkalay (1799–1878).[246] Although born in Sarajevo (Bosnia), Alkalay was raised in Jerusalem. At the age of twenty-eight he became a reader and teacher in the Sephardi community of Semlin (Yugoslavia). Some years later he was appointed rabbi of the community and served in this capacity until 1874, when he emigrated to Eretz Israel.

Rabbi Alkalay's thoughts on Jewish nationalism were derived from such sources as the struggle of the Serbs for independence; the power struggle between the Austrians, Turks, and Serbs for control of Semlin; the theories of Judas Bibas, whom he had met and exchanged views when Bibas visited Semlin; and most importantly, from his interpretation of the the Bible and the Kabbalah. In the introduction to his first major work, a Ladino-Hebrew textbook entitled *Darkhei No'am* ("Pleasant Paths"), published in 1839, Alkalay adopted a revolutionary attitude toward redemption that was completely at odds with tradition. The concept of *teshuvah* (repentance), which according to the Talmud is the precondition for redemption, was seized upon by Alkalay and reinterpreted in a novel way. He noted that *teshuvah* was formed from the root word "shivah," which he felt indicated a return to Eretz Israel. He maintained that *teshuvah* really referred to personal action (*peratit*). Each man therefore, the Rabbi of Semlin declared, shall return from the path of evil according to the definitions of repentance outlined by the early talmudic sages. But the deeper meaning of *teshuvah*, Alkalay insisted, referred to *teshuvah ke lalit*, a general return of the people of Israel to the land of their fathers. Reinforcing his unusual interpretation of *teshuvah*, Alkalay took an even more radical step. He advanced the daring concept that redemption is primarily in the hands of man, and that natural redemption must precede supernatural redemption. These ideas aroused a storm of controversy among religious traditionalists, but in later years paved the way for participation of Orthodox elements in the Zionist movement founded by Theodor Herzl.

In a second book, which he called *Shelom Yerushalayim* ("The Peace of Jerusalem"), Alkalay attempted a rebuttal of his Orthodox critics. He also urged his readers to prepare for redemption, and pleaded with them to give concrete expression to their devotion to Zion by dedicating one tenth of their income (i.e., to pay a tithe) for the support of those Jews already living in Palestine. Alkalay's book *Shelom Yerushalayim* remained largely unknown, and was overshadowed by the outbreak of the Damascus Affair, which riveted the attention of the Jewish world. Stung by the affair's reminder of Jewish insecurity, Alkalay again urged his fellow Jews to strive to return to the Holy Land and not await the advent of the Messiah to achieve this objective. He saw in the Damascus ritual murder trial a symbolic turning point for the Jewish nation on its road to redemption. Alkalay viewed the affair as a clear danger signal intended by providence to arouse the Jewish people to their condition as exiles and as a last warning that they must leave the lands of the Diaspora.

The rabbi of Semlin was particularly encouraged by the united efforts made by Jewish notables from Western Europe to succor the victims of the Damascus Affair. Alkalay took the solidarity as another sign that Jewish restoration in Eretz Israel was now a distinct possibility. He gave expression to this feeling in a booklet entitled *Minhot Yehudah* ("The Offering of Judah"). Published in 1845, the work was a panegyric on the efforts of Montefiore and Crémieux on behalf of their Jewish brethren. It also contained an eloquent appeal for immediate action to hasten final redemption. Commenting on the biblical passage, "Return O Lord, unto the tens of thousands of the families of Israel . . . ," Alkalay rhetorically asked, ". . . upon what should the Divine Presence rest? On sticks and stones?" Replying to his own query, the rabbi stressed, ". . . therefore, [it is essential] that in the initial stage in the redemption of our souls, we must cause 22,000 to return to the Holy Land. This is the necessary precondition for a descent of the Divine Presence among us; afterwards He will grant us and all Israel additional signs of his favor."[247] In a manner reminiscent of Napoleon's Jewish edicts, Alkalay suggested the formation of an Assembly of Notables to serve as the interim representatives of the Jewish people. Organized as a joint stock company, the notables would strive to achieve international recognition to sanction the return of the Jews to Palestine. In a later work, Alkalay suggested that the Assembly of Notables should attempt to induce the Turkish sultan to cede Palestine to the Jews as a tributary territory, on a plan similar to that by which the Danube principalities were governed.

The notables would also be responsible for the rapid colonization of Palestine as well as for the promotion of agriculture, the creation of an army, and the revival of Hebrew as the national language. All of this work would be funded by a special tithe on Jewish incomes. Alert to the instability of the Near and Middle East, Alkalay expressed the hope that Great Britain would play a supervisory role in making his plan a reality.

In all of his writings, but most notably in *Sh'ma Yisrael* ("Hear O Israel," 1834) and in *Goral la-Adona* ("A Lot for the Lord," 1857) Alkalay buttressed his nationalistic arguments with ample quotations from the Bible, the Talmud, and the Kabbalah. He steadfastly insisted that self effort toward the physical and spiritual achievement of redemption was justified by the very proof texts of tradition. Had not the Kabbalah, for example, intimated that the struggle of Jewish common people everywhere would prefigure the coming of the Messiah? It was obvious to Alkalay that the final and supernatural redemption to be brought about by the Messiah must be preceded by the physical return of the Jews to Eretz Israel. The resettlement of the Holy Land, the cultivation of its soil based on biblical laws, even the rebuilding of the Temple were, in the rabbi of Semlin's view, initial stages prior to the arrival of the messianic age. For Alkalay these activities were duties that the Jews were obliged to carry out before the Messiah would come.

In addition to his writings, Alkalay sought to propagate his views through personal contacts with the leaders of various Jewish communities. He traveled extensively throughout Europe, and everywhere he visited he sought to establish societies for the Jewish colonization of Palestine. In 1860 Alkalay joined the Colonisation-Verein für Palästina, a society founded in Frankfurt an der Oder for the purpose of establishing large-scale agricultural settlements in the Holy Land. The guiding spirit behind the organization was Chaim Lorje (1821–78).[248] A doctor of philosophy, educator, and mystic, Lorje claimed descent from the famous sixteenth-century kabbalist, Isaac Luria. Kabbalistic speculation led Lorje to believe that the Messiah would arrive in the 1840s and that all Jews would be gathered into the Promised Land by 1860. When this hope failed to materialize, Lorje concluded that the Messiah would only come if all the Jews were pervaded by a fervent desire to return to Eretz Israel to reawaken its soil and to cleanse themselves of the impurities of the Diaspora. Subsequently to help achieve these objectives he founded the Colonisation-Verein für Palästina.

Although Lorje's society succeeded in enlisting the support of many Jews such as the rabbi of Semlin, it encountered strong opposition from the "old Yishuv" (the Jewish community of Palestine in the pre-Zionist period). The leaders of the "old Yishuv" feared that Lorje's organization would divert part of the charity funds (halukkah) received from abroad. In spite of this opposition, the colonization society managed to survive until 1864 when it disintegrated, largely as a result of Lorje's egocentrism. His adversaries in the society demanded that the headquarters be shifted from Frankfurt an der Oder to a larger Jewish community, and when Lorje objected the dissidents split away and established a new settlement society in Berlin. Other groups with similar goals soon came into being and Lorje's original society faded into obscurity. However, most historians agree that Lorje's creation played an important role in inspiring the growth of the Love of Zion movement in Western and Central Europe.

As a strong supporter for the creation of an international Jewish organization, Rabbi Alkalay welcomed wholeheartedly the founding in 1860 of the Alliance Israélite Universelle. However, when the Alliance proposed the establishment of an agricultural school in Palestine, he opposed the project. Alkalay argued that, despite the need for such a school, it was bound to divert funds away from the main goal of acquiring as rapidly as possible large parcels of land for the establishment of settlements. He was also vehemently opposed to the advocates of the Jewish Reform movement. The rabbi of Semlin was particularly incensed by the movement's abandonment of messianism, and their removal of references to Zion and Jerusalem from their prayer book. He was equally wary of the movement for Jewish emancipation, which he regarded as a diversion completely inimical to the idea of a Jewish restoration in Eretz Israel. Indeed, any individual, group, institution, or movement that suggested alternatives to Jewry's returning to the Holy Land was, in the eyes of Yehuda Alkalay, a betrayal of Jewish religion and history, and in the final analysis self-destructive.

In 1871 Alkalay visited Palestine and was instrumental in the founding of a new settlement. He called the colony "Kol Israel Haverim," the Hebrew translation of the popular Alliance Israélite Universelle. The settlement met with strong opposition from Jerusalem's Orthodox zealots, and when Alkalay returned to Serbia, the colony collapsed. Three years after this failure Alkalay decided to settle in the Holy Land in order to set an example for those of his followers who were thinking about immigrating. One of his disciples who did not choose to emigrate, was Simon Loeb Herzl, the grandfather of Theodor Herzl, the founder of the modern Zionist movement. The link between Alkalay and Theodor Herzl was more than one of historical accident. Both men favored Jewish national unity to be achieved through an all-embracing organization dedicated to Jewish redemption. Similarly, both initially depended on the intercession of affluent Western Jews to play an important role in the struggle to rally the Jews and to build the necessary political and financial institutions. Alkalay as well as Herzl also toyed with the idea of gaining concessions from the Turkish sultan for creating settlements in Palestine. They also looked toward the major powers, especially Great Britain, for support and protection during the transitional period leading to the creation of an independent Jewish entity. On consideration of these parallelisms Alex Bein, in his biography of Theodor Herzl, has noted:

> Simon Loeb Herzl died at a very advanced age, when his grandson Theodor had already reached his twentieth year. It would have been extraordinary if the old man had not, on his annual visits to Pest where his son lived, frequently spoken of Alkalay, and of his plans and dreams. Who knows if it was not then that the seed was sown which after long and invisible subterranean growth broke out in seed and flower in the sight of all men?[249]

Zevi Hirsch Kalischer

From the Polish-speaking city of Thorn in East Prussia came the appeal of Rabbi Zevi Hirsch Kalischer (1795–1874)[250] for a Jewish return to Zion. The recipient of a strict religious upbringing and education (he studied Talmud under Akiva Eger, one of the great scholars of the age), Kalischer was a model of Orthodoxy. In 1824, soon after his marriage, he left his native town (Leszno) and settled in Thorn where he would remain until his death. A fiercely independent soul, Kalischer repeatedly rejected invitations from many communities to serve as their rabbi. Instead, for more than forty years, he occupied the post of acting rabbi (*rabbinatsverweser*) in the Jewish community of Thorn without any remuneration. His meager subsistence was completely dependent upon his wife, the proprietor of a small business.

A prolific scholar, Kalischer wrote extensively on Jewish law and contributed numerous articles to the German-Jewish press and to Hebrew publications such as *Ha-Maggid, Ziyyon, Ha-Ibre,* and *Ha-Lebanon.* Inclined to contemplative speculation, he assiduously studied the works of medieval and modern Jewish and Christian philosophers. The end result of these labors was the publication of *Sefer Emunah Yesharah* ("An Honest Faith"), a two-volume inquiry into the nature of Jewish philosophy. Kalischer's ideas on Jewish restoration, which appeared in these volumes, were later supplemented and expanded on in a small tome bearing the provocative title *Derishat Tziyyon* ("Seeking Zion").[251]

Throughout his lifetime, Kalischer was preoccupied with the idea of a Jewish restoration in Palestine. Like Lorje and Alkalay whose views he paralleled to a remarkable degree, Kalischer believed that Jewish redemption could not come about without human endeavor.[252] Thus in *Derishat Tziyyon* he urged his fellow Jews to hasten the messianic or supernatural consummation through their own efforts, for the Almighty would not suddenly descend from on high and command His people to go forth. The redemption, Kalischer stressed, would only begin by awakening support among the Jewish philanthropists, and by gaining the aid of the major powers in gathering some of the dispersed of Israel and bringing them to Palestine.

In his writings and public statements Kalischer repeatedly emphasized self-help as the key ingredient in hastening redemption. "If the Almighty," he noted, "were to work a miracle, what fool would not be willing to go to Palestine?"[253] However, to renounce home and fortune for the sake of Zion before the coming of the Messiah—that was the real challenge. How could this desirable objective be realized, Kalischer asked? As he had so often in the past, the Rabbi from Thorn believed that it was up to the Jewish philanthropists, who possessed considerable economic and political power, to take the necessary first steps toward achieving the restoration. Current circumstance favored such an endeavor. Kalischer mocked his critics and the faint-hearted, who were fearful and cautioned restraint. He contrasted their passivity with the heroic activism of other people, such as the Italians, Poles, and Hungarians, who had given their lives and possessions in the struggle for independence. Were Jews inferior to these people, asked Kalischer? The children of Israel, he noted, had not always been spiritless and silent, nor had they lacked strong nationalistic feelings in the past, when called upon to defend their ancient homeland. National honor was important, but there were other considerations that the Jews had to take into account. They had received the most glorious and holiest of lands as their inheritance. Should they therefore not exert themselves ". . . for our duty is to labor not only for the glory of our ancestors, but for the glory of God who chose Zion."[254]

Anticipating that some of his Orthodox colleagues would brand his views heretical, Kalischer, in his work *Seeking Zion,* attempted to blunt their opposition. The book, written in classical Hebrew, opens with a series of statements by several renowned religious scholars. The scholars certify that the author, illuminated throughout his life by the study of the Holy Torah, could be trusted even when venturing outside his own field of talmudic legislation. On almost every page of his book Kalischer supported his arguments with an impressive array of proofs from the Bible and Talmud. Shorn of its ritualistic invocations and references to scripture, Kalischer's tome is modern, almost an existentialist piece of writing. Its central message that the salvation of the Jews promised by the ancient prophets, can come about only gradually and by natural means (i.e., through the efforts of the Jews themselves) could not be more clear. Jewish colonization of Palestine must, therefore, begin without further delays. Natural redemption in turn would serve as the initial step in ushering in the miraculous or supernatural redemption at the "end of the days."

Toward the end of his book, Kalischer devoted some space to a discussion of the arguments most likely to be used against his proposals. Would not the property of the Jews in Palestine be insecure? Would not rapacious Arabs rob the Jewish settlers of their harvest? Kalischer felt these and similar problems could be dealt with by training young Jews in self-defense and by encouraging the settlers to organize guard units who would combine farm work with defense against marauding Arab bands.

Yehudah Alkalay, writing on the same theme as the rabbi of Thorn thirty years earlier, had already drawn up a practical program to achieve the return of the Jews to Zion. Kalischer's plan differed ever so slightly from that of his predecessor. He placed greater emphasis on the immediate establishment of farming communities in the Holy Land and on the creation of an agricultural school.

The impact of *Derishat Tziyyon* on European Jewry is difficult to gauge. The book, which was published by the society founded by Chaim Lorje, included an invitation to the reader to join in the Jewish movement to recolonize Palestine. The book was later translated into German and some segments into English and other languages. It eventually found a select audience among Orthodox groups and served as a basic text, justifying from a religious point of view the idea of a Jewish restoration in Eretz Israel.

Kalischer, like Alkalay, traveled throughout Europe in an attempt to enlist the support of Jewish organizations and individuals to rally behind his restoration plan. He also kept his ideas before the general public by writing articles for Hebrew newspapers and periodicals. Remarkably, in spite of this intense activity, Kalischer managed to continue his scholarly writings on *halakhah* (the legal elements in Jewish teachings embodying the religious philosophy underlying Jewish religious life).

Much of his rhetoric was directed at those individuals who, in his eyes, undermined the foundations of Jewish religious tradition, particularly the advocates of reform. Kalischer did not spare the Orthodox rabbis who objected to his nationalistic ideas on religious grounds or the Jewish philanthropists who feared his ideas would jeopardize their struggle for civil rights. The rabbi from Thorn distinguished between philanthropy on behalf of the "old Yishuv" and that devoted to creating new settlements. He adopted a critical attitude to a plan in 1860 to build homes in the old city of Jerusalem, believing it to be a purely private enterprise that diverted sorely needed funds from the objective of quickly developing agricultural colonies. Kalischer was adamant in his conviction that only agriculture, practiced on a large scale, would provide a stabilizing factor for both the Jewish community in Palestine and the Jewish victims of persecution in Eastern Europe.

Kalischer's constant agitation for a return to Zion inspired the founding of several colonization societies. Largely as a result of his propaganda the Alliance Israélite Universelle founded the first agricultural school *Mikveh Israel* (Hope of Israel) near the city of Jaffa in Palestine (1870). For a time Kalischer, at the invitation of Charles Netter (1828–82), entertained the idea of settling at Mikveh Israel to act as the colony's rabbi. However, his advanced age and deteriorating health prevented him from accepting the offer.

Kalischer's legacy was significant for he sowed the seeds of Zionism for those who came after him (particularly the movement known as *Hibbat Zion* (The Love of Zion). In passing, it must be noticed that the rabbi of Thorn's activities occurred during the period that marked the apex of nineteenth-century European liberalism, an era reflecting almost universal optimism, especially in the West, that Jewish emancipation was inevitable. This sanguine feeling was not shared by Kalischer, who firmly believed that a return to Zion was of greater importance than any government's willingness to bestow civil rights on their Jewish subjects. Although he tried desperately to instill a feeling of urgency in his appeals to the Jews of Europe, Kalischer was unable to arouse the Jewish masses. The hostility of the Orthodox rabbinate to his concept of forcing "the end of days" accounted for most of the opposition to his proto-Zion vision. Nevertheless, his nationalistic ideas must be regarded as a modern, but lineally descended, expression of the messianism that had infused Jewish life throughout the centuries.

Elijah Gutmacher

Another advocate of natural redemption was Elijah Gutmacher (1795–1874).[255] Born in Borek, Russian Poland, Gutmacher received a traditional Orthodox education. Like his contemporary, Kalischer, he was a student of the renowned rabbinical scholar, Akiba Eger. At the age of twenty-six, Gutmacher was appointed to his first rabbinical post. From 1841 until his death, he would serve in the city of Graetz (now Grodzisk, Poland). His erudition and saintly way of life earned him the title of "rebbe of Western European Hassidism" and attracted many disciples to his court. Disturbed by the veneration shown him by his followers, he appealed to them to refrain from such behavior as it bordered on idolatry. His pleas, however, went largely unheeded.

Gutmacher's inclination toward mysticism and his fears for the future of European Jewry led him to seriously consider the entire idea of redemption. After much soul searching he came to the conclusion that natural redemption was the only practical solution to the Jewish Question. Gutmacher was thus one of a small group of rabbis who, despite their belief in the Messiah, believed that the Jewish people should not passively await a supernatural redemption. He advocated instead that it was incumbent upon the Jews to hasten redemption by devoting all their energies to constructive work in Palestine. Purchasing, settling, and working the land in Eretz Israel, making it bear fruit, observing the commandments—these were the indispensable components for complete redemption.

Gutmacher reiterated this theme in his sermons, articles, and correspondence. His conception of natural redemption was not the result of a sudden inspiration or insight, but rather the product of a slow evolutionary process. Gutmacher, thinking at first along traditional lines, believed that the redemption of the Jewish people would be accelerated by morally superior individuals who, by their behavior, would restore to Israel the Shekhina (the Divine Presence). The Shekina was believed to have departed from the Jews following the destruction of the second Temple and the beginning of the exile from the Land of Israel. However, after reading Kalischer's *Derishat Tziyyon,* Gutmacher modified his views on redemption. He now felt moral perfection was unattainable outside Eretz Israel. After arriving at this conclusion, Gutmacher devoted himself to encouraging immigration to Palestine, and to the need for rapidly establishing large Jewish agricultural settlements.

In 1860 Gutmacher participated in a conference of rabbis called by Kalischer to promote the idea of self-help and became an active member of the Colonisation-Verein für Palästina. Later on he became involved with that organization's successor in Berlin and provided strong support for the budding Love of Zion movement. Once having arrived at the idea of natural redemption, Gutmacher never slackened in his efforts to bring it about. Although less flamboyant than Kalischer, his exertions on behalf of a Jewish restoration in Palestine gave a certain poignancy to the traditional prayer recited by Jews thrice daily that beseeched the Almighty to "gather us from the four corners of the earth . . . to Jerusalem Thy city. . . ."[256]

Samuel David Luzzatto

The belief in the "ingathering of the exiles" (*kibbutz galuyot*) found an eloquent voice and pen in the polymath, Samuel David Luzzatto (1800–65).[257] Best known by his acronym Shadal, Luzzatto was a poet, philosopher, philologist, translator, biblical exegete, historian, grammarian, and ardent Jewish nationalist. He regarded the Jewish people as a national entity with a common origin, language, and culture. Concerned with his people's survival, he advocated an intensification of the Jewish national consciousness, and in order to further this objective devoted his life to the exposition and interpretation of the literary treasures of Judaism.

Born in Trieste, then part of the Austrian Empire, Luzzatto was the scion of a prominent Italian-Jewish family that had fallen on hard times. His father, Hezekiah, was an artisan (wood turner), deeply religious and inclined toward mysticism. A precocious child, young Samuel received a thorough Jewish education. Instruction by his father and local rabbis was supplemented by attendance in one of the modern Jewish schools set up after the issuance of the Edict of Toleration by the Austrian emperor, Joseph II. The Trieste Talmud Torah, based on the progressive principles laid down by Moses Mendelssohn's disciple Napthali Herz Wessely (1725–1805), incorporated a curriculum of religious and secular subject matter. It included such diverse fields of study as the Bible and Talmud, the natural sciences, and classical and modern languages. While enrolled in this institution, Luzzatto in 1811 received as a prize Montesquieu's *Considerations sur les Causes de la Grandeur des Romains,* which whetted the eleven-year-old's curiosity and contributed much to the development of his critical faculties. His literary activity began that same year with work on a Hebrew grammar and a translation into Hebrew of the life of the Greek fabulist Aesop. Luzzatto also began at this early age to make exegetical notes on the Pentateuch. The discovery of an unpublished commentary on the *Targum of Onkelos* stimulated the young scholar to undertake a study of Aramaic. Years later he would incorporate this knowledge in a work entitled *Oheb Ger* ("Lover of the Proselyte"), an allusion to the conversion of Onkelos to Judaism.

At the age of thirteen, Luzzatto was withdrawn from school to assist his father, whose pecuniary status had further declined. With the death of his mother some months later, Luzzatto's burden and responsibilities increased, as he was now compelled to do the family's housework as well as help his father in his work as a wood turner. However, in spite of these difficulties, the budding young scholar managed to attend talmudic lectures given by a local rabbi and to study Jewish lore on his own.

Refusing to take up his father's trade, Luzzatto became a tutor. For several years he eked out a living giving private lessons, while at the same time writing Hebrew poetry and essays for the Haskalah journal *Bikkurei ha-Ittim* ("First Fruit of the Times"). A radical change in Luzzatto's fortune began in 1821–22 with the publication of his translation of the Ashkenazi prayer book into Italian (to be followed a few years later by a book on the Italian-Jewish rite). His work attracted the attention of the eminent scholar and mathematician Isaac Samuel Reggio (1784–1855), a pioneer of the Haskalah movement in Northern Italy and himself a translator of the Pentateuch into Italian. Reggio had played a leading role in the founding at Padua of the Collegio Rabbinico Italiano in 1829, the first modern albeit traditional rabbinical institution of its kind in Italy. Largely through Reggio's efforts, Luzzatto was appointed to the newly created seminary as an instructor in Bible, philology, and Jewish history. He would remain at the Collegio for the rest of his life.

A product of his age, Luzzatto was deeply influenced by the romantic spirit that had engulfed most of Europe. The new trend marked a dramatic shift from the rationalistic currents of the earlier era that had brought on the French Revolution. Rationalism reverted to the classical pagan thought of antiquity (notably the work of Aristotle) while

Romanticism based itself on the Christian world view of later centuries. To the extent that Romanticism focused on the history of people, it gave impulse to the growth of nationalism. Nationalism was particularly intense in Luzzatto's Italy, which had briefly enjoyed a state of national unity as a result of Napoleon Bonaparte's conquest of the peninsula. However, following the latter's defeat, Italy was transformed by the Congress of Vienna into a mere geographical expression.

The Haskalah (the Jewish Enlightenment) had spawned a renewed interest in the Hebrew language, literature, and poetry, and eventually led to the evolution of the so-called Die Wissenschaft des Judenthums (The Science of Judaism). This movement had as its objective the scientific investigation of Jewish religion, history, and customs. Luzzatto's propensity for research made him a natural ally of the "Science of Judaism," and in fact he carried on a correspondence with almost all the leading Jewish savants of the day, e.g., with Abraham Geiger (1816–74), Moritz Steinschneider (1816–1907), Heinrich Graetz (1817–91), Nachman Krochmal (1785–1840), Solomon Judah Rapoport (1790–1867), Zacharias Frankel (1801–75), and Leopold Zunz (1794–1886).

Although he sympathized with the goals of "the Science of Judaism," Luzzatto was disturbed by the direction toward acculturation in which some of the movement's scholars were moving. He was keenly aware that these individuals, obsessed by the struggle for emancipation and a desire to emulate their Gentile neighbors, were amenable to discarding many Jewish traditions and practices. Indeed, Leopold Zunz, a founding father of "the Science of Judaism," was convinced that the rich Jewish past and its cultural achievement would come to an end with the advent of complete emancipation. He looked forward to the recognition of Jewish culture as part of world culture and dreamt of seeing it introduced as a discipline in the universities. Such a development, Zunz believed, would not only raise the prestige of the Jews in the eyes of Gentiles, but would also speed the granting of civic and political rights. Still other scholars associated with "the Science of Judaism" movement regarded Judaism as an impressive fossil rather than a living faith.

Luzzatto, at home in the Jewish tradition and devoid of any ambivalence about his ties to the Jewish people or Judaism's status as a religion of truth, frequently chided his scholarly contemporaries for their cavalier attitude toward Judaism. Writing to the philologist and philosopher Lazarus Geiger (1829–70) he expressed his disdain for those individuals overly concerned with emancipation at any price.

Shadal was also alarmed by the tendency among German-Jewish scholars to avoid publishing their studies in Hebrew. In a letter to the eminent German-Jewish historian Heinrich Graetz he noted that neither Graetz, nor Zacharias Frankel, the director of a leading Jewish theological seminary, liked to write in Hebrew. What, he asked, will your people do, and where will the language find a home after the demise of the present generation? The complaint was all the more poignant as both Graetz and Frankel were firmly opposed to any attempts to weaken Judaism.

In a letter to Solomon Rapoport, one of the leaders of the Galician Haskalah, Shadal again expressed alarm at the course being followed by some of the German adherents of "the Science of Judaism." He noted that a people living in its own country can exist even without faith, but the sons of Israel, dispersed to the far corners of the earth, have survived only because they have adhered to their faith. However, if they should one day cease to believe in the heavenly Torah, then they would cease to be a people, the name of Israel would be forgotten, and they would suffer the fate of streams that run to the sea. For some, Luzzatto emphasized, this would be a final salvation; such men call it "fusion" (i.e., assimilation).

The wisdom of Israel as it is studied in Germany by several Jewish scholars, Luzzatto insisted, cannot continue to exist, as it is not studied for its own sake. In the last analysis, these scholars respect Goethe and Schiller more than all the *tanaim* (rabbinic teachers mentioned in the Mishnah) and the *amoraim* (interpreters of the Mishnah noted in the Gemara, the second part of the Talmud). They study ancient Israel the way other scholars study Egypt, Assyria, Babylonia, and Persia—for the love of science or the love of fame. They attend, in addition, to increase the honor of Israel in the eyes of the Gentiles; they exalt the role of some of our ancient sages to hasten the first step toward salvation, which is in their eyes emancipation. But this kind of wisdom cannot endure; the wisdom of Israel which will endure is learning grounded in faith.

Shadal, who considered himself a traditionalist, was also an implacable foe of the Jewish Reform movement. He vehemently denounced the attempts of the German-Jewish reformers to replace Hebrew with the vernacular in the synagogues of Berlin; and strongly protested the proposals of the Frankfort Reform Society in 1843 to abolish circumcision as well as other time-honored Jewish practices. Most of all he ridiculed the so-called mission theory of the reformers, which regarded the dispersion of the Jews as a blessing designed to enable them to disseminate the teachings of ethical monotheism to all mankind. Lastly, Shadal resented the readiness of the reformers to abandon the messianic ideals expounded by the Hebrew prophets and in the process Eretz Israel as well.

Luzzatto was also distressed by the so-called biblical school of higher criticism, the creation of Christian exegetes, especially as their work was applied to the foundations of Judaism. He felt that such exegetes as Eichorn, De Wette, Gesenius, and other Christian scholars, strangers to Judaism, did not bring to their studies proper appreciation of the subject matter and still less the necessary devotion. They tended to pursue their studies in a clumsy manner and, for want of real critical ability, had in many instances flung out the true ore as dross. To purify the treasure from the rust of thousands of years, Luzzatto believed, could only be accomplished by individuals imbued with the Jewish spirit and thoroughly familiar with the construction of the Hebrew language even to its most delicate points and grammatical minutiae.

Accordingly, Shadal set out to restore the balance that had been upset by the Christian exegetes. He was among the first to turn his attention to Syriac, considering a knowledge of this language essential for understanding the *Targum* (Aramaic translation or paraphase of a portion of the Pentateuch). He was also a pioneer in enlisting the *Wisdom of Sira* in the service of biblical research. Similarly, after a careful examination of the book of Ecclesiastes, Luzzatto came to the conclusion that its author was definitely not Solomon, but an individual who lived several centuries later. On the other hand, in spite of the opinion of many scholars that some chapters of the book of Isaiah were written after the Captivity, Luzzatto maintained that the whole book was written by one man, Isaiah. Although Luzzatto as an exegete revealed a remarkable gift for the field, he was suddenly frightened by his own boldness, or rather by the possibility that he might misuse his talents. If the walls of the *Masorah* (i.e., the body of traditions regarding the correct spelling, writing, and reading of the Hebrew Bible) were torn down, Luzzatto feared the sacred text would become the prey of incompetent and unending reconstructions, causing confusion among the Jewish people. He did not trust criticism to heal the wounds such a development would cause. As a result of these fears, Luzzatto took up an equivocal position, and re-erected the outworks of the *Masorah,* which he himself had for a time undermined. This sensitivity, however, did not prevent him from producing commentaries on the Pentateuch, as well as on Jeremiah, Ezekiel, Proverbs, and Job.

Roused by the achievements of Krochmal and Rapoport in Jewish history, Luzzatto also delved into the past. He knew that many of the documents and literature of the Franco and Spanish Jewish epochs had been lost, and his zeal was kindled to rediscover them. He was also aware that many Jews, in their flight from Spain, had passed through Italy. Many Jewish literary treasures, Shadal reasoned, must therefore have found their way into Italian archives and libraries, where they were completely hidden from the public eye and from the scholars. His passion for the recovery of these treasures of Judaism was rewarded with great success. Ignoring his financial status, which was never much above the poverty line, and the misfortunes that dogged him throughout his life (the early death of a favorite son, a wife who became insane, the dimming of his eyesight), Shadal spent all of his meager resources to unearth and buy rare Hebrew manuscripts. He would then publish them in scientific journals or as separate works in order to make them available to scholars throughout Europe. He generously shared with others his findings, without any thought of personal gain, and encouraged others to do the same.

Not content with bringing to light historical documents and literature that shed new light on the Jews of Spain, Shadal also composed poetry and produced a number of Hebrew grammatical and philolgical treatises. Although familiar with many languages (Italian, French, Greek, Latin, and a number of Oriental tongues) his favorite throughout life remained Hebrew. He wrote Hebrew belles lettres, treatises, poetry, and books, and contributed numerous articles in that language to almost every scholarly periodical of the day. Luzzatto considered Hebrew to be a national as well as sacred tongue, and frequently referred to the Bible as not only a religious tome, but a national classic as well. Accordingly, he insisted that Jewish literary and cultural enterprises be carried out in their natural medium, the Hebrew language. He believed Hebrew was the chief bond linking the scattered members of the Jewish people, and as both the carrier and guarantor of a revealed national religion embodied its own universalism and humanitarianism.

In addition to his scholarly and literary contributions, Luzzatto was also a prolific letter writer. Some 700 of his letters, on a wide range of subject matter, written to a large circle of friends and colleagues were published under the title *Igrot Shadal* ("The Epistles of Shadal"). Other letters were published by his children after his death in a collection called *Peninei Shadal* ("Pearls of Shadal"). One of Luzzatto's fondest hopes was that some day all of his writings would be disseminated in Hebrew, and that a publishing house would be established to provide an outlet for future Hebrew writers. For Luzzatto, the Hebrew language was to serve as a bridge between the classical and modern cultures of the Jews, and thereby provide the key to the survival of Judaism and its adherents.

In all of his work, Shadal was consistent and unwavering in his views on Jewish nationalism. Although he lived prior to the emergence of modern Zionism, his ideas on peoplehood anticipated some of the important elements of the Zionist movement. As early as 1850 Shadal had urged a prominent rabbi of Jerusalem to use his influence to convince the youth of the Yishuv to return to the soil. If successful, he noted, they would not only rehabilitate themselves, but the Jewish homeland as well. A few years later Luzzatto suggested to Jewish philanthropists that instead of financing the migration of Jewish youth from Asia to Europe, where they would be corrupted by Western civilization and atheism, that they direct their efforts toward bringing them to Eretz Israel.

Many of his thoughts on restoration in the Promised Land he incorporated in a work entitled *Mahzor Roma* (1856), a historical and critical introduction to the festive liturgy according to the Italian version. In a volume bearing the title *Betulat Bat Yehudah* ("The Virgin Daughter of Judah"), Shadal reintroduced to the reading public Jehuda Halevi's (circa 1075–1141) nationalistic poems, the *Zionides*. Not content with resurrecting his favorite bard, Luzzatto shortly before his death completed *Divan*, a work containing annotations, corrections, and comments on eighty-six poems written by the medieval Spanish-Jewish poet. In a poem of his own dedicated in commemoration of the Ninth of Ab, Luzzatto pleaded eloquently for the restoration of the Jewish state, and even for a revival of some of the ancient rituals.

Shadal's scholarly investigations to reacquaint his coreligionists with their religious heritage together with his belief in the restoration of the Jews to Eretz Israel led him to conceive of Judaism in a rather unique manner. In his theological writings, mostly published lectures, such as *Teologia Morale Israelitica,* and *Yesodet ha-Torah* ("Foundations of the Torah"), as well as in much of his correspondence, he evolved a distinct theory of Judaism which stressed the traditional values of God, Israel, and Torah. That Israel's existence had intrinsic and universal worth led Luzzatto to formulate in the sharpest possible manner the antithesis between what he termed Abrahamism ("Judaism") and the other great intellectual tradition of antiquity, Atticism (the heritage of Athens). Atticism, the product of Greek culture and an apotheosis of reason, had given to the world philosophy, science, and art. A clear-cut distinction was made by Luzzatto between creativity whose goal is ethics, and creativity whose highest values are expressed in the manifestation of beauty and its embodiment in the arts and sciences. Although Luzzatto acknowledges that Atticism has helped man to advance technologically, he stresses that it has failed to produce a more humane or morally imbued society. If anything, the rational principles and methods exemplified in Atticism have magnified the horrors of the ancient scourges of mankind—war, poverty, and oppression.

On the other hand Abrahamism's (i.e., Judaism's) goal has been to foster morality, goodness, justice, and compassion. Whereas Atticism is dynamic and progressive, ceaselessly striving for novelty, Abrahamism tends to be static and immutable because morality does not change. Indeed, the latter emphasizes inner sanctity over outer harmony, moral practice over metaphysical and theoretical speculations. The Greek tradition is rational, the Jewish supernatural. Thus, the values that shaped Jewish history transcend human reason. Israel's very survival therefore depends on rejecting the autonomy of reason, which Shadal believed brings into Judaism external criteria that undermine its ethical imperatives, denies the singularity of the Jewish people, and destroys the uniqueness of its religion. By surrendering his particularism and uniqueness, the Jew does violence not only to Judaism, but also deprives mankind of an important ethical force.

Luzzatto's plea for liberating Judaism from the inroads made by Atticism brought him into sharp conflict with many of his contemporaries and colleagues. However, his views on philosophy and rationalism were not based on a lack of understanding of these matters or on blind fanaticism. Shadal claimed to have read all of the ancient philosophers, and said that the more he delved into their works, the more he found them deviating from the truth. What one writer approves, another disapproves; and so the philosophers themselves go astray. Thus, for example, while praising the great Jewish medieval philosopher

Maimonides (1135–1204) for many of his contributions to Judaism, Luzzatto attacks him for being unduly influenced by Aristotelian thought. He stresses that the Greek rationalistic philosophy that Maimonides embraced so wholeheartedly and that was represented in modern times by Baruch Spinoza (1632–77) and Immanuel Kant (1724–1804), was essentially antagonistic to the ethos of Judaism, for it attempted to convert the latter from a religion of the heart to one of the mind.

Rationalistic philosophy, Shadal believed, was also responsible for bringing the negative element of mysticism into Judaism. His disdain for mysticism led him to probe deeply into the literature of the Kabbalah, and to publish his findings in a work entitled *Wikkuah al ha Kabbalah* (1852). Luzzatto's research led him to conclude that the most important kabbalistic tome, the *Zohar* ("the Book of Splendor") was definitely not the product of the second-century *tanna*, Simeon ben Yohai, but had probably been written by the Spanish kabbalist Moses de Leon, an opinion voiced earlier by the Italian rabbi Leone Modena (1571–1648), and the rabbinical scholar Jacob Israel Emden (1697–1776).

Shadal's observations and criticisms, as indicated previously, also brought him into sharp conflict with some of the *maskilim* (Jewish enlighteners) of his day. He was particularly disturbed by the views of Nachman Krochmal, who like Zunz, favored the blending of Judaism with other European cultures. Krochmal in turn was outraged by Shadal's criticism of the medieval thinkers Maimonides and Abraham ibn Ezra (sarcastically, Luzzatto noted that to earn a living, Ibn Ezra wrote a book in every town in which he sojourned, the number of books thus corresponding to the number of towns he visited). In spite of these differences, Luzzatto occasionally agreed with the *maskilim* on the need for slight changes in religious customs; however, he refused to yield on major issues that would radically alter traditional Judaism.

In retrospect, Samuel David Luzzatto's views on religion, culture, and nationalism were central to his personality and were molded by the times in which he lived. A shining example of the best in Hebrew culture, a writer of keen insight and literary sensibility, as well as a slave of the right word and correct form, he was a perceptive interpreter of the Jewish spirit. He gave new impetus to study of the Bible and of the Hebrew language, and forcefully pleaded with his fellow Jews not to abandon their religious traditions or the hope for a restoration in Eretz Israel for the allurements of Western civilization. Although destined like Moses never to dwell in the Promised Land his life work definitely marks him as one who must be numbered among the precursors of Religious, as well as Cultural or Spiritual Zionism. Indeed, his insistence that Eretz Israel become a center from which Judaic ideas of justice and righteousness would flow forth to the entire Jewish Diaspora bears a remarkable resemblance to the views advocated years later by the father of Spiritual Zionism, Ahad Ha-Am (1856–1927).

As fate would have it, the Collegio Rabbinico Italiano, where Shadal had labored for over thirty years and where he had honed his religious and nationalistic concepts, ceased to exist shortly after his death. Nevertheless, the nationalistic seed he had helped sow through his literary contributions and investigations into the foundations of Judaism, survived, took root, and flowered as a new generation less romantically inclined and more practical, renewed the quest for Zion.

23

Simon Bermann: An Agrarian Pragmatist

Into the stifling atmosphere of the Old Yishuv of the 1870s came Simon Bermann (1818–84),[258] a Jew of Polish origin, with a plan for the recolonization of Palestine. A down-to-earth individual with considerable knowledge of agronomy as well as practical experience as a farmer, Bermann, unlike many of his predecessors, was neither a dreamer nor a philosopher. Nevertheless, he was drawn to the Land of Israel by a passionate love that bordered on mysticism.

Born in Cracow, Bermann, while still a youth, played a leading role in the founding of a Jewish agricultural society in his native city. In 1852 he immigrated to the United States, and settled in New York. There and in other cities of the East and Midwest, Bermann attempted to establish agricultural societies on the model of the Cracow group, but received little support from the Jewish public. After spending eighteen years in the United States, and in the aftermath of a personal tragedy he decided to settle in Palestine (1870). Enroute to Eretz Israel Bermann stopped over in London, Paris, and Berlin, where he came into contact with Jewish philanthropists, who at the time were planning to establish an agricultural school in the vicinity of Jaffa in the Holy Land. After his arrival in Palestine, Bermann visited the proposed agricultural site (the future Mikveh Israel), as well as the remains of an American colony near Jaffa that had failed and the settlement of the German Templar Christians, who had taken over the Americans' lands. He also visited the Jewish colony at Petach-Tikva, where he tried unsuccessfully to convince Charles Netter, the representative of the Alliance Israélite Universelle to turn over to him a portion of land, which he proposed to settle and farm scientifically with twenty Jewish families. Undaunted by his rejection, Bermann submitted a formal request to the Ottoman government via the American Consul at Jerusalem, Richard Beardsley, for permission to buy land in Palestine. The petition was granted, and Bermann immediately set about searching for a suitable site. In the account of his experiences in Palestine,

Massot Shimon ("Travels of Simon"), Bermann gratefully acknowledged his debt to Richard Beardsley.

When news of Bermann's successful petition reached Europe, he received messages of encouragement from Rabbi Zevi Hirsch Kalischer and Elijah Gutmacher and promises of funds for the proposed Jewish colony. However, once again the implacable hostility of the Jerusalem rabbinate of the Old Yishuv to any settlement project proved a difficult barrier to overcome. In a letter written to German and Austrian rabbis who had expressed interest in Jewish agricultural settlements in Palestine, Bermann gave full vent to his frustrations. He accused the religious authorities who were responsible for the system of *halukkah* (funds collected in the Diaspora for maintenance of Jewish communities in the holy cities of Eretz Israel) as forming the core of the opposition to his proposed agricultural colony.

The opposition of the rabbinical supervisors of the *halukkah* funds in Jerusalem, Bermann maintained, was motivated by fear that collections for the purpose of establishing an agricultural settlement would seriously affect contributions to the charity fund on which most of the Old Yishuv was dependent for survival. They were also perturbed by the modernism of the group's leader, the Americanized Simon Bermann. Finding himself unable to overcome the resistance of the leaders of the Jewish community of Jerusalem, Bermann departed for Tiberias. Here he was accorded a more sympathetic reception and was successful in convincing a number of individuals to form a society for the colonization of the Holy Land. Bermann's plan was for the society to promote an agricultural cooperative along lines reminiscent of the theories proposed by the French utopian socialist, François Marie Charles Fourier (1772–1837). Elements of Fourier's ideas are particularly evident in Bermann's plans for agricultural and industrial labor in his settlement.

One hundred and fifty people answered the society's call to found a cooperative colony. Bermann at first favored a site near Haifa, where the settlers could profit from the experiences of the prosperous German Templar Christian settlements. He also felt that it was important to be close to the sea so that they could easily obtain from abroad the necessary agricultural implements and at the same time have an outlet for exporting their produce. However, the men from Tiberias, who formed the mainstay of the would-be colonists, insisted on remaining close to their holy city, where according to tradition the Messiah would make his first appearance. The "American", as Bermann was fondly called by this caftan-clad group of settlers from Tiberias, quickly acquiesced to their demands and chose as a site for the settlement a strip of land near the shores of Lake Kinneret (Sea of Galilee) near the Arab village of Abu Shusha.

However, the financial aid necessary to get the colony on a sound footing failed to materialize. Bermann traveled to Europe in an attempt to raise funds, but was unsuccessful. In 1882, disillusioned and broken in spirit, his colony disbanded, he returned to Tiberias, where he spent the remainder of his days. Although his plans were never given a fair trial, Bermann lived long enough to witness the establishment of the first successful Jewish agricultural settlements in Palestine. Some of these early pioneers would acknowledge that it was Bermann's book, the *Travels of Simon*, that had stimulated in them a desire to immigrate to the land of Israel.

24

Moses Hess

The words "socialism" and "socialist" came into common usage in Europe around the year 1830, although the ideas and ruminations that led to this political movement can be traced back to the French Revolution. From its inception, socialism, for a variety of reasons, attracted many Jews. Some regarded socialism as a force for the building of a just society based on the teachings of the Bible and the Prophets, while others were hypnotized by the movement's revolutionary nature. Still other Jews saw in socialism a means of combating anti-Semitism. Many viewed it as a way for discarding their Jewish heritage to best serve the brotherhood of man. Socialism was particularly alluring for those Jews anxious to leave the ghetto behind them and who were disappointed with the slow progress of nineteenth-century Liberalism.

The early European socialists were greatly divided in their attitude to the Jewish Problem. Although some tended to ignore the issue, the vast majority of the rank and file of the movement were imbued with the anti-Semitic prejudices that prevailed in both Western and Eastern Europe. Socialist theoreticians of the Marxist stripe were particularly antagonistic to the idea of a Jewish national movement. Karl Marx (1818–83), and Friedrich Engels (1820–95), the leaders of the so-called scientific socialists were preoccupied with the questions of class and class struggle. They shared the views of the Liberals that cultural, economic, and social progress was gradually overcoming national exclusivity and that the world was moving toward internationalism. However, unlike the Liberals, the Marxists did not believe that all national movements were equal. They considered some such as Zionism to be a dangerous and reactionary form of romantic bourgeois nationalism, drawing the Jewish proletariat away from the revolutionary struggle and separating the Jewish Problem from a universal solution. Not for a moment did Marx and his disciples believe in the existence of a Jewish people per se, and the idea that Judaism and the Jews as a collective had a future must have appeared to them as an aberration typical of people unable to grasp the implications of socialist doctrine.

Among the early adherents of socialism, however, was a small group who were adamantly opposed to the stand taken by the Marxists in relation to the Jewish Problem. Sympathetic to Jewish suffering, they championed the right of Jews to freedom, equality, and nationhood. One of the most outstanding fighters for Jewish national restoration among these opponents to Marxist doctrine was Moses Hess (1812–75).[259] Hess was born in Bonn, Germany, into a family in which religion was very much alive. In 1821 his parents moved to Cologne, where they became the proprietors of a grocery and sugar refinery. Believing that the opportunities in Cologne for a Jewish education were poor, the family left nine-year-old Moses behind in Bonn in the care of his Orthodox grandfather. The latter, a rabbi by training though not by profession, eagerly took on the task of providing his grandson with a traditional religious education (Bible, Talmud, and Hebrew).

At the age of fourteen, Moses was reunited with his family in Cologne, and entered his father's business. Reared in the early post-Napoleonic era, exposed to German literature and culture, Hess as he matured lost interest in religion and ceased to be a practicing Jew. He had become convinced that the ". . . Mosaic religion was dead, its historical role was finished, and could no longer be revived."[260] His religious rebellion led to a bitter quarrel with his father, who finally ejected young Hess from his household and business.

From 1837 to 1839 Hess attended the University of Bonn as a student of philosophy. He did not graduate from there or any other institution of learning. Nevertheless, although basically self taught, he was a quick learner and was able to master a wide variety of intellectual subject matter.

The decade of the 1830s witnessed the zenith of Hegelian and historical philosophy. Hess's first book *Die heilige Geschichte der Menscheit* ("The Holy History of Mankind") clearly reflected these forces. The work by a "young Spinozist", as Hess grandiosely described himself, failed to gain an audience, but was indicative of how far he had strayed from Judaism. Like other intellectuals of his milieu, Hess soon turned from philosophy to ideological politics. He participated in the debates of the Young Hegelians, and played an important role in the dissemination of the theories of the French utopian socialist Pierre Joseph Proudhon (1809–65) in Germany. During this period, Hess also authored a second book, *Die europaenische Triarchie* ("The European Triarchy"), in which he suggested that the three great powers—Great Britain, France and Germany—unite into a single entity, a sort of United States of Europe.

In the same year as the publication of his second book (1840), Hess joined the left wing of the Young Hegelian movement, and became one of the founders, and later Paris correspondent, of the *Rheinische Zeitung,* the first socialist daily in Cologne. With Karl Marx as its chief editor, the newspaper flourished until March, 1843, when it was suppressed by the Prussian government.

Rapidly achieving a reputation in socialist circles as a speaker and writer, Hess was able to exert considerable influence over younger activists, including Marx and Engels. He even collaborated with the latter thinkers in the preparation of two works of critical analysis. In addition, his articles and essays appeared in most of the radical periodicals of the day. In 1845–46, Hess edited the socialist monthly *Der Gesellschaftspiegel,* which provided him with an excellent platform for airing his radical views. Forever restless, Hess eventually moved on to Brussels, where he became deeply involved in the activities of the Kommunistenbund.

His radical activities during the revolution of 1848 alarmed the authorities and he was compelled to flee for his life into political exile. Nevertheless, in spite of his impeccable socialist credentials a serious rift developed between Hess and his former comrades, Karl Marx and Friedrich Engels. The Communist Manifesto of 1848 sealed the break, which had been evolving for a number of years. Indeed, Hess was one of the main targets of what Marx contemptuously referred to ". . . as the 'true socialists' castigated in the Communist Manifesto as those who merely translated French ideas into German; speculative cobwebs,' embroidered with flowers of rhetoric, steeped in the dew of sickly sentiment, a Philistine, foul and enervating literature."[261]

Shorn of invective, the differences between Hess and Marx were fundamental. The former could not reconcile himself to the materialistic interpretation of history or to the doctrine of class war advocated by Marx and Engels. Instead, Hess stressed the moral aspects of socialism as the correct road to free labor and human self development. The conscious will rather than the objective forces of history were therefore all important.

From 1853 until the end of his life, except for a few brief interruptions, Hess lived in Paris. His tumultuous public life was matched by a private life that was indicative of the strong emotional forces which tugged at his soul. Most bizarre was his marriage to Sybille Pesch, a "lady of the night," evidently out of a desire to make personal atonement for the sins of man and the corrupt social system that drove poor women into prostitution. Incredibly, the marriage turned out to be successful, but it further widened the breach between Hess and his family in Cologne.

Although his break with Judaism seemed complete, under the impact of the Damascus Affair Hess was once again compelled to ponder the anomaly of Jewish existence. Years later, reflecting on his innermost feelings during this period, he would recall his shock, agony, and disbelief that such an absurd accusation could still resonate among the masses of Europe and Asia. It seemed that any calumny could be directed against the Jews without fear of retribution. Nothing had happened to change this attitude over the long centuries of Jewry's exile from their ancient homeland.

Hess was also painfully reminded that he belonged to this maligned, despised, and dispersed people. Although Hess at the time had wanted to cry out in anguish as an expression of his Jewishness, the emotion was immediately superseded by the greater torment that was evoked in him by the suffering of Europe's proletariat.

Not long after settling in the French capital, Hess abandoned active politics. The man whom the neo-Hegelian Arnold Ruge had derisively dubbed "the communist rabbi Moses" now devoted all of his energies to a study of the natural sciences, most notably anthropology. Hess, however, could not completely shut out the outside world. Jewish concerns again stirred him as he watched the increase in anti-Semitism throughout Western Europe. In 1857 the writings of Rabbi Kalischer came to Hess's attention. Kalischer's work made a deep impression on Hess's thinking, and he decided to begin a systematic study of Jewish history. Almost simultaneously he became engrossed in the works of the Italian nationalist Giuseppe Mazzini (1805–72) and was deeply moved by the latter's dream of a united Italy. His studies in ethnicity and history as well as the Italian war of 1859 against the Austrians reinforced the view that had gradually germinated in his mind that the national independence of an oppressed people was an essential precondition for social progress.

His sense of identity as a Jew rekindled by his studies and by the national movements of the day, Hess now acknowledged that his original cosmopolitan vision of a single

European entity was an illusion. Each people, he now stressed, nurtured its own traits, ambitions, and mission. The events that had transpired in Italy confirmed this view, for on the ruins of Christian Rome a regenerated Italian people had arisen. What the Italians and others had achieved, Hess felt, must also be attained by the Jews, who represented the last great national problem in Europe.

Rome and Jerusalem

The publication of the early volumes of Heinrich Graetz's *History of the Jews* gave additional stimulus to Hess's changing views on Judaism, and he gave expression to his new-found thoughts in a short volume published in 1862. He originally intended to call the book *The Revival of Israel,* but settled for the title *Rom und Jerusalem, die Letze Nationalitatsfrage* ("Rome and Jerusalem, the Last National Question").[262] This rather discursive work contained echoes of all of Hess's major thoughts on various subjects, including nationalism, socialism, an analysis of the Jewish Problem, as well as his views of science (the latter were published in full posthumously by his wife, under the rubric *Die Dynamische Stofflehre*).

Rome and Jerusalem, written in the form of twelve letters and ten notes, is addressed to a fictional lady mourning the loss of a relative and pondering the problem of resurrection. It opens with the author's confession,

> Here I stand once more, after twenty years of estrangement in the midst of my people. . . . A thought which I had stifled forever in my heart is again vividly present with me, the thought of my nationality, inseparable from the inheritance of my ancestors, the Holy Land and the eternal city. . . . This thought, buried alive had for years throbbed in my sealed heart, demanding an outlet. . . . [263]

Hess goes on to admit how difficult it had been for him to make the transition from his previous beliefs, which had been so far removed from Judaism, and discussed how his new nationalistic ideas had slowly materialized.

A striking feature of *Rome and Jerusalem* was the author's pessimistic assessment of anti-Semitism. Almost all of his contemporaries on the left were convinced that anti-Semitism reflected the dying convulsions of the old order, and that it was reactionary and politically of little consequence. Hess did not share this view. Writing well before modern racial anti-Semitism became a major political force in Europe, he had already realized its dangerous potential. The modern Jew could not hide behind geographical and philosophical abstractions; he could mask himself a thousand times over, change his name, religion and character, but he would still be recognized as a Jew. The Jew might become a naturalized citizen, but he would never convince the Gentile of his total separation from the Gentile's own nationality. The nations of Europe had always regarded the existence of the Jews in their midst an anomaly. In brief, for Hess, the Jew would always remain a stranger among the nations, and even though they might be emancipated, they would never be respected if they put their places of birth above their glorious national memories.

The racial issue, Hess observed was particularly acute in Germany where antagonism toward the Jews was a deep, instinctive force, far more powerful than any rational argument. Reform, education, emancipation, conversion—none of these had changed the

German outlook toward the Jews. It had become not so much a matter of religion as of race hatred. This peculiar view also had supporters elsewhere in Europe.

Since anti-Semitism was based on race and nationhood and would not be eliminated by assimilation or conversion, the Jews, Hess insisted, must accept that they are not merely a religious group, but a distinct separate nation, and seek to restore their independence in Palestine. It was therefore incumbent on the Jews to recognize that homelessness was at the root of the Jewish Problem, and that without a land of their own they would always be considered as strangers and parasites living on the backs of others. Those Jews who refused to accept these obvious facts were traitors to their people, tribe, and race.

All past history, Hess stressed in *Rome and Jerusalem,* was the result of race and class struggle. Race was the primal force, the class struggle secondary. Modern society had been shaped by two historical world races—the Aryans and the Semites. The Aryans aimed at explaining and beautifying life, the Semites at moralizing and sanctifying it. Hess emphasized that between the two races there was variety, but no superiority or inferiority; therefore there was no justification for racial oppression or discrimination. The final aim of history, he felt, would be the achievement of harmonious cooperation among all nations, with each nation expressing in its own way the ethical socialism that for so long had been Hess's quasi-religious faith. To attain this objective, the whole world needed for its revival a fresh restatement of the eternal verities, for the liberal, bourgeois, rationalist revolution had exhausted its historical function and brought mankind to a dead end. The Jews had an important role to play in the required religious rebirth. The function of Judaism as a religion of history and of the Jewish people as a nation in possession of a special talent for social revelation could bring into accord all the forces making for human advancement, and in the process usher in an "eternal Sabbath." It was therefore the historic mission of the Jews, to give the essentially social doctrine of Judaism a new and spontaneous development in free and sovereign self-expression in Palestine.[264]

How could the Jews achieve restoration in Palestine without a central authority, and with their people scattered throughout the world and beset by problems ranging from outright persecution to assimilation and conversion? Religion, Hess believed, was the best means of preserving the nationality of the Jews in the Diaspora. Elaborating on this point, he noted that the dividing line between the West and the East, namely the countries of Poland, Russia, Austria, and Turkey contained millions of Jews. It was these Jews who had preserved Judaism and the sense of Jewish nationalism. More faithful to Judaism than their coreligionists in the West they prayed every day for the Messiah to restore them to the Land of Israel. These religious masses contained the seeds of Jewish nationalism that Hess felt would eventually sprout and give new life to a restoration movement.

The Jewish religion must therefore be left unchanged until the foundations of a political and social establishment had been created in the Holy Land. Only then would a Sanhedrin be chosen that would assume the task of modifying Jewish Law in accordance with the needs of the new society. The main danger to Judaism, Hess emphasized, did not come from the pious Jew, but rather from the Jewish Reform movement, with their newly invented ceremonies and prayers. Not content with working toward the development of Jewish learning on modern scientific lines, they cultivated religious reforms in complete disregard for traditional Jewish practices. These reforms which in many instances aped Christian models, had not the slightest relationship to the essentially national character of Judaism.

In spite of his scathing attack on the religious reformers, Hess was optimistic that the gap between them and the traditional Orthodox could be bridged by the creation of a Jewish state in Palestine. It was therefore essential that the desire for a political rebirth be kept alive until conditions in the Holy Land were ripe for the founding of colonies. Indeed, Hess was convinced that there were signs that conditions were improving. He offered as proof the construction of the Suez Canal and the building of a railroad to link Europe and Asia. France, he felt, would possibly be the Great Power most willing to lend the Jews a helping hand in redeeming their ancient homeland. Such a project would not only enjoy the blessing of the French people, but would also serve the national interests of their country. An acute observer of the contemporary scene, Hess based his conclusions on the rivalry between the European powers to extend their spheres of influence in Asia and Africa. This competition on the part of the great nations was particularly intense between France and England in the Near and Middle East. The Jews, Hess believed, could benefit from this struggle for power. If there were any doubts about his analysis, Hess suggested one had only to look toward developments in France. A recent work entitled *La Nouvelle Question d'Orient* by Ernest Laharanne, a member of Napoleon III's secretariat, had actually proposed the establishment of a Jewish state under French protection. Although the French emperor, occupied with other problems, had not given the proposal official sanction, the idea was discussed and debated in high government circles.

Hess also had definite ideas about the character of the future Jewish state. He had no doubt that, except for a small number of individuals, the majority of Jews living in the civilized West would, even after the creation of a Jewish entity in Palestine, choose not to emigrate. Nevertheless, he was certain that East European Jews, given the opportunity, would gladly immigrate to the Holy Land. Hess also believed that in the final analysis, given modern means of communication, it did not really matter how many Jews lived within the borders of the Jewish state, and how many dwelled in the Diaspora. The important factor was that the Jewish state required a spiritual center around which a nucleus of motivated individuals could build a base for political action. While working on *Rome and Jerusalem,* Kalischer's *Derishat Zion* was published. The old socialist welcomed the Orthodox rabbi's call for the establishment of a society for the colonization of Palestine. He also considered Kalischer's book as additional evidence of his claim that pious Jews and reformers would eventually unite to restore the Jewish nation in Eretz Israel.

Once established, Hess emphasized, the Jewish state must, in general, be based on Mosaic principles. Thus it was essential that the nation as a whole own the land. In addition, legal conditions must be created under which work would flourish. Similarly, agricultural, industrial, and trade societies on the pattern suggested by the French utopian socialist, Louis Blanc, should be established with the help of state credits. Nevertheless, the Jewish state was not to be an end in itself, but merely a means toward achieving a social order to which all right-thinking people aspire.

To Hess's dismay *Rome and Jerusalem* had little if any impact on the reading public. Only 200 copies were sold in the five-year period following its publication. The format employed, the awkward style, and the Hegelian terminology militated against popular acceptance. Most socialists and liberals were unaware of Hess's book, and the handful who did read it rejected the work as a romantic fantasy. Some Jewish nationalists regarded the author's reliance on France and his belief that the Turks could be induced to part with Palestine as political naivete. The Reform Jews, on the other hand, attacked *Rome and Jerusalem* as the work of a charlatan.

Orthodox leaders also had doubts as to the sincerety of Hess's return to the Jewish fold. Only three years prior to the publication of *Rome and Jerusalem,* he had openly opposed all religions as the product of pathological minds. The Orthodox rabbis were also quick to note that while Hess was now preaching the virtues of religious observance, he did not adhere to his own prescription. Although he had convinced himself intellectually that religion, for the time being, was essential to prevent the total disintegration of the Jewish people, Hess nevertheless could not in his private life muster sufficient enthusiasm to live up to his discovery.

In spite of its shortcoming, Hess's book was a work of a prophetic genius. The author's analysis of the Jewish Problem was superior to that of any of his contemporaries. Indeed, Theodor Herzl commenting on Hess's accomplishment noted in his diary (entry of May 2, 1901) the following:

> The nineteen hours of this round trip was whiled away for me by Hess with his *Rome and Jerusalem,* which I had first started to read in 1898 in Jerusalem, but had never been able to finish properly in the pressure and rush of these years. Now I was enraptured and uplifted by him. What an exalted noble spirit! Everything that we have tried is already in his book. The only bothersome thing is his Hegelian terminology. Wonderful the Spinozistic-Jewish and nationalist elements. Since Spinoza, Jewry has brought forth no greater spirit than this forgotten Moses Hess.[265]

Heinrich Graetz the prominent Jewish historian also recognized the brilliance of Moses Hess—a view that the Jewish world at large would only come to share decades later. *Rome and Jerusalem,* which is today considered a Zionist classic was not published in Hebrew until 1899, and was not translated into English until a half century after the appearance of the original version.

In retrospect, Hess's masterpiece was unique in its prefiguration of later and better known Zionist writers. He clearly anticipated, for example, the theories of the future Labor Zionists with his assertion that the return to the Land of Israel and to its soil was indispensable if the Jews were to shed their image as a historical anomaly, a social parasite living in the lands of other people. Similarly, years before the rise of the Love of Zion movement, Hess warned that a national homeland in Palestine offered the Jews their last chance of self-transformation into a normal people, emancipated from the vulnerable phantom status that historically provoked anti-Semitism. Predating Theodor Herzl, Hess foresaw the need for the collaboration of European governments in helping the Jews return to Palestine, and also the need for enlisting the support of Jewish magnates in funding and organizing the settlement of the region.

Although disillusioned by the reception of *Rome and Jerusalem,* Hess continued for a time to take part in Jewish activities. Gradually, however, he drifted back to his earlier interests. Devoting his attentions to the socialist movement, he became a leading figure in the new party formed by Ferdinand Lasalle (1825–64), and later participated in the First International. His views on Jewish nationalism remained constant, but the cause for him had lost its urgency.

In April, 1875, Moses Hess died in Paris, a forgotten man. He was buried according to his instructions in Deutz, Germany (near Cologne). His long-delayed recognition as an authentic visionary of Zionism came in 1961 when his remains were flown from Germany to Israel, and reburied on the shores of Yam Kinneret in a formal state ceremony.

VI

NEW WORLD ZIONS

25

Marrano Zions

The idea of an asylum—a temporary shelter from persecution—has, in the course of Jewish history, often diverted large segments of Jewry from the quest to reestablish a Jewish entity in Palestine. A most notable example of such a development occurred in the wake of the expulsion of the Jews from the Iberian Peninsula. Although a small number of refugees did make their way to the Holy Land, the vast majority did not. Still others preferred a circuitous route to Zion, and dreamed of a territory, a temporary haven, where a scattered and dispirited people could regroup, heal its wounds, and once again become a healthy and vigorous nation. Among this group of refugees were some who visualized the building of a new Zion in the New World, where they could live out their lives peacefully, free from the anti-Semitism of the lands of their birth. To better understand the evolution of this group's thinking, it is essential to digress somewhat to briefly recount some of the highlights of the Jewish (including those designated as New Christians and Marranos) flight from the Iberian Peninsula.

The Columbus Connection

The connection between the Jews and the discovery of the Americas began with the epoch-making voyage of Columbus in 1492. Remarkably, the great admiral seemed to be well aware of the linkage. He began his written account of his first voyage of discovery with the following passage. "In the same month in which Their Majesties issued the edict that the Jews should be driven out of the kingdom and its territories—in that same month they gave me the order to undertake with sufficient men my expedition of discovery to the Indies."[266] He might have added that he actually set sail within a day or two of the departure of the last of the Jewish exiles. As a matter of historical fact, contrary to the legends that have grown up about the expedition, the voyage was very largely financed by funds extorted from the

Jews and by the backing financial and otherwise of a handful of prominent Marranos (derogatory term applied to the descendants of baptized Jews suspected of secret adherence to Judaism) and New Christians (converted Jews who remained loyal to their new religion). Indeed, many historians (e.g., Salvador Madariaga, M. Kayserling, and Cecil Roth) have pointed out that there are strong grounds for believing that Columbus was himself a member of a New Christian or Marrano family, as were some members of his crew (among those most often cited are Alonso de la Calle, Rodrigo Sanches, Mestre Bernal, Rodrigo de Triana, and Luis de Torres). Even more astounding were the patrons of Columbus. They included the Converso (i.e., New Christian) Luis de Santangel, the Chancellor and Comptroller of the royal household, a descendant of an old Saragossan Jewish family; Gabriel Sanchez, the High Treasurer of Aragon, the son of Conversos; Alfonso de la Caballeria, a member of a famous Marrano family; and the noted Jewish scholar Don Isaac Abravanel, advisor and financier to the Spanish rulers Ferdinand and Isabella.

As the end of the fifteenth century neared, the Jews of Portugal, unlike their Spanish coreligionists still felt reasonably secure; they were rendering valuable services to the crown and country. Indeed, when the Spanish rulers instituted their edict of expulsion, over 60,000 Jews fled to Portugal where they were given asylum by King John II. Nor did this state of affairs change with the accession to the throne of his son Manuel I in 1495; the new monarch commenced his reign by reaffirming the policy of leniency toward the Jews. This policy of tolerance, however, proved transitory when it came into conflict with Manuel I's matrimonial and dynastic ambitions. The Portuguese king was eager to marry the infanta Isabella of Castile-Aragon, and to that end he was obliged to bring his policy toward the Jews in line with that of Spain. To ensure the marriage alliance, Manuel I issued an edict (December, 1496) forcibly converting to Christianity all the Jews within his kingdom. This high-handed act greatly augmented the body of Marranos in the country, as well as triggering another wave of migration. Many fled to Italy, North Africa, and Turkey, while others turned their thoughts to finding a haven in the New World.

Colonization of Brazil

When the admiral, Pedro Alvares Cabral, claimed Brazil for Portugal a rare opportunity presented itself to Manuel I. Although unwilling to entirely lose the fruits of Jewish enterprise, he was willing to surreptitiously allow many Jews, New Christians, and Marranos to migrate to the newly discovered land, where their presence was unlikely to be noticed by his prospective Spanish in-laws. Thus in 1502 a consortium of New Christians led by Fernando de Noronha obtained from the King of Portugal a concession to colonize and exploit the resources of Brazil. A majority of the members of this group including their leader Noronha were crypto-Jews (i.e., Marranos). The settlement they founded depended for its survival on the exportation to Portugal of brazil-wood (from which the name of the new land was derived), where it was used extensively to dye textiles. These early colonists experienced severe hardships, but managed to survive in spite of the hostile environment and lack of support from the Portuguese crown. Portugal regarded Brazil as nothing more than a convenient landfall for eastward-bound spice fleets, prior to their sailing into the belt of the northwesterlies that would blow them around the Cape of Good Hope and into the Indian Ocean. Preoccupation with the riches of India precluded any major interest in such a vast and virgin territory as Brazil, and for a long time the Portuguese were content with establishing tiny provision stations at the best harbors and exploiting the dyewood trade.

Soon, however, settlers of a more spirited character began to arrive in Brazil. Noronha's colony received a much-needed boost in 1532 with the arrival from the Madeira Islands of a small band of Marranos. They brought sugar cane plants from Madeira and, with characteristic energy and initiative, speedily introduced the cultivation of cane along the coastal areas. Within a few years sugar far outstripped dyewoods as the settlement's chief export; and by the turn of the century many plantations, and over 100 sugar mills were either owned outright or under the management of Marrano and New Christian settlers.

During this period of commercial expansion, Brazil received numerous New Christians of doubtful orthodoxy as the tribunals of Portugal continued the crown's policy of deporting penitent heretics across the Atlantic. In their new homes the exiles often enjoyed freedom that had been inconceivable in the old country. A Marrano, Thomé de Sonza, for example, served as Brazil's first governor-general. New Christians dominated the medical profession, and were the most important element in the country's agricultural efforts. They encouraged the planting of cotton, tobacco, and rice, as well as sugar cane. Inevitably, the high visibility of the Marranos and New Christians aroused the envy of their Old Christian neighbors and the suspicions of the Church.

When Spain and Portugal were united in 1580, the dreaded tentacles of the Inquisition began to reach out to the Portuguese overseas empire (a similar development had already taken place in such Spanish colonies as Mexico and Peru). Although the Inquisition was never formally introduced into Brazil, inquisitorial powers were conferred on the bishop of Salvador (Bahia). Under his instructions to the secular authorities, all suspects of backsliding from Christianity were to be detained and sent back to the mother country for sentencing. The wave of fanaticism that followed on the heels of this policy led to a rash of interrogations, arrests, confiscations of property, and completely demoralized the New Christian and Marrano population.

The chaotic state of affairs brought about by the persecutions lasted for nearly half a century. It also led indirectly to a trade war that turned out detrimental to the interests of Portugal. Portugal derived little direct benefit from the sugar export trade, the bulk of which was destined for foreign markets—Holland being the most important. Portuguese prohibitions failed to stem the illegal export of sugar to the Netherlands, and by 1620 some 50,000 chests of Brazilian sugar were reaching Amsterdam annually. Through judicious bribery of local officials and the assistance of Marrano agents, this clandestine commerce was able to flourish. This illegal trade in turn provided the impetus for the growth of a great sugar refining industry in the Dutch capital of Amsterdam—a business in which Jews were especially active. From Holland the refined sugar product was exported to England, France, and the Baltic lands. In exchange for its sugar, the Brazilian exporters received Dutch linen and woolen textiles.

The profitable trade between the Marranos and New Christians of Brazil and the Jews of Holland played a major role in the establishment of the Dutch West India Company in 1621. Early in the company's history, the directors, with the blessing of the Dutch government, decided to secure a foothold in Brazil. There can be little doubt that in assessing the risks of such a move, the States-General took into account the support that a military expedition was likely to receive from the Marrano population of Brazil. Thus it was not surprising that when the West India Company eventually launched its military campaign, the Marranos warmly espoused the company's cause. In addition, Jewish volunteers in Holland joined the Brazilian expedition and distinguished themselves repeatedly in the ensuing conflict. Two Marranos, Nũño Alvares Franco, and Manuel Fernandez Drago formulated the attack plans that led to the capture of Bahia in 1623. Similarly, the fall of Pernambuco (Recife) in 1631 was largely the work of several Amsterdam Jews, the most prominent being Antonio Vaez Henriquez (alias Moses Cohen). Still another Amsterdam Jew, Francisco de Camphor, was responsible for the capture of the island Fernando de Noronha.

From its inception, the war turned into a struggle between the Portuguese and Spanish on one hand, and the Dutch supported by the Jews of Amsterdam and the Marranos of Brazil on the other hand. By 1640 the Dutch West India Company had succeeded in winning control of the six northern provinces of Brazil, a region that included the entire sugar-producing area of the country, as well as the heartland of the Marrano settlements.

The Dutch occupation of Northern Brazil greatly affected the Jewish Diaspora. First and foremost, most of the Marranos and New Christians of Brazil renounced the Catholic faith and openly returned to Judaism. In addition, the Jewish community was bolstered by an influx of Jewish immigrants from Holland, as well as from Turkey, the Barbary States, Poland, and Hungary. Typical of this new migration was the arrival in 1638 of a group of 200 Jews led by Manuel Mendes de Castro and in 1642 of a large party of immigrants from Amsterdam. The Dutch group settled in Pernambuco, and included a young scholar named Isaac Aboab da Fonseca (1605–93), who was destined to become the first American rabbi. Born in Castro Daire, Portugal, of a Marrano family, Aboab was brought as a child to St. Jean de Luz in France and later to Amsterdam, where he was given a Jewish upbringing. In Pernambuco the young rabbi organized a congregation bearing the name K.K. Zur Israel (Holy Congregation of the Rock of Israel). The congregation consisted mainly of Marranos who had recently returned to the Jewish faith. By 1644 the Jewish community of Dutch Brazil amounted to one-half of the total white population.

In an attempt to accelerate the exploitation of the region's natural resources, the Dutch authorities not only encouraged immigration to their Brazilian provinces, but also permitted a greater degree of religious freedom than was to be found anywhere else in the western world. During the governorship of Johann Maurits van Nassau (1637–44), in particular, the Jewish community of Brazil flourished and grew in power and size. Their affluence (made especially notable by the building of two synagogues in Pernambuco) aroused certain elements among the Christian colonists, who complained bitterly to the governor about the ostentatious behavior of the Jews. Johann Maurits van Nassau ignored the grumblings of the Christian malcontents, but after the governor's departure from the colony the position of the Jews deteriorated rapidly.

After sixty years of an uneasy political union the Portuguese proclaimed their independence from Spain (1640). The restoration of the House of Braganza made the status of Dutch Brazil uncertain. The directors of the West India Company (about one quarter of the company's shares were controlled by Marranos) became reluctant to invest in long-term projects in Dutch Brazil. They sensed that the Portuguese would sooner or later attempt to recover their former provinces. This policy of retrenchment on the part of the company was, indeed, exploited by the Portuguese, who did their utmost to stir up anti-Dutch feelings among the older colonists of the lost provinces. In Portugal the restoration party, in its efforts to incite the government to take military action in Brazil, did not hesitate to use religion as a cover, and to point to the synagogues, which had been opened publicly in those places under Dutch rule. Ironically, the renewed war, which erupted in 1645, was to a large extent financed, though against their will, by the New Christians of Portugal.

In Brazil the outbreak of hostilities found the Jewish community solidly behind the Dutch government. The rabbi, Aboab, rallied Jews from all over the provinces to come to the defense of Pernambuco, which had come under siege. Jews fought shoulder to shoulder alongside the Dutch soldiers. As the Portuguese tightened their noose around the city, many of its inhabitants fell victim to starvation. The siege was finally broken by a flotilla of eighteen ships under the command of David Peixotto, a Jew. Rabbi Aboab in commemoration of this event wrote a lengthy poem in Hebrew describing the tribulations through which Pernambuco had passed—it was the first piece of Jewish literature composed in the New World. However, after a brief respite, the Portuguese rallied and resumed the siege. Finally, after nine years of warfare, Pernambuco was forced to capitulate. The last major Dutch possession in Brazil had succumbed.

Although the Dutch were granted liberal terms of surrender, the Jewish community of Brazil was doomed. Almost immediately 600 of the most recent Jewish immigrants returned to Holland. Among this group was Rabbi Aboab who had spent thirteen years in Brazil. On arrival in Amsterdam he was appointed *haham* of the Jewish community as well as teacher in the Talmud Torah, principal of the yeshivah, and a member of the *Bet Din* (rabbinic court). In this capacity he was one of the signatories to the ban of excommunication issued against the philosopher, Baruch Spinoza, in 1656.

The greater portion of Brazil's former Marrano population scattered throughout the New World, especially to the West Indies archipelago and the adjacent coast. Many found refuge in the Dutch, English, and French possessions in the Antilles and in Guiana. In many instances these refugees became the founders of communities that would subsequently become important centers of trade. After an adventurous journey one ship-load of twenty-three refugees from Brazil managed to reach New Amsterdam (1654), where they set down roots to become "the Jewish pilgrim fathers of North America." Others obtained a foothold in Jamaica, which was never reached by the Inquisition. Many of these "Portugals," as they were commonly called, had established themselves in Jamaica even before the British conquest of the territory in 1655. On the island of Barbados the refugees from Brazil established the first modern sugar mill and greatly enhanced the territory's economy. Not long after their arrival, they were granted in 1656 full enjoyment of the ". . . privileges of Laws and Statutes of ye Commonwealth of England and of this island, relating to foreigners and strangers."[267] Similar developments occurred on other islands in the Caribbean basin. In Martinique a community of ex-Marranos had settled on the island during the period of Dutch rule and were allowed to remain there after the territory's conquest by the French. The island's first large-scale sugar plantation and refinery was established by Benjamin da Costa with the aid of 900 of his fellow Marranos from Brazil. Santo Domingo, which also received a large contingent of the Brazilian refugees, enjoyed an economic boom similar to that of Jamaica, Barbados, and Martinique.

Curacao

On Curacao the Jewish migration proved to be providential to the island's inhabitants. In March of 1651 the directors of the West India Company had written to Peter Stuyvesant,

the governor of New Netherlands, informing him that they were giving serious consideration to abandoning Curacao. (It had been ceded to the Dutch by Spain sixteen years
earlier.) Curacao was not economically viable. In an eleventh-hour effort to salvage their
investment, the West India Company entered into a contract with Joseph Nunez de
Fonseca (David Nassi), a former Marrano resident of Brazil. Fonseca agreed to provide
colonists for the island, who would attempt to bolster the economy. Under Fonseca's
sponsorship a large group of settlers (mostly Marranos) led by Jan de Illan, a long time
resident of Brazil, who had been denounced for Judaizing, embarked for Curacao.[268] By
December of 1652, Illan and his band had settled in and had begun a trade in logwood with
neighboring islands. However, since this trade was not permitted under the terms of the
contract made with Fonseca, the West India Company attempted to stop it.

The privileges granted to Fonseca under the terms of the contract were exceedingly
generous. He was to be given two leagues of land along the coast for every fifty families he
brought to the island. In addition, the colonists were granted exemption from taxes for ten
years and the right to select the land on which they wished to work and live. Of equal
importance, the colonists were accorded religious freedom. They were, however, restrained from working on Sunday or compelling Christians, should any be among them,
from laboring on that day.

In spite of the liberal concessions, the Curacao colony at first did not prosper and the
directors of the West India Company began to have doubts about the leadership qualities
and capabilities of Jan de Illan. However, a new infusion of Jewish refugees from Brazil
ensured the successful commercial development of the island.

Cayenne

David Nassi (alias Joseph Nunez de Fonseca) also played a key role in bringing Jews to
Cayenne (then Dutch Guiana).[269] Eager to make up for the loss of their Brazilian
territories, the West India Company encouraged the settlement and commercial exploitation of Cayenne. The colonists secured by Fonseca were granted a charter (September 12,
1659) that guaranteed freedom of thought, liberty of conscience, and political autonomy.
Attracted by these generous provisions, Jews from Holland and elsewhere flocked to the
new colony. In 1660 a large party of Jews, including the Marrano poet, David Levi de
Barrios, left Leghorn, Italy for Cayenne. Their water supply ran low enroute, and the ship
was forced to return to Italy, where some of the immigrants abandoned the vessel. Those
hardy souls who continued the voyage finally arrived safely in Cayenne, where they
contributed greatly to raising the spirits of the fledgling Jewish community.

For several years the Cayenne colony flourished, but constant warfare between
Holland and Portugal, and the frequent depredations of the French, to whom the island
was eventually ceded, made it impossible for the colonists to enjoy a normal life. Finally,
a majority of the Jews decided to abandon their settlement. In May of 1664 they
immigrated to the English colony of Surinam (northeastern corner of South America).

Surinam

Jews were present in Surinam as early as 1639.[270] They were reinforced by a group of
Jewish emigrants from England (1652). The latter migration was carried out under the
auspices of Lord Willoughby of Parham, who succeeded in laying the foundation for a

permanent settlement that would later bear his name. A second wave of settlers, led by Fonseca, came to Surinam following the cession of Cayenne to the French. This group was mainly former Marranos who had fled Brazil. Most of them were seasoned plantation owners and farmers, hardened by life under rugged conditions. The English masters of Surinam were keenly aware of the high caliber of manpower that fortune had brought to their colony. They were also conscious of the profits reaped by the Dutch in their various colonies as a result of their grants of liberal charters to the Jews. A letter of the period, written by an Englishman who had come into possession of a Dutch document dealing with the use of Jews as colonists, takes note of this development, and warns his compatriots that Holland is establishing a colony between Surinam and Cartagena for the express purpose of exploiting trade with the Spanish settlements, which are in great need of European commodities. Furthermore, they have invited twenty-five Jewish families to settle in the new colony and as an inducement have offered them many privileges and immunities. The writer ends his letter by advising the English regime on Surinam to follow the wise example of the Dutch and grant their Jews similar privileges.

The Jewish colonists were also aware of their importance to Surinam's economy and felt the time was ripe to assert their claim to be treated as equals with their Christian neighbors. Petitions to this effect were circulated, and the government was notified that further immigration of Jews to Surinam would not be forthcoming until the status of the Jewish settlers was clarified. They did not have to wait long for an answer. In 1665 a sweeping grant of privileges assured the safety of the Jewish colonists, and guaranteed them the full enjoyment and free exercise of their religious rites and usages. To a large extent the provisions of the grant paralleled those given to the Jews by the Dutch on Curacao and elsewhere in the Caribbean. The Surinam charter of rights had the desired effect in encouraging Jewish immigration. In a relatively short time the Jews of Willoughby Land (the name of the territory following the accession of Charles II to the English throne) were forwarding a steady flow of sugar to England and had succeeded in markedly strengthening the colony's economy.

In 1667 Surinam surrendered to the Dutch. Some of the wealthier Jewish colonists, who had by a decree of that year become English citizens, indicated a desire to leave the colony with the English garrison. The Dutch were unwilling to lose these successful planters and attempted to prevent their departure. The incident touched off a bitter controversy within the Jewish community between those who favored the Dutch and those who wished to leave with the English. In the end majority rule prevailed and most of the Jewish planters remained in Surinam. The colony continued to prosper, and the Jewish settlers remained quiescent until 1675, when once again a small group of planters tried to leave Surinam. These planters felt that the Dutch authorities, who had restricted their free exercise of religion following the takeover from the English, had procrastinated in restoring this privilege. Fearing the collapse of the colony's economy, the Dutch forcibly retained the Jewish planters from leaving, and shortly afterward restored all of the privileges the Jewish settlers had enjoyed under the English.[271]

Besides the main settlement of Surinam at Paramaribo, which was located on the seacoast, there were flourishing Jewish colonies inland. The Jews built a city surrounded by plantations on a hillock by the Paramaribo River, deep in the midst of a vast green meadowland (savannah). It became known as Die Joden Savanne (the Savannah of the Jews),[272] and in this territory the settlers enjoyed a remarkable degree of autonomy. Indeed, it came closest to the Maranno dream of a New World Zion. The economy of the settlement was based largely on sugar and other agricultural products and was completely self-sufficient. Die Joden Savanne contained all of the amenities of an urban center, including synagogues and other Jewish institutions. It also boasted its own police force and court system. However, like the rest of Surinam, Die Joden Savanne contained an Achilles heel—the dependence on Negro slave labor to work the sugar plantations.

In 1689 and again in 1712 Surinam was attacked by French forces, and the Jews fought bravely alongside their Dutch neighbors in defense of their adopted homeland. The planters of Die Joden Savanne also played a key role in the attempts by the Dutch authorities to suppress the slave revolts that erupted in the period from 1690 to 1723. These disturbances, coupled with the decline of the sugar trade, ultimately led to the abandonment of the Savannah of the Jews during the course of the nineteenth century. Only ruins and broken tombstones remained to mark the spot where a prosperous community had once existed. The tropical jungle had reclaimed its domain.

Most of the former settlers of Die Joden Savanne drifted toward Surinam's coastal areas, and in particular to Paramaribo. By the eighth decade of the twentieth century, however, few Jews could be found in Surinam. The vision of creating a Zion in the New World, which had begun with the Marrano pioneers of Brazil, had for all practical purposes come to an end with the demise of the Surinam settlement. There would, however, be other attempts to revive this dream, but all would prove ephemeral.

26

Maurice de Saxe

The struggle of the European powers to colonize and exploit the resources of the Americas inspired romantic notions among many adventurous individuals. In one unusual case it awakened dormant dynastic ambitions in a distinguished professional soldier named Hermann Moritz von Sachsen (1696–1750).[273] Although his story is tangential to the quest for Zion and had no impact whatsoever on Jewry or their efforts to regain Palestine, it is, however, important for two reasons: it sheds light on the ferment surrounding the Jewish Question, which was slowly rising to the foreground of European consciousness, and it highlights the efforts to colonize parts of the New World by taking advantage of Jewish immigrants anxious to build a new Zion free from religious and civil persecution.

Moritz von Sachsen was born in Goslar (Germany), the illegitimate son of the elector of Saxony, Frederick Augustus I ("the Strong") later also king of Poland as Augustus II. At age twelve, Frederick launched his son, Moritz, on a military career by sending him to serve in Flanders under the renowned general, Prince Eugene of Savoy. An apt student, Moritz soon revealed a flair for military life. On completion of his apprenticeship, his father conferred upon him the title of Graf (count) and bought for him a German regiment in the service of the French king, Louis XV. Comte Maurice de Saxe (the French equivalent of Moritz's German title and name) rapidly won a reputation as a daring and valorous leader and soon attracted the attention of his superiors for his innovations in the use of musketry and for his training methods. He also won the admiration of the French court, who dubbed him the "Wild Boar" in recognition of his many battlefield and boudoir escapades.

In December of 1725 Maurice de Saxe visited his father in Warsaw where Augustus II was trying desperately to win support for a Saxon succession in Poland. However, the Wettiners ("the Saxon dynasty") were extremely unpopular among the Polish magnates and their followers, and when the gentry of Courland (Latvia) offered their duchy to Maurice, the Polish *sejm* (diet) refused to recognize or assist him in any way. Instead, the *sejm* demanded that Courland be incorporated into the Polish Royal Republic and instructed their hetmans not to oppose the Russians, who were intent on eliminating Maurice and his Saxon forces from Courland and restoring the status quo. Maurice de Saxe did little to help his course when, at the height of the Courland crisis he was caught in an illicit affair, which cost him the support of Anna Ivanova (the future Empress of Russia), who had initially favored his cause. Driven out of Courland by the Russians, the incident left an indelible mark on Maurice de Saxe's ego, which remained with him throughout his life. Decades later he would confide in his memoirs that he had, ". . . never been cured of the throne fever I caught in Courland, I felt born to reign, impelled by ambition to be a sovereign of some state, no matter how small, no matter where situated."[274]

In 1732 the Comte, who had returned to France, won the attention of that country's military establishment with the publication of a treatise on war entitled *Mes Reveries.*[275] The outbreak of hostilities soon diverted Maurice de Saxe's energies to more bellicose activities (the War of the Polish Succession), in which he achieved the rank of lieutenant-general in the French army. His reputation as a master strategist was further recognized during the War of the Austrian Succession, when Maurice de Saxe suggested and personally executed the capture of Prague (November 26, 1741). Nineteen months later he was rewarded with the command of an army in Alsace. However, the jealousy of other French officers, who looked upon Maurice de Saxe as an outsider, a foreigner, and a heretic (he was a Protestant of the Lutheran persuasion), disturbed Louis XV and he transferred the Comte to Dunkerque. In Dunkerque he was given command of an expeditionary force designated to invade England. A sudden storm wrought havoc on the invasion fleet, forcing the French king to order the abandonment of the campaign.

In spite of this unexpected setback, Maurice de Saxe's progress up the French military ladder continued apace. In 1744 he was made a Marshal of France and given command of an army corps in Flanders. When the French king weakened his command by ordering an entire army to the German front, the Comte suddenly found himself in a dangerous situation, as his remaining troops were now greatly outnumbered by the British, Austrian, and Dutch armies arrayed against him. By a series of skillful maneuvers, the resourceful Comte managed to escape encirclement and thus avoid certain disaster. In the Battle of Fontenoy (May, 1745), which followed soon after the restoration of his corps to full strength, Maurice de Saxe won a decisive victory over the allies. Further victories that secured Ghent, Brussels, and Antwerp confirmed the Comte's great military skill. Following these triumphs, the Marshal marched south and capped his amazing campaign by seizing Mons and Namur and soundly defeating Prince Charles of Lorraine at Racoux, near Liege.

A grateful Louis XV conferred upon Maurice de Saxe the rank of Marshal-General of France, an honor held by only two men before him (Turenne and Villars). All of France's military efforts were now concentrated in the hands of the newly created marshal-general who, from his headquarters in Brussels, wielded almost sovereign power over the Netherlands. However, with the Peace of Aix-la-Chapelle, Maurice de Saxe's military career came to an end and he retired to the chateau of Chambord, which had been placed at his disposal by Louis XV along with an income more than adequate for its maintenance. Here the marshal-general lived in a magnificent style. The most sumptuous luxury, the most exquisite delicacy of taste, the rarest productions of art united to embellish the chateau (including tapestries from Gobelin, bronzes by Callini, miniatures by Petitot, fainces by Pallessy, and paintings and sculptures by the great masters of Italy and France). A lover of opera, the Comte maintained his own company, and enjoyed the use of a theater with a seating capacity for 1,000 people located in one of the towers of the chateau. As a special boon, the French king also allowed the marshal-general's old German regiment, the Volontaires de Saxe to be stationed in the chateau's park.

In his retirement Maurice de Saxe exercised boundless hospitality. The elite of the social world of Paris vied with each other to get invited to the marshal-general's table. At Chambord places were laid daily for 140 guests. The Comte who had been insatiably promiscuous throughout his military career now found time for numerous affairs of the heart. One such liaison with a shining star of the Parisian opera presented him with a daughter, Marie Aurore, who was destined to become the mother of the most famous Frenchwoman of her generation, Amandine Aurore Dupin, better known by her nom de plume, George Sand.

However, the splendors of his life at Chambord were not completely satisfying for a man of the Comte's wide outlook and limitless ambition. Forever dreaming of kingdoms and crowns he conceived a plan to colonize the island of Madagascar (chiefly with Germans) and to establish a kingdom there with himself as the ruler. The proposal was placed before the French king and his advisers but rejected as being too costly and impractical. Undismayed by this setback to his dynastic ambitions, Maurice de Saxe looked about for another territory. Finally, he obtained from Louis XV a grant to colonize Tobago, a small island in the West Indies. The smallness of the island provided the enemies of the old soldier with a rare opportunity to ridicule his grandiose schemes. But the very insignificance of Tobago was, in the eyes of the retired marshal-general a decided advantage, for you can ". . . begin with a rock, and if you are intelligent and alert you may finish with an archipelago."[276]

Unfortunately for Maurice de Saxe, the Dutch and the English considered the French king's grant of Tobago to his former commander an infringement of the recently signed Treaty of Aix-la-Chapelle. Louis XV, unwilling to renew hostilities over the disposition of a barren island on the other side of the Atlantic, persuaded the Comte to forgo his ambition to become the ruler of Tobago.

South American Plans

The marshal-general next turned his attention to Corsica, where a Westphalian adventurer had lately reigned for a few months. His scheme to take over the island, however, failed to materialize, as did a second project to conquer the Barbary states of North Africa. Undaunted, the Comte allowed his imagination to take a wilder flight and conceived a plan to transfer all the Jews en masse from Europe to a territory in South America, and then reign over them as king.[277] A contemporary of the marshal-general, the Margravine von Ansbach in her memoirs alludes to his scheme to utilize the Jews of Europe in creating a kingdom in the New World, and emphasizes that the Comte was preoccupied by this project shortly before his demise in November of 1750. Historians, however, remain divided as to how Maurice de Saxe died. The official report listed his death as resulting from pneumonia, but many believe that he was killed in a duel with his enemy, the Prince de Conde, Louis Francois de Bourbon.

Neither the account of the Margravine, or the memoirs of the marshal-general indicate to what extent, if any, Jews knew of or supported the latter's plans. Even more remarkable is the strange quirk of history that a son of Augustus the Strong, whose reign in both Saxony and Poland was marked by indifference toward the Jews, should conceive a plan to create and rule over a kingdom populated by Jews. Even more amazing, there was little in Maurice de Saxe's background or experience to indicate any real sympathy for the plight of European Jewry. On the contrary on the few occasions in his memoirs where he speaks of Jews it is usually in a derogatory manner, referring to them as money lenders, or greedy merchants thinking only of profits. Perhaps the Comte's illegitimate birth, which dogged him all his life, and the burning desire to remove this stain by becoming a monarch and creating a dynasty led him to consider the Jews, the pariahs of European society, as suitable subjects for his proposed kingdom. It is possible that Maurice de Saxe may have met at his father's court some of the court Jews who helped Augustus the Strong outbid his rivals for the Polish throne. These Jews may have left an indelible impression on the young Maurice, and instilled in him a belief that the stock that produced such king-makers could also yield excellent colonists. The Comte may have also felt that the very idea of suggesting the removal of the Jews from Europe would win for him the universal support of the continent's rulers, as well as the gratitude and loyalty of the Jewish people. Lastly, it is more than likely that the marshal-general was familiar with the pioneering efforts of the Jews in Brazil, Cayenne, Surinam, and elsewhere in the Caribbean area, and was confident that with such subjects his project could not possibly fail. Whatever Maurice de Saxe's motives may have been his sudden death brought to an end the grandiose scheme to create a South American kingdom peopled by Jews from Europe. Nevertheless, a century later the dream of a reconstituted Zion in the New World, or at the very least the establishment there of a temporary haven for persecuted Jewry, surfaced once again.

27

North America as a Jewish Haven

Bernhard Behrend's Proposal

Early in December of 1832 a respected Jewish merchant named Bernhard Behrend,[278] living in Rodenberg, Germany, entered into a protracted correspondence with Baron Amschel Mayer Rothschild (1773–1855), the head of the Rothschild family of financiers in Frankfort-on-Main. He proposed to the Baron a plan to purchase land in North America, and to settle there, ". . . our unfortunate oppressed coreligionists . . . especially the Jews of Germany, Poland and Italy."[279] In his letters Behrend pleaded with Rothschild for an audience so that he could explain in detail the colonization plan that he firmly believed would once and for all times remove the Jewish Problem from the agenda of the European nations. Mass migration out of Europe to North America, where cheap land was still available, Behrend felt, would bring a diminution of anti-Semitism for those Jews who chose not to emigrate and offer new hope for those eager to escape the persecutions of the Old World. By financing the initial purchase of land required for the proposed settlements, Behrend emphasized, the Baron would render his fellow Jews a great service, and still be able to realize considerable profit on his investment.

Baron Amschel Mayer Rothschild, the eldest son of the founder of the banking dynasty, and by all accounts the most conservative member of the family, ignored Behrend's correspondence. Refusing to accept defeat Behrend persisted in his efforts to change the banker's mind. However, after the passage of several years without any tangible sign that Baron Rothschild had become more amenable to his proposal or was even willing to grant him an audience, Behrend looked about for another possible benefactor. In 1844 he turned to Gabriel Riesser (1806–63), the leading protagonist of Jewish emancipation in Germany. Riesser's series of memoranda and articles appearing in the journal *Der Jude* demanding civic equality for the Jews had aroused the conscience of German liberals, and earned the writer a reputation as the champion of German Jewry.

Elaborating on the scheme he had originally presented in his correspondence with Baron Amschel Mayer Rothschild, Behrend solicited Riesser's assistance in making the plan a reality. He suggested that the tireless fighter for Jewish rights help found and assume the leadership of an organization to be known as the "North American Colonization Society." Once established the society would issue stock, buy land, and supervise the exodus of the Jews from Europe.

Gabriel Riesser, at the time fully occupied with his struggle with the opponents of Jewish emancipation, rejected Behrend's proposal outright. The civil rights advocate was not in sympathy with the idea of a mass immigration of Jews out of Germany. He feared that a public pronouncement of such a plan would endanger the progress made toward emancipation, as well as place the very continuation of the German Jewish community in jeopardy. Riesser also insisted that the vast majority of German Jews had no desire to leave their native land.

Frustrated by Riesser's rejection, Behrend set out for Frankfort-on-Main in the winter of 1845, determined this time to set his colonization proposal before Baron Amschel Mayer Rothschild in person. His perseverance was finally rewarded and a series of discussions with Rothschild ensued. The Baron, a pious Jew, expressed the traditional view that the redemption of the Jews awaited the coming of the Messiah, and that Palestine, not North America, was the true Zion. Behrend attempted to refute these arguments by stressing the need for an asylum from religious persecution. He also emphasized that by Rothschild taking over the leadership of the proposed colonization society and exodus from Europe he could become a second Moses. The wily financier, at first taken aback by being compared with Moses, quickly recovered his composure and noted that Moses had been sent by God, whereas he had no such mandate. After some additional exchanges, Behrend realized that Rothschild had no faith whatsoever in his scheme, and that he was unwilling to risk his name or capital on a project which he considered neither desirable or feasible.

The failure to convert Rothschild to his views left Behrend with bitter feelings. To clear his mind, he set down in writing a record of his efforts on behalf of Jewry over the previous twelve years. He described in detail the arguments and counter-arguments that had marked his correspondence and interview with Baron Rothschild, and concluded that instead of begging the rich and powerful for help, it would have been a wiser and better tactic to appeal directly to the Jewish masses. Anti-Semitism, Behrend believed, would provide the propelling force for the creation of the colonization society, and the exodus out of Europe. A half century later Theodor Herzl would express similar thoughts, after failing to convince the head of the French branch of the Rothschilds, and other prominent Jewish financiers of the need for a Jewish state.

Seeking a viable outlet to bring his ideas before the Jewish public, Behrend approached Ludwig Philippson (1811–89), rabbi, scholar, community leader and editor of the liberal journal the *Allgemeine Zeitung des Judenthums*. Philippson patiently listened to Behrend's proposals, and bluntly informed the merchant that his plan was nothing less than a chimera. Like Gabriel Riesser, whom he was fond of quoting, Philippson felt that as a fighter for Jewish emancipation he could not in good conscience publish Behrend's appeal to the Jewish masses.

Undaunted, Behrend turned to Dr. Julius Fürst (1805–73) an outstanding orientalist, and founder of the scholarly periodical *Orient*. Fürst proved more sympathetic to Behrend's ideas than Philippson, and published in full the merchant of Rodenberg's colonization plan and his appeal for support in the pages of the *Orient*. The article also specified that Behrend was willing to communicate directly with people interested in his proposals and suggested that a conference of such individuals eventually be called to consider how best to implement the colonization plan. Behrend was particularly anxious to enlist Jewish youth in his proposed society. He called on the youth to prepare for life in North America by acquiring agricultural and mechanical skills, as well as a command of the English and Hebrew languages. In spite of the appearance of Behrend's plan in the prestigious *Orient*, the article and its author failed to find a wide audience.

Neujudaea

Nevertheless, Behrend was not a voice in the wilderness, for others in Germany during these years came up with similar suggestions. Thus in 1840 in Berlin a pamphlet entitled *Neujudaea*[280] appeared, in which the author (he signed his work with the initials C.L.K.) argued strenuously for the uniting of the dispersed Jewish people in a state of their own. Like Behrend, this anonymous author favored North America as the future site of the Jewish state. He proposed several locations, including the American midwest, Arkansas and Oregon. The pamphlet's author also believed that an offer of $10 million would be sufficient to induce the United States to part with the required tracts of land. He also urged speed in negotiating for the land grants, as America was rapidly being populated. The unknown pamphleteer rounded out his thesis with a strong warning to his readers that anti-Semitism was on the rise in Europe, and that Jews were being condemned to lead a parasitic life among people who hated them. In the New World, he felt, the Jews would have an opportunity to demonstrate their real worth and ability, as well as enjoy the blessings of freedom.

One of the most interesting aspects of the scheme outlined in *Neujudaea* was the novel suggestion that, in addition to the proposed settlement on the North American continent, a "spiritual center" be built in the Land of Israel. The imaginative author speculated on the possibility of acquiring the city of Jerusalem, and making it a goal of Jewish pilgrimages just as the ". . . Christians possess Rome and the Mohammedans Mecca."[281]

Unfortunately for the author of *Neujudaea* his appeal to the Jews of Germany came at the height of their struggle for emancipation, and on the eve of the revolution of 1848. Germany's Jews, dreaming of civil rights and equality, showed little inclination to heed the Cassandras among them who warned of virulent anti-Semitism and urged them to abandon their homes for foreign shores in distant America. The heady wine of emancipation had succeeded in dulling the senses of German Jewry, leaving little room for either traditional messianic aspirations for a restoration in the Holy Land, and even less for the startling idea of the creation of a new Zion in North America.

Major Mordecai Manuel Noah's Ararat Project

The most flamboyant of all New Zion advocates was Major Mordecai Manuel Noah,[282] probably the best known and most influential Jew in the United States during the first half of the nineteenth century. In a manner strongly reminiscent of Disraeli, his more eminent contemporary, Noah pursued careers in literature and politics. As one writer has noted Noah ". . . was led by imagination nurtured in both these fields to bring about the eventual resettlement of the Jews in Palestine"—the vision of Disraeli's *Tancred*. However, unlike Disraeli, who for all his Jewish racial pride was a convert to Christianity, Noah remained throughout his life loyal to Judaism, and active in Jewish community affairs and concerns.

Noah was born in 1785 in the city of Philadelphia, the son of a Sephardic Jew and itinerant South Carolinian merchant named Manuel M. Noah. The latter, a Revolutionary War veteran, had served under General Francis Marion (the swamp fox), and as an aide-de-camp to George Washington. Legend has it that Washington was present at Manuel's marriage to Zipporah Phillips, the daughter of an ardent Philadelphia patriot.

Mordecai Manuel Noah's early years were spent in Charleston, South Carolina. At the age of ten, following the death of his mother, he was sent to live with his maternal grandfather in Philadelphia. Although apprenticed to a gilder and carver, Noah nevertheless was able to continue his education by attending school for a few hours each day. His evenings were spent at the theatre and in the Franklin Library, an institution frequented by the most prominent scholars and statesmen of the era (Philadelphia at the time was the capital of the United States).

Young Noah's attraction to the theatre was stimulated by the presence of a playhouse (the American Theatre) in the vicinity of his home. He eagerly joined a troupe of amateur actors associated with this theatre, and to his lot eventually fell the responsibility for writing couplets and casting parts. However, the company of thespians could not meet their expenses and soon dissolved. Noah, by now addicted to the theatre, retained his interest by becoming a regular patron of the better-known Chestnut Street Theatre. In recalling years later his youthful passion for drama, Noah would tell how he never missed a night in the theatre and always returned to bed, after witnessing a good play, gratified and improved. He also felt that his interest in the theatre kept him away from the taverns and the temptations and pursuit of pleasures that frequently allured young men.

At the age of twenty-one, Noah for the first time gave serious consideration to becoming a writer. Following this decision he wrote a number of plays on various historical themes, and produced a volume of Shakespearean criticism. Unable to support himself by his literary efforts, he obtained with the assistance of the financier and senator, Robert Morris (1734–1806), a position as a clerk in the auditor's office of the United States Treasury Department. Upon the removal of the national capital to Washington D.C. in 1800, Noah became a reporter at the sessions of the Pennsylvania legislature at Harrisburg. Here he acquired his first experience in journalism, a profession that he would follow with few interruptions, for the rest of his life.

In 1808 Noah began to show an interest in politics. Along with other so-called Democratic Young Men he strongly favored the candidacy of James Madison for President of the United States. The following year he moved to Charleston, South Carolina, ostensibly to study law. His reputation as a budding writer had preceded him, and he was chosen to fill the post of editor of the *Charleston City Gazette*.

Noah's editorship coincided with the rapid deterioration of relations between the United States and England. A confirmed "war hawk" the young editor, using the pseudonym of Muley Malack, wrote stirring and inflammatory articles attacking British policies, and favoring the rapidly growing anti-British Party. His articles and editorials aroused the ire of a number of Charleston's citizens, and Noah was challenged to several duels. In one confrontation he managed to wound his opponent, and in a second duel he killed his challenger. A third duel, with Joshua W. Toomer, resulted in another triumph for Noah and he was awarded on the spot the honorary title of "major" by the two South Carolinian officers acting as his seconds.[283]

Through influence exerted on his behalf by a wealthy uncle and partly as a reward for the services he had rendered the national administration, Noah was appointed in 1813 American Consul in Tunis. He was also charged to carry out a special mission involving the Algerian government. The Algerines, just prior to Noah's appointment, had committed an act of piracy against the United States by capturing an American vessel out of Salem, Massachusetts, and enslaving the crew. The new consul was instructed to secure the release of the seamen in a manner that would bring honor to the United States, and strengthen American prestige in the Mediterranean. Above all he was to endeavor to make the Algerines believe that the relatives and friends of the captives rather than the American government were interested in liberating the sailors.

On May 23, 1813, Noah sailed from Charleston harbor to assume his North African post. The ship, however, was intercepted by the British, and the newly appointed consul was taken to England, where he was detained for two months. Upon his release he slowly made his way to Cadiz, Spain, where he made arrangements with an American named Richard R. Keene (later accused of treason) to help affect the liberation of the sailors captured by the Algerines.

After the elapse of more than a year from the time of his departure from Charleston, Noah finally reached Tunis. He immediately proceeded to carry out his special mission and accomplished it in a very creditable manner. However, he was compelled in the process to expend a sum exceeding the amount allotted to him by the United States government. Although buoyant over the success of his mission, Noah was not completely satisfied. He was particularly disturbed by the state department's policy, heartily endorsed by his predecessor in office, of paying annual tribute to the Barbary pirates. His reports back to the state department reflected his deep feelings on this subject. By a curious twist of history, a boyhood classmate of Noah named Stephen Decatur would one day exact a humiliating treaty from the dey of Algiers and put an end to these piratical extortions.

Apparently while acting as consul in Tunis, the fact of his Jewishness thrust itself fully on Noah's consciousness. His travels to and from his diplomatic post had given him a rare opportunity to observe first hand the reactionary policies adopted by many European governments following the defeat of Napoleon at the Battle of Waterloo. He was particularly disturbed by the reimposition, in many places, of Jewish disabilities. Noah was also keenly aware of the plight and deplorable conditions under which the Jews of Muslim North Africa lived.

A more shattering personal confrontation with the implications of his origins came in 1815, when Noah was suddenly removed from his consular post. His political enemies at home had raised a clamor over the excessive expenditures incurred in securing the release of the enslaved American sailors, and reference was made to financial irregularities in Noah's official ledgers. Not only were these charges never substantiated, but after two years of audits and litigation the state department acknowledged Noah's claims, and reimbursed him a sum of $5,216.57 for out-of-pocket expenditures made during his term of office.

Most revealing in this disgraceful affair was the the principal reason given in the letter of dismissal of Noah by the Secretary of State, James Monroe. It noted that the consul's religion was not appropriate to a representative of the American people abroad an argument that Noah in no way could find justifiable. It ran counter to everything he stood for as a man, patriot, and Jew. Even more remarkable, it was contrary to everything then known about Noah's actual performance as a consul and was a serious infringement of the spirit of freedom of conscience that marked the young American republic and its leaders. Indeed, the announcement of Noah's removal from office touched off a storm of protest, especially among the Jews of Charleston, forcing President Madison to dispatch a trusted Jewish army officer to the city to pacify the enraged community. In the midst of this uproar, Noah and the diplomatic establishment exchanged charges and counter charges, and in the confusion the relevant documents pertaining to the affair somehow vanished (or were destroyed) from the official archives.

Recent research has uncovered some fascinating material as to the factors that may have motivated President Madison and his Secretary of State, Monroe, to recall Noah from Tunis.[284] The villain of the piece, it is now believed was Tobias Lear, the man who had been consul to the Barbary States prior to Noah's appointment. Lear, socially prominent in Dolley Madison's circle, had been a private secretary and confidant to George Washington and had shared in the first president's estate. Two of his three wives were nieces of Martha Washington. As consul to the Barbary States he had advocated and followed a policy of bribery as the sole means of dealing with the latter's constant acts of piracy and extortion. This policy had early on proved bankrupt. Indeed, Lear's clumsiness in his representations had offended the dey of Algiers, and in 1811 he was ordered to leave the country. His failure as a diplomat dogged him on his return to the United States. Resentment soon turned to rancor when he was not consulted on the selection of his replacement – the Jew from Charleston.

At about the time that Noah was getting started on his mission to rescue the American seamen, Lear received a personal letter from the veteran Swedish consul, John Norderling, who had represented American interests in the period following Lear's abrupt departure and the arrival of Noah in Tunis. Norderling had taken an immediate dislike to Noah who had not thought it necessary to seek out his guidance. In his letter to Lear, the Swedish diplomat included gossip about the difficulties Noah was having in carrying out his rescue mission. In the Washington D.C. circles frequented by Lear, the gossip of the spiteful Swedish consul was embroidered, and magnified by the former consul and treated as information on which complete reliance could be placed.

In delving into this entire affair, author Peter Grose has written:

> No one in that glittering social set [which included the Madisons and the Monroes] would be inclined to speak on behalf of the young and pushy Jew who had taken Tobias Lear's job. . . .
> Noah was sacked . . . because of informal and perhaps malicious distorted reports that reached Madison and Monroe from their social friends. Noah they said was bungling his delicate mission.[285]

Social gossip, however was not enough to justify Noah's dismissal. Additional ammunition was provided when Secretary Monroe learned of the anti-Jewish sentiments encountered by American missionaries on the Barbary coast. Accordingly, he addressed a memo to President Madison indicating that the reason for removing Noah was now stronger than ever before.

On his return to the United States in 1816, Noah settled in New York. His uncle Napthali Phillips was publisher of the influential newspaper the *National Advocate,* and

Noah was invited to join the staff. A facile and witty writer, Noah in time became the newspaper's chief editor and, several years later, its publisher. Throughout his journalistic career he would be associated with several newspapers, including the *New York Enquirer, The Courier and Enquirer,* the *Commercial Advertiser, Times and Weekly Messenger,* and the *Sunday Times.* He also aided James Gordon Bennett (1795-1872), financially and otherwise, when Bennett established the *New York Herald.*

His position as a reporter, editor, and publisher gave Noah access to political circles, and as a Tammanyite, Jacksonian Democrat, and later as a Whig, he held successively the offices of High Sheriff (1822), Grand Sachem of Tammany (1824), Surveyor of the Port of New York (1829), and Judge of the Court of Sessions (1841). Mordecai Manuel Noah's politics were often tempestuous. He did not believe in halfway measures. A cause was either wholly good or utterly hopeless. You were either his friend or his enemy. For example, he broke with Tammany over their opposition to De Witt Clinton, then Commissioner of Canals, and in 1825 supported Clinton for Governor of New York. Critical of President Andrew Jackson's attack on the U.S. Bank, Noah jumped party ranks and aligned himself with the Whigs. Always an individualist he supported the Texas Revolt of 1836 against Mexico; and fervently opposed the abolitionist movement.

His turbulent political career and character however is best illuminated by an incident that occurred in 1822. A yellow fever epidemic threatened the residents of New York City. Noah, in his capacity as high sheriff, fearing the worst, decided to release all of the prisoners confined in the debtors jail located on Manhattan's Ludlow Street. This humane act brought down on him an avalanche of bills and claims for damage from indignant creditors. In the end, Noah and his bond signers were forced to pay these claims. To add insult to injury, he was also denounced by several Christian clergymen who, from their pulpits, insisted that the plague was a divine visitation upon New York for having chosen a Jew as its sheriff.

Similarly, when Noah defected from the Democratic Party, and joined his former enemies, he both baffled and infuriated his former political friends. When questioned about his sudden change of heart, he replied that the party had abandoned its principles, but that he had not. When he found to his surprise that the opposition now stood for what he had always believed in, he had no choice, but in good conscience to change parties.

Political involvement in public affairs in the first half of nineteenth-century America was not for timid souls. Disagreements and petty wrangles often led to fist fights, street brawls and even duels. Noah was a contentious politician; however, there was another side of his character that seemed to belie his natural pugnaciousness. It was mirrored in his work as an author and playwright.

American literature during this period was still in its infancy. It was the generation of James Fenimore Cooper (1789-1851) and Washington Irving (1783-1859), and Noah, who knew these men, also contributed to the literary harvest of the day. In 1819 he published *Travels in England, France, Spain, and the Barbary States,* in which he lucidly described his experiences abroad, and defended the actions he had taken while in charge of the consulate at Tunis. Other books soon followed, including *Gleanings From a Gathered Harvest* (1845), a collection of essays and editorials, and the *Book of Yashar.*

Noah also enjoyed a reputation as the most popular American dramatist of the period. It was his first love, and his passion for the theatre remained a constant factor throughout his life. Many of his plays were based on American history and patriotic themes. Among his better known productions were *Fortress of Sorrento* (1808); *Paul and Alexis,* or the

Orphans of the Rhine (1812); *She Would Be a Soldier,* or the *Plains of Chippewa* (1819); the *Siege of Tripoli* (1820), also staged as *Yussef Caramalli;* and *Marion,* or *The Hero of Lake George* (1822).

Noah's interest in the fate of his fellow Jews, a product of his Sephardic pride and fierce desire to bring succor to a suffering people, reflected still another facet of his complex personality. His travels had opened his eyes to the travails of his coreligionists in various parts of the world. Oppressed and often persecuted, many Jews, especially those in the Levant and North Africa, lived in the memory of their past greatness, nursing the hope of some future messianic miracle that would deliver them from the morass into which they had sunk. Noah, early in his musing about the Jewish Problem, came to the conclusion that the restoration of the Jews in their ancient homeland Palestine was the only viable solution. In 1818 he gave concrete expression to this belief in an address at the consecration of the New York synagogue, Shearith Israel. His eloquent consecration speech was noted and praised by the aged ex-presidents of the United States, John Adams and Thomas Jefferson. Adams, musing on Noah's suggesting that a Jewish entity must be restored in the Holy Land, imagined Noah at the head of an army of 100,000 Israelites marching into Judea, conquering the country, and restoring the Jewish state to its rightful place among the nations of the world.

Jefferson, who was equally moved by Noah's address, was particularly concerned about the inadequacy of mere legal safeguards to protect the Jews, even under a free and democratic government. In a letter to Noah he gave voice to these fears.

> For altho we are free by law we are not so in practice. Public opinion erects itself into an Inquisition and exercises its office with as much fanaticism as fans the flames of the auto-da-fe. The prejudices still scowling on your section of our religion, altho the elder one, cannot be unfelt by yourselves.[286]

Noah, reflecting on how the Jews could reclaim their ancient homeland, came to several conclusions. Although a believer in the Messiah, he, like many before him, was convinced that the restoration of the Jews must come through their own efforts. The first step in this process, Noah believed, had to be the mobilization of world Jewry and public opinion against Turkey's domination of the Holy Land. However, before the persecuted Jewish masses of Europe, the Levant, and North Africa could be made ready for the creation of a state in the Land of Israel, it was essential that they find a temporary haven. This refuge would allow them time to reconstruct their lives and provide the necessary experience on how to live off of the land.

In considering what part of the world was best-suited for a temporary asylum, Noah gave priority to his native land. The free, democratic, prosperous, and still underpopulated United States, he stressed, was admirably suited for the training and preparation of the Jewish masses for the ultimate goal, the permanent settlement and creation of a state in Palestine. By the year 1820 these ideas had become a fixation in Noah's mind.

John Quincy Adams, destined to become the sixth president of the United States, would confide to his diary (September 7, 1820) that Noah had great plans for colonizing Jews in this country, and wanted to be sent as a charge d'affaires to Vienna to promote his ideas in Europe.

In that very same year Noah petitioned the New York state legislature for a grant of land on Grand Island for the purpose of establishing a refuge for persecuted Jews. The island, a fertile wooded area of 17,381 acres and well stocked with wild game, was located in the Niagara River equally distant from Lake Erie and Niagara Falls and not far from Buffalo. Although a committee reported favorably on Noah's petition, the legislature failed to pass the required bill.

Undaunted, Noah continued to lobby for his plan. He also publicized the proposed project among Jewish notables in America and Europe. Letters of encouragement reached him from Edward Gans and Leopold Zunz, two well-known and respected leaders of the "science of Judaism" movement. They complemented him on his initiative, particularly the ". . . meritorious undertaking . . . transplanting a vast portion of European Jews to the United States . . . of those who would prefer leaving their country to escape endless slavery and oppression."[287]

The state of New York in the wake of the interest aroused by Noah's petition, in 1825 surveyed and subdivided Grand Island into lots, and announced through the press that the area was now open for settlement. Major Noah reacted immediately. With the financial assistance of a Christian friend named Samuel Leggett, he purchased from the state 2,055 acres at a cost of $16,985.00. He intended for this acreage to serve as the nucleus for a Jewish city that would eventually encompass the entire island. Noah believed the Erie Canal, which was nearing completion about this time, would greatly benefit Grand Island, as the latter was directly in the path of the new commerce bound to be generated by the "big ditch".

Confident of the inevitable success of his plan, Noah launched an all-out campaign to publicize the proposed "city of refuge." He gave to the haven the name "Ararat," thereby linking it with the biblical account of Noah's ark and with his own name. In the summer of 1825 Noah and an associate (A.B. Seixas) journeyed to Buffalo, then a sleepy village of about 2,500 souls, to prepare for the official dedication of the Jewish refugee city. A cornerstone was ordered for the auspicious occasion. On it was inscribed the following statement:

Ararat
A City of Refuge for the Jews
Founded by Mordecai Manuel Noah in the Month of Tizri
September, 1825 & in the 50th Year of American Independence

On September 15, 1825, the day after the Jewish New Year, the residents of Buffalo were treated to a remarkable scene.[288] Down the main street marched a procession of soldiers, officials, Masonic members, and Indians led by a grand marshal. Directly behind the grand marshal was the central figure of the parade, Mordecai Manuel Noah. He was attired in a judge's robe of black drape covered with a cloak of crimson silk trimmed with white ermine. A gold medal hung around his neck. On reaching the shore of Lake Erie, the column found there were not enough boats available to take all the paraders to Grand Island. After some hesitation Noah led the marchers back to town where they assembled in St. Paul's Episcopal Church, the largest building in Buffalo.

In the church a band blared out the grand march from *Judas Maccabeus* and the Episcopalian minister warmly welcomed the celebrants and introduced Noah to the gathering. Noah delivered an impassioned discourse, in which he reiterated his intentions to build a city of refuge on Grand Island as a preliminary step on the road toward the restoration of a Jewish state in Palestine. In what he termed "A Proclamation to the Jews" he declared the Jews:

. . . are to be gathered from the four quarters of the globe . . . to be restored to their inheritance, and enjoy the rights of a sovereign people. Therefore, I, Mordecai Manuel Noah, citizen of the United States of America . . . and by the Grace of God, Governor and Judge of Israel, have issued this day my Proclamation, announcing to the Jews throughout the world, that an asylum is prepared and hereby offered to them, where they can enjoy that peace, comfort and happiness, which have been denied them through the intolerance and mis-government of former ages.[289]

In his proclamation Noah also called for a number of innovative steps and suggestions to hasten the implementation of his plan. They included a worldwide census of the Jews, the levying of a poll tax on Jews for the support of Ararat, and a plea that Jewish soldiers in European armies continue to serve in their posts and that all Jews who had no desire to settle in Ararat remain in their adopted homes. In addition, Noah recommended certain religious reforms, and that an election be held every four years for a "judge of Israel." The judge would be assisted by deputies stationed in countries containing Jewish communities.

Until elections could take place, Noah declared he would act as the "judge of Israel." As his first act in this capacity he nominated a number of prominent European Jews to be his deputies, and issued an appeal for all Jewish community leaders, rabbis, elders of synagogues to circulate his proclamation and to give it maximum publicity.[290]

Noah's call for Jews to settle in *Ararat* was also directed toward the American Indians, whom he identified with the ten lost tribes of Israel. He conjectured, as had many others (e.g., the Jewish scholar Manasseh ben Israel [1604–57], that after their conquest by the Assyrians, the ten tribes had wandered in a northwesterly direction that eventually brought them to the North American continent. As proof of the Indians' Hebrew origins, Noah pointed out that they worshipped one Supreme Being whom they called the Great Spirit, and they were divided into tribes in a manner strongly reminiscent of the ancient Israelites. Furthermore, he noted, the Indians deemed themselves the select and beloved people of the Great Spirit (i.e., God), and even set aside a Day of Atonement when they dressed in white doe skins and moccasins. In the spring they celebrated the Feast of Flowers, strongly suggestive of the Jewish festival of Passover; at the beginning of summer they honored the Feast of First Fruits, their Pentecost; and in the fall, the Feast of Booths, suggestive of the Festival of Tabernacles. In addition, the Indians computed time like the Jews, dividing the year into four seasons and the months by new moons, which commenced like the ecclesiastical year of Moses after the vernal equinox. Their high priests and prophets, towns of refuge, sacrificial cult, marriage and mourning customs, and even many of their words resembled those of the Jews.[291]

As a result of his convictions that the Indians were the descendants of the lost ten Jewish tribes, Noah was particularly sensitive to the efforts of missionaries to convert them to Christianity. The conversion activities among the Indians of Elias Boudinot, a leading exponent of the lost ten tribes of Israel theory, and president of the board of directors of the American Society for Meliorating the Condition of the Jews, aroused Noah's combative instincts. Ararat, he felt, could serve as a check to the conversion activities of Boudinot and other missionaries by providing the Jews as well as the Indians a haven and an environment immune to proselytism.

Very few American newspapers took Noah's "Proclamation to the Jews" seriously. There were, however, some outstanding exceptions. The *Buffalo Emporium* praised the speech and took pride in "this great work by a fellow citizen."[292] The *Albany Gazette* also had favorable words for Noah's plans, and rhapsodized that in Ararat the Jews would at last have found a refuge free from bigotry and persecution.

In Europe as well as in America many Jews considered the proclamation as the utterance of a madman. The chief rabbi of London immediately declined the title of commissioner conferred upon him by Noah, and considered the latter's project to be sacrilegious. Abraham de Cologne, the chief rabbi of Paris, was also disturbed by Noah's statements and noted that according to Judaic doctrine:

> God alone knows the epoch of the Israelitish restoration; that He alone will make it known to the whole universe by signs entirely unequivocal; and that every attempt on our part to be reasonable with any political national design is forbidden as an act of high treason against the Divine Majesty.[293]

Both the London and Paris religious leaders feared that Noah's activities, and in particular his proclamation, threatened to undermine the status of their communities by bringing into question their loyalty to the governments under which they lived. In spite of such attacks, Noah managed to retain his composure. He replied to all the jeers and verbal abuse with good humor and incredibly did not lose either morally or politically his standing in the eyes of the American general public. Since he had long enjoyed a reputation as an eccentric, the Ararat project was put down as another episode in Noah's erratic career.

Nevertheless, when reality finally intruded (the Jews did not respond to his call to settle Ararat) Noah reluctantly admitted defeat and abandoned the project. He now became convinced that only Palestine could provide the incentive to effect a restoration of a Jewish state, and that any such attempt would require assistance from the Christian world. In analyzing the possibilities of a return to Palestine, Noah felt the situation was far from hopeless. He urged world Jewry not to stand by idly, but to do something for themselves. He also noted with great interest the race by the Great Powers to extend their influence into the vital and strategic Middle East and the importance of Palestine in this power struggle. He was convinced that England was the key to this geopolitical game. Great Britain must possess Egypt in order to secure the route to her possessions in India. Palestine was essential to protect Egypt's flank and as a barrier to Britain's rivals, France and Russia, both of whom had interests in the Levant. In this arena of power politics the Jews, Noah believed, had an opportunity to reclaim their ancient homeland. Not only for England, but also for the contending Christian powers, an independent and enterprising people such as the Jews, placed in Palestine, would provide stability in the region. This would also resolve the Jewish Problem. Every other attempt to colonize Jews in other lands had failed, therefore it was time that the Land of Israel return to its legitimate proprietors.

Even during the height of his drive to create a temporary refuge for Jews on Grand Island, Noah's conviction that a restoration in Palestine was the true solution to the Jewish Problem remained uppermost in his mind. Thus, on October 28th, 1844, some months prior to the official laying of the cornerstone for Ararat, he delivered, before a large Christian audience at the Broadway Tabernacle of New York City, an address entitled a "Discourse on the Restoration of the Jews." The talk, made against a backdrop of mushrooming millenarianism and intensive efforts on the part of missionaries to proselytize Jews, revealed the depth of Noah's feelings and concern for his coreligionists. He appealed to his Christian audience's sense of fair play and justice to help the Jews regain their ancestral lands. He offered a possible plan to achieve restoration. The Christian powers, Noah suggested, should solicit the sultan of Turkey to grant Jews permission to purchase and own land in Palestine. As to the question of whether the Jews of the world would want to move to the Holy Land, Noah's answer was direct and to the point. Jews who seek freedom, he stated, would go, while those who already enjoyed freedom, such as those Jews living in the United States, would have no need to emigrate. However, the latter would feel more secure in their identity knowing that a Jewish homeland existed and were under the obligation to assist those Jews who wished to reside in Palestine, but did not have the means to immigrate. The discourse's interfaith message, political insight, cogency of argument, and scholarship presented in an eloquent and dignified manner mesmerized his listeners, and Noah was compelled to repeat the talk for a second overflow audience on December 2, 1844.

Major Mordecai Manuel Noah continued, during the declining years of his life, to maintain a lively interest in community affairs—Jewish and Christian alike. He was one of the early subscribers to the founding of New York University, and his efforts on behalf of Jewish philanthropy led to the establishment of Mount Sinai Hospital. In 1851 Noah, in his sixty-sixth year, suffered a stroke from which he did not recover. His funeral drew one of the largest crowds of mourners that New York City had yet known.

What had Noah accomplished with his grandiose scheme to create a haven for Jews on Grand Island? In a time when the young republic of the United States was still evolving, when boundaries were stretching and new horizons beckoned, when national conscious-ness quickened the pulse, Noah had dared to raise before the public eye the age-old Jewish Problem. His bold suggestion to create a temporary asylum as a first step on the road towards a Jewish restoration in Palestine fitted in well with the young republic's value system and democratic legacy. Although his scheme failed to materialize, his efforts typified those of the ideal type of American Jew and provided a role model for others who both treasured their Jewish and American heritage to follow.

Emma Lazarus

From the days of the early New England divines, Palestine as theme or in allusion, in book, sermon, or in place name has been present in American life and letters. In some periods it was central; in others only peripheral. But it was always present. Thus, it is not surprising to find that throughout the first half of the nineteenth century there were clear signs of Zionist stirrings in the United States.

Some of the agitation was in response to European visionaries; occasionally it was in answer to Christian philo-Semitism, or anti-Semitism. Lonely figures like Warder Cresson and Mordecai Manuel Noah issued appeals for the revival of a Jewish state. Their ideas were derided and their character and motives questioned. However, the visions of these men, and others like them, did not vanish from Jewish conscience, but would emerge in a more aesthetic form in the oeuvre of a talented young poetess named Emma Lazarus (1849–87).[294] As a muse, she is best remembered by most Americans for the immortal lines of her sonnet *The New Colossus*,[295] affixed in 1886 to the base of the Statue of Liberty, which dominates and ennobles the entrance to New York harbor.

Lazarus was born into a large, wealthy, and devoted Sephardic family in New York City. She passed a pleasant youth. Her education was received entirely from private tutors provided and supervised by her adoring father. A precocious child, Lazarus, while still in her teens, showed poetic talent. Her first lyrical impulse was stimulated by the Civil War. In 1867 a collection of her verse, originally intended for private circulation, was published. The poems revealed a charm of imagery, a command of rhythm, and a rare ability to capture emotion and to render it into a crystallized poetic expression of a mood. The themes of these early poems (written between the ages of fourteen and seventeen) were romantic and melancholic and derived from classical sources.

Lazarus's gift was instantaneously recognized by several eminent poets and essayists, including William Cullen Bryant, Henry Wadsworth Longfellow, and Ralph Waldo Emerson. During her short but brilliant career Lazarus was admired by, and maintained an active correspondence with, such notable contemporaries as Henry George, Edmund Clarence Stedman, William James, James Russell Lowell, William Morris, Laurence Oliphant, and Robert Browning.[296]

A second volume of poems entitled *Admetus and Other Poems*[297] (dedicated to Emerson), followed in 1871 and established her reputation as a talent of the first rank in both America and England. During the decade that followed her poems appeared regularly in such popular periodicals as *Scribner's Monthly* and *Lippincott's Magazine*.

In 1874 Lazarus published her first prose work, *Alide: An Episode in Goethe's Life;* and two years later, a five-act poetic drama, *The Spagnoletto*. These works were followed by more poems, essays, and translations including in 1881 the *Poems and Ballads of Heinrich Heine,*[298] to which Lazarus attached a fascinating biographical sketch of the famous German poet. Thus far Emma Lazarus had shown little interest in Jewish life or affairs. Patriotic, yet internationally minded; a classicist by training and inclination; ostensibly Orthodox in belief, but not zealous in matters of religion, she was representative of her class and station in life. Nevertheless, the winds of change would soon transform the poetess into an ardent Hebraist and, even more startling, into an impassioned champion of Jewish nationalism.

Lazarus's interest in Jewish problems was first awakened by a reading of George Eliot's provocative novel *Daniel Deronda*. Certainly, neither Eliot's sentimental story of a star-crossed love, nor the author's exposition of positivism aroused her enthusiasm. What moved Lazarus was the call for a Jewish national revival and the restoration of an organic center for Judaism in Palestine.

It was the Russian prescriptive May Laws of 1881, however, that converted her from a sheltered poetess into an enthusiastic Jewish activist. She witnessed in horror the mass flight of Jews from Eastern Europe. Over 3 million would seek the shores of America during the years 1881–1920. At first, Lazarus, like others of her social class, expressed concern on the effect that the tidal wave of immigration would have on the older established Sephardic and German-Jewish communities of the United States.

Aware of the apprehensions caused by the newcomers, Lazarus sought the ways and means to assuage these fears, which threatened to split the Jewish community. At first, she considered schemes for stemming the wave of immigration by improving conditions in Eastern Europe. However, after some reflection, Lazarus realized the futility of such plans, and turned her attention to the immediate problem of how to ameliorate the lives of the refugees who had already arrived on America's shores.

Thus, when the Jewish immigrants began to crowd into Ward's Island in 1881, Emma Lazarus volunteered her services. She made numerous visits to the temporary barracks built on the island by the Jewish philanthropist Jacob Schiff (1847–1920) to shelter the refugees, and played a prominent role in organizing social services to help the newcomers adjust to their new environment. Now more than ever the poetess realized that her earlier suggestions for reform based upon education in the "old country" was ". . . a fanciful dream . . . a far more visionary proposition than [George Eliot's novel advocating] the re-colonization of Palestine."[299]

In the process of seeking alternatives to Jewish mass-migration from Eastern Europe to the United States, Emma Lazarus found her theme and genius. Her Hellenic period had come to an end. In the columns of the *American Hebrew*, which had grown into an outstanding Jewish periodical, she kindled the ardor of the Sephardic and German-Jewish communities for the task of training the refugees, particularly the children, in technical arts and trades. Largely as a result of her efforts, the Hebrew Technical Institute was established in New York City and later in Boston, Philadelphia, and Chicago.

In 1882, in the same issue of the *Century Magazine* that carried a study of Disraeli by Emma Lazarus, an article by a Mme. Ragozin, a Russian journalist, appeared. Attempting to justify the pogroms that had swept through her native land, Ragozin accused Russian Jewry of having brought the violence down on their heads by their own behavior.[300] Taking up the challenge, Lazarus, in the next number of the magazine, came to the defense of her maligned coreligionists. In a crushing rejoinder bearing the title *Russian Christianity Versus Modern Judaism* she condemned the Russian excesses and praised her fellow Jews as pioneers of civilization and progress. Warning that the anti-Semitic tirade of Mme. Ragozin contained an important lesson for American Jewry, Lazarus noted, ". . . when the life and property of a Jew in the uttermost provinces of the Caucasus are attacked, the dignity of a free Jew in America is humiliated. . . . Until we are free, we are none of us free."

Inspired by her contacts with the unfortunate refugees from Eastern Europe, Lazarus, in her thirty-fourth year, underwent a dramatic transformation. She immersed herself in studies of the Bible, the Hebrew language, Judaism, and Jewish history. Emerson and some of Emma's other Christian friends admired and encouraged her decision. John Burroughs, the famous naturalist, wrote to inform her that even the work of such literary giants as Walt Whitman and Carlyle contained definite traces of Hebraic influence.

The result of Lazarus's intensive concentration on Jewish subject matter was the publication in 1882 of *Songs of a Semite*.[301] In this collection of poems, she lashed out at both the savage and civilized enemies of her people, those who slaughtered Jews, and those who turned their backs on their suffering. As if aroused from a deep torpor, Lazarus's verses resonated with an unmistakable militancy as they recalled the spirit and glories of ancient Israel. Most notable of the slim volume's contents was *The Dance to Death, A Historical Tragedy*,[302] a powerful poetic drama of five acts, about the burning of the Jews of Nordhausen in Thuringia during the period of the Black Death (fourteenth century). Lazarus dedicated the drama to the memory of George Eliot, ". . . the illustrious writer, who did most among the artists of our day toward elevating and ennobling the spirit of Jewish nationality."[303] *Songs of a Semite* also included poems reflecting the author's newly discovered Jewish nationalistic feelings. Representative of this group was the poem *Banner of the Jews* which called out for Jews everywhere to remember their Maccabean past.

> Oh deem not dead that martial fire,
> Say not the mystic flame is spent!

With Moses' law and David's lyre.
Your ancient strength remains unbent.
Let but an Ezra rise anew,
To lift the Banner of the Jew![304]

Enthralled by the Hebrew language, Emma Lazarus, with the help of the German versions of Michael Sachs and Abraham Geiger, translated excerpts from the Hebrew poets of medieval Spain: Judah ben Ha-Levi, Solomon ben Judah Gabirol, and Moses ben Ezra. She also wrote articles dealing with Jewish themes, including a series of articles on Bar Kochba, and a critique of the French scholar Joseph Ernest Renan's interpretation of Jewish history. However, it was in a prose series entitled, *An Epistle to the Hebrews,*[305] comprising fifteen articles written for the *American Hebrew,* that Lazarus gave full expression to her thoughts on reinvigorating and deepening Jewish life. Her chief purpose in writing these articles, she noted, was to contribute her mite toward arousing the spirit of Jewish enthusiasm. This, she believed, might manifest itself in various ways: in a return to the varied pursuits and broad system of physical and intellectual education favored by our ancestors; in a more fraternal and practical movement toward alleviating the suffering of oppressed Jews in countries less-favored than our own; in a closer study of Hebrew literature and history; and finally in a truer recognition of the large principles of religion, liberty, and law on which Judaism is founded.[306]

In seeking solutions to accomplish her second objective, the alleviation of the suffering of Jews in countries less favored than the United States, Lazarus absorbed ideas from many sources. Warm interest in the fate of Palestine, and particularly in the return of the Jews to their ancestral home, had received considerable attention in Christian circles in America and Great Britain. Many of these Gentile advocates were influenced by religious feelings, others by economic and political considerations, and still others by romantic notions. In Emma Lazarus's case all of the above factors converged and merged with a deep-seated desire to do something for her people that would remove their pariah image and restore them to their rightful place among the nations of the world. Her conclusions, though influenced strongly by George Eliot's *Daniel Deronda,* owed even more to the work of the English religious mystic and proto-Christian Zionist, Laurence Oliphant (1829–88). Motivated by a desire to improve economic and cultural conditions in Asiatic Turkey for the sake of the peace of Europe, Oliphant agitated vigorously for many years for the Jewish settlement of Palestine. Lazarus was particularly impressed by a provocative article of Oliphant's entitled *The Jew and the Eastern Question,*[307] in which the author stressed the moral penalties, such as loss of time-honored customs and sacred beliefs, which would result from Jewish emigration to the United States. Lazarus fully agreed with Oliphant's well-reasoned arguments. She now realized that:

. . . for the mass of semi-Orientalists, Kabbalists and Hassidim who constitute the vast majority of East European Israelites some more practical measure of reforms must be devised than their transportation to a state of society [America] utterly at variance with their time honored customs and most sacred beliefs.[308]

Because educating the Jewish masses in Eastern Europe was out of the question and emigration to America would destroy a traditional way of life, as well as a proven value system, the only viable solution to the Jewish Problem was the establishment of a Jewish entity in Palestine.

Although Emma Lazarus gratefully acknowledged her debt to those Gentiles whose concern for the Jews was both genuine and absorbing, she cautioned her fellow Jews not to look for leadership from them. Jews, she insisted who had provided political leaders for England, Germany, and France can surely furnish a new Ezra for their own people.

Consequently, when Oliphant advised Lazarus that 300 Jewish families stranded in Jerusalem and Jaffa were being provided for by the Christian Missionary Society, she publicly reproached the American Jewish community for failing to take care of its own and for ignoring the biblical commandments of charity and justice.[309]

The conversion of Emma Lazarus to a Zionist solution of the Jewish Problem was greatly abetted by her voracious reading of European literature. In the course of this reading she came across an anonymously published pamphlet in German entitled *Auto-Emancipation: Ein Mahnruf an seine Stammesgenossen von einem russichen Juden.* The author, a Russian–Jewish physician named Leon Pinsker, soon to become a leader of the nascent Love of Zion movement, greatly impressed Lazarus with his eloquence. His appeal for a Jewish restoration, she felt, ". . . was a pregnant indication of the spirit of the times."[310]

The very idea of a nationalistic solution, it seemed to Emma, had become more acceptable to large numbers of Jews. It was a doctrine that in the ". . . minds of mature and thoughtful men, individuals of prudence and of earnest purpose, little apt to be swayed by the chance enthusiasm of a popular agitation, it has taken profound root, and in some cases overturned the theories and intellectual habits of a lifetime."[311]

In the *Revue des deux mondes,* a journal Lazarus read devotedly, she discovered an article by Gabriel Charmes that further confirmed her views on the feasibility of a Jewish restoration in Palestine.[312] Charmes's speculations concerning the possibility of a new destiny for the Jews, a resurgence of their moral energy, aroused Emma's interest. Islam, Charmes believed, had been engulfed by fatalism, Christianity by other-worldly hopes, but Judaism had always sought, and aspired now, to a *félicité générale* on earth. Modern Jews were attempting to realize an ancient dream to build a community in Palestine, where progress and perfectibility would have actual force.[313]

Emma Lazarus was now convinced that Jews, particularly Russian emigrants, possessed the willpower and the ability to carry out a restoration scheme, for they were people:

> . . . who had sacrificed much for an idea, a high spirited aim. By assuming the mask, converting to Christianity, they could have remained in Russia, life and property secure. Surely these people are capable of comprehending the principle of consolidation and desiring a restoration—as indeed, these already do in great numbers desire it.[314]

What of the Jews in the emancipated countries of Europe and those in America? Emma's answer to this question revealed that the refugee problem was still uppermost in her mind. She firmly believed that there was not the slightest necessity for an American Jew, the free child of a republic, to rest his hopes on the foundation of any other nationality or even to decide whether he individually would or would not be in favor of residing in Palestine. All that was required of him was that he have a patriotic and unselfish interest in the suffering of his oppressed brethren of less fortunate countries, sufficient to make him promote by every means in his power the establishment of an asylum. For if the American Jews abandoned their Eastern European coreligionists to their misery, while they enjoyed the benefits of peace and prosperity, they would be guilty of inhumanity, selfishness, and shortsighted materialism. In an article on the Jewish Problem for *Century Magazine,* Lazarus emphasized the point that an individual pitied can never be regarded as an equal. The driven, persecuted, homeless Jew required a fixed address, status, security, and above all to be accepted by others. Only the restoration of a Jewish national state in Palestine could provide for these needs.[315]

Objections to Lazarus's advocacy of a return to the Promised Land were soon forthcoming from the adherents of the Jewish Reform movement. The latter's doctrine of a Jewish mission based on rationalism and ethical monotheism rejected messianism and eschewed any plans for the restoration of Jews in Palestine. Representative of this group, which contained the elite of American Jewry, was Rabbi Isaac Mayer Wise. Deeply concerned that the nationalistic ideas espoused by Lazarus would raise the issue of double loyalty and threaten American Jewry's status he gave vent to his fears.

> If Miss Emma Lazarus and others would lay aside their romantic notions of race, nation, Holy Land, Restoration etc., and assist practical heads in scratching out of their brains the pervert notion of distinctions between a man and a citizen who believes in Moses and the Prophets, and another who believes in Jesus and the Apostles, they could render a good service to their co-religionists and to the cause of humanity. . . . We are citizens of the United States . . . and of no other. . . .[316]

Criticism of Lazarus's nationalistic views also came from the opposite camp of Jewry—the Orthodox, who believed that redemption would come about through Divine intervention and that man's obligation was to wait. The editor of the *Jewish Messenger,* Rabbi Abram Samuel Isaacs, who often reflected the views of the Orthodox was particularly disturbed by Emma Lazarus's Zionistic writings. His reasoning, however, was rather unusual. He believed that the plan advocated by Lazarus was also favored by the German anti-Semitic movement. Isaacs pointed out that at a recent anti-Semitic congress held in Dresden, the delegates had actually adopted a plank in their platform urging Jews to leave Europe and settle in Palestine. The champions of Jewish nationalism, the rabbi felt, were by their writings and statements creating great harm. Unconsciously they were intensifying the mischievous impression, which the anti-Semites give every currency, ". . . that Jews are but Semites after all, strangers and aliens in Europe and America, patriots only in Palestine."[317]

Nevertheless, the picture was not totally bleak. Support for Lazarus's ideas was strong among the Eastern European Jewish newcomers to America, and even among some elements of the Sephardic community. The immigrants had no official voice to express their feelings, as control of most Jewish newspapers and periodicals was in the hands of German reform-minded Jews. However, many of the leaders of the Sephardic Jewish community were far from silent and paid tribute to the poetess whom they considered one of their own. Thus Pereira Mendes, the minister of a Spanish and Portuguese congregation, writing in the same *Jewish Messenger,* whose editor was so adamantly opposed to Emma Lazarus's views, noted that:

> . . . her muse has awakened responsive patriotic vibrations in the Jewish heart. I acknowledge gratefully, very gratefully, that her pen has unveiled the figure of the

martyr-nation of the world, properly poised in such a way as accords with truthful history and will command the admiration of the ages.[318]

Throughout the war of words that greeted her proposal of a nationalistic solution to the Jewish Problem, Emma Lazarus remained calm and continued to urge her views in public and in print. The literary fruits of identification with her coreligionists and with Zion were particularly evident during this period, notably in such poems as "The Choice", "By the Waters of Babylon," and "the Feast of Lights." The latter work, an apt commentary on Psalms 70 and 118 contrasted the desolation of Zion and the rededication with sacred splendor.

> Kindle the tapers like the steadfast star,
> Ablaze on the evening's forehead o'er the earth.
> And add each night a luster till afar
> An eightfold splendor shine above thy hearth
> Clash, Israel, the cymbals, touch the lyre,
> Blow the brass trumpet and the harsh-tongued horn;
> Chant psalms of victory till the heart take fire,
> The Maccabean spirit leap new-born.[319]

Time, however, was running out; Emma Lazarus had but a few years left to sing her songs of Zion. In 1883 she visited Europe and was received everywhere with acclaim, but at the very height of her powers she was stricken with a fatal illness. Although she continued to write and managed, despite her weakened condition, to make a second trip to Europe (1885), the end was near. Returning home, she died at the age of thirty-eight. Paradoxically, at the request of her executors (members of the family) all her works with a Jewish content were deliberately omitted from a collected edition published two years after her death. Fortunately, her Zionist poems and essays escaped oblivion; they had become etched in the hearts of those who believed in the necessity of a return to Zion. During her short life, Emma Lazarus had managed to synthesize all the best traits of her native land and of her faith into a rare combination of lyrical sentiment, compassion, wisdom, creativity, and optimism. She was as one author has written, ". . . a passionate pilgrim in a moment of history charged with drama."[320]

VII

PROGENY OF
THE HASKALAH

28

The Enlighteners

In Eastern Europe, Jewish nationalism gradually took root among a few of the intelligentsia. This development was in a large measure made possible by a *maskil* living in an obscure village in Galicia. His researches into Judaism and Jewish history provided a theoretical underpinning for a modern nationalist (Zionist) philosophy of history. The name of this remarkable scholar was Nachman Cohen Krochmal (1785–1840).[321]

Nachman Cohen Krochmal

Krochmal, often referred to as the "Prince of the Galician *Haskalah*" was born in Brody. It was in this city and in Lemberg and Tarnopol, the major crossroads of the growing commerce with the East, that the influence of the German *Haskalah* first penetrated and took root. Moses Mendelssohn, in his late years, had attracted young Polish, Austrian, and Russian Jewish disciples, eager to expand their intellectual horizons and to become familiar with European philosophy, science, and literature. Among these seekers of knowledge was a well-to-do merchant named Shalom Krochmal, the father of Nachman. The elder Krochmal made a point of maintaining contact with *Haskalah* circles in Germany, while pursuing his livelihood in Galicia.

The father's enthusiasm for enlightenment found a receptive audience in his son. Nevertheless, Nachman was given a traditional Orthodox education (Bible, Talmud, and Hebrew). When barely fourteen years old, Nachman was married to the daughter of a wealthy merchant. Following the ceremony he went to live with his father-in-law in the little village of Zolkiew, near the city of Lemberg and devoted himself entirely to his studies. Placed in a locale in which any deviation from pure Orthodoxy was frowned upon and lacking teachers or formal instruction of any kind, Krochmal found himself completely isolated. Undaunted, he secretly pursued, on his own, various secular studies and slowly acquired an extensive knowledge of philosophy and history. His chief inspiration in Jewish thought came from intensive study of the works of Maimonides, especially *Guide of the Perplexed,* and the writings of Abraham ibn Ezra. He also delved deeply into the strange world of European philosophy, science, and linguistics, devoting considerable time to a study of the German language and the German philosophers Kant, Fichte, Schelling, and Hegel. In addition, Krochmal mastered Latin, French, Arabic, and Syriac literary classics. As a result of these intensive studies, in 1808 the young scholar suffered a nervous breakdown and went to Lemberg to seek medical help. While receiving treatment, Krochmal met and formed a friendship with Solomon Judah Rapoport (1790–1867). Later he would become Rapoport's teacher and mentor, and share with his disciple the honor of being recognized as the outstanding luminaries of the "Science of Judaism" in Galicia.

After recovering from his illness, Krochmal returned to Zolkiew. He resumed his secret secular studies. Aware that the talmudists and heretic-hunting Hassidim of the village were eager to uncover and denounce anyone who occupied themselves with non-Hebrew books or secular studies, Krochmal went to great length to avoid suspicion. Indeed, even his outward appearance was deceptive. He dressed in the robes of an Orthodox scholar and it would have been difficult for anyone to guess the revolutionary thoughts brewing in the mind of such an inconspicuous figure. Fully enjoying the fruit of his stolen pleasures, Krochmal never considered openly challenging the doctrines of the talmudists and Hassidim of his village.

Nevertheless, in spite of his caution, Krochmal on one occasion was accused by certain pious individuals of Zolkiew of hatching a conspiracy against the Talmud, with the help of members of the Karaite sect. The incident was triggered by a harmless correspondence that Krochmal had carried on with a Karaite scholar in a neighboring village. Although he was able to fend off his accusers by means of a circular letter in which he explained his actions, the affair left its mark on his future behavior. Writing to the scholar Samuel David Luzzatto, he confessed that he was hesitant to teach things that might be controversial, and that he greatly feared the wrath of the ignorant and malicious zealots.

Gradually, Krochmal's fame as a scholar of the first rank extended beyond the borders of Zolkiew. Aside from Solomon Judah Rapoport who often visited him, a dedicated band of disciples soon gathered around Krochmal, whom he stimulated to think critically and historically about Judaism. Often, however, because of Krochmal's dread of being misunderstood by his pious neighbors, exchanges of ideas between himself and his disciples were confined to open fields or secluded places, secure from prying eyes and outstretched ears. So timid and cautious was Krochmal, that for years he could not be induced to publish the results of his research.

In 1814, after the death of his wife's parents, Krochmal, *Der ewige student* (the eternal student), as he liked to call himself was compelled to earn a livelihood. He became a merchant and later a liquor tax farmer. Twelve years later he lost his wife and his health deteriorated. Nevertheless, in spite of bad health, family tragedies, business failures, and loneliness, his reputation as a teacher and scholar continued to grow. The little village of Zolkiew, because of Krochmal's presence in the community, soon assumed in Eastern Europe the status held by Berlin in the minds of *maskilim* of the West. Tended an invitation to become the chief rabbi of Berlin, Krochmal refused the offer and accepted instead a position as a bookkeeper in Zolkiew. He would serve in this capacity from 1836 to 1838, when illness compelled him to retire to his daughter's home in Tarnopol, where he died two years later.

When questioned as to why he had turned down the Berlin rabbinate, Krochmal indicated that he feared the prestige that would accrue from such a prominent position. It had never entered his mind, he stated, ". . . to fill the post of a keeper of conscience, or to occupy myself with the conduct of the religious affairs of a community; such a purpose would have been in harmony neither with my theological researches, nor with my whole personality."[322]

Krochmal's fame rests on his Hebrew opus *Moreh Nevukhei Ha-Zeman* ("Guide of the Perplexed of the Time"), which was edited and published in 1851, eleven years after the author's death, by his friend the German-Jewish scholar Leopold Zunz (1794–1886). This single work represented almost all of Krochmal's literary legacy. A considerable part of the text reflects the author's philosophy of Jewish history. Borrowing ideas from the theory of historical development propounded by the eighteenth-century Italian philosopher Giambattista Vico (1668–1744), and to a lesser extent from the German thinker Johann Gottfried Herder (1744–1803), Krochmal maintained that every nation or people passes through three distinct stages. The first step is efflorescence and growth, the second maturity, and the last stage progressive decline and disappearance from the historical scene. Accordingly, it was essential to analyze, in light of these three phases, the economic, intellectual, and cultural factors that affect the life of a nation or people. However, being an idealist, Krochmal hedged on his basic assumptions by subjecting the various factors to a metaphysical principle. God (or to use a Hegelian term the Absolute Spirit), he wrote, is partially realized in every nation through the particular idea or spirit that it represents. The ancient Greeks, for example, represented the spirit of beauty and philosophic speculation, and the Romans, the spirit of law and political administration. Once these ideas or spiritual forms of a people are realized, their original bearers vanish from the historical arena, but the ideas themselves are adopted by other people and continue to operate in history.

The Jewish people, according to Krochmal, were unique. What singled them out from other people was that the idea for whose sake they had come into being, and for which they lived, was neither partial or limited. That idea is the Absolute Spirit itself, i.e., the everlasting God. Since this idea is eternal, as well as universal, the Jewish people are also eternal and universal. Hence Jewish history does not end with a single cycle like the history of other peoples, but continues to rise, flower and decay. Krochmal, however, was careful to point out that the character and causes of the unending Jewish cycle can be explained by the same mechanisms that account for the single historical cycle of other peoples, i.e., by mechanisms and causes that are entirely natural.

In Krochmal's reading of history, the Jewish people had passed three times through the cycles of birth, maturity, and decline. The first cycle had lasted from the era of the patriarch Abraham to the period of the Babylonian exile (586 B.C.E.); the second cycle included the return from exile permitted by the Persian ruler Cyrus (536 B.C.E.) to the suppression by the Romans of the revolt led by Bar Kochba (132 C.E.); the third cycle covered the period of time from the redaction of the Mishnah by Rabbi Judah Ha-Nasi (c. 200 C.E.) to the expulsion of the Jews from Spain in 1492.

At the end of each cycle the Jewish people might have been expected to follow the course of other nations and die, but instead each time it sprang phoenix-like to new life from its own ashes. This occurred because its goal was always to attain the Absolute Spirit, which is the fountain of all ideals and is pure spirituality, by nature imperishable. Although Krochmal did not explicitly assert it, he seems to have believed that in his day the Jewish people were in a stage of efflorescence marking the fourth great cycle of their eternal historical pilgrimage. Assuming that his conjecture was correct, one can, using hindsight, safely state that the fourth cycle ended with the Holocaust, and a fifth cycle began with the birth of the State of Israel.

In addition to Krochmal's philosophy of history the *Moreh Nevukhei Ha-Zeman* also contained a series of chapters exemplifying the use of the critical historical method. He applied this method to explain such diverse subject matter as Alexandrian Jewry, the evolution of *halakhah,* and the relation between Gnosticism and Kabbalah. Throughout the book the author appeals to his readers to remove the excrescences of fanaticism and superstition which have obscured the essence of the Jewish spirit. Krochmal emphasizes that neglect of the moral and rational meaning of Judaism's precepts in favor of mechanical obedience to the letter of the law was demeaning to both the religion and the faithful. It was therefore imperative to go back to the original sources and trace their development in order to recover the genuine and eternal qualities of the Jewish spirit and to distinguish between the transitory and the permanent. However, the enterprise to search out, reveal, and establish all the phenomena of Judaism in and through the actual period of their origin required rigorous critical historical study (the guiding principle of all the adherents of the "Science of Judaism"). Krochmal differed somewhat from followers of the historical school in his insistence that only philosophy could reveal the ultimate purpose of history.

Although Krochmal had scant sympathy for Reform Judaism, leaders of the Reform movement had little hesitation in adopting those of Krochmal's ideas that suited their purpose. It was primarily from him that the reformers took their favorite theme: that Israel was invested by God with a mission to teach the nations of the world the benefits of ethical monotheism. Remarkably, the reformers chose to ignore Krochmal's major thesis that the Jewish people's eternity is assured by a continuous renewal of national life (the Zionists would later accept this idea as a cardinal principle of their movement). It was thus not accidental that the reformers would also reject Krochmal's suggestion that following a period of spiritual stagnation, all efforts must be directed towards strengthening those elements of national consciousness and cohesiveness that would eventually lead to a restoration of the Jewish people in Zion.

By basing his studies on the historical reality of the Jewish people and not solely on theological or philosophical abstractions, Nachman Krochmal, the shy frail scholar of Zolkiew, laid the foundations for a new approach to Judaism and the Jewish tradition. Almost single-handedly he was responsible for launching the Galician version of *Die Wissenschaft des Judenthums.* He taught a new generation of Eastern European scholars how to submit the ancient rabbinic records and literature to the test of modern criticism and showed them the way in which this material could be utilized in historical studies. His concept of a Jewish mission influenced the adherents of the Reform movement, but more importantly, his studies and research provided Jewish nationalists with a historic and philosophical basis for their movement.

Peretz Smolenskin

In the mid-nineteenth century the Jewish masses of the Pale of Settlement experienced for a time what appeared to them to be the dawn of the messianic age. This optimistic mood was brought about by the ascension in 1855 of Alexander II to the czarist throne. The new czar immediately set about launching a vigorous program of domestic reforms. He also initiated a more humane approach to his Jewish subjects. Rejecting his father's harsh Jewish policies, Alexander II early in his reign, abolished the dreaded and hated "cantonist system" (the conscription of Jewish adolescents, some as young as eight-years-old, into the Russian Army for a minimum of twenty-five years, with the implicit intent of converting them to Christianity). A succession of imperial *ukases* followed that allowed Jews to move into the Russian interior, attend universities, and enter the professions. The response of the Russian Jews was at first disbelief, and then gratitude, relief, and self-examination.

With fresh opportunities suddenly opening for Jewish enterprise, elements among the Jewish middle class that had evolved along the border area of the Pale of Settlement began to question their traditional values and customs. They felt that the time had come for all Jews in the Russian empire to modernize and wrest themselves free from parochial Jewish education and religious obscurantism. This secular awakening, known as the *Haskalah* (the Jewish Enlightenment, which began in Berlin and gradually moved eastward) placed its faith in eventual emancipation on Russian soil. On the positive side, it revitalized the Hebrew language, which had long been consigned to the synagogue and the religious school. Negatively, *Haskalah* literature at first tended to play down the traditional messianic yearnings for Zion and to divert a new generation of secular educated Jews from a basic identification with their people's fate and fortune. The result of this paradox was a protracted and often bitter struggle in Eastern Europe between the great majority of the Jewish people, who remained loyal to tradition, and the enlighteners–the so-called *maskilim,* the torch bearers of the Haskalah.

The *maskilim* were confident that they would eventually prevail over their opponents and that the czarist regime constituted a powerful and welcome ally. Indeed, the weakening of Jewish autonomy that began in prepartitioned Poland reached new heights under the predecessors of Alexander II and boded ill for the traditionalists. For generations the latter had exerted control over the Jewish masses, based on the authority of Jewish law and on the support of the government of their leadership. This support was now removed from them to a large extent and transferred to the *maskilim,* who depicted the traditionalists as stubborn rebels unwilling to cooperate with the authorities.

However, by the end of the 1860s, and in the decade of the seventies many of the *maskilim* in the East began to lose faith in the goals of the *Haskalah.* A number of the enlighteners who had taken as their slogan "Be a man in the street and a Jew in your home" discovered that the idea was not feasible. The young people who had been brought up in the spirit of enlightenment and on whom the elder generation of *maskilim* had pinned their hopes for a moral and cultural renaissance of Jewry tended more and more to embrace assimilation and thus completely remove themselves from their people's struggle and traditions. The disillusioned *maskilim* began to ask themselves whether all their efforts had been in vain. The answer was soon forthcoming, and it came like a bolt out of the blue with the assassination of Czar Alexander II in 1881.

Hard on the heels of the czar's death the Jews were subjected to a series of bloody pogroms and to the infamous May Laws that confined them to the towns and townships of the Pale of Settlement and forbade their settling in the villages. The Russian government made it appear as if the excesses (murder, rape, destruction of goods and property, arson) were uncontrollable outbursts of popular indignation against the Jewish exploiters, whereas in reality government circles had planned, organized, and orchestrated the pogroms. The effect of the pogroms was to shatter, for most of the *maskilim,* the illusions of achieving civil equality under czarist rule. Even more unquieting for the enlighteners was the realization that the majority of Russian academicians, liberals, the church hierarchy, and the illiterate peasants had all joined enthusiastically in the government's anti-Jewish campaign.

The Jewish reaction among some of the more Russified *maskilim* was shock, disbelief, horror, and complete disillusionment. Many of them had come to love the Russian language and had introduced it into their homes. They now felt rejected and abandoned, without any hope for a future in the land of their birth.

Among those enlighteners who even before 1881 had warned against the extravagances and dangers of the *Haskalah* was the novelist, essayist, journalist, and editor, Peretz Smolenskin (1842–85). Smolenskin[323] was born in Monastyrschina, in the province of Mogilev (White Russia), into a life of privation, tragedy, and sickness. At age five, he witnessed the press gang recruitment of his elder brother, himself a mere child, into the army of Czar Nicholas I. The young cantonist was never heard of again, leaving a lasting impression in the memory of Peretz Smolenskin that would haunt him all his life. Years later he would include a description of the terrifying event in one of his novels. Peretz's father, who had been a fugitive for several years, died when Peretz was barely eleven. A year later Smolenskin left home to join his brother Leon at the yeshivah of Shklov. He remained at this school for five years.

Introduced to the ideas of the *Haskalah* by his brother, Peretz began to secretly read secular books and study Russian (both of these activities were regarded as mortal sins in pious circles). When Smolenskin's clandestine activities were uncovered he was subjected to harassment and persecution at the hands of the *Mitnagdim,* the ultra-Orthodox element in charge of the yeshivah. Finding further stay at Shklov impossible, Smolenskin, still in his teens, fled to the *Mitnagdim's* bitter foes—the Hassidim. At first he sojourned with the Lubavich Hassidim and then later he went to Vitebsk, where he spent the years 1858–60. Repelled by the intrigues of the Hassidic courts, he moved on to Mogilev and afterwards wandered for a time through Southern Russia and the Crimea. During this period, Smolenskin supported himself by singing in choirs and preaching in synagogues, where the congregations were unaware that the young talmudist was in secret a *maskil.* In 1862 he found himself in Odessa, the most modern Jewish community in Russia and a center of the Jewish enlightenment. Here he remained for five years studying music and modern languages while earning his keep as a Hebrew teacher. It was in Odessa that Smolenskin also embarked upon his career as a literary figure, with the publication of articles in the Hebrew journal *Ha-Meliz.*

Leaving Russia in 1867, Smolenskin traveled through Rumania, Germany, and Bohemia before finally settling in Vienna, Austria. Although he intended to enroll in the Austrian capital's great university, he was compelled by his persistent poverty to abandon all hopes of gaining a systematic secular education. Instead, he took a job as a proofreader in a printing shop. After his marriage in 1875 Smolenskin became manager of the printing establishment, which enabled him to provide for his family's needs, and to devote his free time to the idea of founding a Hebrew periodical. His ambitious dream eventually became a reality with the help of an individual named Solomon Rubin. The end result of their collaboration was the establishment of the monthly journal *Ha-Shahar* ("The Dawn"). Smolenskin managed and edited the periodical while serving simultaneously as proofreader, typesetter, distributor, and contributor of belles lettres, articles, essays, and stories. The journal, which survived for almost seventeen years (indeed, until shortly before Smolenskin's death from tuberculosis in 1885), became the most effective literary platform for the *Haskalah* movement in its later period and for the Jewish nationalist movement in its formative years.

From the outset, Peretz Smolenskin conceived his journal to be an organ dedicated to making the Jewish people aware of their precarious position in Eastern Europe and as an instrument to strengthen the internal resources of the community by fostering the spread of genuine enlightenment and culture. In addition, *The Dawn* was intended to serve as a powerful weapon against certain harmful aspects of traditional Judaism and Hassidism. Smolenskin was equally committed to waging war on the assimilationists, who he believed were undermining Jewish national unity. Above all his journal epitomized its editor's passionate love for the Hebrew language, which he regarded as the core of Jewish nationalism and a substitute for national territory as long as the nation lacked a state. To reject the Hebrew language was, in Smolenskin's eyes, an act tantamount to treachery, for without Hebrew there was no Torah, and without Torah no Jewish people.

As the fame of *Ha-Shahar* spread, its contributions to Hebrew literature became increasingly important. The monthly journal facilitated the publication of many articles in the field of Jewish research, and even printed whole books by major scholars. It also served as a forum for the propagation of ideas and the discussion of a wide range of contemporary issues. Lastly, it provided a hospitable outlet for literary criticism, book reviews, and novels (including those written by the indefatigable editor himself).

Of Smolenskin's many novels, *Ha To'eh Be Darkhei ha-Hayyim* ("The Wanderer On Life's Path") was by far the most interesting. The first three parts of the book were originally published in *Ha-Shahar* in 1876. Rambling, picaresque, and autobiographical in flavor, the novel describes the adventures of a Jewish orphan who wanders though Eastern and Western Europe and eventually dies in a Russian pogrom. The title and the theme of the novel summarized much of its author's early life and that of many of his generation. In spite of the tortuous plot, crudities, exaggerations, and melodramatic flourishes, the author's easily perceived sincerity exerted a considerable appeal to its Jewish readers. The novel became the most widely read book of modern Hebrew in the 1870s, largely because it spoke for many individuals living in a transitional setting between the ghetto and the world of modernity.

Other books by Smolenskin that first appeared in the pages of *Ha-Shahar* were: *Simhat Hanef* ("The Joy of the Godless"), a philosophical and critical account that attempted to trace the dependence of certain aspects of Shakespeare's *Hamlet* and Goethe's *Faust* on the singular spirit informing the biblical books of *Job* and *Ecclesiastes* within the structure of a story depicting the shallow attitudes of many of the ostensibly enlightened Jewish intellectuals of Odessa; *Kevurat Hamo* ("A Donkey's Burial"), a humorous plot permeated with social criticism and fierce invective hurled against certain types of Jewish organizations and community leaders; *Gemul ha-Yesharim* ("The Reward of the Righteous") a work outstanding for its dramatic techniques, as well as for its interesting ideas on nationalism. The book strongly condemned the Poles for their maltreatment of the Jews caught between themselves and the Russians in the ill-fated 1863 uprising; *Ha-Yerushah* ("The Legacy") a story set for the most part in Rumania where Smolenskin had spent three months in 1874 on behalf of the Alliance Israélite Universelle, following a wave of pogroms directed against the Jewish community. These works and others won for their author recognition as one of the outstanding Hebrew novelists of the day. His style of writing was considered unique. He endeavored to model his Hebrew on that of the ancient prophets, and concentrated on character development and description.

In his novels, and even more in his essays, Peretz Smolenskin represented a transition from the period of the Jewish Enlightenment, which for all practical purposes came to an end with the Russian pogroms of 1881 and the rebirth of Jewish nationalism. In most of his early litreary efforts, Smolenskin had stressed the theme that reforming Jewish life was both desirable and inevitable. However, even during this stage of his career he was not an uncritical admirer of modernity. He feared that it would encourage assimilation and would not necessarily lead to personal happiness, or even acceptance by the majority of Jews.

Smolenskin's historical significance is largely due to his advocacy of Jewish nationalism. Long before the pogroms of 1881 he had evolved a theory that he called "spiritual nationalism." The Jewish people, he insisted, were not merely a religious group, as many of the *maskilim* and the adherents of Reform Judaism held, but rather a distinct nation. Therefore if the Jewish people were to reverse the process of disintegration that was consuming their substance, they had to resolutely affirm their nationhood. Only by following this course could the Jews maintain self respect and respond meaningfully to anti-Semitism. Smolenskin tended to view anti-Semitism as a phenomenon resulting primarily from the contempt of the nations for the Jews' deficient national status. In two major studies, *Am Olam* ("The Eternal People"), and *Et Laasot* ("A Time to Act") Smolenskin elaborated on his theory of spiritual nationalism. He stressed that a triple knot bound Jews together throughout the long centuries of their homelessness and dispersion. These knots consisted of the Torah, the Hebrew language, and the messianic hope of eventual redemption.

Of the three binding factors, Smolenskin believed the Torah was the most important. He considered it to be the foundation of Jewish national identity, a tie that created a spiritual nation that took precedence over territory and over political identity. Torah was the basic reason the Jewish people had survived after their kingdom had been destroyed, and the inhabitants dispersed throughout the world.

When a contemporary, Eliezer Ben Jehudah, openly advocated the creation of a Jewish state in Palestine with all the trappings of a modern political entity, Smolenskin, convinced that the essence of Jewish nationalism was spiritual, demurred. "The life of all other nations," he declared, "is bound up with the existence of their state, but the Jews have a spiritual realm. . . . He who wishes to rebuild the ruins of Zion in Jerusalem is like a man who wishes to erect a tower on a rooftop before he has built his house."[324] Smolenskin repeatedly pointed out that the Torah, the key element in his theory of spiritual nationalism, had been received in the wilderness prior to the conquest of Canaan and the founding of a polity.

Apart from the Torah, Smolenskin stressed that Israel had always been sustained by its messianic beliefs and by its loyalty to the Hebrew language. The messianic era, he wrote in his essay *Am Olam*, will be at that point in time when Jews will have received political and moral emancipation. Although declaiming against fanaticism and divisiveness, Smolenkin pleaded with his fellow Jews to strengthen their awareness of being one people. His views led him to regard with hostility the program of enlightenment advocated by many of the disciples of Moses Mendelssohn (the Berlin *Haskalah*), who insisted that Judaism was nothing more than a religious confession. Smolenskin's *bete noir* was the Berlin *Haskalah* movement. The fiery editor of *Ha-Shahar,* in a series of articles, attacked the enlighteners with a vengeance. He was firmly convinced that the *maskilim*'s aim was not to cultivate and spread knowledge among the Jewish people, rather it was a thinly disguised effort to cast off Judaism. Rejection of enlightenment, the *maskilim* insisted, prolonged Jewish suffering. By imitating the Gentiles and abandoning cherished traditions, a new age would dawn for Jewry. As a reward for such an achievement, the *maskilim* stressed, the benefits of western civilization would accrue to the Jews and they would be accepted as equals.

The consequences of such a doctrine, Smolenskin argued, were disastrous. It would destroy the basis of Israel's unity, the belief that the Jews were a nation. Adherence to the ideas of the Berlin enlighteners would, for example, automatically lead to the abandonment of the hope of redemption, for the *maskilim* considered nationhood a serious bar to assimilation. ". . . The memory of the land and sovereignty that was once ours," Smolenskin wrote, "together with a continuing hope that they be restored, make us a nation."[325] All efforts to efface these remembrances must be strongly resisted, for otherwise Jewish life would be extinguished.

The Russian pogroms of 1881 had shocked Smolenskin, but unlike most of his contemporaries, he was quick to realize the nature and depth of the hatred that had been unleashed on the Jews. He believed that these excesses were only the beginning of a deliberate policy of persecution fostered by the czarist government. He noted that the pogroms were the outcome of twenty years of anti-Jewish venom that had spilled from the pages of Russian newspapers, periodicals, and books, as well as from the mouths of officials and rabble-rousers. Even such old medieval canards as the blood libel and the desecration of the host had been revived to vilify the Jews. In addition, every sort of imaginable wickedness and crime was ascribed to the Jews by those individuals intent on exciting the general public to plunder and murder.

The Russian pogroms reinforced Smolenskin's long-held view that political emancipation and assimilation, on which several generations of *maskilim* had pinned their hopes was illusory. Even die-hard enlighteners now understood the fallacy of their views. Smolenskin himself had become acutely aware that spiritual nationalism, and a linguistic revival of Hebrew, which he had fought so hard to encourage, was not enough to resolve the Jewish Problem. Accordingly, he modified his theory of spiritual nationalism and adopted wholeheartedly the idea of a return to Zion and the creation of a Jewish state. In a score of brilliantly argued articles, which appeared in the last three volumes of *Ha-Shahar,* Smolenskin pleaded with Eastern European Jewry to abandon their birthplaces and emigrate to their ancient homeland in Palestine. Once in the Holy Land the immigrants were to undertake as rapidly as possible all the political, economic, and cultural activities necessary for the establishment of a viable state.

Throughout his articles, Smolenskin's percipience is clearly evident. He rails against those individuals and institutions (e.g., the Alliance Israélite Universelle) for encouraging Jews to migrate to the Americas instead of the Land of Israel. This policy, he believes, will only lead to a repetition of the lachrymose cycle of Jewish history. Smolenskin repeatedly emphasizes that the pogroms in Russia, and the recrudescence of anti-Semitism in Germany are not temporary aberrations. These incidents, he felt, were ephemeral manifestations of social regress, and harbingers of far greater horrors yet in store for the Jewish people in the future. The Jews, in brief, were in mortal danger if they did not take steps to rebuild a national life in Palestine. The latter entity would also serve as a place of refuge for those Jews so unfortunate as to be caught in the storms that were certain to break over Europe.

Smolenskin's change of heart in regard to Zion, although strongly influenced by the Russian pogroms, was not wholly a precipitous decision. An analysis of his writing indicates that he was already moving in that direction prior to 1881. However, once having made up his mind, Smolenskin became an enthusiastic advocate of Jewish nationalism. He joined the Love of Zion movement, and played a role in the founding of *Kadimah* (Vienna, 1882) the first Jewish student's organization dedicated to the Jewish settlement of Palestine, and to fighting assimilation in Europe. In addition, Smolenskin worked closely with Laurence Oliphant in the latter's attempt to obtain from the Turkish government permission for the establishment of Jewish colonies in the Holy Land. Most importantly, he devoted his pen and journal to convincing his readers that a Jewish entity in Eretz Israel was essential if the Jews were to survive as a people in a world of national states.

Time and again Smolenskin, as editor of *The Dawn,* would use its columns to extol the virtues of Palestine as a refuge for persecuted Jews. He believed that the land, if properly cultivated, could support a population of millions. Even if only one million would emigrate, that fact would bring new hope into their lives, as well as remove some of the pressure on those Jews who chose to remain in the Diaspora.

The Land of Israel, Smolenskin stressed, had other advantages to offer immigrants besides providing a refuge for the most needy. It was not too distant from their former homes in Eastern Europe; they could live together without abandoning their accustomed traditions; not everyone would be required to work the land, for some immigrants would devote themselves to industry and commerce. Most importantly, the newcomers would help infuse a new spirit in those Jews living in the Holy Land on charity from the Diaspora, and bring pride and dignity to Jewry the world over.

In the course of time, Smolenskin felt, no propaganda would be needed to induce Jews to settle in Palestine. The opportunity to pursue a peaceful and dignified existence would prove irresistible to large numbers of Jews. Nevertheless, in the interim it was essential that Jewish philanthropists do everything in their power to help their less fortunate brethren who were looking for a way out of their miserable existence. The idea of Jewish settlement in Palestine must become the chief topic of conversation among this privileged group. Mere talk, however, was not enough. They should hasten to buy land in Eretz Israel and let Jews settle on it to begin a new life.

Smolenskin foresaw the importance of establishing political, economic, and spiritual footholds in Palestine as essential steps in the process of creating a Jewish state. Agricultural colonies by themselves, he believed, would not be enough to support a mass migration to the Holy Land. Commerce and industry were also needed. It was equally important that Torah and a knowledge of the Hebrew language and literature be widely disseminated among the emigrants so that the restored ancient homeland would once more become a free and highly cultured nation.

The nationalistic writings of Peretz Smolenskin had a great impact on an entire generation of Jewish youth. His imagination, intuitive foresight, breadth of perspective, and clarity of style greatly appealed to their own search for identity in an increasingly hostile environment. Much of what he wrote was tinged with prophecy, notably his conviction that Jews should leave Central and Eastern Europe while they still had an opportunity to do so. Equally remarkable was his insistence that the Jewish state must also be a spiritual center.

The enthusiastic readers of Smolenskin's journal helped swell the ranks of the Love of Zion movement, and converted many former *maskilim* to Zionism. As a result of this shift on the part of many enlighteners, the Zionist movement absorbed some of the fundamental ideology of the *Haskalah*. On the other hand, the tendency of the mainstream of the *Haskalah* adherents to drift toward assimilation received a serious setback. Not all *maskilim,* however, were eager to choose the path leading to Zionism. A considerable number of young Jewish enligteners, in the last decades of the Romanov dynasty, joined the Russian underground revolutionary movements. They were convinced that with the overthrow of the czarist regime Jews would be fully emancipated and accepted by Russian society. A few die-hard *maskilim* continued to uphold the traditional goals of the *Haskalah,* and refused to join either the ranks of the Zionists or the revolutionaries. Nevertheless, many Jews who had been touched by the *Haskalah* in Eastern Europe heeded Smolenskin's advice and found in Zionism a commitment that gave new meaning and substance to their lives.

Eliezer Ben-Yehuda

In the last two decades preceding World War I a linguistic revolution occurred in Palestine. Hebrew, considered by many at the time to be a dead language, underwent a remarkable revival. It was an impressive rebirth, as Hebrew educational institutions in the Holy Land were virtually nonexistent. Until the late 1870s the few Jewish schools in Palestine were almost exclusively religious and Orthodox with Yiddish as the language of instruction. There were a few exceptions to the bleak educational scene, such as the Lämel school (founded in Jerusalem in 1856), which taught courses in German as well as Yiddish. The network of elementary and vocational schools operated by the Alliance Israélite Universelle preferred French as the principal language of instruction.

A similar situation prevailed in the Russian Pale of Settlement, the reservoir of Jewish life that provided the bulk of the immigrants to Palestine, in what later became known as the First and Second Aliyahs. So strong was the czarist government's policy of Russification in the Pale of Settlement during this period, that even the small number of Jews who wrote in Hebrew were not at all certain if the language had a future. Thus in a poem the prominent *maskil* Yehuda Leib Gordon (1830–92) raised the question whether he might not be the last of the writers of Zion—and his audience the last of the readers. What seemed to be lacking was a standard-bearer willing and able to take on the titanic struggle of converting Hebrew into a modern secular language capable of winning the support of the Jews in Palestine and the Diaspora. The man destined to undertake this formidable task was a young philologist named Eliezer Yizhak Perelman (1858–1922), later better known by his adopted surname Ben-Yehuda.[326]

Perelman was born in Luzhky, Lithuania. His father, a Habad Hassid, died when Eliezer was five years old, and at age thirteen the youngster was sent to his uncle who enrolled him in a yeshivah in Polotsk. The head of the school, a secret *maskil,* introduced his young charge to secular literature. Eliezer's uncle removed his nephew from the yeshivah, and sent him to study in the Vilna district of Lithuania. Here the young student made the acquaintance of a Habad Hassid named Samuel Naphtali Herz Jonas, who at the time was writing articles for Hebrew periodicals. Jonas persuaded young Eliezer to prepare himself for a secondary school matriculation, and his eldest daughter Deborah took on the task of teaching him Russian. After months of intensive preparation Eliezer succeeded in entering the Dvinsk Gymnasium (he would graduate from this institution in 1877).

The schools of intermediate and higher education during this period of Russian history were hotbeds of political activity. Eliezer Perelman, like many of his contemporaries, was caught up in the Russian revolutionary ferment prevalent in these schools. He accepted in turn, the programs of the Narodniki and of the Nihilists. Nevertheless, in spite of his radical leanings and his rejection of Orthodox pietism, he did not break with Judaism nor discard Jewish interests. He continued, for example, to be an avid reader of Smolenskin's journal, *Ha-Shahar*, and to follow closely the arguments on behalf of Jewish nationalism formulated by the editor.

The Russo-Turkish War (1877–78), and the long struggle of the Balkan nations for independence aroused in Perelman strong feelings revolving around the possibility of a Jewish revival in Palestine. These thoughts were reinforced by impressions derived from his connections with the Russian Populist movement. Adherents of the latter movement favored a form of Pan-Slavic nationalism, and a large segment of its intelligentsia were willing to use terrorism to achieve their radical aims. Eliezer, drawing inspiration from these nationalistic currents, decided that the Jewish people were no different than other people in their desire to be a free and sovereign nation. Indeed they had a historic land, Eretz Israel, and a historic language, Hebrew. What was lacking was a vital force to actuate the national drive to restore the Promised Land to its rightful owners—the Jewish people. The key to bringing about such a renaissance, Eliezer Perelman believed, was the Hebrew language.

In 1878 Eliezer enrolled as a student of medicine at the Sorbonne in Paris. Here he learned of the important role that literature had played in the growth of French nationalism. Writing to his fiancee (Deborah Jonas) about his discovery, he stressed the point that a national language was essential to hold a people together. For the Jews that language had to be Hebrew. The language could not, however, be the Hebrew of the rabbis, but had to be a language in which people could conduct the business of life.

In an article in *Ha-Shahar* entitled *She'elah Lohatah* ("A Burning Question") written for the first time under the nom de plume Ben-Yehuda (Son of Judah), Eliezer outlined his thoughts on Jewish nationalism. He linked the idea of a Jewish national revival with the general European national awakening. He also emphasized the importance of Palestine as a focal point for the entire Jewish people. Even Jews remaining in the Diaspora would reassess their heritage.

During the winter of 1878, Ben-Yehuda contracted tuberculosis and was compelled to discontinue his medical studies. He decided to emigrate to Eretz Israel. To qualify for a teaching post in Palestine, Ben-Yehuda enrolled in the teacher's seminary of the Alliance Israélite Universelle. While thus engaged he attended lectures given by the Assyriologist Joseph Halevy, who as early as 1860 had advocated the expansion of the Hebrew language through the coinage of new words—a suggestion that would become central in Ben-Yehuda's own thinking.

As his health deteriorated, Ben-Yehuda became a patient in the Rothschild Hospital in Paris. Here he met a Jerusalem scholar, A. M. Luncz, who spoke Hebrew to him using the Sephardi pronunciation. The latter also informed the young convalescent that the Sephardi dialect was the lingua franca of the various Jewish communities in Jerusalem. Ben-Yehuda would later exploit this bit of knowledge in his campaigns to make Hebrew a living language of the home and the workplace.

Finally, Ben-Yehuda's health improved and he was able to embark for the Holy Land. Enroute, he stopped at Vienna, where he was met by his fiancee Deborah Jonas. After a marriage ceremony in Cairo, Egypt, they proceeded to Palestine, arriving in Jaffa in October of 1881. Legend has it that the young couple vowed to speak only Hebrew from the moment they boarded the vessel for Eretz Israel and that this pledge was never broken.

Truth or fiction, it is a fact that Eliezer Ben-Yehuda's household was the first home in Palestine to speak only Hebrew, and that his first-born son Ben-Zion (later called Ithamar Ben-Avi) was the first modern Hebrew-speaking child.

Eliezer's determination to settle in Palestine was indeed an unusual decision, considering his early allegiances and radicalism. Almost none of the Russian *maskilim* writing in Hebrew found their way to Palestine even after the infamous pogroms. The ideological motivations behind Ben-Yehuda's emigration relate directly to his criticism of the *Haskalah* movement. In an open letter written toward the end of 1880 to Smolenskin, he set forth his views. Ben-Yehuda referred to the polemic exchange between Smolenskin and a number of German-Jewish intellectuals regarding the Hebrew language. Some members of the latter group, who were also advocates of the Jewish Reform movement, considered Judaism strictly a religious community and not a national entity. Accordingly, they also felt that the preservation of Hebrew in religious worship was anachronistic and should be discarded in favor of the national language of the country in which the worshipers lived (in their case German). Smolenskin strongly opposed the suggestions of the German-Jewish reformers and in rebuttal argued that there existed a historical uniqueness in Jewish national existence. The Jews, he emphasized, were a universal spiritual people even without a unifying territorial concentration. The Hebrew language was important, as it served as a spiritual bond uniting the various Jewish communities of the Diaspora.

Ben-Yehuda supported Smolenskin's position, but took the debate one step further. He asked why the Hebrew literary efforts of the *Haskalah* had not succeeded in producing masterful aesthetic and artistic achievements? This poor showing was particularly remarkable because in the few decades of its existence the *Haskalah* had been able to bring about a renaissance in Jewish intellectual life in Eastern Europe. Many books, essays, plays, and poems had been produced in Hebrew and the language had reached an ever-widening public. Nevertheless, literary greatness had not been realized, as most of the *Haskalah* literature was stylistically stilted, highly pedantic, mediocre, and derivative. True literature, Ben-Yehuda insisted, could only emerge in a social environment speaking the language in which that literature is being written. Haskalah literature was artificial, alienated from the source of true artistic creativity—life itself. The authors who wrote in Hebrew did not use that language in their daily life. In their work they described in Hebrew a society which did not speak the language, but one that spoke either Yiddish, Polish, or Russian. How, Ben-Yehuda asked, could an authentic Hebrew literature develop under such circumstances? His answer to the question he had posed was straightforward. A viable Hebrew literature was only possible in a society in which a majority of the people spoke Hebrew and used it as the daily language of intercourse and communication. The nation and its tongue could therefore best be revived if the Jews returned en masse to the Land of Israel.

Over and over again Ben-Yehuda hammered away at the theme that the revival of Hebrew must not be limited to an intellectual elite. Those truly dedicated to the regeneration of Hebrew must aim at the creation of a Jewish territorial concentration in Eretz Israel for, ". . . we cannot revive [Hebrew] with translations; we must make it the language of our children, on the soil in which it once blossomed and bore ripe fruit."[327]

Ben-Yehuda's conviction that Hebrew had to be the language of all the Jewish people may have been influenced by his association with the Russian Populist movement prior to his emigration to Palestine. The Russian Populists believed that a social revolution could not succeed if it remained purely a spiritual effort of the intelligentsia. Thus they called on the latter to live among the people, share their suffering, and educate them toward revolutionary consciousness and action.

Similarly, Ben-Yehuda argued a national language was not possible without the social infrastructure of national life. Just as a linguistic renaissance and national political revival had gone hand in hand among other nations in the nineteenth century so must it take place among the Jews. A nation, he believed, could not live except on its own soil, nor could its culture flourish in an alien environment.

Eliezer and Deborah's early years in Palestine were as agonizing and hard as any endured by the agricultural pioneers of the Zionist movement. On several occasions they were evicted from their quarters for lack of rent money. At other times the poverty-stricken couple nearly starved. In Jerusalem, where they settled, Ben-Yehuda managed to eke out a pittance teaching in an Alliance Israélite Universelle school. He had accepted the post only after gaining permission to use Hebrew exclusively as the language of instruction in all Jewish subjects. Other teachers, inspired by Ben-Yehuda's example, followed suit and bravely ventured into uncharted territory by attempting to teach in Hebrew—mathematics, geography, history and other secular subject matter. In the process they were often forced to devise new terminology and textbooks.

In spite of the pressures of earning a living, Ben-Yehuda spent every free moment on his Hebrew language studies, and on editing a succession of Hebrew newspapers and periodicals (circulation of these publications in the early 1880s rarely exceeded a few hundred readers). In his enthusiasm to proselytize all whom he met of his dream of a Hebrew-speaking nation, he tried to ingratiate himself with the Orthodox Jews of Jerusalem. The latter's knowledge of written Hebrew, Ben-Yehuda felt, made them the most likely prospects to learn to speak the language. Thus, the former *maskil* and revolutionary, in order to win over this group, adopted Orthodox garb, grew a beard and earlocks, and prevailed upon his wife to wear a wig, Orthodox style. However, the pious Jews of Jerusalem soon sensed that Hebrew for Ben-Yehuda was not a holy tongue, but rather an instrument to create a secular national language and a political state. A falling-out was inevitable. Eventually, realizing that he was unable to make any inroads with the ultra-Orthodox, Ben-Yehuda stopped posing as a member of their community, and became a bitter critic of the group that he had formerly so ardently courted. He registered as a national Jew "without religion", and turned his pen to mount incessant attacks upon the ultra-Orthodox for their opposition to the use of spoken Hebrew as an everyday language. He also vilified them for their rejection of all attempts to achieve redemption though human efforts (they believed that redemption would have to await the coming of the Messiah). Lastly, he excoriated the leadership of the pious of Jerusalem for fostering the *halukkah* system (the distribution of charity received from the Diaspora for the support of the community's poor, but which, with the passage of years, had become a way of life). Incensed by these attacks, the outraged pietists retaliated. Ben-Yehuda's office was stoned and he was placed under a *herem* (a rabbinical ban of excommunication). So deep was the bitterness of this dispute that when Ben-Yehuda's wife Deborah died of tuberculosis in 1891, leaving behind five children, the Orthodox refused to allow her burial in the Ashkenazi cemetery.

After a brief period of mourning, Ben-Yehuda remarried. His second wife, the younger sister of Deborah, adopted the Hebrew name of Hannah, and more importantly, her husband's strong views on language, religion, and politics. A talented individual, Hannah contributed many translations and original Hebrew stories to Ben-Yehuda's periodicals. She also incited her husband to continue his vendetta against the pietists. Searching for a pretext to rid themselves of their nemesis, the trustees of the *halukkah* system found their opportunity in the 1894 Hannukah issue of Ben-Yehuda's periodical, *Ha-Zevi*. An article in this issue contained the innocent phrase, ". . . let us gather strength and go forward." The Orthodox trustees seized on this line, distorted its meaning, and informed the Turkish authorities that it was a signal to arouse certain Jewish elements to rebellion. Ben-Yehuda was charged with sedition and sentenced to a year in jail. The affair created a stir throughout the Jewish world. An appeal was lodged on Ben-Yehuda's behalf and he was eventually released. Fortunately for the peace of the Yishuv, the incarceration of Ben-Yehuda forced the religious and secular elements to come to an understanding and refrain from interfering in each other's way of life.

In 1881 Ben-Yehuda, in collaboration with Yehiel Michael Pines (1842–1912), the director of the Montefiore Foundation in Jerusalem, and other prominent figures of the Yishuv founded a society called Tehiyyat Israel. This organization devoted itself to reviving "the real Israel" by lifting the community out of its degradation and by fortifying its spirit. The society's programs encouraged work on the land, expansion of the community's productive population, education of the youth, dismemberment of the *halukkah* system, and the revival of the Hebrew language. Emphasizing the latter goal, a key plank of the society's charter read:

> Members living in Israel shall speak Hebrew to one another within the Society and in its hall, nor shall they be ashamed to speak it in the market and the street. And they shall take heed to teach it to their sons and daughters and their whole household. The Society will strive to purify and enrich Hebrew, and make it the language of instruction in the schools.[328]

To avoid Turkish suspicion the society included in its charter a statement of loyalty to the government. However, in their private conversations, the members of the organization frankly acknowledged that what was in their hearts and minds was the reestablishment of the Jewish nation in Palestine. Only in Palestine, where Israel was born and flourished, the members insisted, could the Jewish nation truly exist.

During the years 1882–85, Ben-Yehuda continued to work as a teacher and as the editor of various Hebrew periodicals. Toward the end of 1884 he established his own weekly, *Ha-Zevi*, which later became a biweekly under the name *Ha Or*. The following year he published a geography of Palestine, and from 1897 a magazine called *Hashkafah*. In all of the publications with which he was associated, Ben-Yehuda championed the use of Hebrew in everyday life. He actively contributed to the growth of Hebrew by coining new words and introducing transliterations from other languages.

Financial difficulties constantly plagued Ben-Yehuda's career as a publisher but never deterred him from his goal. Despite many setbacks, Ben-Yehuda's periodicals were the first in the Hebrew language to come up to European standards. His publications covered, insofar as Turkish censorship allowed, all aspects of political and cultural life in Palestine.

Turkish restrictions, although a nuisance, had one positive effect on Ben-Yehuda's work—it forced him to concentrate more on linguistics than on politics. One result of this emphasis was the key role that he played in the establishment of the Va'ad Ha Leshon Ha Ivrit (Hebrew Language Council). The council, over which he presided until his death, was the forerunner of the Academy of the Hebrew Language created by the State of Israel in 1953 to conduct research into the history and development of the Hebrew language. The academy is also Israel's supreme authority for modern Hebrew terminology, usage, and spelling.

By the beginning of the twentieth century, Eliezer Ben-Yehuda's crusade on behalf of spoken Hebrew had achieved amazing results. A large segment of the Palestinian Jewish community had made Hebrew the language of the marketplace and the home. Ben-Yehuda himself had become a voice to be reckoned with in the Yishuv and in the Zionist movement. Nevertheless, controversy seemed to follow in his footsteps. His popularity, for example, took a serious downturn in Zionist circles following his support of the so-called Uganda proposal. This scheme involved an offer by the British government through its Secretary for the Colonies, Joseph Chamberlain to the Zionist leader, Theodor Herzl, for the establishment of an autonomous Jewish colony in British East Africa. When officially presented to the Sixth World Zionist Congress (August 23–28, 1903) the proposal provoked a grave crisis, and split the Congress into opposing factions. Most of the delegates from Western and Central Europe approved the Uganda offer, but the representatives from Eastern Europe and from the Yishuv were opposed to the scheme and considered acceptance a betrayal of the Zionist cause.

Ben-Yehuda's stand on the Uganda proposal was soon forgotten, and he again managed to regain the respect and admiration of the Yishuv. His popularity reached new heights as a result of his bold leadership in the "language *kulturkampf*" brought about by the German-Jewish directors of the Hilfsverein der Deutschen Juden (German Jews' Aid Society). Founded in 1901 this institution maintained a network of schools throughout Palestine. Both German and Hebrew were languages of instruction in these schools.

Ironically, a crisis over what language should predominate in the Aid Society's schools arose as an indirect result of Germany's imperialist ambitions. As unconscious agents of German culture in the Holy Land the directors of the Hilfsverein schools threatened the impressive progress made in the use of Hebrew by offering a number of courses taught exclusively in German. However, the issue of Hebrew versus German did not become urgent until plans were laid to establish a technical institute in Haifa. Funds for such a "Technion" had been made available by the estate of Wolf Wissotzsky, the Russian-Jewish tea magnate. The Jewish National Fund (Keren Kaymet L'Yisrael) established by the Fifth Zionist Congress (1901) had supplied the land (in Haifa), and the Hilfsverein and individual philanthropists contributed additional sums toward the project. As the administering agency, the Hilfsverein was determined that Technion become the very capstone of the Yishuv's educational system, as well as a spectacular example of German culture. In recognition of the latter goal the German undersecretary Arthur von Zimmerman personally sought and obtained from the Turkish authorities approval to erect the school's first building (it was completed in 1913). While construction was under way the German-Jewish members of the Technion board of governors proposed that all technical subjects be taught exclusively in the German language. However, although pride in the land of their birth was involved in their decision, it was widely recognized at the time that German was the language of science par excellence.

The board's proposal produced a wave of indignation among the Zionist settlers, most notably among the immigrants of the so-called Second Aliyah. Ben-Yehuda was outraged, and at his instigation student protest meetings were organized throughout the Yishuv. The Hebrew Teachers Association joined the fray and proclaimed a strike against all of the Hilfsverein schools. Demonstrations were also staged in front of the German consulate in Jerusalem, and a campaign to reverse the board's proposal was begun among the Jewish communities of Palestine. Many individuals feared that the entire Hebraic nature of the Zionist renaissance was being threatened and reacted accordingly. Aroused by the language war, the Zionist organization launched a world-wide drive for funds to immediately establish a dozen new Hebrew schools in Eretz Israel. By February, 1914, much of the tumult had subsided, and the controversy was finally brought to a conclusion when the Technion board of governors reversed its decision and agreed that all courses would be taught in Hebrew. In the aftermath of the language conflict the Hebrew Teachers Association established a board of education to administer the Technion curriculum, and to create guides for all Jewish non-Orthodox schools in Palestine, including those in the Hilfsverein network. Ben-Yehuda's dream had been realized.

The outbreak of World War I placed Ben-Yehuda in a precarious position. Jamal Pasha, the Turkish commander in Palestine outlawed Zionism, and fearing imprisonment, the outspoken editor and philologist was forced to seek asylum in the United States. While in America he continued to pursue his Hebrew language studies. At the conclusion of hostilities he returned to Palestine, where together with other prominent personalities the British high commissioner, Sir Herbert Samuel was persuaded to declare Hebrew one of the three official languages of the country (the other two were Arabic and English). During this same period Ben-Yehuda founded Sefatenu, a society for the propagation of Hebrew. In addition, he served as secretary of the planning committee of Hebrew University.

Throughout his years of residence in Palestine, Ben-Yehuda devoted much of his energy to the compilation of a comprehensive dictionary of the Hebrew language. In pursuing this project he gathered words from the Bible, the Talmud, commentaries, responsa, ancient and modern Hebrew literature, and delved into manuscripts and other writings sent to him by his disciples from every corner of the globe. Relentlessly he tracked down the Semitic roots of words and incorporated them into a contemporary vernacular. Seeking funds for his dictionary, Ben-Yehuda traveled on several occasions to Europe. In 1904 he received modest grants from the Zionist organization and from Baron Edmund de Rothschild, which enabled him to publish the first volume of his dictionary. A monumental work of scholarship, the dictionary was virtually an encyclopedia as well as a thesaurus of the Hebrew language. Ben-Yehuda would manage to complete three more volumes before his death in 1922. Following his demise the project was continued by his widow and son with the assistance of several distinguished linguists. When completed the dictionary would number seventeen volumes and become widely acclaimed as the definitive work on spoken and written Hebrew.

Eliezer Ben-Yehuda's passing was marked throughout the Jewish world in memorials and eulogies. Thirty thousand people escorted his body to its final resting place and the Jewish community of Palestine honored his passage with three days of official mourning. His dream of the Jewish people revived in the Land of Israel and united by the common bond of the Hebrew language became a key factor in Zionist ideology. Indeed, due largely to Ben-Yehuda's zeal, exalted feelings of national pride, and genius for linguistics, Hebrew was able to successfully take its place among modern languages and eventually become the official language of the new State of Israel.

VIII

THE LOVERS OF ZION

29

A Zionist Awakening

The Hibbat Zion[329] (Love of Zion) movement constituted an intermediate link between the forerunners of Zionism and the emergence of modern Herzlian or Political Zionism in the last decade of the nineteenth century. The Hibbat Zion ideology derived its strength from an acute awareness of the anomaly of the Jewish people among the nations, a heightened sense of living in exile, a longing for redemption, and a spiritual attachment for Eretz Israel generated by religion and tradition. Its adherents were at first to be found among Jewish intellectuals of Eastern Europe.

Prior to the emergence of the Hibbat Zion, the question of a Jewish national renaissance had chiefly been discussed by individuals who were motivated by messianic visions or by the national awakening of various European peoples. Most of Eastern European Jewry had little or no experience involving organized political activity and a religious leadership that, with a few exceptions, was hostile to the idea of a movement to restore the Jews to Eretz Israel. The religious leaders believed that such a movement constituted human interference in the ways of Providence. Nevertheless, a few charismatic rabbis such as Kalischer and Alkalay had defied the general consensus of Orthodoxy and had advocated return to the Promised Land as early as the 1840s. Kalischer had even initiated a conference of rabbis and community leaders of German Jewry in 1860 with the objective of forming a company for the Jewish colonization of Palestine. Shortly afterwards, Chaim Lorje of Frankfort on the Oder succeeded in founding the Jewish Company for the Settlement of the Holy Land. However, the activities of Kalischer, Alkalay, and Lorje had little effect on the Jewish masses of Eastern Europe. Similarly, the call of the socialist Moses Hess for the creation of a Jewish state in Palestine had fallen on deaf ears.

The entire issue of Jewish redemption in Palestine took a curious turn as a result of the movement for religious reform in Germany. In a desire to accentuate their patriotism the reformers favored national and cultural assimilation. The more radical proponents of a denationalized Judaism, such as Samuel Holdheim (1806–60), attacked the edifice of Talmudic Judaism and the residue of rabbinical jurisdiction. Holdheim's basic premise was that the law of the state was supreme and therefore Jewish laws must give way to this higher authority. The program of the Frankfort Reform Society, for example, went even further in breaking with tradition. It introduced new additions to the ritual, threw over the Talmud as devoid of dogmatic or practical authority, and rejected the messianic restoration of the Jewish people in Palestine.

Reaction to the Frankfort reformers and their successors was not long in forthcoming. Foremost in the ranks of those opposed to the reformers was the influential editor of the Hebrew monthly *Ha-Shahar,* Peretz Smolenskin, who looked askance at assimilationists. He was convinced that Jewry was in the same camp as other peoples in Europe and elsewhere aspiring toward national liberation (an idea particularly odious to the German-Jewish advocates of reform). Eliezer Ben-Yehuda also decried the reformers' trend toward assimilation, but emphasized that a national revival in Eretz Israel could only be achieved if the Hebrew language was revived as a spoken tongue. Smolenskin and Ben-Yehuda received unexpected support from former *maskilim* (enlighteners) who had become disillusioned with the *Haskalah*'s struggle to obtain civil rights for Jews everywhere and with the drift of many within the movement toward assimilation. This support increased markedly following the so-called southern tempests – the series of pogroms which ensued after the assassination of Czar Alexander II in 1881.

The very fact that there was no section of the Russian society ready or willing to come to defense of the Jews, who had to face the rioters and the hostile authorities alone, came as a severe shock to the *maskilim,* as well as to the entire Russian Jewish community. The new czar's restrictions on the sources of income, government posts, and institutes of learning available to Jews created an ideological crisis among the Jewish enlighteners, and many of them who had grown distant from their people now returned to the Jewish fold. Others who had pinned their hopes on the struggle to change the Russian social system came to the realization that it was a futile effort, and that even if successful it would not resolve the Jewish Problem. Among those who now turned their thoughts to a Jewish national revival the fact soon became obvious that a spiritual and linguistic revival was not sufficient, and that they must set their sights on achieving a territorial base. The panic-stricken flight of thousands of Russian Jews seeking to escape the pogroms and persecution and the suffering of the refugees confirmed for the Jewish intellectuals the dire need for a homeland – preferably in Palestine.

During the winter of 1881–82 associations for the promotion of Jewish emigration to Eretz Israel sprang up throughout the Pale of Settlement. Many of these groups adopted such fanciful names as Ezra, Maccabi, Sons of Zion, and Flag of Zion, but all eventually became known under the generic term Hoveve Zion (Lovers of Zion). In most cases these associations were a mixed lot. Some consisted mainly of Orthodox Jews, others of former *maskilim,* or radical students such as the St. Petersburg society, Ahavat Zion. This organization, for example, welcomed into its ranks any Jew who was willing to support the establishment of a state in the Holy Land.

Some of the groups favored immediate aliyah (immigration to Eretz Israel); still others advocated a slower approach, careful planning, and campaigns to spread the idea of a Jewish return to the ancient homeland among the Jewish masses. The latter approach received the enthusiastic support of the Hebrew journals *Ha-Shahar, Ha-Maggid, Ha-Meliz,* as well as the Russian language publication, *Razvet.* Many of the associations, in the classic pattern of European nationalist movements, championed education. They offered courses in Hebrew language, and Jewish history. Many of the associations were philanthropic in character and dedicated themselves to the task of raising funds for the founding of Jewish colonies in Palestine. Almost all of the Hoveve Zion were in agreement that agricultural colonies were the key to a successful Jewish revival in the Holy Land. Accordingly, priority was given to the goal of acquiring land, either by means of grants from the Turkish government, or by outright purchase from the land owners. In attempting to carry out these objectives the Russian Lovers of Zion, in particular, were well aware of the limits that the Russian government imposed on the scope of their activities. To avoid the baleful eyes of czarist officialdom, which frowned upon minority nationalism of any kind, they were compelled to meet in secret to conduct their affairs undisturbed.

During its formative years the Hibbat Zion movement counted on winning the support of the Alliance Israélite Universelle and other well-established and well-funded Jewish organizations in Western Europe. However, when this support failed to materialize, the Hibbat Zion societies decided to go ahead alone with their plans for establishing agricultural colonies in Palestine.

In the spring of 1882 a few would-be Jewish settlers managed to reach Eretz Israel. Alarmed by this unexpected immigration, the Turkish authorities promptly issued orders prohibiting further immigration. Despite this official ban, the foundations of Jewish agricultural settlement had been laid. Zalman David Levontin (1856–1940) and a handful of his companions from Russia acquired a tract of land near Jaffa on which the colony of Rishon le-Zion (First in Zion) would arise. Shortly afterward, members of the Moinesti society from Rumania set down roots in Rosh Pinna, which had previously been settled and abandoned by Jews from Safed. During this same period the settlement of Petah-Tikva was revived (it had originally been colonized in 1878 by Jews from Jerusalem and abandoned some time later because of an outbreak of malaria). At the end of 1882 a second band of Rumanian Jews settled on a strip of land on the western ridge of Mount Carmel. The colony was named Zammarin (later changed to Zikhron Ya'akov). The following year Lovers of Zion from Poland founded in the Galilee the settlement of Y'sod HaMa'aleh and some months later in 1884 the colony of Mishmar Ha-Yarden (Watch of the Jordan).

The Bilu Vanguard

In the vanguard of these early settlers was an idealistic and enthusiastic group of youngsters from Russia who banded together under the acronym Bilu,[330] the Hebrew initials of the biblical acrostic from Isaiah 2:5, Beit Ya'akov Lekhu ve Nelkhah ("O House of Jacob, come ye and let us go forth"). The Bilu society, which would provide the first organized group to actually go to Palestine, originated following a fast held by the Jewish communities of Russia on January 21, 1882, to mark the infamous pogroms of the preceding year. Israel Belkind (1861–1929), at the time a student at Kharkov University, invited fellow classmates to his home to discuss the status of Russian Jewry, in light of the recent pogroms and persecutions. The students who answered Belkind's invitation represented a curious mixture of Jewish nationalistic fervor and Russian populism. The pogroms had stirred them deeply and had aroused their Jewish consciousness to a fever pitch. They were acutely aware of the plight of those Jews who had become refugees as a result of the persecutions and sympathized with those who had chosen to return to "the land of their fathers" rather than seek a haven in the United States.

The students, after considerable discussion, decided to form an association. They thought of calling their group Davio, the Hebrew acronym from Exodus 14:15 for Dabber et Benei Yisrael ve Yissa'u ("Speak unto the Children of Israel that they go forward." However, on further reflection, they decided in favor of Bilu. The latter appellation seemed more appropriate to their objective, for instead of advising Jews to emigrate to Eretz Israel, they reached a decision to go there themselves:

> Let our lives be an example to our people. Let us forsake our lives in foreign lands and stand on firm ground in the land of our forefathers. Let us reach for shovels and plows. . . . We educated must be the heroes who go into battle at the head of the people.[331]

The spirit of the Bilu was contagious. After a whirlwind campaign to spread their ideas throughout the Jewish communities of Russia, the association's membership grew to over 500 souls—the majority of whom were students. The rapid expansion brought on a division of opinion over how to proceed toward realization of the group's objective. The original members favored immediate immigration to Palestine and the establishment there of an agricultural colony based on cooperative principles. Most of the newer members demurred and advocated a more gradual approach. Accordingly, the ideology of the society began to reflect an individual member's particular views and frequently led to the issuance of contradictory statements. Thus, of the many statutes formulated by the Bilu, some defined the aim of the organization as the creation of a political center for the Jewish people, while other documents proclaimed that the principal goals were economic and spiritual. The original activist nucleus of the Bilu made no attempt, however, to distinguish between political, economic, and spiritual goals. Ze'ev Dubnow (1858–1940), the elder brother of the renowned Jewish historian, Simon Dubnow, and one of the first of this core group to undertake the journey to the Holy Land, best summed up its philosophy. He affirmed that the ultimate goal of his associates was nothing less than the eventual conquest of Palestine and the return of political independence to the Jewish people after a 2,000 year hiatus. To accomplish this long-range objective it was essential that agricultural settlements and industrial enterprises be established. In addition, Ze'ev Dubnow noted, once a foothold in the Holy Land has been achieved, Jewish youngsters should be given military training and supplied with weapons. Only then will the glorious day prophesied by Isaiah come about, for with weapons in their hands the Jews will be able to become masters of their ancient homeland.

With the expansion of the Bilu society, the headquarters was moved from Kharkov to Odessa, a more convenient embarkation point for travel to Eretz Israel. However, the eternal debate within the organization of whether to undertake immediate emigration or to wait for more favorable circumstances raged on for almost two years and greatly weakened the resolve of the original activists. During this period of indecisiveness the society sought support for its objectives from wealthy Russian Jews. Disappointed by the latter's lack of interest the Bilu turned for help to the devout English millenarian, Laurence Oliphant.

Oliphant had witnessed first hand anti-Semitism outbreaks in Rumania (1879) and the suffering of the victims seeking to escape persecution. He was aware of the Rumanian government's devious disavowal of its explicit obligation, made at the Congress of Berlin in 1878, to grant equal rights to all its people, including the Jews. The dispossession by Rumania of large numbers of Jews from their sources of income had become a scandal in all of Europe. Faced with the threat of further pogroms, emigration seemed to be the only viable solution for Rumanian Jewry. Oliphant strongly supported the emigration, and his ideas on this subject were reinforced after attending a Hibbat Zion conference in Jassy. He instantly sensed the potential of the movement. Dedicating himself to helping the Lovers of Zion achieve their objectives, Oliphant traveled to Constantinople in the hope of persuading the Ottoman sultan to grant the Jews a charter to establish colonies in Palestine. His appeal fell on deaf ears. The Turks, who had been angered by Great Britain's policies in the Mediterranean and the Near East, were in no mood to support schemes proposed by an English eccentric. Not only Oliphant, but also Edward Cazalet (1827–83), a prominent industrialist who was also promoting plans for Jewish colonization in the Holy Land, had his proposals firmly rejected by the Ottoman authorities.

Oliphant, refusing to admit defeat, continued to lobby for a Jewish charter. He reiterated many of the arguments he had originally set forth in a book entitled *The Land of Gilead* (1880), written after a tour of the Holy Land. The author advanced the thesis that England, in pursuit of its own national interests, would eventually persuade the Turks to allow Jewish settlement of Palestine under British protection. Oliphant persisted in this belief even after the British government had apprised him that, having occupied Cyprus (an Ottoman possession) some years earlier, they were wary of further provoking the Turks.

Unaware of the state of Oliphant's negotiations with the Turks, the Bilu continued to await word as to whether or not he had been successful. When weeks and then months passed by in silence, their hopes began to fade. By the summer of 1882 news of Oliphant's lack of progress finally reached the Bilu society. At this point a small group of the membership decided to reinforce Oliphant's political and diplomatic efforts in Turkey. Accordingly, seventeen Bilu'im set sail for Constantinople. There, after many inquiries, they received word that Oliphant's failure was not a temporary setback, and that he had literally exhausted all his resources and could do nothing further for them. All but three of the Bilu'im decided to press on to Palestine, without obtaining the desired Turkish charter. Before undertaking their journey to the Holy Land, the group drew up a document outlining their principles. With more than a trace of Russian radicalism, they condemned the system of capitalist land ownership, and warned against transposing this relic of the old order to Palestine. The Bilu'im also agreed that the bachelors among them would serve the Jewish people and the land for three years in a model communal agricultural settlement. Upon completion of this term they would take on the role of instructors in a network of other newer settlements. By following these simple principles, the Bilu'im hoped to create a new society based on social justice.

In July of 1882 thirteen young men and one woman of the Bilu'im who had set out from Constantinople reached Jaffa in Palestine. They were preceded by a few weeks by Ya'akov Shertok, the father of the future State of Israel's second prime minister. The history of the Jewish resettlement of Eretz Israel in modern times is usually dated from the arrival of the Bilu'im in Jaffa (this period of immigration has come to be known as the First Aliyah). The group's initial encounter with the squalid port town and its inhabitants was far from encouraging to the idealistic young pioneers. The Orthodox Jews they met were far from enthusiastic or supportive of the Bilu'im and their objectives. Indeed, they considered the newcomers to be nonreligious and rivals for the distribution of funds sent each year for their support by the Jewish communities of the Diaspora. Even more ominous, the Turkish authorities were suspicious of the Bilu'im. They viewed the group as possible agents of one of the Great Powers and a potential threat to the very existence of Ottoman rule in Palestine.

Undeterred by these formidable obstacles and by their own lack of preparedness, the Bilu'im found work at the Mikveh Israel Agricultural School, an institution to train Jewish farmers, founded twelve years earlier by the Alliance Israélite Universelle. Living as a commune, the young pioneers were set to hard work for a pittance by the school's French agronomists, who cared little for the newcomers' idealism. Laboring in the fields eleven and twelve hours a day, the Bilu'im, unused to physical exertions, suffered terribly.

The morale of the young pioneers was further tested when reinforcements and financial support from Odessa failed to materialize. Nevertheless, although the group had little to be optimistic about during their first months in Eretz Israel, they were not completely without friends in an otherwise hostile atmosphere. They managed to find a sympathetic ear and confidant in Charles Netter (1826–82), one of the founders of the Alliance Israélite Universelle and the Mikveh Israel Agricultural School. Netter adopted a paternal attitude to the Bilu'im, encouraged their efforts, and openly identified with their goals. However, the sudden death of Netter in 1882, once again left the group without a patron or support of any kind. Their dream of developing a model colony – the very raison d'etre for coming to Palestine – seemed more remote than ever.

At this crucial moment in the lives of the Bilu'im, a Hebrew writer and Zionist pioneer named Yehiel Mikhel Pines (1843–1913),[332] came to the assistance of the group. Pines, who acted as a representative of the Mazkeret Mosheh society in Palestine, persuaded some of the Bilu'im to leave the agricultural school for Jerusalem. Calling themselves "Shehu," an acronym derived from the biblical phrase Shivat he-Harash ve ha Masger ("Return of the Craftsman and the Smith"), the Jerusalem group established a carpentry workshop. Lack of experience, however, led to the enterprise's eventual failure.

Help of a sort materialized in the persons of Zalman David Levontin (1856–1940), and Joseph Feinberg (1855–1902). Both men, activists in the Hibbat Zion movement, had managed to collect considerable funds from individuals in Europe and Jerusalem for the purpose of purchasing land in Palestine. Through an intermediary, an Ottoman subject, they managed to circumscribe Turkish restrictions and acquired possession of a tract of land eight miles inland from the port of Jaffa. Here, with settlers recruited mainly from Jerusalem families, a new colony was founded and enthusiastically dubbed Rishon l'Zion (First in Zion).

Touched by the idealistic fervor of the Bilu'im, Levontin and Feinberg persuaded the colonists of Rishon l'Zion to allow the former students to join the new settlement. Eleven of the Bilu'im, under the leadership of Belkind, accepted the invitation and in November of 1882 moved to Rishon l'Zion and took up shelter in a makeshift dormitory set aside for their use. Pooling their remaining worldly goods, the young pioneers set about clearing the soil and planting maize and vegetables. Unfortunately, the season for such crops had already passed, and their efforts proved futile. Soon both food and money were exhausted and the Bilu'im faced the very real threat of starvation. Adding to their troubles, ill feelings between the Bilu'im and the settlers from Jerusalem that had been simmering from the moment of the newcomers' arrival at Rishon l'Zion now erupted into the open. When it became obvious that a reconciliation was impossible five of the Bilu'im decided to return to the Mikveh Israel Agricultural School. Six others chose to return to Russia.

When some of the Bilu members who had remained in Constantinople realized that their compatriots had failed in their efforts to create a model colony, they refused to admit defeat. Instead they felt that another attempt should be made, and in 1884 they left the Turkish capital for Palestine. This second band of Bilu'im encountered the same obstacles as their predecessors as they came face to face with harsh realities resulting from a lack of agricultural skills, a debilitating climate, sickness, insufficient funds, and the hostility of the Orthodox Jews as well as the Arab population. Dismissed from the Mikveh Israel Agricultural School, where they had originally found work as laborers, the Bilu and their dream of securing a foothold in Palestine seemed doomed.

Once again Yehiel Mikhel Pines came to the rescue of the disheartened pioneers. He had acquired land in the vicinity of the Arab village of Qatra, on the coastal plain of Palestine, and after dividing the property into small plots he had sent an envoy abroad to sell the tracts to the Hibbat Zion organization. However, each of the latter's associations that were interested in Pines' offer had to agree as a condition of the purchase that they would turn over their land parcels to the Bilu'im to settle and farm. The conditions were accepted and shortly afterwards the settlement of Gederah was founded. The Bilu'im took possession of their new home in December of 1884. Their problems, however, were far from over. They were obliged to live in a single shack, and lacked even basic farm equipment as well as such essentials as oxen or milch cows. In addition, their funds were scarcely adequate to purchase more than a few months' supply of staples. With the land best suited for viticulture, the Bilu'im also realized they would have to wait at least three years for a paying harvest. In the interim, they hoped to survive on what they could grow, namely on winter wheat and barley and summer dura. Lacking agricultural skills, they misplanted their subsistence crops, and in the end were reduced to meals of radishes and potatoes. Their physical and mental health deteriorated rapidly and they became too weak to protect their land. They watched helplessly as local Arabs grazed their herds on Gederah's fields, and dispossessed them of whole tracts of land. Not content with taking advantage of the Bilu'im's weakened condition, the Arabs began to beat and humiliate the pioneers. The hapless settlers could do nothing in the face of these assaults except swallow their pride and stifle their anger.

In spite of all its difficulties and even some desertions, the Gederah colony clung on to its land. The handful of settlers who remained abandoned completely the notion of a cooperative community, and like other Jewish colonies such as Rishon l'Zion, and Petah-Tikva, sought out cheap Arab labor to help work the land. The original Bilu'im who had made Gederah their home refused to accept this moral surrender and by the end of the decade of the 1880s all of them left the colony.

In Eastern Europe, as in Palestine, the enthusiasm that had been kindled at the onset of the Hibbat Zion movement gradually subsided. The general malaise that had overtaken the settlement efforts and the Turkish restrictions on immigration to the Holy Land played a role in weakening the ardor of the Love of Zion associations. Even more harmful was the lack of central direction that marked all of the movement's activities.

The loosely knit societies of the Hibbat Zion, however, finally found a leader in Leon Pinsker (1821–91), a physician of Odessa. In an anonymously published pamphlet entitled *Auto-Emancipation* (1882) Pinsker called on the Jewish nation to help itself and to return to national consciousness and a life of territorial independence. Anti-Semitism, he emphasized, was a universal peril and would not be solved by Jewish migration to other countries where they would continue to be a minority. Although Pinsker did not originally consider Palestine as the most suitable territory for the Jews to establish a state, he changed his mind after joining the Hibbat Zion. This change was largely due to his coming in contact in the organization with such ardent proponents of Eretz Israel as Moses Leib Lillienblum (1843–1910), Hermann Tzevi Schapira (1840–98), and Max Emmanuel Mandelstamm (1839–1912).

In 1883 a memorandum was circulated calling for the creation of a central executive committee to be elected by a congress of delegates drawn from all the Hibbat Zion societies. The suggestion was not acted upon, but shortly afterwards a new association, the Zerubavel Society was founded in Odessa with Leon Pinsker as the chairman and Lillienblum as secretary. A similar group was established in Warsaw under the leadership of Saul Phineas Rabinowitz (1845–1910) and Isidor Jasinowsky (1842–1917). These societies, because of the stature of their leaders and the cities in which they were located, began to act as clearing houses for contacts with other Hibbat Zion groups. However, it become obvious to most Lovers of Zion that such an ad hoc system of administration was less than perfect. They felt centralization was essential if the objectives of the movement were ever to be achieved, but there was a considerable difference of opinion as to the form it should take and what would best serve the associations.

The younger and more radical elements among the Hibbat Zion societies demanded an organic structure that would place major emphasis on the movement's national aspirations. A more moderate and conservative segment advocated a slower approach and concentration on strengthening the existing colonies in Palestine. The one hundredth birthday of Sir Moses Montefiore provided both sides an opportunity to air their views. The idea took hold to convene an assembly of the Hibbat Zion societies in the philanthropist's honor and to further commemorate the occasion by establishing a Montefiore Society for the Promotion of Agriculture in Palestine. David Gordon, the editor of the Hebrew journal *Ha-Maggid* was selected to travel to Ramsgate, England, the home of Montefiore, to sound out the aged Maecenas on the Hibbat Zion proposals and to secure financial support for the planned agricultural society. Gordon, however, met with an unexpectedly cool reception. Montefiore was too tired and feeble to be receptive to new schemes, and his family and associates would not allow the aged philanthropist to be burdened with new responsibilities. The hope that Montefiore would fund the agricultural society or at the very least serve as a magnet to attract the required funds from other philanthropists thus proved to be still-born.

Kattowitz Conference

In spite of the Montefiore fiasco the Hibbat Zion leaders decided to go ahead with the call for a general assembly of all the associations. To circumvent interference by Russian authorities they chose to meet in Kattowitz, a German-Silesian city located at a point where the three empires of Russia, Austria, and Germany met. Thirty-four delegates attended the sessions, which took place from November 6th through 12, 1884, and were chaired by Leon Pinsker. The conferees, who came from Russia, Rumania, Germany, England, and France were all aware of the obstacles confronting them: Turkish opposition to Jewish immigration to Palestine; the hostility of the Jewish philanthropic agencies to their goals; the inability to attract to their movement the volatile and radical youth who shunned the movement because of its hesitant nature and bourgeois elements; the resentment of many of the more secular-minded Lovers of Zion to the considerable influence wielded by rabbinical leaders within the movement; and lastly the chronic lack of funds for support of the Palestinian colonies, as well as the movement's rather unimpressive record of achievements.

Faced with such a diverse and complex array of problems, the delegates struggled to find solutions that would be equitable to the various factions, and possible to achieve within the limits of the resources available to the Hibbat Zion. Nevertheless, when the conference had ended, consensus was reached on the need to adequately fund the Jewish settlements in Eretz Israel and recommendations made to create a tighter union of associations. Keeping with the original premise to honor Montefiore, Pinsker suggested that the new union be called Mazkeret Moshe be Eretz ha-Kodesh (The Testimonial to Moses in the Holy Land).

To carry out the tightening of the Hibbat Zion's loose organizational structure, the Kattowitz conferees recommended that a central committee be established with head-quarters in Berlin. This proposal was given high priority, as conditions in Russia had made Hibbat Zion activities virtually impossible. In the interim, until the Berlin center could become operational, its functions would be handled by a temporary central committee in Odessa, and by a subcommittee in Warsaw.

During the deliberations of the Kattowitz Conference, its chairman, Leon Pinsker, found himself in a rather awkward position. Instead of the suggestions that he had set forth in his pamphlet to rapidly achieve "auto-emancipation" in a national homeland, he was compelled to accept the decision of the majority, which favored a gradual approach and practical work in Palestine. Ironically, Pinsker at heart was opposed to the piecemeal approach to colonization, and regarded it at best as having minimal value. He would have preferred instead a vigorous propaganda campaign and recruitment drive to strengthen the ranks of the Hibbat Zion in the West, followed by the convocation of an international Jewish Congress to place the Jewish Question before the governments of the world.

Fortune, however, did not smile on the decisions of the Kattowitz majority. Everything seemed to conspire against their great expectations. Thus a protracted search for capable organizers in the West met with little success. Indeed, in Germany not a single personality of any stature could be found to head the proposed Berlin headquarters, thus forcing the Hibbat Zion leadership to abandon the entire idea. Equally disturbing was the fact that the handful of Lovers of Zion in Germany and England seemed to lack the elan and spirit of their Russian counterparts. Only the student society Kadimah (Forward) in Vienna seemed able to overcome the general malaise that marked most of the associations in Western and Central Europe. In Rumania as well the Hibbat Zion movement stagnated until the 1890s, and even the usual energetic Russian groups seemed to have lost their drive. Not only did the movement fail to provide the momentum required to organize new settlements in Palestine, but their ability to support the existing colonies was sorely tested. Funds continually lagged far behind what was required for a successful coloniza-tion program.

The situation of those Jewish settlers who had risked all by making "aliyah", became more and more alarming with the passage of each month.[333] A diary entry dated August 21, 1882, written by one of the pioneers (*chalutzim*) who had settled in Rishon l'Zion, poignantly reveals the state of despondency that overwhelmed many of the colonists of his day and for several years afterwards. The diarist notes that he has been unable for the past ten days to write a word as his hands are covered with blisters and he cannot straighten his fingers. Physically and mentally exhausted, he laments that he has no time for any intellectual activity, and thinks only of throwing himself on his bed and hopefully getting a night's sleep.

Working long hours in the fields, eaten alive by flies, constantly robbed of their livestock by Bedouins, living in wretched hovels, and exposed to the elements, the early Jewish settlers of the Hibbat Zion struggled to survive. Disease and sheer exhaustion took a toll and the original enthusiasm of the pioneers waned. The entire Hibbat Zion movement seemed doomed. When they were at the very brink of collapse, support for the handful of Love of Zion colonies in Palestine came just in time from an unexpected source.

Rothschild and the Palestine Colonies

Rabbi Samuel Mohilever (1824–98) and Laurence Oliphant approached and solicited the help of European Jewry's most celebrated philanthropists—Baron Edmund de Rothschild (1845–1934), and Baron Maurice de Hirsch (1831–96). Hirsch was willing to aid the Palestine colonies, but insisted that Russian Jewry assume part of the rescue effort by contributing 50,000 rubles. When this sum failed to materialize, he decided to concentrate his efforts on creating Jewish colonies in the Argentine.

Edmund de Rothschild, the head of the French branch of the famous banking family, had previously supported efforts to transform the Jews into a "productive normal people capable of laboring once again on the soil." He was receptive to Mohilever's plea for help (the rabbi had been brought in touch with the Baron through the good offices of the chief rabbi of France, Zadoc Kahn [1839–1905]). In the autumn of 1882, Rothschild also granted an audience to still another petitioner, Joseph Feinberg. One of the founders of Rishon l'Zion Feinberg had, at the urging of Charles Netter, returned to Europe to raise funds to succor his languishing colony. Emotionally moved by the appeals of Mohilever and Feinberg, Rothschild immediately contributed 30,000 francs for the purpose of drilling a well at Rishon l'Zion, and promised additional help would be forthcoming. Soon after this initial step the Baron sent an expert agronomist to instruct the colonists and hired the director of the Mikveh Israel Agricultural School to act as an overseer of the settlement at Rishon l'Zion. He also arranged for twelve additional families to study at the agricultural school and promised to set them up with farms of their own when they had completed their courses. These families would eventually form the nucleus of a new settlement called Ekron. In addition, Baron Rothschild took the struggling colonies of Zamarin and Rosh Pina under his wing and rescued them from going under. Zamarin was later renamed Zikhron Ya'akov in memory of the Baron's father. In return for his assistance, Edmund de Rothschild insisted on anonymity. His wish was honored for many years by those individuals who had been instrumental in seeking his help. The colonists, however, were well aware of their rescuer and tended to refer cryptically to the Baron as "that well-known benefactor."

With the passage of time the Zionist colonies in Eretz Israel became Rothschild's major philanthropic interest. Between 1884 and 1900 he spent 6 million francs on the colonies—buying land, providing agricultural training, purchasing farm equipment and livestock, and building housing, waterworks, dispensaries, synagogues, and old age homes for the settlers. Hardly any of the fledgling colonies were denied his largess. Petah-Tikva and Rishon l'Zion greatly benefited from the Baron's philanthropy. Other settlements such as Mishmar Ha-Yarden, Ein Zeitim, Metulla, and Hartuv, were established with the understanding that the "well-known benefactor" would come to their aid if the settlers failed to manage on their own.

Nevertheless, Baron Edmund de Rothschild's support did not come without a price. He did not have complete faith in the abilities of the settlers or the Hibbat Zion and therefore insisted on direct supervision and control of the colonies by his agents. The experts the Baron sent from France and some drawn from the Mikveh Israel Agricultural School became his overseers and were charged with the day to day administration of the settlements. Thus a paternalistic regime was created, which was not at all to the liking of the settlers or the Hibbat Zion movement. It radically affected the ideals of the latter organization, as well as the actual status of the colonists. No longer did the settlers collect subsidies according to the work performed, but rather on the size of their families, or their ability to ingratiate themselves with the overseers. Eventually the colonists were even stripped of all authority to determine what crops to grow.

Rothschild's administrators showed no understanding for the settlers or the ideology which had motivated their coming to the Holy Land. In general they despised the colonists and considered them as nothing more than charity seekers. The end result was a serious demoralization in the settlers' spirit and initiative. Nevertheless, even though aware that they might starve without Rothschild's support, many of the colonists frequently voiced bitterness at their transformation into "serfs." Their youth, they moaned, was passing them by and leaving them more insecure and uncertain of the future. The Hibbat Zion leadership, although sympathetic to the settlers, felt helpless to rectify the situation, for fear of incurring the wrath of the Baron. Indeed, during the decade of the 1880s the Hibbat Zion were able to provide only about five percent of the total funds allocated for the Palestinian colonies – Rothschild provided the remainder of the budget. The major beneficiary of the Hibbat Zion effort was the Bilu colony of Gederah.

The bitter criticism of Rothschild's administrators eventually reached the Baron's ears. After a visit to Eretz Israel in 1898, Rothschild himself recognized the symptoms of demoralization. The Jewish planters, he noted, had lost their pioneering spirit and had become dependent on Arab labor. Accordingly, the Baron decided to phase out his subsidies to the settlements in order to force the colonists to meet their day to day responsibilities on their own. In 1900, he turned over the responsibility for the administration of the settlements to the Jewish Colonization Association (commonly referred to as the ICA). This entity formed a Palestine commission to carry out its new responsibilities. Rothschild, who was still not willing to drop completely the philanthropic projects that had absorbed him since 1882 retained his interest by presiding over the commission's sessions. The ICA was not a newcomer to colonization projects, as it had already had considerable experience in promoting Jewish farming in various parts of the world (particularly in Argentina).

In 1923, as a result of the rapid growth of the Palestinian Jewish community, Baron Edmund de Rothschild decided to establish a new body to better deal with the problems created by the expanding population. The new entity, headed by his son James de Rothschild took over the ICA, and was officially recognized by the British Mandatory authorities in 1924. Known as the Palestine Jewish Colonization Society, or PICA, this organization provided Jewish settlements with various types of assistance, helped fund cooperative ventures, engaged in swamp drainage, afforestation, stabilization of sand dunes, and encouraged farm modernization and agricultural research. It also gave financial support to cultural institutions including the Hebrew University and Technion.

PICA would also play a prominent role in developing industrial enterprises. On the death of James de Rothschild in 1957, PICA wound up its activities and transferred its considerable assets and property to the State of Israel.

Although completely overshadowed by the efforts of the French branch of the Rothschilds on behalf of the Jewish settlements of Palestine, the Hibbat Zion movement was not moribund. In June of 1887 a conference of Russian associations was held in Drushkieniki, Russia. It was called by Rabbi Samuel Mohilever, at the time the head of the Bialystok Society, who attempted to use the occasion to impose an Orthodox authority on the Love of Zion movement. His efforts, however, were foiled by the secular delegates who vehemently opposed any moves to give the movement a religious turn. A divisive split was avoided at the eleventh hour by a compromise. Leon Pinsker, the standard bearer of the secularists, was reelected as head of the Hibbat Zion, and he was provided with an advisory board of six, three of whom were rabbis. On a more positive note, the conference also decided to renew efforts to win legal recognition from the Russian government. Indeed, a breakthrough of sorts came in 1890 as a result of the work of Alexander Zederbaum (1816–93), a pioneer of Jewish journalism in Russia and the editor of the Hebrew weekly, *Ha-Melitz*. Zederbaum obtained government permission for the Hibbat Zion to conduct their activities under the rubric of a Society for the Support of Jewish Farmers and Artisans in Syria and Palestine. The Russian government, which was adamantly opposed to minority nationalistic agitations of any kind, was willing to look aside on a movement that encouraged Jewish emigration. Indeed, such a goal was not unattractive to the anti-Semitic minions of the czar.

The Odessa Committee

The initial conference of the Society for the Support of Jewish Farmers and Artisans in Syria and Palestine was held in Odessa, the city that would become its permanent headquarters. Creation of this entity marked the dawn of a new era for the Hibbat Zion movement. The new society's headquarters became known by the popular sobriquet "Odessa Committee," and increased contributions into its coffers enabled it, during the years 1890 to 1891, to encourage and direct a new flow of immigration to Palestine. The expulsion of the Jews from Moscow (1891) reinforced the importance of the Odessa Committee, and gave additional impetus to its work.

The enthusiasm engendered by the Odessa Committee was paralleled by a rapid growth in the 1890s of Hibbat Zion associations in Europe and the New World. In Rumania, where the status of the Jewish population was at best marginal, the movement took strong root, and many new societies came into being. In the Habsburg empire, the Hibbat Zion, led primarily by Jews living in Vienna, enjoyed a brief renaissance, and produced such outstanding leaders as Smolenskin, and Nathan Birnbaum (pseudonym Mathias Acher, [1864–1937], author, publicist, and originator of the term Zionism). Similarly, in Germany Hibbat Zion associations were formed by Russian-Jewish students at the country's various universities. Among the future leaders to emerge from this environment were Chaim Weizmann (1874–1952), destined to become the State of Israel's first president; Lev Arye Motzkin (1867–1933), a cofounder of the World Zionist Organization; and Shmarya Levin (1867–1935) one of Zionism's greatest orators. Some time later German-Jewish students would follow the example set by the Russian-Jews studying in their country and organize Hibbat Zion societies of their own. From their ranks would come a number of important personalities (e.g., Victor Jacobson, Willi Bambus, and Arthur Hantke). Of course Russia, the very heart and soul of the Love of Zion movement, continued to lead in the number of associations created throughout this period.

Remarkably, even English Jewry experienced a surge of nationalistic consciousness. Here, a Sephardic Jew, Colonel Albert Goldsmid (1846–1903), a promising staff officer from a military family that had almost severed all connections with Judaism established an unusual branch of the Love of Zion. Combining military and romantic tradition, he formed a series of so-called tents to correspond with the ancient tribes of Israel. The tents, which were distributed through various quarters of London and other towns of Great Britain were headed by commanders and vice-chiefs. Each commander of a tent received his commission from the chief of the association.

One of Goldsmid's earliest supporters was Elim d'Avigdor, who also came from a family that was nearly completely assimilated. In the United States the Hibbat Zion was represented by societies largely sponsored by Russian-Jewish immigrants. A handful of distinguished scholars and rabbis, notably Gustav Gottheil (1827–1903), Benjamin Szold (1829–1902), and Marcus Jastrow (1829–1903) also early on identified themselves with the movement.

In an effort to make its operations more efficient, the Odessa Committee established a branch office in Jaffa, Palestine, under the direction of Vladimir Tiomkin (1861–1927), a Russian-Jewish engineer. His assignment was to supervise the distribution of funds to the settlements and to acquire additional land for the committee. Tiomkin initially enjoyed considerable success in carrying out his mission. Unfazed by Ottoman restrictions he managed, through the use of intermediaries, to purchase large tracts of land, which he then resold to prospective settlers or land companies. It was chiefly through these means that the two important colonies of Rehovot and Haderah were founded.

The upsurge of Hibbat Zion activities in the Palestine of the 1890s proved to be ephemeral. Malaria forced the abandonment of some of the settlements. In addition, Tiomkin's enthusiasm for acquiring land frequently exceeded his good judgment and financial resources. His transactions gradually drove up land prices, making it virtually impossible for many of the newly arrived immigrants to acquire a plot of land. An investigatory panel dispatched by the Odessa Committee to determine what could be done to remedy the situation recommended that the Jaffa office be closed. Tiomkin, completely distraught by this decision, returned to Europe a disillusioned man.

Disenchantment again became common among the colonists. The hardships of reclaiming a land that had been neglected for centuries was overwhelming. Recurring epidemics such as malaria and typhoid also took a toll, as did the constant interference in the lives of the settlers by the hostile Turkish administration. In addition to their other woes, the settlers were opposed at every turn by the beneficiaries of the *halukkah* system, who spread unfavorable stories about the colonists.

It also became evident to the pioneers that the Hibbat Zion movement, on whose support their very lives sometimes depended, was riven by dissensions that rendered the organization ineffective. Most divisive was the power struggle between the secularists and the Orthodox. Originally, only a few Orthodox rabbis had shown any interest in the Hibbat Zion, but with the passage of time many reconsidered their position and joined the movement along with their followers. As their number increased, the Orthodox insisted that religion play a greater part in the movement. They were particularly outraged by the lack of religion of the vast majority of the pioneers who had settled in the Holy Land. "There was not a single pair of tefilin ('phylacteries') in all Rishon l'Zion,"[334] an Orthodox rabbi complained.

On several occasions, most notably at the Kattowitz and Drushkieniki conferences, the Orthodox leadership attempted to wrest control of the Love of Zion movement from the secularists. Although the Orthodox leaders failed in each instance, they remained a constant irritant. Indeed, some of the actions of the Orthodox rabbis within the movement threatened the very survival of the Palestinian settlements. A case in point occurred in 1888–89, a year designated as *shemitta* (a sabbatical year). In line with the biblical prohibition the rabbis issued proclamations forbidding the Jewish farmers to work the land during the sabbatical year. Conforming to this edict would have resulted in wide-spread starvation and was therefore widely ignored by the settlers. Equally inimical to the welfare of the colonists was a quarrel which erupted between the Orthodox rabbis within the Hibbat Zion and their ultra-Orthodox colleagues outside the movement over *ethrogim* (the so-called apples of paradise required for the ritual observance of the Feast of Tabernacles). The ultra-Orthodox demanded that the fruit should be imported from the island of Corfu, while the rabbis associated with the Hibbat Zion insisted that only the *ethrogim* grown in Eretz Israel be used.

The Odessa Committee, which had set as one of its major objectives rapid Jewish mass migration to the Promised Land, gradually found itself bogged down with the day to day problems of the settlements. Such items as the condition of the livestock at Gederah, or whether attacks by the inhabitants of a neighboring Arab village on the settlement constituted a serious threat to its existence came to dominate the committee's time and activities. This was not what the founders had envisaged, and the conviction grew among some of the Odessa Committee's members that some corrections were necessary if the original objectives were ever to be attained.

The crisis confronting the Odessa Committee, and indeed the entire Hibbat Zion movement had been perceived at the very outset by Asher Ginzberg (1856–1927), a brilliant essayist who wrote under the nom de plume Ahad Ha-Am (Hebrew for "One of the People"). As early as 1889 he had warned his fellow Lovers of Zion to cease blaming the Rothschild administrators or the supporters of the *halukkah* system for everything that went wrong in Palestine. He was convinced that the tactics for a Jewish national revival employed by the Hibbat Zion were not sound. When Ahad Ha-Am was sent by the Odessa Committee to Palestine in 1891 and again in 1893, his worst fears were confirmed. Accordingly, he employed his literary talents to lash out at the policies of the Hibbat Zion. Piecemeal colonization, Ahad Ha-Am stressed, was not the answer. Colonization could only succeed if it was carefully planned, gradual, practical, and on an adequate scale. His criticism was partially inspired by a belief that Eretz Israel could not absorb large numbers of immigrants and should become a cultural and spiritual center rather than placing all efforts on immediately creating a national state.

Ahad Ha-Am's views won the support of the Odessa Committee members who favored change. The end result was an intensification of the ideological and cultural activities of the committee. Ahad Ha-Am's approach, which became known as "Cultural Zionism," did not win over the rank and file of the Hibbat Zion and in time would be completely overshadowed by a more popular movement known as "Herzlian" or "Political" Zionism.

By the dawn of the twentieth century, the enthusiasm that had marked the early years of the Hibbat Zion movement had ebbed. The movement's ideology had become blurred, and its challenge blunted. The various conferences clearly revealed the organization's lack of cohesion and its weakness. With the passage of the years Hibbat Zion had become more of a philanthropic entity than a political movement and was not very effective in its new role. At the height of its popularity, the Hibbat Zion was only able to collect about 20,000 roubles a year, a paltry sum when compared to the contributions for the Palestinian settlements made by Baron Edmund de Rothschild. Equally disturbing was the fact that, throughout the period of its greatest activity, the movement had only managed to send a few colonists to Eretz Israel. The vast majority of the Lovers of Zion had no desire to emigrate, but preferred instead the role of well-wishers and sympathizers for those who did. After decades of struggle the principles and convictions that had originally motivated the Hibbat Zion pioneers had dissipated. Many of the early settlers had become owners of plantations employing mainly Arab labor. Their children were often sent to France for education, and a fairly high number of these students on graduation spurned a career in agriculture or chose not to return to Palestine. When a new wave of Jewish immigrants reached the Holy Land, they found it exceedingly difficult to obtain employment in the established settlements. The latter preferred the cheaper and more experienced Arab laborers to their fellow Jews. The Hibbat Zion crusade had gradually and unconsciously taken on the attributes of a commercial venture. This development was no doubt preferable to the unproductive existence of the Old Yishuv, which depended on organized begging as a way of life, but it was hardly what the ideologists of the Lovers of Zion had hoped to achieve.

The situation, however, was not completely hopeless. A Jewish beachhead in Palestine had been established. Between 1882 and 1903 fully 25,000 Jews found their way to Eretz Israel, the largest single influx since the decree expelling the Jews from Spain. In addition, twenty-one agricultural settlements had been founded, and the experience gained in the process bode well for the future. Although many of the immigrants had come under the auspices of the Hibbat Zion movement, the vast majority of the newcomers were refugees from oppression or religiously motivated individuals intent on spending their remaining years in study and prayer. Nevertheless, the Hibbat Zion pioneers, although small in number, set the stage for the next act in the age-old struggle for redemption—the dramatic appearance of Theodor Herzl on the Jewish landscape. Within a relatively short span of years, nearly all of the Love of Zion associations joined Herzl's creation—the World Zionist Organization. This shift in allegiance did not eliminate the Hibbat Zion movement, as it continued to exist even after Herzl's concept of Political Zionism had gained the attention of most of the Jewish world. From 1906–19 the Hibbat Zion was led by Menahem Mendel Ussishkin (1863–1941), an early adherent of the Bilu and one of the founders of the Bene Zion society in 1884. When the World Zionist Organization modified Herzl's concept of Political Zionism and accepted the principle of practical work in Palestine, the differences with Hibbat Zion vanished, and the latter began to decline rapidly. The formal end came in 1920 when the Communist regime of the Soviet Union ordered the Hibbat Zion societies to disband.

30

Moses Leib Lilienblum

The evolution of the Hibbat Zion was marked by three distinct stages, with each phase dominated by one or more individuals whose thoughts and actions clearly marked the movement's rites of passage from genesis to maturity to dissolution. Thus the period of birth pangs is best-reflected by the lives of the writer and journalist Moses Leib Lilienblum (1843–1910) and the teacher and author Lev Osipovich Levanda (1835–88); the mature period of the movement by the physician Leon Pinsker (1821–91); and that of decline by the critic and philosopher Ahad Ha-Am (1856–1927). All four men were products of the ferment of Russia in transition and of the Jewish intellectual awakening known as the *Haskalah*.

The reforms of the Russian social order introduced in the early years of Czar Alexander II's reign had wide repercussions among the Jews of the empire. The czar, who had emancipated Russia's serfs, also appeared genuinely interested in ameliorating the lives of his Jewish subjects. He repealed the harsh laws of Nicholas I pertaining to military conscription of Jews and opened up his entire realm to "certain classes of Jews." A new era seemed to be dawning and the Jewish enlighteners (*maskilim*) grasped at the opportunity to participate in the life of the empire. Many of the *maskilim* turned their attention away from sentimental and romantic idealization of the Jewish past to concentrate on the problems of the day confronting their people. Illustrative of this development was a group of *maskilim* and Jewish financiers led by Baron Joseph Günzberg (banker, builder of railroads, and developer of the Siberian gold mines). Organized in 1863, this elite band calling themselves "Hevrat Mefitzei Ha-Haskalah" (Society for the Promotion of Enlightenment) set out to educate the Russian Jewish masses and to prepare them for citizenship. The society encouraged and supported programs for the dissemination of the Russian language among Jews, established night schools and libraries, and published educational books and pamphlets. In addition, it sponsored agricultural training courses and classes in a variety of skills and crafts, and provided financial aid for needy students.

During this same era *maskilim* who had been educated in government schools began to hold rabbinic offices. These government-appointed rabbis were intended by the czarist regime to encourage Russification of the Jewish masses. However, for most Orthodox Jews they remained an anathema. These same years also witnessed the beginning of new periodicals and journals aggressively devoted to spreading enlightenment among Russian Jewry. Among the more prominent were the Russian language journal *Razvet* (Dawn), the Hebrew periodical *Ha-Melitz* (The Interpreter), and the Yiddish *Kol Mevasser* (The Proclaiming Voice). Through these publications a large segment of Russian Jewry, especially the youth, were exposed to secular ideas and values. Many other youngsters were influenced by attendance at gymnasia and universities. The spread of enlightenment produced outstanding literary figures. Some of these fell under the influence of the Russian "positivist" school dominated by such essayists as Tschernishevski, Dobrolyubov, and Pisarev. The positivists railed against all forms of romanticism, aestheticism, intellectualism, and fought vigorously for practical reforms for Russian society. Their emulators among the *maskilim* turned a critical eye on Jewish society and became ardent champions of its reformation. They began by attacking early *Haskalah* literature for its detachment from reality. In place of casuistic hair splitting over literary forms and even words, the positivist-imbued *maskilim* stressed literature that introduced its readers to materialistic thought and social utilitarianism. Not content with these initial sallies, these *maskilim* soon turned their criticism on religion. Traditional Orthodox studies in the modern age, they believed, were worthless. A knowledge of science and secular subject matter on the other hand was essential if Russian Jewry was to emerge from its stupor. An early exponent of these views, a man often considered by many scholars to be the last of the great leaders of the Russian *Haskalah,* was Moses Leib Lilienblum.[335]

Lilienblum was born in the small town of Keidany in the Kaunas district of Lithuania. His first teachers were his father, a cooper, and his maternal grandfather, a man steeped in the Talmud. A perspicacious youth and natural leader, Moses, at age thirteen, organized a group of boys to study the work *En Yaakov* ("Fountain of Jacob") a popular compilation of aggadic passages from the Babylonian and Palestinian Talmuds. The following year, in line with the prevalent custom among the Orthodox of the time, he married and moved with his bride to Vilkomir, the residence of his father-in-law. In Vilkomir, Lilienblum continued his religious studies until a drastic change in the fortune of his wife's family forced him to fall back on his own resources. In 1865 the young scholar established a small school for the study of Talmud. During this pedagogical interlude, Lilienblum became interested in the new Hebrew literature being produced by adherents of the *Haskalah* movement. The writings of the *maskilim,* who for the most part, were opposed to the rigors of talmudic legalism and obscurantism, deeply affected Lilienblum, and wrought a great change in his attitude toward reform. Convinced by his readings that ignorance and superstition had debased Judaism, he decided to personally combat these evils within his own community. The Orthodox townspeople of Vilkomir did not take kindly to Lilienblum's proposals for change. His friends began to avoid him, and even his immediate family looked askance at his new status as a reformer. His sole support came from an enlightened young woman with whom he had become romantically involved.

Undaunted by the rejection of his proposals, and certain more than ever before that moderate reforms were essential in order to harmonize Judaism with the spirit of the age, Lilienblum took up his pen to more fully express his views. In an article written in 1868 entitled *Orehot Ha-Talmud* ("Paths of the Talmud"), he stressed the point that traditional

Orthodoxy was stagnating, and hindering the development of the Jewish people. To break out of the medieval mold in which Judaism seemed entrapped, Lilienblum suggested that the religion be viewed as part of an ongoing evolutionary process. Thus, just as the Talmud had once reformed Judaism in accordance with the needs of the day, Judaism must again undergo reforms to enable it to meet the demands of the modern era. The article ended with an appeal to the Orthodox rabbinate to take the lead in introducing moderate religious reforms, and to begin the process by relaxing the more rigid precepts found in the Talmud, as well as abandoning the tome's many anachronisms.

Lilienblum's article created a storm of controversy, and the author was made to feel the full wrath of the Orthodox community of Vilkomir. He was denounced as a freethinker and atheist. Hounded and scorned by the townspeople, continued residence in Vilkomir became impossible. Forced to flee, Lilienblum in 1869 moved to Odessa, the Mecca of the *maskilim.* Here he hoped to acquire a thorough secular education and find a more enlightened Jewish community, one devoted to Hebrew literature and religious reform. Still smarting from his Vilkomir experience, Lilienblum a few months after his arrival in Odessa, wrote a rhymed satire in which he portrayed the dark side of a small Jewish town. The characters—elders, rabbis, writers, and ordinary folk—were depicted as moving about in the shadow and gloom of a nether-world. The author's message was clear: Vilkomir and hundreds of towns just like it were doomed unless they found the strength to break with the past and find a more reasonable relationship between religion and life.

At first Lilienblum basked in the liberal atmosphere of Odessa and the spirit of the *Haskalah* that dominated the Jewish intellectual life of the city. However, with the discovery of the writings of the Russian positivists and socialists, Lilienblum's views underwent a subtle change. The intellectual crosscurrents he had been exposed to were clearly reflected in a series of articles that he wrote while employed as an editor of the journal *Kol Mevasser* (1871–73). He continued to call for a radical transformation of Russian Jewry, but gradually moved away from his former belief in religious evolution. In its place he substituted the need to close the civil, political, and economic gap between the Jewish and non-Jewish population of Russia. As a first step he advocated the need for the czarist government to accept the Jews as the equals of their other subjects. The spread of secular education among the Jews and Gentiles alike, Lilienblum believed, was the best guarantee for bringing about tolerance and mutual understanding to the diverse population of the Russian Empire.

By 1873 Lilienblum had lost much of his ardor for the *maskilim* of Odessa. He was disillusioned by their general indifference to Judaism, and their cynical careerism. The result was a further turning toward positivism. In an article of this period entitled *Olam ha-Tohu* Lilienblum wrote of the importance of reflecting on life as it really is, without resorting to romanticism, superstition, or mysteries. This materialistic outlook on the human condition continued in his writings well into the 1870s. However, the transformation from religious reformation to positivism was not an easy passage and was accompanied by much soul-searching. This inner struggle emerged sharply in Lilienblum's 1876 autobiography, *Hattot Ne'urim* ("The Sins of Youth"). The work was replete with pathos and insights into the emotional and moral conflicts faced by the author in his attempts to cope with Jewish social mores and tradition. Clearly, Lilienblum's autobiography, although a resounding commercial success, represented the shriek of a wasted soul, which having overthrown the old idols, had failed as yet to find a new God.

Not long after the publication of his autobiography, Lilienblum took the final step toward making positivism his creed. Turning away from the concepts of the *Haskalah* and rejecting as virtually useless and wasteful the concerns of the *maskilim* with Hebrew poetry and religious reform, he now hewed closely to the ideas expressed by the Russian positivists. He was particularly impressed with the theories of Tschernishevski, as outlined in the work *Chto Delat* ("What Is To Be Done"). Practical utilitarian education, the keystone of the Russian author's opus was adopted by Lilienblum as a viable approach to resolving the Jewish Problem. The passage from positivism to socialism, the next step in the evolution of Lilienblum's ideology, was but a matter of degrees. By the end of the 1870s he was convinced that class struggle offered the best hope for Russian Jewry and indeed for the future of mankind.

Lilienblum's logic was gradually moving toward a policy of assimilation when it was suddenly derailed by the emergence of a strong anti-Semitic movement in Russia. Led by such prominent intellectuals as Ivan Aksakov and Dostoevski and encouraged by the czarist regime the agitation culminated with the infamous pogroms of 1881. Rioting, pillaging, rape and murder took place in over one hundred sixty cities and villages. Not even the metropolis of Odessa, where Jews and Gentiles had lived for years in an atmosphere of relative enlightenment, was spared. To Lilienblum, who had believed that the roots of anti-Semitism were embedded in religious prejudice and lack of education, the pogroms came as a rude awakening. The progressive and educated inhabitants of Odessa had not behaved very differently from the most backward Russian villagers in the Pale of Settlement. Indeed, Lilienblum himself barely escaped being numbered among the victims of the pogrom by hiding from the rioters in a cellar. In a series of diary entries later incorporated in a work entitled *Derech Teshuvah* ("Way of Return"), Lilienblum vividly described his ordeal and that of his neighbors.

His Jewish consciousness jolted by his traumatic experience, Lilienblum tried to come to grips with the ideas to resolve the Jewish Problem that he had espoused before the pogroms. One by one he discarded them as untenable. Neither education or assimilation were of any value, as the Russians would always consider the Jews as aliens. There now seemed to him to be only one possible solution: the exodus of Russian Jewry, preferably to Palestine. Almost overnight Lilienblum had become an apostle of Jewish nationalism.

In articles written in Hebrew, Yiddish and Russian, Lilienblum devoted his considerable talents as a writer to propagating the idea of a Jewish return to Eretz Israel. He proposed that land be purchased from the Turkish government for the establishment of settlements, and that a Jewish organization be created, as rapidly as possible, in the newly bought lands to oversee the entire colonization process. Lilienblum also felt that it was not enough to merely establish settlements in Palestine. The final solution to the Jewish Problem, he firmly believed, required the elimination of the Diaspora and the creation of an independent state in Eretz Israel.

Lilienblum's focus on Palestine, like that of Smolenskin, was derived from several sources. It had roots in the talmudic studies of his youth, and in the Hebrew renaissance spurred by the *Haskalah* movement. The catalyst for his acceptance of a nationalistic solution, however, was the rise of Russian anti-Semitism and the pogroms of 1881. By 1883 Lilienblum's views were reinforced when he became better-acquainted with the new racial anti-Semitic literature that permeated much of Europe. He now realized that the Jews were facing a modern phenomenon and not a mere repetition of the traditional religious prejudices. He recognized that the emergence of this new type of racial anti-

Semitism was closely linked with the rise of modern European nationalism. Thus, although traditional religiously inspired anti-Jewish feelings had become weakened by the forces of emancipation and secularization, the Jews were now being confronted with anti-Semitic agitation originating in the wave of European national liberation movements.

One of the key objectives of most of these European nationalistic movements was the total assimilation of the Jews or their expulsion from their territories. In line with these developments Lilienblum understood that a revolution might overthrow the repressive Russian regime and yet not bring freedom to the Jews of the sprawling empire. Indeed, they might still be excluded and hated in a new social order just as they had been in the old order. Not even the proletariat could be relied on, for if they came to power, they would regard the Jews as former rivals who deprived them of their livelihood. Other elements among the revolutionists would look on the Jews as capitalists and cast them in the role of scapegoats—an outlet for the fury of the disgruntled within the new society.

Over and over again Lilienblum, in his articles and essays, emphasized that neither enlightenment, revolution, or socio-political-economic progress would eliminate anti-Semitism. Its foundation was based on the widely held belief that the Jews were a nation within a nation. As a result of this judgment, Jewry had been forced by the Gentile world into a cul de sac. In his article *The Future of Our People,* Lilienblum expanded on this thesis. The opponents of nationalism, he wrote, looked on the Jews as zealous nationalists, with a nationalist God and Bible. Nationalists, on the other hand considered the Jews to be avid cosmopolitans, whose homeland is wherever they were well-off. Freethinkers among the Gentiles believed the Jews were too religious, and held sacred all sorts of nonsense, while religious Gentiles claimed the Jews were devoid of any faith. Conservatives considered the Jews to be liberals, while the liberals said they were too conservative. Some writers and governmental officials saw Jews as the purveyors of anarchy, and insurrection. Anarchists and some socialists said the Jews were capitalists, the bearers of a civilization and culture based on parasitism and slavery. Still others accused Jews of crimes against art and music and of circumventing the laws of the land.

According to Lilienblum the future of Jewry, considering all these accusations, was exceedingly problematic. Jews, he insisted, would remain forever aliens and strangers unless they took their destiny into their own hands. Palestine, the seat of the original Hebrew nation, was sparsely inhabited and could absorb Europe's Jews. If Jews were being uprooted from the lands of their birth, Lilienblum mused, why would they choose to flee to America, where they would still be considered aliens rather than emigrate to Palestine, where they could have the opportunity to rebuild their lives and ancient homeland.

Many of Lilienblum's friends among the *maskilim* were not willing to go as far as their former associate or even to relinquish their long-held beliefs. Representative of this latter group was Yehudah Leib Gordon (1830–92), widely regarded as the poet-laureate of the Russian *Haskalah.* Although accepting in a qualified fashion the idea of a Jewish restoration in the Holy Land, Gordon held fast to the original objectives of the *Haskalah* of the modernization of Judaism and the Jewish way of life. Such reforms, he felt, were essential and the best way to respond to the pogroms. Gordon incorporated these themes in an article entitled *Our Redemption and the Saving of Our Life.* Lilienblum promptly rejected Gordon's thesis as being irrelevant to the main concerns of Russian Jewry. In an essay called *Let Us Not Confuse the Issues* (1882), he emphasized that the primary issue confronting Jewry was not religious reform or modernization, but rather survival as a people.

Against those individuals who desired to create or uphold one normative structure of Judaism, Lilienblum argued that historical Judaism was never uniform or unitary and had always been pluralistic. The criterion for future Jewish existence, therefore, did not hinge on the theoretical question of whether Jews would follow the Orthodox or Reform liturgy or whether they would be religiously or secularly oriented. History has revealed that the Jewish people had always been deeply divided along doctrinal lines, but had always shared the same fate regardless of their differences and squabbles. This pluralism within a common identity, Lilienblum insisted, must be maintained when the Jews return to Eretz Israel. Particular care had to be taken in the restoration not to create a uniformity that would exclude any group of Jews, for where the nation was concerned there are no sects or denominations. Lilienblum called on the factions in the Jewish community to overcome their differences and join in a public action to confront the dangers faced by the community as a whole. This could best be achieved by shunting aside religious questions and not dividing into Mitnagdim, Hassidim, or Maskilim. The single most important aim was Jewish survival, and this could be achieved by concentrating on gathering the dispersed Jews of Eastern Europe and bringing them to Eretz Israel.

How could this exodus from Europe be facilitated? Lilienblum suggested the following scenario. The wealthy individuals among the Jews, although not likely to emigrate, should invest part of their fortune to acquire land in Palestine. On these lands Jews willing to emigrate and cultivate the soil would settle, on terms agreeable to the investors. Those Jews with less capital, but still able to purchase land for themselves or others should immediately do so. Once these people became established, artisans and craftsmen would follow. In time, when conditions had somewhat improved, the masses who have nothing would join their brethren in Eretz Israel.

Lilienblum's call for a return to Zion was by and large well-received. His analysis of the Jewish condition seemed flawless, and his plan to relieve the suffering of the Jewish masses eminently practical. For those individuals who still had reservations, Lilienblum suggested there were only three courses of action open to them. They could remain in their present state, oppressed forever and subject to persecution, pogroms, and even possible extinction as a people (a major Holocaust). Secondly they could assimilate, forsaking Judaism for Christianity. In all probability such individuals would be despised by the Gentiles for many years. This state of affairs would persist until some far off date in the future when their descendants no longer retained any trace of their Jewish origins. The last and most palatable choice was to initiate efforts for the rebirth of Israel in their ancient homeland, Palestine. Only this option offered Jews the opportunity to attain a normal life.

Many young Jews agreed wholeheartedly with Lilienblum's analysis that only Zionism could resolve the Jewish Problem. Thus the former talmudist and *maskil* played an important role in inspiring the first group of pioneers, who left Russia in 1882 to settle in Palestine. Almost overnight, Lilienblum had become the most prominent ideologist of the Jewish national movement in Russia. Not content with his role as a propagandist for Zion, he joined the newly created Hibbat Zion, and moved rapidly into its leadership ranks. Together with Leon Pinsker, the author of *Auto-Emancipation*, Lilienblum helped found the Zerubabel Society of Odessa (1883), one of the key associations of the Lovers of Zion in Russia. He also participated in the Kattowitz Conference of 1884, which strove to unify and give direction to the Hibbat Zion movement. At the conference, Lilienblum was elected secretary of the newly formed central committee, which was to be based in

Odessa. Presided over by Pinsker, the central committee would evolve into the chief organ of the Lovers of Zion for furthering Jewish colonization in Palestine.

As the moving spirit of what came to be known as "Practical Zionism," Lilienblum constantly found himself at odds with other Hibbat Zion leaders (and later with the father of Political Zionism, Theodor Herzl, as well). From 1889 onward he carried on a running debate, in the journals of *Ha-Melitz* and *Ha-Shahar,* with the eminent Jewish historian Simon Dubnow and the essayist–philosopher Ahad Ha-Am, as to the course the Hibbat Zion should chart for itself. In an article entitled *Love of Zion, Zionism and their Enemies* (Odessa, 1899), Lilienblum severely criticized Dubnow's theory of Diaspora nationalism. In particular, Lilienblum rejected the concept that Jews must fight for their national and cultural rights in the countries where they live, rather than strive for political independence in Palestine. With a touch of sarcasm, Lilienblum noted that:

> Dubnow is even a greater dreamer . . . than the founder of modern Zionism [i.e., Theodor Herzl]. If the idea of establishing an independent state in the near future be fantastic, it is nowhere near as ridiculous as the hopes that the Jews dispersed in many countries will finally be given the right to a free inner development in the sense of national freedom as demanded by the Czechs, the Irish, and others.[336]

Lilienblum feared anti-Semitism and felt it posed a dire threat to the Jewish people and might lead to the total destruction of European Jewry. Lilienblum felt Dubnow's national autonomist approach to resolving the Jewish Problem was artificial and unreal and increased the threat of a complete annihilation of Europe's Jewish communities. Similarly, Lilienblum regarded with trepidation the theories of Ahad Ha-Am, the champion of Spiritual Zionism (i.e., the creation of a morally based national spiritual center in Palestine that would foster a colonization inspired by the will for redemption). Such an approach, he believed, would make the existence of the Jewish people completely dependent on metaphysical speculations rather than reality. In refuting Ahad Ha-Am, the former disciple of positivism argued that the Jewish people wanted to live for the sake of living and not for any purpose beyond life.

Lilienblum's censure of Dubnow's and Ahad Ha-Am's ideas clearly reflected the pragmatic attitude that was the hallmark of his Zionism. He considered any deviation from rational logic as a dangerous digression from reality. His realism enabled him to set forth operative ideas that would later for a time guide Zionist activity. Illustrative of this development was Lilienblum's suggestion for funding the purchase of land in Palestine by means of a popular subscription — an idea that became a reality in 1901 with the creation of the *Keren Kayemet le-Yisrael* (Jewish National Fund) by the Fifth Zionist Congress. As originally conceived by Lilienblum, there would be no lack of funds for the acquisition of land in Eretz Israel. He suggested ways in which the required funds could be raised, including a novel scheme whereby all individuals who wished to support the national idea would contribute a kopeck ("Russian penny") a week to be saved for a given period in boxes placed in every Jewish home. In addition a percentage of sums donated to synagogues at weddings, at funerals, and other occasions could be set aside for the national cause. Contributions from the rich and the powerful, as well as a Jewish lottery might also provide the huge sums necessary for the purchase of land in Palestine from the Turkish government. The funds spent on the purchase of large land holdings would be recovered from the rent paid by the colonists, and the money paid by individuals purchasing lots. This in turn would allow for the purchase of additional land, and for the development of the country's infrastructure, as well as provide for such vital needs as afforestation and irrigation systems.

Although Lilienblum called upon Jewish financial magnates to support the Hibbat Zion movement by buying land in Palestine, he was aware that this group favored assimilation in the lands of their residence and had no desire to emigrate to a desolate and backwater region of southwest Asia. Like Moses Hess before him, and Leon Pinsker, his fellow Lover of Zion, Lilienblum placed his faith in the Jewish masses of Eastern Europe as the key to the establishment of a viable Jewish entity in Eretz Israel. Accordingly, in an article entitled *The Future of Our People,* he cautioned his readers not to look to the Jewish plutocrats for leadership, but rather to those who espoused a return and restoration of the Jewish people in Palestine.

Completely dedicated to the nationalistic cause, Lilienblum would remain secretary of the Odessa Central Committee until his death in 1910. In the latter half of his life, when Theodor Herzl burst upon the Jewish scene, Lilienblum, like many of the Lovers of Zion, embraced the charismatic new leader and supported his World Zionist Organization. However, as the paramount theorist of the older Zionist movement, he frequently found himself at odds with Herzl's predilection for political and diplomatic activity. Always a pragmatist, Lilienblum favored a gradual approach to obtaining national objectives. Thus, he placed emphasis on such practical steps as establishing institutions to fund the purchase of land in Palestine, creating new settlements, and propagandizing the Jewish masses in the Diaspora.

During his tenure as a leader of the Hibbat Zion Moses Leib Lilienblum set his stamp of personality on the movement, giving it a rationality and practical outlook that it had previously lacked. Many of his suggestions were adopted by the Zionists. Although like Moses of the Bible, Lilienblum did not live to witness the end results of his life-long struggle, his memory has been perpetuated by a grateful people. In the State of Israel today almost every major community contains a street named in honor of the former *maskil,* who in mid-life became an eloquent spokesman for a return to Zion.

31

The Russophile

The left wing of the Russian *Haskalah*, during the latter half of the nineteenth century, included many prominent intellectuals. Curiously, whereas most of the outstanding writers in Hebrew among these "enlighteners" were products of Lithuania, where Jewish nationalism was particularly strong, those who wrote in Russian were, with one major exception, natives of South Russia. In the latter region two extreme movements, Hassidism and the adherents of Russification, fought for the heart and soul of the Jewish masses.

The lone advocate of Russification who did not stem from the south was Lev Osipovich Levanda (1835–88).[337] Born into a poverty stricken family in Minsk (White Russia), Levanda nevertheless received a traditional religious education (*heder*), which was later supplemented by attendance at a government-sponsored school for Jewish children and by study at a rabbinical college in Vilna. Following graduation from college in 1854 he accepted a position as an instructor in the Jewish crown school of his native town. Some years later his scholastic talents were recognized by the Russian government, and he was appointed Uchony Yevrey (learned Jew, i.e., an expert on Jewish affairs) and assigned to the chancery of the governor-general of Vilna. The young scholar was thus thrust into the very heart of Russian officialdom advocating Russification of the Jews, a circumstance that would leave a lasting imprint on his ideology and life's work.

Although Levanda would spend thirty-two years of his life in Vilna, he never got over the feeling that he had abandoned the aspirations of his youth for a government sinecure. As a boy he had dreamed of attending the University of St. Petersburg, and devoting his life to academic and literary activities. In spite of these misgivings, Levanda did eventually become a leading figure among Russia's Jewish intelligentsia.

During his lifetime Levanda made several trips abroad, and was well-acquainted with European literature. He also was familiar with Jewish life in the West. A sensitive and perspicacious individual, Levanda took a lively interest in everything that affected his fellow Jews. In his capacity as a government official he often came to the aid of his coreligionists. Most noteworthy in this respect was his involvement in defusing an incipient blood libel case brought against several Jews of the Kovno district of Lithuania (1863). However, Levanda's role as a shield for his people was destined to be of short duration. His emotional nature, internal doubts, and passionate idealism would eventually take their toll. Afflicted with a nervous condition that left him an invalid the last two years of his life, he would die a tragic death in a mental sanatorium in St. Petersburg.

Levanda's life spanned three distinct periods of Russian Jewish history. He grew up during the autocratic reign of Czar Nicholas I (1825-55), an era in which the Russian government attempted to assimilate the Jews by the use of draconian measures. In 1827, for example, the czar introduced the barbaric cantonist system, which destroyed the unity of many Jewish families. Later in 1844, the czarist regime abolished the community organizations of the Jews and established secular government schools to hasten the process of Russification. In 1850 the Russian government outlawed the distinctive Jewish garb and dramatically increased the supervision of Jewish intellectual activities. During these years of unrelenting oppression, Levanda, a product of the government school system and a radical *maskil,* strongly supported programs that would help enlighten the Jewish masses.

Under Nicholas I's successor, Alexander II, a period of liberalization was begun, and important reforms were introduced that affected the entire Russian empire. Feelings of great expectation, in particular of genuine improvement in the quality of life, ran high among many of the Jewish enlighteners, who believed that the ultimate integration of the Jews into Russian society was not too far off. During this period Levanda was caught up in this general euphoria, and became a government official. It also marked the beginnings of his literary activity. He became a part time editor of the journal *Vilensky Vestnik* and made regular contributions to many other publications, including *Razvet,* the first Russian-Jewish periodical. Although a creative and witty writer, Levanda lacked the mastery of characterization so essential to a great artist. In a series of articles, belletristic sketches, feuilletons, and novels, Levanda presented a *maskil's* critique of Jewish life in Russia. His pen ranged over such subject matter as poverty, parasitism, the role of women, excessive pursuit of talmudic studies, the negative role of rich and retrograde communal leaders, arranged marriages, as well as the entire gamut of problems—economic, political, and social—confronting Russian Jewry.

Representative of this literary output was his first novel, *The Grocery Store* (1860), which clearly reflected the views of the Jewish *maskilim* of the day. The hero of this tale, a believer in the *Haskalah* is pictured as wearing European clothes rather than traditional Jewish garb and calling himself by a well-sounding German or Russian name. In addition, he cultivates relationships with noble-minded Christians and dares to make a love match unassisted by a marriage broker.

It was during this stage of his development that Levanda became convinced that no educated Jew could escape being a cosmopolitan. In time this belief in the virtues of cosmopolitanism gradually changed into a distinct trend toward Russification and assimilation. He called on Russian Jewry to awake under the scepter of Alexander II and urged the Jews of Lithuania and Belorussia to act as prospective carriers of Russian culture to offset Polish aspirations in their provinces. Jews, Levanda stressed, should become Russians in all respects except religion.

Levanda expanded on his theme of Jews as carriers of Russian culture in a novel entitled *Goryachev Vremya* ("A Hot Time"). Written in 1873, a decade after the czarist regime's brutal suppression of the Polish Insurrection, the book was a clarion call for Russification. The hero of the novel, Sarin, pleads with his fellow Jews to abandon their Polish orientation and become Russians. He stresses that a fusion between Jews and Russians will usher in a new epoch in the history of both people.

In his frantic pursuit of Russification, Levanda continued to ridicule traditional Jewish life. This criticism was particularly pronounced in his work, *Sketches of the Past*, which contained such satiric stories as *The Earlocks of the Melammed,* and *Schoolophobia* (reminiscences of the bitter campaign waged by traditional Jews against the introduction of government schools). Throughout his writings of this period, Levanda upbraided his coreligionists for their apathy and backwardness. He worried over the harmful effects of Jewish concentration in middleman occupations, and urged the need for greater economic diversification and productivity. Levanda was especially incensed by the economic activities of the small group of wealthy individuals of Russian Jewry. He felt that these nouveau riche Jews — bankers, industrialists, speculators — were only noteworthy for their ostentation and greed, and did little or nothing to promote Jewish interests.

The final stage in the evolution of Levanda's ideology coincided with the reign of Alexander III (1881–94), an era of Russian history marked by repression and persecution of the Jews. As in the case of Smolenskin and Lilienblum, the wave of pogroms of the 1880s dealt a staggering blow to Levanda's Russification hopes, and shattered forever his illusions of Jews achieving equality under czarist rule. Expressing his disillusionment in the pages of the journal *Razvet,* he openly admitted his error of judgment in having fought so long and hard for Russification.

Seeking an alternative to his discarded ideology, Levanda now favored emigration as the best response to the abnormal conditions confronting the Jews of Russia, and thought that serious consideration should be given to a return to Zion. In the interim, before immigration could be organized, he proposed that the Jews undertake self-defense measures as neither the Russian government nor their minions could be trusted to provide protection. The amazing transition from a radical *maskil* and believer in Russification to a Jewish nationalist, although precipitous, was an honest conversion, and Levanda threw himself wholeheartedly into his new role. He joined the Love of Zion movement and within a relatively short span of time became one of its leading spokesmen.

Reflecting on his metamorphosis in his private correspondence, Levanda asserted that even in his days as a radical *maskil* he had never considered the dissolution of Jewish group existence or its cultural extinction. His advocacy of Russification, he emphasized, had been a call for a cultural partnership and definitely not an appeal for assimilation.

An early indication that Levanda was willing to consider other solutions to the Jewish Problem if Russification failed was already evident in his novel *A Hot Time.* When the hero of the tale, the advocate of Russification of the Jews is asked, ". . . what if the Russians do not respond to your aspirations," he answers "then we will have to reconsider . . ." the entire matter. Levanda would later recall that while writing this line in his novel he first gave thought to modern Jewish nationalism.[338]

Levanda's career as an ardent Jewish nationalist began in earnest in 1882 with his participation in the founding, in Vilna, of the Love of Zion association *Ohab Zion.* This group originated in the home of Elijah Eliezer Friedman, the editor of the Hebrew journal *Ha-Zofeh.* For security reasons the initial meeting, a secret gathering of a handful of close friends, had carefully chosen the editor's home for their conclave. Friedman, it seems had written an elegy on the death of Empress Marie, the wife of Alexander II, and had received two letters of appreciation from the government. The editor had framed the letters and hung them up in a conspicuous place, so that if the police made a sudden entry they would immediately see convincing evidence of officially acknowledged loyalty to the czarist regime. To further avoid any possibility of arousing the suspicions of the czar's secret police, the assembled group sat around a table on which glasses of tea, a chess board, and several packs of playing cards had been placed. The moving spirits behind this initial meeting were Levanda, who spoke for the secularly and politically minded within the Hibbat Zion movement, and Samuel Joseph Finn, a communal leader and author, who represented the religious elements. Since both leaders held government posts (Finn was head of the charity organization of the Vilna Jewish community, and Levanda was employed in the chancery of the governor-general of Vilna) there was a considerable element of danger in their participation in an obvious illegal gathering.

Under the guidance of Levanda and Finn the society rapidly grew in membership and importance. In order to further protect the group from government harassment and persecution the name of the association was changed to Tikvat Aniyim (Hope of the Poor) so as to make it appear a purely philanthropic body, rather than an entity with a nationalistic program.

Gradually, the Tikvat Aniyim society moved to the forefront of the Hibbat Zion movement in Lithuania. It was largely due to the pressure exerted by the Vilna association that the Kattowitz Conference was convened in 1884. Curiously, circumstances made it impossible for the leaders of the Tikvat Aniyim to be represented at this milestone conference. Since neither Levanda or Finn could attend the meeting because of their government posts, the Hibbat Zion chose an Orthodox rabbi, Yankele Harif, to be their delegate. The latter set out for Kattowitz, but was forced to turn back at the frontier. He was supposed to pose as a commercial traveler, but unwilling to discard his traditional Orthodox costume he could not get past the border officials.

In his role as a spokesman for the Hibbat Zion movement, Levanda concentrated his efforts on awakening the Jewish masses of Russia to the need for immediate emigration, the acquisition of land in Palestine, and the rapid settlement of Jews on the soil of the Holy Land. He cautioned, however, against unplanned and hasty colonization efforts such as those attempted by the youthful members of the Bilu. He also vehemently opposed the philanthropic trend exhibited by some of the Hibbat Zion societies. Unlike most of the Love of Zion luminaries, Levanda had little faith in Western Jewry, and did not hold out much hope that they would play a role in the Hibbat Zion movement.

Although Levanda had never visited Palestine he, like Lilienblum, was keenly aware that the intended Jewish homeland was not unoccupied. Lilienblum had not only noted the existence in the Holy Land of an Arab population, but had emphasized that it was small and backward. Lilienblum also believed that if 100,000 Jewish families were to settle in Palestine over a period of twenty years, they would no longer appear as strangers to the Arabs. Levanda, on the other hand, felt strongly that the Arabs would benefit greatly from the Jewish colonization of Palestine.

Lev Osipovitch Levanda's life in many ways paralleled the various stages in the sociopolitical evolution of a segment of the Russian-Jewish intelligentsia. Originally followers of the *Haskalah,* many of these enlighteners abandoned long-held and cherished ideas and in their quest for a solution to the Jewish Problem discovered Zion. As in the case of Levanda, the transition of these *maskilim* to Jewish nationalism had been a tortuous process. The rise of anti-Semitism in the West and the Russian pogroms had finally convinced the most die-hard Russophiles that the very physical existence of the Jewish people was at stake. Levanda, for example, was quick to point out that in the past the Jews had been frequently subjected to restrictive laws and persecutions, but that now the threat to their lives was far greater. The hope that these threatening forces could be tamed and reeducated had proved to be illusory; it was therefore a much wiser course of action for the Jews to avoid the expected onslaught. Such being the case, it was imperative that Jews reclaim their ancient homeland. This message, as proclaimed by Levanda, found a sympathetic audience among many of the disillusioned *maskilim,* who had traveled a similar road in their search to bring the Jewish masses into the modern world. Prominent among the latter group was a physician of Odessa named Leon Pinsker.

32

Leon Pinsker

Leon Pinsker[339] was born in 1821 in Tomaszow, Russo-Poland, and grew up in Odessa. His father was a distinguished scholar, an authority on the Karaites, and a teacher at the Hebrew school of Odessa, the first such academy permitted by the Russian government. Leon received his early education at his father's school, an institution whose curriculum included secular subjects alongside traditional Jewish studies. On graduation from the Hebrew school, young Pinsker enrolled in a Russian high school (gymnasium), and later attended the Richelieu Academy. For a time he entertained the idea of becoming an educator (he had accepted a post as an instructor of Russian at the Jewish school in Kishinev). Shortly after his initial experience as a teacher Pinsker was attracted to the legal profession. He succeeded in enrolling in Odessa University, (one of the first Jews to gain entrance) but on discovering that his religion would bar any chance of his becoming a lawyer, he decided on a career in medicine. Accordingly, he transferred to the University of Moscow. While still a medical student, Pinsker displayed great personal courage during a cholera epidemic that struck Moscow in 1848. Without thought for his own safety he volunteered to care for hospital patients suffering from the dreadful and usually fatal disease. On completion of his medical studies the young physician returned to Odessa. Highly recommended by government officials, Pinsker was appointed to the staff of the city's hospital. His dedication, skill, and personality soon won the recognition of his colleagues and the admiration of the general public. Within a decade after embarking on his medical career, Pinsker was recognized as one of the foremost physicians in Odessa. During the Crimean War he volunteered to serve as a field doctor with the Russian Army. Following the conclusion of the conflict he was decorated for his service by the czar—an extraordinary honor for a Jewish person to receive in the highly charged anti-Semitic atmosphere of Nicholas I's Russia.

Parallel with his medical career, Leon Pinsker, from 1860 onward, took a lively interest in Jewish communal affairs. An ardent proponent of enlightenment and Russification, he helped found and was a regular contributor to the first Russian-Jewish weekly, *Razvet* (Dawn). This journal dedicated its pages to acquainting Jews with the Russian language and culture. These aims were also those of the publication *Sion*, which eventually replaced *Razvet*, and on whose staff Pinsker served as an editor for some months. In addition, Pinsker was one of the leaders of the Odessa branch of an organization known as the Hervai Marbei Ha-Haskalah be Erez Russia (Society for the Dissemination of Enlightenment Among the Jews of Russia). Founded in 1863, this society was in the forefront of the struggle for Russification of the Jews. A frequent contributor to the society's Russian language weekly, *The Day,* Pinsker displayed considerable originality and talent as a writer and propagandist. His vision of the future of Russian Jewry, at this point in his life, was a rosy one in which he believed that it was possible for his coreligionists to obtain cultural self-expression within the Russian empire.

The violent pogrom that erupted in Odessa in 1881 during Easter week and the subsequent changes in the attitude and policies of the Russian government toward Jewish subjects severely shocked the *maskilim* and the advocates of Russification. The Odessa branch of the Society for the Dissemination of Enlightenment Among the Jews of Russia decided to close down, and the organization's weekly journal ceased publication. Deeply disturbed by the turn of events, Pinsker withdrew from communal affairs and concentrated on his medical practice.

The Russian pogroms of 1881, however, had jolted Pinsker out of his complacency. He was appalled by the fact that it was not only the ignorant rabble that had attacked the Jews. Academicians, journalists, and government officials had sanctioned the bloodbath by whipping the mobs into a frenzy and in many instances by actually participating in the rioting. He now realized that the hopes of the Jews for emancipation through enlightenment and Russification were illusory. Nothing, Pinsker was now convinced, could be expected from an autocratic Russian regime. In addition, it was sheer fantasy to believe that the deep-seated hatred of the Jews by the general populace of Russia could be overcome by education.

Accordingly, Pinsker abandoned his former views. Jews, he declared, required new alternatives if they were to survive. They could no longer afford to wait for a messianic or utopian solution (i.e., the traditional belief in the coming of the Messiah, or the secularized version of a liberal brotherhood of all men). What was needed was a realistic and pragmatic solution—one that started with the premise that the Jews were a nation, one people, and not merely a religious community. Having arrived at the latter conclusion, Pinsker followed closely the debates over what to do that were raging in Russian-Jewish circles. Many leaders, concerned with the immediate problem of survival, urged the creation of self-defense units; many favored emigration, while others spoke of emigration to a country in which a Jewish national center could be created. The recently formed Hibbat Zion societies insisted that all emigration be directed to Eretz Israel. Pinsker agreed with this view.

At age sixty, Leon Pinsker suddenly left Russia ostensibly to seek a cure in Italy for a chronic heart condition. His itinerary, however, included stop-overs in Vienna, Berlin, Paris, and London. In each of these capitals he hoped to meet with leading Jews and to convince them of the need for the Jewish people to create a national home of their own. To his consternation he found few individuals who shared his views. Typical was the reaction of Adolph Jellinek (1821–93), the chief rabbi of Vienna and a close friend of Pinsker's father. After listening to Leon Pinsker's thoughts on Jewish nationalism and the need for a mass Jewish exodus from Europe, Jellinek intimated that the prominent physician was emotionally disturbed and should seek immediate medical attention for his mental malady. Similarly, in Paris the leaders of the Alliance Israélite Universelle spurned Pinsker's ideas. The Alliance favored the emigration of Russian Jews to the United States, and looked askance at any suggestion aiming at the concentration of the bulk of Jewry into a national state of their own.

Auto-Emancipation

One of the few individuals responding favorably to Pinsker's ideas was Arthur Cohen (1830–1914), a member of the British parliament, and the chairman of the Board of Deputies of British Jewry. Cohen, a nephew of Sir Moses Montefiore, like Pinsker, regarded the Jewish Problem as an international issue that could only be resolved with the help of the major powers. He suggested to Pinsker that the latter put his ideas down on paper so that his thoughts could reach a wider audience.

In September of 1882 Pinsker published in Berlin, anonymously, a pamphlet written in German entitled *Autoemanzipation: Mahnruf an seine Stammesgenossen von einem russischen Juden* ("Auto-Emancipation: An Admonition to His Brethren by a Russian Jew").[340] Written in a passionate style, and in many ways reminiscent of a manifesto, the pamphlet forcefully reflected the author's deep anxiety for the fate of his people. Pinsker began his essay with a clear and succinct statement outlining his concerns and his approach to resolving what he considered to be a very ancient problem. The core of the Jewish Question, he stressed, was the fact that the Jews comprised a distinctive element among the nations in which they lived, and as such could neither assimilate nor be readily digested by any nation. Hence the solution lay in finding a means of so readjusting this exclusive element to the family of nations that the basis of the problem would be permanently removed.

Normal relations between people, Pinsker emphasized, was founded on mutual respect. However, it was unlikely that the Jews would ever be accorded such respect, for they lacked the important prerequisite of national equality. Furthermore, the Jews were missing most of the attributes by which a nation is recognized—a common language, common customs, and a common land.

> The Jewish people has no fatherland of its own, though it has many motherlands; no center of focus or gravity, no government of its own, no official representation. It is everywhere a guest, and nowhere at home.[341]

The nations therefore never have to deal with a Jewish nation, but always with mere individual Jews. On the other hand, in seeking to fuse with other peoples, the Jews deliberately renounced to some extent their own nationality, but nowhere did they succeed in obtaining from their fellow citizens recognition as a nation of equal status. The very fact that Jews were not regarded as an independent nation rested in part on their abnormal position among the nations. Merely to belong to the Jewish people was to be indelibly stigmatized—a mark repellent to non-Jews and painful to the Jews themselves.

This state of affairs, Pinsker believed, was the result of a bizarre historical and psychological phenomenon. Like a good clinician, he pointed out that among the living nations of the world the Jews were looked upon as a nation long dead. With their loss of independence following the Roman conquest of Judea a state of decay had set in which was incompatible with the existence of a whole and vital organism. But, Pinsker noted, even after the Jewish people had yielded up their existence as an actual state, they refused to submit to total destruction and lived on spiritually as a nation. Thus, the world saw in this people the frightening form of one of the dead walking among the living. This ghost-like apparition of a living corpse, of a people without unity or organization, without land or other bonds of union, no longer alive and yet moving about was unparalleled in history. It could not fail to make a strange and peculiar impression on the imagination of the nations.

Elaborating on this theme, Pinsker asserted that having become a phantom-like people, the Jews inspired the same dread that ghosts normally evoke, ". . . for there is something unnatural about a people without a territory, just as there is about a man without a shadow."[342] Worse yet, the fear of the Jewish ghost had been handed down through the centuries. It had led to prejudice, which in turn, in conjunction with other forces, paved the way for Judeophobia (anti-Semitism).

Prior to Leon Pinsker, Jews of Western and Eastern Europe were wont to explain anti-Semitism on religious grounds, or on the backwardness of a country and the evil character of its inhabitants. A dispassionate analysis that took into account the anomaly of Jewish existence, with the sole exception of Moses Hess's forgotten book *Rome and Jerusalem,* had never been attempted before. Pinsker's training as a physician made it easier for him than for many of his contemporaries to face unpleasant truths. He was not content to accept the interpretations of anti-Semitism current in his day, and considered Judeophobia to be an illness. Pinsker was convinced that, along with a number of subconscious and superstitious ideas, instincts, and idiosyncrasies, Judeophobia had become deeply rooted and had acquired legitimacy among all the people of the earth with whom the Jews had come in contact. Using clinical terminology to describe the phenomenon, Pinsker called Judeophobia a form of demonpathy. The Jewish ghost, which was not disembodied like other ghosts but was flesh and blood, suffered the most excruciating pain from the wounds inflicted on it by the fearful mob who imagined it threatened them.

"Judeophobia," Pinsker asserted, "is a psychic aberration. As a psychic aberration it is hereditary, as a disease transmitted for two thousand years, it is incurable."[343] The Jewish nation is held responsible for real or supposed misdeeds of its individual members and is libeled and buffeted about shamefully.

Furthermore, Pinsker declared, the charges frequently hurled against the Jews of ritual murder, desecration of the host, poisoning of wells, exploiting the peasantry, conspiring to rule the world, etc., not only made no sense, but clearly reflected the demonological aspect of Judeophobia. These and a thousand other accusations against an entire people had time and again been proved groundless. The accusations had to be trumped-up wholesale in order to quiet the evil consciences of the Jew baiters—to justify the condemnation of an entire nation and to demonstrate the burning of the Jews, or rather the Jewish ghost, at the stake.

Pinsker's dissection of the Jewish Problem was revolutionary. For generations many Jewish reformers and intellectuals had maintained that anti-Semitism could be reduced or even completely eradicated by patient reasoning and education. It had to be shown, they argued, that Jews were willing to accept civic responsibilities, and that they were capable of making positive contributions to the political, economic, social, and cultural life of their countries. This theme had been the basis for the founding of associations for combating anti-Semitism that had come into existence during the waning decades of the nineteenth century. It was also the view, with some modifications, shared by most Jewish socialists. *Auto-Emancipation* cast doubt on these approaches to resolving the Jewish Problem, and led many a Jewish activist to rethink his positions.

In his pamphlet Pinsker was particularly harsh on those who still believed emancipation was the key to resolving the Jewish Problem. He emphasized that it did not matter if Jews lived in a certain country for generations, they would still be regarded by the native population as aliens. Although it was true that Jews were, or would be, in some liberal countries legally emancipated and accorded civil rights, in reality they would never be socially emancipated and accepted as equals. Emancipation, Pinsker insisted, was always the fruit of a rationalist mind and enlightened self-interest and was never the spontaneous expression of the feelings of the majority of the populace. Hence the stigma attached to the Jews could not be removed by legislation imposed from above. The anti-Semites, by their ill will, had proved the case that the Jews were irretrievably and forever aliens, and that assimilation could never be realized because the majority would not let them.

Emigration to other countries was not a viable solution to the Jewish Problem. Pinsker ridiculed the doctrine of the German-Jewish Reform movement, which regarded the dispersion of the Jews throughout the world as essential for the fulfillment of their religious mission to act as an ethical and moral light to all of mankind. Such a scattering of the Jewish people, Pinsker believed, would merely lead to the creation of a new Diaspora. Such a development might suit individual Jews, but would never resolve the plight of the masses, which could only be relieved by a national solution.

Pinsker also reproached the Orthodox Jews who counseled passive acceptance of the status quo until the arrival of the Messiah, whom they believed God would send in time to relieve their suffering and usher in a golden age.

Having diagnosed Judeophobia as a disease, Pinsker in the second half of his book *Auto-Emancipation* considered treatments and a possible cure. The Jews, he insisted, must cure themselves and determine their own future. It was foolish to appeal for justice or to expect of human nature something that had always been of short supply—humanity. What the Jews needed most was self respect. They had waged a long and often heroic battle for survival, but as individuals, not as a nation with a fatherland. In this protracted struggle they had been forced to fall back on dubious tactics, many of which were detrimental to their moral dignity and self respect. As a result the Jewish people had cut a pitiful figure among the nations. They had not counted nor had a voice in the nations' councils, even when the affairs being dealt with concerned the Jews. In place of a fatherland and unity the Jews, in order to survive, had come to depend on flight, humility, and adaptability. What a miserable role for the descendants of the Maccabees!

The only meaningful solution to the Jewish Problem, Pinsker stressed, was to transform the Jewish people into an independent nation living a normal life on its own soil. He was fully aware of the enormous internal and external difficulties involved in attaining such an objective. Drawing on biblical parallels, Pinsker compared the modern plight of the Jews to the traumatic days preceding the Exodus from Egypt. He noted that the Exodus itself was not a mere running away of slaves, but rather a collective enterprise. Acknowledging that modern Jewry did not possess a leader of the caliber of Moses, Pinsker nevertheless felt that the consciousness of the Jewish people had already been raised to a level where decisive action was inevitable. Warning the Jewish people against letting the moment pass by, he urged them once again to take fate in their own hands and adopt the watchword "Help yourselves, and God will help you." Pinsker then turned to the problem of where to begin the drive toward a nationalist solution.

He observed that an infrastructure of sorts already existed in the Jewish societies, clubs, and voluntary associations. These organizations would be called upon to lay the foundations of the future entity. However, in order to carry out this responsibility they had to be completely transformed. Their function would be to convene a national congress of which they would form the center. If they refused to go beyond the limits of their current activities, they must at the very least delegate some of their members to a national board, a directorate that would help develop the unity of the Jewish people, without which the entire national endeavor would be unthinkable. To truly represent national interests, the board must comprise recognized leaders and must energetically take in hand the direction of the national movement. In addition, the ablest individuals in the Jewish communities—men of finance, statesmen, publicists, scientists etc., must join in the effort to attain the common goal. In all planning thought was to be given to creating a secure and inviolable home for the surplus of those Jews who lived as proletarians in the different countries and who were considered by the native population to be a burden on their resources.

In *Auto-Emancipation* Pinsker visualized that immigration to a national territory would not necessarily involve all the Jewish communities of the world. The Jews of Western Europe, living in relative security and liberty, he believed, would probably choose to remain where they lived. Similarly, wealthy individuals, even in countries where they were not tolerated, would be reluctant to leave. Pinsker was convinced that the main stream of immigrants would come from regions of dense population such as Eastern Europe. A certain point of saturation existed in those areas beyond which their numbers could not increase without exposing Jews to the dangers of persecution.

The territory required for a national home, Pinsker maintained, had to be fertile, well-situated, contiguous, and sufficiently large to accommodate the settlement of several million Jews. Selection of this permanent national territory was to be the responsibility of a single body, preferably a committee of experts appointed by the directorate. Only such a committee of experts, after a comprehensive investigation, would be able to render an intelligent opinion on where the national entity should be established. Pinsker left the question open, but had in mind either North America or Asiatic Turkey, notably Palestine.

After a territory had been decided on, the directorate would negotiate with and secure the assent of the European Powers. If Palestine was chosen to be the national home, the approval of the Ottoman government would also be required. Following these diplomatic steps the directorate, working closely with wealthy and influential Jews, would seek to mobilize capital for the creation of a stock company. This institution would buy the land that would form the national territory. The actual settlement of the land would be carried out in gradual stages and in a fixed order.

Under the supervision of the directorate, the land purchased by the stock company would be divided into plots and assigned according to the local conditions for agricultural or industrial purposes. The tracts of land would be leased, but not be sold to individual settlers. The income derived from the leases would, after defraying initial capital expenses, accrue to a national fund. To facilitate the establishment of the fund, the directorate could opt for a national subscription. Ownership of the land, however, would remain in perpetuity in the hands of the national fund. The fund would in turn actively finance the immigration and settlement of those Jews who did not have the means to assume the costs of emigration on their own.

It was typical of Pinsker's intellectual objectivity that in *Auto-Emancipation* the historical bond to Palestine was secondary to his approach to resolving the Jewish Problem. What chiefly motivated his writing the pamphlet was the plight of the Jews in Eastern Europe and elsewhere. He considered the choice of a territorial refuge as requiring a pragmatic solution, rather than one based solely on traditional yearnings. Nevertheless, he viewed the beginnings of Jewish settlement in Eretz Israel as a good indicator of the growing interest among Jews for a national home. What was important in his eyes was not the location of the national home, but the striving to find a solution based on self-realization. In spite of these feelings, Pinsker would, in his pamphlet, return several times to the question of a national home in Palestine or elsewhere.

At first Pinsker's views on a Jewish return to Palestine were negative. After commenting on the historical links of the Jews to Eretz Israel, he informs his readers that if the goal is a secure home, an end to wandering, and rehabilitation of the nation in the eyes of the world, then the dream of restoring ancient Judea should be discarded. He feels it is an error to concentrate on a place where Jewry's political life was once violently interrupted and destroyed. Finding a territory which is secure, and one from which no foreign power can expel its new inhabitants is more important. There the Jews could take their most sacred possessions that were salvaged from ancient Israel — the God idea and the Bible. It is these alone that made the old fatherland the Holy Land, and not Jerusalem or the Jordan.

Immediately following this discourse in *Auto-Emancipation,* Pinsker seemed to have second thoughts about completely eliminating Palestine as a possible site for the national Jewish home. Perhaps, he writes, the Holy Land may after all become a Jewish possession again. If so, all the better. However, first and foremost it is crucial to determine what territories are accessible to the Jews, and best adapted to offer to the Jews who must leave their homes a secure and undisputed refuge, and one capable of being productive.

Whether the territory chosen would be Palestine or a site in North America was immaterial to Pinsker as long as the decision arrived at produced a united Jewish national entity. He felt the eventual choice should be dictated by the territory's economic absorptive capacity and by political considerations. However, Pinsker was quick to point out that if North America was chosen for the national home, then time was of the essence, as the population of that continent was increasing so rapidly that soon open land would no longer be available.

Auto-Emancipation evoked a mixed review among its readers. In some circles it was greeted with vociferous indignation. Orthodox Jews regarded the author, who did not remain anonymous for very long, as irreligious. They could not accept or follow anyone so clearly estranged from traditional Judaism. In addition, the very idea of human efforts to bring about the restoration of the Jewish nation seemed to the Orthodox a repudiation of belief in the Messiah.

There were, however, in the Orthodox camp some individuals who agreed with Pinsker's analysis of the Jewish Problem and recognized the merits of his proposals to resolve the issue. Outstanding in this respect was Rabbi Isaac Ruelf (1831–1902), a native of Rauisch-Holzhausen, Germany. In addition to his rabbinical studies (he was ordained in 1857), Ruelf also received a thorough secular education at the universities of Marburg and Rostock. While serving as a district rabbi in the border city of Memel he became actively involved in relief work for Russian Jewry. Strongly influenced by Pinsker's pamphlet, Ruelf disseminated its message to his congregants, and to Memel's Jewish community. Later on in 1883 he gave voice to his own nationalistic views in a work entitled *Arukhat Bat Ami* ("The Healing of the Daughter of My People"). The rabbi of Memel would also become one of the early supporters of Theodor Herzl and played an important role in the Zionist organization of Germany.

Liberal Jews, especially those living in Western Europe, vehemently attacked Pinsker's *Auto-Emancipation.* In general, they regarded the author as being too pessimistic. They believed anti-Semitism was a temporary aberration that would eventually disappear. By insisting otherwise, the liberals argued, Pinsker betrayed faith in the ultimate victory of humanity over prejudice and hatred. Pinsker, who had written his pamphlet in German with the hope of winning over the Jews of the West to his ideas and to gain their support for the establishment of a national center, was sorely disappointed in their reaction. Hardly any of the prominent leaders of the Jews of Central and Western Europe responded to his appeals for action or showed any inclination to support a Jewish national movement.

The response of Eastern European Jewry was quite the opposite. The pamphlet found a sympathetic audience among many former adherents of the *Haskalah,* and especially among the Love of Zion movement. Indeed, shortly after the publication of *Auto-Emancipation,* prominent members of Hibbat Zion attempted to persuade the author to begin work immediately toward the realization of his plan and not to depend on Western Jewry for support. They also urged him to reconsider his position on Palestine, but despite the pressure placed on him, Pinsker refused to make a definite decision as to the location of the future Jewish homeland. However, a year later he was prevailed upon by Moses Lilienblum and other Jewish nationalists to rethink his position and to dedicate his considerable talents to the Hibbat Zion movement, and to the goal of a Jewish settlement of Eretz Israel. Pinsker accepted the challenge, and in conjunction with Lilienblum founded the Zerubabel Society of Odessa, which in a short span of time became the driving force behind the entire Love of Zion movement.

Almost overnight the former advocate of Russification had become a leading fighter for Jewish nationalism, and one of the most admired men in Russian Jewry. In 1884 Pinsker was chosen to preside over the Kattowitz Conference, which had as its chief objective the unification and centralization of the amorphous and loosely knit Hibbat Zion societies. The personal prestige of Pinsker reached a new height when the conferees elected him chairman of its temporary executive committee. This group was designated to operate out of Odessa until a permanent central bureau responsible for the overall policy of the movement could be created.

When efforts to establish a central bureau of the Hibbat Zion outside of Russia failed to materialize, the Odessa Executive Committee retained its position as the key organ of the Hiobat Zion movement. The Odessa Committee was soon confronted with a series of problems that defied easy solutions. The inability of the Committee to raise adequate funds for the handful of settlements in Palestine, the constant bickering and differences of opinions among the members, and the failure of the Committee to win legal recognition from the Russian government led Pinsker to have second thoughts about his role as a leader. Embittered and in poor health he attended the second Hibbat Zion conference, held at Drushkienski in the summer of 1887, with the intention of resigning his post as chairman of the executive committee. However, the pleas voiced by the majority of the delegates that his resignation would lead to the demise of the Jewish national movement compelled Pinsker to reconsider his position. With considerable misgiving he eventually gave in and agreed to stay on as chairman. Following the conference the ailing Pinsker traveled abroad. In Paris he met with Baron Edmond de Rothschild and persuaded him to provide immediate financial help for the struggling settlement at Petah-Tikva and to acquire additional land for Jewish immigrants eager to settle in Palestine. Rothschild was amenable to these suggestions, but the banker's associates made it clear that they would only collaborate with the Love of Zion as long as Pinsker remained at the helm of the movement. Encouraged by his success in Paris, Pinsker continued on his journey through Western Europe with the intention of persuading other prominent Jewish leaders to actively support the Hibbat Zion movement.

Returning to Russia, Pinsker's health continued to deteriorate, no doubt aggravated by the continuous wrangling with the Orthodox element of the Hibbat Zion. Once again he considered resigning, and in fact did not attend the Love of Zion convention of 1889 held in Vilna, Lithuania. At this meeting Rabbi Samuel Mohilever, who at the second convention had attempted to impose Orthodox authority over the Hibbat Zion, tried to capture the movement by winning over the chairmanship. Alarmed by this development, which inevitably would have taken away the centrality of the Odessa Committee and caused a rift between the religious and secular Love of Zion, Pinsker decided to personally intervene. Accordingly, he sent a letter to the conferees at Vilna suggesting a possible compromise to avoid a split in the organization. He proposed that Abraham Gruenberg, a resident of Odessa, be chosen to share executive power along with Rabbi Mohilever and Joseph Finn. This arrangement was accepted, a schism avoided, and Odessa remained the center of the Jewish national movement.

In 1890 the Hibbat Zion was legalized by the Russian government under the pseudonym Society for the Support of Jewish Farmers and Artisans in Syria and Palestine (for the Lovers of Zion it was still referred to as the Odessa Committee). Pinsker was again called upon to head this supposedly new entity and was privileged to witness the beginnings of large scale Jewish immigration to Palestine. This development took an unexpected turn in 1891 with the expulsion of Jews from Moscow, leaving Pinsker to believe that the scenario he had outlined in his *Auto-Emancipation* was about to be realized. This euphoria on the part of the Love of Zion leader proved short-lived when the Turkish government, reacting to the Russian action, banned Jewish immigration to Palestine. Pessimistic by nature, Pinsker again began to have doubts about the viability of Palestine as a national homeland. This uncertainty received additional reinforcement when the Hibbat Zion Jaffa Bureau was forced to close because of mismanagement. Perhaps after all, he told himself, Baron de Hirsch, who had founded the Jewish Colonization Association (ICA) for the settlement of Jews in Argentina, had the better solution to the Jewish Problem. However, after giving further consideration to the issue, Pinsker concluded that in the long run Eretz Israel would most likely evolve into a spiritual center for the Jewish people. He elaborated on this theme in an article that he wrote and read to Lilienblum a few weeks before his death in 1891. Pinsker had intended this article to serve as a supplement to an English edition of *Auto-Emancipation*. Despite his wishes, the article containing his final views on Palestine, which ran counter to that of most Lovers of Zion, was never published. Nevertheless, his concept of Eretz Israel as a spiritual center was taken up and expanded on by the great critic of Hibbat Zion policies, Ahad Ha-Am.

Leon Pinsker's *Auto-Emancipation* was the first fully formed articulation of a nationalistic solution to the Jewish Problem. It offered the Jewish people an alternative to the earlier proposals made by the advocates of enlightenment, emancipation, and assimilation. The pamphlet, written when the author was past sixty years of age and after a lifetime devoted to integrating Jews into the mainstream of Russian life and culture, lacked the dynamism of youth and the charisma essential to a leader of a national movement. The time was ripe for change, but Pinsker could not and would not be the new Moses to lead his people out of bondage. Nevertheless, his name looms larger in the history of ideas than in the history of Jewish politics. The immediate impact of his nationalistic work was limited. Still, the few who were converted to Zionism as the result of reading *Auto-Emancipation* constituted the very heart and soul of the Hibbat Zion movement in Eastern Europe in the 1890s. Without the support of these individuals, the accomplishments of the generation that followed and of Theodor Herzl, the founder of the World Zionist Organization, would have been virtually impossible. A grateful Jewish nation acknowledged their debt to Leon Pinsker two score and three years after his death by transferring his remains from Europe to Israel where they were laid to rest on Mount Scopus in Jerusalem.

33

Spiritual Zionism

At the very point when the Hibbat Zion was showing definite signs of becoming moribund, a young *maskil*, recently arrived in Odessa from the provinces, would attempt to revive it by charting a new course for the organization. His name was Asher Hirsch Ginzberg (1856–1927), better known by his nom de plume Ahad Ha-Am (one of the people). [344] He lashed out remorselessly at the bankruptcy of the Love of Zion policies and insisted that the establishment of a national homeland in Palestine had to be preceded by the spiritual regeneration of the Jewish people.

The only son of Isaiah Ginzberg, a merchant and the scion of a distinguished Hassidic family, Asher was born in the townlet of Skvira, in the Kiev province of Russia. He received a traditional Jewish education in the home of his father and in the local *heder*. At the age of eight the lad expressed a desire to learn Russian, but his pious family rejected his request, fearing that instruction even in the letters of the Russian language might lead to heresy. The precocious youth ignored the family's decision and surreptitiously taught himself to read Russian from the signs on the store fronts of his town. In Asher's eleventh year his father provided a private tutor for the study of Talmud and the devotional literature of the Hassidic movement.

In 1869 Isaiah Ginzberg leased from an aristocratic Russian family a large estate near the village of Gopitshitz (not far from Berditchev, the principal town in the district of Volhynia, which had a large Jewish population). The property, which had been almost ruined by its owners, was turned into a flourishing and profitable estate under the capable administration of Isaiah, making him in the process fairly affluent. Soon after settling down on the estate, Isaiah presented his son Asher at the court of the Rabbi of Sadagora. Young Asher, however, found the customs and practices of the rabbi's court not to his liking, and would during his lifetime develop a deep-seated antipathy toward Hassidism.

An avid reader, Asher applied himself assiduously to his studies, and at the time of his marriage in 1873, at the age of sixteen, he had achieved a wide reputation as a scholar. His advice was frequently sought by men who were themselves considered prominent religious authorities. Asher was greatly impressed by the works of the medieval Jewish philosophers, most notably by Maimonides's *Guide of the Perplexed.* Not content with an investigation of rabbinical literature, Asher also delved into the forbidden literature of the *Haskalah.* His interest in the literature of the Jewish Enlightenment gradually led him to adopt a form of religious agnosticism without in the least part diminishing his fervent attachment to the cultural and ethical ideals of Judaism.

Following his marriage, Asher continued his independent studies in the privacy of his home. His secular investigations tended toward philosophy and the sciences, but in time also included languages, notably Russian, German, French, English and Latin. In addition, Ginzberg delved into European literature, sociology, and history. Like his contemporary Lilienblum, he was also attracted to the writings of the Russian positivists, and their English counterparts John Stuart Mill (1806–73), and Herbert Spencer (1820–1903).

On several occasions Asher Ginzberg felt a need to escape his surroundings and to go abroad to complete his education at a university. Attempts to enroll at the universities of Breslau, Berlin, and Leipzig all came to nought, largely because of his own self-doubt, family obligations, and an unwillingness to meet certain formal requirements. In the end Asher abandoned his ambition to achieve a formal education and contented himself with being self-taught.

In 1884 Ginzberg decided to once and for all break away from the stifling atmosphere of his small village. Against the wishes of his parents and relatives, he moved with his wife and child to Odessa, the citadel of the Jewish Enlightenment in Russia. His stay in the city proved, however, to be of short duration as unfinished family business compelled him to return to his former village home. Two years would elapse before Asher could return to Odessa, where he would remain, except for a brief interlude, until 1907. The Odessa period would prove to be a turning point in his life, as it brought him into direct contact with Jewish writers, communal leaders, and enlighteners, as well as the fact that Odessa offered a cultural atmosphere charged with excitement. The Hibbat Zion quickly became aware of the talented young man and drew him into their counsels. Eventually, Asher Ginzberg became an active member of the Love of Zion and of the circle of intellectuals who looked to Leon Pinsker for leadership. When Pinsker was instrumental in establishing a central committee, a place was set aside for Ginzberg. Though only an ordinary member of the central committee, he immersed himself in all the facets of its responsibilities and operations. A keen observer, Asher soon found faults with the committee's parent—the Hibbat Zion movement itself. Convinced that it was his duty to report these failings if the movement was to survive, he wrote an article entitled *Lo Zeh ha-Derekh* ("This Is Not The Way").[345] Published in 1889 in *Ha-Melitz* ("The Advocate") under the pseudonym Ahad Ha-Am, the name by which he would henceforth be known, the article pleaded for a radical change in the Hibbat Zion's policies and direction.

Ahad Ha'Am's Criticism of Hibbat Zion

In his article the author hammered away on the theme that the movement had failed to live up to the promise of its early days. The original enthusiasm aroused by the idea of a Jewish return to the ancestral home in Eretz Israel had given way to despondency and internal bickering. Far from attracting new supporters and expanding its colonization efforts, the Hibbat Zion was scarcely able to maintain the handful of settlements already in existence. It was futile, Ahad Ha-Am emphasized, to look for scapegoats to blame for the organization's failures in Palestine. Furthermore, neither the old system of *halukah* (the indiscriminate sending of alms to Palestine, which led to corruption), or the demoralizing patronizing policies of Baron Edmund de Rothschild and his administrators toward the Jewish colonists were entirely to blame for the Hibbat Zion's lack of success.

In his analysis of what had gone wrong with the Love of Zion movement Ahad Ha-Am stressed that the Jewish national idea required a certain amount of spiritual preparation, a strengthening of faith, and a kindling of the will to attain the final goal. Furthermore, the goal itself was national in scope rather than geared to the individual and in this sense reflected the way life in ancient Israel had begun. Thus the Torah, for example, had as its aim the welfare of the whole people; the welfare of the individual being inconsequential. After the destruction of the first Temple, when the nation's fortune was at a low ebb and the situation seemed completely hopeless, the individual came to feel the need of a personal reward for his labor and sacrifices. As there was little hope of this in the present world, the idea of personal immortality found its way into Judaism. Subsequent historical events tended to further weaken the sense of devotion to the nation, and to intensify the belief in the salvation of the individual in the world to come. This trend, according to Ahad Ha-Am, in time evolved among the Jews into a distinct individualism and indifference to the national welfare. In order to swing the pendulum back to its original position, a revitalization of the heart had to be undertaken, and Jews educated once again to a sense of common responsibility.

In these circumstances, what should the leaders of Hibbat Zion have done? Ahad Ha-Am's answer was straight forward and clear. They should have devoted their energies, first and foremost, to the revival of national consciousness and postponed the commencement of actual colonization work in Palestine until they had trained a band of settlers who were properly inspired and capable of carrying out their work efficiently. Instead, the Hibbat Zion had abandoned the appeal to national sentiment as soon as they found that it evoked little or no response and had endeavored to build up the movement on the theme of self-interest. As a result of this policy many of the individuals attracted to Palestine were self seekers who were not prepared for the hardships and sacrifices that settlement in an undeveloped land entailed. When these individuals discovered that they had been deceived by information that had no basis in reality they fled the country. It was therefore not surprising that the Hibbat Zion movement, because of the wrong approach used to reach its goal, had suffered a sharp decline in membership.

The regeneration of the Promised Land, Ahad Ha-Am maintained, required a firm foundation of faith in the hearts of the Jewish people. Unfortunately, the Jews were fragmented, without any sense of unity or common purpose. Therefore it was essential to return to the ideas that first motivated the Hibbat Zion movement.

Ahad Ha-Am's article made a profound impression on its readers. It stirred up considerable controversy among the rank and file of the Love of Zion. In particular, it aroused the anger of those members of a practical persuasion, who favored pushing ahead as rapidly as possible in creating new settlements in Palestine. They felt that the spiritual revival that Ahad Ha-Am advocated would follow later. Lilienblum's reaction to *Lo Zeh ha-Derekh* was similar. He had become a practical Zionist in the narrowest sense of the term. It was said of him that he rejoiced over every single goat and every single dunam of land added to the Jewish holdings in Eretz Israel. Ahad Ha-Am's reasoning made no sense to him, and he did not hesitate to challenge the concept of "spiritual Zionism" in the columns of *Ha-Melitz*. Other critics, more acrimonious, soon followed Lilienblum's lead. In the process of replying to his opponents, Ahad Ha-Am became a highly regarded publicist and a master of the Hebrew language.

The appearance of Ahad Ha-Am's critical essay ushered in a new era in the history of modern Hebrew literature. In spite of the controversy aroused by the author's thesis, almost every one agreed that there was something new about the article's style and presentation. Readers of modern Hebrew had never before encountered such unusual qualities in a writer. His article reflected a passionate sincerity and a dignified restraint, and displayed integrity, strong convictions, and intellectual detachment. In addition, the language and style of the article and the essays that followed it were models of Hebrew construction and clarity. Though these compositions retained some biblical flavor, they were completely free of the flowery language of the early *Haskalah* writers, which most of Ahad Ha-Am's contemporaries had as yet not succeeded in discarding.

Although he had sharply rebuked his fellow Lovers of Zion and had been severely criticized in turn, Ahad Ha-Am had no intention of abandoning the movement. He viewed the differences between himself and the majority of the Hibbat Zion as a friendly debate among brothers—an argument over basic goals and philosophy. The leadership of the movement, he stressed, concentrated too much on the number of colonists, settlements, dunams of land, and livestock, whereas he was concerned about values. The former saw the problem as an economic one, while Ahad Ha-Am visualized it in terms of education. Similarly, while the leadership focused on the needs of the individual and worked for the immediate present, Ahad Ha-Am was more concerned about the nation and the future.

The Sons of Moses

Very early on in Ahad Ha-Am's career as a writer his exceptional gifts of mind and character attracted a coterie of followers among the younger set of the Hibbat Zion in Odessa. Often they met in his home for informal discussions, and it was to the members of this circle that Ahad Ha-Am first tested his novel ideas on how to reform the Hibbat Zion movement. About this same time dissatisfaction with the policies and operations of the organization had arisen among a small group of Jewish settlers in the Jaffa area of Palestine. Eager for reform, the dissidents made contact with Ahad Ha-Am's circle and a consensus was reached to form within the Love of Zion a kind of special fraternity or order, and to call it "B'nai Moshe" (Sons of Moses).[346] The name selected, linking the fraternity with the great biblical leader and prophet of the Jewish people, was intended to stress the lofty ideals and dedication of its members. As a symbolic act the B'nai Moshe was formally inaugurated on the seventh day of the Jewish month of Adar, which according to tradition was the day on which Moses was born and died.

From the very inception of the "Sons of Moses," Ahad Ha-Am was acknowledged as the order's spiritual leader. Aware of the czarist government's suspicion of all Jewish organizations, the founders of the B'nai Moshe decided to function as a secret society. Although Ahad Ha-Am disliked the idea of secrecy, he reluctantly accepted the verdict of the majority of the order's membership. The declared aim of the B'nai Moshe was to create a corps d'elite within the Love of Zion movement dedicated to serve the Jewish national renaissance with absolute unselfishness and with the highest ethical principles. In the introduction to the order's rules and regulations (which may have been modelled on the Order of the Freemasons), Ahad Ha-Am defined its mission.

> The supreme object of our Society . . . is the rebirth of our people in our ancestral land. . . . This effort must be a prolonged one, and there must be no indiscipline, no haste, no beating of drums, but circumspection, moderation and patience, guided always by good organization and settled rules of procedure. . . .[347]

It was Ahad Ha-Am's hope that the society would attract the best elements in Jewish life, which he felt were at present scattered and unorganized. Gathering momentum from generation to generation, the society would progress step by step to secure the attainment of the national objective. This effort would replace the futile isolated activities carried on in Palestine by individuals and groups with no bond of unity except the cash box.

Every member of the B'nai Moshe was expected to be completely devoted to the idea of a Jewish national revival in the Land of Israel, and was required to have a good command of the Hebrew language and culture. Membership was to be limited and reserved to men of high worth and character. The minimum age for entry into the order was set at twenty (later raised to twenty-five). Each member promised to contribute to the B'nai Moshe not less than two percent (later changed to one percent) of the expenses he and his household incurred annually. In addition, rigid standards had to be met by individuals desiring admittance into the B'nai Moshe. These included a thorough investigation of each candidate's moral character. A solemn ceremony preceded formal admission into the ranks of the order, and all members were oath-bound to observe the organization's rules. Discipline, truth, and discretion were to be the order's hallmarks. What Ahad Ha-Am and the B'nai Moshe were striving for was nothing less than a recrudescence of the ancient prophetic concept of the "remnant of Israel," which would become a nucleus for a newer and better Israel.

At the height of its existence, the order consisted of fourteen lodges with a total membership under 200. All of the lodges with one exception were located in Russia. Attempts to enlarge the B'nai Moshe played havoc with its discipline. With an augmented membership, differences of opinion multiplied. Much energy was dissipated in mutual recrimination and essential objectives and projects suffered from this divisiveness. Ahad Ha-Am, as spiritual head of the order, tended to leave actual day to day operations to the membership of the respective lodges. He also avoided as much as possible instituting new binding rules and regulations.

A decision to move the B'nai Moshe headquarters from Odessa to Jaffa brought the order into conflict with the Orthodox element in Palestine. The latter viewed the order as secularists dedicated to undermining Judaism. The intended relocation also created considerable internal dissension within the B'nai Moshe. Many members felt that the dispute with the Orthodox undermined the society's objective of unifying Jews of varying views, religious and secular alike, in seeking the common goal of the regeneration of the Jewish nation. Ahad Ha-Am, frustrated by the Jaffa fiasco and by other setbacks to his plans for the order, resigned his position as moral leader of the B'nai Moshe in 1896. The organization, however, managed to survive for another year, at which time the greater part of its membership was absorbed by the Zionist Organization created by Theodor Herzl.

Although the B'nai Moshe were unsuccessful in influencing the Jewish masses, the order did achieve some notable triumphs. Hebrew culture, for example, was greatly stimulated by the B'nai Moshe's establishment of the Ahiasaph publishing house, and the periodical *Ha-Shiloah*. The order was also instrumental in introducing into Russia the so-called reformed *heder* system (day schools) in which the language of instruction was Hebrew rather than Yiddish. Still other accomplishments included the creation of a national land purchasing fund (later absorbed by the Zionist Organization's Jewish National Fund), the publication of a series of newsletters in Jaffa noted for factual accounts of developments in the Jewish community of Palestine, the founding of a Hebrew school in Jaffa, and the establishment of libraries throughout the Holy Land. In addition, the B'nai Moshe played a role in the formation of agricultural settlements in which the colonists were men of independent means, and thus unlike most of the other colonies, not dependent on the philanthropic assistance of Baron Edmund de Rothschild. In spite of Ahad Ha-Am's strictures the order also revealed a certain amount of political acumen. Representatives of the B'nai Moshe, for example, were stationed in Constantinople, from which they attempted to win over the Jews of the Ottoman Empire to the idea of Jewish nationalism.

In 1891 Ahad Ha-Am visited Palestine. He found it inspiring to see Jews working the land with their own hands, but was repelled by the spiritual vacuum that prevailed among the colonists. He summed up his impressions in a lengthy article entitled *Emet me-Eretz Yisrael* ("Truth from Eretz Israel"), which was published in several installments in *Ha-Melitz*. Once again his article aroused a storm of controversy. Although his survey of the settlements had been undertaken on behalf of the Hibbat Zion, Ahad Ha-Am made no effort to spare his sponsors' sensibilities, or to idealize the organization's accomplishments. Instead, his essay gave a detailed description of the weaknesses in the Hibbat Zion's colonization policies, and the numerous problems confronting the various settlements. Coming at a time when the fortunes of the Lovers of Zion seemed to have taken a turn for the better as a result of the recognition of the Russian government for the so-called Society for the Support of Jewish Agriculturists and Workmen in Palestine and Syria, Ahad Ha-Am's criticism was a bitter dose of truth designed to shatter the prevailing complacency. Ahad Ha-Am's article stressed such disturbing factors as the petty assistance rendered the settlers by the Hibbat Zion, the widespread speculation in land, the bickering and feuding among the colonists, and the negative attitude of many of the settlers toward the Arab population. He was also quick to note that the amount of unoccupied land in Palestine was quite small. Similarly, Ahad Ha-Am felt that the Jewish community (the Yishuv) should not be built exclusively on viticulture. The settlers, he believed, were rashly pushing ahead with planting vines without waiting for the results of the first experiments designed to test if such cultivation was feasible.

Even more alarming to Ahad Ha-Am was the Hibbat Zion policy of increasing the number of Jewish settlers in the Holy Land by surreptitious means in direct defiance of the sovereigns of the country, the Ottoman Turks. Correspondingly, the blatant publicity that often accompanied Jewish purchases of land in Palestine was foolish and dangerous. It attracted the attention of the government, and it was an illusion to believe that the Turks did not care what was going on behind their backs in Palestine. Ahad Ha-Am conceded that although bribery and baksheesh was rampant among the Turks, there were Turkish dignitaries who were ardent patriots who, when dealing with Palestine issues, would enforce their government's laws honestly and could not be swayed by bribes from carrying out their duties.

The publicity that frequently accompanied land purchases had another harmful side-effect. It caused prices to soar and speculation to thrive, which in turn left an indelible mark on the social and economic fabric of the Jewish community of Palestine. On his visit to the Holy Land Ahad Ha-Am had been repelled by the get-rich schemes he had witnessed of men wildly pursuing speculative investments (a direct result of the real estate boom touched off by the establishment of the Odessa Committee). Almost completely lacking, according to Ahad Ha-Am, were settlers willing to sacrifice for a cause or a high ideal. Nevertheless, he felt that the day of reckoning for the land speculators was close at hand. The Turkish government, alarmed by developments in Palestine, had decided to cut off further Jewish immigration, thereby setting into motion forces which would inevitably lead to the collapse of the real estate boom.

A distinguishing feature of Ahad Ha-Am's analytical account of the Jewish colonies was his perception of the problem that would later confront the Zionist movement as a result of the presence of an Arab population in Palestine. Writers have frequently claimed that Zionism overlooked the very existence of the Arabs in the territory considered to be the Jewish homeland. Historically, these assertions are false. Moses Hess, for example, thought that the emergence of a Jewish commonwealth in the Holy Land would go hand and hand with a renaissance of Arab nationalism and the establishment of independent Arab states in Syria and Egypt. Theodor Herzl, in his novel *Altneuland,* presented a humanitarian proposal to integrate the Arab population of the Holy Land into the universalist society that would arise with the return of the Jews to their ancient homeland.

Ahad Ha-Am in his article, *Emet me-Eretz Yisrael,* differed from Hess and Herzl's approach to the Arab problem and presented a more pessimistic view. He clearly foresaw the possibilities of a clash between the Jewish and Arab nationalist movements — this at a time when there were few signs of a rising Arab nationalistic movement anywhere. Jews, Ahad Ha-Am insisted, must not harbor the illusion that Palestine was an empty country, a noncultivated wilderness where people could come to buy as much land as they pleased.

In reality this is not the case. It is difficult to find anywhere in the country Arab land which lies fallow; the only areas which are not cultivated are sand dunes, or stony mountains which can only be planted with trees, and even this after much labor and capital would be invested in clearance and preparation.[348]

Faced with these facts it was incumbent on the Hibbat Zion that they seek a realistic policy for dealing with the Arab population of Palestine. An attitude of superiority toward the Arabs and their culture would only exacerbate relations between the two communities. Ahad Ha-Am was convinced that many Zionists believed that the Arabs were barbarians. He believed this view was a cardinal mistake and dangerous. The Arabs, especially the city dwellers, were fully aware of what was going on around them. If they did not seem to take notice of Zionist activity in Palestine, it was because at present they did not see any danger for themselves and their future in what the Jews were doing. However, Ahad Ha-Am warned that the day would come when the number of Jews and their activities in the Land of Israel would have increased to such a degree that they would tend to push aside the local population and the situation would drastically change. The Arabs would not submit easily to this pressure or give up their place.

In spite of this gloomy prediction, Ahad Ha-Am by no means intended to draw the inference that there was no future for the Jews in the Holy Land. As a realist, he was trying to dispel the illusion that the Arabs would continue to be indifferent to Jewish colonization and therefore could safely be ignored by the Hibbat Zion movement. He continually cautioned Jewish settlers to avoid humiliating the Arab population, and to treat them with love, respect, and justice.

To those Jewish pioneers who insisted that the Arab respects only those individuals who show valor and fortitude, Ahad Ha-Am suggested that this was only the case when the Arab feels that the others have justice on their side. The opposite was true when the Arab thinks his opponent's actions are unlawful. In such a case the Arab may keep his anger to himself for a long time, but eventually he will seek retribution and vengeance.

Throughout his essay *Emet me-Eretz Yisrael,* Ahad Ha-Am emphasized that the Hibbat Zion movement must change its policies and direction if it had any hope at all of achieving its objective. If the status quo continued, the movement at best might, in the course of time, settle a few thousand on the land. However, it was certain that they would never get near the goal of finding a conclusive and final solution to the Jewish Problem.[349]

Another leitmotif of the essay was Ahad Ha-Am's sharp distinction between spiritual and material problems, between the "plight of Judaism" and the "plight of Jewry." These issues were at the core of his criticism of the Hibbat Zion movement and later with the adherents of Herzlian, i.e., Political Zionism.

Convinced that the policies followed by the Love of Zion were incapable of bringing economic and social redemption to individuals or to the Jewish people as a whole, Ahad Ha-Am suggested an alternative course of action. The colonization of Palestine, he advocated, had to be carried out slowly and with great care. Not quantity but quality had to be the determining factor; not the expansion of existing colonies, but rather their improvement. Above all, the true objectives of the Hibbat Zion movement would not be achieved, as Lilienblum and others believed, by a mass action to colonize Palestine. What was required was a cultural revival accompanied by policy reforms introduced by a carefully chosen elite (e.g., the B'nai Moshe). Ahad Ha-Am was convinced that the redemption of the Land of Israel could only be accomplished by men who lived in complete freedom and honor, men who were willing to shed the habits of the Diaspora, and who were not afraid of hard work, if they could obtain spiritual satisfaction thereby. The role of Hibbat Zion was to actively engage in preparing hearts for the spiritual and moral resurrection of the Jewish people. Palestine, however, must not serve as a balm for the trials and tribulations of the Jews. A national center served by an elect group could provide a model for the Jews of the Diaspora and greatly strengthen Jewish pride and nationalism.

Critique of the Palestinian Colonies

In 1893 Ahad Ha-Am paid a second visit to Palestine. His worst fears were confirmed by the mood of despair that he encountered throughout the Yishuv (Jewish community of Palestine). He was shocked to discover that he could not even land at the port of Jaffa without paying baksheesh to the Turkish officials and was forbidden by them to visit Jerusalem. On returning to Russia, he again resorted to the pages of *Ha-Melitz* to express his views on the situation in the Holy Land. This time, however, his criticisms, although similar to those expressed after his first visit to the Holy Land, were more tempered in tone. Ahad Ha-Am reiterated the need to obtain the consent of the Turkish government for any Jewish actions or projects in Palestine. Underhanded methods and schemes designed to bypass the Turkish officials were to be avoided; and subventions to settlers, as well as fiscal assistance to individual merchants and craftsmen, discontinued. In addition, Hebrew education in the colonies should be encouraged, settlers should place greater emphasis on quality rather than numbers, a shift should be made from viticulture to the growing of corn, and lastly, Jews should realize that Arab nationalism in Palestine had, in the wake of the Young Turk Revolution, become a potent force that could no longer be ignored by the Hibbat Zion.

Ahad Ha-Am, in his critique, also stressed the need to mobilize the help of Western Jewry in organizing an international society dedicated to building up the Yishuv. Such a body, he believed, would best be suited for negotiating with the Turks for a charter permitting the Jewish settlement of Palestine. The society would also have the responsibility for buying land in Palestine and systematically preparing for its colonization. Ironically, Ahad Ha-Am, who would later become the most vocal opponent of Theodor Herzl for emphasizing the need for a charter to achieve an autonomous Jewish homeland, was at this point advocating a similar approach. Indeed, he was the first authentic voice speaking from the depths of the Jewish tradition, and in the Hebrew language itself, to anticipate the climactic Zionist vision of the founder of modern Political Zionism, Theodor Herzl.

Ahad Ha-Am's second critique of the Palestinian colonies, although no less devastating than its predecessor, aroused less animosity. He had become accepted by many in the Jewish world as a critic of independent mind and as a writer possessed with an extraordinary literary talent.

To foster educational work, which he considered fundamental to his Spiritual Zionism, Ahad Ha-Am planned to produce and publish an encyclopedia on Jews and Judaism (it was to be called *Ozar ha-Yahudat*). The project, however, failed to materialize due to a succession of personal setbacks including the collapse of the business in which he was a partner with his father. The business failure compelled Ahad Ha-Am to seriously consider writing as a profession. With a wife and three children to support, and with no other resources available to him, Ahad Ha-Am accepted a position in Warsaw (1896) as manager of the Ahiasaph Publishing Company (he had previosly served the company as an unpaid literary advisor). Later that same year he left Poland to accept the offer of the philanthropist Kolonymus Ze'ev Wissotzsky (1824–1904) to edit the Hebrew monthly *Ha-Shiloah*. Under Ahad Ha-Am's guidance the periodical would become the most important organ of Jewish nationalism and Hebrew literature in Eastern Europe. However after six years of journalistic toil, exhausted and depressed by the burdens of his editorial post, he decided to resign and seek new fields for his talents (1902). *Ha-Shiloah*'s illustrious career would continue under his successor Joseph Klausner (1874–1958) and would enjoy another quarter of a century of existence. The last issue of the periodical would appear in 1927 in Jerusalem, a few months after the death of Ahad Ha-Am.

It was in the pages of *Ha-Shiloah* that Ahad Ha-Am's first collection of essays, entitled *Al Parashat Dirachim* ("At the Crossroads"), appeared. Between 1895 and 1914 three more volumes bearing the same title would be published. These four volumes, together with an anthology of his letters and some autobiographical reminiscences would constitute the sum total of Ahad Ha-Am's literary output. His legacy remains that of a great publicist and critic. Ahad Ha-Am had never intended to present a unified social and political philosophy. His essays always dealt with concrete problems and were always imbued with a lofty idealism. His original approach and brilliant style inevitably won many readers, even though many of them did not subscribe to his views.

In Ahad Ha-Am's approach to the Jewish Problem the individual was subordinate to the people, the bearer of the creative spirit, and the source of national creativity. In the ghetto, which maintained the Jewish spirit, it was cramped by limitations of space and means; in the open fields of emancipation, where it had attained access to the world, it suffered from inner want of freedom, from the mortification of all hopes for the future. Recovery could be expected only through the reawakening of the national, ethical, and spiritual ideal of prophecy and its return to its central position in Jewish life and by the creation of a spiritual center for its preservation and cultivation in Palestine.

The numbers in the spiritual center could even be insignificant; it only needed to effect a quickening of the heart of Jews everywhere. Indeed, Ahad Ha-Am considered the spiritual center to be the key for turning Jewry toward a productive national life. Using biologic imagery to stress this point he wrote:

> When all the scattered limbs of the national body feel the beating of a national heart, restored to life in the home of its vitality, they too will once again draw near one to another and welcome the inrush of living blood that will flow from the heart. . . . [350]

While Ahad Ha-Am was producing his critical essays and expounding his theory of spiritual nationalism, Theodor Herzl, the correspondent in Paris of the Vienna newspaper the *Neue Freie Presse,* was writing his book *Der Judenstaat* ("The Jewish State", 1895). The effect of this small volume would eventually transform the Jewish scene and lead to the creation of a new national movement known as "Herzlian" or "Political Zionism." Ahad Ha-Am, as he had in the case of the Hibbat Zion, would become Political Zionism's most vociferous opponent. Indeed, the clash of ideologies and personalities that marked Ahad Ha-Am's dispute with the new movement's leader, Theodor Herzl, was inevitable. Herzl represented a conception of nationality that was prevalent among some elements of Western Jewry who had been brought up in the heady atmosphere of nineteenth-century European liberalism and humanitarianism. His Zionism was an attempt to apply to the Jewish Question the principle of nationalities, which had set its imprint on the political struggles of Europe in the wake of the French Revolution. From this principle, which saw in statehood an essential feature of nationality, it followed that Jews could not be a real nation unless they had a state of their own. Therefore, Herzl's Zionism was from the start a purely political movement concerned solely with the restoration of the Jewish state as the best means to eliminating anti-Semitism and *Judennot* (Jewish misery, i.e., the suffering of the Jews caused by civic, economic, and social disabilities).

Ahad Ha-Am, on the other hand, viewed the Jewish Question from an entirely different perspective. As a result of his early upbringing and training he was deeply imbued with the religious and historical traditions of the Jewish people. His nationalism was therefore substantially formed by Jewish ideals and ethics rather than by purely political considerations. Accordingly, the essence of Ahad Ha-Am's nationalism expressed itself in a distinct outlook on life, and in the ideas, institutions, and customs that constituted what he believed to be the particular character of Jewish national culture. The worth of a nation, he insisted, was to be found in its individual contribution to the spiritual development of humanity. What mattered most in the life of a nation was the preservation and the full unfolding of the inner impulses and capacities that are the mainsprings of its cultural creativeness, and which in turn best reflect its national spirit. Statehood was not in itself therefore an essential element of nationality. However, it was an important factor in the formation of a nation, furthering its people's unity, strengthening its powers of resistance, and facilitating the unhindered expression of the national spirit.

For Ahad Ha-Am, a far more important aspect to the Jewish Question than creating a state, or resolving *Judennot* was the "problem of Judaism." He found most intolerable in this issue the dissolving consensus of the Jewish people resulting from the loss of faith among the enlightened, and the apparent irrelevance to modernity of the faith of the Orthodox. To reestablish a consensus among the Jewish people, Ahad Ha-Am believed the primary objective of the nationalist movement had to be the encouragement of a secular Jewish culture through the medium of the Hebrew language. This goal, however, could best be achieved within the framework of a return to Palestine, under conditions of relative autonomy, by a small nucleus of dedicated individuals who would establish the basis for a well-rooted Jewish society. Ahad Ha-Am aimed at making the soul of the Jewish people whole again, whereas Herzl strove to make the body normal.

At the First Zionist Congress convened by Herzl in 1897, Ahad Ha-Am attended as a visitor, although invited to be a delegate. He was thoroughly alarmed by the sessions of the Congress, which were marked by ebullient scenes of almost hysterical joy and enthusiasm. He would later write that he sat in gloom like a mourner at a wedding feast, and was deeply disappointed to hear only discussions of politics and diplomacy, and nothing of inner generation or culture. It seemed to Ahad Ha-Am that the leading figure at the Congress, Theodor Herzl, was little better than a well-meaning confidence trickster. "Be careful" he admonished his followers, "the salvation of Israel will come through prophets, not diplomats."[351]

Ahad Ha-Am's public reaction to the Zionist Congress was no less biting. He acknowledged the value of the convention as a proclamation to the entire world without parallel since the dispersion of the Jews, and he paid tribute to Max Nordau (1849–1923), whose address on the status of the Jews was the highlight of the Congress. However, for the rest of the proceedings he had not a good word. He was convinced that in the aftermath of the Congress disillusionment would set in that would even eclipse the extravagant hopes generated some years earlier by the Hibbat Zion movement. In addition, he stigmatized the Congress delegates as mostly inexperienced youngsters, and belittled their demands for a petty Jewish state as a poor substitute for the true goals of Jewish nationalism, the universal ideals propagated by the ancient Hebrew prophets.

Some months after the First Zionist Congress, Ahad Ha-Am expanded on his objections to Herzl's call for a Jewish state in an article entitled *Jewish State and Jewish Problem*. In this piece echoes of the German philosophers Johann Gottfried von Herder (1744–1803) and Georg Wilhelm Friedrich Hegel (1770–1831) are clearly evident in the author's belief that the creation of a body politic is the apex of the cultural and spiritual force of a people. A state, Ahad Ha-Am emphasized, is not created out of thin air, or through a diplomatic coup. Indeed, such a state would inevitably prove to be an ephemeral phenomenon for the socio–cultural infrastructure essential to a viable polity would be lacking.

Accordingly, diplomatic efforts to secure a Jewish state by means of a charter or by similar devices were futile. An entity thus constituted would lack a solid foundation and without cultural roots would be certain to fail. The cultural shallowness and spiritual one-dimensional aspect of Herzl's political structure as described in *Der Judenstaat* struck

Ahad Ha-Am as being superficial and dangerous. Herzl's state, he wrote, ". . . may perhaps be a State of the Jews. . . . but it will not be a Jewish State."[352]

On practical as well as ideological grounds, Ahad Ha-Am found fault with Herzl's blueprint for a Jewish state. He felt that Herzl's Zionism was much too exacting in its demands on the Jewish people as a whole, as well as on the individual Jew. He disliked the idea of the establishment of an entity in which the victims of anti-Semitism in its cruder and more violent forms would find refuge and scope for a freer life, while the emancipated Jews of the West remained for the most part in the countries of their birth or adoption to be peacefully absorbed into the general populace. Although Ahad Ha-Am believed that Palestine could not take in more than a fraction of the number of Jews living at the time, he was not prepared to accept the disappearance of the rest of the Jewish people as inevitable.

Ahad Ha-Am was convinced that what was really required was not a refuge for the persecuted, but a truly Jewish state that would be established after a long process of national self-education. Such a development would give the Jewish people time to purge themselves of the evil effects of centuries of Diaspora life. It would enable Jews to get rid of the shiftlessness and stagnation associated with the ghetto, as well as emancipated Jewry's attenuated Jewish consciousness and slavish acceptance of Gentile standards and ways of thinking. Such a process could be accelerated by a national spiritual center in Palestine that would also enable the Jewish people to again contribute creatively to human progress. In order for the Jewish center to successfully carry out its functions, preparatory work preceding its establishment had to take place in the Diaspora. Instead of being allowed to lay down the burdens of Judaism, the Diaspora Jews had to be made aware of their rich tradition and infused with a sense of belonging to a Jewish nation. Once created, the national center would encourage and accentuate these feelings. Ahad Ha-Am was thus demanding nothing less than a restructuring of Judaism in order to make possible a national Jewish cultural revival.

Particularly disturbing to Ahad Ha-Am was the fact that the Political Zionist movement had been created and was largely led by assimilated secular Jews of the West (e.g., Theodor Herzl and Max Nordau) who were spiritually far removed from the vast majority of the Jewish people. He disagreed with the new movement's leadership's emphasis on diplomacy and mass colonization of Palestine – the very antithesis of the policies pursued by the Hibbat Zion. Ahad Ha-Am also felt that the Political Zionists tended to make extravagant and baseless promises, exaggerated their successes, and covered up their failures. The noisy propaganda employed by the followers of Herzl irked Ahad Ha-Am, who looked askance upon such methods. He was convinced that Jewish freedom and self-emancipation could only be achieved by inner discipline and definitely not by public demonstrations. Equally galling to Ahad Ha-Am was the fact that his Herzlian opponents appeared to be using every possible device to prevent free discussion of the fundamental problems confronting Zionism, for fear of bringing into the open the conflicting views between Eastern and Western European Jewry on how best to resolve these vexing issues. Most unforgivable to Ahad Ha-Am was his sense that Herzl and his circle were not interested in the Hebrew language and culture. For Ahad Ha-Am these were the very breath of life of true Jewish nationalism. Last but not least, he was piqued by the knowledge that so many of his friends and colleagues shared the enthusiasm generated by Theodor Herzl, and had, without a second thought, abandoned the ideals that he and they had fought for so long as members of the Hibbat Zion.

With the passage of years the rift between Ahad Ha-Am and Theodor Herzl increased in intensity. The 1902 appearance of Herzl's utopian romance *Altneuland* ("Old-New Land") elicited a critical and satirical review by Ahad Ha-Am. He played up the many absurdities in the novel, most notably the idea of millions of penniless Jews being rapidly settled in barren Palestine and achieving prosperity practically in the twinkling of an eye. Ahad Ha-Am also raised a question as to the Jewish content of the cosmopolitan society described by Herzl in his novel. *Altneuland* contains theaters where plays could be heard in several European languages, an opera house, and a learned academy modeled on France's famous institution. In Jerusalem there is a Temple strongly reminiscent of the type favored by the German-Jewish Reform movement; there are also newspapers in several languages, as well as museums, concert halls, and all other institutions normally found in a highly civilized society. But there is no sign of the Hebrew language except in the synagogue service and in a song of welcome sung by school children to admiring visitors. Indeed, as Ahad Ha-Am pointed out, there is in *Altneuland* no trace of Hebrew literature or culture. Nothing whatever, he stresses, distinguishes this particular "Jewish society" from that which might be created by bushmen if they had the means and set about to build themselves a new life modeled on the latest ideas and inventions of western civilization.

Following his scathing review of Herzl's novel, Ahad Ha-Am's popularity declined dramatically. He became for many Zionists the "enemy within." Some of Herzl's more zealous supporters vented their fury by burning the critic's writing in public. Nevertheless, not all Zionists were willing or anxious to condemn a writer who refused to buckle under the pressure exerted by the majority of the adherents of Jewish nationalism. Many Russian Zionists, in fact, had misgivings about Herzl and his lieutenants. They did not like the elegance, sophistication, and worldliness that characterized these men; it seemed to belie the folk democracy of the Pale of Settlement. Moreover, Herzl's constant pursuit of princes, kings, and powerful ministers whom he believed would help the Jews gain Palestine struck the Russian Jews as being naive and a chimera. Of great concern for many of the Russian Jews, who had formerly been associated with the Hibbat Zion movement, was the palpable lack of Jewish spirit in the activities of Herzl and his followers. This uneasiness would in time cryatallize into an organized party within the World Zionist Organization; among the more prominent leaders of this party would be Leo Motzkin (1867–1933), Berthold Feiwel (1875–1937), Chaim Weizmann (1874–1952), and Martin Buber (1878–1965). At the Fifth Zionist Congress (1901) the Democratic Fraction, as this dissenting party was called, succeeded in pushing through the Congress a resolution affirming the need to educate the Jewish people toward the creation of a national spirit (Ahad Ha-Am's original suggestion).

Herzl recognized that many Eastern European Jews shared Ahad Ha-Am's views and he was deeply moved by their inner unity and commitment to Judaism. Nevertheless, he was unwilling to forsake his own views and in the years immediately preceding his untimely death in 1904 the gap between himself and the Russian Zionists widened. Matters came to a head during the Sixth Zionist Congress, which met in Basle, Switzerland, during August of 1903. Herzl's hope of obtaining a charter from the Turkish government for the mass Jewish settlement of Palestine under international guarantees had come to nought. Haunted by the spectre of Jewish misery and insecurity in Russia (the infamous Kishinev pogrom had occurred a few months prior to the convocation of the Congress), Herzl changed tactics and tried to find a haven for those Jews fleeing persecution. The British government answered his prayers with an offer of a territory in East Africa for Jewish settlement, which the Zionist leader promptly brought before the Sixth Zionist Congress.

The proposal, which became known as the "Uganda Scheme" aroused a storm of opposition among the Russian delegates. For many of them, former Lovers of Zion, the very idea of a Jewish national settlement other than Palestine was unthinkable. They refused to believe the Zionist leadership's assertions that the East Africa scheme was intended to provide a temporary haven for persecuted Jews and that Palestine remained, and would always remain, the goal of the movement. Equally disturbing for the Russian delegates was the shock of realization that Ahad Ha-Am had spoken the bitter truth when he had pointed out that the Zionism of the West and their own version of Jewish nationalism rested on different philosophies and value systems.

A resolution to send out a commission to investigate the territory offered by the British government and to report the findings to the next Congress mustered a substantial vote in favor. However, 178 delegates—basically the entire Russian contingent—had cast their votes against the resolution. When the result of the vote was read, the Russians walked out of the hall in protest, and held a separate meeting of their own at which cries of betrayal were raised and tears were shed for a "lost Palestine." Eventually, Theodor Herzl's personal entreaties persuaded the reluctant Russian delegates to return to the Congress.

Ahad Ha-Am regarded the entire affair as a natural consequence of the detachment of the Herzlian Zionists from Jewish values. He spelled out his reactions to the events of the Sixth Zionist Congress in his personal correspondence and in an article entitled *Those Who Wept*. He saw in the East Africa proposal confirmation of the forebodings he had expressed following the First Zionist Congress.

> In Basle, on the first of Ellul, 5657, this Zionism [Political] was born, and in Basle, on the first of Ellul, 5663 its soul departed from it, leaving nothing but a name emptied of all meaning and a program with a new far-fetched interpretation . . . [353]

Angered by what he considered a betrayal of Zionism, Ahad Ha-Am at one point urged his followers to consider the creation of a new organization that would dedicate itself to the furtherance of Jewish culture in Palestine and the Diaspora. However, cooler heads prevailed, as many of the men who shared Ahad Ha-Am's views also believed in the necessity for political, as well as practical and cultural work and felt that these objectives could best be attained by remaining in the World Zionist Organization. In the years following the death of Theodor Herzl these individuals, most of whom were members of the Democratic Fraction, were able to successfully incorporate practical and cultural items into the World Zionist Organization's program.

Even prior to the East Africa crisis, Ahad Ha-Am had engaged in a war of words with the Political Zionists over the issue of establishing a Zionist bank. The prospectus of the proposed bank (the future Jewish Colonial Trust) had been approved by the Second Zionist Congress (Basle, 1898), which had also suggested that the activities of the institution be limited to Palestine and the countries of the region. However, the prospectus was loosely drafted and seemed to allow the proposed bank permission to carry on colonizing and other activities in any part of the world. Ahad Ha-Am saw in this prospectus a deliberate attempt on the part of the Zionist leadership to use the resources of the bank for the establishment of a state elsewhere if Palestine proved unobtainable. This view was shared by a large segment of the rank and file of the Zionist Organization and the issue remained unresolved until the Seventh Zionist Congress (Basle, 1905). The Seventh Congress decided that the articles of the association of the bank must be altered, as originally intended, to restrict the institution's activities exclusively to Palestine and Syria. It also officially rejected Great Britain's East Africa offer.

In 1903 Ahad Ha-Am decided to retire as editor of *Ha-Shiloah* in order to enter the world of commerce. He joined the Wissotzky tea firm as an inspector of the organization's far-flung branches throughout Russia. However, he continued to write and engage in Jewish public activities. In 1908 he accepted a position as manager of the tea company's recently opened office in London. He would remain a resident of the English capital for fourteen years before permanently settling in Palestine (1922). During his entire stay in London he remained aloof from the largely assimilated segment of the Anglo-Jewish community, as well as from the Orthodox and the advocates of Yiddish. Uprooted and separated from his old friends, the English experience proved more wrenching than Ahad Ha-Am had anticipated. Unable to adjust to the English climate, his health gradually deteriorated. Nevertheless, in spite of his isolation and health problems, Ahad Ha-Am managed, during his British period, to actively participate in several events that vitally affected the cultural and political future of Zionism.

Foremost from a cultural point of view was his involvement in the so-called language war. When the tea magnate Kalman Wissotzky died in 1904 his will stipulated that an institution to commemorate his name be established once every five years. The first such entity was scheduled to be created in 1909. A year or so earlier Ahad Ha-Am, one of the trustees of the late Wissotzky's charitable bequest, suggested to the testator's son, David Wissotzky, the creation of an institution in Palestine. The latter at first rejected the suggestion, but was later convinced by Dr. Paul Nathan (1857–1927), one of the leaders of the German philanthropic organization, the Hilfsverein der deutschen Juden and by Shmarya Levin (1867–1935), a prominent Zionist writer, to establish a technical school in Palestine. Eventually an agreement was reached between the Wissotzky trust and the Hilfsverein in which both parties accepted joint responsibility for the implementation of the technical school project. A *kuratorium,* i.e., a board of governors composed of representatives of the two sponsoring bodies was created to oversee the project. Included on the *kuratorium* as charter members were Ahad Ha-Am, Shmarya Levin, Paul Nathan and several other members of the Hilfsverein der deutschen Juden. Later, after a notable contribution to the project by the philanthropist Jacob Schiff (1847–1920) of New York, the *kuratorium* was enlarged by the addition of some prominent American Jews.

From the outset the board agreed that if the project was to succeed, it was essential to establish a secondary school that would act as a conduit or feeder of students to the technical school. Plans were made to build both schools in Haifa, Palestine, on the slopes of Mount Carmel. Construction of the buildings proceeded smoothly (the cornerstones were laid in 1912), but as the date approached for the opening of the technical school an ideological struggle between the Zionist and non-Zionist members of the *kuratorium* erupted. Ahad Ha-Am at first attempted to act as a mediator between the Zionists and their opponents, who included the Wissotzky heirs and the German-Jewish representatives of the Hilfsverein. His efforts, however, proved futile as the breach between the two parties grew wider and more bitter. The key divisive issue confronting the *kuratorium* involved the question of the language of instruction to be used in the Technikum (the German name for the technical school). The Zionist members of the board insisted that

Hebrew be the sole language of instruction in both the feeder and technical schools. Ahad Ha-Am, in an attempt to find a compromise, suggested that Hebrew should be the language of instruction in the feeder or secondary school, but felt it unwise and impractical that instruction in the technical school be limited to Hebrew. The representatives of the Hilfsverein, on the other hand, favored German as the only language of instruction for both schools, and refused to compromise on this issue. As a result the Zionist members and Ahad Ha-Am resigned from the *kuratorium* in protest. The language controversy then became a public issue, arousing fierce passions among the Jewish population of Palestine. Meetings were held throughout the country and resolutions favoring Hebrew over German were passed by practically every Jewish institution and organization in the Yishuv. In addition, the Hebrew Teachers Association forbade their members from accepting posts with the Technikum institution, and at the same time launched a campaign to discourage students from registering for the school. Simultaneously, Hebrew teachers and pupils at the various Hilfsverein schools in Palestine went on strike in support of the advocates of Hebrew instruction for the Technikum.

Ahad Ha-Am objected to some of the tactics employed by both sides in the bitter struggle, but was by and large ignored. Eventually, the Zionist Organization entered the fray and established a network of Hebrew schools to compensate for the breach in education caused by the strike against the Hilfsverein schools. The language controversy, however, continued unabated, further delaying the opening of the technical school. When in the midst of this debate World War I broke out, the unoccupied school was converted into a military hospital, first by the Turks and later by the British. After the cessation of hostilities the Zionist Organization acquired the property, and the first university level classes were held in Hebrew in the winter of 1924 (today this institution is the widely acclaimed Technion, Israel's Institute of Technology). The protracted battle over the language of instruction had ended with a complete victory for the advocates of Hebrew.

A second issue that disturbed the Jewish community of Palestine was the question of religion. It was easier for Ahad Ha-Am to compromise on religious matters than on the language issue. His position on religion was that of a highly sympathetic and understanding agnostic. Disclaiming adherence to any particular Jewish religious sect or movement, he nevertheless retained a reverence for the "holy things of the nation" equal to that of the most conservative traditionalists. In his view a good Jewish nationalist was bound to respect these things, independent of his personal faith or nonbelief. In reality, however, Ahad Ha-Am more often than not sided with moderate traditionalists rather than with the followers of Reform Judaism, whom he considered misguided and essentially assimilationists. Opposed to mysticism and distrustful of emotion, Ahad Ha-Am sought and found a balance between his native skepticism and some of the less negative elements of his spiritual makeup such as his passion for individual freedom and his strong sense of the importance of historical continuity in Judaism.

These convictions motivated Ahad Ha-Am to intervene in a religious versus secularist conflict that threatened the peace of the Tel Aviv High School, better known as the Gymnasia Herzlia (opened in 1907 by Jewish nationalists; it was the first Hebrew language secondary school in Palestine). The school's chief benefactor and patron had become disturbed by reports of extreme secularist tendencies on the part of some of the institution's staff and threatened to withdraw his support. Ahad Ha-Am agreed with the patron's complaints. In particular he disapproved of the introduction of the disputable theories of the German school of "higher criticism" into the teaching of the Bible, and he ridiculed the objections of the more rabid antireligious teachers to students having their heads covered during Bible lessons.

Ahad Ha-Am's opposition to extreme secularism was matched by his strong resistance to those who insisted that a Jewish nationalist must necessarily profess religious faith. He firmly believed that the Jewish religion was national in nature, that it was a product of the national spirit rather than the other way around. Therefore it was impossible to be a Jew in the religious sense without acknowledging Jewish nationality. It was, however, Ahad Ha-Am felt, possible to be a Jew in the national sense without accepting many things in which religion required belief. He believed that traditional *halachah,* the religious law of Judaism, required modification, and that the changes would evolve naturally with the renewal of Jewish life in Palestine.

Ahad Ha-Am's sojourn in London was also marked by an ongoing debate with Simon Dubnow, the eminent Jewish historian, on the relation of the Diaspora to a Jewish national spiritual center or a state in Palestine. This controversy, which had begun in Ahad Ha-Am's Odessa period, continued unabated for many years in the correspondence between the two men, as well as in the columns of various periodicals. In spite of their basic differences, Dubnow and Ahad Ha-Am admired and respected each other. Indeed, Dubnow would note that, ". . . in the field of national ideology I am closer to Ahad Ha-Am than to any other writer of our times."[354] In a similar manner Ahad Ha-Am would reciprocate by acknowledging that Dubnow was much closer to him in spirit than those newly arrived Zionists whose entire nationalism was based upon the creation of a Jewish state.

Both men were convinced that even after the establishment of a national center in Palestine, the majority of Jews would choose to remain in the Diaspora. Dubnow, commenting on this point, gave his reasons why he was adamantly opposed to those individuals who completely negated the value of the Diaspora. It was not because he recognized some intrinsic good in a Galut existence. On the contrary, Dubnow stressed that if he had the power to transfer the entire Diaspora to a Jewish state, he would do it with the greatest joy. Because such a scenario was unlikely and realistically impossible, he considered the Diaspora to be a historical necessity. As such the importance of the Diaspora was to preserve and develop the national spirit of the greater part of the Jewish nation that chose to remain there.

Reasoning along similar lines, Ahad Ha-Am queried whether the establishment of a state in Palestine did not automatically result in the "ingathering of the exiles" and the end of Diaspora history. In answering his own question he reiterated his belief that the end of the Diaspora and the restoration of the Jewish people to their ancient homeland was still a matter of the distant future. Zionism was therefore only a step forward in the long and thorny road toward national redemption. However, the very idea that it would be possible in the future to restore the entire Jewish people to the Holy Land was a dangerous delusion, and the inevitable failure to achieve this goal would drive the disillusioned masses to despair. Ahad Ha-Am felt the Diaspora would be a reality for a considerable time into the future. Ahad Ha-Am also believed that the Diaspora was important to the Zionist movement. If Eretz Israel was to become a spiritual center, it needed the Diaspora as a periphery satellite. The two were interdependent and inseparably connected. The center in Palestine, which Ahad Ha-Am pictured as a small but elite group, would play an active part as the cultural vanguard of the nation. Diaspora Jewry, the more passive partner, would be the spiritual recipient of the influences emanating from the homeland

and would build up the national center in Palestine and strengthen relations between a revitalized Judaism and the Jewish communities of the Orient and the Occident.

Dubnow was in full agreement with Ahad Ha-Am's conviction that it was essential to maintain the national consciousness of the Jews living in the Diaspora. On the other hand, Ahad Ha-Am was quick to point out what he believed were serious ambiguities in Dubnow's doctrine of national autonomy (the concept that the Jewish Problem in the Diaspora could only be resolved if the Jews were granted national and cultural autonomy in the states where they lived). He had grave doubts as to the likelihood of such a scheme succeeding, considering the repressive regimes of Eastern Europe under which most of Jewry lived. Ahad Ha-Am's assessment of the weak link in Dubnow's doctrine was prophetic, as all the experiments to impose Diaspora nationalism in Europe by treaty following World War I ended in failure.

The real divergence of views between Dubnow and Ahad Ha-Am was not one of basic theory but rather of subtle differences in emphasis. Dubnow, closer to the Jewish masses with his historical approach and with his all-inclusive view of the Jewish community, was deeply concerned about the fate of the millions of Jews living in the Diaspora. Ahad Ha-Am, the thorough intellectual, was more concerned with the fate of Judaism and less about the formulation of a program for saving the Jews of the Diaspora, other than by creating a cultural spiritual center in Palestine. He believed that Palestine was important, not as a political entity or a refuge for Jews, but rather as a spiritual center for Judaism and Jewish national culture. With the achievement of an independent Jewish society in Palestine, the Jews, Ahad emphasized, would no longer suffer from the constraints of being a minority in a non-Jewish world. As a consequence, they would be able to build a moral social order with cultural values that would inspire all the Jews of the Diaspora and guarantee their continued survival and unity as a people. When, in time, the Jewish national culture in Palestine reached the highest level of perfection of which it was capable then, ". . . we may be confident that it will produce men . . . who will be able [presented with] a favorable opportunity to establish a state which will be truly a Jewish state and not merely a state of Jews."[355]

Ahad Ha-Am's activities during his residence in England reached a high-point during World War I. The conflict overturned earlier convictions and theories and radically affected the Jewish national movement. For all practical purposes, the war put an end to Ahad Ha-Am's literary career and greatly magnified his responsibilities as the manager of a foreign-owned business in a society that had become highly patriotic and xenophobic. His physical health, always sensitive to emotional disturbances, suffered a setback from which he never fully recovered. Nevertheless, the war that caused him so much suffering and grief was also the source of renewed hope for a brighter future for Jewish nationalism. This development came about when Turkey, the master of Palestine, entered the conflict as an ally of Germany. Ahad Ha-Am saw in this the possibility that the situation could be exploited to benefit the Jewish national cause. Chaim Weizmann, a disciple of Ahad Ha-Am and a lecturer in chemistry at the University of Manchester, realized at the outbreak of hostilities in August of 1914 the importance of identifying the Zionist movement with the Allied powers. Like Ahad Ha-Am, Weizmann was convinced that an Allied victory was inevitable. Thus Weizmann, on his own initiative, embarked on a series of discussions with British statesmen and leaders of public opinion, for the purpose of winning support for the Zionist goal of a Jewish restoration in Palestine. From the outset, Weizmann included his mentor, Ahad Ha-Am, in his confidence. Throughout the three years that elapsed before the issuance by the British government of the Balfour Declaration (November 2, 1917), which pledged support for the establishment in Palestine of a national home for the Jewish people, Ahad Ha-Am was consulted by Weizmann on every issue of consequence. Ironically, the one-time implacable opponent of Herzlian diplomacy and Political Zionism thus played a part of some importance, although in an unobstrusive and mainly unrecorded role, in the molding of Zionist policy during the period that culminated in the first great triumph of the movement in the political field since the East Africa offer.

Ahad Ha-Am, however, was not overwhelmed by the British government's issuance of the Balfour Declaration. He perceived its limitations, especially as it related to the Arab Question and feared that the Zionist movement's enthusiasm for the document would blind them to the realities of the situation in Palestine. Even prior to the Balfour Declaration, Ahad Ha-Am was frequently consulted on matters pertaining to the Zionist cause. This is particularly evident in his involvement in the debate over the formation of a Jewish Legion.

With Turkey's entry into war on the side of the Central Powers, the attitude of its government toward the Jewish development of Palestine, previously passively obstructionist, now became one of active hostility. Many of the leading members of the Yishuv were imprisoned or driven into exile. Accordingly, some of the younger and more daring spirits in the Yishuv expressed a desire to participate as Jews in the military operations of the Allies against Turkey. Six hundred of the Palestinian Jewish refugees who had fled to Egypt formed themselves into a "Zion Mule Corps" and after a brief training embarked in 1915 for the Dardanelles. There they fought through the whole ill-fated Gallipoli campaign, under the command of a soldier sympathetically disposed toward Jews and Zionism, Colonel John Henry Patterson. The "Zion Mule Corps" shared with the stout-hearted Australians and New Zealanders in the feat of the difficult evacuation of the Gallipoli peninsula from November, 1915, to January, 1916. On the corps disbandment, Joseph Trumpeldor (1880–1920), a former officer in the Russian Army launched a campaign to form a Jewish Legion to fight alongside the Allied forces. Visiting London in the latter half of 1916, he asked Ahad Ha-Am for advice and support in furthering the Jewish Legion project. Although not a pacifist Ahad Ha-Am disliked military solutions to complex problems. Nevertheless, he listened to Trumpledor's plans and expressed no objection, in principle, to the formation of a Jewish Legion. He insisted, however, that the legion must be available on any front (not only Palestine) and that it must not be aimed exclusively at Turkey.

Trumpledor's initial efforts to win Allied support for his scheme came to nought, but in the following year the idea was again brought before the Jewish public and the British government by Vladimir Jabotinsky (1880–1940), a journalist and the future founder and leader of the Zionist Revisionist Organization. His proposal eventually found its way onto the agenda of the Executive Committee of the English Zionist Federation, and its leading member Chaim Weizmann wrote to Ahad Ha-Am asking for his opinion on this sensitive issue. Ahad Ha-Am promptly responded and urged Weizmann and the Federation to act immediately on the legion project, i.e., either to accept or reject the idea, but under no circumstances to remain neutral. He reasoned that the public would automatically assume that the British government could not possibly have failed to consult the Zionists on a proposal of this kind put to them by a free lance journalist (Jabotinsky). Ahad Ha-Am also offered his own views on the proposed Jewish Legion, which had apparently undergone radical changes since his meeting with Trumpeldor. He noted:

... although it is highly advisable to have Jewish soldiers at the Palestine front, they should be in British (or if possible American) units and not in separate Jewish regiments. I consider the latter to be an empty demonstration, the result of which may prove disastrous both to Palestinian and, generally Turkish Jewry, and to our future work in Palestine if after all, it is not occupied [by the Allied forces].[356]

Ahad Ha-Am's opinion of the dangers involved in the creation of a Jewish Legion closely paralleled the views of the majority of the members of the English Zionist Federation. However, this outlook changed dramatically after the British government decided to recruit for their army Russian-Jewish subjects resident in Great Britain. The announcement of this policy strengthened the hands of the advocates of a Jewish Legion, and enabled them to win over to their cause the reluctant English Jewish establishment, as well as British officialdom. Late in 1917 the first Jewish fighting battalion was formed. In the following year the battalion left for Egypt, where it was reinforced by Jews from the liberated areas of southern Palestine and by others coming from the United States and Canada. The units eventually expanded in size to three battalions and elements of these units played a prominent role in the campaign to dislodge the Turkish forces from Palestine.

The cessation of hostilities brought with it a renewal of Zionist efforts to push for a Jewish settlement of Palestine. The door of Zion had opened wide. The charter that had seemed a visionary thing in 1900 had become a reality with the issuance of the Balfour Declaration. The resolve of the Allies to recognize Jewish rights in Palestine was in turn sanctioned by the League of Nations. The very heart of Ahad Ha-Am's pre-war concept of an evolutionary development of a Jewish cultural center in Palestine, to some extent separate and apart from the establishment of a political state, was derailed by the course of events. With the Allied victory, the Jewish world saw a rare opportunity to bring immediate succor and consolation to those Jews who had suffered most from the ravages of the Great War. For the first time Ahad Ha-Am found himself in harmony with the Zionists, who desired to find a home for these victims and refugees in the Promised Land.

As early as his third visit to Palestine (1912), Ahad Ha-Am had tried to come to an arrangement with the Wissotzky firm that would have permitted him to spend most of his time in the Holy Land while maintaining his post in London. That design had failed, and it was only after World War I, when he had reached the age of retirement and his pension was ensured, did relocation to Palestine become a concrete reality. Illness, however, prevented his departure until 1921. Ahad Ha-Am, with his wife and son, settled in Tel Aviv, the first truly Jewish city of the modern era.

It now seemed to Ahad Ha-Am that his forecasts of Jewry and Judaism's future were being justified by events. He had become more optimistic about Eretz Israel and believed that the Zionist movement was in fact creating there the spiritual center that he had labored so long to bring about. This trend, which Ahad Ha-Am had detected, would continue during the early years of the British mandate for Palestine. But then came the Arab disturbances of the 1930s, the destruction of European Jewry during World War II, the abandonment of the Palestinian mandate by Great Britain, and the establishment of the State of Israel. Ahad Ha-Am did not live long enough to witness these crucial events. He died January 2, 1927, without seeing the realization of his hopes for the spiritual regeneration of Diaspora Jewry, which he had considered essential prior to the creation of a Jewish state.

The Holocaust, however, which wiped out the heartland of the Diaspora—from which many of Jewry's spiritual and cultural leaders would have most likely come—conversely created the conditions favoring the creation of the State of Israel. The latter, in turn, by focusing the attention of world Jewry on its struggles and accomplishments, fulfills to a great extent the function of the spiritual and cultural center originally conceived by Ahad Ha-Am.

In retrospect, Ahad Ha-Am's impact on his contemporaries and on the Jewish world was considerable, although always controversial. He was neither a popular leader, nor a politician in the strict sense of the word. He did not create a political party, yet he influenced individuals who did. It is difficult to point to any hard and fast program in his teachings. Ahad Ha-Am possessed an extraordinary critical gift and was without a doubt the most austere of all Zionist thinkers. The effect of his criticism of the Love of Zion and Political Zionism was far-reaching despite persistent misunderstandings and misinterpretations. From the early days of the Hibbat Zion down to the postwar days of the Yishuv, his advice was often sought, though often ignored. Always a seeker of the truth and unwilling to be deflected from its path, even when it seemed to contradict and run counter to popular opinion, Ahad Ha-Am remained an example of moral integrity and rectitude.

His theory of Spiritual Zionism was unique. He often confessed that he had no panacea for the salvation of Jews as individuals, but was more concerned with the rescue of Judaism as a spiritual and cultural force. Many of Ahad Ha-Am's contemporaries were annoyed with what they believed was his conviction that the existence of a Jewish majority in Palestine was not an essential element for the creation of a national spiritual center. Some of his followers went so far as to adopt as an alternative to a Jewish state the concept of a Jewish Vatican. This was definitely not what Ahad Ha-Am had intended. In a letter written in 1903 he succinctly states, "Palestine will become our spiritual center only when the Jews are a majority of the population and own most of the land."[357] Such statements, however, were rarely to be found in his published essays, and if his contemporaries misunderstood his position, it was above all his own fault. Ahad Ha-Am's chief concern was the development of a national spiritual center; he took everything else for granted. Thus, he never made it clear how the political and economic infrastructure of the center was to be created.

There were other weaknesses in Ahad Ha-Am's thought. His concept of nation and nationalism were not in the Jewish tradition. His reflections on these subjects had largely been shaped by western philosophical and political theories. As a result of this indoctrination, he was one of the first thinkers who tried to present a philosophy of Judaism not based on religious dogma, or metaphysical postulates, but rather one designed to resolve problems of social behavior. Judaism for Ahad Ha-Am meant a specific national expression of universal values. It included certain basic ethical principles derived from Jewish tradition and practically applied to the life of the nation. In a sense Ahad Ha-Am was attempting to link Jewish tradition and humanitarianism by disengaging the ethical elements of Judaism from religious and theological roots, and using the synthesis to form the spiritual basis of a secular nationalism.

Opponents of Ahad Ha-Am's Theories

This philosophic theorizing provoked the ire of many of the prominent Hebrew writers of the day (e.g., Micah Joseph ben Gorion, Joseph Hayim Brenner, Joseph Klatzkin), who contended that Ahad Ha-Am's conception of national culture was based on a one-sided interpretation of Jewish history. These critics saw Ahad Ha-Am's ideas as similar to a narrow-minded rabbinism such as had prevailed in the darkest hours of the Diaspora epoch. These writers maintained that the original Hebrew culture that had flourished in ancient Israel was not confined to ethical or spiritual values, but rather had included the entire range of human activities. Accordingly, it was of utmost importance that Jewish nationalism allow for absolute freedom of thought and not be bound to a specific conception of spiritual values.

Other critics of Ahad Ha-Am stressed that he had built his ideology on shaky grounds and had described the future of Jewish culture in complete isolation from political and economic factors. Many of these same men reluctantly agreed with Ahad Ha-Am's belief that only a relatively small part of the Diaspora would find shelter in Palestine, but were at the same time convinced that he had not foreseen the large number of Jews who would actually settle in the Holy Land. David Ben-Gurion, Israel's first prime minister commenting on this point has written:

> If events had followed the course that Ahad Ha-Am had predicted, there would have been neither a Jewish state nor a spiritual center. Luckily, Ahad Ha-Am was wrong, and that was not his only mistake. The great philosopher of Hibbat Zion was a shrewd observer, but imagination and vision were not among his virtues. He did not perceive a people's capacity to respond to historic needs which can turn any current reality upside down.[358]

Most of the individuals who considered themselves disciples of Ahad Ha-Am were at times opposed to some of his doctrines. For example, the loose constituency within the Zionist Congresses known as the Democratic Fraction in general accepted Ahad Ha-Am's diagnosis of Jewry's ills, but refused to endorse his views on the character of Judaism and the Jewish people. Still less were they willing to apply his exacting standards for the Zionist development of Palestine. Nevertheless, it is important to note that that many of those individuals who either openly or secretly acknowledged Ahad Ha-Am to be their guiding light played a decisive role in influencing the course of Zionism. From his creation, the B'nai Moshe, emerged some of the leaders of Russian Zionism who were largely responsible for the shift in the policies of the Zionist Organization after the death of Theodor Herzl. Ahad Ha-Am's role as a mentor of Chaim Weizmann and his followers among the English Zionists to some extent influenced the course of events that led to the issuance of the Balfour Declaration. In the United States, Ahad Ha-Am's doctrine of Spiritual Zionism was best represented by Judah Leon Magnes, and Louis Dembitz Brandeis. The former would become a major player in the founding of the Hebrew University in Jerusalem, while the latter, in the aftermath of World War I, would provide leadership for the American Zionist Organization before accepting an appointment as a United States Supreme Court Justice.

Other persons, in one way or another influenced by Ahad Ha-Am's philosophy or swayed by his critical writings reads like a Who's Who of Zionism. They include such prominent figures as Menahem Mendel Ussishkin, one of the founders of the Bilu in 1882, of the Bene Zion Society in 1884, head of the Hibbat Zion in Russia from 1906 until its dissolution in 1919, and chairman of the Jewish National Fund from 1923 until his death; Yechiel Tschlenow, a physician by profession and one of the first Lovers of Zion in Russia;

Shmarya Levin, one of Zionism's most persuasive and elegant orators; Sir Herbert Samuel, the first high commissioner of Palestine under the British Mandate, and his chief secretary, Sir Wyndham Deedes; and Mordecai Kaplan, rabbi, author, philosopher and founder of the Reconstructionist movement of Judaism.

Ultimately, much of Ahad Ha-Am's ideology was swept away by the force of events. The actual rebuilding of Palestine, which he observed during the last years of his life provided the tireless critic with some solace, but he was never able to achieve a total reconciliation with the mainstream of Zionist thought. He was particularly pleased with and greatly admired the spirit that animated the men and women of the Third Aliyah (1919–23) to Palestine, which combined spiritual values with hard physical labor. He lived long enough to witness how the young Jewish pioneers were transforming the land and to take pleasure in the cultural highlight of the era—the founding of the Hebrew University. Equally gratifying to the great critic was the fact that in his declining years he found himself admired and endeared by all, regardless of party and ideology, and widely respected as a sage and teacher. Not only was the street in Tel Aviv on which he lived named in his honor, but during his afternoon rest hours it was closed off to traffic so that he would not be disturbed. In Ahad Ha-Am's sunset years the rancor that he had once aroused was forgotten, and the old agnostic had reached an apotheosis of sorts as a "secular rabbi," with admirers in the Jewish community of Palestine and in the Diaspora.

34

Nathan Birnbaum

The leaders of the Love of Zion, in spite of their many efforts, were never really able to consolidate the loosely knit organization. Financial instability, internal bickering, and differing ideologies plagued the movement. Pinsker and Lilienbaum, secularists in their outlook, were continually confronted with the steadfast opposition of the Orthodox rabbinate. Indeed, only a handful of rabbis expressed any interest at all in the movement and its objectives. Most notable among them were Ruelf of Memel, Zadok Kahn of Paris (a close friend of Pinsker), and Israel Hildesheimer, a leader of German-Jewish Orthodoxy. With the passage of time, however, many rabbis reconsidered their positions and indicated a willingness to drop their opposition if the Hibbat Zion adopted a more religious tone. Adding to the disarray of the Lovers of Zion were the supporters of Ahad Ha-Am and Simon Dubnow. Their theories of Spiritual Zionism and Diaspora nationalism, which emphasized the importance of the Diaspora, diverted attention from the main objective, the restoration of the Jewish people in Palestine. These conflicting ideologies and goals weakened the Hibbat Zion, and seriously hindered the movement from becoming a truly viable political force.

Nevertheless, throughout its existence, many of the movement's most ardent supporters, particularly elements of the Jewish student population of Eastern and Central Europe, continued to harbor hopes and actively work for a restoration in Palestine. A moving spirit among this group was Nathan Birnbaum (1864–1937),[359] better known by his pseudonym, Mathias Acher. He was born in Vienna to Hassidic parents of Galician and Hungarian stock and into a family with rabbinical roots reaching back to the Middle Ages. A man of great talents and a mercurial temperament, Birnbaum tended to veer to the extreme in every cause or enterprise that he espoused. He had protean obsessions and rarely remained constant even to his own ideas. Nevertheless, once having adopted a cause of action, Birnbaum would for the short term concentrate on it with great enthusiasm and

322

passion. Possessed of a sharp tongue, a penetrating mind, and a facile pen, he served all the issues that he made his own with great skill, zeal, and self-abandon.

While still a student he became estranged from Judaism. He did not, however, follow the assimilationist path so common to Jews of this period who had lost their faith. Instead, while enrolled in the University of Vienna he began to propagate the idea among the student body that the Jews were a distinct ethnic people. In 1882 he succeeded, together with a few students of Eastern European background, in founding a Jewish nationalist-oriented fraternity called "Kadimah." The name of the brotherhood, a Hebrew word meaning both "forward" and "eastward" was derived from a suggestion by Peretz Smolenskin. Involvement in the fraternity stimulated Birnbaum's animus toward assimilationists and led to the publication of his first important work, a pamphlet attacking the ideology and motivations of those individuals who sought to escape their ethnicity through assimilation.

Coins the Word Zionism

In 1885 Birnbaum founded and edited the first Jewish nationalist journal in the German language. The journal, which appeared fortnightly was named *Autoemanzipation* in honor of Pinsker's famous pamphlet, and was dedicated to promoting the objectives of the Hibbat Zion movement. In the decade that followed its initial appearance, the journal made its publisher the most distinguished intellectual personality in the Jewish nationalist circles of Germany and Austria. It was during this period that Birnbaum is credited with coining the name *Zionism* (presumably after Jerusalem's Mount Zion) to designate the movement for the restoration of an independent Jewish state in Palestine. He is believed to have first used the term publicly at a meeting in Vienna in the winter of 1892. Some historians, however, point out that the word *Zionism* had already appeared in print even earlier, but without any clear political connotation.

In a pamphlet of 1893 entitled *Die nationale Wiedergeburt de Juedischen Volkes als Mittel zur Loesung des Judenfrage, Ein Appell an die Guten und Edlen aller Nationen* ("The National Rebirth of the Jewish People in its Own Country as a Means to Resolve the Jewish Question: An Appeal to all Noble Minded Men of Good Will"), Birnbaum summed up his Zionist philosophy. The central theme of the essay was a call for the renaissance of the Jewish people in their ancient homeland. Anticipating Theodor Herzl's classic *Der Judenstaat* by two years, Birnbaum outlined a plan for the establishment of a Jewish state. To achieve this goal he recommended the convening of an international Zionist congress that would be charged with the task of designing the institutions and the political movement necessary for creating a viable state. Soon after the publication of Birnbaum's pamphlet a conference of various Zionist organizations met in Paris (1894), but failed to find the unity necessary to launch a mass movement. However, the way had been prepared for the appearance of Theodor Herzl on the Zionist stage. A charismatic leader, Herzl was totally unaware of the work of such men as Birnbaum, Pinsker, Lilienblum, and earlier Jewish nationalists such as Moses Hess. Nevertheless, he was able, in a relatively short span of time, to forge a loyal following and to successfully convoke a Zionist congress, which created the institutional framework (the World Zionist Organization) that Birnbaum and others had failed to achieve.

Unlike most Lovers of Zion, Birnbaum, like Herzl, understood the importance of political action. It was not sufficient, he believed, to establish in Palestine a handful of settlements, whose economic and political existence were at best doubtful. It was more important therefore to gain the confidence of the sovereign power in the Holy Land, the Turkish government, and the backing of those major powers with interests in the Near and Middle East. Birnbaum also differed with many of his colleagues on the nature of anti-Semitism. Although his early advocacy of Zionism would soon be tinted by socialist ideas, he did not believe that anti-Semitism was primarily an economic phenomenon. He felt that a revolution in the social structure would not by itself eradicate the evil. Indeed, it was possible, Birnbaum stressed, that a millennium might elapse before national hatred such as anti-Semitism would fade away. Socialism simply did not have the answers to the hatred of the Jews or to the Jewish Question.

Differences with Theodor Herzl

Birnbaum was an early supporter of Theodor Herzl, and played a prominent role at the First Zionist Congress. Eventually, he became chief secretary of the Central Zionist Office headed by Herzl in Vienna. Having early on earned a reputation as a fiery orator and polemicist he had every reason to expect that he would be included in the leadership of the World Zionist Organization. However, because of certain factors, mostly of his own making, this did not happen. Beset by constant financial difficulties (he was always on the edge of absolute poverty), and saddled with a terrible temper and jealous nature, he tended to irritate friend and foe alike. These flaws in his character led inevitably to a falling out with the World Zionist Organization's charismatic leader, Theodor Herzl. The latter, in his diaries chronicled the gradual change in their relations. Herzl was particularly disturbed by Birnbaum's frequent requests for money and by his attempts to involve him in the petty squabbles of the Austrian and German Zionists. A diary entry of March 1, 1896, clearly reveals Herzl's disgust with Birnbaum's inexcusable behavior:

> . . . Birnbaum is unmistakably jealous of me. What the baser sort of Jews express in vulgar or sneering language, namely that I am out for personal gain is what I catch in the intimations of this cultured, refined person. . . . I regard Birnbaum as envious, vain and dogmatic.[360]

A few days later Herzl would record in his diary that Birnbaum had written him a letter bemoaning his financial straits, and that he had sent him twenty guilders, in spite of his obvious hostility. In addition, in a Zionist meeting Birnbaum had given a socialist speech that contained a barb against a discussion of *Der Judenstaat,* which was on the agenda. It seems, Herzl recorded, that Birnbaum wants to become the socialist leader in Palestine. In closing the diary entry Herzl wryly observed, ". . . we haven't got the country yet, and they already want to tear it apart."[361]

Gradually, Birnbaum began to openly challenge the aims of Political Zionism and the rift between him and Herzl widened. Following the Second Zionist Congress (1898) Nathan Birnbaum attached increasing importance to the national-cultural content of Judaism. He vigorously attacked the "inorganic nature of the Zionist movement," and criticized Herzl's diplomatic efforts, as well as his negation of the Diaspora. Birnbaum also believed that it was a mistake to base the case of the Jewish people on the existence of anti-Semitism. He saw the main task of Jewish nationalism being the improvement of conditions in the Diaspora, but also recognized the national duty of the Jews to rebuild

Palestine because the masses were deeply attached to the Holy Land. Israel, he insisted, must come before Zion and the quest to return to the Promised Land must not entail neglect of the Jewish people. In elaborating this theme, Birnbaum repudiated the idea that Palestine should become a center of emulation for the Diaspora. Instead, he stressed that all of Jewry were equally important for the nation.

Somewhat later in a complete reversal of his former Zionist and socialist positions, Birnbaum became a leading spokesman for a variant form of Diaspora nationalism – a concept that he had previously dismissed as impossible to achieve. He visualized an interterritorial nation composed of all existing Jewish groups that had a cultural life of their own. This doctrine found expression in Birnbaum's demand for the cultural autonomy of the Jews in the Diaspora in a manner similar to the autonomy principle for the various nationalities gaining ground in the Austro-Hungarian empire.

One of the cornerstones of such a policy was language, and in the case of Eastern European Jewry (in Birnbaum's view the most important Jewish group), the mother tongue was Yiddish. Accordingly, the former staunch advocate of Hebrew became a fervent supporter of Yiddish in spite of the fact that most Zionists regarded it as a barbarous jargon. Never one to stop at half measures Birnbaum set about learning Yiddish and working for its recognition as a legitimate language. A quick study, he was soon adept at using Yiddish to propagate his ideas in articles and lectures. In 1908, while on a visit to America, he proposed that a world conference on Yiddish be convened. His appeal found wide support, and a conference was convened that same year in Czernowitz, Rumania. Many prominent journalists, authors, and linguists attended the meeting, which culminated with the passage of a resolution declaring Yiddish to be a (not the) national language of the Jewish people.

From 1908 to 1911 Birnbaum made Czernowitz his home. This exposure to and deepening acquaintance with East European Jewry gradually led to another radical change in his philosophic outlook and life style. The materialist philosophy and secular nationalism of his student days, as well as his short-lived flirtation with Socialism, gave way to a deep-seated conviction that the destiny of the Jewish people could not be separated from religion. The turning point seems to have come in 1908, when Birnbaum underwent a traumatic religious experience and found God. During the years immediately preceding World War I his writings and lectures were almost exclusively devoted to religious matters. Birnbaum returned to the traditions and way of life of his forefathers. He joined the ranks of the Orthodox and became a pious and observant Jew. However, his restless mind was not completely content with the status quo. Birnbaum protested that Orthodox Jewry was not fulfilling its mission as an exemplary people living on the basis of God's word (an idea perhaps borrowed from Reform Judaism). To correct this shortcoming he proposed a program designed to effect changes in the attitude and practices of Orthodox Jews. First and foremost, Birnbaum stressed that all things in the life of the Orthodox, i.e., in their environment, occupations, and customs, that were barring the way to spiritual enrichment had to be altered or discarded. The highest authority of the Jewish nation, he believed, should be invested in an elite body called the "Guardians of the Faith." In addition, Birnbaum suggested the establishment of select orders of Hever Olim (literally, Those who Ascend), whose members would be dedicated to the messianic ideal of a Jewish community based on Torah. The saintly mode of life of the Hever Olim would serve as a model and inspiration for all Jewry. Birnbaum gave expression to these ideas in a series of articles and brochures, most notably in an essay entitled *Et La'asot* ("The Time

Has Come For Action") and in one called *Divrei ha-Olim* ("The Words of Those Who Want to Ascend"). Completing his own metamorphosis from doubter to believer, he also authored a work entitled *Gottes Volk* ("People of God," 1917), in which he repudiated his former pagan life. Two years later he recounted his spiritual development in an auto-biographical work called *Vons Freigeist zum Glaeubigen.*

By 1919 Birnbaum had moved still further to the religious right. He joined the ultra-Orthodox Agudat Israel (Union of Israel). This organization had been founded in 1912 in Kattowitz by German, Polish, and Ukranian Jews seeking to resolve in a religious spirit and framework the problems confronting Jewry. They viewed the Torah, as interpreted by traditional commentators throughout the ages, as the only code of laws binding on the Jew as an individual and on the Jewish people as a whole. The Agudat Israel drew much of its inspiration from the school of neo-Orthodoxy founded by Samson Raphael Hirsch (1808–88) and was violently opposed to Political Zionism. During World War I, German rabbis organized large numbers of Polish Hassidim into an association that subsequently merged with the Agudat Israel. Birnbaum became affiliated with this enlarged organization and subsequently assumed a leading role in it.

In the turbulent period following the Great War—years marked by revolution, po-groms, and epidemics—Nathan Birnbaum turned his attention to the problem of Jewish refugees from Eastern Europe. He played an important part in the effort to regulate and organize the panic-like flight of the Jews from this vast region, and endeavored to enlist world-wide support to ease their suffering.

In the waning years of his life the mercurial Birnbaum continued to expound and expand on his version of Judaism. In a book called *Im Dienste der Verheissung* ("In the Service of the Promise") he called on Orthodox Jewry to create the atmosphere necessary for effecting a religious revolution. Nearness to God, he believed, could only result from a complete inner transformation of the Jewish masses. Birnbaum insisted that such an objective could only be achieved by a sociological restructuring of Jewry in favor of an agrarian life and by colonization of a sparsely populated or uninhabited territory. The Jewish Problem therefore could not be solved by the state creating institutions favored by the Political Zionists. Instead, for Birnbaum the solution was to be found in an "inter-territorial all Israel congregation" under the authoritative spiritual leadership of an elite such as his proposed Guardians of the Faith. Perhaps remembering his Zionist past, Birnbaum was unwilling to completely negate the importance of Eretz Israel in Jewish thought and religion. He called on the Jewish people to work in and for Palestine out of love for the Holy Land, but without political aspirations toward the creation of a state.

With the Nazi rise to power in Germany, Birnbaum, who had been living in Berlin (from 1930 to 1933 he published the journal *Der Aufsteig* in the capital city) was forced to flee. He settled in Holland where he continued his career as an editor and publisher of *Der Ruf* ("The Call") until his death in 1937. At every stage of his erratic intellectual odyssey, Nathan Birnbaum articulated and defended his views with great vigor and skill. Neverthe-less, in spite of his brilliance and qualities of leadership, his capricious nature and insatiable ambition severely limited his effectiveness. Indeed, his turning away from Zionism led many to forget that he had been an early advocate of Jewish nationalism, as well as one of the first supporters of Theodor Herzl. Paradoxically, when Birnbaum's name is recalled by Jews, it is not in the context of his socialistic ideas, his struggle on behalf of the Yiddish language, or even his advocacy of Orthodoxy. Rather, as fate would have it, for his coinage of the word Zionism—a movement that he eventually rejected.

35

Aaron David Gordon:
A Jewish Tolstoy

The first major wave of Jewish immigration to Palestine in modern times, commonly referred to as the First Aliyah (1882–1903), took place under the shadow of Russian pogroms. It was spearheaded by a small group of student pioneers known as the Bilu. In 1882 300 Jewish families and some additional small bands of immigrants arrived in the Holy Land from Russia. Their numbers were further augmented by 450 pioneers from Rumania and a few dozen individuals from Yemen. In an attempt to coordinate this immigration to the Land of Israel, the Hibbat Zion in 1884 convened the Kattowitz Conference. Throughout these early years, in spite of the barriers to immigration placed before them by the Turkish government the percentage of Jews making their way to Palestine steadily increased, as did the number of agricultural settlements in Palestine. A new wave of pogroms in 1890 sent thousands more Russian Jews to seek new homes in Eretz Israel.

Following the infamous Kishinev pogrom of 1903 and the failure of the Russian Revolution of 1905, another Jewish wave of immigration, the so-called Second Aliyah made its way to Palestine. Although not a homogenous group, almost all of these immigrants were young, unmarried, and motivated by Socialist ideology. Many of the newcomers actually felt a sense of guilt for being alienated from the soil in the land of their birth. Their reaction was the direct result of a back-to-the-soil movement which had gained considerable adherents among Russian intellectuals, writers, and activists. From the popular Narodniki (literally, men of the people) to the universally venerated Count Lev Nikolaevich Tolstoy (1828–1910), it had become stylish to extol the peasant, the tiller of the soil, as the repository of all virtue. Amazingly, in spite of the Russian peasants' affinity for pogroms, a goodly number of the Jewish intelligentsia subscribed to this romanticized image of the peasantry. The obsession of these Jews with the soil also reflected an unconscious resentment against the toll that the industrial revolution, which had belatedly come to Eastern Europe, had exacted upon their people's economic status. Indeed, the industrial revolution had caused a radical social transformation of the Jewish communities and had unleashed against them the vicious ant-Semitism peculiar to the Russian urban lower middle class. Thus agriculture alone seemed to offer for some Jews a means to escape the hostility directed against them.

In an effort to correct the lopsided occupational structure of the Jews and to counter the assertion of the Marxists, who constantly cited the absence of a Jewish peasant class as evidence that the Jews were not a nation, some of the young pioneers of the Second Aliyah formed in 1905 a Palestinian Zionist Labor Party called Ha-Poel Ha Tzair (The Young Worker). The name of the party was carefully chosen in order to distinguish it from the "old workers" of the First Aliyah, most of whom had become overseers or independent farmers. Almost from its very inception Ha-Poel Ha Tzair found itself in opposition to the Poalei Zion (Workers of Zion), a Socialist-Zionist party that had originated in Russia and had established a branch in Palestine in 1906. Poalei Zion's goal was to create a Jewish society in the Holy Land based on socialist doctrines. Their advocacy of the concept of the class struggle in particular irritated the supporters of Ha-Poel Ha Tzair. The latter rejected the theory of class struggle on the basis that the Jewish society and its economy in Palestine was still in a precapitalist stage. The two parties also disagreed bitterly over what language Jewish settlers should favor. Ha-Poel Ha Tzair championed Hebrew while the Poalei Zion leaned toward Yiddish.

Central to the philosophy of the Ha-Poel Ha Tzair was the idea of "the conquest of labor," a belief that the Jews alone (they had rejected adherence to the international workers' movement) should carry out all of the economic tasks necessary to create a new society. This concept was in turn inextricably linked with a strong belief in pioneering (*halutziyyut*). The party members dedicated to these principles were willing to support national renewal by undertaking any work, however arduous or dangerous. Strongly influenced by revolutionary workers' movements in Russia, as well as by the Zionist dream of redemption, the pioneers fought for the right to work as farm laborers on the soil of Eretz Israel. Indeed, they regarded their transformation into manual farm workers as part of the national revolution of the Jewish people and a precondition for the establishment of a self-sustaining society. They met, however, with considerable resistance from many Jewish farm owners (mostly men of the First Aliyah) who preferred to use cheap Arab labor to work their land.

If any one individual can be said to have symbolized the spirit of the Second Aliyah, especially as reflected by the objectives and activities of the Ha-Poel Ha Tzair, it was Aaron David Gordon (1856–1922).[362] Although not a predecessor of Theodor Herzl (his arrival in Palestine took place some years after the publication of *Der Judenstaat* and the convocation of the First Zionist Congress), and therefore outside the parameters of this treatise, it is of value to include his story. In a sense Gordon was a transitory figure between the pre-Herzlian forerunners of Zionism, and those who came to the foreground in the first quarter of the twentieth century. A spiritual guide to the pioneers of the Second Aliyah, his legacy influenced many of the leaders of the State of Israel, which emerged from the Middle East maelstrom of 1948.

Aaron David Gordon was born in Troyanov, a small village in the province of Podolia (then Russo-Poland). His grandfather was a noted scholar, and his father managed an estate for his relative, Baron Günzburg, one of the greatest financial magnates in the Russian Empire. Like most Jewish children of his day, Gordon received a traditional education in Bible, Talmud, and Hebrew grammar. On his own, following the path set by numerous others before him who were caught up in the *Haskalah* movement, he picked up a knowledge of western languages and explored secular subject matter. His parents, who had lost four children, were anxious to have their sole surviving child exempted from military duty, but Gordon insisted on presenting himself for examination. Found medically unfit, he married and entered the employ of his wealthy relatives, the Günzburgs. The latter assigned him as an official on a large tract of farming land that they had recently leased. Here A.D. Gordon would remain for twenty-three years (1880–1903). During this period he won the respect of the farm workers, whose interests he tried to protect, often at the expense of his own welfare. Throughout these years of almost complete isolation Gordon read avidly, and was active in educational and cultural work, especially among the farm youth. He also, at this juncture, began to develop unique ideas on the nature of society. The sources contributing to this intellectual growth were many and diverse: they included the religious ethics of Judaism, the romantic optimism of Rousseau, the semi-anarchistic theories of the Russian Social Revolutionaries, the teachings of Count Tolstoy, the writings of Nietzsche, and the Zionism of the Hibbat Zion.

When the Günzburg lease on the farm expired in 1903, the land was sold to a new owner, and Gordon was forced to seek new employment. His relatives offered suggestions and business opportunities, and there was even talk of emigration to the United States. Gordon, after months of indecision (he was troubled by the duty he owed his wife and children), decided to break completely with the past and to settle in Palestine. Thus, in 1904, over the objections of his parents and his wife's family, he set out alone for the Holy Land (five years would elapse before his wife and a daughter would be able to join him).

Arriving in Palestine at age forty-eight, the sickly former white collar worker was determined to devote his remaining years to physical agricultural labor. After some initial setbacks, Gordon found day labor in the vineyards and orange groves of Petah-Tikva and Rishon le-Zion and after 1912 in various villages of the Galilee. Like many others before him, he suffered all the tribulations encountered by the early Jewish pioneers: malaria, unemployment, hunger, and insecurity.

A.D. Gordon's sincere hope that his family would share his dreams was shattered by the death of his wife of malaria shortly after her arrival in Palestine. The tragedy was compounded by the demise of his only surviving son in postwar Russia. In spite of these personal losses, Gordon never wavered in his resolve to achieve redemption through physical labor on the soil of Eretz Israel. A contemporary, attempting to explain Gordon's zeal during these early years of exhausting drudgery on the land, recalled that there were many individuals of the Second Aliyah that worked just as hard and even exceeded him in their labors. However, there was a difference in motivation. For Gordon labor was a kind of worship, a prayer, and a key to life itself, whereas for most of his fellow laborers the desire to excel was a way of proving that Jews as well as Arabs knew how to work.

Within a relatively short span of years Gordon's figure, with his great Tolstoyan beard, and his unique philosophy of labor became known throughout Palestine. He was recognized as the spiritual father of the halutzim (pioneers). The latter came from all parts of Eretz Israel to visit Gordon at his humble lodgings, to talk to him about their hopes and frustrations, and to confirm their faith in the value of the enterprise they had embarked on. From 1909 Gordon made a point of devoting his few spare hours, usually at the expense of sleep, to writing essays on Labor-Zionism and Jewish destiny, a theme that became popularly known as "the religion of labor." The last years of his life were spent at the *kevutzah* (cooperative settlement) of Deganyah, near the Jordan River. In 1921 Gordon fell ill. The malady was diagnosed as cancer, and he was sent to Vienna for treatment. Realizing that the disease was terminal, he returned to Deganyah, where he died early in 1922.

A.D. Gordon's legacy was his idealization of labor and its application to Zionism. He considered tilling the soil of Eretz Israel as the ultimate ethical value and the only way to achieve redemption. All schemes that diverted the Jews from this objective, Gordon believed, should be avoided. He felt strongly that the Jewish pioneers were engaged in a creative endeavor unique in the history of mankind. It was nothing less than an attempt to rehabilitate a people that had been uprooted from their homeland almost 2,000 years earlier and scattered to the four corners of the earth. This objective, Gordon emphasized, could only be achieved through intensive labor in Eretz Israel, for here was the original mainspring of Jewish life and the vital redemptive force of our cause.

The Religion of Labor

Gordon's philosophy of "the religion of labor" became the cornerstone of the Zionist non-Marxist labor movement in Palestine. It was a doctrine replete with popular agrarianism, nationalism, socialism, and mysticism. The heart of this creed, the idealization of labor, assumed an almost transcendental value. Gordon himself literally worshipped on its altar. Central to his philosophy was the idea that although culture was the high point of human achievement, the distance that separated the cultured individual from nature was detrimental to human life. Man therefore must return to nature (the source of his very existence) and give expression to his attachment by physical labor, particularly in the form of tilling the soil. The land, however, must not become the property of individuals, but belong instead to the community as a whole. In an essay entitled *Logic for the Future* Gordon gave an eloquent presentation of this theme and in particular of his belief in the redemptive powers inherent in nature.

When a people are torn away from agricultural work, Gordon stressed, they become deracinated and ultimately lose their homeland. This, he believed, is what had happened to the Jewish people. They had become completely separated from nature and forced into a marginal existence, notably in trade and commerce. In the centuries of exile following the loss of their homeland the Jews had become a distorted, emasculated, unnatural people with a value system totally out of focus. They were missing the principal ingredient for national life – the habit of labor, the kind of labor that binds a people to its soil and to its natural culture. To overcome this rift caused by historical circumstances, Gordon called for a new spirit in the struggle for a national renaissance, a spirit created and nourished in Palestine, and given meaning and direction by Jewish "zealots of labor."

A Jewish national renaissance, Gordon believed, demanded more than a migration of Jews to Palestine. It also called for a radical change in the social structure of Jewry. If immigration took place without change, it would merely result in a transference of the evils of the exile to Eretz Israel. In an article called *Some Observations*, Gordon insisted that there was only one road that would lead to a national renaissance that would be natural and beneficial, namely "the way of labor." A people, he believed could only acquire its land by its own effort, and by unfolding and revealing its inner self. However, for Gordon, a parasitical people was not a living people. Thus the Jewish immigrants coming to Palestine must recreate themselves through labor and a life close to the land. Should they fail to achieve rehabilitation, it would be up to the next generation or the one thereafter to complete the process.

In Gordon's philosophic musings, as expressed in his numerous essays and articles, man and nature, or the cosmos as a whole, are an essential unity. Man is molded by the cosmos through his intuitive perception of the world. He feels instinctively that he is an organic part of creation, and that this is the heart of religious sentiment. God cannot be approached through the intellect, but man can reach God in an immediate living relationship.

Gordon's fellow worshipers of the virtues of labor found it difficult to accept his religious notions. For most of them religion had become irrelevant. The apostle of labor attempted to meet their objections by making a distinction between form and content in religion. He conceded that as far as form was concerned religion had lost much of its vitality. The content of religion, on the other hand, originated in the religious individual and was an expression of his sense of cosmic unity and purpose. Gordon felt that although present religious thinking might be dead, God himself could never die. Although a hidden mystery, God is encountered in all that a person experiences. Accordingly, religion will not die as long as men live, think, and feel. True religion, however, is of the future. Through the medium of labor man could discover religion and regain a sense of cosmic unity and holiness.

Although Gordon concentrated much of his thought on the individual, he did not neglect the social matrix within which personal fulfillment must occur. Individual and social regeneration, he held, are independent of each other. Genuine social renewal could only be achieved by an organically inter-related community, i.e., a people or a nation. Indeed, the nation is the force that creates the spirit of man and is the link that unites the life of the individual to the life of mankind and to the world at large.

A nation is therefore a natural community. It exemplifies a living cosmic relationship, the result of the interaction between man and nature and its particular expression in one place, by which the unique soul and history of the group is formed. No matter what may happen to a nation once it is created, nothing can change the fact of its existence. Thus, Gordon noted, in the case of the Jews in which the nation was torn from its roots and exiled, both its corporate soul and the souls of its individuals are stunted until they are returned to their original habitat. Any endeavor to bypass the specific historic nation in which one is born to achieve the status of a citizen of the world is an illusory undertaking. In the place of such cosmopolitanism Gordon substituted the idea of *Am Adam* (literally man-nation, or people embodying humanity) as the key to the spirit of the Jewish nation. To realize this principle was the task of the Zionist movement. In terminology suggestive of some of the tenets of the Reform movement in Judaism, Gordon maintained that the Jews had to become a nation in the highest meaning of the word, a moral force and a spiritual leader among the peoples of the world, becoming a "light onto the nations," providing a model and a challenge for others to emulate. As to why the Jews should assume such a role, Gordon's answer was direct and basic to his philosophic outlook. Because the Jews were the first to state that man was created in the image of God, they must now go further and proclaim that the nation must be created in the image of God. Furthermore, because of the torments suffered by the Jews through the long centuries, they had bought the right to be the first in this mode of creation.[363]

The remarkable resemblance of much of A.D. Gordon's thought and life to that of Count Tolstoy has been pointed out by many writers. Both men were mystics and romantics, as well as believers in nature and the virtues of physical labor (especially agrarian labor). Even more striking is the similarity of the major event in the lives of these two men. Gordon abandoned his family, in middle age, in order to get closer to nature in Palestine. The Russian aristocrat, Count Tolstoy, in late life fled to his estate at Yasnaya Polyana to work the soil and to write tracts extolling the redemptive powers of physical labor. Both men also idealized the natural man and the belief that man is inherently good, but corrupted by society (a concept originally made popular by Rousseau). The acceptance of the this theory inevitably led Tolstoy and Gordon to reject urban society because of its alienation from nature. This doctrine also fitted neatly into the neoromantic atmosphere that pervaded late nineteenth-century Europe.

In Gordon's case his thought also encompassed the preceding century's criticism of the ghetto system as detrimental to the Jewish spirit and largely responsible for the Jews' stunted economy. Let the Jews, the doyens of the European Age of Enlightenment declared, cease earning their livelihoods by their wits and return to the soil in order to acquire a normal economic profile. Gordon agreed with this thesis; however, unlike Tolstoy his advocacy did not dissolve into a mere literary protest or an attempt to recreate a primeval world of innocence as envisaged by Rousseau. Instead, Gordon's ideology became the very basis for a practical program of social change, with the reformer himself as the first practitioner of the new creed, exhorting others to follow in his footsteps. Thus while confining his literary efforts to the hours of nighttime, Gordon used his daylight hours as the proving ground for his ideology by laboring in the fields alongside the pioneers of the Second Aliyah.

In spite of his ideology, activities, and associations, Gordon never saw himself as a doctrinaire socialist. He scorned Marxism and considered it to be nothing less than an appeal to the herd instinct in man. It aimed solely, he believed, at the reorganization of the social order, and cared nothing for the renewal of the human spirit. Marxism sought to change man by changing regimes instead of changing regimes by changing man. Where individual commitment and involvement did not exist there could be no community of interests. For these reasons Gordon did not favor linking the Jewish labor movement in Palestine with the struggle of international Socialism. Jewish labor, he felt, faced tasks that no other labor movement in the world had ever faced, and so had to find its own way of combining social goals with national aspirations. Because the problems faced by Jewish labor in Palestine were so different from those of Europe's industrial working class, it was essential that the Jews not become sidetracked by extraneous issues. This principle led Gordon to strenuously oppose such political parties as the Poalei Zion and the Ahdut ha-Avodah, both of whom had ties with international Socialism. It was to combat these parties that Gordon's followers organized the Ha-Poel Ha Tzair.

Although A.D. Gordon held no official post in either the Jewish Labor Movement, or the Zionist movement, he nevertheless exercised a profound influence on both entities. On many occasions his views ran contrary to the institutions. He strongly opposed, for example, the immigration to Palestine of Jews whose only motive was to escape persecutions and preferred that they seek asylum elsewhere. His rationale for this view was that he ardently desired that Palestine be built by individuals who were motivated to devote themselves body and soul to the "religion of labor." They must, Gordon insisted, do all work with their own hands and not fall back upon Arab labor. Furthermore, it did not matter whether the work involved skilled, or unskilled labor.

Gordon expected that the number of individuals dedicated to his philosophy of the "religion of labor" and choosing to come to Palestine would at first be very small. He seemed oblivious to the fact that even if many Jews could be inspired by the example of a handful of zealots to abjure forever their parasitic lives in the Diaspora, his requirements were so stringent that it is doubtful that most individuals could meet his standards for admittance into Palestine.

Gordon repudiated almost every outside agency or institution that might help the Palestinian Jewish community grow (including even funds raised in the Diaspora to ease the worker's lot in the Holy Land). This attitude, coupled with a strong pacifist outlook, led Gordon to assume strange positions in relation to Palestinian politics. His horror of all bloodshed and of the use of force in general prompted him to argue vociferously against Jewish participation as a quasi-ally in the military effort of either the Allied Powers or the Central Powers in World War I. He also objected to the formation of the Jewish Legion, and later even to the acquisition through diplomatic means of a legal title to build a Jewish national home in Palestine (the Balfour Declaration). Always steadfast in his pacificism, Gordon refused to participate in the founding of the Palestinian Jewish defense organization, Hashomer. Nevertheless, in spite of his abhorrence of politics he occasionally made some exceptions. He participated in the Eleventh Zionist Congress in 1913 and the Ha-Poel Ha Tzair conference of 1920 held in Prague.

Gordon's activities in Palestine fully exemplified the idea of self-fulfillment (Hag'shama Atzmit) which he so ardently advocated in his writings and personal life. Labor-Zionist parties such as the Ha-Poel Ha Tzair in Palestine and the Tzeire Zion (Young Men of Zion) in the Diaspora considered Gordon to be their mentor and reflected his ideology to a high degree. Gordon's considerable influence also extended to other groups within the Palestinian labor movement whose social orientation was directly opposed to many of his key conceptions. These groups frequently adopted Gordonian suggestions in their practical work while rejecting his philosophy.

Prior to Gordon's arrival in Palestine respect for work and worker had been a hallmark of the First Aliyah. However, physical labor had been equated with the pastoral ideal of a return to the Land of Israel, and had been fused with the biblical promise of life under one's own vine or fig tree. Only with the Second Aliyah did the concept of labor as social redemption, Gordon's basic premise, become an imperative.

Similarly, Gordon's emphasis on the regenerative effect of physical agricultural labor and his ethical and cultural vision of Jewish nationhood were significant factors in stimulating the growth of cooperative settlements in Palestine. The first such collective or *kevutzah* was Deganyah (Gordon's last home) established in 1909. In Deganyah, as in the *kevutzot* that were later formed and based on its model, all property was jointly owned by the members of the settlement, who came together voluntarily for the purpose of establishing a truly viable democratic society. Hired labor was to be strictly avoided, as the members of the *kevutzah* themselves were obligated to perform all work, as well as share all tasks. Meals were served in a community dining room. The children of the collective were raised in a common nursery and spent only a few hours a day with their parents. Another type of collective village, the kibbutz was developed, which early on distinguished itself from the *kevutzah* by incorporating industry as well as agriculture into its economy. The kibbutz, which originated during the Third Aliyah (1919–23) also permitted wage labor and removed restrictions on the size of the community.

A.D. Gordon's championship of a pioneering movement for Jewish youth also bore fruit in Palestine and the Diaspora. Recognition of his contribution in this area came in 1925, three years after his death, with the founding in Poland of the pioneer scouting movement, Gordonia. This movement grew rapidly and gradually spread to other countries (in 1928 it held a world conference in Danzig). Ideologically, Gordonia was identified with the Ha-Poel Ha Tzair in Palestine.

The consequences of Gordon's work and theories were far-reaching. His call for transferring the focus of the Zionist movement and the Jewish people from the Diaspora to Eretz Israel became a reality in the 1930s. During these years the leadership of the Zionist movement shifted from the Diaspora middle class to the Labor movement in Palestine. For the skeptics the very idea that large numbers of Jews could and would gather in Palestine, under the conditions specified in A.D. Gordon's writings, seemed impossible. Nevertheless, the skeptics and critics of Gordon were wrong, as his life and work in the long run provided inspiration to a new generation of Labor-Zionists destined to become the most effective force in Palestine in the trying period before the establishment of the State of Israel.

IX

THE SOCIALISTS

36

The Revolutionaries

The rise of Jewish nationalism was also accompanied, particularly in the Russian Empire, by a dramatic turning of many Jews toward a competing ideology, Socialism. The earliest roots of this development can be traced back directly to the tumultuous reign of Czar Alexander II (1855–81). The spread of discontent triggered by Russia's defeat in the Crimean War had encouraged Alexander, upon his assumption of the throne, to inaugurate a comprehensive program of reform. While his zeal lasted he emancipated some 40 million serfs, created provincial and district assemblies, overhauled the judicial system, stimulated public education, relaxed censorship of the press, permitted Russians to travel abroad more freely, and treated Jews and other minorities with greater leniency than any of his predecessors. But the chorus of criticism from the advocates of autocracy, orthodoxy, and nationalism that greeted his endeavors soon discouraged the reform-minded czar.

Following the outbreak and suppression of the Polish Insurrection of 1863, Alexander II realized that in tampering with the status quo he had opened the door to anarchy; and accordingly, hearkening to his reactionary advisers he turned his back on any further reforms. Thenceforth, the law courts, the journals, and the schools found their privileges steadily curtailed; vigilant police spies circulated once more among all ranks of society; and teachers, writers, and others who had hailed the czar's reforms now felt the chill of imperial disfavor.

Placed on the defensive, the reformers tried to counter the administration's change of heart, but they lacked any constitutional means of action and their petitions to the czar brought no response. Desperate, they decided to take their case directly to the Russian masses, whose dense ignorance and superstition they considered to be the chief obstacle to progress. Hundreds of ardent young Russian intellectuals dedicated themselves to the task of instructing the peasantry, hoping by daily contact and personal example to inculcate a gospel of enlightenment. Early on a split developed in this agrarian populist (Narodnik) movement. The more moderate members remained committed to the belief that improvements would have to be introduced slowly through education of the masses. However, the more radical element, losing patience, favored more desperate measures and embraced violent modes of revolutionary activity. The latter group soon spawned terrorist organizations such as the Narodnaya Volya (People's Will), who were convinced that only the assassination of the czar would bring about the desired reforms. Indeed, they would make a half dozen attempts upon the life of Alexander II before they succeeded in killing him on March 1, 1881.

Few Jews were represented in the Russian revolutionary movement of the 1860s and early 1870s. In the Pale of Settlement (the provinces of czarist Russia where Jews were permitted permanent residence) there had always been a tradition of abstinence from political affairs and of obedience to the establishment. The leaders of the *Haskalah* (the Jewish Enlightenment) movement on the other hand were far too absorbed in the struggle against cultural and religious obscurantism to give serious attention to the problems of the Jewish working masses. Yet it was the *Haskalah* that was largely responsible for the rise of Jewish socialist activity, for the enlighteners (*maskilim*) had secularized the outlook of thousands of their fellow Jews. They had also supported the state sponsored schools for Jews (a key element of the czarist government's policy of Russification).

At first, socialist activity among the Jews was limited to young intellectuals who became involved in the Russian agrarian populist movement. The most active of these would-be *narodniki* were enrolled as students in the government-supported rabbinical seminary of Vilna (better known as the Teachers' Seminary), which nurtured a spirit of hostility to traditional society. Their sympathies were aroused less by the disabilities and suffering of their Jewish brethren than by the romantic desire to ally themselves with those elements in the empire dedicated to relieving the misery of the Russian masses.

Aaron Samuel Liebermann

Representative of the latter group of individuals was Aaron Samuel Liebermann (1845–80)[364] who, after his death would be recognized as "the father of Jewish Socialism." Born in the small town of Lunna, Lithuania, Aaron was the son of Eliezer Dov Liebermann, a Hebrew scholar and *maskil*. While Aaron was still a youngster the family moved several times and eventually settled in Suwalki. In 1867 he graduated from the Vilna Teachers' Seminary. While at that institution he came under the spell of the Russian agrarian populist movement, but did not participate actively. Following graduation he returned to Suwalki where he received an appointment as secretary of the community. Three years later, seeking new challenges, he enrolled as an occasional student in the Technological Institute of St. Petersburg. Here he authored a geography of Palestine, which was somehow destroyed before it could be published. Distressed by the incident, Liebermann left for Vilna where he found employment as a draftsman and later with an insurance company. The return to the Lithuanian capital proved to be a transitional phase in his life. From 1872 onward Liebermann dedicated himself to radical courses. He joined a local revolutionary group, and became one of its most active members. From among the ranks of this group would come many of the future prominent figures of the Narodnaya Volya (the Russian terrorist party dedicated to eliminating the czar). Among Liebermann's associates in this radical circle were Lippe Ben-Zion

Novakhovich, who would become his disciple and closest friend; Joseph Elijah Tri-wosch, a future Hebrew writer; Vladimir Jochelson, who would later achieve fame as an ethnologist; Anna Epstein, a medical student at St. Petersburg University who had associated with such leading Russian revolutionaries as Prince Peter Kropotkin and Nicholas Tchaikovsky; and the fiery radical student leader Aaron Zundelevitch. Besides propagandizing their cause among the student bodies of the state supported Jewish schools and some of Lithuania's outstanding yeshivot, the Vilna circle also facilitated the escape abroad of individuals who were hunted by the police and arranged for the smuggling of forbidden literature into the Russian Empire from the West.

Some members of the group, such as Zundelevitch, nurtured a spirit of hostility to traditional Jewish society. Although receiving a rabbinical education, he was strongly inclined toward assimilation. Zundelevitch scorned the idea of a separate Jewish identi-fication within the Russian radical movement and considered nationalism of any kind a vestige of outmoded capitalism. Liebermann, on the other hand, despite his *maskil* outlook and his involvement with the Russian *narodniki* — who had an exclusive passion for the peasantry — had already begun to give thought to the need for Jewish autonomy within the revolutionary movement. For initiating his socialist ideas among the Jews he favored the use of Hebrew over Yiddish. He was firmly convinced that Hebrew would prove more appealing to the yeshivah students and the *maskilim,* and that written propaganda in that language would have a better chance of getting past the government censors.

Liebermann's personal campaign and that of the Vilna circle to win over the yeshivah students met with little success. Some years later, while engaged in a conversation with Peretz Smolenskin, editor of the Hebrew monthly *Ha-Shahar* ("The Dawn"), he remi-nisced about this failure. He felt that the yeshivot of Volozhin, Mir, and the others had consumed the best of the Jewish youth. The young people were buried alive in these deserts without dew or sunshine. Study of the Torah in these academies, Liebermann believed, congested the heart and the mind and withered every blossom. What was needed instead was institutions to educate people with uplifted heads who would have the spirit and courage to oppose despotic government. Liebermann then informed Smolenskin that he had once tried to liberate these unfortunate yesivah students from their dark institu-tions. He had published a proclamation in Hebrew entitled *To The Young Men of Israel* and had copies distributed among the students of the Volozhin yeshivah, and believed that its message would stir them, touch their hearts, and point them in the right direction. Instead, weeks and then months passed without a response from the student body.

In 1875 the Russian police discovered the existence of the secret Vilna circle, swooped down on the Teachers' Seminary, made a search of the premises and of some of the homes of the students, and effected several arrests. Among the apprehended were Zundelvitch, who during his radical career was destined to spend twenty-six years in various prisons, and Jochelson, who was exiled to northern Siberia where he whiled away his time studying the life of the region's aborigines. Liebermann and a few others managed to escape the dragnet and fled abroad. Liebermann made his way to Berlin and then to London, where he found work as a typesetter for the socialist periodical *Vpred* ("For-ward"). The editors of the publication, Peter Larov and Valerian N. Smirnov, familiar with Liebermann's views, encouraged him to write a series of articles for *Vpred* on the harsh conditions under which Jewish workers labored in Russia.

Heartened by the milieu in which he found himself, Liebermann in 1876 drew up regulations for the establishment of a socialist organization to serve the Jews of Russia. In the spring of that same year he founded in London the Aggudat ha-Sozyalistim ha-Ivrim (Hebrew Socialist League). It was the first organization of its kind in England. The members of the League, chiefly workers and students, discussed social problems, produced political manifestoes, and in general urged workers to unite in a common cause for their own betterment.

Lippe Ben-Zion Novakhovich

At the beginning of 1877 Liebermann moved to Vienna and, with the assistance of his disciple Lippe Ben-Zion Novakhovich (1856–1932),[365] later known by the alias Morris Vinchevsky, founded a monthly paper called *Ha-Emet* ("The Truth"). The journal created considerable excitement, as it was the first Jewish socialist publication to appear in the Hebrew language. The prospectus for *Ha-Emet* attacked the existing Hebrew press, which at the time was, according to Liebermann, "treating only religious and national questions and other nonsense." Smirnov, one of the editors of the *Vpred* and a non-Jew criticized *Ha-Emet* as a symptom of Jewish nationalist separation, thus casting doubts on its creator's socialist credentials. This was a common theme among doctrinaire Russian socialists. Jewish intellectuals attracted by Socialism often, like Liebermann, found themselves in a dilemma. Their desire to put an end to a corrupt Russian regime and to participate in building a new classless society clashed with the idea of many of their fellow Jews who advocated the restoration of the Jewish nation. Although they believed the latter to be embarked on a futile quest, some were reluctant to sever all ties with the Jewish community. However, the hard core of Jewish socialists considered all nationalism as outmoded vestiges of capitalism. They insisted that capitalism had created anti-Semitism and only Socialism could effectively eradicate this evil. The majority of these socialists thus remained unconcerned about the question of Jewish survival as a people, and resented any energies expanded on activities other than the class struggle and the inevitable proletarian revolution. Others among the various socialist factions looked forward to the day when the Jews as a distinct group would vanish. Still others like Liebermann viewed the Jewish worker as a distinct group within the Socialist movement with an agenda of its own. All the factions rejected parties or movements not based upon the class struggle theories advanced by Karl Marx and Friedrich Engels. Zionism, as a Jewish nationalist movement, would fall within this category. Indeed, for the socialists, the Zionist objectives and philosophy represented an anathema, a deviation from the true path, and a mirage compounded of religious romanticism and chauvinism. It threatened the best interests of the Jewish working class, which according to socialist doctrine had to be international rather than national in character.

Liebermann, angered by Smirnov's attack on his socialist credentials, responded in kind. He accused Smirnov of knowingly distorting his international bona fides, and emphasized that he was not ashamed of his Jewish origin. He loved that segment of humanity that national and religious principles designated as Jews. However, Liebermann was careful to point out in his reply to the Russian editor that he did not love all Jews, but only the suffering masses, and those fit to join us (i.e., the socialist cause). Otherwise he would not be worthy of the name socialist.

The lifespan of Liebermann's journal *Ha-Emet* was exceedingly short. Only three issues appeared. Difficulties in obtaining financing and in getting the monthly into Russia (the last issue was actually seized by the Russian censors) were the chief reasons for its failure. Left without a periodical of his own, Liebermann wrote articles for the newspapers published by Peretz Smolenskin. Subsequently, both he and Novakhovitch became regular contributors to the Hebrew journal *Ha'Kol* ("The Voice") put out by a young socialist named Michael Radkinson. Gradually, both men realized the futility of writing socialist and revolutionary articles in Hebrew. They had hoped to arouse the masses, but there were no Hebrew speaking masses; this meant that one had to choose to write for the Russian masses in their language or for the Jewish masses in their language, Yiddish. Liebermann and Novakhovitch decided in favor of the latter course and founded a Yiddish supplement to *Ha'Kol*. It was the first regular vehicle for socialist ideas published in Yiddish.

In 1888 Liebermann was arrested, tried, and imprisoned by the Austrian authorities for his revolutionary activities. Upon his release he was expelled to Germany, where he was immediately detained and ordered to leave the country. He made his way to London, then a major place of refuge for Russian revolutionaries. Novakhovich, following Liebermann's arrest by the Austrians, had fled to Koenigsberg where he found employment as a bank clerk. During his sojourn in this city he managed to publish a Hebrew socialist journal entitled *Asefat Hakhamim* ("Assembly of the Wise") – a continuation of sorts of the earlier *Ha-Emet*. However, the periodical was doomed by the passage of Bismarck's antisocialist legislation and by the sudden arrest of Novakhovich by the Prussian police. He was charged among other things with carrying on a correspondence with a known revolutionary, Aaron Samuel Liebermann. On the verge of being extradited to Russia, the Jewish banker for whom Novakhovitch had worked helped him to escape to Denmark. From there he made his way to Paris and eventually to London, where his old collaboration with Liebermann was resumed.

The two young radicals were now convinced that socialist agitation of the masses required the extensive use of the Yiddish jargon, and they made plans for a series of pamphlets in that language. At the same time, in conjunction with some exiled German Social Democrats, they organized in London the Jewish Workers' Benefit and Educational Society (Verein). The founders confronted some initial difficulties in their efforts to extricate the Verein from the pervasive German atmosphere that set the tone of all radical immigrant activity in the English capital. Novakhovich, for example, discovered that the Russian Yiddish-speaking members had trouble understanding the highly Germanized Yiddish that he had acquired while residing in Koenigsberg. However, as an offspring of a Lithuanian *shtetl*, authentic Yiddish speech soon returned to his lips, ending the temporary linguistic crisis.

The initial success of the Jewish Workers' Benefit and Educational Society was tempered by a tragedy that would eventually result in the organization's disintegration. Liebermann and other socialist exiles frequented a restaurant run by a cousin of Novakhovich named Rachel Sarasohn. She was a young *agunah*, i.e., a woman whose husband had disappeared but had not yet been proven dead and who, according to Jewish law, was not eligible to remarry. Liebermann, a thirty-six year old bachelor, fell deeply in love with the beautiful Rachel. She did not reject his affections, but remained hesitant in considering a second marriage. In the fall of 1880 a letter arrived from Rachel's missing husband indicating that he was living in Syracuse, New York, and wanted his wife to join him. A steamship ticket for passage to America was enclosed with the letter. Rachel decided to rejoin her husband, and Liebermann followed her all the way to Syracuse. When Rachel refused to leave her husband, Liebermann committed suicide by shooting himself.

Stunned by his friend's death, Novakhovich withdrew from active political life. For the next four years he earned his livelihood as a clerk for the Seligman Bank. During this period the Jewish Workers' Benefit and Educational Society, deprived of the guidance of its founders fell apart. The Russian pogroms of the eighties, which resulted in a wave of Jewish immigration to England as well as the United States, reawakened Novakhovich's social consciousness, and he resumed his calling as a socialist agitator among the Yiddish speaking workers of London.

A socialist poet, polemicist, educator, and editor, Novakhovich's entire life was dedicated to bringing about change, especially for Jewish workers in Russia and elsewhere. Born in Lithuania in 1855 he came from a family that had a tradition of community activity. His paternal grandfather had been killed fighting in the Polish uprising of 1831, and his widowed grandmother had devoted her remaining years to community work for the poor. Novakhovich's father was of a similar bent of mind. Although superficially an opponent of Hassidism, he admired their spirit of brotherhood and their devotion in principle to the notion of poverty as an outward form of spiritual purity. His unorthodox attitudes were absorbed by his son Lippe.

In 1884, Lippe, in conjunction with William Morris, the author of the utopian novel *News From Nowhere,* and other prominent socialists helped found the British Social Democratic Federation. During this same time frame, Novakhovich gathered together a group of like-minded individuals and began publication of a Yiddish weekly worker's newspaper entitled *Das Poilische Yidl* ("The Polish Jew"). This transition from Hebrew to Yiddish as the language of socialist propaganda reflected the new thinking that Novakhovich and Liebermann had mulled over, prior to Liebermann's death, on how best to win over the Jewish working masses. Incredibly, the newspaper's title offended the Anglo-Jewish establishment as well as many immigrant workers and ignited a barrage of criticism. In a move to curtail further faultfinding, Novakhovich condescended to changing the masthead's title to the more conventional Judeo-German *Die Zukunft* ("The Future").

Encouraged by the modest success of his paper, Novakhovich concentrated on a project to write a series of socialist pamphlets in Yiddish. The first to appear in print was *Yehi Or* ("Let There Be Light"). Written in the form of a dialogue between two workers, the pamphlet portrayed socialist ideas and programs in simple everyday terms in the conversational Yiddish of the immigrant masses. Novakhovich named the two workers of his pamphlet "Morris" and "Hyman" and to complete his assumption of a working class persona for literary purposes, he fictitiously designated the former as the author of the work, which was signed "Morris Vinchevsky." This was the first use of the nom de plume by which he was to become exclusively identified in both England and America.

Despite its relative success, *Die Zukunft* came to an abrupt end a year after its initial appearance. Novakhovich was compelled to cease publication as a result of a bitter dispute with the paper's printer and landlord, who insisted on accepting advertisements that the editor and his collaborators considered improper for a socialist newspaper.

In 1885 the Yiddish-speaking radical element in London began publication of a monthly called *Der Arbeiter's Freint* ("The Worker's Friend"), and Novakhovich was asked to be its editor. Fearing that the editorship of a paper openly sponsored by anarchists as well as socialists might threaten his position at the Seligman Bank, he declined the offer. Nevertheless, he recommended Philip Krantz for the job and generously contributed poems, essays, and articles to *Der Arbeiter's Freint* (his contributions included the popular "London Silhouettes").

When a falling out between the anarchists and the socialists on *Der Arbeiter's Freint* turned into a bitter struggle for control of the monthly, Novakhovich and other nonpartisan contributors reluctantly withdrew their support and decided to found a paper of their own (spring of 1891) to be known as *Die Frei Velt* ("The Free World"). By this time Novakhovich (alias Vinchevsky), now in his late thirties and married, had become a kind of elder statesman to the Jewish workers of London. His poems, feuilletons, and articles were celebrated among them, and his lectures drew large audiences. In the summer of 1893 he was sent by the workers as a delegate from London to the Third Congress of the Second International in Zurich.

A year later Novakhovich resumed his pamphlet series and produced a sequel to his *Yehi Or* entitled *Der Alef-Beys fun Trade Unionism* ("The ABC of Trade-Unionism"). It proved to be a greater success than its predecessor, and the grateful Jewish workers of London took to referring to Vinchevsky, their teacher, as *Der Zeyde* ("The Grandfather"). The title, honoring his contributions to the cause of labor, would remain with him for the remainder of his life.

In 1894, following the example of many of his compatriots, Novakhovich emigrated to the United States. He continued to avoid involvement in *Der Arbeiter's Freint* controversy, which had crossed the ocean along with its main participants. However, he continued writing and his articles appeared in various Jewish journals (notably in the *Morning Freiheit*). He also played a prominent role in the founding of the *Jewish Daily Forward*.

In May of 1895 Novakhovich moved to Boston, where he edited a new socialist weekly journal called *Der Emmes* ("The Truth"), a name rich with connotations for him because it was the Yiddish form of the journal begun by his mentor and friend Aaron Samuel Liebermann nearly two decades earlier.

In the immediate aftermath of World War I, Novakhovich was appointed to the Committee des delegations juives, which represented Jewish interests at the Versailles Conference. In the years that followed his political outlook changed. Novakhovich broke with his socialist friends and turned more to the Soviet Union as the possessor of the key to resolving both the workers' difficulties and the Jewish Problem. During 1924–25 he visited the Communist state and eulogized its accomplishments. Two years later his health failed. Although paralyzed and broken in body and spirit, Novakhovich clung to life for several more years. His heart finally gave out in 1932, and he was buried in the cemetery of the Workmen's Circle in New York. Two years later the remains of Aaron Liebermann were disinterred and placed alongside those of Novakhovich, his old comrade in arms.

Jewish socialism and the labor movement are deeply indebted to the pioneering work of Liebermann and Novakhovich. The very concept that Jewish workers had their own special agenda as well as sharing a common interest with other working people was a revolutionary idea. It would stimulate elements that had arisen phoenix-like in the Pale of Settlement to press for an organization that would unite all Jewish workers in a struggle to achieve their rightful place in society. By a strange twist of fate, the very same year that witnessed Theodor Herzl's convening of the First Zionist Congress (1897), representatives from Jewish socialist intellectual circles, clandestine political clubs, workers associations and unions met secretly in Vilna and founded the Bund. This organization, dedicated to Social Democracy, was destined to become the major rival of Zionism in the Jewish world. Both Liebermann and Novakhovich, ensconced in their socialist heaven, must have looked down and smiled at this development.

37

The Jewish Bund

The first stirrings of the Jewish labor movement in Eastern Europe occurred in Lithuania, i.e., in the heavily populated six northwestern Lithuanian-Belorussian provinces, and in the districts surrounding the city of Vilna. From this region also came the early leaders of the Bund. In this vast geographical area the Jewish element among the proletariat, especially in the cities and towns, was higher than elsewhere in the Pale of Settlement. This was also a region in which the trend toward assimilation was weakest, as a result of the endless conflict among the Lithuanian, Russian, Polish, and Belorussian inhabitants, none of whom appealed to the Jewish population. The Jews of this region had attained independently a high cultural and religious standard that was best exemplified by their celebrated academies.

The pre-Bund Jewish labor movement had drawn its support from several sources. The most important source was the hired-workers who had gained corporate consciousness and cohesion as a result of the capitalization of the crafts and the breakup of the traditional craft associations (*hevrot*). Next in significance were the circles of radical intelligentsia who combined enlightenment ideas with Marxist ideology, while retaining strong feelings for their Jewish identity and a sense of responsibility for the fate of the Jewish proletariat. Finally, there were the so-called semi-intellectuals who, though lacking a formal education, were deeply rooted in Jewish culture and sympathetic to the plight of the worker.

The atmosphere of tension that pervaded in the Pale of Settlement, the growing anti-Semitism, and the social, economic, and political restrictions under which the Jews of the overcrowded *shtetls* toiled forced the pre-Bund labor leaders to the conclusion that an organization was needed that would represent all the Jewish workers. The idea for such an entity seems to have been first broached in a speech delivered in Vilna (1895) by a young radical named Lev Tsederbaum (1873–1923), who in later years under the pseudonym

Julius Martov, would become one of the preeminent leaders of the Social Democratic Party of Russia (prior to the Bolshevik-Menshevik split). However, the actual initiative for creating the Jewish labor organization would come from Arkady Kremer (1865–1935), the son of an "enlightened" Hebrew teacher. Kremer had made his way back to a Jewish identification after having been almost totally assimilated. By 1896 he had become the leader of a loose federation of Jewish unions in Lithuania. That same year he had traveled to Geneva, Switzerland, to visit the spiritual leaders of Russian Marxism—Georgy Plekhanov, Vera Zasulich, and Paul Axelrod, who at the time were editing the underground newspaper *Iskra* ("The Spark"). Kremer, who had previously written a pamphlet entitled *Ob agitatsu* ("On Agitation"), in which he issued a call for socialist action among the masses, had a special request to ask of the *Iskra* editors. He wanted to know if they would open the pages of their newspaper to rally Jewish labor in a campaign to improve working conditions, and to raise the Jewish workers' political consciousness. The editors of *Iskra* were sympathetic, but suggested that Kremer instead concentrate his efforts on organizing the Jewish unions and mutual aid societies into a single entity. Kremer agreed and issued a call throughout the Pale of Settlement for a conference to bring about the proposed union.

The secret gathering took place in an inconspicuous wooden house in Vilna on three days in October, 1897. It was attended by only thirteen individuals, as a spate of recent house searches and arrests had made a fuller attendance virtually impossible. The delegates, which included two women, came from such prominent Jewish centers as Vilna, Warsaw, Minsk, Bialystok, and Vitebsk. The deliberations took place in a sparsely furnished room containing a small table and a few chairs, and for lack of space, some of the delegates were compelled to stand or sit on the floor. In spite of these bleak surroundings, and the ever-present danger of being discovered by the czarist police, the proceedings were spirited and constructive. The conference ended with a unanimous decision to found an organization to be known as the Allgemeine Yiddisher Arbeterbund in Poilen un Russland (General Federation of Jewish Workers in Poland and Russia).[366] Within a few years this organization, more commonly known by the acronym Bund, would grow tremendously in membership and achieve a reputation for its audacity and energy on behalf of the Jewish working man. Later its title would be amplified to include the word *Lite* (Lithuania).

Structurally, the Bund comprised sixteen district committees in various parts of the Pale of Settlement, all under the control of a Central Committee. The committee acted as the chief political and administrative body of the organization. Periodically the Central Committee would call for conventions of the membership to discuss problems, accomplishments, and goals. It also played a key role in nominating candidates for the district committees, particularly those committees responsible for large populated centers. In December of 1898 a group of workers and students who had left Russia established a "Committee Abroad." This committee served as the Bund's representative to the Internationalist Socialist Movement and raised funds, published propaganda, and organized transportation for members attending Bundist meetings. Considerable assistance was also provided to the parent organization by its network in the United States of *Landsmanschaften* (societies composed of persons originating in the same town or province in the country of their origin).

During the early years of its existence the Bund did not have a clear national program. Originally it was intended to be the spokesman of the Jewish proletariat and the defender of the its economic interests. The Bund fought for better working conditions and tried to instill in its membership the belief that labor was paramount in the economic system. Gradually, the Bund's leadership enlarged the scope of the organization's activities when they realized that, in spite of some gains in working conditions, the Jewish worker remained subject to czarist oppression. The Bund did not hesitate to join forces with the organized agitators among the Russian populace for political liberty and constitutional government.

In the beginning the Bund did not consider itself a separate party, but rather as a part of the Russian social democratic movement. The Bund played a key role in the establishment of the Russian Social-Democratic Party in March of 1898. The conference creating the latter entity was held in Minsk, a Pale of Settlement town in which the Bund had strong roots. The conferees recognized the contribution of the Bundists to their cause and agreed to allow the Bund to enter the Russian party as an autonomous body, independent on all questions relating to the Jewish working class (this would later become a point of dissension within the Russian Social-Democratic Party).

Shortly after the Minsk conference, the czarist police succeeded in arresting the Central Committee of the Russian Social-Democratic Party and some of the Bundist activists. However, their detainment did little to stifle the rapid growth of either organization. The Bundists in particular proved adroit at outwitting the authorities. Meetings were held secretly in synagogues in the guise of religious services, or in cemeteries, or in secluded forest areas with patrols stationed at the outskirts to give warning of approaching police. Leaflets were also distributed in market places and showered down from the gallery of theatres during performances. Agitation and propaganda campaigns were carried out at military recruiting centers and even within the prison system. In this manner adherents to the Bund were won over not only from the Jewish working class, but also from students in the Yeshivot (academies) who were induced to abandon the Talmud for the teachings of Karl Marx.[367]

The Bund in its formative years faced a series of tensions from within and from without its ranks. Foremost among these stresses was the question of its exact relationship with the Russian Social-Democratic Party and its policies. The latter, for example, at its first conference had proclaimed as part of their program the right of every nation to self-determination. The Bund at this stage had no Jewish national demands, other than a request for civil liberties. Thus, from its inception it was brought face to face with the basic conflict between socialist and nationalist ideology.

Nationalism based on the consciousness of historical continuity and on the unity of tradition tended to disregard the social differences and economic conflicts inherent in the life of a national community. Socialism, on the other hand, was based on the common economic concerns of workers. By appealing to their class solidarity, the socialists believed they could overcome national and religious differences within the labor movement. This in turn, would lead to a social order that would transcend national divisions, as well as state boundaries. The Socialist Movement, in general, inclined toward a cosmopolitan ideology motivated by the idea of a homogenous and undifferentiated humanity. Imbued with this philosophy, the early socialist thinkers minimized the value of nationalism, viewing it as an impediment to human progress.

The Bund, as a workers' organization, tended to accept the Marxist views on nationalism and the primacy of the class struggle. Thus, for the Bundists, the natural ally of the Jewish proletariat was the proletariat of other peoples, and its principal enemy (apart from the czarist regime) was the capital class, including the Jewish bourgeoisie and the nationalistic Zionists. As a consequence, the Bund found it difficult to define an ideologically correct relationship to the Jewish people as a whole. Early Bundists followed the usual Marxist position that the Jews had survived in history as a distinct group only because of their unusual economic roles and legal status. Therefore, after the socialist revolution, the Jews would inevitably assimilate because the economic substructure that maintained their identity would disappear.

In addition to opposing Zionism, the Bund was also extremely hostile to the use of Hebrew, the language of the rabbis, the Zionists, and a handful of visionaries. In its place they favored Yiddish, the language of the Jewish masses, and therefore the medium best suited for propagating the Bund's ideological message. Their opponents, the Zionists, had in turn rejected Yiddish as a caricature of a language, a jargon that embodied the spirit of the ghetto. Hebrew alone, they insisted, incorporated the heart and soul of the Jewish people. Nevertheless, most Zionists were willing to concede that the Bund, through the use of Yiddish, had been able to make great educational strides among the backward Jewish masses. Often, in spreading their ideology, the Bund fell back on methods originally developed by Liebermann and his followers. A former yeshivah student, Liebermann had adopted the practice of writing his socialist tracts in the style of the sacred texts of the Jews, especially that of the biblical prophets. He had on occasions even imitated the order of prayer. Similarly, Bundist publications frequently simulated synagogue practice by printing in Yiddish the "portion of the week." However, in place of the traditional passages from the Torah they substituted socialist doctrine. They also often quoted from biblical texts to support their revolutionary message. Even the Bund's hymn was carried out as a ceremonial act akin to a Jewish ritual. Some of the more radical Bundists went so far as to sing the "oath" while wearing traditional prayer shawls

In time, as the political and social struggle in Russia deepened, the Bund was compelled by circumstances to modify its rigid ideology. In the case of the Jewish people, it appeared impossible to maintain an irreconcilable antithesis between the socialist and national ideal. The Jewish people had never disassociated their own cause from that of humanity. The Jewish hope for a messianic future encompassed all peoples without depriving them of their national individuality. On the other hand, the Jewish Problem was unique; its urgency and worldwide implications could not be ignored by any movement that took its stand on the principles of humanity and advocated the universal realization of social and economic democracy. Least of all could it be disregarded by a socialist organization that desired to rally the Jewish masses under its banner.

The peculiar situation of the Jewish people as a nation without a territory of its own complicated the task of the Jewish socialists theoretically as well as practically. The national problem for peoples and ethnic groups living in their historic homelands was basically a question of political freedom (i.e., full national sovereignty or national autonomy). The problem could thus be resolved by justly delimiting the political rights of the contending national and social groups and by eliminating from the society those social and economic factors that favored a policy of national domination and aggression. However, the Jewish people did not fit the mold. Their national problem could not be solved by the mere formal recognition of a right to self-determination. The conditions for the existence of a Jewish nation had to be created.

From its very inception the Bund was confronted with the vexing problem of whether the Jews were a nation and with the competition of the Zionists for the hearts and minds of the Jewish masses. Unexpectedly, the flowering of Yiddish literature had aroused among many Jewish socialists a powerful spirit of nationalism that threatened to splinter the unity of the Bund. This development led the leadership of the Russian Social Democratic Party to regard the Bund as being dangerously tainted with the bourgeois and chauvinist attitudes of the Zionist movement.

At the same time, many young Bundists were antagonized by what appeared to them as gross indifference on the part of their Russian counterparts to the specific needs of the Jewish people. The Russian Social Democrats concentrated their efforts on industrial workers, while Russian populists were above all interested in the fate of the peasants. Most Jews, however were neither peasants nor industrial workers. Some Russian socialists may have sympathized with the suffering of the Jews, but from their point of view it was a marginal issue. They had no advice to offer the Jews except to insist that the socialist revolution would eventually resolve the Jewish Problem. Most Russian socialists would not acknowledge the sad fact that anti-Semitism had strong roots in their movement. The infamous Kishinev pogrom further weakened the link between many Bundists and their Russian counterparts, whom they suspected of something less than brotherly love.

The Bund, faced with an internal and external threat to their survival as an organization, had to decide whether to adhere strictly to doctrinaire socialist ideology, which frowned on Jewish nationalism as a betrayal of the interests of the Jewish proletariat, or to abandon this principle and join in the drive toward nationhood (a territorial solution) outside of Eastern Europe, or to strive for an autonomous national life within Russia itself.

For a long period the leaders of the Bund sought to straddle the issue by adhering to a policy of "neutralism" enunciated by the organization's ideologist Vladimir Medem. Neutralism avoided the need to take a positive stand on any of the alternative policies, and emphasized instead the task of fighting for a political framework that would allow all trends to evolve according to the "laws of history." At the Third Conference of the Bund held in Kovno (December, 1899) some of the participants voiced the view that national rights should be demanded for Jews. However, the suggestion was rejected by a majority of the delegates. In spite of this setback, the clamor within the Bund's ranks for a change in policy did not subside. The call for change was renewed at the Fourth Conference of the Bund held in Bialystok in May of 1901. This meeting turned out to be a milestone in the history of the Bund. The conferees decided on intensification of the political struggle and treatment of it as a separate issue from the economic objectives. They also considered the national question and passed a resolution demanding the transformation of Russia into a "federation of nations," each people possessing national autonomy independent of the territory on which they resided. For the first time the conferees agreed that the term nation should be applied to the Jews. However, the delegates rejected the call for Jewish communal rights apart from political emancipation as individuals. They feared that a campaign for Jewish autonomy would arouse Russian nationalists and socialists and blur the class consciousness of the proletariat, leading to chauvinism. In advocating a federation of nations, the Bund delegates drew heavily on the ideas advanced by the Austrian Social Democratic Party, which under the influence of its leading theorists Karl Renner and Otto Bauer had come out for a federal-nationalist arrangement as the basis for a constitution in a multinational state.

The restrictions placed on campaigning for Jewish autonomy were largely ignored and were officially removed at the Sixth Conference of the Bund held in Zurich in 1905. Even prior to this conference, the Bund, unable any longer to disregard the fact that Eastern

European Jewry had distinct ethical and cultural characteristics, began to recognize the need for a more forceful national policy. Thus at the Fifth Conference of the Bund in Zurich in 1903 the delegates endorsed a demand for Jewish cultural autonomy—an idea that had received much attention in the writings of the socialist Chaim Zhitlowsky (1865–1943), and the historian Simon W. Dubnow (1860–1943). Expanding on the views expressed earlier, the Bund now defined Jewish national cultural autonomy as the separate existence of a nationality with the right of self-determination in all matters pertaining to culture and education. The Russia of the future, they stressed, should be composed of a federation of nationalities, and the Jews must be considered one of those component nationalities. Jewish peoplehood and culture did not require a particular geographic center (i.e., a state). "Historic destiny," declared a Bundist leader, "has made the Jewish people into a stateless nation—whether we like it or not—it is bound to remain so."[368]

The goal of cultural and social autonomy became widely accepted among Russian Jewry as the only solution in a multinational state, and as a result of this policy the Bund gradually began to include Jews more deeply rooted in *Yiddishkeit* (the Ashkenazic folk ethos). In adopting this policy, the Bund again reaffirmed its opposition to Zionism by limiting its demands for rights and autonomy to Russian Jewry. Indeed, the Bund vehemently rejected (in the name of class warfare) any collaboration with other Jewish parties, even in situations involving organizing for self-defense against pogroms.

Although most Russian Social Democrats regarded Bundist ideology as "inconsistent Zionism", and the Marxist philosopher Georgi Plekhanov went so far as to sarcastically refer to the Bundists as "Zionists afraid of a sea voyage," the Bund for its part continued to regard the Zionists as reactionary bourgeois. It continually hammered away on the theme that the settlement of a few Jews in Palestine could not resolve the Jewish Problem. Secondly, if Zionism had ambitious plans for the resettlement of the whole Jewish people, or a large part of it, in the Promised Land, it had to be fought as a dangerous utopian vision bound to deflect the working masses from the struggle for political and economic rights in Russia, as well as weaken their class consciousness.

The Bund's demand as recognition as the sole representative of the Jewish workers in Russia and its call for cultural autonomy within a federation of nations encountered vigorous opposition from the Russian Social Democratic Party. Matters came to a head at the latter's second congress, in 1903. A new generation of leaders younger than the Iskra group, which had urged Arkady Kremer to organize a Jewish central labor organization in the first place, had now come to the foreground in the Russian Social Democratic Party. One faction (later known as the Bolsheviks), led by Nikolai Lenin (1870–1924) refused to accept a separation of any kind within the party's ranks and were determined to squash the Bund's call for a federation of nations and their appeal for cultural autonomy. Lenin rejected the ethnocentrism of the Bund and was firmly convinced that the Jews, lacking a territory of their own within Russia, could not be considered a nation. He believed that the Jews should be assimilated into the Russian nation. However, unwilling to be accused of anti-Semitism, Lenin and his followers assigned the task of repudiating the Bundists on the floor of the second congress to the two foremost Jews in their group, Julius Martov who had abandoned his earlier ideas on autonomy, and Lev Davidovich Bronstein (1879–1940), later known as Leon Trotsky. The Bundists were roundly denounced as reactionaries and deviationists, and their demands were overwhelmingly rejected by the majority of delegates (a crushing defeat, as out of the forty-five delegates attending the conference, twenty-five were Jewish). Outraged by the rejection of their demands, the

Bund seceded from the Russian Social Democratic Party, and reconstituted itself as an independent party.

Now more than ever before, the Bund concentrated its efforts on the political sphere. Demonstrations and strikes became the organization's weapons of choice, but brought little amelioration to the Jewish workers of Russia. Indeed, the change in tactics brought on even more suppression on the part of the czarist regime. The Bund exploited the anger aroused by the government's actions to make additional inroads among the Jewish working class, but carefully avoided open clashes with the authorities.

A year prior to their break with the Russian Social Democratic Party feelings among the Bundists had reached a flashpoint when Von Wahl, the Governor of Vilna, had Jewish workers flogged for taking part in a May Day demonstration. A twenty-two-year-old Jewish shoemaker named Hirsch Leckert, a member of the Bund, was incensed by the governor's brutality and sought revenge. He fired several shots at Von Wahl as the latter came out of a circus, but injured him only slightly. Tried by a military court, Leckert was given a death sentence. His execution aroused furious indignation in the ranks of the Bund, as well as in all the socialist and revolutionary parties. However, the tendency toward combating violence with violence that evolved in the Bund following the Leckert affair proved short-lived.

The pogroms at the beginning of the twentieth century in Russia intensified Jewish awareness of the dangers confronting their survival as a community, and led to the development of a self-defense movement. The Bund, which had gained considerable experience in this area, became one of the principal promoters and in some places the main organizer of self-defense units.

During the Russian Revolution of 1905 the Bund reached the apex of its power and influence, with a membership exceeding 35,000. This period also marked a radical change in the attitude of the Russian Social Democratic Party toward the Bund. In 1905–06 the Bund had sided on many issues with the Bolsheviks. In return, the support of the latter at the Russian Social Democratic Party Congress held in Stockholm in 1906 enabled the Bund to reconsider rejoining the all-Russian party. This decision assumed a more positive outlook when the Russian Social Democratic Party agreed to refrain from coming to a final conclusion on the question of a national program. On the basis of this resolution, which implied belated recognition of the autonomous status of the Bund, the latter's membership at their seventh conference in Leipzig in 1906 voted to return to the Russian Social Democratic Party.

In the reaction that followed the failure of the Russian revolution of 1905, the Bund, along with all other revolutionary parties suffered a serious decline in political activity. Government-sponsored campaigns of terror together with massive emigration considerably reduced the ranks of the Bund. Forced by these events to once again change tactics, the Bund began to concentrate its major effort on culture. It organized literary, musical, and theatrical events, as well as evening courses to raise the educational level of their members. Renewed emphasis was placed on the use of Yiddish. At the eighth conference of the Bund held in Lvov in 1910, a call was issued to fight for Yiddish as the language of the Jews. The conferees also decided to promote secularization by participating more fully in Jewish communal life. Lastly, they appealed to the czarist regime to allow the population of the empire to choose their own day of rest (Saturday for the Jews, Sunday for the Christians, and Friday for the Moslems).

During the years 1910–11 the Bund made strenuous efforts to strengthen its organization. It once again began to play a pivotal role in socialist politics. In 1912 the Bund, along with other socialist groups within the Russian Social Democratic Party, called for a special convention to curb the Bolsheviks, who had declared that their faction constituted the mainstream of the party. The meeting was held in Vienna (August, 1912), and led to a split between the Bolsheviks and the Mensheviks with the Bund siding with the latter. The convention did, however, finally recognize the principle of cultural national autonomy, the concept for which the Bund had been fighting for ten years.

In November of 1914, with the threat of a German invasion of Poland imminent, the Central Committee of the Bund formed a coordinating committee to cope with the emergency. The fighting on the Eastern Front forced a loosening of the links with the Russian Social Democratic movement, which was further weakened by the resurgence of Polish nationalism. Adjusting to the changing circumstances, the Bund in Poland reconstituted itself as an independent body. The more moderate regime of the German occupation authorities enabled the Bund, though still functioning clandestinely, to set up Jewish trade unions, worker kitchens, and cooperative enterprises and to strengthen their network of cultural institutions.

Following the Bolshevik Revolution of 1917, conventions of various Jewish groups in Russia called for Jewish autonomy. The Bund, however, was content to strive solely for cultural autonomy. The rapid march of events that marked this turbulent period of Russian history soon made a mockery of the Bund's struggle to maintain its independence. From the autumn of 1918 onwards the Bund membership, especially in the Ukraine, the site of bloody pogroms, began to favor the Communists. In the following year the Ukrainian Bund split apart. The left wing of the organization, now the majority, took the name "Kombund," and some months later joined the United Jewish Communist Party to form a new entity called the Komfarbund. In August of 1919 the latter amalgamated with the Communist Party of the Ukraine.

A similar development took place in White Russia where a compromise between those Bundists favoring Jewish activity within a special framework and those opposed resulted in the so-called Communist Union of Russia and Lithuania. The request of a Bundist minority that the Jewish sections of the Communist Party constitute an autonomous body within the party structure was summarily rejected at the Third All-Russian Conference of the Jewish Sections held in July of 1920. In the following year the Communist leaders of the Soviet Union turned down a last appeal for autonomy and the Russian Bund ceased to exist.

Only the Polish Bund remained independent. During the first years of the newly revived Polish state, it suffered considerable persecution because of its opposition to the war against the Soviet Union. The question whether or not to affiliate with the Comintern (the Communist International) also disturbed and divided the Bund. Still another cause of dissension was the Bund's relationship with the Polish Socialist Party, an organization that many Bundists regarded as anathema because of its extreme nationalism. However, with the passage of time and as the situation in Poland stabilized and conditions improved, the Bund itself adopted a firm anti-Communist stand.

Among the Jewish communities of postwar Poland, the Bund continued its relentless campaign against Zionism and religious Orthodoxy. Nevertheless, despite its secularist philosophy, the Bund became an important factor in the *kehillot* (the elected boards of the Jewish communities), which had received government recognition as official bodies. The Bund also managed to establish an extensive school system, with Yiddish as the language of instruction, throughout Poland. The Bund continued to play a prominent role in the perennial struggle against anti-Semitic forces and displayed considerable initiative and energy in safeguarding the Jewish communities by organizing a network of self-defense units.

On the eve of the Nazi invasion of Poland, the Bund was probably the largest Jewish party in the country. Smaller Bundist parties still existed in Rumania, Lithuania, and Estonia (the Holocaust, however, would completely eliminate these splinter groups). During and in the aftermath of the German blitzkrieg, the Bund participated in the Polish resistance movement. One of its most prominent members, S. Zygelbojm, represented the Bund on the National Council of the Polish Government in Exile in London. His suicide in 1943 was a heroic symbolic act of identification with the Jewish martyrs who had fallen victim to Hitler's forces and a protest against the silence and apathy of the world in the face of the Nazi annihilation of the Jews of Europe.

At the conclusion of World War II, despite the utter destruction of Poland's Jewry, the Bund attempted to renew its activities among the surviving remnant. However, with the establishment of a Communist regime in Poland (1948), the Bund was liquidated. A handful of Polish Bundists managed to make their way to the United States, where they joined fellow socialist sympathizers to form an American counterpart to the old Bund. In 1947 a world conference was held in Brussels, and a World Coordinating Committee of Bundist and Affiliated Socialist Jewish Organizations was created, with headquarters in New York City. Still committed to an ideology that had changed little since the last quarter of the nineteenth century, the policies of the Bund had become anachronistic and seemed completely irrelevant in the aftermath of the Holocaust, the birth of Israel, and events in the Communist Soviet Union. For all practical purposes the Bund no longer constituted a significant factor in Jewish life. Their rivals, the Zionists, had succeeded to their mantle of leadership.

38

Synthesis of Socialism and Zionism

Between Zionism and Socialism, during the waning years of the nineteenth century, there appeared to be an unbridgeable chasm (in spite of the early efforts of the so-called "communist rabbi," Moses Hess to fuse the two ideologies). For most Zionists, Marxism or "scientific socialism" was anathema. Orthodox Marxists, on the other hand, considered the nation-state to be an outmoded relic, and nationalism an evil force used by capitalists to divert the proletariat from their true interests. Proletarians, they insisted, have no homeland. Both Jewish and non-Jewish Marxists also vehemently denied that there was a specific Jewish Problem; the socialist revolution, they asserted, would eliminate anti-Semitism, and the Jews would then be able to disappear within the ranks of the proletariat.

It was therefore with considerable hesitation that the Bund, the largest and best organized socialist organization within the Russian Empire, acknowledged the uniqueness of the Jewish Problem. After much debate and soul searching the Bundists came to believe that the emancipation of the Jewish masses would have to take place within a social and cultural framework specifically related to Jewish concerns and experiences. Having arrived at this decision, the Bund threw its full support behind Yiddish, which it saw as the language of daily Jewish life and the instrument that best expressed the struggle of the toiling Jewish masses.

The theoreticians of the Bund were also firmly convinced that a Jewish proletariat conscious of its own cultural heritage, could be integrated within the general Russian revolutionary movement. Following this line of reasoning, the Bund remained hostile to Hebrew as the language of the modern Jewish renaissance and strongly opposed the Zionist movement as a dangerous form of romantic bourgeois nationalism drawing Jews away from the revolutionary struggle in Eastern Europe, and separating the Jewish Problem from a universal solution.

Dov Ber Borochov

However, not all Jewish socialists were willing to accept the stand taken by the Bundists or the rosy future portrayed by the Marxists. A few socialist intellectuals were convinced that a synthesis of Zionism and Socialism was desirable. These thinkers were not opposed to the creation of a Jewish state, but were adamant that such an entity had to be erected along socialist lines, i.e., a society in which all class distinctions would be erased. The chief proponents of this school of thought were Nachman Syrkin (1867–1924) and Dov Ber Borochov (1881–1917).[369] Borochov, in particular, attempted to find and develop a concept along Marxist lines that would take into account Jewish nationalism. In the process, he evolved not only a special theory explaining Jewish history, but an expansion of Marxist principles totally unforeseen by its founder.

Dov Ber Borochov was born in Zolotonosha, a small town in the Ukraine, and grew up in the city of Poltava. For some unknown reason the czarist regime favored Poltava as a place of exile for revolutionary agitators and radicals. Among the exiles were such prominent figures as the writer Korolenko and the fiery orator Martov, editor of the revolutionary paper *Iskra* and later a leader of the Menshevik Party. The concentration of these revolutionaries in Poltava with little to do but write and engage in endless debates created a radical ferment among the Russian, Ukranian, and Jewish youth of the city. Indeed, Poltava was also among the earliest communities in the Russian Empire in which a branch of the Hibbat Zion was founded. Ber Borochov's father, a *maskil* (advocate of the Jewish Enlightenment), was one of its most active members.

Borochov's enlightened parents tried to provide him with a secular education. He attended a Russian High School and early on displayed a distinct preference for philosophic thought. However, Borochov's educational plans received a setback when he was denied entrance to a Russian university. Undaunted by the anti-Semitism that was the basis for his rejection, Borochov undertook a strenuous program of independent study that included a variety of subject matter (e.g., European literature and languages, philosophy, and sociology). He also became involved in politics and at the age of nineteen joined the ranks of the Russian Social Democratic Party (1901). However, the latter entity's negative attitude toward Jewish nationalism led him to break ranks with the leadership, and expulsion from the party as a "Zionist deviationist" quickly followed.

Soon after his ouster from the Russian Social Democratic Party, Borochov established in the city of Yekaterinoslav the Zionist Socialist Workers Union. The newly formed union became active in Jewish self-defense and in promoting the interests of Jewish workers. Borochov's creation was bitterly opposed by the Russian Social Democratic Party and by most Zionists. The latter disliked the association of Zionism with Socialism, and the Russian Social Democrats refused to recognize the need for any independent Jewish workers' movement.

Borochov's organization reflected the new mood that had come over many Jewish workers at the dawn of the twentieth century—namely a disposition to regard Jewish nationalism in a more favorable light. Although only a handful of socialists had attended the First Zionist Congress in 1897, they were not representative of the mainstream of the socialist movement. In the years immediately following the Zionist Congess, the situation radically changed as Jewish worker groups, study circles, clandestine clubs, and societies sprang up throughout the Pale of Settlement. Calling themselves Poalei Zion (Workers of Zion) these groups, for the most part, remained independent of each other.

Many of these associations were composed of former socialists who disagreed with the stand taken by the Russian Social Democratic Party toward resolving the Jewish Problem. Others had withdrawn from the Bund after it had adopted a resolution in 1901 stating that membership in the Zionist Organization was incompatible with Bundist doctrine. Other Poalei Zion, like the so called "Minsk Group," did not regard themselves as socialists and held themselves aloof from those elements of the Jewish intelligentsia who fostered ideologies that did not take into account the plight of the workers and the common man.

The first conference of the Minsk Group was held in December of 1901 in the city from which it took its name, and was closely linked with the Fifth Zionist Congress, which convened shortly afterwards in Basle, Switzerland. Most Poalei Zion societies, however, in spite of their rapid growth throughout the Russian Empire, remained hopelessly divided over ideological issues. The diversity of views espoused by these societies reflected their make-up, which included Marxist and non-Marxist socialists, anarchists, syndicalists, Yiddishists and Hebraists, Zionists and territorialists, and religious and agrarian reformers.

The Uganda crisis, which resulted from England's offer of a territory in East Africa to Theodor Herzl, exacerbated the divisions among the Poalei Zion societies. One schismatic group, the so-called Vozrozdheniye (Renaissance) favored the development of Jewish life in the Diaspora within an autonomous setting. Others felt that the interests of Jewish workers would best be served in a land other than Palestine. However, most groups remained true to the concept of a restoration in the Holy Land. The struggle over these issues in the period 1904–06 resulted in the emergence of three distinct parties from the Poalei Zion movement.

At the Seventh Zionist Congress (1905) a faction appeared that broke sharply with the other Poalei Zion groups. They called themselves the Zionist Socialist Workers' Party (more commonly known as the S.S. from their Russian designation, Sionisty-Sotsialisty), and were led by Nachman Syrkin (1868–1924). Syrkin was the first theoretician of Socialist Zionism, according to which there had to be a territorial solution to the Jewish Problem in the form of a cooperative society based on economic justice and productive labor. The Zionist dream could only succeed if the Jewish commonwealth was based on socialist values; conversely Zionism alone could end the distorted economic situation of the Jewish proletariat. Unlike most socialists, Syrkin insisted that the triumph of Socialism throughout Europe would not end anti-Semitism. Jewish survival could only be ensured if the East European Jewish masses, deeply rooted in traditional ethnic values, refused to emulate the assimilated Western Jewish bourgeoisie, whose pursuit of individual enrichment led to ethical bankruptcy.

Syrkin and his followers acknowledged that the main goal of the party was to solve the Jewish Problem. They were convinced that there was not the slightest possibility for the normal economic development of the Jewish people in Russia. Syrkin also believed that immigration to more highly developed countries would not benefit the Jewish workers, as they would only be absorbed in the marginal fields connected with consumption and commerce and not by the nation's basic industries. Only if the Jews evolved their own economic framework from the ground up could desirable economic development be ensured. Hence it was essential to search for a territory outside of the great industrial nations (the party agreed with other groups such as the Zionists that a territory was essential, but were for a long time hesitant to include Palestine as the ideal locale for a

Jewish renaissance). Nevertheless, they also felt that as socialists they had other responsibilities. Syrkin also advocated that the Russian Jewish working class was morally
obligated to participate in the struggle to overthrow the repressive and brutal czarist
regime. Later joined by the Minsk Group, the Zionist-Socialist Workers' Party exerted
considerable influence over Jewish workers, particularly during the turbulent days of the
Russian Revolution of 1905.

Syrkin's ideology was in many ways similar to that of Moses Hess, whom he greatly
admired. Indeed, for Syrkin and his party, socialist values were not alien to ancient
Judaism; they were a rediscovery in a modern context of the biblical concern for social
justice found in Mosaic legislation and the message of the Prophets. Through a socialist
Jewish homeland, the messianic hope, which was always the greatest desire of exiled
Jewry, would be transformed into political action.

Another faction of the Poalei Zion, known as the "Sejmists" (Jewish Socialist Workers
Party), was in direct opposition to the policies of the Zionist-Socialist Workers' Party.
This group promulgated ideas similar to the Vozrozheniye, whose membership they
largely absorbed. The Sejmists did not favor Marxism, and tended to cooperate closely
with the Russian Social Revolutionary Party. Although the Sejmists did not deny the
desirability of an independent territory for the Jewish workers, they felt that this aspiration was unattainable in the foreseeable future. Accordingly, the party emphasized
national autonomy within the framework of the Russian Empire. They hoped the latter
entity would become a loose federation composed of various national states with each
state having its own Sejm (Diet) and enjoying wide powers. Jews would form one of these
autonomous states in the Russian Federation from the territories in which they were
heavily concentrated. The Sejmist ideology reflected to a large extent the theories of
the historian Simon Dubnow (1860–1941) and the theoretician Chaim Zhitlowsky
(1865–1943).

At the Seventh Zionist Congress (Basle, 1905) Ber Borochov headed a group of the
Poalei Zion that remained faithful to the concept of a Jewish restoration in Palestine.
During the acrimonious debates over the territorial issue and autonomism that marked the
sessions of this congress, Ber Borochov laid the foundations for a third Poalei Zion party.
This party's program was based on ideas that Ber Borochov had first outlined in a work
entitled *The National Question and the Class Struggle*.[370] In this treatise he rejected the
sentimental and ethical utopianism of Hess and Syrkin and attempted to formulate a
theory that would encompass the relationship between nationalism and the class struggle
within the framework of Marxist ideology.

In his search for "scientific socialist" legitimacy Borochov drew heavily on the
sociological studies of the Austrian theoreticians Otto Bauer, Max Adler, and Karl
Renner. These individuals had argued that in the context of multinational societies, class
emancipation may have to go hand in hand with national emancipation because so many of
the oppressed were also persecuted for their nationality. Borochov seized on this idea and
greatly expanded the theme to suit his needs.

Realizing that most Marxists at the turn of the century were cosmopolitan interna-
tionalists, Borochov had first to defend the principle that nationalism was not necessarily
reactionary. He proposed, alongside the "relations of production" as the primary cause of
the formation of classes and conflict, that Marxist Socialism should acknowledge the
importance of the geographical "conditions of production" that brought nations into
being. Nations existed long before modern social classes, Borochov argued, because a

common past would give rise to a feeling of common kinship. This sense of kinship, resulting from the sharing of a historic heritage and common conditions of production, Borochov labeled nationalism. Such sentiments of national unity, quite real in their effect, were not "spiritual" because they had material causes in earlier times. Marxists therefore must realize that nations would not fade away after the proletarian revolution.

According to Borochov, the validity of each form of nationalism depended on the social class whose economic interests it reflected. The nationalism of the landowning gentry and the bourgeoisie was reactionary and chauvinistic. True nationalism did not obscure class consciousness. Indeed, genuine nationalism ". . . was to be found only among the progressive elements of oppressed nations"[371] The revolutionary proletariat within these nations expressed their nationalism in firm and lucidly formulated terms, demanding as a minimum program the establishment of a nation under normal conditions of production. Proletarian nationalism furthered the economic interests of the nation's workers, forced frequently to compete with other nations, by defending the "strategic base" (i.e., the homeland) on which the working class supported itself. Borochov felt strongly that only after being emancipated from foreign subjugation could the proletariat of an oppressed nation wage a real class war within its own society. National liberation was therefore essential for carrying out a successful class war. Giving nationalism its place in a nation's historical development was not a deviation from Marxist doctrine, but rather a correct application of history, involving one of the most important forces in modern society.

From this analysis, Borochov drew specific implications for the Jews. Socialization of the means of production alone would not solve the Jewish Problem because the Jewish proletariat would continue to be pressed into an increasingly narrow, stunted, and marginal place in Diaspora society. Earlier, the Jews had been financially useful to the ruling classes of European society, but now they were superfluous, excluded from the basic industries from which a normal proletariat emerges. Escape by immigration to America, Borochov stressed, was not the answer, because in the course of time the same cycle of discrimination and anti-Semitism would be repeated. The Jewish workers would find themselves resented as intruders by other working class immigrant proletariat. Unable to integrate into a productive labor force, the Jews would be pushed into marginal occupations, creating again, in the New World, an inverted pyramid of the Jewish social structure—a narrow base and a top heavy with middle class and intelligentsia.

The solution to this problem, Borochov believed, was concentrated Jewish immigration into an undeveloped country. Instead of being limited to the final level of production, as was the case for Jews in most countries, they would now be able to assume a leading role in developing the economy of the new land. Jewish flight from persecution, in short, must be transformed from immigration to colonization, for only a territorial solution could resolve the Jewish Problem.

After considering various options, Borochov reached the conclusion that Palestine was the best choice for Jewish colonization. Why the Holy Land? Besides the obvious religious and historical connections, Borochov felt that there were other factors that would draw the emigrating Jewish masses to Palestine. As the basic industries of the capitalistic nations became barred to Jews, and as the capacity of the latter to absorb immigrants gradually decreased, forcing them to close their borders to all immigrants, there would remain only one place for the Jewish masses seeking a home to go—their ancient homeland, Palestine. Palestine would be the only territory where they would be able to enter all branches of production and enjoy a normal economic life. Palestine, in fact, met all the demands that the future homeland of the Jewish people required. It was a semiagricultural country, thinly populated and politically undeveloped—an area unlikely to attract non-Jewish immigrants. It would thus be possible to create a strategy that would eventually lead to a Jewish socialist society.

Syrkin's ideology had emphasized ethical freedom and moral idealism. Borochov adhered to the Marxist principle that Socialism must be modeled on the deterministic laws of natural science. Concentration of the Jewish masses in Palestine, he believed, was a "stychic" process, a result of elemental, spontaneous, and unconscious factors not dependent on human will. Borochov was convinced that normalization of the material conditions of Jewish existence was an inevitable result of the dialectical laws of history. Religion for him as for Karl Marx was "the opiate of the masses"; human desire alone could not create a just society if the objective forces of history were not headed in that direction. The views expressed by Borochov became the platform for a new party—the Jewish Workers' Social Democratic Party Poalei Zion, which he formed in 1906 following a conference held in Poltava. Its curious mixture of nationalism and Marxism made it in time one of the most determinedly anti-religious forms of Jewish secularism to emerge in the twentieth century.

Critics of Borochov's theories were quick to point out some flaws in his reasoning. Almost all of his opponents emphasized that his views betrayed a certain dogmatism, and a totally unhistoric approach to the complex phenomena of social life. The rigidness of his theory was most apparent in Borochov's attempt to explain, rather skillfully but with obvious difficulty, why the purely economic forces underlying historic development must and will select Palestine and no other territory as the final goal of a Jewish mass emigration from the Diaspora.

Borochov's analysis of the economic status of European Jewry, according to his detractors, also suffered from a tendency to engage in sweeping theoretical generalizations. His assumption, for example, that a landless national minority cannot gain a foothold in the basic industries of a host nation was challenged by many scholars (in recent years by the prominent Israeli biblical scholar Yehezkel Kaufmann). Still other critics have taken issue with Borochov's assertion that Jews entered Europe when all the economic vantage points had already been occupied. But perhaps the sharpest criticism of Borochov's theories for most scholars was his failure to fully appreciate the importance of the spiritual factor in Jewish history.

In 1907 Borochov's activities resulted in his arrest by the Russian authorities. Upon his release he left the country and went to the Hague where he participated in the Eight Zionist Congress. Soon after the conclusion of the Congress, Borochov suggested that the Russian Poalei Zion withdraw from the World Zionist Organization in order to preserve the proletarian independence of Socialist Zionism. During this same period he played a key role in the founding of the World Union of Poalei Zion. Until the outbreak of World War I, he would dedicate himself to furthering the aims of the Union (he would serve as the organization's secretary until his death in 1917).

Immigrating to the United States in 1914, Borochov not only remained active in Poalei Zion affairs, but also campaigned vigorously on behalf of the American Jewish Congress and for the establishment of a Jewish Legion. In addition, he continued his philosophical studies and research on the Yiddish language and literature and worked as an editor for the New York daily, *Die Warheit.*

With Russia rapidly drifting toward revolution, Borochov decided to return to the land of his birth. Enroute he stopped off at Stockholm to join a Poalei Zion delegation who were participating in an international socialist conference. At this meeting Borochov helped formulate a manifesto spelling out the demands of the working classes (including the Jewish proletariat) in the postwar era. When he finally arrived in Russia, the fiery theoretician immediately became immersed in the political turmoil that marked the stormy period preceding the October Revolution. Borochov participated in the Congress of Minorities convened by the Kerensky regime, and presented before this body a concise analysis of the economic and social structure of Russian Jewry.

In a speech before the Russian Poalei Zion (August, 1917) he again elaborated on the Marxist-Zionist theories he had so carefully developed over the course of a lifetime. Contact, however, with the Jews of Western Europe and the United States had considerably broadened his outlook. Indeed, during his American interlude, Borochov had begun to write, for the first time, of the need for Zionism to include a total partnership of all the Jewish people and of Palestine as a home for all the Jews. In his essays and articles of this period the term "Jewish masses" replaced the "proletariat," and the ancient designation "Eretz Israel" instead of Palestine. Nevertheless, in his August address to the Russian Poalei Zion, Borochov remained loyal to his earlier beliefs, declaring himself to be an anarchist-socialist, i.e., a Marxist opposed to both materialism and idealism. "There must be unity," he asserted, "between all those who strive for abolition of capitalism be they socialists, anarchists, Marxists, or revolutionaries in the spirit of Isaiah."[372]

The Poalei Zion, Borochov stressed, must take the lead in encouraging Jews to return to their ancient homeland if a concentration of the Jewish masses was ever to be achieved in the Land of Israel. Almost apologetically, he explained to the Russian Poalei Zion audience why the party had previously ignored the emotional element inherent in the idea of a Jewish restoration in the Holy Land. The reason for this strange behavior, Borochov believed, was largely due to the party's immaturity in its early years, and to its conception of policies and programs in strictly materialistic terms. He noted, however, that with the expansion and consolidation of the party, more attention was being given to esthetic and cultural factors.

Missing in Borochov's explanation was the fact that the party's policies were to some extent influenced by its confrontation with other Jewish factions. In the struggle with the Bund, for example, Borochov's party was compelled to purge their programs of all romantic elements so as not to be accused, in Marxist terminology, of being "non-scientific," or of being confused with mainline Zionist parties.

Shortly after the conclusion of the Russian Poalei Zion conference, Borochov embarked on a speaking tour. While fulfilling an engagement in Kiev he contracted pneumonia and quickly expired. He was thirty-six years old at the time of his death in December, 1917.

In retrospect, Ber Borochov's message had great appeal for the intensely class-conscious Jewish workers of Eastern Europe in the early years of the twentieth century. He had devised a theory of Zionism that evolved deductively, almost mathematically, from Marxist premises. As a result, he made Zionism intellectually respectable to thousands of Jewish workers and youth who were uneasy about the claims of the orthodox Marxists that Zionism and "scientific Socialism" were incompatible. This was a considerable achievement in a generation in which, for many individuals, it was almost de rigueur to be a socialist and a revolutionary and to believe wholeheartedly in historical materialism and the mission of the industrial proletariat. The writings, for example, of Karl Johann Kautsky (1854–1938) were regarded by many Jewish socialists with the same awe that religious believers showed for holy writ. Borochov helped to change this dogmatic outlook. Yitzhak Avner (better known as Ben Zvi, the second President of the State of Israel), who worked closely with Borochov during the early Poltava days of Poalei Zion, would note in his memoirs that the fiery theorist was the teacher of a whole generation of Zionists, and was considered the patron saint of left-wing socialist groups within the Zionist movement—the discoverer of the synthesis between Zionism and Socialism.

The Socialist-Zionist parties that adopted many of Ber Borochov's doctrines played a major role in the creation of the State of Israel. Always volatile in their politics, they constantly split and united to form new groupings. Among the parties spawned by these shifts were the Mapai, the Mapam, and the Ahdut Ha-Avodah. However, it would be the Left Poalei Zion, formed in 1920, that would adhere most closely to the theories of Ber Borochov. The latter's contribution to Zionism would receive its final recognition in 1963 when his remains were removed from the Soviet Union for reinterment in Israel alongside the graves of other notables of Socialist-Zionism.

X

UTOPIANS, AUTONOMISTS, AND TERRITORIALISTS

39

Utopian Novels

Der Judenstaat

Many of the ideas articulated by Ahad Ha-Am and Theodor Herzl were also anticipated by several utopian novelists. Herzl's *Der Judenstaat*, which was responsible for the launching of the modern Political Zionist Movement was considered by many of his contemporaries to be an example par excellence of a utopian tract in spite of the author's efforts to forestall such claims. Herzl wrote:

> I must guard my plan from being treated as a utopia. Actually in doing so I am only keeping superficial observers from possibly committing a silly blunder. . . . I could achieve an easier literary success — and as it were avoid all responsibility — if I presented my plan in the form of a novel . . . [but] I think the situation of the Jews in various countries is bad enough to render such introductory dalliance superfluous.[373]

Herzl believed that his book, unlike utopian novels, contained nothing suggestive of a perfect society, nor did it reveal any tendency to mold individuals into uniform creatures devoid of all emotions and passions. Similarly, in the proposed Jewish state individuality was not to be crushed on either esthetic or moral grounds. Private property and the family were to remain intact. Finally, *Der Judenstaat* dealt with concrete territories and lacked the symmetry so beloved by utopian writers, who tended to neglect natural regions in favor of perfectly round islands and perfectly straight rivers.

Altneuland

Nevertheless, in spite of Herzl's protestations, *Der Judenstaat* was not completely free of the detailed proposals that he himself recognized as a distinguishing feature of most utopian works. Some years after the appearance of *Der Judenstaat* he would make full use of this literary genre to produce a truly utopian novel entitled *Altneuland* ("Old-New Land"). The Hebrew translation of this novel by Nachum Sokolow would bear the title *Tel Aviv* ("Hill of Spring"). In this utopian novel, Herzl went far beyond the ideas of nationalism and Jewish statehood that had marked his earlier work, *Der Judenstaat*. He visualized Palestine as it would appear in 1923 and depicted a new society, created by the Jews, based on the cooperative principle. Enjoying the fruits of a highly developed technology and living in peace with their neighbors the new society looked forward to providing a model for the improvement of all humanity.

Herzl's *Altneuland* was one of many books dealing with the need to rebuild or reform society along modern lines—a popular theme of many nineteenth-century writers. Some works in this category such as the writings of the French socialists Cabet, Fourier, Blanc, Saint-Simon, and Proudhon were intentionally dubbed utopian by the self-styled "scientific socialists" Karl Marx and Frederich Engels in an effort to discredit their authors and their theories. Eventually the term *utopian* was applied by the Marxists in a derogatory manner to all reformers who did not accept the division of society into classes, the inevitability of class warfare, and social revolution.

Herzl's vision of a Jewish entity based on cooperative institutions clearly reflected his debt to the French utopian socialists, especially to the work of Charles Fourier (1772–1837) and Etienne Cabet (1788–1856). Herzl was also familiar with the utopian novel *Looking Backward* by Edward Bellamy (1850–98), the experiments of Robert Owen (1771–1858), the Rochdale Weaver Cooperative Movement, and the short-lived Rahaline agricultural venture.

A Journey to Eretz Israel in the Year 5800

Some of Herzl's contemporaries also fell back on the utopian novel to reveal their ideas on Jewish nationalism and statehood. Ten years prior to *Altneuland's* appearance in 1903, a Hebrew author named Elhanan Leib Levinsky dealt with the theme of redemption of the Jews in Palestine in a work entitled *A Journey to Eretz Israel in the Year 5800* (i.e., the year 2040). Levinsky was a firm believer in Hebrew culture and language, and like Ahad Ha-Am he portrayed Israel in his utopian novel as the spiritual center of a regenerated Jewish nation.

Ein Zukunftsblick

Another book, bearing the intriguing title *Ein Zukunftsblick* ("A Vision of the Future") written in 1882 and published in Vienna three years later, contained many of the elements later to be found in Theodor Herzl's utopian novel. A copy of *Ein Zukunftsblick* was in fact later found among the books in Herzl's library following his death. The author of this little-known work was Edmund Menahem Eisler (1850–1942), who was born in Tyrnau, Slovakia, into a family of enlightened merchants and scholars. Several members of his family, including a brother and uncle had written on Jewish themes, and Edmund himself was active for many years in the fields of Jewish journalism and literature.

Eisler's motivation in writing a Jewish utopian novel remains obscure. Although probably purely coincidental, the preface of his book is dated October, 1882—a period corresponding to some of the major pogroms in Russia and to the publication of Pinsker's *Auto-Emancipation*. The writer Shlomo Avineri, speculating on Eisler's motivation, has suggested that he may have been influenced by events closer to his home in Slovakia, in the Hungarian orbit of the Hapsburg monarchy.[374] One such event was the infamous Tiszla-Eszlar blood libel that caused a shock wave among Hungarian Jewry. Equally disturbing was the emergence of an anti-Semitic movement in Hungary in the wake of the Congress of Berlin. A deputy in the Hungarian parliament, named Count Geza Istöczy suggested that the Berlin Congress, in its deliberations on the future of the Ottoman Empire, should give serious consideration to the possibility of establishing a Jewish state in Palestine. Istöczy would later become leader of Hungary's anti-Semitic party.

Eisler's novel begins with a description of persecutions and pogroms directed against the Jews in an unidentified European country. Out of this vortex of violence emerges a young Jewish hero named Abner. A product of the philosophy of humanism and the Enlightenment, he decides to forge for himself and his people a new course of action, a radical departure from traditional Jewish passiveness and perpetual exile. Abner proposes a mass exodus of Jews out of Europe and their return to the ancient homeland in Eretz Israel.

Prompted by Abner and other like-minded Jewish leaders, the European Powers initiate an extensive debate on the entire Jewish Problem. Desiring to rid themselves of their Jewish populations, the European nations express support for Abner's plan. After considerable lobbying on the part of the Great Powers, the Turks, the masters of the Holy Land, agree to grant the Jews a charter for the creation of a Jewish state in Palestine. With the achievement of the charter a mass immigration of Jews from Europe occurs and within a relatively short time Palestine is transformed by the emigres from a barren desert to a viable modern technological society. Abner is rewarded for his leadership by being chosen king of the new state, a constitutional monarchy. As in the biblical account, the new state is called Judea and its population divided into twelve tribes. The tribes, however, are based on cultural and linguistic criteria rather than on ancient territorial divisions. Thus Russian speaking Jews form one tribe, German speakers another, etc.

A considerable portion of Eisler's utopia is devoted to a detailed description of Judea's constitution—a document containing 1,500 separate clauses and provisions. In general, the constitution incorporated a curious amalgam of biblical concepts and liberal ideas common to the Europe of his day. It begins by declaring all citizens equal before the law, including the king who can be removed for malfeasance in office. Hebrew is made the official language of the state, and all legal documents must be rendered in that language. However, in recognition of the polyglot population of the tribes of Judea, the constitution grants parties to any litigation the right to request a verdict be translated into their respective mother tongue. Ownership of land by a single individual is limited. If an individual through inheritance finds himself in possession of land above the allowable limit he is obligated to turn the excess land back to the state. The latter bears the responsibility of selling the excess property, but the former owner is entitled to its cash value. Universal military conscription is required by the constitution of all male citizens up to the age of fifty. The state is also responsible for the welfare of the aged, the infirm, orphans, and widows. Revenue for the state coffers is to be derived chiefly from a five percent tax on all incomes. Much space in *Ein Zukunftsblick* is devoted to the role of religion. Although freedom of religion is guaranteed to all citizens, special emphasis is given to the place of Judaism in the new state. On this issue Eisler seemed to be walking a tightrope. His basic commitment was definitely directed toward the creation of a secular state, but he was keenly aware that such an entity had to include some recognition (symbolic or realistically) of the Jewish religion and heritage. His solution to this problem was rather simple. Eisler proposed that the king symbolize in his person and office both religious and secular power. Other than this suggestion, and that of the restoration of the Temple, religion in Judea was to be stictly a private affair, reserved for the home and synagogue. Public religious ceremonies were to be prohibited except on Independence Day, when religious rites would form part of the celebration. Although the Jewish Sabbath would be made an official day of rest, marriage and divorce would fall under the jurisdiction of secular authorities. In addition, religious injunctions could not be used to prevent the burial of a suicide in a public cemetery; and children born out of wedlock would be entitled to all the legal rights enjoyed by legitimate offspring. In court a citizen had the right to take an oath prescribed by his religion. For those individuals who claimed not to belong to any religious community the oath could be based on the happiness of their children or parents.

In a chapter of *Ein Zukunftsblick* devoted to the European scene, Eisler ridiculed the anti-Semites who attributed all of the continent's problems to the Jews. The author's description of Europe following the Jewish exodus belies the arguments of the anti-Semites. The inhabitants of Europe are portrayed as having become more coarse and brutal. The social, political, and economic tensions between nations and classes, which in the past had been glossed over by using the Jews as scapegoats had now intensified and become more pronounced. In passages reminiscent of the ancient Hebrew prophets, Eisler predicts some of the more horrendous events of the twentieth century. He foresees the emergence of a militaristic and more aggressive Germany—"a hob-nailed boot regime," which has combined nationalism with a pseudo-Socialism. The attempts of France to counter the expansionist policies of its powerful German neighbor are frustrated by internal bickering as republicans, monarchists, Catholics, socialists, anarchists, and communists vie for power. The end result is that France falls an easy victim to German aggression. England fails to resolve the Irish Problem and is beset by terrorist campaigns on the part of Protestants and Catholics alike. The constant bloodshed takes its toll and Great Britain's power is gradually diminished. In the East the Russian bear hovers over all of Europe as it seeks to expand its power and frontiers.

Eisler's depiction of the relationship between the new state of Judea and its immediate neighbors is equally prophetic. He predicts the outbreak of war and the advance of a host of invaders toward the heartland of Judea. Although Eisler does not directly name the invaders, it is obvious from the terms he uses to describe them, such as the "children of the desert," that it is Judea's Arab neighbors he is portraying. From this unsought struggle, Judea emerges victorious, and King Abner informs the vanquished enemy that his people crave only peace and have no territorial ambitions. Eventually, Judea's neighbors accept Abner's offer of amity, and tranquility is restored to the region. Eisler ends his novel with the Judeans and their former foes enjoying peace and brotherhood, while Europe is engulfed by internal conflicts and wars.

Ein Zukunftsblick did not enjoy a wide audience, and with the passage of time the book and its author were forgotten. Both, however, were rediscovered in the middle years of the twentieth century, and Eisler's novel was reprinted in a Hebrew translation in an anthology of Zionist utopias entitled *Hezyonei Medinah* ("Visions of Zion").

Das Reich Judaea in Jahre 6000

Still another example of a utopian work with a Zionist theme appeared in 1893. *Das Reich Judaea in Jahre 6000* ("The Jewish State in the Year 2441") was written by Max

Austerberg-Verakoff, a non-Jew, although probably of Jewish extraction. Like Eisler, the author pictured a mass exodus of the Jews out of Europe, the colonization of Palestine, and the establishment of a Hebrew-speaking state. Greatly influenced by the writings of the American utopian-socialist Edward Bellamy, Austerberg-Verakoff depicts how the Jewish state had gone about resolving the troublesome problems of political and economic equality. The most unique feature of the novel, however, is the author's attempt to define the relationship of the immigrants with their coreligionists, who had remained behind in the Diaspora—a problem that still vexes Israeli and Diaspora leaders.

Looking Ahead

Edward Bellamy's literary classic *Looking Backward* also inspired a Zionist utopian novel entitled *Looking Ahead* (1899). The author, Henry Pereira Mendes (1852–1937), was born in Birmingham, England, into a prominent Sephardi family. He received a thorough religious and secular education. In is early youth he attended Northwich College, a boarding school founded by his father. Mendes continued his education at the University College of London. Some years later he would also receive a medical degree from the University of the City of New York. From 1874 until 1877 Mendes served as a rabbi to a Sephardi congregation in Manchester, England. Offered a post as a *hazzan* (cantor) and rabbi by the Shearith Israel congregation of New York City, Mendes eagerly accepted and immigrated to the United States in 1877. He would serve this congregation for nearly half a century.

A dynamic individual, Mendes represented an enlightened type of Orthodoxy, and used his influential post at Shearith Israel to work closely with all sectarian and social elements of Jewish society. His accomplishments on behalf of the American Jewish community were legion: Mendes was one of the founders of the Union of Orthodox Congregations of the United States and Canada (1897), as well as the *New York Kehillah* (1908) and the Young Women's Hebrew Association of New York (1902). Together with Sabato Morais (1823–97), Mendes was also instrumental in establishing the Jewish Theological Seminary of New York (1885). On the centennial of the birth of Sir Moses Montefiore, the rabbi of Shearith Israel appealed to his congregation to mark the event by supporting a pragmatic community project. As a result of his request, which involved many of the leading Jewish personalities of New York City, the Montefiore Home for Chronic Invalids was founded in 1884. In a similar manner the energetic rabbi also promoted the establishment of a branch of the Jewish Guild for Crippled Children.

Mendes was among the first of American Jewish leaders to respond favorably to Theodor Herzl's Zionist movement. At Herzl's personal request, Mendes helped create the Federation of American Zionists. He also served as a member of the Zionist Actions Committee from 1898 through 1899.

A prolific writer, Mendes produced numerous articles, pamphlets, and books on Jewish themes. Many of his essays appeared in the *American Hebrew,* which he and his brother Frederic De Sola Mendes (1850–1927) helped establish. Among his better-known works is *Looking Ahead,* in which Mendes expressed the essence of his Zionist vision, namely a mass exodus of Jews from Europe to Eretz Israel, and the creation of a Jewish state with Jerusalem as its capital. Like Herzl in his novel *Altneuland,* he envisaged Jerusalem's emergence as a center for world peace. Mendes also expressed the belief that if the nations of the world supported the national restoration of the Jews in their ancient homeland, that support would go a long way toward redressing the wrongs perpetrated against the Jewish people throughout the ages. A thorough Herzlian in his approach to Zionism, Mendes took special pains in his utopian novel to caution those Jews who chose to remain in the Diaspora to be loyal citizens of their country, but never to lose awareness of the temporary nature of their residence.

In general, in confronting the problems affecting Jewry, Henry Pereira Mendes adhered closely to the principle of *kelal Yisrael* (the totality of Israel); and it was this concept that dominated his Zionist utopia, as well as his life. His activities enriched the American Jewish community, just as his remarkable personality touched all who crossed his path. His character was best summed up by one of Mendes' former students, Supreme Court Justice, Benjamin N. Cardoza (1870–1938), who, while delivering the eulogy on the occasion of Mendes' death in 1937, stated:

> What can I say, save that I have loved and honored him? His sweetness was unique and beautiful. Now that the life is finished it is the personal phase of it which is uppermost in my thoughts. The larger achievements will be measured by the world.[375]

40

Simon Dubnow
and Diaspora Nationalism

At a time when Jewish communal self-government had virtually disappeared from Europe, the idea of making it the basis for Jewish survival in the Diaspora resurfaced in the minds of a handful of thinkers. The concept of Jewish autonomism, in its modern form, originated in the early years of the twentieth century. However, indications of this trend were already apparent some years earlier in the writings of such individuals as Bernard Lazare (1865–1903), Nathan Birnbaum (1864–1937), and Chaim Zhitlowsky (1865–1943). The idea also took root among socialist and nationalist groups. The latter were to a large extent influenced by the multicultural and political struggles of the Austro-Hungarian Empire. In this great empire the regime was compelled to search for way to enable the various nationalities that composed the state to coexist in peace, while at the same time satisfying some of their nationalistic and cultural claims. Of special significance in this connection was the work of the socialist party of Austria, which advocated a system of government for the empire in which each national minority would be able to enjoy the fruits of autonomy, i.e., self-rule.

A similar suggestion had been made by Chaim Zhitlowsky. Originally a participant in the revolutionary activities of the Russian *narodniki,* he broke with the group when they advocated assimilation as a solution to the Jewish Problem. After joining the Russian Socialist Revolutionary Party, Zhitlowsky founded a Jewish section, and stressed a program that included national emancipation and Yiddish as the preferred language of the Jewish people. Forced in 1888 to flee from Russia, he went to Switzerland where he edited a publication called the *Russian Worker.* Following the Russian Revolution of 1905, Zhitlowsky returned to his native land and founded a new party, the Sejmist. Although elected to the Russian parliament (the Duma), he was not permitted to take his seat because of his past radical activities. In 1908 Zhitlowsky immigrated to the United States (New York), and as editor of *Dos Neie Leben* ("The New Life") rapidly became the outstanding spokesman for Socialism, Yiddishism, and Jewish autonomism.

Many of his ideas, especially those pertaining to cultural autonomy, were gradually accepted by Jewish socialists, notably by the Bund, and various Zionist-Socialist factions. In the case of the Bund this approval represented a complete turnabout from their original policy. In its early days the Bund, with its Marxist orientation, had rejected the idea of Jewish national and cultural rights. For many years the leaders of the Bund had tried to justify its existence as a separate socialist party on the grounds that it alone through the medium of the Yiddish language was able to reach the Jewish working masses. In time the party's policy gradually changed as more of the membership agreed with Juli Martov (1873–1923) that:

> . . . a working class which is content with the lot of inferior nationality will not rise up against the lot of an inferior class. . . . The growth of national and class consciousness must go hand in hand.[376]

Accordingly, in spite of the steadfast opposition of the Russian Social Democratic Party, the Bund eventually insisted on the right of Jewish self-determination in all matters pertaining to culture and education.

By far the most eloquent spokesman for Jewish autonomism was the eminent historian Simon Dubnow (1860–1941).[377] He was born in the small town of Mstislav, in the province of Mohilev, White Russia, into a family whose ancestry included a long line of scholars. Simon was one of nine children. His parents lived on the edge of absolute poverty and constantly struggled to survive. The patriarchal head of the family, Simon's paternal grandfather, had rejected the world of business to devote himself exclusively to study (he was a great admirer of the Elijah ben Solomon, the Gaon of Vilna). Although Simon would eventually rebel against the traditional Orthodoxy of his grandfather, the latter's piety and intense devotion to study left a lasting mark on his own life. Throughout his later years Simon Dubnow would refer with great reverence to his grandfather, conscious of the fact that he himself had inherited many of the traits which had characterized the old sage.

As a young child, Simon was initiated into the traditional education process then customary among Orthodox Jews. He attended a *heder* and studied Bible and Talmud. At age nine he began to question this conventional Jewish pattern of education. He came upon a copy of the medieval Hebrew chronicle *Josippon* and devoured its contents. Sometime later Dubnow discovered Moses Mendelssohn's *Biur,* which he avidly read and secretly shared with some of his classmates. While still continuing his talmudic studies, Simon clandestinely sought out the works of various *Haskalah* writers. From an older brother and from local *maskilim* he secured such works as Eugene Sue's *Mysteries of Paris* (in Hebrew translation), Abraham Mapu's romance, *Avit Tzavua* ("The Hypocrite"), the poetry of Micha Joseph Lebenson, and issues of Peretz Smolenskin's periodical *Ha-Shahar* ("The Dawn").

Simon Dubnow's exposure to *Haskalah* literature had a profound effect on his development as an independent thinker. At age twelve he composed in Hebrew a diatribe against religious fanaticism. Assigned as his bar-mitzvah discourse a pilpul-type exercise (i.e., a sort of mental gymnastics, consisting in establishing artificial analogies between divergent themes, or in creating distinctions between related parts) Simon demurred and refused to deliver the speech. These acts, as well as his pursuit of secular subject matter, soon gained him a reputation among the Orthodox townspeople as a heretic.

In 1874 Dubnow enrolled in the official government school in Mstislav and for the first time was exposed to the language and culture of Russia and the literature of the West. He became enamored with the poetry of Alexander Sergeevich Pushkin (1799–1837) and Mikhail Yurievich Lermontov (1814–41), and formed a deep attachment for Russian literature that would remain with him throughout his lifetime. Indeed, he would later adopt the Russian language as his vehicle of expression as a writer and historian. It was also during his formative years that Dubnow encountered the writings of Ludwig Börne (1786–1837), an essayist and member of the Young Germany Movement. He greatly admired the fact that Börne had also rebelled against his traditional background and had immigrated to Paris in order to be able to freely express his libertarian convictions.

However, unlike many of the Jewish youths anxious to escape the confines of traditional Orthodoxy, Dubnow did not espouse radicalism or any of the reform movements of his day. He was not impressed with Aaron Liebermann's efforts to organize a Jewish socialist movement or with those Jews who enlisted in the Russian revolutionary parties. His cosmopolitan outlook led him to reject the Hibbat Zion movement led by Lilienblum and Pinsker. Instead, in these early years he dreamt of a synthesis of the Jewish and Gentile worlds, although crystallization of these ideas did not come until later in his career.

Refused admission to the Vilna Jewish Teachers Institute, he moved to Dvinsk and enrolled in that city's gymnasium. Life in Dvinsk was hard and Dubnow suffered great privation. After completing his studies in Smolensk he prepared for entrance into a university, but was unable to pass the examination in mathematics. Depressed by his failure, Dubnow would never again attempt to receive a university education. Instead, he continued his studies on his own, amassing in the process an extraordinary amount of knowledge. It was during this stage in his life that he was attracted by the culture of France and England. The positivism of Auguste Comte (1798–1857) and the classic liberalism of John Stuart Mill (1806–73) were much more to his liking than the German metaphysical systems of Georg Wilhelm Friedrich Hegel (1770–1831) and Karl Marx (1818–83). Dubnow also read and studied the works of the English historian Henry Thomas Buckle (1821–62) and the naturalist Charles Robert Darwin (1809–82) and avidly absorbed the writings of the French philosophers François-Marie Arouet (a.k.a. Voltaire 1694–1778), Denis Diderot (1713–84), and Marie Jean de Condorcet (1743–94). At the same time Dubnow also broadened his knowledge of languages by mastering Latin, Greek, English, and French to complement his fluency in Yiddish, Hebrew, and Russian.

On June 20, 1880, at the age of twenty, the young scholar found himself in St. Petersburg, the capital city of the Russian Empire. Because Jews were forbidden to live in the capital without a special residence permit, he was forced to assume the fictitious status of a domestic servant to an attorney. His residency became more complicated a few years later after a brief romance and marriage. Nevertheless, it was during his stay in the czarist capital that he began in earnest his literary and scholarly career. Fascinated by history, he strove to find his way through the treasure trove of the Jewish experience. In pursuit of this goal he became a regular contributor to the *Russki Yevrei* after the latter journal published his first article on the development of Jewish thought. During this same period Dubnow also headed the foreign news department of the Russian-Jewish periodical *Razvet*. In 1882, after a falling out with the paper's pan-Palestinian policy, he transferred his allegiance to the *Voskhod* ("Sunrise"), an association that would endure for a quarter of a century.

The *Voskhod* occupied a unique role in the life of Russia's Jewish intelligentsia and numbered among its contributors some of the great Jewish literary figures of the day. Dubnow's input was considerable and included essays on the false Messiahs Shabbetai Zevi and Jacob Frank, as well as original studies that would later become the basis for his major works, a philosophy of history, a history of Hassidism, and a multivolume world history of the Jews.[378]

In 1890 Dubnow shifted his residence to Odessa, the mecca of Russian-Jewish intellectual life. The thirteen years that he would spend in this city would be the happiest in his life and the period in which he matured into a great scholar and public figure. In Odessa he came in contact with a galaxy of the leading personalities in Hebrew and Yiddish literature. Foremost among the latter was Ahad Ha-Am, whose friendship he would greatly cherish. Gradually, an informal circle of Jewish literati and activists developed around Dubnow and crystallized into a group dubbed "the National Committee." The major aim of this entity was to combat assimilation among the Russian-Jewish community. Dubnow now shed his earlier cosmopolitan views and moved closer to the ideas of Jewish nationalism and self-government. Out of this radical change in outlook emerged his famous *Letters on Old and New Judaism*. These originally appeared in *Voskhod* during the years 1897 through 1903, and then in book form in 1907. The letters laid the theoretical foundations for Dubnow's theory of Diaspora Nationalism (also sometimes called Galut Nationalism, Spiritual Nationalism, or Autonomism).

Although many of his contemporaries favored some form of Jewish nationalism, Dubnow's theory was unique. Unlike the Orthodox who favored the past, the Zionists who were concerned primarily with the Jewish future, or the socialists who were preoccupied with the Jewish present, and for whom Jewish history began only with the emergence of the Jewish proletariat, Dubnow, with his profound historical approach, wove into his theory all the strands of the Jewish past, present, and future.

Applying himself in his letters to the question of nationalism, Dubnow postulated three stages of national life in human society—the tribal, the political territorial, and the cultural historical, or spiritual. The lowest stage was that of the tribal whereas the highest and most sophisticated level was that of the spiritual. In the latter the connection between state and nationality disappears, and the nation becomes a purely cultural historical society. Only the Jewish people, Dubnow claimed, had succeeded in attaining the spiritual stage.

> We have many examples in the history of nations that have disappeared from the scene after they lost their land and became dispersed among the nations. We found only one instance, however, of a people that has survived for thousands of years despite dispersion and the loss of their homeland. This unique people is the people of Israel.[379]

In spite of loss of political independence and national territory followed by dispersion and even loss of its unifying language, the Jews had shown a stubborn determination to carry on autonomous development. This had enabled them to reach the highest stage of cultural historical individuality. Dubnow emphasized that this remarkable development was not a miracle, but rather the product of historical evolution. The Jews in the Diaspora had indeed lost many of the attributes that normally ensured the continuous existence of a nation. However, as a compensation for these losses they had evolved a special social system and communal ideology. Through these adaptations, the Jewish people were able to survive in foreign lands with a semblance of judicial autonomy and spiritual independence. In every period since the dispersion from Eretz Israel a Jewish community existed that managed to be more successful than others in maintaining self-rule and national creativity. The flourishing community would in turn act as a center for the Jewish communities outside its borders. In the early Middle Ages, Babylon replaced the Palestinian center. Later Spain and the Rhineland came to the foreground. In the late Middle Ages and the beginning of the modern era, Poland and Lithuania became the major centers. In the interim, the Jews became for the most part a European people. In the course of 2,000 years, Dubnow stressed, the Jewish people were converted from an ordinary nation into the very essence of nationhood — i.e., pure spirituality, the highest stage of nationalism. Accordingly, Jewish history proved that it was possible to establish in modern times an entity enjoying internal independence within the framework of a foreign country. Such an entity would rest on firmer ground and be more highly developed than its Middle-Ages predecessors. Cultural autonomy in those countries where compact Jewish communities existed was therefore feasible as well as desirable and, Dubnow insisted, was the best way to resolve the Jewish Problem.

In presenting his theory of Diaspora Nationalism, Dubnow clearly had in mind the Jews of Eastern Europe and the Austro-Hungarian Empire. However, many of his ideas reflected theories derived from the European West, particularly from the writings of the philologist and historian Ernest Renan (1823–92) and from the pen of Adolphe Hippolyte Taine (1828–93). Both French thinkers were concerned with the so-called organic concept of the nation, which they termed *race*. From Taine, Dubnow took the concept that the particular situation of a people and its aspirations are faithfully reflected in the spiritual attributes of its great men. Renan's historical writings made it easier for Dubnow to change his earlier antagonistic assessment of Jewish religion into a positive evaluation of it as the revelation of the Jewish national spirit. The religion of Israel, he was convinced, had until the nineteenth century been an important element of Jewish nationalism, a means of self-defense used by a people who possessed none of the defense mechanisms of other nations. Elaborating on this point, Dubnow noted that when the Jewish people, by virtue of its belief in monotheism, became a distinct group within the pagan, and later the Christian, world its leaders, in order to combat assimilation, were forced to make use of religion as a weapon for survival. In the nineteenth century, however, a Jewish renaissance had occurred that tended to liberate individuals and to stimulate a secular interest in Jewish national life. The development of the Wissenschaft des Judenthums movement in Germany, Dubnow believed, was one the manifestations of this Jewish renaissance. Religion, he insisted, was a discipline that had been imposed on the national organism, and that it was only necessary as long as Jewish culture remained isolated and unrelated to the cultures of other peoples. Once emancipation was achieved, the religious discipline would no longer be desirable.

In Hassidism Dubnow saw still another sign of the creative power of the Jewish religion. In Eastern Europe Hassidism had helped to preserve traditional values among the Jews, but the Hassidics had remained aloof from the cultures of the peoples among whom they lived. Cooperation with the latter, Dubnow felt, would enable Jewry to exist as a European people, enjoying cultural autonomy in this vast region, although destined to remain forever a permanent minority.

In regard to the Diaspora, Dubnow felt it represented a challenge to the Jewish people to measure up to its fullest potential as a spiritual nation. Far from considering the

Diaspora an unmitigated tragedy, or an anomaly, he believed it provided an important stage in the development of Jewish nationalism, as it proved conclusively that a nation could exist without a territorial base, just as it could without bonds of blood. The decisive factor was the will of the nation to exist, without being artificially separated from the people among whom it lived and without the danger of assimilation. National, as distinct from religious, autonomy was the best way to achieve this goal.

However, even a spiritual nation needed a structural framework to hold it together. Besides stressing the theme that the Jewish people, as a result of their long experience in the Diaspora, had reached the highest stage of national life (the spiritual), Dubnow added a corollary to his historical research. He proposed that the Jewish people be formally recognized as a nation within the confines of those states in which they lived in considerable numbers. The host states would be responsible for guaranteeing the Jew's rights to preserve their own language and culture, and that they be allowed to live as a respected minority sharing fully the privileges and responsibilities of citizenship and free from all discriminatory restrictions. Thus, a network of Jewish autonomous communities rather than a Jewish national home (i.e., state) would finally resolve the Jewish Problem.

Diaspora Nationalism aroused a storm of opposition from various groups. It ran counter to the advocates of assimilation whom Dubnow often accused of preaching treason and moral defeat. The theory was equally disturbing to the original position taken by the Bund, and Dubnow did not rejoice when the latter reversed its stand and adopted a variant form of cultural autonomism. Unlike the Bundists, he was irrevocably hostile to the idea of a Jewish state. A realist, Dubnow adopted a position that fell somewhere between the Bundists and the Zionists. He would often note that if the power existed to transfer the entire Diaspora to a Jewish state he would support it without hesitation. However, because such a development was highly unlikely his acceptance of the Diaspora was based solely on historical necessity. Preserving and developing the national existence of the greater part of the nation, which, even if a Jewish state was created, would remain in the Diaspora was of the utmost importance.

Dubnow's ideas also differed to some extent to those in the socialist camp who looked to Zhitlowsky as their mentor. Chronologically, many of Zhitlowsky's ideas had preceded Dubnow's theories. Vague hints of autonomism were already evident in Zhitlowsky's first work, published in 1887, in which he also expressed the need to raise the status of the Jewish people to that of a normal nation. Dubnow's approach was somewhat different, as he believed that cultural and spiritual fulfillment could only be achieved to the extent that a people were able to transcend the normality of territorial nations.

Zhitlowsky also believed that it was possible to be a Christian by faith and a Jew by nationality. Dubnow believed that a Jew could be potentially or actually a member of the Jewish faith, or without religion at all. But exit from Judaism by acceptance of the Christian faith meant exit from the Jewish nation. Dubnow also rejected the idea of religion as the supreme criterion of Jewish nationalism. He considered Judaism to be not merely a religion, but a system of culture. Nevertheless, he realized that the religion of Judaism was an integral part of Jewry's national culture, and that anyone seeking to destroy it undermined the very basis of national existence.

Dubnow and Zhitlowsky also differed to some extent on the role of language in nationalism. The self-taught scholar did not share some of his critic's beliefs in the power of mysticism and romanticism in furthering nationalism. He thus had no strong feelings for those theorists who imputed mystical attributes to land and language. He was reluctant to completely accept the views of intellectuals who considered the connection between a people and its language as an essential, if not the most important, factor in defining nationalism; hence, his tolerant attitude in the language struggle between Hebrew and Yiddish that ensued in Jewish circles during his lifetime. In illustrating his neutrality on the question of language, he fondly compared Hebrew and Yiddish to the two legs of an individual. Hebrew as a natural leg, and Yiddish was a wooden leg grafted onto the Jewish national body after the amputation of one of the original legs. For the socialist Zhitlowsky, Yiddish was the centerpiece of modern Jewish culture, the language of the proletariat, and the cornerstone of Jewish survival as a progressive people.

Although in his heart of hearts Dubnow considered Hebrew the true Jewish national language, he did not belittle or underestimate the value of Yiddish. In fact he considered the jargon spoken by 7 million Jews in Eastern Europe to be a vital bastion against cultural assimilation. In addition, he believed it would be foolish to abandon Yiddish, one of the foundations of:

> . . . national unity in the very hour that the languages of the people around us rob our people of thousands and tens of thousands of its sons, so that they no longer understand the language [Yiddish] used by their parents. . . .[380]

Dubnow's theory of Diaspora Nationalism was vigorously opposed by the Zionists, who insisted that the Diaspora must be liquidated. Dubnow responded by pointing out that in seventeen years the Hibbat Zion movement had only managed to assist 3,600 Jews to settle in Palestine. At this rate, even if the Zionists succeeded in settling half a million more within the next century, it would be no more than the number of Jews living in the Kiev district of Russia—a fraction of Russian Jewry.

Political Zionism, Dubnow declared, was merely a renewed form of messianism that was transmitted from the enthusiastic minds of the religious kabbalists to the minds of the political communal leaders. In the excitement generated by the idea of a Jewish rebirth, messianism had passed over from the religious to the secular political arena.

Dubnow's view of Political Zionism would with the passage of time evolve from outright skepticism to reluctant acceptance. He would regard the issuance of the Balfour Declaration by Great Britain and the Jewish efforts to rebuild Palestine as miracles of Jewish history. As early as 1901 he began to entertain some doubts about his earlier assessment of Political Zionism. He wondered if the movement might possibly be able to succeed in settling 1 million Jews in Palestine. Such a development, Dubnow felt, would help smooth the way for the achievement of Jewish autonomy in the Diaspora.

Although Dubnow credited the Zionist movement with containing many positive elements, he could not accept its continual denial of the Diaspora. Zionism, he stressed, could only be a healthy movement if it understood that the return to Judaism was the primary goal and not merely an indirect objective that might result from the restoration of a Jewish state. The Diaspora in turn could not be ignored or dismissed if Jewry was to survive. Zionism had to acknowledge reality and could be helpful if it served as a transition to the higher principle of spiritual nationalism, the product of countless generations of the Jewish people's historical and religious experience.

In their quest for a Jewish state the Zionists had brought to the foreground the issues of Palestine and the Diaspora. On these vital questions Dubnow and Ahad Ha-Am carried on a debate for many years. It had begun in their Odessa days, and continued later in the columns of the leading Jewish periodicals and in their private correspondence. As a result of this extended debate, both men were able to clarify their views and in the process draw closer to the position of the other.

Dubnow, like Ahad Ha-Am, eventually came to share the view that even after the establishment of a center in Palestine, the majority of Jews would remain in the Diaspora. Ahad Ha-Am had been quick to point out that Dubnow's initial theory contained a serious flaw. He had neglected to clarify whether he thought that the Jews who remained in the Diaspora would be able to carry on a full and complete national life. As a result of Ahad Ha-Am's criticism, Dubnow was forced to reevaluate his theory and recognize the possibility that total autonomy might be unobtainable.

The divergence between Dubnow and Ahad Ha-Am was not over basic theory, but rather over a reflection of the subtle differences in their personalities, which affected their outlook on the Jewish Problem. Dubnow, with his historical approach, was much closer to the Jewish masses and their suffering than was his friend and rival, Ahad Ha-Am. He could not help being deeply concerned over the future of Diaspora Jewry. Ahad Ha-Am, an intellectual elitist, was more concerned with the fate of Judaism and with the need to establish a cultural center in Palestine than with formulating a program for Jews who chose to remain in the Diaspora.

Dubnow agreed with the idea that the handful of Jews in the Holy Land would live a fuller national life than those in the Diaspora, but he was unwilling to abandon the latter. He feared that, ". . . the Land of Israel might be converted into a Noah's Ark in which only a portion of Jewry will be saved from the great flood, while the rest sink in its waves."[381]

Dubnow's theory of Diaspora Nationalism added to his luster as a Jewish historian and thinker. Nevertheless, he was far from being a cloistered scholar and was constantly torn between his love for the solitude of the study and the public battle for Jewish civil rights. Inevitably, the latter objective diverted much of his time and energy from scholarly pursuits. His public activity intensified following the notorious Kishinev pogrom of 1903. Dubnow banded together with other Jewish leaders in organizing self defense and in launching a campaign to offset the anti-Semitism sweeping across Russia.

In the aftermath of the pogroms, Dubnow decided to leave the city of Odessa and accepted a position to lecture on Jewish history in an institute for higher learning in Vilna, Lithuania. He would remain in Vilna for three years (1903–06), a period that witnessed tumultuous events, including the Russo-Japanese War and the Russian Revolution of 1905. The military defeat and the revolution compelled the czar to consider granting his subjects some semblance of constitutional government. Indeed, the promulgation of a constitution for Russia in August of 1905, and the subsequent elections for the first parliament ("Duma") aroused great hopes among the Jewish population of the empire. Opinions were divided in the Jewish community as whether the best cause of action would be to concentrate on going it alone in the struggle to obtain civil rights or to throw the whole weight of Jewish support behind the progressive Russian parties in their struggle against the reactionary government. Most of the Jewish intellectuals favored the latter alternative. The Jewish people, they believed, would automatically benefit from a triumph of Russian liberalism and ought therefore to submerge their particular interests for the greater objective. Dubnow however thought otherwise. Along with Vladimir Jabotinsky (1880–1940), the future leader of the Zionist Revisionist Movement, he participated in the creation of the League for the Attainment of Equal Rights for the Jewish People in Russia.

Dubnow was elected to the Vilna section of the League, and was especially pleased by the organization's adoption of many of his ideas. The League, which rapidly gained support among various segments of Jewish society, included among its goals a demand for Jewish national rights and cultural autonomy.

At the second conference of the League in November of 1905 a resolution was proposed that an all-Russian Jewish national assembly be convened to decide what form Jewish self-determination should take. This resolution was followed several months later by a suggestion by Dubnow that the Jewish delegates elected to the Russian Duma organize themselves into a caucus. The proposal received the backing of the Zionist parties, but alienated those Jewish League delegates active in the Russian K.D. Party (Constitutional Democrats). When the latter individuals threatened to withdraw from the League, Dubnow and his supporters retracted their proposal. For his part in this affair Dubnow was attacked by the Russian-Jewish press and accused of being incapable of looking beyond his own narrow interests.

In September of 1906 Dubnow moved to St. Petersburg to occupy a special chair for Jewish history in a newly created Russian progressive university. As the early winds of revolution drifted off and gave way to reaction, the university was an early victim. By July of 1907 the counter-revolution was in full swing, and had for all practical purposes annulled all of the democratic freedoms brought about by the Revolution of 1905. Among the casualties was the League for the Attainment of Equal Rights for the Jewish People in Russia. Dubnow was disheartened by the turn of events, but resolved to remain in the Russian capital to continue to struggle for Jewish national autonomy. The result of his renewed efforts was the creation of a movement that became known as "Volkism" and entered the political arena as the Volks Partei (Peoples' Party).[382] The party adhered closely to the principles outlined by Dubnow and emphasized a program built around the Jewish *kehillah,* the legal recognition of Yiddish; and a system of free education. These planks were designed to allow maximum communal autonomy for the Jewish population of Russia. The Volks Partei would prove to be Dubnow's sole attempt at political leadership. Although party branches were established in Lithuania, Poland, and the Ukraine, the movement was not very successful. The party lasted until 1918, when it dissolved in the aftermath of the Russian Revolution.

Throughout this turbulent period of Russian history, Dubnow somehow managed to devote long hours to historical research and to the Jewish Historical Ethnographic Society (for ten years he edited the organization's quarterly, *Yevreiskaya Starina*). The Russian Revolution of 1917, which overthrew the Czarist regime, marked a turning point in Dubnow's life. The Provisional Revolutionary government issued an official manifesto proclaiming Jewish emancipation, and the hopes of the Jewish communities for the future soared. Dubnow shared in the general enthusiasm. The triumph of the Bolsheviks in November, 1917, dampened much of the original optimism as it brought with it considerable suffering, both physical and spiritual, to traditional Jewry.

Paradoxically, the defeat of the Central Powers and the dismantling of the Russian and the Austro-Hungarian empires cleared the way for a testing of Dubnow's autonomist theories. Independent national states emerged from the Versailles Peace Conference that were based on the principle of self-determination (Poland, Czechoslovakia, Yugoslavia, Lithuania, Latvia, Rumania). In practice this Allied policy had its drawbacks as it was not possible under the ethnic and geographic conditions then prevailing in Europe to bestow on all nations the right to self-determination. Several of the newly established states,

Czechoslovakia and Yugoslavia for example, were multinational from the outset (i.e., they were intended to be partnerships of several peoples). In others that in theory encompassed one nationality there existed large national minorities (e.g., Poland where minorities accounted for one third of the total population). Complicating matters was the fact that among some of the nations that gained independence, extreme nationalist sentiment was rife and frequently accompanied by violent anti-Semitism and pogroms. As a result of these developments the victorious Allied Powers looked about to find a way to safeguard minorities and minority rights in the newly created states.

The quest for means to stabilize the new European order was in line with the expectations of the Jewish political parties, particularly Dubnow's Volks Partei. All of the Jewish parties placed their hope in the survival and expansion of the corporate Jewish minorities in the newly created national states. The demands at the Paris Peace Conference for Jewish national minority rights had been energetically supported by the American Jewish Congress and the Comite des Delegations Juives. The Allies, sensitive to these demands, had agreed to regard the Jews as a religious or ethnic minority entitled to protection and even autonomy. Pressure exerted by the American Jewish Congress and the Comite on the Allies was largely responsible for not only the inclusion in the international treaties signed by the new states of guarantees for the Jews, but also of guarantees for all minority groups in the former territories of Russia, Austro-Hungary, and Germany.

The first attempt to provide minorities with autonomy was made in the Ukraine and preceded the decisions of the Paris Peace Conference. In the days following the outbreak of the Russian Revolution the Ukraine had declared itself an independent state and had granted autonomy to the three major minority groups in its territory – the Jews, the Poles, and the Russians. Shortly afterwards, a Ministry of Jewish Affairs was established. In addition, a Jewish National Council composed of representatives of the Jewish communities was organized. However, the civil strife that marked the new state and its occupation by the Red Army in 1919, followed by the incorporation of the Ukraine into the Soviet Union, prevented a successful outcome to the experiment in autonomy that had begun so promisingly.

National autonomy for Jews in Lithuania was granted in 1919. It was based on a union of Jewish communities, with a Jewish National Council and a Ministry for Jewish Affairs as the key institutions. The Lithuanian experiment fared no better than its Ukraine counterpart. It managed to survive for a few years, but was abolished by the ultranationalist regime that came into power in 1922. Of the original programs instituted during the period of autonomy, only state support of Jewish schools survived until the end of Lithuania's independence in 1940. A similar fate befell the Baltic states of Latvia and Estonia. Here too, support of Jewish schools continued until both entities were absorbed into the Soviet Union.

Much more significant was the story of Jewish autonomy in Dubnow's native Russia. With the establishment of the Soviet Union, autonomy was granted to the Jews along with other nationalities in the country. Aware of their dispersion throughout the Soviet Union, the government proclaimed a few districts in the Ukraine and the Crimea containing Jewish majorities to be Jewish autonomous districts. The government eventually added to these autonomous districts urban and rural communities in which Jews were predominate in the population. In all of these places Yiddish was recognized as an official language. Later, the Soviet regime decided to have one of the remote provinces of the country turned into an autonomous Jewish territory. The eastern province of Birobidzhan was chosen for this purpose and was proclaimed a Jewish national territory in 1934. Immigration of the Jews to Birobidzhan preceded slowly and a majority was never achieved within the general population of the province.

Governments in the West did not favor granting Jews autonomous rights, nor were the Jewish populations interested or eager to embrace the principle. Although Jewish communities existed in many western nations, their status was quite different from that of their brethren in Eastern Europe. For the most part they were fully emancipated and enjoyed the fruits of citizenship, with its full range of benefits and privileges. Only in Latin America, and especially in Argentina, did the Jewish population find it necessary to embrace some form of communal government. In doing so they chose the Eastern European *kehillah* as their model, differing only from the latter in that membership was voluntary.

The institutions of Jewish self-government in Europe broke down during the years of Nazi domination, but revived to some extent in the aftermath of World War II. In the Soviet Union, however, nothing remained of the national autonomy of the prewar years, apart from the failed experiment in Birobidzhan.

Soon after the Bolsheviks had assumed power in Russia, Dubnow was asked by them to participate in the work of committees assigned to prepare publications on various Jewish themes. He accepted the offer, but his contributions were never published. Although seemingly in favor with the Bolshevik regime and holding down a post at the government-sponsored Jewish People's University, Dubnow felt ill at ease. He was alarmed at the increasing signs of a Bolshevik dictatorship and by the reign of terror initiated by the party's leader. For the first time Dubnow began to give serious thought to leaving his native land. Through the intervention of friends in the newly established state of Lithuania he was offered a position as a professor of Jewish history at the University of Kovno. After considerable delay and red tape, Dubnow managed to leave for Lithuania (April 23, 1922) and soon after began teaching at the university. He did not remain long in Kovno, however. Opposition to his appointment on the part of the Lithuanian faculty and the limited intellectual climate compelled him to emigrate again. Dubnow settled in Berlin, where he was soon surrounded by a circle of devoted followers and former students. During his residence in Germany he completed his great historical works, notably the ten-volume *Weltgeschichte des Judisches Volkes* and a history of *Hassidism*. He also participated in the creation in Vilna of the Yiddisher Visenshaftlikher Institut (Institute for Jewish Research), better-known by its acronym "YIVO."

The rise of Hitler to power in Germany (1933) brought the aging scholar face to face with the need to move once again. Urged by friends to go to Palestine, Dubnow balked and chose instead to settle in Riga, Latvia. His decision not to leave Europe reflected his reluctance to abandon the Jews of the Diaspora, as well as his long-held views as spiritual leader of the Volkist movement.

The founder of the Volks Partei and chief advocate of Diaspora Nationalism thus bravely adhered to his principles, even when he knew his personal safety was at stake. He continued to resist the pressures of his friends to immigrate to Eretz Israel, or even to another part of the Diaspora, the United States. On July 1, 1941, the Nazis entered Riga and Dubnow's fate was sealed. By October, the Germans had decided to liquidate the ghetto, and a month later they carried out their first "action." With the help of some friends who managed to conceal him, Dubnow escaped the initial roundup. On the night of December 8, 1941, the Nazis launched a second "action" against the Jews of Riga. All of the old and sick, as well as the women in advanced stages of pregnancy were rounded up and herded into waiting buses for deportation to a death camp. Dubnow, now eighty-one years old and sick and feverish, was among those caught and designated for deportation. Unable to move quickly enough to his assigned bus he attracted the attention of a drunken Latvian soldier who was advancing along the line of deportees. Without hesitation, the soldier raised his rifle and fired a bullet into the old man's back. The venerable scholar died instantly. The next day some of his friends who had survived the "action" found Dubnow's body and buried him in the old cemetery in the heart of Riga's ghetto. Legend has it that the last words that the old historian uttered as he was being led out for shipment to the death camp were: "Brothers, don't forget! Recount what you hear and see! Brothers make a record of it all!"[383]

41

Territorialism

Criticism of Zionism by the Bundists and the Volkists was echoed by still another group, the Territorialists. This group came to the foreground of Jewish politics in the wake of Theodor Herzl's frantic diplomacy. The Fifth Zionist Congress held in Basle in 1901 marked a turning point in Herzl's negotiations and in the evolution of the World Zionist Movement. Despairing of obtaining a charter from Turkey, Herzl changed tactics and looked to England for support of his movement and its objectives. The first opportunity to test this new strategy came in 1902 when Herzl was invited to testify before the British Royal Commission on Alien Immigration. Lord Nathaniel Mayer Rothschild (1840–1915), a member of the commission, met privately with the Zionist leader, and the groundwork for future Zionist contacts with the Anglo-Jewish community was firmly established. In addition, Herzl gained access to the British Colonial Secretary, Joseph Chamberlain and the Foreign Secretary, Lord Henry Lansdowne, and was able to pass on to these officials his ideas for a Jewish settlement in the Sinai Peninsula at El Arish. The project, however, failed to materialize when it encountered the opposition of Lord Cromer, the British Consul General and Minister Plenipotentiary to Egypt.

The Uganda Offer

Although dismayed by the setback, Herzl continued to negotiate with the British officials, who eventually suggested a possible alternative settlement site in East Africa (the Uganda Scheme). Without awaiting the final resolution of these sensitive negotiations, the Zionist leader departed for Russia, where he hoped to persuade the rabid anti-Semitic czarist regime to permit Zionist activity throughout the empire. Profoundly disturbed by the condition of Russian Jewry and still reeling from the aftermath of the infamous Kishinev pogrom, Herzl began to give serious thought to finding a short-term solution to their plight. While in the city of Vilna, he received a letter (August 16, 1903) from Leopold Jacob Greenberg (1861–1931), his liaison with the British officials. Included with the letter was a communique sent to Greenberg by Sir Clement Lloyd Hill, Chief of the Protectorate Department of the British Foreign Office. It indicated that Lord Lansdowne, the Secretary of State for Foreign Affairs was prepared to entertain favorably proposals for the establishment of a Jewish colony or settlement on conditions that would enable the members to observe their national customs. Furthermore, the Secretary was prepared to discuss, if a suitable site had been found and subject to the views of his advisers in East Africa, the details of the colonization scheme. These would include the grant of a considerable tract of land, the appointment of a Jewish official as the chief of local administration, and permission for the colony to have a free hand in regard to municipal legislation and the management of religious and purely domestic affairs. However, such local autonomy was to be conditional upon the right of His Majesty's government to exercise a general control.

The letter created a profound impression on Herzl, although he was not entirely happy with its contents. Greenberg had written him that Joseph Chamberlain was considering a territory in East Africa between Nairobi and the Nan escarpment, and Herzl was not certain if this region was suitable for Jewish settlement. Nor was it clear whether the British government was willing to grant the Jewish colonists the independence that Herzl considered essential to any settlement scheme. He also had doubts about the reaction of the Zionist Organization to an offer of territory in East Africa. However, after his initial hesitation, Herzl decided to bring the British proposal before the Sixth Zionist Congress, which was scheduled to convene in Basle, Switzerland, shortly following his return from Russia.

The Uganda proposal came as a shock to the delegates of the Congress, who knew nothing of the negotiations with the British officials. In his opening address to the Congress, Herzl emphasized that Uganda was not and could never become Zion. He portrayed the British offer of territory as a way out of a desperate situation, a temporary solution to help Jewish refugees from Eastern Europe find a haven and in the process avoid dispersion throughout the world. This view found strong support among the delegates from Western Europe and America. The chief spokesman for these delegates was Max Nordau (1849–1923), a physician who had achieved fame as the author of several volumes exposing the foibles and hypocrisies of contemporary European society. Although Nordau himself was at heart unenthusiastic about the Uganda proposal, he followed Herzl's lead and in his address to the Congress stressed that Palestine remained the final goal of the Zionist Movement. The East Africa territory, he declared, would merely serve as a *nachtasyl* (refuge for the night) for the hundreds of thousands of persecuted Jews who could not yet enter Palestine. Nordau informed the delegates that the offered territory would not only provide a shelter for the refugees, but would serve as a training ground for the greater task ahead (i.e., the colonization of Palestine).

When the various factions composing the Congress withdrew to consider the British offer, opposition to the scheme surfaced among the Russian delegation who had not been asked by the leadership to decide between Uganda and Palestine, but merely to give approval to the dispatch of an investigation commission to East Africa. Tempers ran high and the excitement mounted hourly as one after another of the Russian delegates expressed their antagonism toward the British proposal. Finally, when the Congress had reassembled, Herzl's tremendous prestige prevailed and a resolution to create an investigation commission was passed (the vote was 295 for the commission, 178 against, with 132 abstentions). The Russian delegation had voted against the creation of the commission. Led by one of their leaders, Jehiel Tschlenow (1864–1918), they left the Congress hall en masse and gathered in another room, where some of them wept and sat on the floor as if in mourning for what they considered to be the death of Zionism. Fearing that the walkout of the Russian delegation would lead to an irreparable split in the Zionist Organization Herzl pleaded with the dissidents to return to the Congress sessions. After considerable persuading, the nay-sayers agreed to return, but their opposition to the Uganda proposal remained firm.

The rift was far from healed. Protest demonstrations among Zionist groups in Russia and Austria occurred in the wake of the Sixth Zionist Congress (it would become known as the Uganda Congress). In Paris a disenchanted Russian Jew attempted to assassinate Max Nordau (Herzl's most prominent spokesman). At a meeting held in Kharkov (October, 1903) chaired by Menahem Ussishkin, a leader of the Hibbat Zion, a resolution was made to send Herzl an ultimatum demanding that the Zionist Organization refrain from considering any territorial project outside the borders of Palestine and Syria. Some months later (April, 1904), Herzl, still smarting from the recriminations raised by the Uganda issue, delivered an emotional speech at a Zionist executive meeting, in which he reaffirmed his loyalty to the Basle Program (namely, the establishment for the Jewish people of a publicly and legally assured home in Palestine). Peace was thus temporarily restored to the Jewish national movement. The internal bickering however had taken its toll on the Zionist leader's already weakened heart, and shortly thereafter on July 3, 1904, he died.

The Uganda proposal again emerged as the central issue at the Seventh Zionist Congress (Basle, July, 1905). The commission sent to investigate the territory reported that it was unsuitable for large-scale colonization. Accordingly, several delegates who had favored the Uganda offer proposed a search for new territories outside of Palestine because for the time being it was not available for mass settlement. These views were rudely brushed aside by the "Zionists for Zion"—the majority of delegates attending the Congress, who were determined to extirpate every trace of "territorial heresy" and to reaffirm the Zionist Organization's loyalty to the Basle Program. To ensure this goal the Congress delegates in quick order formally rejected the Uganda offer and passed resolutions aimed at increasing the pace of practical projects in Palestine. British officials were greatly relieved by the actions of the Seventh Zionist Congress. A steady stream of protests from the East African Protectorate had reached the government in London and had led to second thoughts as to the wisdom of a Jewish settlement in this region. The offer was, for all practical purposes, dead even prior to the Zionist Congress vote on the proposal.

A small group of twenty-eight delegates dissented to the decisions taken by the majority of the Seventh Zionist Congress (they were later joined by a dozen more delegates) and withdrew from the sessions. They refused to accept the rejection of the British offer as final, and meeting separately decided to secede from the World Zionist Organization. The dissidents or territorialists as they came to be called were determined to continue the search for a territory suitable for Jewish colonization. They were firmly convinced that a break with the Zionist Organization was inevitable, as the latter, committed as it was to Palestine, was a captive of the past and therefore insensitive to practical proposals for Jewish settlement that might arise in other parts of the world. The territorialists felt it was of the uttermost importance to direct their efforts to finding a land in which climate and geography, as well as political and socio-economic factors, were right for a mass settlement of Jews.

Israel Zangwill and the Jewish Territorial Organization

Led by the prominent Anglo-Jewish writer Israel Zangwill (1864–1926),[384] the territorialists formed a new association, the Jewish Territorial Organization, better known by the acronym I.T.O.[385] Although Zangwill had at first opposed seceding from the Zionist Organization, he had a change of mind when its institution, the Anglo-Palestine Bank, refused to expand its activities beyond Palestine. He had also come to believe that the Jewish Problem demanded a solution that could only be rationally resolved by territorial concentration and autonomy in any region of the world that was suitable for settlement and available. Like Herzl, Zangwill felt that such colonization projects could bring about a rebirth of the Jewish people and prepare them for the possibility in the future of a return to Palestine. He summed up his position with the slogan ". . . better Zionism without Zion than Zion without Zionism."

The first conference of the I.T.O., which met in Basle from July 30 to August 1, 1905, defined its objective as follows: to procure a territory upon an autonomous basis for those Jews who cannot, or will not remain in the lands in which they at present live. To achieve this end the I.T.O. proposed to unite all Jews who were in agreement with this goal and to enter into relations with governments and public and private institutions to create financial organs, labor bureaus, and other instruments that might be found to be necessary.

Israel Zangwill, the driving force behind the I.T.O., was born in London into a poor Russian-Jewish immigrant family. He was educated in the English capital's East End Jews Free School and later became a teacher there. He began his literary career writing humorous short stories. However, his early upbringing provided him with material for more serious subject matter. Early in life, Zangwill had begun to record in notebooks his observations, along with descriptions and anecdotes of the world of London's East End Jews. This subject matter later served as the basis for his famous ghetto novels: *Children of the Ghetto* (1892), *Ghetto Tragedies* (1893), *Dreamers of the Ghetto* (1898), *Ghetto Comedies* (1907), and *King of the Schnorrers* (1894).

In addition to his novels, Zangwill's mordant essays on Jewish themes were collected in a volume entitled *Voice of Jerusalem*. Similarly, his verse translations of liturgical poetry as well as the poetry of Solomon Ibn Gabirol (c.1021 to c.1056) made his name known throughout the Jewish world. A prolific talent, Zangwill also wrote works for the general non-Jewish reading public. Most notable in this category are *The Master*, a tale of an immigrant child who succeeds in becoming a famous artist; *The Mantle of Elijah*, a story based on the events of the Boer War; and *Jenny the Carrier*, a novel set in mid-nineteenth-century rural England.

Playwright as well as novelist, Zangwill's plays included *The War God* (1911), *The Cockpit* (1921), *The Forcing House* (1922), and *The Melting Pot* (1909), which enjoyed a long run on Broadway.

The Anglo-Jewish writer's interests were not confined to literature, and thus it was not surprising that Theodor Herzl, on the suggestion of Max Nordau, decided to visit Zangwill and to get his opinion on an essay he had written (*Address to the Rothschilds*) posing a solution to the Jewish Problem. They met in London in November of 1895. Zangwill immediately recognized the significance of his visitor's ideas and became an enthusiastic supporter of the charismatic Herzl. The sophisticated Zangwill was so impressed with Herzl's appearance and personality that he would later, during the sessions of the First Zionist Congress, describe him in the following terms:

> . . . a majestic oriental figure, not so tall as it appears when he draws himself up and stands dominating the assembly with eyes that brood and glow—you would say one of the Assyrian kings whose sculptured heads adorn our museums.[386]

Zangwill also introduced Herzl to some of the leading figures of British Jewry. Included among the latter personalities were the Chief Rabbi of the British Empire, Dr. Hermann Adler, his half brother, Elkan Adler, who had helped draw up the constitution of the Hibbat Zion of England, and his brother-in-law, Nathan Solomon Joseph; Simeon Singer, a renowned preacher and spiritual leader; Asher Myers an influential intellectual and editor of the *Jewish Chronicle*; Colonel Albert Edward Williamson Goldsmid, a professional army officer and commander of a Welsh regiment; and Sir Samuel Montagu, a banker and liberal member of parliament (he would later be known as Lord Swaythling).

Montagu, who was also a prominent member of the English Hibbat Zion, would antedate by several years Herzl's Turkish diplomatic efforts on behalf of Zionism. In 1892 he had petitioned the Turkish sultan for a grant of land in the Hauran district of Palestine, east of the Jordan River, for the purpose of Jewish colonization. The plan was said to have received the blessings of William Gladstone, the British Prime Minister, but was derailed by the opposition of Lord Rothschild.

Zangwill also brought Herzl to the attention of the Maccabean Club, an association of intellectuals dedicated to the spread of Jewish culture. In a speech before this club Herzl provided for the first time in public his blueprint for the creation of a Jewish state. His talk was courteously received, but failed to generate the excitement he had expected. Nevertheless, stimulated by the reception he had received in England, Herzl returned to Vienna, where he set about pruning and reorganizing his *Address to the Rothschilds* into a compact sixty-page essay. The end result was the pamphlet *Der Judenstaat* ("The Jewish State"), which would radically change the course of Jewish history.

In 1896 Herzl revisited London, and Zangwill again arranged for him to speak before the Maccabean Club and used his influence to gain for the Zionist leader and his cause a sympathetic hearing. The following year Zangwill joined other members of the Maccabean Club on a pilgrimage to Palestine. He also attended the First Zionist Congress (August 29–31, 1897) as an observer. A scintillating and witty speaker, Herzl invited the Anglo-Jewish writer to participate in some of the Congress debates, in spite of the fact that he was not an official delegate. In the Congresses that followed during Herzl's remaining years, Zangwill, now an ardent Zionist and delegate, adhered closely to the policies enunciated by the Zionist leader. He strongly favored the Uganda offer, but with its rejection by the Seventh Zionist Congress and the tragic death of Herzl, Zangwill saw no alternative other than to resign from the World Zionist Organization.

With his usual zeal and energy, Zangwill systematically set about seeking support for his creation the I.T.O. From its inception the new entity represented a preference for pragmatism over ideology. Among the early champions of the territorial organization were many prominent Western European Jews. Some, such as Sir Francis Montefiore (1860–1935) and other members of the Anglo-Jewish establishment, had assisted Herzl in his negotiations with the British government. Equally supportive of the I.T.O. were such

individuals as Israel Jasinowski (1842–1917), one of the organizers of the Katowitz
Conference of 1884; Professor Emanuel Mandelstamm (1839–1912), a close friend of
Pinsker and Herzl as well as a former member of the Zionist Actions Committee; Alfred
Klee (1875–1943), a leader of German Zionism; and Nahum Slousch (1872–1966) the
author of the first history of Hebrew literature, and later lecturer at the Sorbonne. For a
time even Nathan Birnbaum (1884–1937), the founder of the first Jewish student's
fraternity (Kadimah) and the individual credited with coining the term *Zionism* was an
active member of the Jewish Territorial Organization. A few anti-Zionist stalwarts also
favored the I.T.O. Most notable were Lucien Wolf (1857–1930), an influential journalist;
James Simon (1851–1932), and Paul Nathan (1857–1927), founders of the Hilfsverein der
deutschen Juden.

Other supporters of the I.T.O. came from the ranks of the Socialist-Zionist Workers
Party of Russia, headed by Nachman Syrkin. In 1906 a branch of the latter party calling
themselves Socialist-Territorialists was established in New York and eventually spread to
other cities across the United States. Like the parent organization in Russia, the American
branches eliminated Palestine as a possible site for a Jewish homeland because of its lack
of natural resources and the political instability of the region. The Socialist-Territorialists
considered Palestine to be a historical anomaly totally unsuited for the requirements of a
modern state.

Encouragement and support for the I.T.O. was also strong among the elite of the
American-Jewish community. In the forefront of this contingent were such luminaries as
the banker and philanthropist Jacob Henry Schiff (1847–1920), the civic leader and
diplomat Oscar S. Straus (1843–1926), Cyrus L. Sulzberger (1852–1932), and Mayer S.
Sulzberger (1843–1923), a judge of the Court of Common Pleas of Philadelphia. In April
of 1906 these individuals and others coalesced to form in New York an American
federation of the Jewish Territorial Organization.

On a visit to the United States, Zangwill lobbied hard to gain additional adherents and
funds. In his many appearances he emphasized that, after a hiatus of two millennia, the
Jews needed some place to start relearning the art of self-government. Zangwill's ideas
were in general well received by his American audiences. However, on one occasion
when he suggested the possibility of anti-Semitism becoming a reality in the United States
in the distant future, the audience reacted negatively to his remarks. It was during this tour
that Zangwill received a most unusual offer from the Philadelphia naphtha soap king,
Joseph F. Fels. The industrialist was so impressed by Zangwill's presentation that he
offered the latter 100,000 dollars if and when he succeeded in gaining a territory and if the
Jewish colonists would adopt the single tax concept of the American economist Henry
George (1839–97).

Blessed with an influential membership, the I.T.O. within a relatively short time
became a world-wide organization. In Russia alone Zangwill's entity created 200 emigration centers. Headquartered in London, the actual operations of the I.T.O. were carried
out by several commissions. Territories deemed suitable for settlement were selected by a
geographical commission. An international council composed of thirty-one members
attended to political and administrative problems.

Within weeks after the formal establishment of the I.T.O., Zangwill attempted to
reopen negotiations with the British government regarding a settlement in East Africa. In
a letter to the British colonial secretary (Joseph Chamberlain's successor), he asked that
the site in the East African colony originally offered to Herzl not be removed from

consideration until his organization had an opportunit[...]
the secretary and his advisors. In his reply to Zangwi[...] the matter with
informed him that in view of the official rejection of the [...]olonial secretary
Organization, he had already instructed the commissio[...]he World Zionist
torate that the subject was closed and not to reserve th[...] Africa Protec-
settlement. Zangwill, however, remained confident that h[...]nger for Jewish
several prominent members of the British government (Lord [...]en the issue, as
among others) had publicly expressed sympathy for the idea [...]nston Churchill
Africa. These hopes rapidly dissipated with the fall o[...]he Conse[...] colony in East

Frustrated by the turn of events beyond his cont[...], Zang[...]rty from power.
defeat, and to abandon all hopes of reviving the East A[...]ica [...]er [...]forced to admit
that he dropped the scheme out of fear that the neo-Jewi[...] civ[...][...]ould later claim
the region if the territory was gained would be based on [...]ack[...][...][...]a would rise in

During the early days of the I.T.O. it appeared that [...]pe[...]ful [...]oxistence with the
World Zionist Organization was still possible or that [...]e[...]ery le[...][...][...]differen[...]
could be papered over. In this spirit of compromise the[...]nist Org[...]zation in[...]ed the
I.T.O. to a meeting in Brussels (January 29, 1906) calle[...]eek co[...]ructive solutions to
the problem of Jewish immigration. However, the c[...]ence produced no tangible
results and heightened the tensions between the two or[...]ations causing them to drift
still further apart. Subsequently, the Zionists perceived I.T.O. to be a definite threat
and engaged it in a propaganda campaign marked bitter recriminations and
harsh polemics.

The I.T.O.'s Search for a Territory

During the years of its existence, the Jewish Territorial [...]ganization made numerous
searches for a territory that could be converted into what [...]ermed an "I.T.O. Land." In
1905 they considered Surinam as a possible area for Jew[...]settlement; and in 1908 the
I.T.O. sponsored an expedition to Cyrenaica (Libya), le[...] the distinguished explorer
John W. Gregory. Both attempts ended in failure. The foll[...]ing year an expedition was
dispatched to Mesopotamia (now Iraq), but political nego[...]ons with the Turkish rulers
proved fruitless. That same year (1909) John W. Gregor[...]eaded another exploratory
party to the Portuguese African territory of Angola. Zan[...]ll, in connection with this
venture, went to Portugal to discuss settlement possibilitie[...]ith the nation's president,
who seemed favorably disposed to the project. After the com[...]tion of his investigation of
the Angola territory Gregory was asked to submit his [...]dings to an international
assemblage of the I.T.O. scheduled for the fall of 1914 i[...]Zurich, Switzerland. The
outbreak of World War I caused the meeting to be canceled [...]nd the Angola project was
abandoned. The territorialist organization also gave seriou[...] consideration to Canada as a
viable settlement area, only to be informed by the Prime Minister, Sir Wilfred Laurier
that the request had come two years too late. Similar effort[...] to find a suitable territory for
Jewish settlement led the I.T.O. to consider Mexico, Honduras, Australia, and even
Siberia. Nothing, however, came of these endeavors. In each case the territory was found
unsuitable because of climatic conditions, or lack of water and natural resources, or more
frequently by opposition from the government and the indigenous population of the
territory being considered.

...ting, Zangwill began to consider practical
...members. This turn to pragmatism strongly
...Jacob Schiff, who proposed to the I.T.O. an
...ir ideological goal. Schiff explained to Zangwill
...Jews enjoying civil rights and freedom in their
...ing persecutions drastic action was required. He was
...had to be immediately found to help those Russian
...ssion. Schiff suggested to Zangwill, that in view of the
...orial organization put aside its policy of finding a separate
...live under autonomous conditions and concentrate
...ca... ently practical and feasible. This project would enable
...rend a great service to those Jews seeking asylum.

To keep his organizati... projects that would raise... appealed to the American... undertaking directly at... that his greatest desire... native land, but in view... of the opinion that w... Jews who wished to... existing crisis, the Je... land of refuge who... instead on a scheme... Zangwill's organi...

The Galveston Project

The pra... undertaking... ff had in mind was a novel emigration project to help
individual Jews an... their lies find refuge in the New World. Zangwill accepted
Schiff's suggestion as a while secondary objective for his territorial organization.
Accordingly, an I.T.O. Emi...ion Regulation Department was established and promptly
took over the direction of...-called Galveston Project. This scheme, the brainchild of
a group of Berlin philant...ts led by Arthur Myerowitz, the assistant director of the
North German Lloyd Stea... Company, had begun its activities in 1906. The aim of the
Galveston Project was to ... t Jewish immigration from Eastern Europe away from the
slums of the large cities ... east coast of the United States and to channel them to the
less-crowded southern an... tern parts of the country or even to South America. Instead
of a mass immigration of ... to a given territory, which usually provoked anti-Semitic
feelings on the part of ... digenous population, the immigrants were to be widely
dispersed throughout the ...ericas. To facilitate this policy the North German Lloyd
Steamship Company pu... operation a special passenger service that took Jewish
immigrants to Galveston, as, instead of to the usual east coast ports of entry such New
York, or Boston. In Gal...n a Jewish Immigration Information Bureau was created,
which cooperated closely... h the agencies of the United States government to advise and
assist the immigrants. F...cial support for the Galveston Project came largely from a
handful of philanthropist... otably Jacob H. Schiff, Lord Rothschild, and Baron Edmond
de Rothschild). Between ...06 and 1914 some 10,000 Jews landed in Galveston, which
served as an assembly po... for distribution of the immigrants to locales throughout the
southern and western regi... of the United States. The project came to an end several weeks
before the outbreak of W...d War I. Its demise was hastened by the sudden scarcity of
transportation facilities, an... the unsympathetic attitude of the newly created United States
Department of Labor, whi... had assumed authority in all matters relating to immigration.

The Great War would also bring about a major change in Zangwill's ideology, which
would vitally affect the fortunes of the Jewish Territorial Organization. The transition in
his thinking, however, was a gradual process, and was not initially evident in the early
years of the war. As the war clouds gathered over Europe, Zangwill still held fast to the
views that had led him to withdraw from the World Zionist Organization. Most revealing
in this respect is an exchange of correspondence between Zangwill and the English
novelist and historian, H.G. Wells (1866–1946). In an open letter to Zangwill, published

in the *London Daily Chronicle* a few days after Turkey's entry into the war on the side of the Central Powers, Wells posed the question: ". . . and now what is to prevent the Jews from having Palestine and restoring a real Judaea?"[387] Why the English novelist had addressed his letter to Zangwill, the titular head of the I.T.O., and not to the Zionists is not quite clear. Nevertheless, Zangwill, annoyed by Wells's letter and by articles of a similar nature appearing in the English press, was quick to answer his critics. In a letter to Wells he again outlined his fundamental concerns and ideology. He acknowledged that the idea to create a Jewish state in Palestine was in the air, but pointed out the numerous obstacles to achieving such a goal. These difficulties had led him to suggest a new Judea in Canada and elsewhere. However, it would be helpful if Englishmen of Wells's caliber would work to ensure British suzerainty for a new state in Palestine. All Jews would welcome such assistance, but could only accept it if its motive was pro-Jewish and not based on hatred of the Jews. In fact Palestine could only receive and support a Jewish immigration in small installments, thus requiring the majority of the Jews to continue in their present homes for a long time. An offer of Palestine coupled with a desire or worse a policy for the clearance of Jews from other countries, such as Poland, as had been suggested by a journalist specializing in Eastern European affairs, could lead to a disaster of major proportions. No bait of Palestine, Zangwill informed Wells, would lessen the demand of his organization for equal rights for the Jews in Russia, Rumania, or wherever anti-Semitism dragged down civilization.

The World Zionist Organization also tried to enlist Zangwill's cooperation on behalf of a Jewish return to Palestine. Chaim Weizmann, the rising star of the Zionists active in England, wrote a letter to Zangwill in which he pleaded with the I.T.O. leader to forget past disagreements. He noted that the time was ripe:

> to put forward our claim for the establishment of an organized, autonomous Jewish community in Palestine and that if all the mental, moral and physical forces of Jewry concentrated on one aim, the building up of a Jewish community would certainly not lag behind and could stand comparison with any modern highly civilized state.[388]

Weizmann's appeal for cooperation did not persuade Zangwill to change his mind. Rapprochement seemed virtually impossible after so long a rift and the hardening of positions. Everything however changed with the British government's issuance of the Balfour Declaration in November of 1917. The document for which the Zionists had labored so hard brought about a radical shift in the hearts and souls of the rank and file of the I.T.O membership and led many of the territorialists to rejoin the Zionist Organization. Although skeptical of the vague wording of the Balfour Declaration, Zangwill considered the document a historic achievement of Zionism in the field of diplomacy. Addressing a mass meeting at the London Opera House (December 2, 1917), he offered the Zionist Organization the full cooperation of the I.T.O. However, he retained his suspicions of the British government and felt that it had not given the declaration the interpretation originally intended by David Lloyd George and Arthur James Balfour. His apprehension grew two years later as he reviewed the behavior of the Zionist representatives who had appeared before the Allied Supreme Council (February 27, 1919). Zangwill was disturbed that the Zionists (Weizmann, Sokolow, and Ussishkin) had not pressed hard enough for an autonomous Jewish state in Palestine. Instead, they had argued for the immediate encouragement of immigration and settlement, recognition of a Jewish council or agency to represent the Jews of Palestine and of the Diaspora, and recognition of the prior rights of the Jews for concessions in the Holy Land. These proposals, Zangwill argued, would create a Jewish National Home that would in fact be a British crown colony with a predominantly Arab population. It would therefore be, ". . . neither Jewish, nor National, nor a Home."[389]

In spite of his misgivings, Zangwill believed that because of the importance of the Balfour Declaration, the Palestine effort had to be fully supported. In time however this initial conviction gave way as the I.T.O. leader witnessed the difficulties encountered by the Jewish settlers, the growing Arab opposition, and the failure of the British government to fulfill its obligations. Finally, completely disillusioned, Zangwill resorted to bitter criticism of the Zionist leadership for accepting the whittling down of the Balfour Declaration.

No longer bound by the need to cooperate with the Zionist Organization, Zangwill made a valiant attempt to revive the I.T.O., which was suffering from lack of funds and a loss of membership. He was particularly hopeful that the Galveston Project could be reactivated, but this expectation was dashed by the death in 1920 of Jacob H. Schiff, its main financial backer. Undaunted, Zangwill continued for a few more years to seek new supporters and projects for the I.T.O. Finally, in 1925, realizing that he was unable to breathe new life into the organization, he gave up the struggle, and dissolved the Jewish Territorial Organization. Only in Eastern Europe, where territorialism was maintained by a small but tightly knit ideological movement, did its partisans keep the flame alive.

Curiously, Zangwill's last years (he died in East Preston, England, in 1926) were notable for his advocacy of a population transfer of Palestinian Arabs to other Arab countries.[390] The concept of an Arab population transfer had first occurred to him during the period immediately following the issuance of the Balfour Declaration. Zangwill expanded on this concept in his writings and speeches in the postwar years. The Arabs, he emphasized, must not be forced to leave Palestine. Zangwill pointed out that there were many examples in history of mass migrations that had been voluntarily and peacefully carried out (e.g., the migration of the Boers to the Transvaal). He was convinced that the Arabs would realize that it was in their best interests to abandon Palestine.

Zangwill fully expected that the postwar world would be reconstituted on a basis of reason and understanding. The Arab inhabitants of Palestine, for whose kinsmen several new states were being created, he believed would sympathize with the aspirations of the Jews and be magnanimous enough to leave a few thousand square miles to the nation that had preserved its dream of a return to their ancient homeland for 2,000 years.

Independent of the I.T.O. and lacking its organizational ability, was another territorialist entity—the Allgemeine Juedische Kolonisation Organisation (abbreviated as A.I.K.O.)[391] founded by Alfred Nossig (1864–1943), a highly gifted but erratic individual who was, at various stages in his life, a philosopher, playwright, sculptor, statistician, historian, demographer, author, and musician. Born in Lemberg, Nossig in his youth was active in assimilationist circles. He later became fascinated by the Jewish nationalist movement and abandoned his earlier fondness for assimilation. In 1887 Nossig published *An Attempt to Solve the Jewish Problem,* the first Zionist book to appear in the Polish language. The work had a great impact on the Jewish intelligentsia of Galicia, and marked for the author the beginning of an intensive period of Zionist activity.

Orient Colonising Company

Nossig participated in the First Zionist Congress. However his artistic temperament and eccentric personality made it difficult for him to work closely with other people and invariably led to a falling out with the Zionist leadership. A parting of the ways came in the wake of the Young Turk Revolution of 1908 when Nossig, on his own initiative, turned up in Constantinople with a grandiose plan for the settlement of Jews both in Palestine and elsewhere in the Ottoman Empire. Publicly reprimanded by the Zionist organization for his unauthorized activities, Nossig resigned from the movement. To further his own settlement scheme he founded the A.I.K.O., which made a point of ridiculing the efforts of the Zionist leadership to resolve the Jewish Problem. The A.I.K.O. also differed with the Jewish Territorial Organization insofar as it preferred a compact settlement only in Palestine, Syria, and the Sinai Peninsula. However, the A.I.K.O. also stressed that autonomy must not be rejected if it developed through gradual immigration into the areas of settlement. At its inception, Nossig's organization managed to attract a handful of prominent Zionists, including a future president of the World Zionist Organization, Otto Warburg (1859–1938); Moses Gaster (1856–1939), the Haham of the Sephardi community of England, and vice-president of the First Zionist Congress; and Selig Eugen Soskin (1873–1959), an agronomist and an original member of the 1903 Zionist Commission sent to investigate El Arish as a possible site for a Jewish settlement. The anti-Zionist polemics of Nossig soon alienated many of these individuals and led them to shy away from the A.I.K.O. Although the A.I.K.O. never became a real threat to the Zionist Organization, it did create some institutions that challenged the latter's supremacy in resolving the Jewish Problem. Most notable in this respect was the organization's creation of the Orient Colonising Company, based in London; as well as the Juedische Hilfskommittee Roter Halbmond fuer Palestine and the Deutsch-Israelitish-Osmanische Union, headquartered in Berlin.

Nossig tried valiantly in 1911 to reopen negotiations with the British government regarding a Jewish colony in the Sinai Peninsula. When these efforts failed he used his Berlin base to disseminate suggestions that Jews seriously consider establishing a foothold in Mesopotamia. These intimations aroused British suspicions, as in no other part of the Turkish Empire in the pre-World War I period were British and German interests so near to colliding. An ardent supporter of Germany, Nossig, prior to and during the Great War, tried to get the Kaiser's government to apply pressure on their Turkish ally to accept a compact Jewish settlement in Palestine. The issuance of the Balfour Declaration, which was followed a year later by the military defeat of the Central Powers, put an end to Nossig's plans and to his base of power (he had apparently worked for German intelligence during the war). Without any real successes to its credit, the A.I.K.O. gradually atrophied, and was officially disbanded in 1920.

Nossig continued to live in Berlin until the Nazi rise to power, at which time he was expelled to Poland. Here, he followed his many interests, including the design of a monumental piece of statuary called "The Holy Mountain" which he hoped to place on Mount Carmel in Palestine as a symbol of world peace. After the Nazi occupation of Poland and the establishment by the Germans of the Warsaw Ghetto, Nossig drew up plans for Jewish emigration. He submitted several memoranda on this subject to the German authorities. On orders of the Nazis, the chairman of the Warsaw Judenrat (Jewish Council), Adam Czerniakow, nominated Nossig as a member of the Council in charge of the Department of Art (which existed only on paper). Suspicious that Nossig was collaborating with the Nazis he was condemned and sentenced to death by the Jewish resistance movement. On February 22, 1943, he was shot to death by a member of the latter movement.

The Freeland Movement

Ten years after the demise of the I.T.O., a new territorial movement came into being as a direct result of British restrictions on Jewish immigration to Palestine, and the growing need to find places of refuge for those Jews seeking to escape Germany. In an attempt to cope with these problems, a group of English Jews established in 1935 the Free Land Movement, A League for Territorial Organization, which subsequently became known as The Freeland League for Jewish Territorial Colonization.

The Freeland League, like its predecessor the I.T.O., soon spread to other countries, including France and the United States. The League's objective was to find and obtain, for the purpose of Jewish settlement, land on a large scale, preferably in a sparsely populated area of the world. The League did not expressly demand autonomy for the settlements, but did not exclude it as a possible goal. In an effort to clarify its position on Zionism and Palestine, the Freeland League stressed that its efforts were directed solely to those Jews who sought a new home and did not want to go to Palestine.

The Zionist Organization did not oppose the activities of the League, as they recognized the need for some temporary alleviation for Jewish victims of persecution. Negotiations were instituted by the League with the governments of Angola, Ecuador, Surinam, and Australia. These talks went nowhere, as all of the governments approached refused to accept large numbers of Jewish settlers in their countries.[392]

The League survived World War II and welcomed the birth of the State of Israel, but remained convinced that Israel's small land area could not possibly resolve the problem of Jewish homelessness. Accordingly, the League did not think it advisable to disband and allow the future of the Jewish people to depend solely on the viability of the State of Israel. Although it would not publicly admit it, the League for all practical purposes had lost its raison d'etre.

Shortly before World War II, efforts were made to coordinate all territorial and settlement activities under one umbrella organization. The result was the creation in 1938 of the International Colonization Society. Several groups, including the Freeland League, and the Jewish Colonization Association (I.C.A.), founded in 1891 by Baron Maurice de Hirsch to assist the Jews of Russia and Rumania to settle in Argentina, agreed to cooperate with the International Colonization Society. Beyond the basic premise of coordination, the Society was charged with the responsibility of financing Jewish settlements in various parts of the world, including Palestine. Although some substantial sums were raised for carrying out the Society's mandates, the outbreak of World War II brought its activities to an abrupt end.

42

The Mesopotamian Project

The territorialist alternative appealed to a handful of individual non-Jewish thinkers and academics. Among the latter was the Bible scholar, philologist, theologian, and assyriologist Paul Haupt (1858–1926).[393] Born in Görlitz, Germany, Haupt received his education in Leipzig and Berlin, and later taught at the University of Göttingen. In 1885 he was appointed head of the recently formed "Oriental Seminar" at Johns Hopkins University in Baltimore. Haupt, however, continued to lecture at Göttingen each summer until the outbreak of World War I.

Besides being a prolific writer with over 500 publications to his credit, Haupt was also a great teacher. His training of several generations of Semitic philologists contributed significantly to biblical scholarship. Some of Haupt's most notable essays dealt with Hebrew metrics. This subject was thoroughly explored in the following publications: *The Oldest Semitic Verb Form* (1878), the *Song of Songs* (1902), *Ecclesiastes* (1905), *Nahum* (1907), *Esther* (1908), and *Micah* (1910). In another work entitled *Purim* (1906), Haupt attempted to explain the origins of the holiday. Similarly, in a commentary called *Midian and Sinai* (1909), he elucidated the cultural and historical background of the Mosaic era. Haupt also from time to time accepted editorial assignments and participated on various biblical projects, such as the publication of the *Polychrome Bible*. He also collaborated with W.R. Harper on the early volumes of *Hebraica*.

A product of his age, Haupt on several occasions unwittingly rendered a disservice to the very people whose religion, religion, rituals, history, and language he had devoted his life's work. Caught up by the racial myths prevalent at the time, he attempted in some of his articles to prove the "Aryan ancestry of Jesus Christ." Years later these articles would be exploited by the Nazis in their propaganda campaign against the Jews.

Paradoxically, Haupt himself was deeply disturbed by the suffering of Russian Jewry and in 1882 published a pamphlet suggesting a possible solution to the problem. It was entitled *Uber die Ansiedlung der russichen Juden in Euphrat und Tigris-Gebiete; Ein Vorschlag* ("A Proposal for Settling Jews in the Euphrates-Tigris Region"). The central theme of the pamphlet was strongly reminiscent of imperial Germany's geopolitical master plan for the Near and Middle East. As early as the 1880s Germany, in its drive to become a world power, had succeeded in penetrating the region by supplying a military mission to Turkey to help reorganize the latter's army. By 1896 the real work of German economic penetration took a giant step forward with the construction of railways in Anatolia. The building of this transportation network enabled the German Kaiser to proudly boast that his nation's commerce, industry, and military might had come abreast with that of Great Britain. A few years later in 1899 the Ottoman regime granted the Deutsche Bank the long sought concession to build a Berlin to Baghdad railroad. If completed, this railway would have opened up the Persian Gulf and India to German economic and political exploitation. It was in response to this threat that England, France, and Russia composed their differences over Persia, Morocco, and Egypt and entered into an alliance, the so-called Triple Entente.

Haupt's proposal seemed to parallel the German geopolitical plan for the Middle East.[394] It is possible that he considered the Yiddish speaking masses of Eastern Europe (a language which owed much to German) as a sort of bridgehead for German culture. Whatever his underlying motives, humanitarian or political, Haupt advocated a mass settlement of Russian Jews in the region between the Euphrates and Tigris Rivers of Mesopotamia (now Iraq) to resolve the Jewish Problem. Once established in this strategic region, Haupt visualized future Jewish commercial (his critics would say German) expansion in the direction of the Persian Gulf, the Mediterranean Sea, the Black and Caspian Seas. A railroad would tie together the entire area, which in turn would be integrated into the network of world trade and provide an alternate route to the Suez Canal.

According to Haupt, using modern technology, the Jewish settlers would make the sparsely populated areas of ancient Babylonia and Assyria bloom again. The region was large enough to accommodate the settlement of over 16.5 million people. Compact settlements and a strong militia would frustrate any attempts by the Arabs to hinder the process of mass colonization. To test the feasibility of his plan, Haupt suggested that a scientific expedition be organized under the auspices of the Smithsonian Institution and sent to Mesopotamia to thoroughly investigate the entire region.

As a result of his biblical studies, Professor Haupt had developed cordial relations with Jewish circles and numbered among his friends such distinguished personalities as the orientalist Cyrus Adler, Judge Mayer Sulzberger, and Oscar Straus.[395] All three men were destined to play a role in the dissemination of Haupt's Mesopotamian plan. Straus, in particular, was fascinated by the professor's proposal. Author, diplomat, public servant, and jurist, Oscar Solomon Straus was the scion of one of the great mercantile families of the nineteenth century. While his father and brothers were expanding their crockery stores into a far flung commercial empire, he was drawn through his law practice into political circles advocating reform. A "mugwump" who worked for the election of Grover Cleveland in 1884, he was rewarded by the Democratic administration with the post of Minister to Turkey. He served at this post from 1887 to 1889, and during two subsequent appointments (1898 to 1900 as Minister, and 1909–10 as Ambassador).

During the period of his first term as Minister to Turkey, Straus brought Haupt's scheme to the attention of the philanthropist Baron de Hirsch. The latter had wide experience dealing with the Turks and had actually as early as 1869 received a railroad concession from the Sublime Porte. He had also played a key role in helping the Alliance Isráelite Universelle establish Jewish schools in Turkey. In spite of Straus's enthusiasm, Baron de Hirsch rejected Haupt's plan as unrealistic. He was convinced that it was impossible to deal in a rational manner with the Turkish sultan and his government when it came to a question of sovereignty or the diminution of Ottoman territory.

The Baron, whose philanthropy—especially to Jewish causes—was proverbial, had his own ideas of how to alleviate the suffering of Eastern European Jewry. In 1888 Hirsch offered to raise considerable funds for the purpose of creating craft and agricultural schools for Russian Jews. When the Russian government objected to his proposal, the Baron decided that nothing remained but to get the Jews out of Russia. Accordingly, he caused to be created in London the Jewish Colonization Association (I.C.A.), which he endowed with a capital of 2 million pounds (at his death it received a further legacy of 6 million pounds). At the same time he established, under the laws of New York, the Baron de Hirsch Fund, with an initial capital of 2.5 million dollars, for the aid of Jewish immigrants from Russia and Rumania and another fund of 12 million francs in Galicia for the relief of Jews there. Many of the immigrants were directed by the I.C.A. to Argentina, but by the end of the nineteenth century the wave of immigration from Eastern Europe would reach flood proportions beyond the control of any relief organizations. The largest number by far would go to the United States, many to Great Britain and her colonies, and a small body to Palestine.

For a number of years following Baron de Hirsch's refusal to support the Haupt plan, the plan seemed to have become a dead issue. It was revived by Judge Sulzberger, who gave a copy of the Johns Hopkins professor's pamphlet to Israel Zangwill, who in turn, through the good graces of Cyrus Adler, sent it along to the Zionist leader, Theodor Herzl. In his correspondence with Herzl, Adler, a non-Zionist, stressed the advantages to be gained from a Jewish settlement in Mesopotamia. On a trip to Turkey, Cyrus Adler had actually broached the subject of Jewish settlements in the Euphrates-Tigris region with the Ottoman Empire's Grand Vizier, Kamil Pasha (1832–1912). The wily Turkish official intimated that his government might indeed look with favor upon an immigration into Mesopotamia of 5,000 Jews annually. However, like many other schemes involving Turkey, nothing came of this proposal.

In the immediate aftermath of the Third Zionist Congress, Theodor Herzl's attention was again drawn to the Haupt Mesopotamian scheme by Oscar S. Straus. On his way home on leave from the Turkish capital, Straus received Herzl during a stop over in Vienna (December 28, 1899). The Zionist leader, who had been anxiously awaiting word for weeks from one of his paid intermediaries, who was supposed to arrange an audience with the Turkish ruler, tried to extract from Straus whether the Sultan had ever spoken to him about Zionism. Straus responded that the Sultan had not brought the subject up as he knew that it was not an American issue. However, it had on occasions entered into their conversations indirectly in connection with Turkish efforts to exclude American Jews from Palestine because of the "Zionist infiltration" into the country. The American minister, although a non-Zionist, had on those occasions insisted on the rights of his countrymen, irrespective of their race, religion, or political beliefs, and had fought hard to overcome Turkish resistance on each individual case that came to his attention.

As the conversation with Herzl progressed, Straus was drawn into a general discussion of the Jewish Problem and the Zionist plan to resolve it. Straus considered it unfortunate that so many Jews considered Palestine as a refuge. There was, he stated, dire poverty in the Holy Land and no opportunities for employment. It was chiefly for these reasons that as minister to Turkey he had advised against further immigration into Palestine. Herzl listened to this frank confession, and noted that he too was opposed to infiltration of Palestine by small groups and was desperately trying to obtain from the Ottoman government a charter for a mass immigration and settlement of Jews into the region. He informed Straus of his modus operandi for dealing with the Turkish regime. In essence he planned for the Zionists to arrange a loan for the Turks of several million pounds in exchange for a charter granting Jews settlement rights in Palestine. Herzl would spend the last frantic years of his life shuttling back and forth between the Turkish court and Jewish bankers in Western Europe. He often exaggerated to the Sublime Porte the amount and availability of the loan, while telling the Jewish financiers that the Palestinian charter was about to be granted if only the money for the loan was immediately forthcoming. In reality the two key elements of Herzl's plan never coalesced.

Straus was not impressed by Herzl's outline of his plan. The very idea of the Jews eliminating the Turkish debt in exchange for a charter seemed to him to be completely unrealistic. He could not visualize how a chartered company would be able to secure the concessions essential for the creation of a Jewish state. The minister also perceived deep-rooted opposition to the Palestine settlement from quarters much more powerful than the Turks. He was convinced that from its very inception it would encounter the hostility of the respective Christian denominations, as well as the enmity of various governments with interests in the Middle East, notably Russia and France. Finally, Straus informed Herzl that the Ottoman ministers and officials were mostly cowardly and venal fellows, and that the sultan was the worst of the lot. Nothing therefore could be gotten from the sultan by appeals to humanity, but it might be possible by bribes and money loans to win the ruler over for granting specific territorial concessions in areas of the Ottoman Empire other than Palestine.

Since he felt that Palestine was out of the question for Jewish settlement, Straus tried to persuade Herzl to take a closer look at the Haupt plan for colonizing Mesopotamia. That region, he argued, was a vast territory inhabited only by nomadic tribes and had played an important role in Jewish history from time immemorial. All that was needed to restore the land to the position it had in antiquity was irrigation and a people dedicated to the task of building a viable community. Herzl was favorably impressed by the minister's presentation and promised to consider the Mesopotamian alternative more seriously. He also recalled that this was the same scheme that Cyrus Adler had written him about and was rather astonished that a number of prominent New York Jews were strongly in favor of the Haupt plan.

Although Herzl remained committed to Zion, he did not shrink from using the Mesopotamian card in his later negotiations with the Turkish sultan. In February of 1902 the sultan would indeed tempt the Zionist leader with an offer of a charter for one of three territories—Mesopotamia, Syria, or Anatolia (but not for Palestine). A charter that did not include Palestine was for Herzl now inconceivable and he was compelled to reject the Turk's offer.

Oscar S. Straus and Theodor Herzl would never meet again. The former diplomat would go on to become a member of the International Court of Arbitration at the Hague (an appointment that would be renewed four times), and the first Jew to hold a cabinet post in an American administration. Straus would serve as Theodore Roosevelt's secretary of commerce and labor from 1906 through 1909. In 1912 he would follow Roosevelt into the Progressive Party, and would run as the its candidate for governor of New York. Throughout his long career, Straus displayed a strong sense of responsibility to Jewish interests. As minister and later ambassador to Turkey he interceded on numerous occasions on behalf of the persecuted Jews of Russia and Rumania. In 1906 he helped found the American Jewish Committee. Although opposed to Political Zionism, he nonetheless contributed and otherwise supported numerous projects for the physical rehabilitation of Palestine.

Professor Haupt's Mesopotamian plan continued to arouse support among various prominent individuals. The banker and philanthropist Jacob H. Schiff (1847–1920)[396] like Straus favored the scheme and valiantly tried to convince his wealthy colleagues and friends of its merits. Among those whom Schiff approached was the British banker, and executor of the estate of Baron de Hirsch, Sir Ernest Joseph Cassel (1852–1921).[397] Schiff also wrote to Lord Nathaniel Rothschild (1840–1915),[398] head of the English banking house of Rothschild and a director of the Bank of England. He urged Rothschild to throw his considerable influence behind the Haupt Mesopotamian plan.

Israel Zangwill, while still a loyal follower of Herzl, was also inspired by Haupt's pamphlet. He wrote to the Zionist leader suggesting that Mesopotamia be considered as an alternative goal if there was no way to obtain Palestine. This view assumed greater importance following the increasing persecution of Eastern European Jewry, and the death of Theodor Herzl. Indeed, soon after the formation of the Jewish Territorial Organization, Zangwill began his quest for an "Itoland," and Mesopotamia was high on his list as a possible suitable territory for Jewish colonization. Haupt's plan was clearly on Zangwill's mind, but his approach to implementing it was somewhat different. He solicited the powerful bankers and philanthropists who had expressed interest in the scheme to provide financial assistance in gaining from Turkey a controlling interest in the Baghdad railroad. Such a move, Zangwill believed, would give the Jews entry into the Mesopotamian region—a first step toward achieving a settlement without arousing Turkish suspicions. The Turkish Revolution of 1908, for a time upset Zangwill's plans, but a year later he returned to the idea and attempted to form a company to carry out his version of the Haupt proposal. The I.T.O. leader approached Oscar S. Straus to head up the proposed company, but the latter who had just been named United States ambassador to Turkey, declined the honor. Zangwill then turned to Sir Ernest Cassel who also balked as he now believed that the Mesopotamian scheme was no longer feasible. At this juncture, Jacob Schiff advised Zangwill to draw key staff for his proposed company from existing Jewish institutions such as the I.C.A., the Deutsche Hilfsverein, and even the World Zionist Organization. Once recruited these experienced people would go about establishing and operating a settlement company, and manage it as it were an ordinary business enterprise. Five million pounds would be raised and placed at the company's disposal as seed money. Zangwill liked Schiff's suggestions, but when he pleaded with the philanthropist to take the lead in establishing the company the latter refused.

The Mesopotamian option continued to surface among various territorialist groups until the outbreak of World War I, but never again with the intensity that had marked its early years. Other territorialist schemes arose to claim the spotlight, and Professor Haupt's plan was relegated to the scrap-heap of historical curiosities.

43

The Greater Palestine Controversy

Almost from its inception, the World Zionist Organization was subjected to the pressures of territorialists, who split away from the movement when the Zionist leadership was unable to obtain a charter from the Turkish government for the Jewish colonization of Palestine. The need to find an immediate asylum for the persecuted Jews of Eastern Europe also contributed to the Zionist Organization's distress. The urgency of the situation led many Zionists who preferred to remain within the framework of the movement to seriously consider the possibility of establishing colonies contiguous to Palestine if the latter objective proved unattainable. Among the locations most often discussed were El Arish, the Sinai Peninsula, and Cyprus. The proponents of these schemes, in an effort to overcome those who opposed any departure from the Basle Program, argued that the lands suggested for settlement were near enough to Palestine and could serve as a jumping-off point for a later expansion into the Holy Land. Of equal importance, such settlements appeared to their sponsors to be politically feasible.

A leading advocate of this approach was Davis Trietsch (1870–1935),[399] author, editor, publisher, and statistician. He was born in Dresden, Germany, and educated in Berlin. Trietsch subsequently moved to New York where he lived from 1893 to 1899. Soon after his arrival in the United States he became fascinated by Jewish migration patterns, and immersed himself in a study of the subject. In the course of his studies his attention was drawn in 1895 to a newspaper article describing the controversy raging in British government circles on the issue of whether England should remain in Cyprus or abandon the island altogether. Others wanted to return the island to Turkey, or to Greece, or establish an autonomous Cyprus ruled as an independent republic. The article struck a responsive chord in Trietsch's mind and an idea was born. Recollecting the incident years later he would write:

. . . here was a land which the English did not know what to do with, while on the other hand Jews everywhere were searching for a place of settlement for their brethren. . . . Furthermore Cyprus was in the vicinity of Palestine. . . . It appeared to me that the natural and beautiful idea of a return to the Old Land [Eretz Israel] could well be combined with colonization in Cyprus—whether or not England remained there.[400]

At first Trietsch did not know what to do about his idea. He had no desire to be active publicly. The idea however remained fixed in his mind. One day while sitting in the Cafe Boulevard on New York City's Second Avenue he read:

. . . in Bloch's *Oesterreichische Wochenschrift* about a *Judenstaat!* This was the first mention of *Political Zionism*. . . . Immediately I hoped to combine my project with those expressed in the *Judenstaat.*[401]

While Trietsch mused about Cyprus, Theodor Herzl, the moving spirit behind Political Zionism, was also giving some thought to the island. After a futile attempt in 1896 to gain an audience with the Turkish sultan he had been advised by the latter's chamberlain, Izzet Bey to seek a territory in the Ottoman Empire other than Palestine for Jewish colonization. The wily Turkish official had also intimated that once such a territory was gained it would be possible, with some additional monetary considerations, to exchange the land grant at a later date for Palestine. In recording this conversation in his diary Herzl noted, "I immediately thought of Cyprus."[402]

The following year the First Zionist Congress convened in Basle, Switzerland, and among the delegates from the United States was Davis Trietsch. Although enthusiastic about his Cyprus proposal, he was unable to bring it before the Congress because of the latter's preoccupation with the formulation of the Basle Program, and the establishment of the key institutions that would create the entity henceforth to be known as the World Zionist Organization. On his return to New York City, Trietsch wrote to Herzl about his Cyprus scheme. Herzl responded that the plan had merit, but that the time was not propitious to bring it to the foreground, as there were better prospects on the horizon. Nevertheless, Herzl in his diary noted:

I am thinking of giving the movement a closer territorial goal [while] preserving Zion as the final goal. The poor masses need immediate help, and Turkey is not yet so desperate as to accede to our wishes. In fact, there will probably be hostile demonstrations against us in Turkey, in the immediate future. They will say that they have no intentions of giving us Palestine.
    Thus, we must organize for a goal attainable soon, under the Zion flag and maintaining all our historic claims. Perhaps we can demand Cyprus from England. . . .[403]

At the Second Zionist Congress, Trietsch was again denied the opportunity of presenting his Cyprus plan before the assembled delegates. He did however manage to air his ideas informally with various delegates, many of whom felt that he should bring his scheme to the attention of Baron Maurice de Hirsch's Jewish Colonization Association. After some initial hesitation, Trietsch contacted Association officials in Paris and submitted to them a memorandum on his Cyprus plan. As a first practical step he suggested to the I.C.A. the immediate settlement on the island of a group of Jewish laborers from the Galician city of Boryslaw. Trietsch's recommendation of this particular group of workers was dictated by several factors: they were unemployed and living in an anti-Semitic climate, they were miners accustomed to hard work and therefore excellent pioneering material, and they had indicated to the First Zionist Congress their willingness to emigrate.

When the I.C.A. did not respond to his memorandum, Trietsch decided to again approach Theodor Herzl, who had previously indicated some interest in the Cyprus scheme as a possible alternative to Palestine. The Zionist leader again advised patience, but Trietsch chafed at being restrained and was eager to take some practical steps toward the realization of his plan. In this respect he had much in common with other Zionists, who in contrast to Herzl's political approach, favored immediate practical work in Palestine. Trietsch, however, was unable to muster any support from these practical-minded Zionists (later to be known as the "Democratic Fraction"), as they were vehe-mently opposed to the colonization of any territory other than Palestine.

Fully aware that he could not carry out his scheme without the backing of an organization and without proper funding, he decided to do his utmost to bring the Cyprus alternative to the attention of the Third Zionist Congress, which was scheduled to meet in Basle in the summer of 1899. Anxious to avoid being rejected as in the two previous Congresses, Trietsch embarked on an intensive publicity campaign to make his ideas known to the rank and file of the Zionist Organization. His public airing of the Cyprus issue forced Herzl's hand, and the Zionist leader decided that the time had finally arrived to bring the matter before the Congress and test the reaction of the delegates. Accordingly, Herzl arranged for Trietsch to address the plenum of the Third Zionist Congress (August 18, 1899). From the start of his speech, Trietsch was confronted by a hostile and noisy group of delegates, mostly former Hibbat Zion members who did not take kindly to any suggestion of an alternative territory to Palestine. His presentation was cut short, and he was compelled to leave the platform. Although disappointed, Trietsch left Basle deter-mined more than ever to go ahead with his plan without the help of the Zionist Organiza-tion, or the I.C.A. If there was no representative Jewish body to support him, he would create one.

In a relatively short time after reaching this decision, the indefatigable Trietsch succeeded in forming a committee in Berlin consisting of several prominent Jewish personalities. It included, among others, Professor Otto Warburg (1859–1938), a botanist and future President of the World Zionist Organization; Professor Martin Philippson (1846–1916), an eminent historian and rector of Brussels University, as well as chairman of the Deutsch Israelitischer Gemeindebund; Professor Leopold Landau (1848–1920), a physician and lecturer at the University of Berlin; and Dr. Heinrich Meyer Cohn (1855–1905), a banker, philanthropist, and member of the Hibbat Zion. Soon after the committee's creation, Professor Warburg was dispatched to Cyprus to survey conditions on the island. While awaiting the professor's report, Trietsch traveled to Boryslaw to select suitable colonists for the proposed Jewish settlement on the Mediterranean island. Following his mission to Boryslaw, Trietsch visited Rumania. Here as a result of the constant persecution directed against the Jews he found great interest in his Cyprus plan. In a letter to Herzl describing the terrible conditions he found in Rumania and the desperate need to provide the Jews of that nation with an immediate haven, Trietsch again pleaded with the Zionist leader to recognize the merits of his Greater Palestine proposal and to amend the Basle Program to include it.

Although Herzl sympathized with Trietsch, he knew that any attempt to change the wording of the Basle Program would split the membership of the World Zionist Organization. Nevertheless, he did not hesitate to use the Cyprus scheme as a bargaining chip in his diplomatic efforts with Turkey to gain a charter for the Jewish colonization of Palestine. In a letter to Nuri Bey, the Turkish chief secretary for foreign affairs, Herzl informs Bey that the last Zionist Congress showed signs of leaning toward a Cyprus project because the island being under the control of England was accessible. It was therefore up to the Turks to understand that by not allowing a Jewish establishment in Palestine, an opportunity was slipping away that could bring the Ottoman regime great benefits, such as financial stability, industrial and commercial life and a modern fleet. Herzl concluded by intimating that he was still in control of the situation, and that there was still time for the Turks to come to an arrangement over Palestine until the next Zionist Congress met. However, if there was nothing to show at that occasion, Zionist plans would definitely shift toward a consideration of Cyprus for Jewish colonization.[404]

Trietsch, totally unaware of the Zionist leader's use of the Cyprus card and believing that Herzl was now adamantly opposed to his scheme, decided to act on his own. He traveled to Cyprus to meet with Warburg, only to find that the latter had left for Palestine. Anxious to learn the contents of Warburg's report, Trietsch followed him to Palestine. The meeting between the two men did not go smoothly. Warburg had doubts about the feasibility of a Jewish settlement on Cyprus. He had lost his enthusiasm for the proposal after being escorted around the Mediterranean island by officials of the I.C.A. Disappointed with Warburg's conclusions, which had definitely been influenced by the negative attitude of his I.C.A. guides, Trietsch journeyed to Cyprus to see for himself whether or not conditions on the island were suitable for colonization. His assessment was favorable, and he summed up his findings in a memorandum which he forwarded to the British High Commissioner of Cyprus. In this document he elaborated on his primary objective–the immediate establishment of a pioneer Jewish colony on Cyprus–with the intent to gradually expand this initial effort through further Jewish immigration. The memorandum also included practical suggestions: ways to increase agricultural production, a moratorium on taxing factories for a period of ten years, renting land to colonists with the option of subsequent purchase, expansion of the island's salt industry, the cultivation of tobacco as a cash crop, and the construction of a railway network to link the entire island with its ports.

The high commissioner, on receipt of the memorandum, sent it on to the Colonial Office in London for further consideration. Unable to accomplish anything more until hearing from London, Trietsch decided to return to Germany. Before leaving Cyprus, he made arrangements for the employment, in the island's water works, of a small number of Jewish laborers whom he intended to bring over from Boryslaw, Galicia.

After a brief stay in Berlin, Trietsch traveled to Boryslaw, where he recruited eleven laborers for his Cyprus project. He then went to Rumania only to find that the anti-Semitic government had adopted a hostile stand toward allowing Jews to emigrate. In addition, a decree was issued by the government expelling Trietsch as a potential troublemaker. In January of 1900 the peripatetic traveler was in London, where he tried to enlist support for his Cyprus scheme from Jewish organizations and government officials. The following month, Trietsch made his way to Vienna ostensibly to discuss cooperation with the governors of the Jewish Colonial Trust, a Zionist Organization institution.

Meanwhile, the Berlin Committee, which Trietsch had created, without informing him, took the first step toward implementing the Cyprus scheme. The eleven laborers from Boryslaw, under the auspices of the committee, were instructed to go directly to

Cyprus. Two more Boryslaw men financed by the Galician society Ahawath-Zion were to join them on the island. Red tape delayed the group of laborers sponsored by the Berlin Committee; however, the two individuals backed by the Galician society arrived on the island without incident and were met by Trietsch. He was shocked to discover that a group of Rumanian refugees had also reached Cyprus and were anxious to come under Trietsch's patronage. However, the group did not fit into the Trietsch's plans. He had not provided for such a contingency (the refugees had not been part of his or the committee's sponsorship), and he had always stressed that no settlement should be undertaken without careful planning. Nevertheless, he managed to find employment for the Rumanians, while awaiting the arrival of the group of laborers from Boryslaw. On April 12, 1900, the Boryslaw contingent, consisting of nine individuals reached Cyprus (two members of the original group of eleven had decided to return home during a stopover in Trieste).

Almost as quickly as the settlement project had begun, it began to unravel. Dissension between the Boryslaw laborers and the Rumanian refugees became commonplace. In addition, the climate, the food, the lack of family life, and the abysmal working conditions took a toll and finally erupted into an open revolt against Trietsch's leadership. His dream of establishing a Jewish foothold on Cyprus was shattered. After realizing that the would-be pioneers were not amenable to reason, he acquiesced to their demands to be sent home, and arranged for their departure from the island.

The collapse of the settlement project opened Trietsch to severe criticism from various quarters. His bruised feelings led him to believe that he was being made a scapegoat for a failure that was caused by circumstances beyond his control. He could not understand, for example, why he was being blamed for the actions of the Rumanian refugees who had come to Cyprus without his knowledge or blessings. Disillusioned, Trietsch returned to Berlin. The German capital soon provided him with a new venture. He became an editor of *Ost und West* (1901), an illustrated monthly for modern Judaism that quickly won universal recognition as an outstanding periodical. During his tenure as an editor, Trietsch watched with growing interest the development of independent factions within the Zionist Organization and the tendency of some of these groups to move in the direction of the Greater Palestine concept. Encouraged by these signs, he decided to make another attempt at the Fifth Zionist Congress to win over delegates to his colonization ideas. At the Congress, Trietsch's efforts to amend the Basle Program to include the neighboring lands of Palestine again aroused the ire of the majority of delegates. Herzl, like most of the delegates, believed that Trietsch was deliberately trying to destroy the Basle Program, the very cornerstone of the Zionist Movement. Accordingly, the Zionist leader responded in a negative manner, and with a satirical tone to Trietsch's resolution to change the Basle Program. When Trietsch took the floor again to elaborate on his concept he was roundly assailed by a chorus of boos and was hissed until he left the hall. Two days later, however, during a debate on the Jewish Colonial Trust, he was allowed to ascend the rostrum and address the delegates. This time, Trietsch was able to complete his speech without interruptions and to clarify his previous statements. He began his address by emphasizing that Palestine, at the moment, was not open for colonization, and therefore it was vital to have an alternative such as his Greater Palestine proposal. The speech was greeted with applause, and although Trietsch did not achieve any concrete results at the Fifth Zionist Congress, he now knew that his ideas were beginning to take hold.

Shortly before the Fifth Zionist Congress, Trietsch embarked on new literary ventures. He entered into a close collaboration with Martin Buber (1878–1965), one of the leaders of the Democratic Fraction (Herzl's opposition at the Zionist Congresses) and editor of the official Zionist organ, *Die Welt*. Trietsch together with Buber, Berthold Feiwel (1875–1937), and the artist Ephraim Moshe Lilien (1874–1925), combined their talents and founded in Berlin a Zionist publishing house, the Juedischer Verlag (1902). The new enterprise soon attained the highest standards in its field and the respect of the Jewish world. Davis Trietsch's association with the publishing house helped enormously to enhance his reputation and status. Nevertheless, to propagate his Greater Palestine concept, Trietsch turned to Alfred Nossig, who also held strong views on the narrowness of official Zionism. Together they founded a periodical entitled *Palestina: Zeitschrift fuer die kulturelle und wirtschaftliche Erschliessung des Landes* (1902) as an outlet for their opinions on how to resolve the Jewish Problem.

The very same year that the first issue of *Palestina* appeared, Herzl was again toying with the idea how best to use the Cyprus card in his diplomatic game to create a Jewish state. An opportunity presented itself when he was invited to England to testify as an expert witness before the Royal Commission on Alien Immigration. While thus engaged, he met several times with Lord Rothschild, a member of the commission and one of the leaders of England's Jewish community. During the course of their conversations, Herzl informed Rothschild of his hopes for establishing a Jewish colony, preferably under British auspices and protection. Rothschild suggested Uganda as a possible site, but Herzl demurred and wrote on a slip of paper his own choices of suitable territories—the Sinai Peninsula, Egyptian Palestine, and Cyprus. Although Lord Rothschild expressed interest in Herzl's selections, he qualified his support by indicating he would oppose any scheme that visualized large-scale colonization. He also requested that the Zionist leader provide him with a detailed memorandum on the subject. Herzl obliged and in his letter described in some length his colonization plans (the political aspects in English and the financial part in German) for the settlement of destitute Jews in one of the three sites he had suggested. In addition, Herzl pressed the point that to obviate any misunderstanding he had drawn up this plan for Lord Rothschild because of the latter's declared opposition to Palestine. However, whether he could personally assist in the execution of such a project or whether he could make the Zionist Organization available for it depended solely on the decision of the movement's members.

Herzl's plan, which Lord Rothschild eventually rejected because of the Zionist leader's insistence on a large-scale colonization, was amazingly similar to the program advocated by Davis Trietsch. Undismayed by the Anglo-Jewish banker's refusal to go along with his ideas, Herzl decided to directly approach the British government. His efforts met with success, and he had audiences with a number of key officials, including the Colonial Secretary, Joseph Chamberlain. Herzl disclosed to Chamberlain his understanding of the Jewish Problem and his proposed solution. He also informed Chamberlain of his negotiations with the Turks for Palestine. Herzl also spoke of possible alternatives such as Cyprus, El Arish, or the Sinai Peninsula if Palestine proved unattainable. The colonial secretary was sympathetic, but questioned Herzl's choices of alternatives to Palestine. He noted that he could only speak for Cyprus, as the other sites fell under the jurisdiction of the foreign office. Chamberlain then went on to describe the problems Jews would face if their objective was Cyprus. The island's population was composed of Greeks and Moslems and as colonial secretary he could not crowd them out for new immigrants. Similarly if the Greek inhabitants, perhaps with the support of Greece and Russia, decided to resist Jewish immigration, there would be real difficulties for Great Britain. In Cyprus, the secretary continued, the influx of foreign workmen would without a doubt lead to economic strife just as had occurred in the East End of London and in Australia. In any case he could not do anything against the will of the indigenous population.

In reply to the dismal picture presented by Chamberlain, Herzl noted that not everything in politics is disclosed to the public—only results. He then unfolded his plan for creating favorable public opinion for a Cyprus colonization project. Among Herzl's suggestions was a scheme to create a Jewish Eastern Company with 5 million pounds capital, ostensibly for settling Sinai and El Arish. When the Cypriots got wind of it, Herzl believed, they would want some of the golden rain on their island too. The Moslems would probably move away and the Greeks would gladly sell their lands for a good price, or migrate to Athens or elsewhere. Chamberlain seemed impressed by Herzl's plans, but once again he emphasized the difficulties inherent in a Cyprus project, and reiterated that he could not make any statement in regard to El Arish and Sinai.

Like most supporters of the Zionist Organization, Trietsch had no knowledge of Herzl's diplomatic forays. Neither did he have any way of knowing that Herzl, on the advice of Chamberlain, had dropped the Cyprus scheme in favor of El Arish and the Sinai Peninsula. Frustrated by his inability to get anything done, Trietsch tried another approach. He suggested the creation of an emigration office, under the auspices of the World Zionist Organization, the I.C.A., B'nai B'rith and the Alliance Israélite Universelle. This office would be responsible for providing information on, and support of, refugees, and seek territories for Jewish colonization. When his suggestion remained stillborn, Trietsch changed course and successfully created a new entity, Die Juedische Orient-Kolonization Gesellschaft (The Jewish-Orient Colonization Society). Incorporated on March 30, 1903, the Society had as its main objective colonization, based on cooperative principles, for Jews forced by persecution and economic hardships to flee from Eastern Europe. The new organization's master plan, influenced to a large degree by the eminent economist and sociologist Franz Oppenheimer (1864–1943), contained many novel features. It envisaged, for example, the Society's issuance of shares with the right for each shareholder to acquire up to 100 shares (each share was fixed at a value of 100 marks). Payment for shares could be made in small installments of at least two marks per month. The money thus gained would be applied by the Society to buy land, build homes, and plant trees. Actual construction of homes would be done by paid laborers under the supervision of a group of experts provided by the Society. The settlers would lease rather than own the land they worked, as the land itself would belong forever to the Society. Each lease, however, would be a perpetual one, and the rental charged the settlers would be used to cover costs and expenses. The ultimate aim was to make the settlers completely independent of the Society. As soon as the settlers were able to pay back part of the original investment, the Society was obliged to turn over to them the entire colony, which would then function as a giant cooperative. The money returned to the Society would then be reinvested in establishing new colonies.

Soon after its creation, the Jewish-Orient Colonization Society was confronted with its first challenge. Thousands of Jewish refugees from Eastern Europe were fleeing westward seeking asylum from persecution and a resurgence of virulent anti-Semitism. The Society attempted to help. It began rescue operations in Breslau, near the Polish, Galician, and German borders. While the Society was thus engaged, Trietsch, through various news reports learned of Herzl's negotiations with the British government, and that a Zionist commission was to be sent to investigate El Arish and the Sinai Peninsula as possible sites for colonization.[405] These news items were soon followed by a report that Herzl himself had traveled to Cairo to discuss the proposed projects with Lord Cromer, the British Agent and Consul General and Minister Plenipotentiary to Egypt. Outraged that he had been bypassed and not given any credit for his Greater Palestine concept, Trietsch made a fatal decision, which would subsequently lead to a complete personal rupture between Herzl and himself. He resolved to openly challenge Herzl for the leadership of the World Zionist Organization. The Jewish-Orient Colonization Society, he believed, would provide him the means and the instrument for his battle with the Zionist leader.

Once again Trietsch badly misjudged his support. Almost immediately after announcing his candidacy, he was attacked in the pages of the Zionist newspaper, *Die Welt,* which informed its readers that the Jewish-Orient Colonization Society was a private enterprise and did not represent the Zionist Organization or its policies. In the same vein, the Zionist leaders of Germany circulated a letter drawing attention to the fact that Trietsch's Society could in no way be considered a Zionist agency, as it had not accepted as a precondition for its activities the principle of a publicly legally guaranteed security for any proposed settlement. Angered by these accusations, Trietsch struck back. If Herzl could negotiate in Cairo with British and Egyptian officials, why couldn't he reopen his contacts with the British authorities on Cyprus? Accordingly, he wrote a letter to the High Commissioner of Cyprus, W.F. Haynes Smith, inquiring about the availability of certain state-owned lands on the island, and the conditions that must be met to obtain these tracts for a settlement project. Trietsch also informed the high commissioner of the existence of the Jewish-Orient Colonization Society and its goal to create cooperative settlements composed of Jewish immigrants from Eastern Europe.

Receiving no reply from the high commissioner, Trietsch traveled to London to deal directly with the officials of the colonial office. Although given an opportunity to be heard, his request for information regarding land purchases on Cyprus went unanswered. While awaiting a decision from either Cyprus or London, Trietsch made plans for carrying his struggle to the Sixth Zionist Congress, which was scheduled to meet the week of August 23–28, 1903. In preparation for the Congress he made vigorous efforts to rally support for his claim to the leadership of the Zionist Organization. As the originator of the Greater Palestine concept, which Herzl by his negotiations over El Arish and the Sinai had for all practical purposes adopted, Trietsch felt that he was entitled to the Zionist leadership.

However, not even the stalwarts of Herzl's opposition in the Democratic Fraction such as Buber, Feiwel, and Lilien, men whom Trietsch had collaborated with in the creation of the Juedischer Verlag, were willing to go beyond mere expressions of sympathy for his course. Trietsch's campaign for the Zionist leadership suffered still another blow when the prominent sociologist Franz Oppenheimer suddenly resigned from the Jewish-Orient Colonization Society. Similarly, an attempt by Trietsch to win support from the Conference of the Zionist Federation of Germany also ended in failure.

At the Sixth Zionist Congress, Herzl, in his opening address informed the delegates that the El Arish–Sinai scheme had to be abandoned. The unwillingness of Cromer, Britain's top official in Egypt, to divert water from the Nile for the proposed settlement, plus the objections of the Egyptian authorities, had proved too difficult to overcome. Nevertheless, Herzl stressed, all was not lost, as the British had suggested an alternate territory in East Africa (the Uganda proposal).

Trietsch, like most of the delegates, was taken aback by Herzl's speech. Given the floor, he launched into a personal attack against the Zionist leader and his policies. The so-called experts, he insisted, were wrong about El Arish and the Sinai Peninsula. Water in these areas would not be a problem if instead of colonizing a large territory, a beginning was made on small tracts of land. Furthermore, it was unthinkable to give up part of one's country (i.e., the southeastern sector of Palestine) because of a supposed water shortage. In conclusion he reminded the delegates of his long struggle to gain acceptance for the Greater Palestine scheme, and the advantages of occupying a territory close to Palestine, namely Cyprus.

In the debate that followed only Alfred Nossig came to the defense of Trietsch. Herzl, in his rebuttal, ignored the personal attacks that he had been subjected to and defended the conclusions of the Zionist commission experts who had also, after investigating El Arish and Sinai, rejected the areas as settlement sites. Dramatically, Herzl completed his reply by reading the statement of a woman from Galatz, Rumania, who described in vivid terms her ordeal as a pioneer on Cyprus (presumably after having followed Trietsch's advice to immigrate). In the uproar that followed this presentation, Trietsch realized that he had lost his bid to replace Herzl. However, he still felt that a great injustice had been done to him in being blamed for the misadventures of the Rumanian refugees on Cyprus. Accordingly, he appealed to the Congress for redress, and a special committee of delegates was formed to air his complaints. The committee met, listened, and absolved Trietsch of any responsibility for the plight of the Rumanian woman and of her fellow countrymen, who had on their own immigrated to Cyprus. Herzl himself declared to the Congress delegates that he never for a moment doubted the personal integrity of Davis Trietsch, but he never forgave the latter for his slanderous attacks on his character.

Following the Congress, an embittered and disillusioned Trietsch returned to Berlin. This mood soon passed and his combative spirit returned, along with his confidence. He knew that a large contingent of the Zionist organization would never accept the East Africa proposal, and that since the El-Arish–Sinai negotiations had collapsed, and Palestine was still inaccessible, only Cyprus remained a viable alternative. Having never received an official reply to his original inquiries regarding Cyprus, he wrote to the British colonial office reiterating his proposal for establishing a Jewish settlement on the island. The colonial office passed the letter on to the high commissioner of Cyprus with instructions for the latter to forward to London any information they might have on Davis Trietsch and particularly on the financial status of the Jewish-Orient Colonization Society. On receiving these instructions, the high commissioner ordered his chief secretary to answer Davis Treitsch's original inquiry of June 6, 1903. This done, a dispatch was forwarded to the colonial office headquarters in London. It indicated that Trietsch had not specified what type of Jews he intended to introduce into Cyprus. There were however no openings for laborers, tradesmen, or miners, or for any immigrants who were not skilled agriculturists. The dispatch also pointed out that there would be strong opposition from the Orthodox Christian community to any large settlement of foreign Jews. In addition, the general question of immigration into Cyprus of persons without property was regulated by a proclamation of 1898 that was still in force. It prohibited any such persons to land unless and until provision had been made for their support to the satisfaction of the high commissioner.

Enclosed with the dispatch was a letter sent by Trietsch inquiring at what rates or conditions a colonization society could obtain government lands. He had been informed that land was available in the Messaoria Plain at a price of six pounds an acre, or two pounds a dunam, with the condition that the land had to be placed under cultivation within a specified time period. Half of the purchase money was to be paid before entry on the land and the balance in two equal payments.

The dispatch concluded with a warning that a colonization society, before bringing settlers to the island, would have to build housing for them and that it was unlikely that they could obtain any housing accommodations in the neighboring villages.

Upon receipt of the high commissioner's letter, the colonial office transmitted a copy to the foreign office. At this juncture a bureaucratic tangle occurred as both the colonial office and the foreign office were dealing with Jewish issues involving various organizations and individuals, as well as proposed sites for Jewish settlements. The roots of this confusion could be traced back to the Sixth Zionist Congress at which, after a bitter debate, the delegates had agreed to dispatch a commission to investigate the British offer of a territory in East Africa. When news of the offer and the commission reached East Africa, rigorous opposition was voiced by the British settlers of the region. The upshot of these complaints was a voluminous correspondence and exchange of views between Sir Charles Eliot, the British Commissioner in Mombassa and the colonial office, and between the latter agency and the foreign office. In the midst of this correspondence Davis Trietsch's Cyprus proposals became intermingled with the exchange of dispatches between the various ministries and officials of the British government. Indeed, the parallel efforts of Herzl and Trietsch, sometimes contradictory and sometimes identical, were to a large measure responsible for the confusion of the British authorities, who had trouble distinguishing between the two rivals and their movements. The bureaucratic muddle deepened when the colonial office wrote the foreign office asking for information on Trietsch and their thoughts on his Cyprus plan, as well as the current status of the East African proposal. When the foreign office received the inquiry, it was delegated to the department responsible for African affairs (because of a brief reference to East Africa) instead of being forwarded to the section responsible for handling matters pertaining to Cyprus. This error gave the impression that both the Cyprus and East Africa proposals had originated with Trietsch and his organization.

The foreign office, acting on the colonial office's request, inquired of the British embassy in Berlin what it knew about Davis Trietsch's background. After a preliminary investigation the embassy reported back that Trietsch was a respectable citizen who was occupied mainly with literary work of a Jewish political nature. Although he enjoyed a fairly good income, he did not possess any means worthy of note. On receiving this information, the foreign office passed it on to the colonial office, which then drafted an official reply to Trietsch indicating their final decision on his settlement proposal. The document clearly reflected the advice the high commissioner of Cyprus had given to his superiors. It informed Trietsch that because of local feelings in Cyprus the colonial office could not see its way to move the government of the island to grant any exceptional terms to Jewish settlers. Therefore any settlers introduced under Trietsch's plan would be subject to the ordinary regulations as to the purchase of crown lands and to the Proclamation of 1898 in regard to destitute immigrants.

The colonial office's letter, coupled with the internal disarray in the Jewish-Orient Colonization Society resulting from Dr. Oppenheimer's resignation and the perennial shortage of funds severely curtailed Trietsch's plans for a "Greater Palestine." Nevertheless, he continued to devote his energies to the problem of Jewish refugees. In 1905

Trietsch opened an Information Office for Immigration in Jaffa, with branches in several other cities of the Holy Land. When financial difficulties slowed the effectiveness of the operation, the irrepressible Trietsch organized and participated in an exploratory expedition to El Arish, with a view to reopening negotiations with the British for this territory.

Throughout these tumultuous years Trietsch never completely severed his ties with the World Zionist Organization. In 1907 the organization finally recognized his considerable talents, and he was made a member of the Zionist Actions Committee, a post that he would occupy through 1911, and again from 1920 to 1921. Many of his earlier proposals regarding practical work in Palestine were adopted by successive Zionist Congresses. Trietsch's abrasive personality and zealotry for the causes he espoused, however, irritated many Zionists throughout his long career and probably led to his never attaining the top leadership of the movement.

The outbreak of World War I presented Davis Trietsch with an unusual opportunity to air his views. At the beginning of the conflict both the Allied and the Central Powers, in their desire for a total victory, gave consideration in their war plans to the Jews and their age-old dream of returning to Eretz Israel. In England Chaim Weizmann would work diligently, in the name of the Zionist Organization, to overcome the prevalent view that the Jews were pro-German. In fact, many educated Jews of Central and Eastern Europe and elsewhere considered the German language as the mark of high culture. In addition, the majority of Jews in Eastern Europe and America tended to sympathize with the Central Powers, not so much out of fondness for Germany, as out of hatred for czarist Russia, a member of the Allied Powers.

On the other hand, Zionists such as Davis Trietsch were convinced that the future of Zionism would be enhanced by a German victory. Extreme patriots, the German Zionists initially sought from their government the protection of the Jewish population of Palestine from the malevolence of a Turkish regime implacably hostile to Jewish nationalism and bent on mischief. The German Zionists reasoned that it would be difficult for the Turks to turn a deaf ear to the remonstrations of their principal ally at a time when the Germans were at the height of their military power and prestige. Although the starting point of the German Zionists was the emergency in Palestine, their approach to their government soon broadened to include other issues. The German regime, these Zionists felt, might be induced to come to the rescue of the Jews in Palestine in the interests of their war-time propaganda campaign, or better still if they could be persuaded to see long-term advantages for Germany in favoring Zionist aspirations to return to the Holy Land. For some of the German planners and strategists, the belief that the war could end with Turkey a satellite and its considerable Asiatic territories thrown wide open for commercial exploitation made the the idea of using Zionism to achieve these goals seem especially appealing.

The above concept received its fullest expression in a brochure by Davis Trietsch entitled *Die Juden der Türkei* ("The Jews of Turkey"). Trietsch, who served in the Great War as a member of the statistical department of the German army, wrote the brochure in 1915 as part of the ongoing propaganda campaign. In this work he systematically enumerated all the arguments in favor of collaboration between the Imperial German Government, the Zionist movement, and world Jewry. He pointed out, for example, that about 13 million out of 14.5 million Jews in the world spoke German or Yiddish as their mother tongue, and that in their cultural orientation the Jewish population of Eastern Europe was a definite asset to the spread of German influence and commercial interests.

Hitherto, Trietsch noted, Germany had concerned herself very little with Jewish emigration from Eastern Europe. It had not realized that the annual exodus from the region of about 100,000 Yiddish speaking Jews to the United States and England and its colonies had greatly enlarged the economic potential of the latter nations, as well the spread of Anglo-Saxon culture. At the same time a possible German asset was being proportionately depreciated. The beginning of the war, Trietsch wrote, had found Eastern European Jewry in the process of being uprooted, and the conflict had accelerated the catastrophe. Particularly hard-hit were the western provinces of Poland and Galicia, where more than half of the Jews of the world lived. Hundreds of thousands had been displaced, their homes destroyed. As a result, Trietsch predicted there would be an emigration of East European Jews on an unprecedented scale into Germany.

> It will no longer do simply to close the German frontiers to them, and in view of the difficulties which would result from a wholesale migration of Eastern Jews into Germany itself, Germans will only be too glad to find a way out in the emigration of these Jews to Turkey – a solution extraordinarily favorable to the interests of all three parties concerned.[406]

Elaborating on this theme, Trietsch argued that because nine-tenths of Jewry spoke Yiddish or German and that a large proportion of the remaining population lived in the Islamic world, it was in Germany's interest to take these factors into their overall geopolitical strategy. Indeed, once victory was achieved, German policy should give serious consideration to creating a protectorate for the Jews of the East. In his vision of the postwar era, Trietsch was clearly suggesting the use of Jews as a stalking horse for German imperialism. He bolstered his thesis by pointing out that smaller groups had in the past been able to render Germany vital service. Although the Jews had no national state, their dispersion over the whole world and their peculiar abilities gave them a weight that was worth more in the balance than many larger populations who enjoyed a compact territory of their own. Underlying Trietsch's exposition was a firm belief that the German policy he was advocating would gain for the Jews entry into Turkey's Asiatic provinces, notably Palestine and its environs.

Trietsch's brochure and similar works by German Zionists succeeded in influencing Germany's Near East and Middle East policies. In November of 1915 the German government instructed its consuls in the Ottoman Empire to look favorably on Jewish activities designed to promote the economic and cultural progress of the Jews of Turkey and also to facilitate the immigration and settlement of Jews from other countries into the region. These decisions were still far short of Trietsch's grand design or that of the German Zionists, but it seemed to suggest that Germany was tentatively embracing their cause.

The Allied Powers were quick to take note of the efforts of the German Zionists to influence their government. The English, in particular, slowly began to revise their earlier views of Zionism, and launched an intensive propaganda campaign to offset the work of Trietsch and the other German Zionists. At the request of the British government, Arnold J. Toynbee, the eminent historian, was given the task of countering the arguments presented by Trietsch in his provocative brochure, *The Jews of Turkey*. In a work entitled *Turkey: A Past and a Future* (1917), Toynbee pleaded for cooperation with the Zionists. His efforts were applauded by the leaders of British Zionism who rallied fully behind

Great Britain's war effort. Indeed, under the inspired leadership of Chaim Weizmann, Great Britain recognized Zionist aims with the issuance of the Balfour Declaration. The Allies had clearly outplayed the German government in the propaganda war to win the hearts of Jewry. The conquest of Palestine by General Edmund Allenby, which followed soon after the issuance of the Balfour Declaration, completely silenced the German Zionists. They now realized that the British propaganda and military victory had opened wide the door to the age-old dream of a Jewish restoration in Palestine.

With the cessation of hostilities, the World Zionist Organization was once again united. Among the thorny issues that confronted the movement was the form and rate of Jewish immigration and settlement in Palestine. Arthur Ruppin (1876–1943), an economist and sociologist who had been deported from Palestine in 1916 by the Turks, had returned to the country after the war as director of the Zionist Executive's colonization department. He envisaged a yearly immigration into Palestine of 20,000 Jewish families. This estimate was the lowest put forth at the time by various experts. Ruppin's main critic was Davis Trietsch, who favored a policy that would become known as "Zionist Maximalism," i.e., the immigration and settlement of hundreds of thousands of Jews into the Holy Land as quickly as possible. This stand was a complete reversal of his earlier position in relation to Cyprus, El Arish, and the Sinai Peninsula. Trietsch fought strongly for his maximalist idea, but in the end it was Arthur Ruppin who won out. The latter's immigration estimates, over the course of a few years, proved to be more realistic than those of his opponents. Trietsch's maximalist program contained many suggestions, however, weighty of consideration. He favored, for example, intensive agriculture in the settlements, contrary to the advice of most of the experts, and felt that the agricultural methods approved by the Zionist organization were inadequate and inefficient. Moreover, in view of the general lack of agricultural experience among Jews, Trietsch insisted on the importance of developing industry to absorb the large number of immigrants. He also advocated the building of small garden cities in conjunction with the projected industrial expansion. Whereas Ruppin and others thought that an investment of 1,000 to 1,500 pounds sterling was needed for the absorption of one immigrant family, Trietsch felt that funds of such magnitude would be hard to come by, and, therefore, it would be wiser to search for ways of cutting the costs of settling immigrants, and of the construction of settlements. Trietsch constantly advanced these views at the Zionist Congresses and in numerous publications, especially in *Volk und Land,* a Berlin weekly, which he founded and edited.

In 1932 Trietsch settled permanently in Eretz Israel. In the few years remaining him he continued unabated his struggle for a change in Zionist immigration policies. Throughout his long career, his critics considered this fighter for Jewish survival as "the bad boy of Zionism" – an unruly, insubordinate, refractory, contumacious individual. However, even his most vociferous detractors could not deny his talents, nor his overwhelming devotion to the Jewish people.

44

Paul Friedmann's Midian Experiment

The year 1891 ushered in a new era of adversity and tribulation for the Jews of Eastern Europe and the handful of Jewish settlements in Palestine. The expulsion of the Jews from Moscow plus the continuing anti-Jewish actions on the part of the czarist regime forced thousands of Jews to leave Russia and seek new homes in other lands. At the same time the settlements established in Palestine, largely through the efforts of the Hibbat Zion movement, faced mounting fiscal crises, and had become dependent for survival on the munificence of the philanthropist, Baron Edmund de Rothschild. Adding to this atmosphere of impending doom, Hibbat Zion's guiding spirit Leon Pinsker, the author of the pamphlet *Auto-Emancipation* had passed away, and anti-Semitism was on the rise in Germany, Austria, France, and throughout Eastern Europe.

In an effort to deal with the flood of refugees streaming out of Eastern Europe, relief committees were established in London, Berlin, Vienna, and Paris. Almost all of these Jewish committees believed that some form of organized immigration was required to resettle the refugees. In England, the Hibbat Zion approached Lord Nathaniel Mayer Rothschild, the doyen of the Jewish community to use his influence to get the government to open negotiations with Turkey. The purpose of these talks would be to obtain from the Turks permission for Jews to immigrate to and colonize Palestine. Abdul Hamid II, the Turkish Sultan of the Ottoman Empire, however, reacted negatively to the pressures brought to bear on him. He tightened his policy of barring Jewish immigration to the Holy Land. This setback led to an intensification of the efforts on the part of various Jewish territorialist groups to find a suitable land for the ever-swelling number of refugees. One immediate result of this activity was the creation in 1891 of the Jewish Colonization Association (I.C.A.) by Baron Maurice de Hirsch. Its objective was to assist Jews to emigrate from countries where they were being persecuted or economically depressed and to settle in the New World, especially in Argentina. The same year in which the

I.C.A. was born, Baron Maurice de Hirsch was approached by an individual named Paul Friedmann who suggested a plan for establishing a Jewish settlement in the general vicinity of Palestine. "It is my hope," Friedmann informed the philanthropist, "to convert the weak, and bad elements into strong active men, and to build up a tribe around which the nation can rally."[407]

The Baron considered Friedmann's plan to be impractical, and refused to back it with either his money or name. A few years later, the great philanthropist would, in a similar manner, reject another visionary – Theodor Herzl.

Who was Paul Friedmann? A dossier compiled by the Berlin police described him as being a person of independent means; born on April 26, 1840, in Konigsburg, Prussia; Protestant; single; and an individual of good repute and worthy of esteem and confidence. Although not Jewish, he evinced a great interest in sheltering Jews being deported from Russia. However, he had not joined the international rescue committee formed by Baron Maurice de Hirsch, but preferred instead to work on his own. Accordingly, his charitable plans could not be assessed since his connections with authorities and key people remained unknown. The dossier also indicated that he lived quietly in an apartment that was in keeping with his income, and that because of his frequent absences he was not well known among the local population.

In fact, Paul Friedmann was a convert to Christianity. He was the scion of an old Jewish family, which claimed descent from Veitel Heine Ephraim, master of the mint under Fredrick the Great of Prussia and head of the Berlin Jewish community. Possessor of a considerable personal fortune (the police estimated that his annual income was somewhere between 21,600 to 25,200 marks), Friedmann traveled extensively. He frequently visited Vienna, Paris, and London, where he pursued historical studies and research in the great libraries of these European capitals. These intellectual labors eventually culminated in the publication by Friedmann of several historical works, the best known being *Les Dépêches de G. Michiel, Ambassadeur de Venise en Angleterre pendant les années 1554 à 1557,* and a two-volume work entitled *Anne Boleyn: A Chapter of English History 1527–1535.*

Much exercised over the persecution of Russian Jewry, Friedmann, the converted Jew, suddenly became acutely aware of his roots and began an all-out search for a viable solution to the Jewish Problem. His attention, at first, was drawn to Palestine, and he closely followed the numerous accounts of the Holy Land appearing in various publications of the day. He was particularly impressed by the work of a relative named George Ebers (1837–98), who had written historical novels set in Palestine and the Sinai Peninsula. In his research Friedmann also came upon the books and reports of the British explorer and orientalist Sir Richard Burton (1821–90), dealing with the ancient land of Midian (Arabia). He became convinced that the sparsely settled region described by Burton was ideal for the establishment of a Jewish colony.

Midian, at this time, was somewhat of an enigma to the West. Its early history was shrouded in mystery. The ancient Pharaohs of Egypt had held sway over the region, and Midian was frequently mentioned in the Bible. Abraham's fourth son by his wife Keturah was named Midian, and seemingly was the eponymous ancestor of the Semitic tribe that inhabited the land. Moses had fled from Egypt to Midian and had married Zipporah, the daughter of Jethro, the Midianite priest. King Solomon had absorbed part of Midian into his realm. Midian eventually came under Roman rule, and centuries later was conquered by the forces of Mohammed. For a short time it was occupied by the Christian Crusaders.

In the first half of the sixteenth century Midian became incoroporated into the Ottoman Empire, which allowed the province to be administered by its vassal, Egypt. By the nineteenth century, the name Midian had come to stand for the region that stretched from Aquaba in the north to the port of El-Wijh some 200 miles to the south on the Red Sea coast of the Arabian Peninsula. In this territory of approximately 9,000 square miles the total population, mostly Bedouins, numbered about 23,000.

In 1890 Paul Friedmann visited Midian to see for himself if the information he had gleaned from his readings was accurate and if the territory was suitable for colonization. The following year he published his findings in a small pamphlet entitled *Das Land Madian*.[408] The eighteen-page booklet dealt almost exclusively with statistics on Midian's population, climate, economy, natural resources, and potential for supporting a number of colonies. Friedmann pointedly avoided indicating that his prospective colonists would be Jews. Also left unsaid was that beyond his immediate objective of finding a haven for persecuted Jews, he was ultimately considering the creation of a Jewish state.

Having published his thoughts on Midian, Friedmann now turned to the task of winning over Jewish leaders and organizations to his colonization scheme. In rapid succession he conferred with representatives of the Alliance Israélite Universelle of Paris, the Anglo-Jewish Association of London, the Israelitische Alliance of Vienna, and with other Jewish relief organizations. Almost all of these entities had reservations about Friedmann, as they suspected his plan to be a thinly disguised plot for Christian missionary activities. A similar fate had befallen Laurence Oliphant, the author of the *Land of Gilead,* a few years earlier. However, Friedmann persisted in his efforts and eventually his enthusiasm and sincerity overcame the fears of the Jewish organizations. The fact that he did not ask these agencies for financial help, but only for moral support was an important factor in their tacit approval of his colonization plans. Nevertheless, similar appeals by Friedmann to the great Jewish philanthopists of the day, such as Baron de Hirsch, were less successful.

Friedmann also cultivated the representatives and diplomats of Great Britain, Germany, Austria-Hungary, as well as the countries most essential to his project, Turkey and Egypt. Some years prior to the publication of *Das Land Madian* he had made the acquaintance of Lord Cromer (Evelyn Baring), the British Minister Plenipotentiary and Consul General for Egypt. Cromer not only represented the British government's point of view, but for all practical purposes that of the Egyptian government as well. In a memorandum sent by Cromer to the British prime minister and to the foreign secretary he described his first encounter with Paul Friedmann. According to Cromer, he had met the Berlin man of letters some years earlier, perhaps in 1889, while in London during a summer leave from his Egyptian post. He had previously received correspondence about Friedmann from Sir Louis Mallet, the Permanent Under-Secretary of State for India. In a description reminiscent of the Berlin dossier, Cromer noted that Friedmann possessed a considerable private income, a large portion of which he devoted to benevolent works, and that, although not a Jew, he took a great interest in everything that affected the Jewish race. In a word, he was an intelligent and honest man, somewhat eccentric and very tenacious in his opinions.

Lord Cromer's memorandum went on to state that Friedmann had informed him that he intended, at his own cost, to establish a small colony for Jewish refugees on Egyptian soil, and asked whether Her Majesty's government would object to his plan. Cromer had tried to dissuade Friedmann from undertaking the project. He had told Friedmann that it did not appear to be a matter that concerned the English government, and that he would have to deal directly with the Egyptian government. Furthermore, although Cromer, as minister plenipotentiary and consul general for Egypt, would not take any hostile action against him, Friedmann should not expect any effective support either.

Toward the end of 1890 Friedmann again called on Lord Cromer, this time in Cairo, and was advised to establish direct contact with Riaz Pasha (1835–1911), the Prime Minister of Egypt. Although a severe critic of European expansion into the Middle East, Riaz Pasha did not object too strenuously to Friedmann's settlement proposal. He would later inform Lord Cromer that his intention was neither to encourage nor discourage the project.

In May of 1891 Friedmann was again in London. He called at the foreign office, where he submitted a copy of his pamphlet, *Das Land Madian,* and requested of the British officials a promise that no obstacles would be placed in the way of his colonization scheme. He also addressed a memorandum containing the details of his plan to the Marquis of Salisbury.[409] It began with the observation that the Jewish Question was keeping the Russians in a state of ferment that was dangerous to the peace of Europe. Jews seeking to escape persecution were trapped. The only country, Friedmann stressed, where Jews could possibly go in large numbers was Arabia, where they would meet no race hatred, as the Arabs were a younger branch of their own stock.

The memorandum went on to explain that Friedmann intended to go in the fall with about eighty picked Galician and Hungarian Jews to found a colony in the Egyptian province of Midian on the coast of the Arabian Peninsula. The colony would rely for its substance on the settlement's artisans providing skills that the Bedouins lacked, in fishing, trade with turquoise (found in the mountains of the region), and on the working of mother of pearl, which is found in the waters along the coast. Once established, the memorandum continued, the settlers would plant small vegetable gardens, as well as fruit trees and vines for the climate and soil were admirably suitable for these purposes. The Bedouins, if properly treated or bribed, would probably not object to these undertakings. However, once the colony reached a population of 300 men, who would be properly trained and armed, there would be little to fear from the Bedouin tribes. So that the colony might grow and prosper and attract many Jews from Russia, Rumania, and elsewhere, it was also essential to introduce new industries into the region, such as shipbuilding and cotton spinning.

Friedmann's memorandum to Salisbury acknowledged his understanding that his colony could not expect any protection from the government, and that in all dealings with the Bedouin the settlers were on their own. Nevertheless, Friedmann posed several situations for the English statesman to consider, which might arise if the colony prospered. First, who should rule the country, which, although in Egyptian territory, was actually in the hands of the Bedouin? Expanding on this issue, Friedmann suggested that if the Jewish colony was granted more autonomy, they would prove that they could keep the Bedouins in order. In addition, such authority would prevent an influx of adventurers from flocking into the region and bringing in their wake disorder, quarreling, and anarchy.

Secondly, if the colony prospered greatly and achieved a super-abundant population, Friedmann hinted, he would like to extend his colonization program to the remainder of the Arabian Peninsula. The Turks, he understood, cared only for the holy areas (Mecca and environs) and their pilgrims' road to these places. The rest of Arabia was of no consequence to them, and they might prefer to see it in Jewish rather than European hands. Continuing in this vein, Friedmann noted that his hope was that Jews might eventually settle right across the peninsula in Oman and Hadramant, and then try to build a railroad that would shorten the route to India by several days. He then asked the English statesman that if the Jews could carry out such a plan, would the British government object or hinder it.

The Marquis of Salisbury confirmed the receipt of Friedmann's memorandum, but gave no indication if he approved or disapproved of the proposed colonization project. Pursuing other British leads, Friedmann also met with Arthur Godley, First Baron Kilbracken (1847–1932), the private secretary to Gladstone, and with Sir Francis Grenfell (1841–1925), who had in 1885 been appointed Commander-in-Chief of the Egyptian Army. Not content with these British diplomatic overtures, Friedmann also sought support for his scheme in the chancelleries of Berlin and Vienna.

A confidential report to the Imperial German Chancellory by Prince Ratisbon speaks of a petition by Friedmann in which he outlined his Midian plans and asked for the German government's blessings. Prince Ratisbon then notes that the petitioner is quite aware that the government cannot give direct support to his project. He hopes, however, that wherever his scheme appears compatible with German interests he will be given whatever small assistance that can materially facilitate his task, e.g., information from consular officials, and special privileges from Egyptian local, port, tourist, and health authorities. Because Egyptian Arabia borders on three sides the vilayets of Damascus and Hejaz, Friedmann also deemed it important that at some later date he be assisted in gaining an audience with the Grand Vizier at Constantinople, to tell him he was not scheming against Turkey.

Prince Ratisbon's report to his superiors received considerable attention and was circulated by the chancellory to the German embassies in Constantinople and Vienna, as well as to their representatives in Egypt. Although no formal German assistance was promised Friedmann, all of the officials contacted were made to understand that they were free to show him personal considerations.

A similar approach was made by Friedmann to the Austro-Hungarian government and to such prominent members of the realm as Feldzeugmeister (General) Ferdinand Freiherr von Bauer, and the diplomat Count Welsersheimb. Diplomatic dispatches from Vienna relating to Friedmann revealed a general consensus of opinion that the philanthropist was a man of integrity and an idealist willing to make personal sacrifices to achieve his goals. However, like the British and the Germans, the Austro-Hungarian reports indicate a willingness not to place any obstacles in Friedmann's path, but also a serious doubt as to the chances of the colonization plan succeeding.

Friedmann was particularly anxious to have the help of Germany and the Austro-Hungarian Empire in gaining access to the Turkish authorities. Although he made plans to visit Constantinople, he was compelled by unexpected circumstances to postpone the trip. This diplomatic lapse would later come back to haunt him, and in a way contributed to the eventual failure of his colonization scheme.

Nevertheless, having touched bases with the various governments, Friedmann now began to implement his plan. He hired a former Prussian army officer named Lothar von Seebach to be his chief aide, and together they traveled to Cracow (1891) to recruit an elite force of Jewish pioneers. The selection process proved more difficult than Friedmann had anticipated. He would later complain that his recruitment efforts had been hampered by the constant interference of certain leaders of the Cracow Jewish community. As a result of this unexpected opposition, Friedmann was forced to accept individuals that did not quite come up to the standards he had originally proposed as essential for strenuous pioneer work. Most of the Jews selected were artisans from Galicia and Russia, totally unaccustomed to hard labor and lacking in discipline. The group chosen numbered seventeen men, six women, and four children. All of the men signed contracts that stipulated that besides pioneer work, they would be expected to render other services. Friedmann was adamant that each pioneer was expected to undergo military training and to abide by his rules and that of von Seebach for two years.

After leaving Cracow, Friedmann began to work out the details for his expedition to Midian. He spared no expense and purchased only the best of equipment and supplies. He acquired a steam-driven yacht in Scotland, which he promptly registered under the Austrian flag, and renamed the vessel the "Israel". From an Austrian ministry he obtained 100 rifles, which he stashed away aboard the Israel. A meticulous planner, Friedmann saw to it that the yacht was well-stocked with kosher food for his Jewish recruits, and that the children of the pioneers were supplied with toys.

To oversee the expedition, the philanthropist acquired a small staff, which, in addition to the ex-Prussian officer Lothar von Seebach, included two noncommissioned officers, a Viennese physician, a Scot private secretary, and a ritual slaughterer from England. Finally, in the fall of 1891 the Israel set sail from Southampton for Egypt. Arriving in Alexandria, Friedmann, after consultations with the leaders of the city's Jewish community, added eight more people to the expedition, including an Arabic interpreter and a native of Odessa named Abraham Rasnowitch.

All together, the expedition now numbered forty-six individuals. Continuing the journey, the yacht reached Suez on December 1, 1891. Given a warm welcome by the local Jewish residents, the pioneers were in a festive mood, happy to have left Eastern Europe and impatient to see their future home. Leaving the women and children behind at Suez with the understanding they would follow later, the Israel sailed on. Twelve days later (December 13th), a landing was made at Sharm al-Moza in territory theoretically under Egyptian control. Here the would-be colonists pitched their tents and transported to sheds especially provided for this purpose their stores and provisions. At this juncture, Friedmann placed the pioneers under the strict supervision of Lothar von Seebach and his noncommissioned officers. Military discipline was immediately instituted and assignments meted out to each of the settlers. At first the colonists were enthused by a sense of mission, and the required labors were performed willingly. Many of the settlers felt they were carrying out a historic work for the Jewish people, and that the Almighty had chosen them for the task of creating a permanent home for their suffering coreligionists. Some of the pioneers had agreed to participate in the expedition because they felt it would take them close to the borders of Palestine.

To Friedmann's surprise, the colonists were not molested by the local Bedouins. This circumstance may have been largely due to the efforts of the commander of the Egyptian Army, Sir Francis Grenfell. Fearing for the safety of Friedmann and his settlers, Grenfell had taken the precautionary step of issuing the philanthropist a notice of protection. The notice advised all Arab sheiks within the boundaries of Egyptian territory of Paul Friedmann's identity and requested that they give him free passage.

News of the expedition was reported in the Egyptian and Turkish press without editorial comment. The first critical account appeared in Europe in a Jewish periodical published by Nathan Birnbaum. The author of the article, Saul Raphael Landau

(1869–1946), had met Paul Friedmann when the latter had visited Cracow. Landau, at the time a student in Vienna University, was spending his vacation in his native town. He felt that Friedmann's Midian plan was sheer fantasy and posed great danger for the expedition's participants. Accordingly, Landau put his fears into writing and persuaded Birnbaum to publish a series of articles attacking the Friedmann enterprise.

In the meantime the initial glow that had marked the preliminary work of establishing a settlement at Sharm al-Moza had dissipated. Two incidents, in particular, were destined to upset Friedmann's carefully laid plans. One affair was of an internal nature and the other was the result of a political conflict between Turkey and Egypt.

The first incident resulted from the strict discipline imposed on the colonists by the former Prussian officer, Lothar von Seebach. Tension developed between Von Seebach and his charges and led to open defiance when Abraham Rasnowitch, the Russian Jew who had joined the expedition in Alexandria, refused outright to obey the Prussian's orders. Lothar von Seebach, fearing a general mutiny, punished Rasnowitch by expelling him from the encampment. However, the unrest had already spread to other colonists, and Rasnowitch was joined by another malcontent named Schwarz. After being forcibly ejected twice and prevented from reentering the settlement, the two outcasts wandered off into the desert. Somehow, the dissenters became separated. Schwarz managed to reach safety after three days in the wilderness. Rasnowitch was less fortunate and lost his way in the desert. He was found semiconscious seven days later by some monks, and died soon after, as a result of his exposure.

The death of Rasnowitch aroused great indignation among the colonists. Friedmann, in an attempt to retain the loyalty of the pioneers, promised to release from contractual obligation anyone who desired to leave the settlement. However, he made the mistake of giving the colonists too much time to mull over their decision, thus playing into the hands of the few dissidents who were determined to defy Friedmann and his Prussian henchman. The agitators skillfully exploited the consternation produced by Rasnowitch's death, and sixteen settlers declared their intention to leave the colony. Friedmann, after failing to persuade them to change their minds, kept his word and released them from their contracts.

The Rasnowitch affair received considerable attention in the Egyptian press, especially in the French-language newspapers *La Phare d'Alexandrie* and *Le Bosphore*. These journals treated the incident in a sensational manner calculated to excite, alarm, and provoke readers. Paul Friedmann, in particular, was vilified, and made the butt of scurrilous attacks and outright lies. *The Herald of New York* would later report that the slanderous charges directed against Friedmann were first published in *Le Bosphore,* after the philanthropist had been approached by the newspaper and told that such calumnious stories would be printed unless he submitted to blackmail.[410]

The adverse publicity also provided an opportunity for other parties interested in undermining Friedmann's project. The Russian consul in Cairo ordered an investigation of the Rasnowitch affair (Rasnowitch had been a Russian subject), and the Turks suddenly awoke to the threat to their interests posed by the Midian settlement. Certain diplomatic elements in Egypt were also alarmed by the respect and friendship that the philanthropist had acquired among the Bedouins, and were determined to destroy this relationship to preserve their own narrow interests in the region.

The horror stories that appeared in the sensational Egyptian press were reprinted with alacrity by non-Jewish and Jewish publications in Europe. Saul Raphael Landau, for example, renewed his attacks against Friedmann. He reiterated his earlier forebodings, and in a surge of hyperbole compared the colonists of Sharm al-Moza to white slaves. He also did not hesitate to repeat the Egyptian press's calumny that the Prussian, Lothar von Seebach, Rasnowitch's presumed murderer, had returned to the camp "in bloodstained clothing after wiping his dagger clean in the sand."[411]

In spite of the rash of accusation hurled at him, Friedmann remained optimistic about his project's future. He made plans to abandon the Sharm al-Moza camp in favor of settlement further down the Red Sea coast of the Arabian Peninsula. In this connection the philanthropist made new efforts to recruit Jews to replace those who had abandoned Sharm al-Moza. In addition, he hired a few Sudanese soldiers to help in the preparatory work of establishing the new colony. While thus engaged, he was, at the instigation of the Russian diplomats, indicted for the death of Rasnowitch, and summoned before a German consular tribunal in Cairo. The court eventually dismissed the charges as unfounded, and Friedmann was free to devote his full attention to his colonization project.

Fate, however, again intervened to foil the philanthropist's plans. The sultan of Turkey decided to exploit Friedmann's presence in Midian to stir up an old border dispute with Egypt. Press reports on Friedmann's activities were suddenly followed with great interest by the Turkish government. Ostensibly, the Turks suspected that there was a Great Power support behind Friedmann's venture. They believed that it was unlikely that the philanthropist would risk bringing Jews in large numbers to Midian without such backing. In addition, they feared that the Arabian settlement was merely an attempt to gain a foothold in the region for a later expansion into Palestine. Lastly, the Ottomans believed that Friedmann's colony might evolve into a Jewish state, which would threaten their interests in the region, especially the need to keep the pilgrim routes to the Muslim holy cities of Mecca and Medina free from foreign infiltration. Overriding all of these concerns was the fact that the Turks had striven for many years to regain full control of the entire Arabian coast, from the Hejaz boundary at Ras Churkuma to Aquaba. The province of Midian, however, was at this time nominally under the supervision of Egypt. An Egyptian officer stationed at Suez would spend a few months each year in Midian. The Arab governors of Aquaba and Mweilah were directly under the command of this official and a garrison of twenty-seven soldiers was responsible for the security of the entire province. Two hundred miles south of Aquaba, the Egyptians had reluctantly tolerated the establishment of a Turkish garrison at El Wijh of about 150 soldiers.

The Egyptian's administration of the Midian province was inefficient and showed little concern or understanding for the native population. Nevertheless, the Arabs preferred the Egyptians to the Turks at El Wijh, whom they feared and hated. Toward the close of 1891, the Turkish regime decided to act more aggressively. The governor of El Wijh, an individual named Mohammed Bey, was instructed to occupy the Midian town of Dubbah. Accordingly, he dispatched a contingent of Turkish soldiers who promptly seized control of the town. This event coincided with Friedmann's arrival in the area to establish his new colony. The Bedouins of the region welcomed the philanthropist warmly, as they were convinced that he had the backing of a Great Power and would use his influence with the latter to oust the Turks from the region. Incredibly, Friedmann himself also toyed with the idea of launching a military attack against the Turkish contingent occupying Dubbah. He had, after all, expressly chosen the Midian site for his settlement because it was under Egyptian control. However, Friedmann was forced to reconsider military action against the Turks when he realized that his colonists would not be willing to participate in such a drastic step.

Returning to Cairo, the philanthropist met with Lord Cromer and gave him a full account of what had transpired at Sharm al-Moza and at Dubbah. He also called on the sirdar (Commander) of the Egyptian army (Grenfell). The latter intimated that the Turks would soon be expelled from Dubbah. A contingent of Anglo-Egyptian troops, Grenfell informed Friedmann, were already on their way to Midian. On his return to Dubbah, Friedmann found that nothing had changed—the Turkish troops had not withdrawn, and no effort had been made to forcibly dislodge them. Instead, the entire affair had become a full blown diplomatic crisis.

Turkey had asked Egypt to explain by what right it had granted permission for the establishment of a Jewish colony in Midian. At the same time, the Turks launched an inquiry to ascertain whether Friedmann was harboring arms and whether his yacht was in reality a warship. The increase in pressure on Egypt and a demarche directed at Great Britain by the Turkish government brought a sudden halt to Friedmann's activities. He was instructed by the British and Egyptian governments to suspend his Midian colonization project, and to leave the province.

Disappointed, disillusioned, and embittered, Friedmann reluctantly abandoned his colony. He was convinced he had been betrayed by the British and Egyptian authorities. The Midian project had cost him a fortune (over 170,000 marks). A broken man spiritually as well as financially, Friedmann would never again return to Midian. The colonists who had remained with him following the Rasnowitch incident were released from their contracts and brought back to Europe (some chose to stay in Cairo).

Friedmann, for a time, considered seeking compensation for his losses from the Egyptian government, but was persuaded by the German diplomats in Cairo not to pursue this course of action. Later on, however, he did initiate a court action against the Egyptian newspapers that had slandered him. The litigation dragged on for years without a resolution.

The gambit of the Turkish regime to extend their authority in Midian proved equally inconclusive. For a short time the demarcation of the borders of the Sinai Peninsula and Midian became a burning issue between Great Britain, Turkey, and Egypt. In the end Lord Cromer refused to give in to Ottoman pressure, and the frontiers remained unchanged. The only party to suffer from this tempest over the borders was Friedmann, whose dream of a Jewish colonization of Midian had been sacrificed on the altar of power politics.

Paul Friedmann gradually disappeared from the public eye, but his failed experiment was to have unexpected repercussions on the course of Jewish nationalism. It is certain, for example, that Theodor Herzl, the father of the World Zionist Organization was aware of Friedmann's Midian venture. The articles describing the colony appeared in the same issues of the *Vienna Freie Presse* as Herzl's reports from Paris, where he served as the newspaper's foreign correspondent.

On October 22, 1902, Herzl was received by Joseph Chamberlain, the British Colonial Secretary. The Zionist leader suggested to the secretary a scheme for establishing a Jewish settlement at El Arish on the Sinai Peninsula. Chamberlain, although sympathetic, indicated that he would put the matter before Lord Cromer. In the discussions that followed in Cairo between Herzl's representative Leopold J. Greenberg and Cromer, the Friedmann episode was recalled. Both Cromer and the Egyptian Prime Minister Boutros Ghali Pasha fell back on the failure of the Midian colony as an excuse for not favoring a Jewish settlement at El Arish. In particular, they stressed the political and diplomatic disputes that the incident had created with Turkey.

In rebuttal, Greenberg pointed out the different character of the Zionist proposal, which he insisted could not be compared in any way with the ". . . ill executed fancy of an ambitious assimilated Jew."[412] Herzl, in a letter dated November 12, 1902, to the Marquis of Lansdowne, the British Secretary for Foreign Affairs also defended the El Arish proposal and attempted to explain why the Friedmann experiment had failed. A copy of Herzl's letter was forwarded to Lord Cromer, who in turn felt it necessary to write to Lansdowne that he had serious doubts that the Zionist Movement would find much favor with the Turkish sultan. Cromer noted that it was certainly a fact that the Friedmann venture, to which Herzl briefly referred to in his letter, had caused considerable anxiety in Constantinople. Lord Cromer would eventually rule against the El Arish project. Although many reasons were given for the rejection, there can be little doubt that the memory of Friedmann's failure played a pivotal role in Lord Cromer's unwillingness to support the proposed Zionist colony.

Today, looking back over the more than ten decades that have elapsed since the ill-fated Midian settlement, it is fairly easy to cite the reasons for its failure. First and foremost, the tacit approval that Friedmann thought he had gained from Great Britain, Egypt, and Germany proved to be without substance. In addition, without Turkey's assent, there was little possibility of the colony surviving. Strangely, Lord Cromer, Boutros Ghali Pasha, or the various diplomats of the other countries that Friedmann had approached were not able to correctly gauge Turkey's position in regard to a permanent Jewish settlement on the Arabian Peninsula.

Aside from the fact that Friedmann's project was doomed, the moment it became a pawn in an international dispute over borders, a situation over which he had no control, his failure was also largely due to his own errors of judgment. Placing the Jewish settlers under rigid military discipline and subjecting them to the will of a Prussian martinet was inexcusable. Similarly, it was utopian to believe that a Jewish state could arise from the efforts of one man, no matter how much wealth he possessed and was willing to expend in furthering his cause. Only a mass movement could provide the political, cultural, and financial resources required to build a modern state. Instead of asking Jewish organizations not to oppose him, he should have sought their active help. In fairness, it is possible that Friedmann realized that as a baptized Jew he could never win their trust. Lastly, the settlers that he recruited may have respected Friedmann as a well-meaning philanthropist, but they were not prepared, as some of the pioneers who fled the Sharm al-Moza colony intimated, to acknowledge him as a king or pasha.

Epilogue

The unique and unparalleled attachment of the Jews to the Land of Israel and the conviction that the separation from the ancient homeland was of a temporary nature permeated Jewish thought and life throughout most of the nineteen centuries of the nation's exile. From time to time, in every period and place, this allegiance was challenged by those who despaired of ever achieving redemption in the Promised Land, and who sought instead alternative solutions to resolve the so-called Jewish Problem. The nineteenth century, in particular, marked the apogee of such efforts, as in the wake of the *Haskalah* and the drive for emancipation there arose a host of movements, all of which promised to bring an end to the suffering of the Jewish people. In this category could be found the Assimilationists, the Socialists, the Bundists, the Communists, the Volkists, the Territorialists, the Lovers of Zion, and the Political and Cultural Zionists. Nevertheless, in spite of this plethora of movements, a large percentage of Jewry, although dispersed in many lands, remained faithful to the messianic vision of redemption and a return to the ancient homeland.

The moral and spiritual strength of these Jews to resist the hardships, as well as the temptations, of exile was bolstered by religious rituals and customs, the Hebrew language, the Bible and the Talmud, belief in the Messiah and the promise of national redemption, and an almost mystic attachment to Eretz Israel. Orthodox Jews in the Diaspora prayed three times a day for redemption, turned in the direction of Jerusalem when praying, offered prayers for rain when the rains were due in the Promised Land, and celebrated Israel's seasons of first fruits and harvests. When painting their dwellings, Jews often left an unpainted patch in memory of the destruction of Jerusalem, and when a son was married, ashes were placed on his head and a glass crushed underfoot to remind him of that eventful day long ago when the Temple was destroyed by the Romans and the ancient homeland lost. Many Jews preserved in their homes little bags of the Promised

Land's soil, which were buried with them if they were interred outside of Eretz Israel. Dozens of customs of a similar nature helped Jews keep alive the memory of the Land of Israel. It was not accidental that the cry "Next Year Free Men" heard in Jewish homes on Passover night, followed the annual call of "Next Year In Jerusalem."

The appearance on the world stage of Theodor Herzl in the last decade of the nineteenth century marked the high point of a drama that had begun almost 2,000 years earlier, with the destruction of the Temple and Jerusalem. Herzl, an assimilated Jew, a would-be modern Messiah in top hat and evening clothes, had little knowledge of Jewish religious practices or traditions. Even more astounding, he was completely unaware of the men and movements that had preceded him in the quest for Zion and was frequently surprised to learn that his ideas had been anticipated by others. Nevertheless, in spite of his assimilationist background, Herzl, a talented playwright and journalist, in a short span of years became Jewry's leading advocate of Jewish nationalism. In his new role as political theorist, diplomat, and organizer, he was able to create a viable worldwide movement and the institutions required to make it operable. He negotiated with the great and near great, and initiated a new chapter in the history of the Jews—one that eventually led to the creation of the State of Israel and to a renewal of the hope of the ancient prophecy that this land and its people, nestled in the heart of the turbulent Middle East, would again become "as a light to the nations."

References and Notes

1. On the life and times of Theodor Herzl see Alex Bein, *Theodor Herzl*, trans. Maurice Samuel, (Philadelphia: The Jewish Publication Society of America, 1943). See also Joseph Adler, *The Herzl Paradox: Political, Social and Economic Theories of a Realist* (New York: Herzl Press/Hadrian Press, 1962) and Amos Elon, *Herzl* (New York: Holt, Rinehart, and Winston, 1975).

2. *Stenographisches Protokoll der Verhandlungen des I. Zionistenkongresses in Basel vom 29. bis 31. August, 1897* (Prag: Selbstverlag Druck von Richard Brandeis, 1911), p. 131.

3. Herzl's charismatic personality is thoroughly explored in *Theodor Herzl: A Memorial,* ed. Meyer W. Weisgal (New York: The New Palestine Official Organ of the Zionist Organization of America, 1929).

4. Theodor Herzl, *The Jewish State*, trans. Harry Zohn, (New York: Herzl Press, 1970).

5. Psalm 137:5. Trans. Rev. Dr. A. Cohen. See *The Psalms* (London: The Soncino Press, 1945), p. 448.

6. Chaim Herzog, *Who Stands Accused? Israel Answers Its Critics* (New York: Random House 1978) pp. 5–6. For another explanation of the meaning of the word Zionism see Alex Bein, "The Origin of the Term and Concept of Zionism," *Herzl Year Book,* vol.2 (New York: Herzl Press, 1959), pp. 1–27.

7. On the activities of Menahem ben Judah the Galilean see Flavius Josephus, *The Jewish War,* book 2, trans. H. St. J. Thackeray, (Cambridge: Harvard University Press, 1927), pp. 493–499. See also Heinrich Graetz, *History of the Jews,* vol 2, trans. Bella Lowy et al. (Philadelphia: The Jewish Publication Society of America, 1956), pp. 258–61.

8. On the subject of the "teacher of righteousness" see Edmund Wilson, *The Scrolls from the Dead Sea* (New York: Oxford University Press, 1955), pp. 54–76. Yigael Yadin, *The Message of the Scrolls* (New York: Simon and Schuster, 1957), pp. 94–99, 104–113, 170; and Cecil Roth, *The Historical Backgrond of the Dead Sea Scrolls* (New York: Philosophical Library, 1959).

9. On the rise and fall of Bar Kochba see Yigael Yadin, *Bar Kochba* (New York: Random House, 1971); and Heinrich Graetz, vol 2, op. cit., pp. 409–19.

10. Numbers 24:17. See *The Soncino Chumash: The Five Books of Moses with Haptorah,* trans. A. Cohen. (London: The Soncino Press, 1947), p. 926.

11. Yadin, *Bar Kochba,* p. 23.

12. Ibid., p. 26.

13. Ibid., p. 24.

14. Dio Cassius, *Roman History,* LXIX, trans. E. Cary. (Cambridge: Harvard University Press, 1925), pp. 12–14.

15. Abba Hillel Silver, *A History of Messianic Speculation in Israel, from the First Through Seventeenth Centuries* (New York: Macmillan Co., 1927), p. 30; Graetz, vol 2, op. cit., pp. 610–11.

16. Heinrich Graetz, *History of the Jews,* vol 3 (Philadelphia: Jewish Publication Society of America, 1956), pp. 120–22. See also Salo Wittmayer Baron, *A Social and Religious History of the Jews,* vol 5, (New York: Columbia University Press, 1957), pp. 380–382.

17. Graetz, vol 3, op. cit., pp. 124–126; Silver, op. cit., pp. 55–56; Baron, vol 5, op. cit., pp. 192–92.

18. Psalms 119:164. See The Psalms, op. cit., p. 414.

19. Baron, vol 5, op. cit., pp. 182, 185, 379; Graetz, vol 3, op. cit., pp. 149–150; and Leon Nemoy, *Karaite Anthology,* vol 7, (New York: Yale University Press, 1952), pp. 10, 51, 334, 336, 391.

20. Graetz, vol 3, op. cit., p. 150.

21. On Karaite schism see Baron, vol 5, op. cit., pp. 209–285; Gretz, vol 3, op. cit., pp. 127–138, 156–158, 181–182, 203–207; and Daniel Jeremy Silver and Bernard Martin, *A History of Judaism,* vol 2, (New York: Basic Books, 1974), pp. 333–42.

22. On the life and times of David Alroy see Graetz, vol 3, op. cit., pp. 430–433; Silver, op. cit., pp. 79–80; Baron, vol 5, op. cit., pp. 203–04, 385.

23. Benjamin Disraeli, *The Wondrous Tale of Alroy* (Philadelphia: Carey, Lea, and Blanchard, 1833).

24. Cecil Roth and Geoffrey Wigoder, eds., "David Alroy," *The New Standard Jewish Encyclopedia* (Garden City: Doubleday & Company, 1970), p. 82.

25. Benjamin of Tudela, *Sefer ha Massa'ot,* translated from Hebrew under the title *The Itinerary.* (London: H. Frowde, 1907).

26. Graetz, vol 3, op. cit., p. 433.

27. Samuel Abu Nasr ibn Albas' tract is entitled *The Silencing of the Jews and the Christians Through Rational Arguments.* This Arabic polemic in manuscript form is in the Khedival Library in Cairo, Egypt. An English translation of the portion dealing with David Alroy appears in Jacob R. Marcus, *The Jew in the Medieval World: A Source Book: 315-1791* (New York: Athenum, 1978), pp. 247–50.

28. Ibid., pp. 249–50.

29. Isaiah 60:8. See *Isaiah,* trans. I.W. Slotki. (London: The Soncino Press, 1961), p. 293.

30. Marcus, op. cit., p. 249.

31. Gershom G. Scholem, *Major Trends in Jewish Mysticism,* (Jerusalem: Schocken Publishing House, 1941), pp. 119–55; Silver, op. cit., 87–90; Heinrich Graetz, *History of the Jews,* vol 4, trans. Bella Lowy and others (Philadelphia: The Jewish Publication Society of America, 1956), pp. 4–8.; See also Ben Zion Bokser, *The Jewish Mystical Tradition* (New York: The Pilgrim Press, 1981), pp. 97–106.

32. Moses ben Maimon, *Guide to the Perplexed,* trans. Shlomo Pines. (Chicago: University of Chicago Press, 1963).

33. Louis Ginzberg, "Sefer Yezirah", *Jewish Encyclopedia,* vol 12 (New York: Ktav Publishing House), pp. 602–606; Bokser, op. cit., pp. 65–68.

34. Scholem, op. cit., p. 127.

35. Graetz, vol 4, op. cit., pp. 6–7; and *Standard Jewish Encyclopedia,* p. 19.

36. Scholem, op. cit., p. 128.

37. *Ibid.* See also Graetz, vol 4, op cit., p. 7.

38. Silver, op. cit., pp. 143–45.

39. Isaac Broyde, "Asher Lemmlein", *The Jewish Encyclopedia,* vol 7 (New York: Ktav Publishing House), p. 680.

40. Joseph Ha-Kohen, *Emek ha-Baka* (Cracow: 1895); A.Z. Aescoly, "David Reubeni in the Light of History", *Jewish Quarterly Review* vol 28 (1937), pp. 1–45; Silver, op. cit., pp. 145–49; Graetz, vol 4, op. cit., pp. 491–511; Cecil Roth, *A Short History of the Jewish People* (Hartford: Hartmore House, 1969), pp. 263–64; Marcus, op. cit., pp. 251–55; Cecil Roth, *The Jews in the Renaissance,* (New York: Harper & Row, 1965), pp. 23–24; Brod's work is a historical novel, however in Part I of the book the author attempts to assimilate all known historical data pertaining to Reubeni. Max Brod, *Reubeni, Prince of Jews,* trans. Hannah Waller. (New York: A.A. Knopf, 1928).

41. Elkan Adler, *Jewish Travelers,* the latter pages contain a translation of Reubeni's diary. (London: G. Routledge & Sons, 1930), pp. 251–328.

42. Roth, *A Short History of the Jewish People,* op. cit., pp. 122, 263. The author examines the possibility that Reubeni may have been on a genuine mission on behalf of the Indian Jews of Cranganore.

43. Marcus, op. cit., p. 251; Graetz, vol 4, op. cit., p. 492.

44. Roth, *The Jews in the Renaissance,* op. cit., p. 23; Graetz, vol 4, op. cit., p. 493.

45. On Diogo Pires (Solomon Molcho) see Solomon Schechter, *Studies in Judaism,* Second Series (Philadelphia: Jewish Publication Society of America, 1908), pp. 222–26; Bernard Martin, vol 2, op. cit., pp. 148–50; Marcus, op. cit., pp. 252–255; Roth, *A Short History of the Jewish People,* op. cit., pp. 263–264; Graetz, vol 4, op. cit., pp. 495–511; and Joan Comay, *Who's Who in Jewish History* (New York: David Mc Kay Company, 1974), p. 293.

46. Schechter, op. cit., p. 224; and Graetz, vol 4, op. cit., p. 496.

47. Roth, *A Short History of the Jewish People,* op. cit., p. 263; Graetz, vol 4, op. cit., p. 502; Martin, vol 2, op. cit., p. 149; Roth, *The Jews in the Renaissance,* op. cit., p. 23.

48. Graetz, vol 4, op. cit., p. 498.

49. Ibid.

50. Martin, op. cit., p. 149; Roth, *A Short History of the Jewish People,* op. cit., p. 254.

51. On the legends that arose following Molcho's death see Marcus, op. cit., p. 255.

52. How Reubeni met his end is not known. Graetz believes he was poisoned in his cell, while Cecil Roth was convinced that he was burned at an auto-da-fé. Other historians believe he committed suicide. See Graetz, vol 4, op. cit., p. 511, and Roth, *A Short History,* op. cit., p. 264.

53. Abba Eban, *My People* (New York: Behrman House/Random House, 1968), p. 236.

54. On the life and times of Shabbeti Zevi see Gershom Scholem, *Sabbetai Sevi, The Mystical Messiah* (Princeton: Princeton University Press, 1973); also Scholem, *Major Trends in Jewish Mysticism,* op. cit., pp. 287–324; Bernard D. Weinryb, *The Jews of Poland* (Philadelphia: The Jewish Publication Society of America, 1973), pp. 206–35; Heinrich Graetz, *History of the Jews,* vol 5 (Philadelphia: The Jewish Publication Society of America, 1956), pp. 118–166, 207–11; Marcus, op. cit., pp. 261–269; Werner Keller, *Diaspora: The Post Biblical History of the Jews* (New York: Harcourt, Brace & World Inc., 1969), pp. 334–38.

55. Gershom G. Scholem, "Shabbetai Zevi", *Encyclopædia Judaica,* vol 14 (Jerusalem: Keter Publishing House, Ltd., 1971) p. 1222.

56. Keller, op. cit., p. 335.

57. Scholem, "Shabbetai Zevi", *Encyclopædia Judaica,* op. cit., p. 1222.

58. Ibid., p. 1223.

59. Ibid.

60. Keller, op. cit., p. 336. For a contemporary account of what transpired in Smyrna see Paul Rycaut, *The History of the Turkish Empire from the Year 1623 to the year 1677* (London: 1687), pp. 174–184.

61. Scholem, "Shabbetai Zevi", *Encyclopædia Judaica,* op. cit., p. 1228.

62. Henry Malter, "Shabbetai Zevi", *The Jewish Encyclopedia,* vol 11 (New York: Ktav Publishing House, Inc.), p. 221.

63. Roth, *A Short History of the Jewish People,* op. cit., p. 331.

64. *The Memoirs of Gluckel of Hameln,* trans. Marvin Lowenthal. (New York: Shocken Books, 1977), p. 46.

65. Keller, op. cit., p. 337.

66. Marcus, op. cit., pp. 263–64.

67. Graetz, vol 6, op. cit., p. 135.

68. H.H. Ben-Sasson and others, eds., *A History of the Jewish People* (Cambridge: Harvard University Press, 1976), p. 702.

69. Roth, *A Short History,* op. cit., p. 332.

70. H.H. Ben-Sasson, op. cit., pp. 449–50.

71. Baron, vol 5, op. cit., pp. 185–86.

72. On Judah Halevi see David Druck, *Yehudah Halevy, His Life and Works* (New York: Bloch Publishing Co., 1941); Graetz, vol 3, op. cit., pp. 321–43; Yitzhak Baer, *A History of the Jews in Christian Spain,* vol 1 (Philadelphia: The Jewish Publication Society of America, 1961), pp. 67–77; also Jehudah Halevi, *Selected Poems,* trans. Heinrich Brody. (Philadelphia: The Jewish Publication Society of America, 1974).

73. David Druck, op. cit.

74. Ibid.

75. Jehudah Halevi, *Kitab al Khazari,* trans. Hartwig Hirschfeld. (London: Cailin Gold, 1905). See also the abridged *Kuzari, the Book of Proof and Argument* (Oxford: East and West Library, 1947).

76. S.D. Goitein, "The Biography of Rabbi Judah ha-Levi in the Light of the Cairo Geniza Documents," *Proceedings of the American Academy for Jewish Research* vol 28 (1959), pp. 41–56.

77. See Solomon Schechter, *Studies in Judaism,* 1st ser, (Philadelphia: The Jewish Publication Society of America, 1896), pp. 99–141; Graetz, vol 3, op. cit., pp. 531–62, 598–609; Silver, op. cit., pp. 83–85; Baer, vol 1, op. cit., pp. 102–06, 143–44, 152–59, 245–49, 281–305.

78. Ibid. p. 153.

79. Graetz, vol 3, op. cit., p. 601.

80. Baer, op. cit., p. 159.

81. Graetz, op. cit., p. 606.

82. Ibid.

83. Elkan N. Adler, *Jewish Travellers* (London: G. Routledge & Sons Ltd., 1930), pp. 209–50; Graetz, vol 4, op. cit., pp. 567–68.

84. Roth, *A Short History,* op. cit., p. 281.

85. On the Nasi-Mendes family see Cecil Roth, *The House of Nasi: The Duke of Naxos* (Philadelphia: The Jewish Publication Society of America, 1948); Graetz, vol 4, op. cit., pp. 572–628; Sasson, op. cit., pp. 636–37, 667–68; Marcus, op. cit., pp. 320–22, 415–16; Keller, op. cit., pp. 272–75; Roth, *The Jews in the Renaissance,* op. cit., pp. 55–56; Martin, op. cit., pp. 143–44; Roth, *A Short History,* op. cit., pp. 277–78; Joachim Prinz, *The Secret Jews* (New York: Random House, 1973) pp. 131–49; Cecil Roth, *A History of the Marranos* (Philadelphia: The Jewish Publication Society of America, 1932), pp. 202–03.

86. Prinz, op. cit., p. 134.

87. Roth, *The Jews in the Renaissance,* op. cit., p. 55.

88. Marcus, op. cit., p. 416.

89. On the Ancona Affair see Sasson, op. cit., pp. 668–69; Graetz, vol 4, op. cit.,pp. 577–81; Prinz, op. cit., pp. 142–46.

90. Prinz, op. cit., p. 595.

91. Keller, op. cit., p. 274. See also Meyer Kayserling, "Joseph Nasi, Duke of Naxos", *The Jewish Encyclopedia,* vol 9 (New York: Ktav Publishing House), p. 173

92. Graetz, vol 4, op. cit., p. 610.

93. On the Tiberias experiment, see Roth, *The House of Nasi,* op. cit., pp. 97–135; and Marcus, op. cit., pp. 320–22.

94. On Judah Hassid and Hayyim Malakh see Graetz, vol 5, op. cit., pp. 212–14; Weinryb, op. cit., pp. 233–34; Martin, op. cit., pp. 136–137; S. M. Dubnow, *History of the Jews in Russia and Poland,* vol 1 (Philadelphia: The Jewish Publication Society of America, 1916), pp. 208–10, Max Seligsohn, "Hayim Mal'ak," *The Jewish Encyclopedia,* vol 6 (New York: Ktav Publishing House), p. 275; and Gershom G. Scholem, "Judah Hasid," *Encyclopædia Judaica,* vol 10 (Jerusalem: The Macmillan Company, 1971), p. 373.

95. Raphael Mahler, *A History of Modern Jewry, 1780–1815* (New York: Schocken Books, 1971), p. 657.

96. Gershom Scholem, *Major Trends in Jewish Mysticism,* op. cit., p. 423 and note 13.

97. R.J. Zwi Werblowsky and Geoffrey Wigoder, ed: *The Encyclopedia of the Jewish Religion* (New York: Holt, Rinehart and Winston, Inc., 1965), p. 218.

98. Benjamin Klar, *Rabbi Hayim Ibn Attar* (Jerusalem: Mossad Ha Rav Kook, 1951).

99. Moses Beer, "Hayyim ben Moses ibn Attar," *The Jewish Encyclopedia,* vol 2 (New York: Ktav Publishing House), p. 290.

100. "Hayyim ben Moses Attar," *Encyclopædia Judaica,* vol 3 (Jerusalem: Keter Publishing House, 1971), p. 834.

101. Ibid., p. 835.

102. Mahler, op. cit., pp. 430–535; Martin Buber, *Hassidism* (New York: Philosophical Library, 1948); Martin Buber, *The Origin and Meaning of Hasidism* (New York: Horizon Press, 1960); Harry M. Rabinowicz, *The World of Hassidism* (Hartford: Hartmore House, 1970); Aryeh Rubenstein, *Hasidism* (New York/Paris: Amiel Publishers, 1975); Scholem, *Major Trends in Jewish Mysticism,* op. cit., pp. 325–50.

103. Dan Ben-Amos and Jerome R. Mintz, trans., ed., *In Praise of the Baal Shem Tov: Earliest Collections of Legends About the Founder of Hasidism* (Bloomington: Indiana University,1970; Martin Buber, *The Legend of the Baal Shem Tov* (New York: Harper, 1955); Scholem, *Major Trends in Jewish Mysticism,* op. cit., pp. 330–34; Rubenstein, op. cit., pp. 10–22; Elie Wiesel, *Souls on Fire: Portraits and Legends of Hasidic Masters* (New York: Random House, 1972), pp. 3–39.

104. *The Encyclopedia of the Jewish Religion,* op. cit., p. 54.

105. Martin, op. cit., p. 173.

106. Weinryb, op. cit., p. 325.

107. Ibid., p. 325.

108. Esther Lieber, "Nachman of Horodenko," *Encyclopædia Judaica,* vol 12 (Jerusalem: Keter Publishing House, 1971), pp. 787–788.

109. Avraham Rubinstein, "Menachem Mendel of Przemyslany," *Encyclopædia Judaica,* vol 11 (Jerusalem: Keter Publishing House, 1971), pp. 1309–10. See also *In Praise of the Baal Shem Tov,* op. cit., pp. 153–55, 330–32.

110. Weinryb, op. cit., p. 401.

111. Avraham Rubenstein, op. cit., p. 1309.

112. *The New Standard Jewish Encyclopedia,* op. cit., p. 1317.

113. Avraham Rubinstein, op. cit., p. 1309.

114. On Shneur Zalman of Lyady, the founder of Habad Hassidism see Mahler, op. cit., pp. 482–95; Weinryb, op. cit., pp. 286–97, 322–32, 391–94; Martin, op. cit., pp. 180–86; and Gershon Kranzler, *Rabbi Shneur Zalman of Ladi: A Brief Presentation of the Life, the Work and the Basic Teachings of Chabad Chassidism* (Brooklyn: Kehot Publishing Society, 1948).

115. On the Seer of Lublin see Rabinowicz, op. cit., pp. 99–101; and Avraham Rubinstein, "Jacob Isaac Ha Hozeh Mi-Lublin," *Encyclopædia Judaica,* vol 9 (Jerusalem: Keter Publishing House, 1971), pp. 1227–28.

116. Zvi Meir Rabinowicz, "Simha Bunem of Przysucha," *Encyclopædia Judaica,* vol 14 (Jerusalem: Keter Publishing House, 1971), pp. 1570–71; and Harry M. Rabinowicz, *The World of Hassidism,* op. cit., pp. 99–100.

117. M.A. Lipschutz, *Hassidic School of Gur* (Dissertation, University of Wisconsin, 1964); Rabinowicz, *World of Hassidism,* op. cit., pp. 148–53.

118. On the Gaon of Vilna see Israel Cohen, *Vilna* (Philadelphia: The Jewish Publication Society of America, 1943), pp. 211–52; Weinryb, op. cit., pp. 285–95, 389–91; Schechter, *Studies in Judaism,* 1st ser, op. cit., pp. 73–98; Graetz, vol 5, op. cit., pp. 389–94; and Louis Ginzberg, *Students, Scholars and Saints* (Philadelphia: The Jewish Publication Society of America, 1928), pp. 115–24.

119. Cohen, op. cit., p. 213.

120. Martin, op. cit., p. 137.

121 Joan Comay, *Who's Who in Jewish History After the Period of the Old Testament* (New York: Mc Kay Company, 1974), p. 147.

122. *The World of Hassidism,* op. cit., p. 56.

123. Joshua Kaniel, "Menachem Mendel of Shklov," *Encyclopædia Judaica,* vol 2 (Jerusalem: Keter Publishing House, 1971), p. 1310.

124. Ibid.

125. Avraham Ya'ari, "Israel ben Samuel of Shklov," *Encyclopædia Judaica,* vol 9 (Jerusalem: Keter Publishing House, 1971), pp. 1059–60.

126. Mahler, op. cit., p. 113.

127. Ben Halpern, *The Idea of the Jewish State* (Cambridge: Harvard University, 1969), p. 254.

128. Mahler, op. cit., pp. 611–15; Halpern, op. cit., p. 254; Haim Z. Hirschberg, "Land of Israel", *Encyclopædia Judaica,* vol 9 (Jerusalem: Keter Publishing House, 1971), p. 290; Ben Halpern, "A Note on Ali Bey's Jewish State Project," *Jewish Social Studies,* vol 18, pp. 284–86.

129. Halpern, "A Note on Ali Bey," op. cit., pp. 284–86.

130. On the attitude of some of the leaders of the European Enlightenment toward the Jews see Arthur Hertzberg, *The French Enlightenment and the Jews* (New York: Columbia University Press, 1968). The section on Voltaire's views can be found on pp. 280–308.

131. Natan Michael Gelber, *Zur Vorgeschichte des Zionismus, Judenstaatsprojekte in den Jahren 1695–1845* (Wien: Phaidon Verlag, 1927), pp. 223–40.

132. On Langallerie see Natan Michael Gelber, "Quelques documents relatif aux projets juifs du Marquis de Langallerie," *Revue des Etudes Juives,* vol 88–89 (July, 1929–June, 1930), pp. 224–36; David Kaufmann, "Relations du Marquis de Langallerie avec les Juifs," *Revue des Etudes Juives,* vol 28, no. 56 (Paris, 1894), pp. 193–211.

133. On Moses Mendelssohn see Alexander Altman, *Moses Mendelssohn: A Biographical Study* (Philadelphia: The Jewish Publication Society of America, 1973); Herman M.Z. Meyer, *Moses Mendelssohn Bibliographie* (Berlin: Walter de Gruyter & Co., 1965); and Moses Mendelssohn, *Gesammelte Schriften,* 8 vols (Leipzig: F.A. Brockhaus, 1843–45).

134. On Mendelssohn's first meeting with Lessing see Altman, op. cit., p. 36.

135. Keller, op. cit., p. 357.

136. Meyer Kayserling, "Mendelssohn," *The Jewish Encyclopedia,* vol 8 (New York: Ktav Publishing House), p. 481.

137. Graetz, vol 5, op. cit., p. 302.

138. On the 'man of rank' see Altman, op. cit., p. 424.

139. Ibid. See Alfred Jospe and Leni Yahil, "Moses Mendelssohn," *Encyclopædia Judaica,* vol 11 (Jerusalem: Keter Publishing House, 1971), p. 1335.

140. Moses Mendelssohn, *Gesammelte Schriften,* vol 5, op. cit., p. 494; Altman, op. cit., pp. 424–26.

141. On Seyfart's activities on behalf of the Jews see Gelber, *Zur Vorgeschichte des Zionismus,* op. cit., pp. 94–124.

142. Natan Michael Gelber, "A Pre-Zionist Plan for Colonizing Palestine: The Proposal of a Non-Jewish German American in 1852", *Historia Judaica,* vol 1, no 2, trans. Guido Kisch. (September, 1939), pp. 81–90.

143. Kenneth Scott Latourette, *A History of Christianity* (New York: Harper & Brothers, 1953), p. 1185.

144. Frank S. Mead, *Handbook of Denominations in the United States: Their History, Doctrines, Organization, Present Status,* 6th ed. (Nashville: Abingdon, 1975), pp. 75–76; B.R. Wilson, *Sects and Society* (Berkeley: 1961).

145. Joseph Fielding Smith, *Essentials in Church History* (Salt Lake City: Deseret Book Co., 1953); Leonard J. Arrington and Davis Bitton, *The Mormon Experience: A History of the Latter-Day Saints* (New York: Alfred A. Knopf, 1979); Bernard de Voto, *The Year of Decision 1846,* (Boston: Little, Brown and Company, 1943).

146. For additional material on the life and times of Joseph Smith see Harry Markle Beardsley, *Joseph Smith and his Mormon Empire* (Boston: Houghton Mifflin Co., 1931).

147. *The Book of Mormon, An Account Written by the Hand of Mormon Upon Plates Taken from the Plates of Nephi* (Salt Lake City: The Church of Jesus Christ of Latter-Day Saints, 1951); see also Harold I. Velt, *The Sacred Book of Ancient America* (Independence: Herald House, 1952).

148. Howard W. Goodkind, "Lord Kingsborough Lost His Fortune Trying to Prove the Maya Were Descendants of the Ten Lost Tribes," *Biblical Archaeology Review,* vol 11, no 5 (September/October, 1985), pp. 64–65.

149. *The Book of Mormon,* op. cit., Jacob 7:26.

150. Joseph Fielding Smith, *The Doctrines and Covenants of the Church of Jesus Christ of Latter-Day Saints, Containing Revelations Given to Joseph Smith the Prophet With Some Additions by his Successors in the Presidency of the Church* (Salt Lake City: The Church of Jesus Christ of Latter-Day Saints, 1951).

151. On Hyde's mission to Palestine see Marvin Sidney Hill, *An Historical Study of the Life of Orson Hyde, Early Mormon Missionary Apostle, 1805–52* (Thesis presented to the Dept. of History of Brigham Young University, August 1955).

152. Hill, op. cit., p. 56.

153. Mead, op. cit., pp. 17–23; Elmer T. Clark, *The Small Sects in America* (New York: Abingdon Press, 1949); Yonah Malachy, "Seventh Day Adventists and Zionism," *Herzl Year Book*, vol 6 (New York: Herzl Press, 1964–65), pp. 265–301; and F.E. Hamilton, *The Basis of Millennial Faith* (Grand Rapids: Eerdmans, 1942).

154. C.L. Feinberg, *Premillennialism or Amillennialism* (Wheaton: Van Kampen Press, 1954); W.A. Arnett, "The Second Coming, Millennial Views," *Christianity Today*, vol 6, no 23 (August 31, 1962); Malachy, op. cit.; For a comprehensive work setting forth Adventist beliefs see Le Roy Edwin Froom, *The Prophetic Faith of Our Fathers*, 4 vols (Washington D.C.: Review and Herald Publications, 1954).

155. Abraham J. Karp, "The Zionism of Warder Cresson," *Early History of Zionism in America* (New York: American Jewish Historical Society & Theodor Herzl Foundation, 1958), pp. 1–20; See also Frank E. Manuel, *The Realities of American-Palestine Relations* (Washington D.C.: Public Affairs Press, 1949), pp. 10–11.

156. Ibid., p. 11.

157. E. Cecil Mc Gavin, "Apostate Factions Following the Martyrdom of Joseph Smith," *The Improvement Era*, vol 67 (August, 1944); and Alex Bein, "American Settlement in Israel," *Israel: Its Role in Civilization* (New York: Harper Brothers, 1956).

158. Colonel Sir Charles R.E. Wilson, ed., *Picturesque Palestine, Sinai and Egypt*, vol 2 (New York: D. Appleton Co., 1883), pp. 96–98.

159. Elihu D. Stone, "American Approval of Zionism: The Governmental Attitude from President Harrison to Hoover," *Theodor Herzl, A Memorial* (New York: The New Palestine, 1929), p. 272; See also Manuel, op. cit., pp. 71 and 163; Anita Libman Lebeson, "Zionism comes to Chicago," *Early History of Zionism In America*, op. cit., pp. 165–70.

160. Lebeson, op. cit., p. 165.

161. Ibid.

162. Ibid., p. 166.

163. A reprint of the memorial can be found in the article by David A. Rausch, "The Evangelicals as Zionists," *Midstream*, vol 31, no 1 (January, 1985), p. 14.

164. H. L. Meites, ed., *History of the Jews of Chicago* (Chicago: 1924), p. 692.

165. Getzel Kressel, "Hechler", *Encyclopædia Judaica*, vol 8 (Jerusalem: Keter Publishing House, 1971), pp. 237–39; "Herzl, Hechler, the Grand Duke of Baden and the German Emperor," *Herzl Year Book*, vol 4, Article based on documents found by Hermann and Bessi Ellern, trans. Harry Zahn. (New York: Herzl Press, 1961–62), pp. 207–70; See also S. A. Yahuda, "Reverend Hechler and Dr. Herzl", *The Jewish Forum*, vol 30 (March, 1947), pp. 54–56; Amos Elon, op. cit., pp. 187–94, 265–74.

166. Mahler, op. cit., pp. 682–85.

167. Ibid.

168. Ibid., p. 687.

169. On Napoleon's Jewish policies see Robert Anchel, *Napoleon et les Juifs* (Paris: Les Presses Universitairies de France, 1928); Sasson, op. cit., pp. 761–63; Gelber, *Vorgeschichte des Zionismus*, op. cit., pp. 42–48.

170. Anchel, op. cit., pp. 126–225.

171. Ibid.

172. Ibid. pp. 253–84.

173. See *The Letters and Memoirs of the Prince de Ligne*, trans. Leigh Ashton. (London: G. Routledge & Sons Ltd., 1927). Prince Charles Joseph de Ligne's ideas on Jewish restoration can also be found in Gelber, *Zur Vorgeschichte des Zionismus,* op. cit., pp. 33–38; and in Joseph Schulsinger, "Un precurseur du sionisme au XVIII siecle: Le Prince de Ligne," Tome 17, *Annales Prince de Ligne* (Paris: 1936), pp. 59–87.

174. Ernest Laharanne, *La Nouvelle Question d'Orient; Empires d'Egypte et d'Arabie; reconstitution de la nationalité juive* (Paris: E. Dentu, 1860).

175. Nahum Sokolow, *History of Zionism, 1600–1918,* vol 1 (London: Longmans Green, 1919), pp. 199, 203, 251–52.

176. Gabriel Salvador, *Joseph Salvador, sa vie, ses oeuvres et ses critiques* (Paris: Calmann Levy, 1881).

177. Joseph Salvador, *Paris, Rome, Jerusalem, ou la Question religieuse au XIX Siecle* (Paris: Michel Levy Freres, 1860).

178. Alexis Rancois, *Aspects d'Henri Durant: le bonapartiste, l'affairiste, le sioniste* (Geneve: Librairie de l'universite, 1948); Rene Sonderegger, *Jean Henri Dunant—Revolutionar* (Zurich: Reso-Verlag, 1935); Sokolow, *History of Zionism, 1600–1918,* vol 2 (London: Longmans Green, 1919), pp. 259–61, 265–67.

179. Getzel Kressel, "Jean Henri Dunant," *Encyclopædia Judaica,* vol 6 (Jerusalem: Keter Publishing House, 1971), p. 270.

180. Alexandre Dumas-fils, *La Femme de Claude,* trans. Charles Alfred Byrne. (New York: F. Rullman 1905).

181. On Muhammed Ali see Emil Ludwig, *The Nile: The Life Story of a River* (New York: The Viking Press, 1937); Philip K. Hitti, *History of the Arabs,* 10th ed. (New York: St. Martin's Press, 1970), pp. 722–26; Desmond Stewart, *The Middle East; Temple of Janus* (New York: Doubleday & Co., 1971), pp. 19–26.

182. Herbert C. F. Bell, *Lord Palmerston,* 2 vols (London: [n.p.], 1936; Reprinted: Hamdon, CT: Archon Books, 1966).

183. Sir Charles Kingsley Webster, *The Foreign Policy of Palmerston, 1830–41,* vol 2 (London: Bell, 1951); Sir Harold Willian Vazeille Temperly, *England and the Near East* (London: Longmans, 1936).

184. An excellent account of the blood libel can be found in Graetz, vol 5, op. cit., pp. 632–66. See also Keller op. cit., pp. 399–401; Albert M. Hyamson, "The Damascus Affair-1840," *Transactions of the Jewish Historical Society of England,* 16 (1945–51), pp. 47–71.

185. Graetz, vol 5, op. cit., p. 652.

186. *Public Records Office* (London) FO 78/392. See also Leonard Stein, *The Balfour Declaration* (New York: Simon and Schuster, 1961), p. 6.

187. Webster, vol 2, op. cit., pp. 762–63, note 1; Stein, op. cit., pp. 6–7.

188. Ibid. p. 7.

189. Temperly, op. cit., , p. 444 citing *Public Records Office* (London), FO 78/427. See also Stein, op. cit., p. 7.

190. Lucien Wolf, *Diplomatic History of the Jewish Question* (London: Longmans, 1919), p. 102.

191. Ibid., p. 106.

192. Ibid., p. 106.

193. Ibid., p. 86.

194. Simon Marcus, "David Pacifico," *Encyclopædia Judaica,* vol 13 (Jerusalem: Keter Publishing House, 1971), p. 6.

195. Speech of Lord Palmerston in *Hanard's Parliamentary Reports,* June 25, 1850, cols 380–444.

196. On Anthony Ashley Cooper's life see Edwin Hodder, *The Life and Work of the Seventh Earl of Shaftesbury* (London: Cassell & Company, Ltd., 1887).

197. Ibid., pp. 328–29.

198. The history of this organization can be found in an article by Mel Scult, "English Missions to the Jews – Conversion in the Age of Emancipation," *Jewish Social Studies,* vol 35, no 1 (January, 1973), pp. 3–17.

199. Stein, op. cit., p. 178.

200. Ibid., p. 11.

201. Sokolow, vol 1, op. cit., p. 123.

202. On Shaftesbury's plan see Barbara Tuchman, *Bible and Sword: England and Palestine from the Bronze Age to Balfour* (New York: New York University Press, 1956), pp. 113–33; Franz Kobler, *The Vision Was There: A History of the British Movement for the Restoration of the Jews to Palestine* (London: Lincoln-Prager, 1956), pp. 58–65. See also Albert Montefiore Hyamson, *British Projects for the Restoration of the Jews* (Leeds: Petty & Sons Ltd., 1917).

203. Kobler, op. cit.,

204. Hodder, op. cit., p. 493.

205. Philip Henderson, *The Life of Laurence Oliphant, Traveler, Diplomat and Mystic* (Toronto: Mc Graw, 1965); Margaret O. Wilson Oliphant, *Memoir of Laurence Oliphant and Alice, His Wife,* 2 vols (New York: Harper & Brothers, 1891).

206. Laurence Oliphant, *Episodes in a Life of Adventure; or Moss from a Rolling Stone* (New York: Harper & Brothers, 1887).

207. Laurence Oliphant, *The Land of Gilead* (New York: Appleton, 1881).

208. Ibid.

209. Laurence Oliphant, *Haifa, or Life in Modern Palestine* (Edinburgh: Blackwood, 1887).

210. Louis Lipsky, *Memoirs in Profile* (Philadelphia: The Jewish Publication Society of America, 1975), pp. 178–81.

211. Wolf, *Diplomatic History of the Jewish Question,* op. cit.,pp. 119–21; Gelber, *Zur Vorgeschichte des Zionismus,* op. cit., pp. 140–41, 169–74, 192.

212. Lucien Wolf, *Sir Moses Montefiore* (New York: Harper & Brothers, 1885); and Sir Moses Montefiore, *Diaries of Sir Moses and Lady Montefiore,* 2 vols (London: Griffith Farran Okedun and Welsh, 1890).

213. Franz Kobler, "Charles Henry Churchill," *Herzl Year Book,* vol 4 (New York: Herzl Press, 1962) p. 23.

214. Charles Henry Churchill, *Mount Lebanon: A Ten Years' Residence, 1842–1852,* 3 vols (London: 1853).

215. Charles Henry Churchill, *The Druse and the Maronites Under the Turkish Rule from 1840 to 1860* (London: 1862).

216. Charles Henry Churchill, *The Life of Abdel Kader, Ex-Sultan of the Arabs of Algeria* (London: 1867).

217. Rufus Learsi, *Fulfillment: The Epic Story of Zionism* (New York: The World Publishing Company, 1951), pp. 24–28; Sokolow, *History of Zionism,* vol 1, op. cit., pp. 123 and 175; Christopher Sykes, *Two Studies in Virtue* (London: Collins, 1953), p. 151.

218. Kobler, "The Vision Was There," op. cit., pp. 76–81; Edward L. Milford, "A Time for Mighty Changes," *Midstream,* vol 7 (1961), pp. 17–31.

219. Sokolow, *History of Zionism,* vol 1, op. cit., pp. 206–09, and vol 2, pp. 267–69.

220. On Warren in Palestine see Moshe Pearlman, *Digging Up the Bible* (New York: William Morrow & Company, 1980), pp. 111–21; Watkin Wynn Williams, *The Life of General Sir Charles Warren* (Oxford: B. Blackwell, 1941).

221. On Conder see Pearlman, op. cit., pp. 45–47, 122–23. On his work in Palestine see Claude Reignier Conder and Horatio Herbert Kitchener, *The Survey of Western Palestine: Memoirs of the Topography, Orography, Hydrography and Archaeology,* vol 1–3 (London: The Committee of the Palestine Exploration Fund, 1881–83). See also Claude Reignier Conder, *Palestine* (London: G. Philips, 1891).

222. William Flavelle Monypenny and George Earle Buckle, *The Life of Benjamin Disraeli, Earl of Beaconsfield.* 6 vols (London: 1910–20).

223. George Eliot, *Daniel Deronda* (New York: Harper & Brothers, 1876).

224. Ibid.

225. For this quote and a description of the repression under Czar Nicholas I see Thomas G. Masaryk, *The Spirit of Russia,* vol 1 (New York: Macmillan & Co., 1919), pp. 106–09, 111–13.

226. An excellent account of the Decembrist conspiracy can be found in the book by Bernard Pares, *A History of Russia* (New York: Alfred A. Knopf, 1951), pp. 313–18. See also Simon M. Dubnow, *History of the Jews in Russia and Poland,* vol 1 (Philadelphia: The Jewish Publication Society of America, 1916), pp. 410–13.

227. Pares, op. cit., p. 313.

228. Yehuda Slutsky, "Gregory Peretz," *Encyclopædia Judaica,* vol 13 (Jerusalem: Keter Publishing House, 1971), p. 279.

229. On Pestel and the Jews see Gelber, *Zur Vorgeschichte des Zionismus,* op. cit., pp. 56–61. On Pestel's views in general see Jenny Schwartz-Sachar, *Pavel Ivanovich Pestel: The Beginnings of Jacobin Thought in Russia* (Assen, Netherlands: Royal van Gorcum, 1958).

230. Joan Haslip, *Catherine the Great* (New York: G.P. Putnam's Sons, 1977), pp. 276–77.

231. Moshe Ishai, "Benedetto Musolino," *Encyclopædia Judaica,* vol 12 (Jerusalem: Keter Publishing House, 1971), p. 716.

232. Benedetto Musolino, *Gerusalemme ed il Popolo Ebreo* (Roma: La Rassegnamensile di Israel, 1951).

233. Graetz, *History of the Jews,* vol 5, op. cit., pp. 701–02; Sasson, op. cit., pp. 849–50; Arthur Francis Day, *The Mortara Mystery* (London: Catholic Truth Society. 1930); Ismar Elbogen, *A Century of Jewish Life* (Philadelphia: The Jewish Publication Society of America, 1960), pp. 30–31.

234. Elbogen, op. cit., p. 31.

235. Andre Chouraqui, *L'Alliance israélite universelle et la renaissance juive contemporaine, 1860–1960; cent ans d'histoire* (Paris: Presses universitaires de France, 1965); Simon R. Schwarzfuchs, "Alliance Israélite Universelle," *Encyclopædia Judaica,* vol 2 (Jerusalem: Keter Publishing House, 1971), pp. 648–54; Narcisse Leven, *Cinquante ans d'histoire israélite universelle, 1860–1910,* 2 vols (Paris: Librairie Felix Alcan, 1911).

236. Elbogen, op. cit., , p. 34.

237. Montefiore, *Diaries,* vol 1, op. cit., pp. 198–204.

238. Monteriore, *Diaries,* vol 2, op. cit., pp. 107, 285; Halpern, op. cit., p. 122.

239. Material on the Love of Zion Movement is voluminous. See Nahum Sokolow, *Hibbath Zion* (Jerusalem: L. Mayer, 1934); Adolf Boehm, *Die Zionistiche Bewegung,* vol 1 (Berlin: Juedischer Verlag, 1935), pp. 96–150; Israel Klausner, *Hibbat Zion l'Rumania* (Jerusalem: Ha-Sifria ha Zionit, 1958); Ben Zion Dinaburg et al., eds., *Chibat Zion,* 2 vols (Tel Aviv: 1922–24); Alter Druyanov, *Documents for the History of the Love of Zion and the Colonization of Palestine,* 3 vols (Odessa/Tel Aviv: 1910–32); Sasson, op. cit., pp. 894–98, 918 20; Elbogen, op. cit., pp. 245 72; Jacob Kabakoff, "Beginnings of Hibbat Zion in America," *Herzl Year Book,* vol 6 (New York: Herzl Press, 1964–65), pp. 253–55.

240. Lev Semenovich Pinsker, *Road to Freedom,* trans. Benzion Netanyahu (New York: Scopus Publishing Co., 1944); Israel Klausner, "Kattowitz Conference," *Encyclopedia of Zionism and Israel,* vol 2 (New York: Herzl Press/Mc Graw Hill, 1971), p. 656.

241. Natan Michael Gelber, "Abraham Benisch," *Encyclopædia Judaica,* vol 4 (Jerusalem: Keter Publishing House, 1971), p. 521; Goodman Lipkind, "Abraham Benisch," *The Jewish Encyclopedia,* vol 3 (New York: Ktav Publishing House), p. 21; *Jewish Chronicle,* (July 31, 1879), and jubilee issue (Nov., 1891).

242. S.B. Freehof, "Moritz Steinschneider," *Yearbook of the Central Conference of American Rabbis,* 26 (1916); A. Marx, *Essays in Jewish Biography* (1947), pp. 112–84; G.A. Kohut, *Bibliography of the Writings of Professor M. Steinschneider in Festschrift zum 80 sten Geburtstage Steinschneider's,* 1896.

243. Laqueur, op. cit., p. 17.

244. Israel Klausner, "Ha-Rav Yehuda Bibas," *Ha'Olam,* vol 32, no 69. See also T. Preschel, *Sinai,* 53 (1963), pp. 174–75.

245. See Andrew A. Bonar and Robert M'Cheyne, *Narrative of a Mission of Inquiry to the Jews from the Church of Scotland in 1839.* (Philadelphia: Presbyterian Board of Publication, 1843), p. 392.

246. Arthur Hertzberg, ed. *The Zionist Idea: A Historical Analysis and Reader* (New York: Athenum, 1970), pp. 103–07; Sokolow, *History of Zonism,* vol 2, op. cit., p. 297; "Yaakov Yehudah Alkalay, 1799–1878: The Pioneer of Political Zionism." *The South African Menorah,* vol 16, nos 9–10 (September-October, 1943), pp. 10, 20; Getzel Kressel, ed., *Ha Rav Yehuda Alkalay, Ha Rav Zvi Kalischer* (Tel Aviv: Mivchar Kitveihem, 1943).

247. Howard M. Sachar, *A History of Israel: From the Rise of Zionism to Our Time* (New York: Alfred A. Knopf, 1976), p. 6.

248. Getzel Kressel, "Chaim Lorje," *Encyclopædia Judaica,* vol 11, (Jerusalem: Keter Publishing House, 1971), pp. 493–94, and article by same author in *Zion,* vol 7 (1942), pp. 197–205.

249. Alex Bein, *Theodor Herzl: A Biography,* op. cit., p. 5.

250. Kressel, *Ha Rav Zvi Kalischer,* op. cit., See also Laqueur, op. cit., pp. 54–55; Getzel Kressel, "Kalischer," *Encyclopædia Judaica,* vol 10 (Jerusalem: Keter Publishing House, 1971), pp. 708–09; Martin, vol 2, op. cit., pp. 329–30; Hertzberg, op. cit., pp. 111–14.

251. Zevi Hirsch Kalischer, *Drischath Zion, Order Zions Herstellung* (Berlin: L. Lamm, 1905).

252. Hertzberg, op. cit., p. 11; Sacher, op. cit., p. 7; Martin, vol 2, op. cit., p. 329.

253. Laqueur, op. cit., p. 54.

254. Hertzberg, *The Zionist Idea,* op. cit., p. 114; Martin, vol 2, op. cit., pp. 329–30.

255. Sokolow, *Hibbath Zion,* op. cit., pp. 17–28; Getzel Kressel, "Elijah Guttmacher," *Encyclopædia Judaica,* vol 7 (Jerusalem: Keter Publishing House, 1971), pp. 991–92.

256. David De Sola Pool, ed., trans., *The Traditional Prayer Book for Sabbath and Festival* (New York: Behrman House, Inc., 1960), pp. 14 and 16.

257. Sabato Morais, *Italian Hebrew Literature* (New York: Jewish Theological Seminary of America, 1926), pp. 78–152; Noah Rosenbloom, *Luzzatto's Ethico-Psychological Interpretation of Judaism* (New York: Yeshiva University Press, 1965); Martin, vol 2, op. cit., pp. 259–60.

258. Manuel, op. cit., pp. 44–46; Avraham Ya'ari, "Simon Bermann", *Encyclopædia Judaica,* vol 4 (Jerusalem: Keter Publishing House, 1971), p. 667; Simon Bermann, *Reisebeshreibung im Hailegen Land* (Cracow: 1879).

259. Isaiah Berlin, *Life and Opinions of Moses Hess* (London: Jewish Historical Society of England, 1959); *Moses Hess, Prophet of Zionism* (New York: Thomas Yoseloff, 1963); John

Weiss, *Moses Hess, Utopian Socialist* (Detroit: Wayne State University Press, 1960); August Cornu and Wolfgang Monke, eds., *Moses Hess, Philosophische und sozialistische Schriften, 1837–1850,* (Berlin: Akademie Verlag, 1961); Edmund Silberner, *Moses Hess, Der Geschichte seiner Lebens* (Leiden: 1966); and Hertzberg, *The Zionist Idea,* op. cit., pp. 116–39.

260. Silberner, op. cit., pp. 23–24. Quoted by Hess in his diary.

261. Laqueur, op. cit., p. 46.

262. Moses Hess, *Rome and Jerusalem,* trans. Meyer Waxman (New York: Bloch Publishing Co., 1918).

263. Ibid., p. 40; see also Kressel, op. cit., p. 433.

264. Moses Hess, *Rome and Jerusalem,* op. cit., pp. 118–26, 141–59.

265. Raphael Patai, ed., *The Complete Diaries of Theodor Herzl,* vol 3, trans. Harry Zohn (New York/London: The Herzl Press and Thomas Yoseloff, 1960), p. 1090.

266. Cecil Roth, *A History of the Marranos* (Philadelphia: The Jewish Publication Society of America, 1932), p. 271.

267. Roth, *A History of the Marranos,* op. cit., p. 290.

268. On the Jewish settlement in Curacao and the activities of David Nassi and Jan de Illan see Herbert Friedenwald, "Curacao", *The Jewish Encyclopedia,* vol 4 (New York: Ktav Publishing House), pp. 386–89; Charles Patrick Daly, *The Settlement of the Jews in North America* (New York: p. Cervan, 1893), pp. 9–11.

269. On Cayenne settlement see George Alexander Kohut, "Cayenne or French Guiana," *The Jewish Encyclopedia,* vol 3 (New York: Ktav Publishing House), pp. 634–35. See also Cardoza de Bethencourt, "Notes on the Spanish and Portuguese Jews in the United States, Guiana, and the Dutch and British West Indies during the Seventeenth and Eighteenth Centuries," *American Jewish Historical Society,* pub 29 (1925), pp. 7–38; Meyer Kayserling, *Sephardim* (Leipzig: U. Mendelssohn, 1859), pp. 265–66; Samuel Oppenheim, "An Early Jewish Colony in Western Guiana 1658–1666, and Its Relation to Jews in Surinam, Cayenne and Tobago," *American Jewish Historical Society,* pub 16 (1907), pp. 95–186.

270. Oppenheim, op. cit., See same author's material "An Early Jewish Colony in Western Guiana: Supplemental Data," *American Jewish Historical Society,* pub 17 (1909); also Richard J. H. Gottheil, "Contributions to the History of the Jews in Surinam", *American Jewish Historical Society,* pub 9 (1901), pp. 129–46; Anita Libman Lebeson, *Pilgrim People: A History of the Jews in America from 1492 to 1974* (New York: Minerva Press, 1975), pp. 50–52; p. A. Hilfman, "Notes on the History of the Jews in Surinam," *American Jewish Historical Society,* pub 18 (1909), pp. 179–207; Bernhard Felsenthal and Richard J.H. Gottheil, "Chronological Sketch of the History of the Jews in Surinam," *American Jewish Historical Society,* pub 4 (1895). See also Jacob Beller, *Jews in Latin America* (New York: Jonathan David, 1969), pp. 105–14.

271. J.H. Hollander, "Documents Relating to the Attempted Departure of the Jews from Surinam in 1675," *American Jewish Historical Society,* pub 6 (1897), pp. 9–29.

272. John W. Vandercook, "Jungle Jews," *The Menorah Journal,* 14, no 3 (March, 1928), pp. 238–46; Gottheil, *Contributions to the History of the Jews in Surinam,* op. cit., pp. 129–46.

273. On Maurice de Saxe see W.R.H. Trowbridge, *A Beau Sabreur* (London: T. Fisher Unwin, 1910); Lesle Heber Thornton, *Campaigns Grave and Gay: Studies of Four Soldiers of the Eighteenth and Nineteenth Centuries,* pp. 1–83; ed. and trans. Brigadier General Thomas R. Phillips (London: Cambridge University Press, 1925); Comte Maurice de Saxe's *Reveries on the Art of War* (Harrisburg, Pennsylvania: The Military Service Publishing Co., 1944); Majorie Bowles, *Sundry Great Gentlemen: Some Essays in Historical Biography* (Freeport, N.Y.: Books for Libraries Press, 1968); Rene de Castries, *Maurice de Saxe, 1696–1750* (Paris: Fayard, 1963); Edmund Basil Francis D'Auvergne, *The Prodigious Marshal* (London: Selwyn

and Blount, 1928); John Ewbank Manchip White, *The Life and Times of Maurice Comte de Saxe 1696–1750* (London: H. Hamilton, 1962).

274. Trowbridge, op. cit., p. 315.

275. Maurice de Saxe, *Reveries on the Art of War,* op. cit.

276. Trowbridge, op. cit., p. 316.

277. Ibid.

278. On Behrend see Natan Michael Gelber, *Zur Vorgeschichte des Zionismus,* op. cit., pp. 85–90.

279. Ibid.

280. Ibid., pp. 176–83. C.L.K's pamphlet was entitled *Neujudaea Entwurf Zum Wiederaufbau eines selbstandigen jüdischen Staates* (Berlin: L.A.D. Hairm, 1840).

281. Ibid.

282. Isaac Goldberg, *Major Noah: North American Pioneer* (Philadelphia: The Jewish Publication Society of America, 1936); George A. Kohut, "A Literary Autobiography of Mordecai Manuel Noah, With An Introduction," *American Jewish Historical Society,* Pub 6 (1897), pp. 113–21; Harold Sharfman, *Jews on the Frontier: An Account of Jewish Pioneers and Settlers in Early America* (Chicago: Henry Regnery Co., 1977), pp. 209–16; Lebeson, op. cit., pp. 119–210, 296–97, 305–06; Robert Gordes, "Mordecai Manuel Noah: A Centennary Evaluation," *America Jewish Historical Society,* pub 6 (1951), pp. 1–26; Melvin I. Urofsky, *American Zionism from Herzl to the Holocaust* (Garden City: Anchor Press/Doubleday, 1975), pp. 44–6; Gelber, *Zur Vorgeschichte des Zionismus,* op. cit., pp. 62–84.

283. Sharfman, op. cit., p. 210.

284. Peter Grose, *Israel, In The Minds of America* (New York: Alfred A. Knopf, 1983), pp. 17–19, 320.

285. Ibid., p. 18.

286. Manuel, op. cit., p. 2.

287. Joseph L. Blau and Salo W. Baron, *The Jews of the United States, 1790–1840, A Documentary History,* vol 3 (New York, 1963), pp. 892–93.

288. Sharfman, op. cit., p. 213; Urofsky, op. cit., pp. 44–46.

289. On Noah's proclamation see *American Jewish Historical Society,* pub 21 (1913), pp. 229–52; on Ararat see Bernard D. Weinryb, "Noah's Ararat Jewish State in Its Historical Setting," *American Jewish Historical Society,* pub 63, no 3 (March, 1954) pp. 170–91.

290. Urofsky, op. cit., p. 45.

291. Mordecai Manuel Noah, *Discourse on the Evidence of the American Indians Being the Descendants of the Lost Ten Tribes of Israel* (New York: James Van Norden, 1837). See also Sharfman, op. cit., p. 213; S. Joshua Kohn, "Mordecai Manuel Noah's Ararat Project and the Missionaries," *American Jewish Historical Society,* pub 55, no 2 (December, 1965), pp. 174–87.

292. Milton Plesur, "The American Press and Jewish Restoration During the Nineteenth Century," *Early History of Zionism in America* (New York: Jewish Historical Society and Theodor Herzl Foundation, 1956), p. 61.

293. Urofsky, op. cit., p. 86.

294. Arthur Zeiger, "Emma Lazarus and Pre-Herzlian Zionism," *Early History of Zionism in America* (New York: Jewish Historical Society and Theodor Herzl Foundation, 1958), p. 78.

295. The poem can be found in the work by Joseph Herman Hertz, *A Book of Jewish Thoughts* (New York: Bloch Publishing Co., 1941), p. 40.

296. Ralph L. Rusk, *Letters to Emma Lazarus* (New York: Columbia University Press, 1939).

297. Emma Lazarus, *Admetus and Other Poems* (New York: Hurde and Houghton, 1871).

298. Emma Lazarus, *Poems and Ballads of Heinrich Heine* (New York: Perma Giants, 1950).

299. Emma Lazarus, "An Epistle to the Hebrews," *American Hebrew* (February 9, 1883), Epistle XV, p. 149.

300. Z. Ragozin, "Russian Jews and Gentiles: From a Russian Point of View," *Century Magazine,* vol 33 (April, 1882), pp. 905–20.

301. Emma Lazarus, *Songs of a Semite* (New York: Office of the American Hebrew, 1882). Republished in 1970 by Literature House, an imprint of The Gregg Press, Upper Saddle River, New Jersey.

302. Ibid., pp. 5–48.

303. Ibid., p. 3 (dedication page).

304. Ibid., p. 56

305. These articles appeared in the *American Hebrew* from November 3, 1882 to February 23, 1883. Their dates of publication are as follows:

Epistle I, (Nov 3, 1882), vol 12, p. 141.

Epistle II, (Nov 10, 1882), vol 12, p. 151.

Epistle III, (Nov 17, 1882), vol 13, pp. 4–5.

Epistle IV, (Nov 24, 1882), 13, pp. 16–17.

Epistle V, (Dec 1, 1882), vol 13, p. 28.

Epistle VI, (Dec 8, 1882), vol 13, p. 40.

Epistle VII, (Dec 15, 1882), vol 13, pp. 52–53.

Epistle VIII, (Dec 22, 1882), vol 13, p. 64.

Epistle IX, (Dec 29, 1882), vol 13, p. 76.

Epistle X, (Jan 5, 1883), vol 13, pp. 88–89.

Epistle XI, (Jan 12, 1883), vol 13, pp. 100–101.

Epistle XIII, (Jan 26, 1883), vol 13, p. 125.

Epistle XIV, (Feb 2, 1883), vol 13, p. 137.

Epistle XV, (Feb 9, 1883), vol 13, p. 149.

Epistle XVI, (Feb 23, 1883), vol 14, p. 17.

An article written for another journal entitled, "The Jewish Problem," is sometimes listed as one of the epistles, but is not included in the above list. Portions of that article appeared in the *American Hebrew,* January 19, 1883, and have been considered by some historians to be Epistle XII.

306. Lazarus, Epistle XVI, op. cit., p. 17.

307. Laurence Oliphant, "The Jew and the Eastern Question," *Nineteenth Century*, vol 12 (August, 1882), pp. 242–55.

308. Lazarus, Epistle XV, op. cit., p. 149.

309. M. U. Schappes, ed., *Letters of Emma Lazarus* (New York: 1949), p. 146. The letter originally was sent to the editor of the *American Hebrew* and was printed May 11, 1883, vol 14, p. 146.

310. Lazarus, Epistle VI, op. cit., p. 40.

311. Ibid.

312. Gabriel Charmes, "Voyage en Syrie," *Revue des deux mondes* (June 15, 1882), pp. 888–912.

313. Ibid. pp. 911–12.

314. Lazarus, Epistle VII, op. cit., pp. 52–53.

315. Emma Lazarus, "The Jewish Problem," *The Century Illustrated Monthly Magazine,* vol 25, new series iii (1882–1883), p. 611.

316. Dean Wilansky, ed., *Sinai to Cincinnati: Lay Views on the Writings of Isaac M. Wise, Founder of Reform Judaism in America* (New York: 1937), p. 189.

317. Abram Samuel Isaacs, "A Problematic Champion," *Jewish Messenger,* vol 52 (January 26, 1883), p. 4.

318. Pereira Mendes, "Miss Lazarus and the Restoration of the Jews," *Jewish Messenger,* vol 52 (February 9, 1883), p. 5.

319. Hertz, *A Book of Jewish Thought,* op. cit., p. 259.

320. Lebeson, op. cit., p. 359.

321. Simon Rawidowicz, "Was Nachman Krochmal A Hegelian," *Studies in Jewish Thought* (Philadelphia: The Jewish Publication Society of America, 1974), pp. 350–84; and Simon Rawidowicz, ed., *Kitvei Nachman Krochmal* (Berlin: Verlag Ajanoth, 1924). See also Solomon Schechter, "Nachman Krochmal and the Perplexities of Time," *Studies in Judaism,* first series (New York: The Jewish Publication Society, 1896), pp. 46–72; A.I. Katsh, "Nachman Krochmal and the German Idealists," *Jewish Social Studies,* 8 (April, 1946), pp. 87–102.

322. Leopold Zunz, *Gesammelte Schriften* (Berlin: L. Gerschel, 1876), p. 158.

323. Charles H. Freundlich, *Peretz Smolenskin: His Life and Thought* (New York: Block Publishing Co., 1966); Reuben Brainin, *Smolenskin we-Toledotav* (Wilna: M. Katznelenbogen, 1901); Dubnow, *History of the Jews in Russia and Poland,* vol 2, op. cit., pp. 233–36; Hertzberg, *The Zionist Idea,* op. cit., pp. 143–54.

324. Aryeh Rubinstein and Raphael Posner, eds., *The Return to Zion* (New York/Paris: Leon Amiel, Publisher, 1974), p. 12.

325. Hertzberg, op. cit., pp. 154–55.

326. Robert St. John, *The Tongue of the Prophets: The Life Story of Eliezer Ben-Yehuda* (New York: Doubleday & Co., 1952); Hertzberg, op. cit., pp. 159–65; Sachar, op. cit., pp. 82–85; Avineri, op. cit., pp. 83–87.

327. Ibid., p. 85.

328. David Ben-Gurion, *Israel: A Personal History* (Tel Aviv: Sabra Books, 1971), p. 24.

329. On Love of Zion movement see Footnote 239.

330. On the Bilu see Samuel Kurland, *Biluim: Pioneers of Zionist Colonization* (New York: Scopus Publishing Company, 1943); Sokolow, *Hibbath Zion,* op. cit., ch 42.

331. Amos Elon, op. cit., p. 71.

332. On Pines see Geulah Werfel, *Rabbi Yehi'el Mikha'el Pines* (Jerusalem: Zionist Organization Youth Division, 1943). On Mazkeret Mosheh see Dubnow, *A History of the Jews in Russia and Poland,* op. cit., p. 376; Sasson, op. cit., p. 896.

333. On the struggle of the early colonies to survive see Hannah Trager, *Pioneers in Palestine* (London: George Routledge & Sons, 1923).

334. Urofsky, op. cit., pp. 18–19.

335. Leon Simon, *Moses Leib Lilienblum* (Cambridge: Cambridge University Press, 1912). Lilienblum prepared his own works for publication and they appeared posthumously in four volumes. See Moses Leib Lilienblum, *Kol Kitvei Lilienblum* (Odessa: 1910–13); see also Hertzberg, The Zionist Idea, op. cit., pp. 166–77; Elon, op. cit., pp. 64–69; S. Rosenfeld, "M.L. Lilienblum," *Reflex,* vol 3 (August, 1928), pp. 31–39; and Shalom Spiegel, *Hebrew Reborn* (New York: Macmillan Co., 1930), pp. 199–205.

336. Simon Dubnow, *Nationalism and History* (New York: Athenum, 1970), p. 173.

337. J.G. Lipman, "Lev Osipovitch Levanda", *The Jewish Encyclopedia,* vol 8 (New York: Ktav Publishing House), pp. 238–41.

338. Moshe Perlman, "Lev Levanda," *Encyclopædia Judaica,* vol 11 (Jerusalem: Keter Publishing House, 1971), pp. 67–68.

339. Leon Pinsker, *Road to Freedom,* trans. David Blondheim (New York: Scopus, 1944), pp. 74–106. See also Hertzberg, op. cit., pp. 178–98; Sachar, op. cit., pp. 10–17; Laqueur, op. cit., pp. 70–83; Martin, vol 2, op. cit., pp. 330–33.

340. Leon Pinsker, *Auto-Emancipation: An Appeal to His People by a Russian Jew* (New York: Zionist Organization of America, 1948). Based on a translation from German by D.S. Blondheim published by the Federation of American Zionists in 1916.

341. Ibid., p. 4.

342. Sachar, op. cit., p. 15.

343. Pinsker, *Auto-Emancipation,* op. cit., pp. 6–7.

344. For an excellent biography of the life and times of Asher Ginzberg see Leon Simon, *Ahad Ha-Am* (New York: Herzl Press, 1960). See also Norman Bentwich, *Ahad Ha-Am and his Philosophy* (Jerusalem: Keren Hayesod, 1927); Jacob S. Golub, *Ahad Ha-Am, Nationalist* (New York: Zionist Organization of America, 1939). On Ahad Ha-Am's writings see Leon Simon, ed., *Ahad Ha-Am Essays, Letters, Memoirs* (Oxford: East and West Library, 1946); Ahad Ha-Am, *Ten Essays on Zionism and Judaism,* trans. Leon Simon (London: G. Routledge and Sons, 1922). See also Hans Kohn, *Nationalism and the Jewish Ethic: Basic Writings of Ahad Ha-Am* (New York: 1962); Ahad Ha-Am, *Al Parashat Drakhim,* 4 vols (Berlin: Juedische Verlag, 1930); Ahad Ha-Am, *Igrot Ahad Ha-Am,* 6 vols (Tel Aviv: 1923–25); Leon Simon, ed. and trans., *Ahad Ha-Am, Selected Essays* (Philadelphia: The Jewish Publication Society of America, 1912).

345. For an analysis of this essay see Simon, *Ahad Ha-Am* (Herzl Press edition, 1960), op. cit., pp. 45–56.

346. See Elbogen, op. cit., pp. 266–68; Leon Simon, *Ahad Ha-Am: A Biography* (Philadelphia: The Jewish Publication Society of America, 1960), pp. 76–94; Richard J. H. Gottheil, *Zionism* (Philadelphia: The Jewish Publication Society of America, 1914), pp. 75–76.

347. Simon, *Ahad Ha-Am: A Biography,* op. cit., p. 78.

348. Ahad Ha-Am, "Emet me-Eretz Yisrael," *Kol Kitvei Ahad Ha-Am,* ed. H.Y. Roth (Tel Aviv: 1946), p. 23.

349. Simon, *Ahad Ha-Am: A Biography,* op. cit., p. 64.

350. Elbogen, op. cit., pp. 271–72.

351. Laqueur, op. cit., p. 108.

352. Avineri, op. cit., p. 117.

353. Simon, *Ahad Ha-Am: A Biography,* op. cit., p. 186.

354. Dubnow, *Nationalism and History,* op. cit., p. 55.

355. Avineri, op. cit., p. 116.

356. Leonard Stein, *The Balfour Declaration* (New York: Simon & Schuster, 1961), p. 494.

357. Simon, *Ahad Ha-Am: Essays, Letters, Memoirs,* op. cit., p. 282.

358. Ben-Gurion, op. cit., p. 39.

359. On Birnbaum's life and career see Adolf Boehm, *Die Zionistische Bewegung: Eine kurze Darstellung iher Entwicklung,* vol 1 (Berlin: Juedischer Verlag, 1935); Nathan Birnbaum, *Ausgewahlte Schriften zur judische Frage,* 2 vols (Czernowitz: Birnbaum and Kohut, 1910); Josepf Fraenkel, "Mathias Acher's (Nathan Birnbaum's) Fight for the Crown of Israel," *The Gates of Zion,* vol 8, no 3 (April, 1954), pp. 513.

360. Raphael Patai, ed., *The Complete Diaries of Theodor Herzl,* vol 1 (New York/ London: Herzl Press and Thomas Yoseloff, 1958), pp. 307–08.

361. Ibid., pp. 308–09.

362. Aaron David Gordon, *Kitvei A.D. Gordon,* 5 vols (Tel Aviv: Ha-Poel ha-Tza'ir, 1925–29); Herbert H. Rose, *The Life and Thought of A.D. Gordon,* trans. Frances Burnce

(New York: Bloch Publishing Co., 1938); Hertzberg, op. cit., pp. 368–86; Nathan Ro-
tenstreich, *Jewish Philosophy in Modern Times* (New York: Holt, Rinehart and Winston,
1968); Martin, vol 2, op. cit., pp. 340–42; Shlomo Avineri, *The Making of Modern Zionism:
The Intellectual Origins of the Jewish State* (New York: Basic Books Inc., 1981), pp. 151–58.

363. Joseph Heller, *The Zionist Idea* (New York: Shocken Books, 1949), p. 137.

364. Michael Berkowitz, *Aaron Samuel Liebermann* (Tel Aviv: Dovor, 1928); Moshe
Mishkensky, "Aaron Samuel Liebermann," *Encyclopædia Judaica,* vol 11 (Jerusalem: Keter
Publishing House, 1971), pp. 220–21.

365. Ronald Sanders, *The Downtown Jews: Portraits of an Immigration Generation* (New
York: Harper & Row, Publishers, 1969), pp. 137–46, 171–72, 177–78, 372–73; Henry Tobias,
"Morris Vinchevsky," *Encyclopædia Judaica,* vol 16 (Jerusalem: Keter Publishing House,
1971), pp. 153–54; N.B. Minkoff, *Pionern fun Yiddisher Poezye in Amerike* (New York: 1956).

366. On the origins of the Bund and its organization, ideology and politics see A.L.
Patkin, *The Origins of the Russian-Jewish Labor Movement* (Melbourne: F.W. Cheshire Pty.
Ltd., 1947), pp. 136–276; Charles Bezalel Sherman, *Bund, Galuth Nationalism, Yiddishism*
(New York: Theodor Herzl Institute, 1958); Koppel S. Pinson, "Arkady Kremer, Vladimir
Medem, and the Ideology of the Jewish Bund," *Jewish Social Studies,* vol 7, no 3 (July, 1945),
pp. 233–64: Emanuel Scher, "The Bund," in *Struggle for Tomorrow,* eds. Felix Gross and Basil
Vlavianos (New York: Arts Inc., 1954), pp. 135–96; Bernard Johnpoll, *The Politics of Futility:
The General Jewish Workers Bund of Poland, 1917–1943* (Ithaca: Cornell University Press,
1967); Ezra Mendelsohn, *Class Struggle in the Pale: The Formative Years of the Jewish
Workers Movement in Tsarist Russia* (Cambridge: University Press, 1970); and J.S. Hertz,
"The Bund's Nationality Program and Its Critics in the Russian, Polish and Austrian Socialist
Movements," *YIVO Annual of Jewish Social Science,* 14 (1969), pp. 53–67.

367. Cohen, *Vilna,* op. cit., pp. 342–43.

368. Urofsky, op. cit., p. 35.

369. Dov Ber Borochov, *K'tavim,* 3 vols (Tel Aviv: Ha-kibbutz Ha-Menhad, 1955–1956);
Hertzberg, *The Zionist Idea,* op. cit., pp. 352–66; Dov Ber Borochov, *The National Question
and the Class Struggle,* trans. L. Jessel (Chicago: 1935); Avineri, op. cit., pp. 139–50; Elon,
op. cit., pp. 76–77, 166–68; Laqueur, op. cit., pp. 274–77; and Dov Ber Borochov, *Sozial-
ismus und Zionismus* (Vienna: 1932).

370. Borochov, *The National Question and the Class Struggle,* op. cit.

371. Ibid.

372. Heller, op. cit., p. 134.

373. Theodor Herzl, *The Jewish State,* op. cit., pp. 27–28.

374. Shlomo Avineri, "Edmund Eisler's Zionist Utopia," *Midstream,* vol 31, no 2 (February, 1965), pp. 50–53.

375. Lebeson, op. cit., p. 469.

376. Leo W. Schwarz, ed., *Great Ages and Ideas of the Jewish People* (New York: Random
House, 1956), p. 356.

377. Aron Zakharovich Steinberg, ed., *Simon Dubnow, the Man and His Work* (Paris:
French Section of the World Jewish Congress, 1963); Josef Fraenkel, *Dubnow, Herzl and Ahad
Ha-Am* (London: Ararat Publishing Society, 1963); Israel Friedlander, *Dubnow's Theory of
Jewish Nationalism* (New York: Maccabean Publishing Company, 1905); Simon Dubnow,
Nationalism and History: Essays On Old and New Judaism, ed., trans., Koppel S. Pinson
(Philadelphia: The Jewish Publication Society of America, 1958); and Koppel S. Pinson, "The
National Theories of Simon Dubnow," *Jewish Social Studies,* vol 10, no 4 (October, 1948).

378. Dubnow, *Nationalism and History,* op. cit.; Friedlander, op. cit.; Pinson, *National
Theories of Simon Dubnow,* op. cit.

379. Dubnow, *Nationalism and History,* op. cit., p. 43.

380. Ibid., p. 51.

381. Ibid., p. 56.

382. M. Balberyszki, "Volkism and the Volk's Partei" in *Struggle for Tomorrow,* eds. Felix Gross and Basil Vlavianos (New York: Arts Inc., 1954), pp. 236–43; Dubnow, *History of the Jews in Russia and Poland,* vol 3, op. cit., pp. 145–48.

383. Dubnow, *Nationalism and History,* op. cit., p. 39.

384. Maurice Wohlgelernter, *Israel Zangwill: A Study* (New York: Columbia University Press, 1964); Joseph Leftwich, *Israel Zangwill* (London: J. Clarke, 1956); Maurice Simon, ed., *Israel Zangwill: Speeches, Articles and Letters* (London: The Soncino Press, 1937); and Israel Zangwill, *The Voice of Jerusalem: A Collection of Essays* (London: W. Heinemann, 1920).

385. Gottheil, *Zionism,* op. cit., pp. 135–42; Oskar K. Rabinowicz, *Winston Churchhill on the Jewish Problem: A Half Century Survey* (London: Lincoln-Prager, 1956), pp. 185–95; Halpern, *The Idea of a Jewish State,* op. cit., pp. 154–57; Leftwich, *Israel Zangwill,* op. cit., pp. 216–39; and David Isaac Marmor, "Negotiations of the JTO and the Reasons for Their Failure," *Zion,* vol 11 (Jerusalem, 1946), pp. 109–40, 175–208.

386. Laqueur, op. cit., p. 98.

387. Ronald Sanders, *The High Walls of Jerusalem* (New York: Rinehart and Winston, 1983), p. 60.

388. Weizmann, *Trial and Error,* op. cit., p. 160.

389. Sasson, op. cit., p. 994.

390. Oskar K. Rabinowicz, "Zangwill's Plan for Population Transfer," *Jewish Observer and Middle East Review* (April 24, 1963), p. 23.

391. Richard Lichtheim, *Die Geschichte des Deutschen Zionismus* (Jerusalem: R. Mass, 1954), pp. 104, 204; Boehm, *Die Zionistische Bewegung,* vol 1, op. cit., p. 496.

392. For a typical example of the efforts made by the Freeland League see Isaac Nachman Steinberg, *Australia, the Unpromised Land: In Search of a Home* (London: V. Gollancz, 1948).

393. On Haupt's life and accomplishments see *Oriental Studies in Commemoration of the Fortieth Anniversary 1883-1923 of Paul Haupt as Director of the Oriental Seminary of the Johns Hopkins University* (Baltimore/Leipzig: 1926). Of special interest in this collection honoring Haupt is the article by his most famous student, William F. Albright entitled "Professor Haupt as Scholar and Teacher," pp. 21–32. See also Zev Garber, "Paul Haupt," *Encyclopædia Judaica,* vol 7 (Jerusalem: Keter Publishing House, 1971), pp. 1475–76.

394. For a detailed account of Haupt's proposal see Moshe Perlmann, "Paul Haupt and the Mesopotamian Project, 1892-1914," *American Jewish Historical Society,* vol 67, no 3 (March, 1958), pp. 154–75.

395. Cyrus Adler, *I Have Considered the Days* (Philadelphia: The Jewish Publication Society of America, 1941); Louis Lipsky, *A Gallery of Zionist Profiles* (New York: Farrar, Straus and Cudahy, 1956), pp. 208–13; Herbert Parzen, *Architects of Conservative Judaism* (New York: Jonathan David, 1964), pp. 79–127. On Sulzberger see Louis Edward Levinthal, *Mayer Sulzberger* (Philadelphia: 1927). On Straus see Oscar Solomon Straus, *Under Four Administrations, From Cleveland to Taft* (New York: Houghton Mifflin Co., 1922), and Naomi Cohen, *A Dual Heritage, The Public Career of Oscar Straus* (Philadelphia: The Jewish Publication Society of America, 1969).

396. Cyrus Adler, *Jacob H. Schiff: His Life and Letters,* 2 vols (New York: 1928).

397. Paul Herman Emden, *Money Power in the Nineteenth and Twentieth Centuries* (London: S. Low, Marston and Co., 1937), pp. 331–42; Cecil Roth, "Court Jews of Edwardian England" *Jewish Social Studies,* vol 5, no 4 (October, 1943); and Brian Connell, *Manifest*

Destiny: A Study in Five Profiles of the Rise and Influence of the Mountbatten Family (London: Cassell, 1953), pp. 53–87.

398. Cecil Roth, *The Magnificent Rothschilds* (London: Robert Hale & Co., 1939), pp. 119–38.

399. Adolf Boehm, *Geschichte der Zionistische Bewegung,* vol 1, op. cit., p. 247, vol 2, pp. 20–21; Alex Bein, *Theodor Herzl,* op. cit., pp. 412–14; Oskar K. Rabinowicz, "Davis Treitsch," *Encyclopædia Judaica,* vol 15 (Jerusalem: Keter Publishing House, 1971), pp. 1394–95.

400. Oskar K. Rabinowicz, "Davis Trietsch's Colonization Scheme in Cyprus," *Herzl Year Book,* vol 4 (New York: Herzl Press, 1961–62), pp. 121–22.

401. Ibid.

402. Raphael Patai, ed., *The Complete Diaries of Theodor Herzl,* vol 1 (New York: Herzl Press/Thomas Yoseloff, 1958), p. 383.

403. Raphael Patai, ed., *The Complete Diaries of Theodor Herzl,* vol 2 (New York: Herzl Press/Thomas Yoseloff, 1959), p. 644.

404. Raphael Patai, ed., *The Complete Diaries of Theodor Herzl,* vol 3 (New York/London: Herzl Press, 1960), pp. 883–84.

405. On Herzl's El Arish negotiations see Alex Bein, *Theodor Herzl,* op. cit., pp. 441–52; S.D. Levontin, "The El Arish Project: The Origin and Failure of a Jewish Colonization Scheme," *Theodor Herzl: A Memorial,* ed. Meyer Weisgal (New York: Zionist Organization of America, 1929), pp. 71–72; Raphael Patai, "Herzl's Sinai Project," *Herzl Year Book,* vol 1, 1958, op. cit., pp. 107–27 and in Appendix, pp. 128–44.

406. Oskar K. Rabinowicz, *Arnold Toynbee on Judaism and Zionism* (London: W.H. Allen, 1974), p. 226.

407. Alex Bein, *Theodor Herzl,* op. cit., p. 84.

408. Paul Friedmann, *Das Land Madian* (Berlin: Druck von G. Bernstein, 1891).

409. See Jacob M. Landau, "Documents from British Archives on the Attempt of Jewish Colonization in Midian," *Shibat Zion,* vol 1 (Jerusalem: 1950), pp. 169–78.

410. *The Herald of New York,* May 1, 1882.

411. *Die Juedische Presse* (Berlin), February 18, 1892.

412. Alex Bein, *Theodor Herzl,* op. cit., p. 421.

Index